PATERNOSTER BIBLICAL MONOGRAPHS

The Pauline Concept of Supernatural Powers

A Reading from the African Worldview

PATERNOSTER BIBLICAL MONOGRAPHS

A full listing of titles in this series and Paternoster Theological Monographs series appears at the end of this book

PATERNOSTER BIBLICAL MONOGRAPHS

The Pauline Concept of Supernatural Powers

A Reading from the African Worldview

Kabiro wa Gatumu

Foreword by James D. G. Dunn

WIPF & STOCK · Eugene, Oregon

Wipf and Stock Publishers
199 W 8th Ave, Suite 3
Eugene, OR 97401

The Pauline Concept of Supernatural Powers
A Reading from the African Worldview
By Gatumu, Kabiro wa
Copyright©2008 Paternoster
ISBN 13: 978-1-60608-472-4
Publication date 2/20/2009
Previously published by Paternoster, 2008

"This Edition Published by Wipf and Stock Publishers
by arrangement with Paternoster".

Series Preface

One of the major objectives of Paternoster is to serve biblical scholarship by providing a channel for the publication of theses and other monographs of high quality at affordable prices. Paternoster stands within the broad evangelical tradition of Christianity. Our authors would describe themselves as Christians who recognise the authority of the Bible, maintain the centrality of the gospel message and assent to the classical credal statements of Christian belief. There is diversity within this constituency; advances in scholarship are possible only if there is freedom for frank debate on controversial issues and for the publication of new and sometimes provocative proposals. What is offered in this series is the best of writing by committed Christians who are concerned to develop well-founded biblical scholarship in a spirit of loyalty to the historic faith.

Series Editors

I. Howard Marshall, Honorary Research Professor of New Testament, University of Aberdeen, Scotland, UK

Richard J. Bauckham, Professor of New Testament Studies and Bishop Wardlaw Professor, University of St Andrews, Scotland, UK

Craig Blomberg, Distinguished Professor of New Testament, Denver Seminary, Colorado, USA

Robert P. Gordon, Regius Professor of Hebrew, University of Cambridge, UK

Tremper Longman III, Robert H. Gundry Professor and Chair of the Department of Biblical Studies, Westmont College, Santa Barbara, California, USA

Stanley E. Porter, President and Professor of New Testament, McMaster Divinity College, Hamilton, Ontario, Canada

*Dedicated to my wife Wanjirũ and my children Mũrĩmi and Wawĩra
in love and gratitude for their love, care and support*

Contents

Foreword by James D. G. Dunn	xv
Preface	xvii
Acknowledgments	xix
Abbreviations	xxi

Chapter 1
Introduction: Problem Formulation and Analysis — 1
1:1. Definition of Key Terminology and Concepts — 1
1:2. The Problems of the Concept of Religious Phenomena — 11
1:3. Background, Motivation and Significance — 15
1:4. The Statement of the Problem and Basic Assumptions — 18
1:5. Theoretical Framework and Method — 19
1:6. The Ambiguity of Cross-cultural Communications — 21
1:7. Scope and Delimitation — 22

Chapter 2
A Collision of Two Worldviews: The History and Legacy of the Problem of Supernatural Powers in Africa — 25
2:1. Introduction — 25
2:2. The Missionary Legacy and the African Response — 25
  i. *Condemnation of African Culture and Worldview* — 25
  ii. *The Translation of the Bible* — 37
  iii. *African Christians and Supernatural Powers* — 39
2:3. A Critical Appraisal of the African and Western Worldviews — 43
  i. *A Need for Dialogue* — 43
  ii. *Understanding Worldviews* — 44
    a. *The African Worldview* — 44
    b. *The Western Worldview* — 49
    c. *Can the African and Western Worldviews Meet?* — 54
2:4. Conclusion — 58

Chapter 3 The African Context of Reception: Analysing the Diverse Perceptions of Religious Phenomena Prompting Beliefs in Supernatural Powers — 60

3:1. Introduction — 60
3:2. Africans' Perceptions of Supernatural Powers — 60
   i. Supernatural Powers as the Cause of Human Existence — 60
   ii. Hierarchical Structures and Categories of Supernatural Powers — 61
      a. The Ancestral Spirits — 62
      b. Spirits that were Initially Human but not Ancestral — 63
      c. Non-human Spirits from the Beginning — 64
3:3. Rituals and Practices used to Control Supernatural Powers — 65
   i. Magic, Witchcraft and Sorcery — 66
   ii. Divination — 67
   iii. Accommodation and Expulsion of Possessing Spirits — 68
3:4. Anthropological Interpretations of African Beliefs — 70
   i. Spiritual Powers are Illusions — 71
   ii. Belief in Spirits Symbolizes Lack of Scientific Knowledge — 72
   iii. Belief in Spirits is an Expression of Psychological Disorders — 73
   iv. Belief in Spirits is an Expression of Socio-cultural Identity — 76
   v. Deprivation and Marginalisation Causes Spirit Possession — 77
   vi. Beliefs in Spirits are Symbolic Cultural Texts — 80
   vii. Beliefs in Spirits are the Basis of Religious and Moral Values — 81
   viii. Belief in Spirits is a Way of Political and Economic Protest — 83
   ix. Reactions to the Anthropological Interpretations — 84
3:5. The Views of Comparative Religionists and African Theologians — 87
   i. Traditional Beliefs as the Basis of the Postulate of Affinity — 87
   ii. Reflecting on the Postulate of Affinity — 88
3:6. Conclusion — 91

Chapter 4 The Context of Production: A Critical Appraisal of the First Century CE Beliefs in Supernatural Powers — 93

4:1. Introduction — 93
4:2. Jewish Perceptions of Supernatural Powers — 95
  i. *Jewish Beliefs* — 95
    a. *The Heavenly Court* — 95
    b. *The Angel of Nations* — 96
    c. *Evil Spirits and Demons* — 97
  ii. *Jewish Rituals and Practices* — 100
    a. *Magic and Divination* — 100
    b. *Astrology* — 103
4:3. Graeco-Roman Perceptions of Supernatural Powers — 104
  i. *Graeco-Roman Beliefs* — 105
    a. *Gods and Goddesses* — 105
    b. *Demons and Spirits* — 108
    c. *Spirits of Dead Heroes* — 110
  ii *Graeco-Roman Rituals and Practices* — 111
    a. *Magic and Witchcraft* — 111
    b. *Astrology* — 113
    c. *Divination, Oracles and Dreams* — 116
4:4. Graeco-Roman Reservations about Supernatural Powers — 120
4:5. Conclusion — 124

Chapter 5 The Context of the Literary Genre: Evaluating the Pauline Concept of Supernatural Powers within its First Century CE Milieu — 128

5:1. Introduction — 128
5:2. An Exegetical Treatise — 129
  i. Ἐξουσίαι/ἄρχοντες — 129
  ii. Δυνάμεις — 133
  iii. Κυριότης — 135
  iv. Θρόνοι — 135
  v. Κοσμοκράτορας — 136
  vi. Ἄγγελοι — 137
  vii. Τὰ Στοιχεῖα τοῦ Κόσμου — 138
  viii. Δαίμων — 141
  ix. Σατανᾶς/διάβολος — 142
  x. *The Pauline Terminological Framework* — 149
  xi. *The Pauline Conceptual Framework* — 152

5:3. Theological Reflections: The Evidence for Christ's
    Supremacy over Supernatural Powers 159
    i. Christ is Pre-eminent, Supernatural Powers are Created 159
    ii. The Existence and Resistance of the Church 161
    iii. The Defeat of Supernatural Powers 163
5:4. Conclusion 166

Chapter 6 Previous Interpretations: Interacting with Some Selected Scholars who deal with Supernatural Powers from the Perspective of Myth 168

6:1. Introduction 168
6:2. Understanding Myth and Its Truth 171
    i. The Problem of Definition 171
    ii. The Indispensability of Myth 175
    iii. The Problem of Myth as to the New Testament 177
6:3. The Twentieth Century Treatment of Supernatural
    Powers in Paul 179
    i. Rudolf Bultmann: Interpreting the Myth Existentially 179
    ii. Walter Wink: Structuralist Reading of the Powers 181
        a. The Powers are Structures in Disguise 181
        b. Supernatural Powers as Death, Sin, Law and the Flesh 186
    iii. Some Key Considerations as to Demythologisation 191
6:4. Understanding Metaphor 195
    i. The Relationship Between Myth and Metaphor 195
    ii. The Problems of Definition and Distinction 196
    iii. The Problems of Interpreting Metaphor 200
    iv. The Referential Problem of Supernatural Powers 202
6:6. Conclusion 208

Chapter 7 Conclusion: The African Church and Supernatural Powers with Regard to Christ's Supremacy 209

7:1. Towards a Retrospective Glance 209
7:2. What Can the African Church Do Concerning Supernatural
    Powers? 211
    i. Underline Christ's Supremacy 212
    ii. Use of and Reliance on Cultural Resources and Tools 223
    *iii. Coming to Terms with Other Dimensions of
        Supernatural Powers* 231
7:3. A Summing-up Analysis 238

Bibliography 241
Primary Sources: Text and Translations 241

Secondary Sources: Dictionaries and Encyclopaedias   244
Secondary Sources: Commentaries, Books and Articles   245
Reports   287

Scripture Index   **289**
Author Index   **293**

Foreword

When Dr. Gatumu first proposed his thesis topic, I confess to having experienced some foreboding. The topic was one of the most challenging that I had ever encountered as a supervisor. He wanted to make a fresh study of Paul's understanding of principalities and powers, with a view to how Paul's teaching on the subject could be better communicated in an African setting. The problem and challenge is that Paul's worldview would seem to be very close to the traditional African worldview, in which demons and possession are regarded as a common feature of every day experience. So, from one perspective, it could be all too easy to let Paul speak directly to the African situation. But Dr. Gatumu saw clearly the challenge, that for a PhD in Western Europe, he had to run the line of communication through, or at least take adequate account of the post-Enlightenment worldview on supernatural powers. The challenge is so severe that I was dubious that anyone could hope to pull it off successfully. However, it soon became clear to me that if anyone could do so, that person was Kabiro wa Gatumu.

In the event, he succeeded as fully as I had hoped – as readers will see from the following pages. His solution is to use the concept of metaphor as developed by Paul Ricoeur and others, that is, metaphor as *referential* but *not literal*, referring to but not defining the reality in view. To interpret Paul's language of principalities and powers as metaphor in this way enables Dr Gatumu to build an impressive bridge between the three worldviews (first century Mediterranean, modern western European, and sub-Saharan African), and to do so in a way that can speak powerfully to his own culture, without compromising his integrity and professionalism as a New Testament scholar. I should add that I have rarely had a postgraduate student who read so voraciously in the relevant literature, so that his thesis was as well researched as one could have wished for, in New Testament scholarship, in literary theory and in previous attempts to take seriously the African worldview by social anthropologists. I was particularly pleased that Dr Gatumu's hard-headed examiners were equally impressed by what he had achieved and that the degree of PhD was recommended very strongly – an outcome not always achieved by PhD candidates from outside the Western academic tradition. I was equally delighted when Kabiro told me that the thesis had been accepted for publication by the well respected Paternoster Press in the UK. I expect it to attract a good deal of attention from those who are seriously engaged in cross-cultural communication. And I hope and pray that it will achieve its goal of facilitating the sound words of 2,000 years ago to speak with clearer and better effect to the challenges and concerns of the present.

James D. G. Dunn
Durham
2008

Preface

This book first appeared as a PhD dissertation[1] presented to the University of Durham, UK, in June, 2004. It demonstrates that the Pauline concept of supernatural powers underlines the supremacy of Christ over supernatural powers. They were created in him, through him and for him (Col 1: 16–20). Christ's death was not only their defeat, but also their humiliation (Col 2: 15). Christ's resurrection and exaltation clearly speak of his supremacy (Eph 1: 20-1; Phil 2: 9-11). Christ is also supreme since supernatural powers cannot separate believers from the love of God (Rom 8: 38-9) or thwart the existence of the church, through which the manifold wisdom of God is made known to them (Eph 3: 10).

However, the Pauline teachings about the powers in relation to Christ's supremacy do not seem to have had much sway in the African context. This happens due to two opposite but related errors: that of believing supernatural powers exist and allowing them to determine human existence and that of denying they exist. Yet the Pauline concept neither denies their existence nor allows them to be given allegiance or worship as if they are equal to Christ. Due to these two errors, which also represent the missionary legacy and the African response to it, most African believers hold a dual religious heritage that causes pastoral problems for the African church. Rather than engaging the dual religious heritage, most of the studies on supernatural powers seem to have complicated it.

The trend among anthropologists has been to deny that supernatural powers exist and/or to reduce them to psychological or social or political or religious functions. Several biblical scholars, who deal with supernatural powers from the perspective of myth, maintain that supernatural powers were marginal in Paul's thinking and are irrelevant for modern Christians. They maintain that Paul demythologised supernatural powers so as to refer to existential realities such as sin and death or to the structures of human existence. As a result, most of the anthropological and biblical treatises on supernatural powers do not seem to engage the full measure of the African beliefs in the same. This is largely because the interpretations of supernatural powers are shaped by the Western

---

[1] "Paul and the Powers in Relation to Christ's Supremacy: Re-Visiting the Pauline Concept of Supernatural Powers from as African Worldview Perspective".

worldview and are mainly from a Western perspective. But the interpretation of reality as people perceive it is usually shaped by their worldview. For that reason, this book re-visit the Pauline concept of supernatural powers from an African perspective, taking into consideration that Paul initially spoke to a context similar to the African context with regard to the beliefs in, and fear of supernatural powers .

Acknowledgements

Suffice to say that the completion of this book was not just my own effort. Many people contributed to its completion in one way or the other. Though it is not possible to mention all by name, nevertheless, I acknowledge their support with heartfelt gratitude. They stood by my side through prayers, spiritual, moral and financial support. Colleagues in the Department of Theology New Testament Seminar at the University of Durham provided immeasurable contribution. Their constructive criticisms were really inspiring and beneficial. To them I say thank you. Innermost thanks go to the Langham Partnership for sponsoring my studies at the University of Durham. We especially pay tribute to The Rev. Canon Paul Berg, the then Director of the Langham Scholarship Programme, for his commitment and pastoral care. Not only did Paul take care of financial needs but also the pastoral needs. His letters always concluded, "with my prayers and good wishes". A University of Durham Postgraduate award and a University of Durham Hardship Allowance scheme also made the financial side of my study considerably manageable. Heartfelt appreciation goes to the bishop of the A. C. K Diocese of Kirinyaga, the Rt. Rev. Daniel M. Ngoru for granting me study leave, without which this study could not have begun. My gratitude is also due to my blood brothers and sisters for the support they provided and sojourned with me in this project. I also express unreserved thanks to my wife Catherine Wanjiru and children Vic Preston Murimi and Fiona Nessy Wawira who sacrificed much of their comfort for the sake of this study. Many times they endured separation and loneliness. Despite that, they were a source of encouragement when things seemed to have come to a dark end. Lastly but not the least, I express unlimited appreciation to the Lightfoot Professor James D. G. Dunn for his help throughout the time of research and beyond. His support and constant encouragement were of remarkable quality. He faithfully walked with me in this project even in his retirement. May the Almighty God bless everyone who contributed to the completion of this work in one way or the other according to his riches in glory.

Abbreviations[1]

Technical Abbreviations
E. A. E. P	East African Educational Publishers
LXX	Septuagint (the Greek OT)
NT	New Testament
OT	Old Testament

Apocrypha Citations
Tob	Tobit
Wis	Wisdom of Solomon
Sir	Sirach
1, 2, 3, 4 Mac	1, 2, 3, 4 Maccabees

Old Testament Pseudepigrapha Citations
Asc. Isa	Martyrdom and Ascension of Isaiah
1 En	1 Enoch (Ethiopic Apocalypse)
2 En	2 Enoch (Slavonic Apocalypse
Jub.	Jubilee
L.A.E	Life of Adam and Eve
Test. Abr	Testament of Abraham
Test. Lev	Testament of Levi
Test. Sol	Testament of Solomon
TrShem	Treatise of Shem.

Dead Sea Scrolls and Related Texts
Q	Qumram
1Qap Gen^{ar}	Genesis Apocryphon
1QH	Hodayot or Thanksgiving Hymns.
1QM	Milhamah or War Scroll
1QS	Serek Hayyaad or Rule of the Community,

---

[1] The form in which most abbreviations appear follows Alexander, Patrick H (*et al, eds.*) *The SBL Handbook of Style: for Ancient Near Eastern, Biblical, and Early Christian Studies* (Peabody, Massachusetts: Hendrickson Publishers, 1999) pp. 68-152, and Craig A. Evans and Stanley E. Porter *Dictionary of New Testament Background* (Downers Grove/Leicester: Intervarsity Press, 2000) pp. xii-xxix.

1QSa	Manual of Discipline / Appendix A, Messianic Rule, to 1QS
4QEn^{a-g}	1 Enoch Fragments (4Q201–202, 204–207, 212)
11QPs^a	Psalms Scroll
11QT	Temple Scroll
CD	Cairo Genizah copy of the Damascus Document.

Rabbinic Works

b.	Babylonian tractates
m.	The tractates of the Mishna
t.	The tractates of the Tosefta
y.	Jerusalem tractates
Ber	Berakot
Hull	Hullin
Mek.	Mekilta
Sanh	Sanhedrin

Nag Hammadi Codices

Treat. Res	1, 4 Treatise on the resurrection
Tri. Trac.	1, 5 Tripartite Tractate

Magical Texts

PGM	Papyri Graecae Magicae or Greek Magical Papyri

Classical and Hellenistic Writers in Alphabetical Order[2]

Aeschylus

Ag	Agamemnon
Prom	Prometheus Bound

Cicero

Somn.Scipi.	Somnium Scipionis

Euripides

IPh.Taur	Iphigenia in Taurus

Dio Cassius

Hist	Roman History

---

[2] Citations from classical and Hellenistic writers that are not abbreviated are not included in this list of abbreviations.

Abbreviations xxiii

Diodorus Siculus
bib.Hist Biblioteca Historica

Diogenes Laertius
Vit. Phil Lives of the Philosophers

Josephus
Ant. Jewish Antiquities
J.W. Jewish War

Juvenal
Sat Satires

Pausanias
Graec. Descr Description of Greece

Philo
De Abr De Abrahamo
De Aet. Mund De Aeternitate Mundi
De Agr De Agricultura
De cher De Cherubim
De conf De Confusione Linguarum
De Ebr De Ebrietate
De fuga De Fuga et Inventione
De Gig De Gigantibus
De Leg.Ad.Gai Quod Est De Legatione Ad Gaium: De Virtutibus Prima Pars
De mig De Migratione Abrahami
De mut De Mutatione Nominum
De Op.Mun De Opificio Mundi
De plant De Plantatione
De post De Posteritate Caini
De sac De Sacrificiis Abelis et Cain
De Sobr De Sobrietate
De som De Somniis or Quod a Deo Mittantur Somnia
De spec leg De Specialibus Legibus
De virt De Virtutibus
De vit.Mos De Vita Mosis (I & II)
Frag. Ser CIV Fragments preserved by Antonius
Leg. Alleg, I–III Legum Allegoriae, I–III
Quis rer Quis Rerum Divinarum Heres
Quod.Det.Pot.Ins.Sol Quod Deterius Potiori Insidiari Soleat
Quod deus Quod Deus Immutabilis Sit

Plato
Theaet	Theaetetus
Tim	Timaeus

Plotinus
Enn	Enneads

Plutarch
Cam	Camillus (Vitae Parallelae)
De. Def.Orac	De Defectu Oraculorum
De Is.et Os	De Iside et Osiride
Mor	Moralia
Sept.Sap.Conv	Septem Sapientium Convivium
Ser.Num.Vind	De Sera Numinis Vindicta
Thes	Theseus

Pliny the Elder
Nat. Hist	Naturalis Historiae or Natural History.

Xenophon
Anab	Anabasis
Mem	Memorabilia
Eq. Mag	De Equitum Magistro
Symp	Symposium

Livy
Hist	History of Rome

Early Christian Writers
Cyril of Jerusalem
Epist. Apost	Epistola Apostolorum

Ignatius
Mag	Letter to the Magnesians
Symr	Letter to the Smyrneans
Trall.	Letter to the Trallians

Justin Martyr
1 Apol	1st Apology
Dial	Dialogue with Trypho the Jew

Origen
Contra Cels	Contra Celsum or Against Celsus
de Princi	de Principiis or The first Principles

Shepherd of Hermas

Herm. Sim	Hermas, Similitude(s)
Herm. Vis	Hermas, Vision(s)

Tatian

Orat	Oratio

Tertullian

adv. Marc	Adversus Marcionem
de Idol	De Idololatria
ad. Scap	Ad Scapulam
de Spect	De spectaculis
de Test.an	De Testimonio Animae

Journals and Major Reference Work

AGJU	Arbeiten zur Geschichte des antiken Judentums und des Urchristentums
ANRW	*Aufstieg und Niedergang der römischen Welt*
BWANT	Beiträge zur Wissenschaft vom Alten (und Neuen) Testament
CBQMS	Catholic Biblical Quarterly Monograph Series
CRAIBL	Comptes rendus de l'Académie des inscriptions et belles-lettres
CRINT	Compedia rerum iundaicarum ad Novam Testamentum
Def.Tab	Defixionum Tabellae (Audollent)
EPRO	Etudes préliminaires aux religions orintales dans l'empire
HNTC	Harper's New Testament Commentaries
ICC	International Critical Commentary
JSNTSup	*Journal for the Study of the New Testament Supplement Series*
JSPSup	*Journal for the Study of the Pseudepigrapha and Related Literature Supplement Series*
ÖTKNT	Ökumenischer Taschenbuchkommentar zum Neuen Testament
RILP	Roehampton Institute London Papers
SAHM	Sudhof Archiv Heft Medizin
SBLSBS	Society for Biblical Literature Sources for Biblical Studies
SNT	*Studien zum Neuen Testament*
SNTSMS	Society for the New Testament Studies Monograph Series
STDJ	Studies on the Texts of the Desert of Judah

TBC	Torch Bible Commentary
TD	Theology Digest
TDNT	*Theological Dictionary of the New Testament*
WBC	Word Biblical Commentary
WUNT	Wissenschaftliche Monographien zum Alten und Neuen estament

Churches and Para-church Organisations

ACK	The Anglican Church of Kenya
CHIEA	Catholic Higher Institute of East Africa
C.M.S	Church Missionary Society

CHAPTER 1

Introduction: Problem Formulation and Analysis

1:1. Definition of Key Terminology and Concepts

It is desirable to specify the meaning of key words and concepts in a study right from the beginning. Communication theories unremittingly remind us that people ascribe meaning to messages they read or hear. It does not always follow that the ascribed meaning is the speaker's or the writer's intended meaning because words prompt different memories and experiences to different people. One cannot be sure that the intended meaning of a word is received exactly as it is transmitted without interference or distortion. If the intended meaning and the ascribed meaning do not coincide, what occurs is a breakdown of communication.[1] Again, Turner rightly observes,

> Our approach to any range of phenomena is both revealed and influenced by the names we bestow upon it. Serious study cannot dismiss the issue with the offhand popular remark, 'What is in a name'? A name may prejudice the issue by saying too much or fail to delineate the field concerned by being too vague.[2]

Paul does not use the term supernatural powers and so it needs some additional explanations. This is necessary if as Wink avers in relation to spiritual realities such as angels, spirits, principalities and powers,[3] "the modern world threw out the reality with the words and now finds itself without an adequate vocabulary for the powers even more real today than two thousand years ago...we have no single language for speaking of the total phenomena the ancients knew as 'the powers'".[4] A key consideration is that the subject of supernatural powers confronts contemporary scholars with the problem of language, which this study cannot claim to be capable of eliminating but which it cannot ignore. People can experience the same phenomenon but disagree

---

[1] See G. B. Caird, *The language and Imagery of the Bible* (London: Duckworth, 1980), p. 40.
[2] H. W. Turner, *Religious Invasion in Africa: Essays on New Religious Movements* (Boston, MA: G. K. Hall, 1979), p. 49.
[3] See Walter Wink, *Unmasking the Powers: The Invisible Forces that Determine Human Existence* (Philadelphia: Fortress Press, 1986), pp. 1-8.
[4] Wink, *Unmasking the Powers,* p. 4.

over or interpret differently what it is or looks like. Therefore, it is not only possible to be familiar with the Pauline terms identified in this study as supernatural powers but also to "project them into a wholly different world of meanings"[5] than the meaning that Paul intended and which ancient readers were familiar with. This could also be imposing our own mental constructs on the first century CE world.[6]

It then follows that what Wink regards as the total phenomena the ancients recognised as 'the powers', which this study identifies as supernatural powers, could be inexact. A people's religion attributes events to supernatural powers. But must these be regarded as supernatural powers? Walsh's description of religion as "a system of beliefs and practices resting on the assumption that events within the world are subject to some supernatural power or powers, such that human needs, either physical or psychological can be satisfied by entering into relations with such powers"[7] casts doubt on the idea that 'the powers' are the phenomena. He argues that supernatural powers are personal and impersonal. These are not practically the same as the twelve religious institutions he identifies, involving a whole complex of beliefs, attitudes and practices.[8] The institutions Walsh identifies include belief in powerful impersonal supernatural forces that pervade nature, belief in disembodied personal spiritual beings ranging from the gods to the shades of the dead, the cult of the dead and magic in its various forms.[9] Supernatural powers ought not to be confused with or simply identified with the phenomena if the phenomena are credited to supernatural powers that Wink believes, "largely determine personal and social existence".[10]

This study therefore uses the term supernatural powers as a heuristic reference to the personal or impersonal invisible forces outside or within human beings. These, according to the beliefs in the African context and in the ancient world, determine human existence to one degree or other and can be placated or invoked for good or evil purposes. The term is used as a hermeneutical key to refer to the forces behind or manifested in natural events, influential institutions and traditions, powerful personages and states, which are not readily amenable to scientific analysis. It is also used as a general category for the Pauline terms and phrases, which will be dealt with in chapter five and probably refer to the same forces. It will be seen in chapter five that the referents of the Pauline terms identified as supernatural powers could literally refer to human structures of power or personal spiritual beings that were thought to embody or wield

---

[5] Walter Wink, *Naming the Powers: The Language of Power in the New Testament* (Philadelphia: Fortress Press, 1984), p. 4.
[6] See Colin E. Gunton, *The Actuality of Atonement: A Study of Metaphor, Rationality and the Christian Tradition* (Edinburgh: T & T Clark, 1988), p. 33.
[7] George Walsh, *The Role of Religion in History* (New Brunswick, New Jersey: Transaction Publishers, 1998), p. 3.
[8] Walsh, *The Role of Religion*, pp. 3-5.
[9] Walsh, *The Role of Religion*, pp. 6-15.
[10] Wink, *Unmasking the Powers*, p. 4.

Introduction

extraordinary power within the first century CE religio-cultural and socio-political/economic background. Therefore it would be misleading and unwisely restrictive to reduce the concept of supernatural powers to a single entity or function. Yet in the context of the literary genre where these terms appear, as Dunn notes, "in every case what seems clearly to have been in mind were heavenly beings, subordinate to God and his Christ, with the potential to intervene between God and his creation, and hostile to his purpose and people".[11] For that reason, the term supernatural powers will be used referentially to signify the invisible and spiritual forces that some people regard as the determinants of human existence.

However, the adjective supernatural with regard to African religion and worldview is somewhat imprecise and problematic; hence it has raised a considerable debate among scholars. Several scholars, as a consequence of the Western dichotomy between natural and supernatural, are of the opinion that the adjective can distort the understanding of African religion and worldview. According to some anthropologists, when supernatural is applied to African worldview and religion, it is ethnocentric and misleading, as many African people do not think of supernatural as separate from natural. Some of those who hold this view regard the natural as real while the supernatural is unreal. Klass's assumption is that applying supernatural to a people who do not distinguish natural from supernatural is being polite to naïve beliefs in non-existent beings.[12] Saler argues that the concept of supernatural presupposes that the natural world is separate from a supernatural creator.[13] But probably the merit of using supernatural cannot be denied if supernatural is understood as inseparable from natural. The problem, according to Saler, is that some researchers use supernatural without defining what they mean, possibly to appear respectful of local beliefs that they, however, consider erroneous.[14] His remark, "if by 'supernatural beings' we mean imaginary ones, we should say so",[15] ought to be taken with the approbation it deserves.

Without a precise definition of what one intends supernatural to mean, what may come to mind are the definitions found in most dictionaries. Most conventional definitions of supernatural give an impression of that which exists outside the natural world. Most English dictionaries define supernatural as that which belongs to, or relates to an order of existence beyond the observable universe; that which departs from what is usual or normal, especially so as to appear to transcend the laws of nature. In contrast, natural is that which is in

---

[11] See J. D. G. Dunn, *Romans 9–16* 38b, WBC (Dallas, Texas: Word Books Publishers, 1998), p. 106.
[12] M. Klass, *Ordered Universe: Approaches to the Anthropology of Religion* (Boulder, Colorado: Westview Press, 1995).
[13] B. Saler, *Conceptualizing Religion: Immanent Anthropologists, Transcendent Natives and Unbounded Categories* (Leiden: Brill, 1993), pp. 122-125.
[14] B. Saler, "Supernatural as a Western Category" in *Ethos* 5, 1 (1977), p. 34.
[15] Saler, *Conceptualizing Religion*, p. 125.

accordance with or determined by nature; not marvellous or supernatural.[16] The problem with this understanding is that it removes the natural from the domain deserving awe and reverence by saying that the natural is not marvellous. It makes the supernatural and the natural to refer to two unrelated realms. It accepts that supernatural and natural represent mutually exclusive ideas, and so if an event is described as natural then it has no supernatural components. Similarly, if an event is described as supernatural, then it defies natural description. Arguably, the problem arises from definitions that detach supernatural from natural and vice versa. This dichotomy, however, is confusing, if supernatural indicates that which relates to divine power(s) or the miraculous. This immediately gets us into a problem, such as that which has been given to us by various dictionaries' definitions of supernatural and natural.

Perhaps all that which relates to human existence should be defined and considered in two ways, that is, the natural perspective and the supernatural perspective. This is more useful especially when we talk of the power(s) or force(s) that allegedly determine human existence. It is true that the African worldview and religion, as this study will repeatedly show, do not dichotomise natural and supernatural as these perspectives work together. However, there is awareness that the power(s) or force(s) that purportedly determine human existence are not humans, even though they could be human in origin. Attaching the adjective supernatural to these powers is to recognise that they are more-than-human powers; hence, it would be better to regard the phrase supernatural powers as interchangeable with superhuman powers. These superhuman being(s) could be a single god, many gods, spirits, ancestral spirits, or other powerful beings or personages that rise above mundane humans. These powers or forces are not natural, if natural could be taken to mean that which is susceptible to scientific investigation. It should be noted that supernatural has been defined as something "beyond the potential reach of science as opposed to the natural which can be understood by science".[17] As such, it would mean that to refer to the powers or forces that determine human existence as supernatural is to claim that no relevant scientific description can be given to them. But could it be that the idea of scientific investigation also creates a dichotomy between the natural and the supernatural? We cannot disregard the laws of science in the analysis of any phenomena. Nevertheless, to say that an event is susceptible to scientific investigations does not mean that scientific descriptions supply all the information on an event. It means that some information about an event can be gained from a scientific inquiry. Again, to focus on a supernatural description for the powers that supposedly determine human existence is to look for a description that does not depend on scientific analyses. It is to seek for an explanation from a context beyond a scientific description within which

---

[16] *Webster's ninth New Collegiate Dictionary*, Merriam—Webster. See also *The Chambers Dictionary*, (Edinburgh: Chambers Harrap Publishers, 1998).
[17] Diane Vera *The Existence of the Supernatural*, available at http://www.angelfire.com/ny5/dvera/philos/supernatural.html, accessed 22.06.04

Introduction

human existence could also be viewed.[18] Consequently, this study considers the adjective supernatural useful in determining if the powers that determine human existence can be analysed through scientific investigations.

While it is appropriate to describe the natural through a scientific analysis, is it right to describe the natural from the perspective of the supernatural? It will be argued that the manifestations of the powers that determine human existence in Africa are identified with natural phenomena. In that case, every natural phenomenon could be interpreted within a supernatural framework as well as a natural one. For example, the cause of rain can be described in terms of air pressure and temperature. It can also be described in terms of answered prayers. At any rate, events that take place in the created universe, in terms of the African mind-set, could be the manifestation of the free activity of divine power(s). In terms of Western thinking, that which is natural and susceptible to scientific analysis could be, in terms of African thinking, viewed within supernatural perspectives. In terms of Western thinking, that which is inherently supernatural and not susceptible to scientific analysis could be, in terms of African thinking, natural but bringing out the revelation of divine power(s).[19] It then appears that the forces that determine human existence can be described from the perspectives of the natural or the supernatural. They are supernatural since they are believed to exist outside the world of human habitation, violate or go beyond the physical world. They are natural since they could inhabit the material world, interact and network with natural phenomena and intervene in the course of natural laws. If there is no dispute in applying natural to African religion and worldview, perhaps we can apply supernatural in the same way we apply natural. As such, the attempt to distinguish natural and supernatural could be vague. If used devoid of the Western dichotomy, both natural and supernatural could expediently make clear the dynamic intersection, interaction and networking of the spirit world and physical world. The adjective could be useful in the analysis of power(s) or force(s) that is/are usually felt to be invisible but present in our everyday physical world. Could this mean that the best way is to understand the phrase supernatural powers as metaphorical, bearing in mind, as we shall see in chapter six, the metaphorical "is" both signifies "is like" and "is not"?

Perhaps regarding supernatural and natural as complementing each other could create an awareness that is not too vaguely tied to a worldview. Alternatively, supernatural could gainfully and accurately describe particular worldviews so as to understand the belief in spirits as ubiquitous in human existence. The belief or disbelief in supernatural can be viewed as a universal assumption or as a unique reality of a given culture. Perhaps supernatural and natural, if they complement each other, could describe a universal human

---

[18] See Richard H. Bube, "Penetrating the Word Maze" in *Perspective on Science and Christian Faith*, available at http://www.asa3.org/ASA/PSCF/1989/PSCF6-89Bube.html, p.41, assessed 22.06.04.

[19] Bube, Penetrating the Word Maze pp. 109-10, available at http://www.asa3.org/ASA/PSCF/1989/PSCF6-89Bube.html, assessed 22.06.04.

experience that is explained differently in different traditions. This could provide a bridge between the assumptions of Western and African worldviews as to their different perceptions of the universe. To all intents and purposes, worldviews, whether Western or African, simultaneously enable people to create naturalistic and supernaturalistic models of the world. There is a widespread cognate human tendency to build both natural and supernatural models regardless of culture.[20] It seems that what is natural may not make sense without an interface with the supernatural and vice versa. As Lohmann notes, "a farmer who prays for a successful crop also plants, weed and harvests".[21] This analogy understands prayer from a supernatural perspective and planting, weeding and harvesting from a natural perspective.

Perhaps regarding supernatural and natural as compatible could deal with the belief that everything that exists is part of the material world, and so no supernatural or spiritual realm exists independently. This is to deny a reality, which the African worldview does not deny. In chapter three, it will be argued that Africans recognise powerful spirits that are not human. These spirits reside in the spirit world but naturally permeate the physical world, making it possible for the spirit world and the material world to intersect, interact and network dynamically. As a result, supernatural is used not to refer to a transcendent domain separate from the natural world of human habitation. But it is used to refer to the powers or forces that determine human existence, which in the African context are not, by nature, human and subject to human limitations. These powers seem to isolate or go beyond natural forces and for this reason Africans do not deny the supernatural aspects of spirits, though not in Western categories that tends to separate the supernatural from the natural. So the adjective supernatural is used to qualify the powers that determine human existence and it is intended to highlight the lucid fact that, according to the African worldview, these powers are preternatural, that is above the order of human nature. The intellect and speed of these powers, as the majority of Africans would agree, are far greater than the corresponding human powers.

The use of the adjective supernatural with regard to the African context should not be disregarded with the argument that it may distort the Africans' understanding of reality and the universe. It is often said that the African perception of reality is "this worldly" in orientation. This is true if the perimeters of "this worldly" are not limited to the material phenomenal world of the Western discourse. The African mind-set is that "this worldly" stands at the frontier of human and spiritual activity, which are in constant interaction. If "this worldly", which perhaps according to the Western mentality is the equivalent of the natural world, could encompass the "other worldly", which according to Western thinking is the supernatural world, then speaking about the natural or the supernatural from the African worldview is to speak about the

---

[20] See P. Boyer, *The Naturalness of Religious Ideas: A Cognitive Theory of Religion* (Berkeley: University of California Press, 1994).

[21] Roger Ivar Lohmann, "The Supernatural is Everywhere: Defining Qualities of Religion in Melanesia and Beyond" in *Anthropological Forum* Vol. 13 No 2 (2003), p. 180.

same reality. It is to speak about the head and the tail as two sides, which make up one coin. Citing the example of a farmer who gives an offering to the deceased first owner of a field and paying rent to the absentee landlord, Klass wonders why the former act of the farmer should be classified as supernatural and the latter as natural when the first owner and the landlord are both invisible. This distinction, he concludes, simply underlines disbelief in the efficacy of the offering, and it is an ethnocentric insult and a misconception of the farmer's worldview.[22] If we are interpreting Klass rightly, it follows that in seeking a natural explanation of an event; one should not disregard or disrespect the supernatural one. Alternatively, in seeking a supernatural explanation, one must not disregard or disrespect the natural one. As a result, it is not a distortion of the African worldview to suggest that Africans can distinguish between dealing with spirits and human beings. While Klass serves us well in emphasising that this distinction may not be salient to the believer (in our case to the African), it is possible for the Africans to differentiate that which is supernatural from that which is natural although both occur simultaneously and mix freely. Arguably, even if traditional Africans might not think about the differences between the natural and the supernatural, they could make that distinction were it relevant for their task.

In view of the aforesaid, there is a possibility of speaking of supernatural as well as the natural in the African context in the attempt to understand physical causes and effects. As a matter of fact, we are dealing with modern Africa, which, as this study will show in chapter two, has had an interface with the Western world. This has made the African worldview experience some changes but which have been modified so as to fit into the categories of the African primal worldview.[23] Undeniably, almost every modern African person knows that crops do not grow by offering and prayers alone but must be tended. They also know that crops do not grow by tending alone without divine intervention, which is beyond unaided human intellect. In fact, arguments against the use of supernatural with regard to the African worldview do not expose a problem with the adjective, rather they point to the problem caused by the definitions of natural and supernatural. Any definition that would represent supernatural as contradicting the natural can prevent the idea of supernatural from illuminating a major source of religious behaviour and improving our ability to understand African religion and worldview. All people, including Africans, can distinguish supernaturalistic ideas from naturalistic ones, even if Africans may not find the distinction salient.

However, it would be foolhardy to be simplistic in the use of supernatural, especially when the secularisation of modern Western civilization has created a

---

[22] Klass, *Ordered Universe*, p. 28-33.
[23] The term primal does not refer to the primitive, but to a people's basic and prior thoughts and views of the world. The term has of late been considered as an important theological category, which conveys a theological meaning and if used more persistently and widely would implant a theological agenda into what attempts to be an empirical science.

gulf between the natural and the supernatural. This happens because of the modern perception that the physical universe is controlled by scientifically knowable and predictable laws and exists devoid of supernatural intervention. This gives the impression that the natural world is a profane reality, wholly separated from the sacred and the supernatural. This Western dichotomy is not found in the primal African worldview as well as in the worldviews of the first century CE. In the African worldview and in the worldviews of the first century CE, the supernatural lies at the centre of what is natural for the Western worldview. But since the forces that determine human existence in the African context of reception and the first century context of production are described in language that shows the superiority of the powers that determine human existence over unaided humans, it is probably justifiable to use supernatural with regards to these powers. Nevertheless, supernatural could operate within the perimeters of natural, though moving beyond natural due to the sacrality and power bestowed upon it. Nevertheless, the phrase, supernatural powers, is problematic. It is more nuanced, that is, it is more than meets the eye.

This could imply that the Pauline concept of supernatural powers is best understood as a metaphor, bearing in mind that a metaphor is referential. Caird's assertion that we have no other language, however inadequate it may be, beside metaphor or analogy with which we speak about God[24] may apply to supernatural powers. To be more precise, the language with which we speak of the referents of supernatural powers is like that of referring to God as father or king or husband. Therefore, in using a metaphor, people attribute character and quality to God, which is not best comprehended in literal anthropomorphic terms as it conveys more than what the literal term means to us. Likewise, the concept of supernatural powers is a metaphor for forces we cannot characterise effectively but which resist reduction to the materially and anthropomorphically conceived spiritual beings. As mentioned above, supernatural powers refer to forces without or within human beings, or rather, to what we human beings often experience—forces that impinge upon us and push us in certain directions. These forces can be experienced through natural phenomena that we have no ability to control or within culturally inured attitudes, inherited inhibitions, spirit of greed, love of money and power, corruption, tribalism, anger, malice, dreams and all that. In short, these forces are experienced as constraints and impulses upon us, which come through, or are within our traditions or society, that is, the structures of human existence. Chapter six will discuss the problems of metaphor and also fill out the understanding of metaphor outlined above.

The term 'African context' could remain ambiguous without further explanations because Africa is a vast continent with different cultural shades. It "presents pictures of diversity, unity and variety... precisely because Africa has a rich and varied complexity of cultural, economic, political, linguistic, social

---

[24] Caird, *The Language and Imagery*, pp. 144, 174.

and religious ideas, practices and rites".[25] However, 'African context' refers to Africa south of the Sahara. But this does not imply that Africa south of the Sahara has an identical culture. It brings together rich and diverse, but related cultures and worldviews. But as Magesa asks, "Is what is seen as multiplicity to be considered realistically and accurately as absolute or merely as various elements and expressions of one reality"?[26] Alternatively, can we speak of the religious worldview of Africa south of the Sahara in singular or in plural terms? The fact that each and every society in Africa has its own supreme god, nature spirits, ancestral spirits and different rituals and practice has led some writers to regard the African religious worldview in the plural rather than in the singular. N. S. Booth argues,

> Our reading and observation turn up a profusion of phenomena to which we may attach such labels as supreme gods, nature spirits, ancestor rituals, initiation practices, divine kings, secret societies, sorcerers and demons with considerable variety from one place to place. Perhaps we will decide that there is no such a thing as "African religion" but only "African religions".[27]

This question therefore is of long standing duration and different scholars have applied different approaches to it.

In his earlier work, Mbiti insisted that we should speak of African *religions* in the plural since there are many people in Africa who have different religious system of beliefs, ceremonies, rituals and each religion has its own leaders and religious specialists. But on the other hand, African philosophy is different. While religious expressions in Africa are concrete and observable, one cannot claim the same thing about the thinking behind them provided by the African worldview. Mbiti argued that the philosophy behind the religious expression of African people is a philosophy in the singular.[28] Even so, by positing a philosophy and not *philosophies* behind all African religious expressions, was Mbiti indirectly admitting what he sought to explain away?[29] Whereas there are variations in the religion and religious worldview of Africa south of the Sahara, there are unmistakable similarities that bring out a common human tendency to

---

[25] Edward W. Fashole-Luke, "Introduction" in Edward W. Fashole-Luke, R. Gray, A. Hastings and G. Tasie (eds.) *Christianity in Independent Africa* (London: Rex Collings, 1978), p. 357.

[26] Laurenti Magesa, *African Religion: The Moral Traditions of Abundant Life.* (Maryknoll, New York: Orbis Books 1997), p. 24.

[27] N. S. Booth, "God and the Gods in West Africa", in N. S. Booth *African Religion: A Symposium* (New York: Nok Publishers 1977), p. 3.

[28] J. S. Mbiti, *African Religions and Philosophy* (London/Nairobi: Heinemann Educational Books, 1969) pp. 1-2. See also E. Ikenga-Metuh, *Comparative Studies of African Traditional Religions* (Onitsha, Nigeria: Imico Publishers, 1987), pp. 5-10.

[29] It should be noted that Mbiti changed his view that we should speak of African religions. This is evident in the title of his book, *Introduction to African Religion*, which is used to teach African Traditional Religion in Kenyan secondary schools.

assume that spirits and the spirit world exists. The common idea in African south of the Sahara is that spirits and the spirit world exist in a hidden realm inside the world of human habitation. The belief in the existence of the Supreme Being and the fact that the God of the Bible has a vernacular name in nearly all African society shows a mutual understanding among different African societies with regard to the transcendent world.

There is documented evidence that would allow the generalisation of African religion and worldview of Africa south of the Sahara. A study conference of missionaries held at Le Zoute Belgium in the 1920s noted the unity of the African religion as well as a diversity that mark Africa geographically, linguistically and even in the physical appearance of its various people. But it concluded that "underlying all the divergences that mark pagan [sic] Negro tribes, there is a fundamental unity of belief and out look upon the world ... Africa is a unity – a unity in diversity. Nothing is lost, and much is gained, by trying to look at the new Africa as a whole".[30] The Vatican Secretariat for Non-Christians noted that between the African societies, in addition to apparent diversity, there are bonds of symmetry, of contrast and of complement. Ritual manifestations, even though different, are based on the same religious beliefs and proceed from a common structure.[31] E. W. Smith is cited in G. Parrinder as having stated,

> In spite of... cultural diversities there is, I believe, an underlying identity in religion. I do not deny or minimize the differences you may find between the highly organized Yoruba or Baganda, with their hierarchy of gods, on the one hand, and the simple peoples, on the other hand. But the difference is one of emphasis and development, not of essence. There is sufficient identity to warrant our speaking of African religion.[32]

Sundkler regards the Haya people of Northern Tanganyika (now mainland Tanzania) as "representing characteristic tendencies in the traditional African milieu; at the same time it is clear that Papuans and Dayaks, Karens and Santals would feel themselves on familiar grounds in most of its [Haya society] features".[33]

It could be logical therefore to generalise the religious worldviews in the societies in the Africa south of the Sahara and regard it as an African religious worldview. Although the varieties of African culture and religion cannot be wished away, as J. V. Taylor asserts, there is a "basic world-view which

---

[30] E. W. Smith, *The Christian Mission in Africa* (London: The International Missionary Council, 1926), p. 7.
[31] The Roman Secretariatus Pro Non-Christianis, 1968 p. 7
[32] See E. G. Parrinder, *West African Psychology: A Comparative Study of Psychological and Religious Thoughts* (London: Lutterworth Press, 1951), p. 4.
[33] Bengt G. M. Sundkler, *The World of Missions* (London: Lutterworth Press, 1965), p. 184.

fundamentally everywhere is the same".³⁴ But it should be said that the African worldview, which is fundamentally the same everywhere, refers to the popular and primal worldview, which interprets data and reality through a spiritual lens.³⁵ This worldview is not uniquely African since people from other non-Western worldviews and some Western people may share its aspirations while a few Africans may reject it. Horton decries the besetting sin of many writers on African thought-systems, which he describes as the tendency to treat many features that are in fact widely shared and universal as uniquely African.³⁶ These include experiences attributed to supernatural powers supposedly affecting life for better or for worse but which are universal phenomena. The Western worldview refers to the intellectual worldview that interprets data through a scientific and materialistic lens. Not all Western people approve the intellectual worldview, while some Africans may do so.

Other terms that require explanation are, 'the context of production', 'the context of the literary genre' and 'the context of reception'. The 'context of production' refers to the social and cultural context from which Paul's letters emerged and were read/heard for the first time. The 'context of reception' refers to the social and cultural context in which Paul's letters are received and read/heard currently. The 'context of the literary genre' refers to the text and the narrative in which the text appears. These are depicted as the contexts within which this study seeks to examine the Pauline concept of supernatural powers.

1:2. The Problems of the Concept of Religious Phenomena

This study will refer to some religious phenomena that lead or led people to believe in supernatural powers. The term religious phenomena however, need explanation. It refers to observable events or manifestations that are directly apprehended by human senses and experienced as part of existence. This could be anything that manifests the sacred, ultimately indicating "supernatural values or beings".³⁷ But the concept of religious phenomena is problematic, as the phenomena this study typifies as religious may not correspond exactly to

---

[34] J. V. Taylor, *Primal Vision: Christian Presence amid African Religion* (London: SCM, 1963), p. 19.

[35] The term spiritual could have a wide range of meanings and so it can be ambiguous. In this study, it refers to that which is not tangible and corporeal. It refers to incorporeal and immortal celestial powers understood to have a real existence apart from matter. So the spiritual lens implies that the majority of African people interpret normal behaviour and abnormal phenomena as having been caused by spiritual beings, which act independently or through people, especially religious specialists.

[36] Robin Horton, *Patterns of Thought in Africa and the West: Essays on Magic, Religion and Science* (Cambridge: Cambridge University Press, 1993), p. 2.

[37] M. Eliade, "Methodological Remarks on the Study of Religious Symbolism" in M. Eliade and J. M. Kitagawa *The History of Religious Essays in Methodology* (Chicago/London: The University of Chicago Press, 1959), p. 95.

what may be termed as religious. A perfect example is magic, which some scholars would say is not the same as religion. J. G. Frazer, while noting that in some cases magic is "tinged and alloyed to religion"[38] since both assume the operation of spirits, sturdily advocates their total separation.[39] He insists that magic is closer to science than to religion, regarding it as the "next of kin to science".[40] But to draw a dividing line between religion and magic could be problematic. Julian Pitt-Rivers notes, "the two fields of activity are in fact better viewed as aspects of a single conceptual system offering two causes of conduct to deal with the problem of personal fate, which may be pursued either alternatively or simultaneously".[41] Several scholars would agree that magic is an integral part of religious thought and that it never exists apart from religion.[42]

Magic is complicated by the fact that its definition is open-ended and elusive. Several scholars regard magic as an occult art or science based on superstitious folklore. Others regard it as a practice lacking objectivity since it cannot be constructed as a proper scientific term.[43] As a result, magic and the related practices of witchcraft and sorcery are viewed in purely sociological terms. J. G. Gager avoids using the word magic claiming, "magic as a definable and consistent category of human experience, simply does not exist".[44] But Luck considers magic as

> A technique grounded in a belief of powers located in the human soul and in the universe outside ourselves, a technique that aims at imposing the human will on nature or on human beings by using supersensual powers. Ultimately, it may be a belief in the unlimited power of the soul.[45]

Magic is also the practice of communicating with, and/or controlling supernatural powers using ritual action so as to affect the course of present or

---

[38] J. G. Frazer, *The Golden Bough: A Study in Magic and Religion* Vol. 1 (London: Macmillan, 1926), p. 220.

[39] Frazer, *The Golden Bough*, p. 220-243.

[40] Frazer, *The Golden Bough*, p. 222.

[41] Julian Pitt-Rivers, "Spiritual Power in Central America" in M. Douglas (ed.), *Witchcraft Confession and Accusations* (London: Tavistock Publications, 1970), p. 183.

[42] See J. Middleton, *Lugbara Religion* (Washington, D. C/London: Smithsonian Institution Press, 1987), p. 82; M. Eliade *Patterns in Comparative Religions* (London/New York: Sheed and Ward, 1958), p. 23.

[43] L. Thorndike, *A History of Magic and Experimental Science* 8 vols. (New York: Macmillan 1923-58), Vol. 1, p. 2; Alan F. Segal, "Hellenistic Magic: Some Questions and Definitions" in Brown Judaic Studies 127 *The Other Judaism of Late Antiquity* (Atlanta: Scholar's Press, 1987), p. 81.

[44] J. G. Gager, *Curse Tablets and Binding Spells from the Ancient World* (Oxford: Oxford University Press, 1992), p. 24-5.

[45] George Luck, *Arcana Mundi: Magic and the Occult in the Greek and Roman Worlds* (Baltimore: John Hopkins University Press, 1985), p. 3.

future events. It is a technique by which some people seek to control and to command supernatural powers in order to gain necessary security and favourable providence. It uses symbolic imitation meant to guarantee the results the magician intends. It also uses formulaic recitals that explain the desired result at the same time invoking gods, demons or spirit to quicken the desired outcome. Aune elucidates that magic could be used for protective or apotropaic, aggressive and malevolent aims, or as a technique of acquiring love or power. It could also be used for divinatory or revelatory purposes.[46]

There are two types of magic that have been identified, namely, white and black. White magic is purportedly beneficial to human life while black magic is supposedly detrimental. But this adds more ambiguity to magic, equally evident in the New Testament and in Philo. In Acts 13: 8 the term μάγος refers to a 'wise man' or 'magician' while in 2 Timothy 3: 13 the term γόητες refers to cheats, impostors and charlatans, implying magic was evil. Philo identifies those who practised genuine magic especially kings. He also identifies adulterated magic, the wicked imposture pursued by quacks, cheats, buffoons and the vilest women and slaves.[47] This means that there is acceptable and detestable magic and magicians could be genuine practitioners or people of dubious character. It is not easy therefore to establish when magic is white or black as protective magic can be used destructively. In sum, the basic rationale of magic is the need to communicate with and to manipulate supernatural powers that allegedly determines human existence. It accepts the existence and reality of invisible spiritual powers such as gods, intermediary spirits, angels and demons.[48]

Together with magic, other religious phenomena under consideration (witchcraft, sorcery, divination and 'spirit-possession', and its related practices of exorcising destructive spirits or accommodating beneficial spirits) are linked together by the belief in spiritual beings that purportedly function as mediators, providers and protectors of those who believe in them. The dominant tendency is to unite belief with rituals and practices performed to exorcise or domesticate spirits supposedly possessing people for malevolent or benevolent intentions. These religious phenomena have a common factor: to induce people to believe in more-than-human powers that directly control nature and human existence. Spiritual power is therefore central to the social system and spiritual sanctions eclipse everything else in human existence. Conspicuously, these phenomena have two related elements. The first is theoretical and it is concerned with beliefs in supernatural powers. The second is practical and it seeks to appease supernatural powers through rituals and practices so as to avert their hostile influence, to cope with their pressure and to win favours from them.

---

[46] David E. Aune, "Magic; Magician" in G. W. Bromiley (ed.), *The International Standard Bible Encyclopaedia* vol. 3 (Grand Rapids, Michigan: Eerdmans, 1986), p. 218.
[47] Philo, *De Specialibus Legibus III*. XVIII.100-101
[48] Hans-Josef Klauck, *The Religious Context of Early Christianity* (Trans. Brian McNeil; Edinburgh: T & T Clark, 2000b), p. 214.

These phenomena are sometimes regarded as labels for social phenomena that radically differ from society to society.[49] It will be seen in chapter three that some people, mainly Western academics, do not read these phenomena religiously but anthropologically, or sociologically or psychologically. It is held that these phenomena represent diverse techniques people use to deal with social realities.[50] Yet they seem to be more religious than anything else as they fuse religious ideas, faith, ritual and practice. They not only express mystical power but also form an infinite source of power and sanctity. They are mutually connected by the belief in, and recognition of superior, invisible and envious power or powers that are soothed by means of rituals and practices. However, these religious phenomena and the powers they are attributed to are complex. They have a long historical evolution; hence their interpretations are diverse and intricate. This means that they can be and have been lived and interpreted differently by different people. The trend has been to regard these religious phenomena "as unique, unrelated and even mutually exclusive"[51] but Lewis's holistic approach is estimable. His study shows that to understand the nature of spiritual power, we need to recognize how these seemingly disparate mystical manifestations belong to a single but complex phenomenon that has collective, authoritative and protective tasks. Such seemingly contradictory phenomena as spirit-possession, witchcraft, cannibalism and shamanism, usually attributed to separate cults and cultures, not only reveal their interconnectedness but also their link with world religions such as Islam and Christianity.[52] It would be misleading and unwisely restrictive to regard these phenomena "as mutually exclusive in any given society or culture" as they "coexist and sometimes even blend into a hybrid entity".[53]

This study thus refers to these phenomena as religious since they interlock so intimately with religion that it might be impossible to discuss one without reference to the other. At least the attempt to draw a distinction between them "is not always satisfactory".[54] On the other hand, their analysis is intricate probably because they are full of metaphors. In chapter six, it will be seen that metaphors are socio-cultural and context sensitive. This complicates their

---

[49] T. O. Beidelman, "Towards more Open Theoretical Interpretations" in M. Douglas (ed.), *Witchcraft Confession and Accusations* (London: Tavistock Publications, 1970), p. 351.

[50] But in the African context, socio-political/economic phenomena are viewed from a religious perspective. Mbiti rightly notes, "for Africans the whole of existence is a religious phenomenon; man is a deeply religious being living in a religious universe" (Mbiti, *African Religions*, p. 15).

[51] I. M. Lewis, *Religion in Context: Cults and Charisma* (Cambridge: Cambridge University Press, 1996), pp. i, ix.

[52] Lewis, *Religion in Context,* p. i.

[53] I. M. Lewis "A Structural Approach to Witchcraft and Spirit-possession" in M. Douglas (ed.), *Witchcraft Confession and Accusations* (London: Tavistock Publications, 1970), p. 299.

[54] T. O. Beidelman, "Towards more Open", p. 351

Introduction

interpretation and it could also cause a referential problem with regard to the metaphor of supernatural powers. It is, however, fundamental to explain the background, motivation and significance of this study.

1:3. Background, Motivation and Significance

Despite the widely held view that Christianity is growing rapidly in Africa south of the Sahara,[55] there is a pastoral and doctrinal problem facing the African church. The factors credited to the rapid growth of Christianity and the pastoral and doctrinal problem form the background and motivation of this study. The first factor credited with this growth is the missionary enterprises, which, as it will be shown in chapter two, is a Pandora's Box in relation to African beliefs in supernatural powers. The second is the African primal religion and worldview that Mbiti insists has prepared the religious and spiritual ground for the Africans to listen to the teachings of the Bible, to reflect upon them, and in many cases to convert to Christianity without feeling any sense of spiritual loss but to the contrary thereby gaining a new outreach in their religious experience.[56] Conversely, the requirements of African primal religion and worldview often undermine the Pauline concept of supernatural powers with regards to Christ's supremacy. These demands have been too strong to allow Christ's supremacy to take indisputable authority in the life of many African Christians. The third factor is simply the Bible itself, especially in its availability in the African languages. Mbiti maintains that none of the Christian agents, missionary or even African catechist, "can exert or has exerted as great impact upon the church as the Bible in the local language".[57] Even if this could be true in some areas of human existence, it may not be so concerning the beliefs in supernatural powers. The loyalty given to supernatural powers purportedly because they are connected to each and every dimension of human life has not diminished or vanished in the African context.

Many African people, including some Christians, perform what they regard as significant precautionary rituals before any public and individual event takes place.[58] This indicates the pastoral and doctrinal problem facing the African

---

[55] J. S. Mbiti, *The Bible and Theology in African Christianity* (Nairobi: Oxford University Press, 1986), p. 6 reveals that the annual rate of Christian growth (2.81%) in Africa in the 1970-1980 decade was higher than the population growth (2.38%) in the same period.
[56] Mbiti, *The Bible and Theology*, p. 7.
[57] Mbiti, *The Bible and Theology*, p. 28.
[58] In 2003, a Kenyan legislator and a traditional healer died while on a mission to 'cleanse and protect' the home of the MP from people who may wish to plant evil spirits and guests with ill intentions against the MP or his family on the occasion of his homecoming party. Some Kenyans, who certainly perceive reality through the lens provided by the Western worldview, could not understand how and why an honourable member of parliament could revert to such outdated and superstitious practices. Even so, the newspaper that reported this incident cited another traditional healer, who implicated

church. The recurring problem for most African people who turn to Christ more than anything else arises from the belief that supernatural powers inhibit or enhance human life. As Arnold observes, they struggle with the same issues as Christians in the days of Paul. A common issue in these different contexts in time and space is the belief that spirits/demons cause illness. They also make a curse work and crops grow weak and they cause plagues, earthquakes and natural disasters. The chief concern for African Christians is whether to reject ancestral spirits when one becomes a Christian, or to be a Christian and still remain loyal to them. The belief that to ignore ancestral spirits would bring disaster to the society complicates the whole issue. The question is; do Christianity and biblical scholarship have answers to people who believe in the reality and existence of spirits and demons?[59] There are two options, to deny their reality and existence and to stigmatise such beliefs, or to present Christ as one who is able to meet their felt needs within their cultural milieu. The latter option seems gainful as it allows interaction between African beliefs, fears and aspirations and the Pauline concept. Sadly, as Abijole asserts, biblical scholars have not done this persuasively.[60]

The African church too has not tackled the pastoral and doctrinal problem attributable to supernatural powers as Paul does. Yet the subject of supernatural powers is of great interest in Africa. Turner's research, which collected and classified 8000 sermons preached in African churches, concluded that the majority of these sermons emphasised the power encounter between the superior power of God or Christ and the inferior power of supernatural powers. These sermons derived from biblical concepts, texts and themes on 'power encounter' with, or 'works of power' against supernatural powers and their effects on human life.[61] The interest in the supernatural, as Mbiti notes, draws a picture of God working wonders and miracles, making the impossible to happen.[62] The preacher's interest in the supernatural aims at making "the gospel

---

some Kenyan politicians as highly superstitious (Sunday Standard online, http://www.eastandard.net, accessed 04:05:2003).

[59] Taylor in his *Primal Vision*, 1963 p. 16 avers that Christ has been presented as the answer to the question a white man would ask, the solutions to the needs that a Western man would feel, the Saviour of the world of the European worldview, the object of the adoration and prayer of historic Christendom. He then asks, but if Christ were to appear as the answer to the question that Africans are asking, what would he look like?

[60] Bayo Abijole, "The Pauline Concept of Principalities and Powers in the African Context", in *African Theological Journal* Vol.19, No.2 (1988), p.118.

[61] H. W. Turner, *Profile through Preaching* (London: Edinburgh House Press, 1965), pp. 14-23.

[62] Mbiti, *The Bible and Theology*, pp. 41, 43. Also see H. W. Turner ("The Contributions of Studies on Religion in Africa to Western Religious Studies" in M. E. Glasswell and E. W. Fashole-Luke (eds.), *New Testament Christianity for Africa and the World* (London: SPCK, 1974), p. 174 who notes an "Overriding African concern for spiritual power from a mighty God to overcome all enemies and evils that threaten human life and vitality".

Introduction

message manifest and immediately applicable in a particular situation of crisis or need by means of specific "works of power" which demonstrate the lordship of Christ over the satanic forces of evil".[63] The main objective of this study is to show the lordship and supremacy of Christ in a context where supernatural powers supposedly determine human existence. If the belief in supernatural powers threatened the faith and life of the first century CE church as it does in the African context, the effort to make the Pauline concept of, and the African beliefs in supernatural powers speak to each other is significant. This is largely because the fear of supernatural powers in Africa exists where freedom in Christ should reign.

Another motivation is a personal desire to read the Bible with reference to the African worldview. Indeed, biblical interpretation must resonate with cultural issues if "religious ideas and meanings ... exist for living men and women who keep struggling through the ups and downs of their individual lives with multiple needs and interests".[64] It is therefore desirable to interpret the Bible with reference to a people's worldview and culture. This perhaps allows for a profitable interaction, wherein people would receive biblical themes and concepts within their own culture using cultural symbols familiar to them. In the history of Christianity, people have often received the Bible in situations where different cultures intersect and interact. It is arguably in this line of thought, Sanneh argues, that the success of transmitting biblical faith is grounded on the capability to translate the biblical message into the culture and language of people receiving it. He cites a deep link between translatability of the Bible and cultural self-understanding, vernacular pride, social awakening, religious renewal, transmission and recipiency, cross-cultural dialogue and reciprocity in mission.[65] In that case, believers ought to interact with biblical texts in their religio-cultural and socio-political context. This must not occur without caution because, as Hesselgrave notes, "although the creator made provision for culture...still culture is a human product...it is also the arena of continued divine and satanic intervention and penetration".[66] This may also imply that the Bible is not, culturally and ideologically, an innocent text. Though it is the word of God, it is also expressed in human language, culture and worldview that inevitably generate diverse interpretations. However, it is unfortunate that biblical interpretation from a cross-cultural and an African worldview is a latecomer in African Christianity.

The significance of this study therefore is to have the African and Pauline

---

[63] E. R. Wendland and Salimo Hachimba, "A Central African Perspective on Contextualizing the Ephesians Potentates, Principalities and Powers" in *Missiology: An International Review* Vol. 28 No 3 (July 2000), p. 341.
[64] Walter Burkert, *Ancient Mystery Cults* (Cambridge: Harvard University Press 1987), p. 30.
[65] Lamin Sanneh, *Translating the Message: The Missionary Impact on Culture.* (Maryknoll, New York: Orbis Books, 1989), pp. 1-2.
[66] D. Hesselgrave, *Communicating Christ Cross-Culturally* (Grand Rapids, Michigan: Zondervan, 1991), p. 105.

concepts of supernatural powers interact with each other. The working assumption is that this interaction could be the way forward to criticise, reaffirm, rediscover, abandon or modify the mind-set of African Christians as well as the African culture and worldview with regard to supernatural powers. As the Lausanne Covenant noted, "the Gospel does not presuppose the superiority of any culture to another, but evaluates all cultures according to its own criteria of truth and righteousness, and insists on moral absolutes in every culture". However, "because man is God's creature, some of his culture is rich in beauty and goodness (Matthew 7: 11, Genesis 4: 21, 22). Because he is fallen, all of it is tainted with sin and some of it is demonic".[67] This equally applies to the African culture and worldview as some of its basic assumptions may threaten the faith and life of the African church. If the Pauline concept was meant to intensify the faith and life of a church that emerged from a context that believed in supernatural powers and this belief threatened the life and faith of this church, the concept might be the best point of entry linking the New Testament and the African context.

1:4. The Statement of the Problem and Basic Assumptions

The aim of this study is to re-visit the Pauline concept of supernatural powers, which appears in most of the epistles attributed to Paul, from an African worldview and to let it speak to the African context afresh. The purpose also forms the statement of the problem, that is, whether re-visiting the Pauline concept of supernatural powers from an African worldview could help sort out the pastoral problem facing the African church. This immediately begs the question of why should the Pauline concept speak to the African context afresh. The assumption is that most of the African believers do not pay attention to Paul's central teaching as to supernatural powers. This is surprising if there is an affinity between the New Testament context of production and the African context of reception, particularly with regard to beliefs in supernatural powers. The assumption is that the Pauline concept initially addressed a situation akin to that of the African context. However, Paul suggested different means of engaging the unseen forces that are understood to determine human existence than the one encouraged by the two similar contexts. So, why do the majority of Africans, who certainly read the Pauline concept, fail to pay attention to its teaching? It is assumed that this has been caused by a clash between the African and Western worldviews. The clash occurred because of the missionary legacy of denying and reducing the beliefs in spirits and the African response to it. Another assumption is that people's knowledge and interpretation of reality is largely shaped by their culture and worldview. The interpreter's worldview and the prevailing situation inevitably shape the interpretation of the Pauline concept of supernatural powers.[68] Yet the previous interpretations of the

---

[67] Cited in Hesselgrave, *Communicating Christ*, pp. 118-119.
[68] A. B. Ntreh, "Towards an African Biblical Hermeneutics" in *African Theological Journal* Vol. 19 No 3 (1988), p. 248 observes, "Theological and Biblical interpretations

Pauline concept of supernatural powers and the African beliefs in them have essentially been shaped by the Western worldview. The problem is that Western and African worldviews are different. The Western worldview is sceptical as to the existence of spirits but the African worldview is convinced of their existence. This implies that the previous interpretations do not meet the expectations of African Bible readers. This has grave implications if people are to find the meaning of a concept through interpretation.

A central teaching of the Pauline concept is the supremacy of Christ over supernatural powers. The assumption is that the aim of the Pauline concept was to help its original readers to exist as a social group. It was also intended to help them enjoy the fullness of life in Christ without fearing supernatural powers. It is also assumed that there are rich resources from the social sciences and the African context that may help us read the concept for an African audience. The African worldview can allow the theme of Christ's supremacy to supplant the belief in spiritual beings that purportedly determine human existence. If these assumptions can be proved to be true, then it is vital to re-visit the Pauline concept from an African worldview. It is critical to establish if the introduction of the Bible, and by extension the Pauline concept of supernatural powers in the African context, was clothed with the assumptions of the Western worldview and if owing to this, its African recipients pretend to believe its teaching while still clinging to traditional beliefs in supernatural powers. It is also necessary to find out if there is an affinity between the African context of reception and the context of production from which the Pauline concept emerged. It is significant to examine what the Pauline terms identified as supernatural powers meant within the context of production and what message the Pauline concept conveyed to its original readers. Since most of the previous interpretations approached the Pauline concept from the perspective of myth, it is critical to find if myth is a useful tool in dealing with supernatural powers. Finally, it will be essential to show how the Pauline concept can speak to the African context and if it can allow the theme of Christ's supremacy to displace the belief in, and the fear of supernatural powers.

1:5. Theoretical Framework and Method

Inculturation hermeneutics, an alternative mode of interpreting the Bible in the African context, is the theoretical framework of this study. This method seeks to consciously and overtly study biblical texts with regard to indigenous socio-

---

by westerners reveal that biblical interpretations have been likewise diverse and have been culturally determined". Similarly, David Burnett (*Unearthly Powers: A Christian Perspective on Primal and Folk Religion* (Eastbourne, Sussex: MARC, 1988), p. 22 notes, "our own understanding of the Bible is shaped by our particular historical and cultural context. Western readers, for example, are often oblivious to certain portions of the Bible merely because they are irrelevant to their own life experience... On the other hand, people from primal societies would already find these passages particularly relevant" political/economic and religio-cultural context. Rather than being universal it is contextual, and rightly so, since biblical texts are best interpreted within a given context. It is therefore related to contextualisation and it holds two underlying principles. The first induces believers to internalise biblical teachings and live by them (inculturation). This allows believers to apply biblical teachings to their socio-political/economic and religio-cultural background, challenging their fears and aspirations (contextualisation). The concern is to actualise "the theological meaning of the text in today's context so as to forge integration between faith and life, and to engender commitment to personal and social transformation".[69] The second principle seeks to attain the meaning of a text through the interaction between the text in its context and the interpreter in his/her context.[70] The concern is not only to render the social-cultural context the subject of interpretation but also to examine the context in which the texts were originally written and read/heard. So it analyses the text within the context of the literary genre and the context of reception. After that it correlates these contexts in an attempt to open up the meaning of the text. The correlation of these contexts, which West explains with epithets, 'behind the text' 'in the text', and 'in front of the text',[71] is crucial to the completion of the hermeneutical process. The inculturation framework and method therefore gives equal value to the three contexts and also to the interpreter.

Inculturation augments the historical and literary methods that are mainly attracted to the world that produced the text and the text respectively. It does this by seeking to answer new and real life questions arising from the context of reception after reading the Bible. It is overwhelmingly likely that the aforesaid methods paid less interest to such questions. Inculturation uses resources from people's culture and life experience as complementary to conventional critical tools of biblical exegesis. It uses different methods as servants not as masters simultaneously or separately to further its aim. It is now clear that its aim is to facilitate communication of the biblical message within a given context, and to evolve a clear understanding of biblical texts and concepts so as to enhance a Christian life that is contextual and biblical. To accomplish this aim, historical criticism is used to examine the context of production and social-scientific criticism is used to analyse the context of reception. As a result, inculturation hermeneutics is interdisciplinary. It demands an intercultural hermeneutical method that is informed by the perspectives and concerns of ordinary readers. It is a new model for cross-cultural hermeneutic that most likely makes pastoral concerns the heart of theology. Yet cross-cultural communications are at the same time confusing and captivating.

---

[69] J. S. Ukpong, "Development in Biblical Interpretation in Africa: Historical and Hermeneutical Directions" in Gerald O. West and Musa W. Dube (eds.), *The Bible in Africa: Transactions, Trajectories and Trends* (Leiden: Brill, 2000), p. 24.
[70] See Ukpong, "Development in Biblical Interpretation in Africa", pp. 24-25.
[71] Gerald West, *Biblical Hermeneutics of Liberation* (Pietermaritzburg: Cluster, Maryknoll, New York: Orbis books, 1991), pp. 131-155; Gerald West, *Contextual Bible Study* (Pietermaritzburg: Cluster 1993), pp. 27-50.

1:6. The Ambiguity of Cross-cultural Communications

Rohrbaugh rightly notes that a cross-cultural reading of the Bible is inescapable since the Bible is a document initially written for Mediterranean readers and it presupposes cultural resources and a worldview open to a reader socialized in the Mediterranean world. For all non-Mediterranean people, reading the Bible is a cross-cultural interaction.[72] However, Cross-cultural communication could be tricky due to the regrettable trend of judging another culture through the grids of one's own culture, despite a culture's implicit and explicit prejudices[73]. Biblical themes and concepts also have meaning but the conceived meaning in one culture may not agree with the meaning in another. Davies convincingly exposes the problem met when trying to verify the meaning of a concept once it is realised that cultures hold different notions, social recognition and validation of what ideas and values are worth. He avers that any term used cross-culturally must have general features, which admit comparison while allowing specific variation.[74]

The issue is how to use and to make a term viable in a cross-cultural context. This may be extremely elusive if people perceive and interpret reality and daily life experience in their world through language and patterns of communication provided by their worldview. It could also be specifically elusive if meaning is sought in relation to the external route that religious behaviour takes. Weber observes, "External courses of religious behaviour are so diverse that an understanding of this behaviour can only be achieved from the viewpoint of the subjective experience, ideas, and purposes of the individual concerned".[75] Interpreters too do not approach the Bible with an empty mind. They bring insights from their culture and worldview, which encase the interpretative task with possible bias. This, as Davies insists, may subject religious phenomena to a variety of "interpretations at a number of different levels of analysis".[76] Chances are that biblical texts would suggest divergent ideas to different peoples entailing diverse social consequences if the meaning of a text depends on what the interpreter wants to know. This is indeed walking on a landmine as it seemingly portrays the hermeneutical task as parochial, constrained and subjective.

yet cross-cultural communication may perhaps make durable connections of loose ends. The story of Israel in exile could serve as an illustration. During this period, Israel came into contact with Ancient Near East religious articulations, such as the creation narratives. This cross-cultural encounter of religious beliefs

---

[72] Richard L. Rohrbaugh (ed.), *The Social Science and New Testament Interpretation* (Peabody, Massachusetts: Hendrickson Publishers, 1996), p. 1.

[73] See Paul Strelan, *Paul, Artemis and the Jews in Ephesus* (Berlin: Walter de Gruyter 1996), p. 25.

[74] Douglas James Davies, *Meaning and Salvation in Religious Studies* (Leiden: Brill 1984), p. 63.

[75] Max Weber, *The Sociology of Religion* (Trans Ephraim Fischoff; London: Methuen & Co Ltd 1965), p. 1.

[76] Davies, *Meaning and Salvation*, p. 62

moved the Jews to re-work their theology as the people of God, the creator of everything that is. They traced the history of Abraham the father of their nation to God who created the first human, Adam. The creation itself was seen as having happened through the Word and the Wisdom of God, which were recognized as God's agent in creation.[77] Therefore, as Kee notes, "the cultural factor that led to this development is probably the influence of the Egyptian goddess Maat as the divine instrument of creation and of the maintenance of order within the creation".[78] If this is correct, the Jewish theology of creation matured only after a cross-cultural interaction. It is not only the theology of creation that matured through a cross-cultural interaction but also other theological themes. Worth mentioning is the doctrine of evil and suffering within the wider context of theodicy. Kee once again notes, "it is almost certain under Iranian influence, however, that a real ethical dualism appears, according to which God's chief adversary, Satan, sets out to thwart the divine purpose".[79] Though it may be erroneous to stress dualism when God's power basically surpasses that of Satan, nevertheless, the responsibility for evil and suffering was associated with Satan and his host of darkness. In that case, a cross-cultural reading of the Bible must not be underrated because some theological themes that may be constructed from the Bible are basically cross-cultural.

Generally, a cross-cultural reading of the Bible could be complicated, albeit desirable and inevitable as it may not only enrich the hermeneutical discourse but also defuse the explosive situation. It could be "a great aid in avoiding the erection of graven images and theological idols in the Northern hemisphere or the Southern".[80] Perhaps a cross-cultural approach could help interpreters to develop critical awareness of their own cultural milieu. This may enable them to see their own conventions as a potential stumbling block. Listening to what other cultures say about supernatural powers and critically assessing one's culture may lessen the problems of cross-cultural communication. This may inspire dependable theological, exegetical and hermeneutical debates within the church. A cross-cultural hermeneutics based on an inculturation framework and method is thus necessary in the modern world where the reading of the Pauline concept is largely shaped by culture and worldview.

1:7. Scope and Delimitation

The second chapter examines the history of the problem of supernatural powers in African Christianity. Assuming that the problem survives due to a collision

---

[77] Helmer Ringgren, *Word and Wisdom: Studies in the Hypostatization of Divine Qualities in the Ancient Near East* (Lund: H. Ohlsson, 1947), pp. 45-49; Gerhard von Rad, *Wisdom in Israel* (Nashville, Tennessee: Abingdon Press, 1972), p. 73.
[78] Howard Clark Kee, *Christian Origin in Sociological Perspectives* (London: SCM Press 1980), p. 35.
[79] Kee, *Christian Origin*, p. 36.
[80] Harvie M. Conn, "Contextualisation: A New Dimension for Cross-cultural Hermeneutic" in *Evangelical Missions Quarterly* 14 (1978), p. 46.

Introduction

between two different worldviews, the chapter attempts to make the African and the Western worldview explain themselves to each other. This includes a critique of both worldviews, albeit not polarizing them or judging one as better than the other. The expected conclusion is that worldviews can prejudice the hermeneutical discourse. Chapter three explains the background of the African context so as to be familiar with the context wherein the Pauline concept is being re-visited. This is limited to beliefs, rituals and practices through which human beings seek to control or communicate with supernatural powers and the different readings credited to the phenomena attributed to supernatural powers. The chapter evaluates anthropological readings of African belief in supernatural powers and the related rituals and practices of domestication and exorcism of spirits, divination and magic. It also includes a critical appraisal of the views sanctioned by the phenomenologist of religion who insist on the postulate of affinity between the African worldview and the Bible.

The fourth chapter looks at the context of production from which the Pauline concept of supernatural powers emerged. It is limited to Jewish and Graeco-Roman beliefs, rituals and practices as to supernatural powers. It shows that Jewish and Graeco-Roman beliefs differed but had points of intersection and interaction. It also shows that Graeco-Roman views on supernatural powers were not identical. While the masses had fixated belief in gods, demons and spirits, the approach of the elite was antagonistic and agnostic. Some believed in the existence of supernatural powers but others denied they existed and that they were involved with human affairs. The fifth chapter examines the Pauline terminology and conceptual framework within its first century CE milieu. This involves an exegetical treatise on terms and phrases identified as supernatural powers and an investigation on what background(s) may have influenced Paul's understanding of supernatural powers. Chapter six assesses previous readings that largely favour demythologisation. It shows that the quest to demythologise is complicated by the problems of myth. It also shows that even if metaphor has its own problems, it is better placed to handle the subject of supernatural powers than myth. Demythologisation therefore is unsuitable for reading the Pauline concept within the background of and for the African context and ought to be thrown out with myth. Rather than looking at all previous interpretations, the chapter interacts with selected scholars who believe Paul was involved in demythologisation. Finally, the seventh chapter concludes with an attempt to discern a theology of supernatural powers for the African church, which is based on the findings of the preceding chapters. This chapter invites the African church to underline the supremacy of Christ and to rely on cultural resources and/or tools in explaining Christ's supremacy. It also challenges the African church to recognise other dimensions of supernatural powers, specifically because of the positive implications of the metaphorical tension of the verb *to be*, discussed in chapter six.

Scholars classify the Pauline epistles that contain the concept of supernatural powers, between the disputed and undisputed, giving room for divergent views on authorship. But engaging in that debate as important as it is may widen the scope of this study, which time and space dictate against. The rationale for the study allows us to bypass the issue of authorship. What matters most is not the author but the concept that seems to fortify and intensify the life and faith of believers within the united body of Christ. We recognise the divergent views about authorship[81] but adopt the traditional position that regards all epistles as Pauline.[82] The position of this study is that the distinction between the personal and impersonal may have not been the intention of Paul and his first century CE readers. The distinction may have had no clear meaning perhaps because the so-called impersonal and personal forces could bring about similar religious experiences, which people in the African context of reception and in the context of production access(ed) only by some sort of personification or embodiment. It could be that the so-called personal or impersonal point to the same reality. As a result, the Pauline concept most likely signifies the interlocking of personal and impersonal forces. The result of this interlocking is only discernible in tropes and figures since it may sometimes defy a sole description, spiritual or material. This study therefore does not wish to debate whether supernatural powers are personal spiritual beings or impersonal material aspects of the structures of human existence. It will be noted, however, that the personal aspect of supernatural powers may have played a central role given that impersonal and abstract qualities could be personified.

---

[81] See F. C. Synge, *Philippians and Colossians,* TBC (London: SCM, 1951), pp. 51-57.

[82] See Clinton E. Arnold, *The Colossian Syncretism: The Interface Between Christianity and Folk Belief at Colossae*, WUNT 77 (Tübingen: J. C. B. Mohr [Paul Siebeck] 1995), p. 7 especially the list of scholars who considers Colossians as penned by Paul in footnote 10; Gordon D. Fee, *God's Empowering Presence: The Holy Spirit in the Letters of Paul* (Peabody, Massachusetts: Hendrickson, 1994), pp. 659-660; Ralph P. Martin, *Colossians: The Church's Lord and Christian's Liberty* (Exeter: The Paternoster Press, 1972), pp. 160-164. For a summary of the authorship debate on Ephesians and Colossians and accompanying bibliography, see Guthrie *New Testament Introduction* (Leicester: Apollos, 1990), pp. 496-528; 572-577.

CHAPTER 2

A Collision of Two Worldviews: The History and Legacy of the Problem of Supernatural Powers in Africa

2:1. Introduction

This chapter demonstrates the differences between the African and Western worldviews and the distinct lenses by which these worldviews provide for their people to perceive reality. But the different lenses provided by the tow different worldviews deepen the problem of supernatural powers in the African context. The early missionaries who introduced the Bible in Africa and the African recipients did not share a similar worldview and they did not perceive reality through a similar lens. The missionaries perceived reality through a lens shaped by the Western intellectual worldview, which habitually denies the real existence of supernatural powers. The Africans perceived reality through a lens produced by the African primal worldview, which typically grants supernatural powers real existence. The majority of Africans not only agree to the existence of supernatural powers but also allow them to influence human existence. They have always given supernatural powers a phobic allegiance, which persists despite the rapid growth of Christianity and the frequent use of the Bible. Documented evidence reveals that many African Christians covertly observe traditional beliefs, rituals and practices linked to supernatural powers. Publicly, they repudiate these beliefs, rituals and practices so as to appear as if they are orientated to the official position of the church. Such Christians live between two worlds, probably due to the clash between the Western and African worldviews. This chapter explains and evaluates the missionary legacy and the African response to it, critically appraising African and Western worldviews.

2:2. The Missionary Legacy and the African Response

i. Condemnation of African Culture and Worldview

During the nineteenth century, a number of missionary movements sought to evangelise the world within a concise period.¹ It seems that some missionaries agreed with the philosophy of European enlightenment that assumed European culture was superior to other world cultures. As a result, Western missionaries regarded African culture and worldview as inferior. Several scholars have cited diverse but somehow related factors that led to the assumption that the Western culture was superior to other cultures. Davies claims that this attitude may be traced back to Durkheim's classic work on the nature of primitive religion that influenced later traditions in this area. He argues that the problem is one of anthropological hermeneutics and the reductionism that occurs in the process of analysis and interpretation. He persuasively insists that the power of systematising western academic traditions tends to impress itself upon the analysis of other cultures despite the familiar problem of ethnocentricity and the recognized need to understand religious notions in terms apposite to them.² Hiebert notes that the rise of colonialism, the theory of cultural evolution and the triumph of science added to the belief in the superiority of Western cultures.³ Bediako convincingly illustrates that the Great Chain of Being and the Four Stages Theory strengthened the belief in European supremacy and the abasement of Africans to a lower level of existence. The Great Chain of Being was based on the principles of plenitude, continuity and gradation originally propounded by Plato and Aristotle. This theory arranged the creation hierarchically and so it situated the Africans between the white human race and the highest species of animals. The Four Stage Theory alleged that all societies developed through successive stages based on different modes of survival. The first stage was that of hunters, then that of shepherds and of agriculture respectively. The fourth and most developed stage was that of commerce. Africans were still in the stage of hunters and slowly moving to the stage of

---

[1] Samuel Ling, in his article, "An Independent, Pioneering Spirit: Christian Individualism West and East" in http://www2.ccim.org/~reformata/Individualism.htm, accessed on 23.04.04, notes, "Missionaries were the fruit of revival, especially those revivals in the 1830s and 1860s. They had a strong sense of personal sacrifice for the sake of the gospel, and an independent spirit to go where Christ had not been named". The emphasis on missionary enterprises abroad was certainly tied to the rising influence of Pre-millennialism among the missionary movements and potential missionaries. Samuel J. Stoesz, *Sanctification: An Alliance Distinctive* (Camp Hill: Christian Publications, 1992), p. 43 notes that the Keswick movement took upon a distinctly dispensational flavour by the turn of the 19th century owing to the great focus on the imminent return of Christ. The pre-millennial element of Christ's imminent return gave the missionary movement a strong impulse to overseas missions. It was this sense of imminence that propelled the Keswick movement and perhaps other missionary societies to send abroad those who had responded to missionary call during conventions.
[2] Douglas James Davies, *Meaning and Salvation in Religious Studies* (Leiden: Brill, 1984), p. 69.
[3] Paul G. Hiebert, *Anthropological Reflections on Missiological Issues* (Grand Rapids, Michigan: Baker Books, 1994), pp.76-80.

shepherds.⁴ The Africans were regarded to be lesser than Europeans and slightly higher than apes. They were members of a somewhat disconnected species, more or less halfway between Europeans and orang-utans.⁵ Such unscientific ideas influenced the judgement of theologians and philosophers to rate the African people as primitive and backward and to rate the white people as the pure and super race. This attitude is clearly spelt out in the works of the eminent Scottish philosopher David Hume.

> I am apt to suspect the Negroes, and in general all other species of men (for there are four or five different kinds) to be naturally inferior to the whites. There never was a civilised nation of any other complexion than white, nor even any individual eminent either in action or speculation. No ingenious manufactures amongst them, no arts, no sciences.... Such a uniform and constant difference could not happen, in so many countries and ages, if nature had not made an original distinction betwixt these breeds of men.⁶

It is not surprising therefore that the missionaries did not appreciate the African religious past, which they demonised. According to their judgment, such a background could not offer any preparatory foundation for reading the Bible and appreciating biblical faith.

The Edinburgh 1910 World Missionary Conference, which took place during the high-colonial period in Africa, seems to have welcomed the idea that Africans stood on "a low stage of human development". This, as most missionaries who attended the conference supposed, was an "intellectual hindrance" to Christianity.⁷ The Conference based its conclusion on the reports from the missionaries and on the work of anthropologist E. B Tylor, who had concluded that the religion of primal societies, such as in Africa, was animism. Tylor wanted to understand the difference between European and animistic people's thoughts. Under the term 'animism', he sought to probe the doctrine of spiritual beings representing the core of spiritualistic as opposed to materialistic philosophy.⁸ The rationale behind his study was the evolution theory, which held that "humankind was in a process of development from primitive to

---

⁴ Gillian M. Bediako, *Primal Religions and the Bible*. (Sheffield: Sheffield Academic Press, 1997), pp. 49-57.
⁵ Tudor Parfitt, *The Lost Tribes of Israel* (London: Weidenfeld & Nicolson, 2002), p. 176; A. D. Roberts (ed.), *The Cambridge History of Africa c 1790 – c 1870* vol. 5 (Cambridge: Cambridge University Press, 1986), p. 474; E. Long, *The History of Jamaica* vol. 2 (London: Frank Cass & Co, 1774), pp. 353-356.
⁶ David Hume, *Essays: Moral, Political and Literary*, 2 vols edited with preliminary dissertation and notes by T. H. Green and T. H. Grose (London: Longmans, Green & Co, 1875), vol. 1 p. 252.
⁷ World Missionary Conference 1910: *Report of Commission IV: The Missionary Message in Relation to non-Christian Religions* (Edinburgh & London: Oliphant, Anderson & Ferrier, 1910), p. 13.
⁸ E. B. Tylor, *Primitive Culture* (London: John Murray, 1871), vol. 1 p. 425-6.

civilised; from a belief in magic and religion to an understanding of science".[9] The missionaries accepted the cultural evolution theory. This led them to catalogue the African culture as primitive, animistic and uncivilized.[10] As a result, the Edinburgh 1910 Missionary Conference Commission IV's report depicted the so-called animistic people as "ignorant, apathetic, indolent and indifferent", who due to their low intellectual state had but little sense of natural causation. They were also "a dark degraded company of pagans" who practised the "lowest form of heathenism"[11] based on the belief in the existence of spirits. On the strength of correspondence from missionaries, the report insisted that there was no religion in a belief system that was "simply heathenism".[12] The report also reveals that many missionaries denied the presence of any religious help or consolation in "animistic beliefs and rites".[13] While some missionaries held that "there is a modicum of truth in all religious systems", the general attitude was that there was no religious content in animism.[14] In that case, the so-called animism was not a religious system but a set of superstitions and superstitious observances.[15] Therefore, according to the report, several missionaries felt that they were bringing the Gospel of Jesus Christ to "dirty, degraded fellow-members of the human race". However, the Africans gave the missionaries an "outward obedience" with no respect and without opening their hearts to them.[16] Imasogie observes that Africans could not admit the denial or arrogant condemnation of their worldview as a valid solution to the problem of spirits and the spirit world.[17]

Most of the missionaries denied "the existence of any point of contact or preparation for Christianity", alleging that there was no religious content in animism since it lacked a religious vocabulary.[18] Other missionaries, who at least allowed some points of contact, hesitated to apply the term "preparation for Christianity" to the African culture, religion and worldview. In areas where they recognised some points of contact, it was concluded that these had no influence. Such contacts could not prepare the reception of the biblical message because they meant nothing to the African religious life, which was based on the fear of spirits.[19] Commission IV acknowledged that the entire African culture, religion and worldview were absolutely not *praeparatio evangelica* but demonic and immoral. The correspondence of most missionaries indicated that

---

[9] Burnett, *Unearthly Powers*, p. 15.
[10] Hiebert, *Anthropological Reflections*, pp. 77-8.
[11] *The Missionary message*, pp. 14, 22, 35.
[12] *The Missionary message*, p. 6.
[13] *The Missionary message*, p. 10.
[14] *The Missionary message*, p. 22.
[15] *The Missionary message*, pp. 8, 11, 16.
[16] *The Missionary message*, p. 22.
[17] Osadolor Imasogie, *Guidelines for Christian Theology in Africa* (Achimota, Ghana: African Christian Press, 1993), pp. 81-2.
[18] *The Missionary message*, p. 24.
[19] *The Missionary message*, pp. 25, 27.

a very low moral awareness existed in African religion, culture and worldview. There was no sense of sin and conscience seemed hardly to exist.[20] Immorality was a virtue and the entire belief system was evil and base. Some missionaries noted a rudimentary moral sense and a dim awareness of sin.[21] The Conference, however, concluded that there never existed any "preparation for Christianity" or "religious content in Animism".[22] The idea was that African religion, culture and worldview represented "the religious belief of more or less backward and degraded people".[23] As Kenyatta notes, "as far as religion was concerned the African was a clean slate on which anything could be written".[24]

The missionaries' principal aim was first to civilise the Africans so that they may be easily Christianised. The native world was to be reconstructed, first and foremost, in the name of European civilisation and then in the name of God. A. F. Walls maintains that the missionaries wanted the church in Africa to look like the English parish churches in villages called Leicester, or Gloucester, or Kent, or Sussex, or Wilberforce, or Bathurst, or Waterloo, or Wellington.[25] The missionaries, it seems, accepted the indispensable link between civilization, commerce and Christianity. This, popularly known as the three Cs, was the legacy of pre-colonial missionaries, and it is rightly associated with David Livingstone and Thomas Buxton. It was meant to counter the slave trade and slavery in Africa; hence, according to Livingstone, the cure of slave trade lay in civilisation, commerce and Christianity in that order[26]. But this, as Livingstone

---

[20] C. Cagnolo, *The Akikuyu* (Nyeri: The Mission Printing School, 1933), pp. 253-257 cites Rev. P. Perlo, the earliest Consolata missionary among the Gĩkũyũ people, who after explaining the extreme depravity of their morality and of the whole culture asked, "how could morals be found among this people who in their age-long abandonment have become so corrupt as to raise practice openly immoral to be a social institution". Perlo thus concluded "in short, every moral principle in which our civilization glories and which our religion commands is here, at least in practice, simply reversed in its terms: and that is enough to argue that whatever inference is drawn in this connection it must always confront us with a state of things essentially deplorable, barbarous, inhuman" So Cagnolo describes Rev. Perlo as one who had the opportunity of witnessing "in its crude reality the atrocious and pitiful conditions of the Akikuyu". But Western civilisation was the canon to judge morality.

[21] *The Missionary message*, pp. 12-3, 23, 27.

[22] *The Missionary message*, p. 24.

[23] W. H. T. Gairdner, *Edinburgh 1910: An Account and Interpretation of the World Missionary Conference* (London: Oliphant, Anderson & Ferrier, 1910), p. 139.

[24] Jomo Kenyatta, *Facing Mount Kenya* (London: Secker & Warburg, 1938), p. 269.

[25] A. F. Walls, *The Missionary Movement in Christian History: Studies in the Transmission of Faith* (Maryknoll, New York: Orbis Books, 1996), p. 103.

[26] Livingstone favoured the indirect method of "spreading better principles" than by the direct seeking after conversion. His aim was to fuse "Commerce and Christianity". In his own words, he stated that the duties of the missionary "are not so contracted as those whose ideal is a dumpty sort of man with a Bible under his arm" and proposed that "if we can introduce a system of free labour into Africa, it will exercise a decisive influence on slavery the world over" (cited in Bengt G. M. Sundkler, *The World of Missions*

believed, could only happen if Britain colonised Africa. However, his well-intentioned call for colonialism as an antidote to the horrors of slavery paved the way for colonialism and the era of the colonial missionary represented by the 1910 Edinburgh Missionary Conference.

The missionaries of the high-colonial era (1900s-1960s) took over the noble pre-colonial missionaries' three Cs approach in their effort to convert Africans to Christianity. During this time, missionaries cooperated with colonial officers. As A. F. Walls notes, "the missions, irrespective of their national origin, became part of the colonial state... When power manifestly lay with Whites, there was little point in distinguishing one set of White people from another".[27] The missionaries' assumption that their nationality was crucial in relation to the colonial government was, in fact, a very negative appraisal of their status. This made them change their position regarding secular affairs and as the missionaries tended to conform to the demands of colonial officials, Africans recognised the domination by Europeans as synonymous with the spread of the Gospel. Commenting on the relations of C.M.S missionaries with the Kaguru people of Tanzania, Beidelmann notes,

> Many C.M.S. missionaries of this period (1891–1961) assumed that their nationality was a crucial issue for them; but, ironically, this very negative appraisal of their status proved more significant... The C.M.S. had to follow the secularizing trends, despite misgivings that these might betray the ideals associated with the previous years of heroic evangelism.[28]

(London: Lutterworth Press, 1965), p. 151. Thomas Buxton, *The African Slave Trade and Its Remedy* (London: Murray, 1839–40), p. 511 proposed the way to strangle slave trade was by the development of agriculture. The missionary and schoolmaster, the plough and the spade were to go together for agriculture to flourish. This would finally open the avenues for legitimate commerce and civilisation, which would advance as the natural effect and Christianity would operate as the direct cause of this happy change. But it should not be assumed the three Cs was the favourite of all and sundry during the pre-colonial era. In 1897, Rev. Isaac Taylor announced to a British audience that Christianity had failed not only to civilise the "savage, barbarous Africans", but also commerce had extended "drunkenness and vice and the degradation of the [African] people" (cited in Thomas Prasch, "Which God for Africa: The Islamic-Christian Debate in Late Victorian England" in *Victorian Studies* 22 (1989), p. 51. See also Jessica Powers, *Christianity vs. Islam: A 19th Century Debate*, 2000 available at http://www.islamfortoday.com/africadebate.htm, accessed on 22.06.04.

[27] A. F. Walls, *The Cross-Cultural Process in Christian History* (Maryknoll, New York: Orbis Books/Edinburgh: T & T Clark, 2002), p. 103. Walls' observation is validated by a saying, which the Gĩkũyũ of Kenya coined during the colonial era with regard to the Roman Catholic missionary priests and the Colonial officials. The saying goes, "Gũtirĩ Mũthũngũ na Mũbiĩa (which literally mean, there is no distinction between a Roman Catholic priest and a Colonial Administrator).

[28] T. O. Beidelmann, *Colonial Evangelism: A Socio-Historical Study of an East African Mission at the Grassroots* (Bloomington: Indiana University Press, 1982), p. 72.

Even so, it would be a distortion of facts to claim that all missionaries during the colonial period agreed that Christianity, commerce and civilisation were inseparable. As noted above, even during the pre-colonial missionary era not all and sundry saw the three Cs as relevant to the spread of Christianity[29]. Some missionaries saw their main task as preaching, teaching and conversion, though they found their hours and days taken up by tending gardens that supplied them with food and taking care of the sick that came to their door[30]. That some missionaries saw their main task as preaching the Gospel so as to convert Africans implies that not all missionaries regarded commerce and civilisation as the guide to Christianity. In fact, missionaries during the colonial era were divided over the issue of evangelism and social responsibility. Beidelmann observes,

> The most observant missionaries recognized serious dangers in the growing endorsement of social services... Their fears were rooted in questions about the relations between the missions and other aspects of society. Some missionaries saw the church as properly concerned with spiritual matters; others observed that all social life, from religion to agriculture is of one piece... but many C.M.S thought that religion should exclude many other aspects of everyday life... The C.M.S opposed development of "non-religious" services, however practical or humanitarian, if they did not directly bear on evangelism.[31]

Loram also noted the difficulties the missionaries faced in relation to the three Cs, though they could not avoid it. "How difficult this is every experienced missionary can tell. To attempt to co-operate with an evil-living official or with a rapacious trading company is indeed hard, and yet there is no other way to achieve the adjustment prescribed by such authorities".[32] Some missionaries were thus suspicious of anything, commerce and civilisation included, that could distract their efforts from evangelism. As evangelicals, some C.M.S missionaries were deeply suspicious of all materialistic and secular influence from the colonial government and business.[33] But this created a problem while trying to avoid another because for the Africans, there was nothing material or secular, according to missionary definitions, as everything was perceived through the spiritual lens.

According to Sundkler, Christian missions during the colonial era appeared

---

[29] See footnote 26 above.
[30] See "A New Generation of Missionaries" in *African Christianity: A History of the Christian Church in Africa*, in http://www.bethel.edu/~letnie/AfricanChristianity/SSA-ColonialProtestants.html, accessed 23.06.04.
[31] Beidelmann, *Colonial Evangelism*, p. 119. See also H. Morris, "The Relations of Missions to Government" in *Church Missionary Review*, 62 (1911), pp. 129-136.
[32] C. T. Loram,. "Education in Africa" in *Church Missionary Review*, 74 (1923), p. 159.
[33] Beidelmann, *Colonial Evangelism*, pp. 121-123.

largely to be a religious auxiliary of political, economic and cultural expansion of the West. Nevertheless, the missionaries knew they had been sent for the sake of the kingdom, which belongs not to this world. But the land of birth—England, Scotland, Holland, Germany, France, America and Scandinavia—had inevitably left its traces upon them. They took with them many of their countries' ideals to the mission field.[34] As a result, even if converting Africans to Christianity was the missionaries' principal aim; it could not happen until the Africans were removed from their long-established ethical and moral values and belief systems. This aimed at conforming them to the Victorian Christian morality and civilisation, which could not occur without Western education. It seems that Buxton and Livingstone's concept of three Cs was taken beyond what it was originally intended to accomplish. Commenting on a chapter about Africans, "The Civilising Work of Missions among the Child-Race of the Empire" in a missionary publication, *Our Empire's Debt to Missions* of 1924, Walls notes,

> The implication is clear: child races needed a firm, patient tutor. Nothing could indicate how far both missions and missionary language had travelled since the days of Buxton and Livingstone. Much as they believed in what they called "civilisation", that generation never saw Africans as children".[35]

The African people, having been degraded to an inferior status, and subsequently having been regarded as children, were projected as *tabula rasa*; an empty mind that needed imprinting and improvement using Western education. The missionary founded church was surely nurtured and conditioned in such a mind-set. John Pobee notes that all the historical churches applied the doctrine of *tabula rasa*, that is, there is nothing in the non-Christian culture on which missionaries can build. Every aspect of traditional non-Christian culture had to be destroyed before Christianity could build up.[36] Now the problem is that African

> Churches have tended to avoid the question and have presented the Gospel as though it was concerned with an entirely different compartment of life, unrelated to traditional religious piety. As a result many of our people are uncertain about how Jesus of the church's preaching saves them from the terrors and fears, which they explain in their traditional worldview.[37]

This has left several African Christians betwixt and between, simultaneously

---

[34] Sundkler, *The World of Missions,* p. 121.
[35] Walls, *The Cross-Cultural Process,* p. 98.
[36] J. N. Pobee, "Political Theology in the African Context", in *Africa Theological Journal* 11 (1982), pp. 168-172.
[37] Kwame Bediako, *Jesus in an African Culture: A Ghanaian Perspective* (Accra: Asempa publishers, (1990), p. 12.

clinging to both the Christian faith and traditional religiosity. The problem is that such Christians, by deed if not by word, regard Christ as unable to redeem them from the phenomena attributed to supernatural powers. One sad result of this is that the African church has not earnestly developed her own identity and she has frequently been burdened with pastoral problems, especially those linked with beliefs, rituals and practices as to supernatural powers.[38]

As Hiebert comments, missionaries do not enter cultural vacuums since they go to people who have their own customs, beliefs and practices with regard to supernatural powers. But the missionaries believed that all the phenomena attributed to supernatural powers were primitive. When the Africans spoke of the fear of evil spirits, the missionaries denied their existence and failed to claim Christ's power over them.[39] As a result, many Africans regarded Christ as powerless in meeting their daily needs or developed a dual religious heritage. They perhaps assumed that Christ had little or nothing to say to their deepest concerns and was only partially relevant to the fundamental issues of life. The Africans held that in denying the existence of supernatural powers the religious conscience of Christianity had no place for them. At first, these assumptions hindered conversion since the Bible was seen as a tool for spreading European interests and Christianity was regarded a white man's religion. The Bible was regarded as an imperialist tool meant to deprive them of their culture and land. The Africans' encounter with the Bible is retold with the words, "when the white man came to our country he had the Bible and we had the land. The white man said, 'let us pray'. After the prayer, the white man had the land and we had

---

[38] J. S. Mbiti, "Theological Impotence and the Universality of the Church" in Gerald H. Anderson and Thomas F. Stransky *Mission Trends*, 3: *Third World Theologies* (Grand Rapids, Michigan: Eerdmans, 1976), p. 8 notes that traditional theology is embarrassingly impotent in the face of human questions in the churches of Africa, Latin America, parts of Asia and the South Pacific. He laments that theologians are incapacitated by European education from dealing with supernatural powers.

[39] Hiebert, *Anthropological Reflections,* pp. 75, 197. But, not all missionaries who failed to proclaim the supremacy of Christ over supernatural powers in Africa. A pre-colonial missionary in Uganda, Alexander. M. Mackay had a fervent zeal to convince the Baganda king Mutesa and his chiefs to break down their superstitions and receive the word of God as their guide. He writes, "I had my Bible in my hand, and had carefully considered how I might show from the scriptures the evil of dealing with familiar spirits (Alexander M. Mackay, *The Story of A.M. Mackay—Pioneer Missionary of the C.M.S to Uganda—Told by His Sister* (London: Hodder & Stoughton, 1878), p. 147. Responding to Kabaka (the royal title of Baganda kings) Mutesa's explanation that *lubare* was the spirit that preserved the remains of the ancestors and the guardian of that spirit was Mukasa (the name of the person who was regarded as the spirit-medium or diviner) Mackay said that spirits or mediums do not exist and those who said they possessed familiar spirits were only liars (Mackay, *Pioneer Missionary,* p. 149). In 1914, E. Price preached at the very centre of M'Bona shrine about the great sacrifice of Christ for the world and God's love for mankind. (E. Price, "The Defeat of M'Bona, the Rain Chief" in *The South African Pioneer* XXIX (1916), p. 82.

the Bible".[40] The implication of this saying is that the Bible now belongs to Africans, though this is debatable.

The Africans' response to the biblical message as missionaries preached it was gradual and multifaceted. It began with complete resistance, even if there were a few cases of acceptance. As Smith notes, the indigenous religion and customs gave little immediate prospect of positive response to Christian preaching. The Africans were prepared to accept the worth of the Gospel but they also rejected a message that cut across their way of life so severely. Their imprecise attitude to the Gospel and their evasion of its demands arose from the nature of those demands, which the missionaries propagated with the call to break with traditional clan and family ties. Many would have liked to accept the teaching of the missionaries but the claims of ancestral spirits and the duties and fidelity to them were too strong.[41] Afterwards, the Africans accepted the Gospel but the response of the majority was betwixt and between. As will be shown below, one foot was in the traditional way of life while the other was in the new way of life the missionaries were introducing. It then appears that there was little success in deterring African converts from regressing to traditional ways of dealing with what they experienced and interpreted as pressure, constraints and assaults attributed to supernatural powers.

Nowadays at the popular level, many Africans continue to deal with concerns of life in the traditional ways. The fear of spirits is felt across the continent. The missionary founded churches officially censure beliefs, rituals and practices linked to supernatural powers. Nonetheless, Christianity in Africa is increasingly nuanced as some Christians read the Bible and worship in indigenous ways. They respond to problems they attribute to supernatural powers using a framework that reveals continuity with the traditional mindset.[42] These African Christians respond to Western Christianity by disconnecting themselves from the missionary founded churches.[43] There are several religious groups, which claim to be restoring what the Western form of Christianity has lost, that is, the power of the Holy Spirit.[44] These groups regard the Western

---

[40] T. Mofokeng, "Black Christians, the Bible and Liberation" in *Journal of Black Theology* 2 (1988), p. 34. I remember these words being used by school children to ridicule us, we who followed the 'church of the white man' (meaning the Anglican church – which the colonists and settlers, i.e. European farmers who had occupied the African land attended) as opposed to them, who followed the church of the African (meaning the African Independent Church – which supported the Kenya Land and Freedom fighters Army, aka Mau Mau).

[41] Smith, N., *The Presbyterian Church of Ghana, 1835-1960* (Accra, Ghana University Press, 1966), pp. 47, 92, 10.

[42] See A. M. Howell, *The Religious Itinerary of a Ghanaian People: The Kasena and the Christian Gospel* (Frankfurt am Main: Peter Lang, 1997), p. 166-189.

[43] See Bengt G. M. Sundkler, *Bantu Prophets in South Africa* (London: Oxford University Press, 1961) p. 168-179.

[44] See Nahason Ndung'u, "The Role of the Bible in the Rise of the African Instituted Churches: The Case of the Akurinu Churches in Kenya" in Gerald O. West and Musa

form of Christianity as academic and book centred, lacking the power to deal with the real issues of life. They purportedly depend on the power of the Holy Spirit to deal with the problems and fears they attribute to supernatural powers. Nevertheless, these groups are flawed since some of their leaders behave like traditional witch hunters and diviners, [45]creating untold fear among their group. This sadly motivates the followers to give more loyalty to the leaders than to Christ[46]. The Bible, as Ndung'u notes, is used as a religio-magical power that frightens and even wipes out spirits, making it difficulty to discern the symbolism and the reality the Bible stands for.[47] These groups also overstress the spirit world and allocate superfluous importance to angels in worship.[48] There is also a tendency to see a particular group as the one protecting people from evil supernatural powers but which in the final analysis appears to be promoting demonic activities.[49]

The African context has witnessed major diversities in the expression of Christian faith.[50] But the missionary legacy perseveres[51] since the missionaries neglected an area that Hiebert calls the "excluded middle".[52] As Burnett insists, missionaries underlined philosophical religion on one level and technology on the other, disregarding the daily application of religion.[53] Unfortunately, as

---

W. Dube (eds.), *The Bible in Africa: Transactions, Trajectories and Trends* (Leiden: Brill, 2000), pp. 241, 245.

[45] See J. S. Mbiti, *African Religions and Philosophy* (London/Nairobi: Heinemann Educational Books, 1969), p. 168.

[46] See Howell, *The Religious Itinerary of a Ghanaian People*, p. 174.

[47] Ndung'u, "The Role of the Bible", p. 243-4.

[48] See Samuel O. Abogunrin, "The Total Adequacy of Christ in the African Context (Col. 1: 13-23; 2: 8–3: 5) in *Ogbomoso Journal of Theology* 1 (1986), pp. 9-16.; Rebecca M. Owanikin, "Colossians 2: 18: A Challenge to Some Doctrines of Certain Aladura Churches in Nigeria" in *African Journal of Biblical Studies* 2/ 1 & 2 (1987), pp. 89-96; Walls, *The Cross-Cultural Process*, p. 126.

[49] Howell, *The Religious Itinerary of a Ghanaian People*, pp. 175-179. Daily Nation on the web, http://www.nationaudio.com accessed on 30:01:2002 reported the investigations of Kenyan Police in relation to an allegation that the leader of "The Will of God" sect was detaining people illegally for faith healing. Another sect expelled two pastors accusing them of introducing 'devil worship in the church, misleading the members and plunging the church into problems' (Daily Nation on the Web, http://www.nationaudio.com accessed on 8:02:2002).

[50] See Ndung'u, "The Role of the Bible", p. 236.

[51] See Lionel Caplan, "The encounter of Global Fundamentalism and the Local Christianity in Urban South India" in Wendy James (ed.), *The Pursuit of Certainty: Religious and Cultural* Formulations (London & New York: Routledge, 1995), pp. 92, 95-6; Rebecca Yawa Ganusah "Pouring Libation to Spiritual powers Among the Ewe-Dome of Ghana: An Indigenous Religious and Biblical Perspective" in Gerald O. West and Musa W. Dube (eds.), *The Bible in Africa: Transactions, Trajectories and Trends* (Leiden: Brill, 2000), pp. 278, 282.

[52] Hiebert, *Anthropological Reflections*, pp.335-347.

[53] Burnett, *Unearthly Powers*, p. 218.

Lesslie Newbigin asserts, Western Christian mission grew to become one of the greatest secularising forces in history.[54] Even so, the Africans became more and more interested in education offered by Christian missions as a means of learning how to deal with the power of the Europeans. The problem is that, even with such as opportunity, Christian missions did not delve deeply enough to the belief in supernatural powers so as to build up a real threat to the spirit cults.[55] As a result, some Africans, by deed if not by word, regard missionary Christianity as "an impotent religion"[56] without power to tackle the belief in supernatural powers. There is indeed a deep discontent with the missionaries' perception of supernatural powers among the majority of the so-called third world Christians.[57]

However, the missionaries were children of their own age. It would be naïve to deny that they significantly contributed, and readily sacrificed their lives towards the development of African nations. Rather than passing any value judgement on the activities of Western missionaries, we are simply stating the facts of experience.[58] But their faults that persist in modern Africa are not negligible and trivial. In our own era, Thomas Jonsson, who is referred to as 'missionary, pastor, Bible teacher, author and motivational speaker', and who has founded churches and Bible schools in modern Africa claims, "the African people have lived in darkness in many areas, especially in the truths of the Word of God". They thus lack God's blessings since they have "lived in hunger and poverty and believed that this has been their destiny, and if you are living in a poor country, you are doomed". He further claims, "God wants to prosper his people, not only the Europeans or the Americans but God wants to prosper all his people, including the poorest nation in Africa".[59] This shows that the

---

[54] Lesslie Newbigin, *Honest Religion for Secular Man* (Philadelphia: Westminster Press, 1966), p. 18; Cf. Burnett, *Unearthly Powers,* p 116-7; Elmer S. Miller, "The Christian Missionary: Agent of Secularisation" in *Missiology* Vol. 1 (January 1973), p. 99-107.

[55] Matthew Schoffeleers, "The Interaction of the M'Bona Cult and Christianity" in T. O. Ranger and John Weller *Themes in the Christian History of Central Africa* (London/Naairobi/Ibadan/Lusaka: Heinemann Educational Books, 1975), p. 21.

[56] David Tuesday Adamo, "The Use of Psalms in African Indigenous Churches in Nigeria" in Gerald O. West and Musa W. Dube (eds.), *The Bible in Africa: Transactions, Trajectories and Trends* (Leiden: Brill, 2000), p. 339.

[57] P. T. O'Brien, "Principalities and Powers: Opponents of the church" in D. A. Carson (ed.), *Biblical interpretation and the church: Text and Context* (Exeter: Paternoster Press, 1984), p.130; Stanley Benson, "The Conquering Sacrament: Baptism and Demon Possession among the Maasai of Tanzania" in *The African Theological Journal* 9/2 (1980), p. 58-9.

[58] See Samuel G. Kibicho, "The Continuity of the African Conception of God into and Through Christianity: A Kikuyu Case Study" in Edward W. Fashole-Luke, R. Gray, A. Hastings and G. Tasie (eds.),*Christianity in Independent Africa* (London: Rex Callings, 1978), p. 357.

[59] Thomas Jonsson, *Pastor: You can get Your Church to Prosper: The Law of Giving and Reaping* (Uppsala: TJTM, 1998), p. 2.

African church still feels the missionary impact, although no longer under the control of missionaries. It also shows the extent with which some missionaries may have had an extremist view of God and of the Bible. As Parratt insists, European missionaries penetrated Africa with a fundamentalist view of the Bible. Such a method is still characteristic of African Christians and it hinders biblical studies in the continent. It imposes upon the Bible an fake viewpoint instead of allowing the Bible to speak for itself.[60]

It seems that the missionaries erred since they stressed discontinuity between Christianity and African cultures and religion to such that they excluded the aspects of continuity. They condemned African religious beliefs and practices without a proper evaluation and substituted Western cultural and religious practices with Christianity. This made it impossible for a person to be a faithful Christian and remain fully African. The missionaries thus "failed to perceive the new in the old and the old in the new. They failed to see authentic inspiration in African Religion and its importance for humanity's search for God".[61] The real tragedy was the imposition of western cultural trappings that were wrongly equated with Christianity. Even so, the missionaries' pioneering work is a significant landmark in the history of African Christianity. They certainly made significant contribution towards the development not only of the African church but also of the African nations. As Walls observes, "In fact, the missions had an important place in the colonial state, for they provided a high proportion of education and medical infrastructure. The missions were thus major agents in producing in Africa the organs of modern states, with literacy, technology and technological based communications".[62] This, to all intents and purposes, was a one of the missionaries' positive achievement in addition to the translation of the Bible into African vernacular languages, to which we now turn.

ii. The Translation of the Bible

The African Christians' knowledge of the Bible, though imparted rather selectively, was mainly derived from missionaries. The missionaries pioneered the translation of the Bible into African languages and this brought a new phase of appropriating Christianity. But during the translation process, the missionary translators left out some African words that were a direct equivalent of a biblical word, so that the Bible may not appear to be backing the alleged demonic nature of African culture and worldview.[63] According to the British

---

[60] John Parratt, *Reinventing Christianity: African Theology Today* (Grand Rapids, Michigan: Eerdmans, 1995), p. 62-3.
[61] Magesa' *African Religion*, p. 21. See also Fashole-Luke, "Introduction", p. 357.
[62] Walls, *The Cross-Cultural Process*, p 103.
[63] See John K. Karanja, *Founding an African Faith: Kikuyu Anglican Christianity 1900–1945* (Nairobi: Uzima Press, 1999), pp. 134-5; R. S. Sugirtharajah, *The Bible and the Third World: Precolonial, Colonial and Postcolonial Encounters* (Cambridge: Cambridge University Press, 2001), pp. 58-9.

and Foreign Bible Society Report, Bible translator H. C. Withey alleged that a South Western African Bantu language had "a full vocabulary for vices, but a limited one for virtue".[64] He reported, "Not only the heathen, but the speech of the heathen, must be Christianized. Their language itself needs to be born again. Their very words have to be converted from foul meanings and base use and baptized into a Christian sense, before those words can convey the great truths and ideas of the Bible".[65] Indeed, there was a correlation between missionaries' theology, attitude to culture and its choice of terms for biblical translation. Yet Western education imparted by missionaries hoping it would give African converts the full measure of civilisation, enabled them to read the Bible for themselves. Ukpong notes that when the Scriptures were translated into African languages, African Christians, now able to read for themselves, gained a deeper awareness of a different Jesus than the Jesus taught by their churches. They met a Jesus who confronted spiritual powers and cast out demons that impeded human life and caused cosmic chaos. They encountered a Jesus who healed the sick and who proclaimed release to the captives and liberty to the oppressed.[66] African Christians now could see that the texts clearly mentioned the devil (the god of this world) and the powers of darkness (demons, principalities, powers, world rulers of this present darkness, spiritual hosts of wickedness in the heavenly places and evil spirits).

The translation of the Scriptures thus enabled the Africans to see and hear an affirmation of their own cultural, social and religious life in the pages of the Bible. In reading the Bible, now available in their own languages, the Africans recognized God was speaking to them using their own language and in their cultural milieu. This then was the end of an era wherein the message of the Bible was imparted selectively. The African Christians could now identify what the missionaries had inaccurately condemned as incompatible with the Bible, among which was the reality and existence of supernatural powers. This raised questions on the relationship between people, Jesus Christ and evil supernatural powers. The problem is that the missionaries answered these questions with laughable answers. The missionary-founded churches, more often than not, answer these questions lamentably. A. F. Walls notes,

> As for missionary influence, missionary Christianity was largely disabled from giving clear guidelines on the mater of ancestors, since there was no precise equivalent in Western experience either of ancestors or the family and kinship system to which the ancestors belonged. The more protestant strands of missionary teaching tended simply to proscribe any form of ancestral cult as inconsistent with the sole worship of God; the more Catholic ones offered reinterpretations of ancestor veneration in terms of the Latin Christian doctrine of the communion of the saints. But neither of

---

[64] *The Word among the Nations*, p. 13.
[65] *The Word among the Nations* p. 14.
[66] J. S. Ukpong, "Re-reading the Bible with African Eyes: Inculturation and Hermeneutics", in *Journal of Theology for Southern Africa*. No 91 (June 1995) p. 3.

these procedures could abolish, absorb, or fully re-place the religious consciousness from which ancestor cult arose.[67]

Adamo also notes that the missionaries and later the missionary-trained African church leaders made African Christians throw away cultural paraphernalia and techniques of protecting and liberating themselves from evil powers. They only left them with the Bible but without teaching them how to use it to protect themselves from evil spirits.[68] So, in reality, even though the Bible has had a dynamic impact on African Christianity as the basic source of theology, biblical scholarship has not tackled thoroughly the pastoral problem caused by belief in supernatural powers. African Christians may be piously convinced that Christ is the Lord of all creation. But are they convinced Christ is the all-powerful Lord of their day-to-day life where they meet the pervasive influence of supernatural powers understood to be the forces behind human existence? As Imasogie notes, an authentic Saviour must be capable of destroying the cause of fear and anxiety of African Christians, since no religion can be applicable to a people if it neglects any area of their total experience, as they perceive it.[69]

iii. African Christians and Supernatural Powers

The great majority in the African context, including Christians, believe that spiritual and material aspects of creation interlock and work together to influencing human existence. The popular conviction is that supernatural powers shape institutions and that human beings sometimes respond to them consciously and at times unconsciously. This happens despite the fact that African Christians have had an age-old historical link with the Bible, which portrays supernatural powers as real but weak in comparison to God and Christ. Beliefs and fears allied to, and the obsessive loyalty given to spirits still dominate the African way of life.[70] It seems that, in real life and to a certain degree, African Christians satirize the theory of several African scholars that the Bible commands a central place in the life of African Christians and that it

---

[67] Walls, *The Cross-Cultural Process*, p 127.
[68] Adamo, "The Use of Psalms", p. 336.
[69] Imasogie, *Guidelines*, pp. 81-2.
[70] The cremation of the wife of a former Anglican Church of Kenya Archbishop the Most Rev. Manasseh Kuria triggered a wave of controversy since many retain sentimental and emotional ties with the spirits of the dead. A University of Nairobi Institute of African Studies lecturer opposed cremation saying that the spirit of the dead would not simply accept it. He insisted that the African burial ceremony was important for it prepared the body's journey to the spirit world after death. Cremation would destroy the human spirit since there is a physical and spiritual life. It would affect the resurrection of the dead and it is a taboo to cremate an African person. (Daily Nation on the Web, http://www.nationaudio.com, accessed on 10.07. 2002).

is the pillar of their faith.[71] Yet, these scholars definitely put the Bible right at the heart of African culture, where it is read, listened to and even discussed so as to speak to the African Christian way of life. But the question is, to what extent is the Bible at the heart of African culture when it comes to the subject of supernatural powers? In fact, several African Christians fail to adhere to the teachings of the Bible, and specifically to the Pauline teachings on the subject. They prefer traditional ways of dealing with issues threatening and upsetting life, which they assign to supernatural powers. Research has persuasively shown that many African Christians are customarily devoted to intermediary spirits as recognised by their culture and worldview.

Howell reveals a dual religious bequest at the heart of the Kasena Christians of Northern Ghana. As her study reveals, "in times of crisis and illness some Christians would seek help by means of divination and participate in traditional sacrifice and ritual as well as requesting prayer or mass". Citing a Kasena priest, Father Augustine Kazaresam, Howell reveals that the Kasena people "are Christians on Sundays and for the rest of the week they are 'real' Kasena" because God's Spirit had "not permeated the Christians' daily life".[72] Congdon shows that 69.6 per cent of Zulu Christians believe in ancestral spirits, which accompany, protect and bring them good fortune. His research concludes,

> Fewer professing Christians affirmed the deity of Christ than (*those who*) expressed dependence upon the ancestral spirits for problems connected with daily living... Where formalized Christianity has proved powerless, African church members have resorted to nativistic religion in seeking to meet felt needs... A resurgence of cultic magical arts and witchcraft in Black Townships has been associated with the desire for protection from crime and violence.[73]

DomNwachukwu notes that the Igbo embrace the white man's God recognising him as their traditional God *Chukwu*. But they still retain allegiance to, and fear of, traditional deities through whom they communicate with their Supreme

---

[71] M. Sibeko and B. Haddad, "Reading the Bible "with" Women in the Poor and the Marginalized Communities in South Africa" in *Semeia*, 78 (1997), p. 85; M. Masenya, "Proverb 31: 10–31 in a South African Context: A Reading for the Liberation of African (Northern Sotho) Woman" in *Semeia* 78 (1997), p 55; Zablon Nthamburi and Douglas Waruta "Biblical Hermeneutics in African Instituted Churches" in H. Kinoti and J. Waliggo (eds.), *The Bible in African Christianity* (Nairobi: Acton Press, 1997), p. 51 Emanuel Obeng, "The Use of Biblical Critical Methods in Rooting the Scriptures in Africa" in H. Kinoti and J. Waliggo (eds.), *The Bible in African Christianity* (Nairobi: Acton press, 1997), p 8; J. S. Mbiti, "The Bible in African Culture" in Rosino Gibellini (ed.), *Paths of African Theology* (London: SCM Press, 1994), p. 38.
[72] Howell, *The Religious Itinerary of a Ghanaian People*, p. 1.
[73] Dal G. Congdon, "An Investigation into the Current Zulu Worldview and its Relevance to Missionary Work" in *Evangelical Missions Quarterly* 21 (July 1985), p. 297-8. See also Gailyn Van Rheenen "Animism, Secularism and Theism", in *International Journal of Frontier Mission*, Vol 10. 4 (October 1993), p. 171.

Being *Chukwu* in daily life. The Igbo believe that the white man's God is not authoritative enough to deal with issues emanating from the spirit world. Igbo Christians often return to the traditional deities and ancestors so as to contact *Chukwu*, who competently deals with spirits and demons that are part of their daily experiences.[74]

Magesa notes that the belief in spirits continues to exert a more profound influence over African spirituality than many Christian leaders and Western or 'Westernised academics' care to admit. He notes that one of the widespread complaints among Christian leaders concerns the "duality" of African Christians' way of life. African Christians do not always adhere to religious and ritual demands that are formulated and expressed by the leaders of their churches. Many times they do not exactly demonstrate the inculcated and expected response their leaders await, because they seek comfort in their own religious symbol systems and rituals, which church leaders explicitly condemn. Similarly, Shorter notes that African Christians disown little of their former non-Christian outlook at baptism. They are asked to repudiate some traditional practices that have been rightly or wrongly damned by the church but they are not asked to recant a religious philosophy. They therefore return to the banned practices on occasion with remarkable simplicity. Conversion to Christianity is for African Christians a sheer gain, an "extra" for which they have opted. It is an "overlay" on their original religious culture. Apart from the official criticism of African Traditional Religion, Christianity has had little impact on the same in the way of serious judgements of value.[75] Tutu rightly recapitulates the state of affairs with regard to African Christians.

> The African Christian has suffered from a form of religious schizophrenia. With part of himself he has been compelled to pay lip service to Christianity as understood, expressed and preached by the white man. But with an ever greater part of himself, a part he has often been ashamed to acknowledge openly and which he has struggled to repress, he has felt his Africanness was being violated. The white man's largely cerebral religion was hardly touching the depths of his African soul; he was being redeemed from sins he did not believe he had committed; he was being given answers, and often splendid answers to questions he had not asked.[76]

The available evidence therefore suggests that the majority of African Christians operate within two belief systems that are closed to each other and

---

[74] Chinaka S. DomNwachukwu, *Demons are Real* (Lagos: Integrated Press, 1990), pp. 71-2.

[75] See Aylward Shorter, "Problems and Possibilities for the Church's Dialogue with African Traditional Religion" in *Bulletin of the Pontifical Council for Interreligious Dialogue* 28-29 (1975), pp. 111-121.

[76] D. M. Tutu, "Whither African Theology?" in Edward W. Fashole-Luke, R. Gray, A. Hastings and G. Tasie (eds.), *Christianity in Independent Africa* (London: Rex Collings, 1978), p. 366.

only superficially modified by the other. As Nürnberger insists, many Africans faithfully attend church on Sundays but at night they will be in secret vigils where magic rites are performed, or where an "independent" prophet offers healing powers.[77] The waning of the traditional beliefs in supernatural powers among African Christians is only on what Scott calls the 'public transcript', while it continues to operate within the 'hidden transcript'.[78] The belief in supernatural powers has incessantly perpetuated doctrinal and pastoral concerns in the African church, which Ferdinando adeptly explicates.[79] But it seems that this occurs because of a clash between two different worldviews. The popular Christianity is predominantly influenced by the primal African worldview's imagination and perception of reality. The official Christianity originates from a theology influenced by the Western intellectual worldview.[80] The official reading of the Bible is also inclined to the Western intellectual worldview that repeatedly regards African belief in spirits as figments of a human mind influenced by a primitive worldview. Yet as Ricoeur observes, "never, in fact, does the interpreter get near to what his text says unless he lives in the *aura* of the meaning he is inquiring after".[81]

---

[77] K. Nürnberger, "*MODIMO:* The Sotho Notion of the Supreme Being and the Impact of the Christian Proclamation" in *Journal of Religion in Africa* vol. II (1974), p.195.

[78] The 'hidden transcript' "represents a critique of power spoken behind the back of the dominant" (James C. Scott, *Domination and the Arts of Resistance: Hidden Transcript* (New Haven/London: Yale University Press, 1990), p. xii and is the discourse including speech act and a whole range of other practices that subordinate groups create in response to their ordeal of domination. So 'the hidden transcript' is a self-disclosure that power relations normally exclude from the official transcript. The 'public transcript' refers to actions that are openly avowed to the other party in the power relations. It is a "way of describing the open interaction between subordinates and those who dominate" (Scott, *Domination and the Arts of Resistance* p. 2. Cf. his footnote 1). Thus Scott opens his study with an Ethiopian proverb, 'when the great lord passes the wise peasant bows deeply and silently farts' to show the relationship between, the 'hidden transcript' and the 'public transcript', and between domination and resistance.

[79] Keith Ferdinando, *The Triumph of Christ in African Perspective: A study of Demonology and Redemption in the African context* (Carlisle, Cumbria: Paternoster Press, 1999), p. i.

[80] Official Christianity refers to the teaching sanctioned by church leaders while popular Christianity refers to daily life and faith of ordinary Christians, which negates the official teaching.

[81] Paul Ricoeur, *The Symbolism of Evil* (New York: Harper & Row, 1967), p. 351.

2:3. A Critical Appraisal of the African and Western Worldviews

i. A Need for Dialogue

So far, it is clear that the African and Western worldviews perceive and interpret reality differently. The missionaries explained what the African people experienced as pressure and constraint attributed to supernatural powers as superstitious animistic beliefs. This occurred precisely because the missionaries and the Africans were reared in different social worlds. Also, modern African and Western scholars come from different socio-cultural backgrounds. When two persons, as Berger and Luckmann note,[82] arrive at their meeting place from social worlds that have been historically produced in isolation from each other, their interaction occurs in a situation that has not been institutionally defined for both. Each person first observes the activities of the other, assigning a motive to them. When these activities occur again, the observant typifies the motives as regular, saying to himself, 'Aha there he goes again'. At some stage in their interactions, these typifications will be expressed in specific patterns of conduct. Each person will begin to play roles vis-à-vis each other and each will inwardly receive the reiterated roles of the other and make them the models for his/her own role-playing. The consequence is that each will take the role of the other and 'Aha there he goes again' becomes 'there we go again'.[83] Berger and Luckmann argue, "This relieves both individuals of a considerable amount of tension... Each action of one is no longer a source of astonishment and potential danger to the other".[84] The two individuals successfully construct a background, which serves their separate actions and mutual interaction. It is this social interaction that is disseminated to the third party such as children. Yet the interaction between the two individuals produces the institutional world known very well to the two. As the institutional world thickens and hardens for them and for their offspring, what was 'there we go again' becomes 'this is how these things are done'. "A world so regarded attains firmness in consciousness; it becomes real and in an ever more massive way and it can no longer be changed so readily".[85]

Something akin to this may be said with regard to the African and Western readers of the Bible who have been nurtured in social worlds that have been historically produced in isolation from each other. They have watched each other perform for a long time and 'Aha, there he goes again' has become exhausting and nauseating. They would rather now be saying, 'there we go again' and then 'this is how these things are done'. This will most likely remove the source of astonishment and potential danger hitherto seen in the

---

[82] P. L. Berger and T. Luckmann, *The Social Construction of Reality: A Treatise in the Sociology of Knowledge* (London: Penguin Books, 1967), pp. 74-77.
[83] Berger and Luckmann, *The Social Construction of Reality*, p. 74
[84] Berger and Luckmann, *The Social Construction of Reality*, pp. 74-5.
[85] Berger and Luckmann, *The Social Construction of Reality*, p. 77.

other. It can also help to critique the African and Western worldviews, as there is no pure and absolute worldview in itself as to the meaning of a subject or concept. This dialogue may help Bible readers to recognise their long-held views as a potential obstacle to other genuine interpretations.

ii. Understanding Worldviews

Arguably, deep-level assumptions, values and commitments that worldviews generate and are held dearly by a society are learned for the most part unconsciously.[86] But a worldview may act back and affect the interpretation and meaning of phenomena. Yet it may be exacting to understand a worldview although it can be analysed by describing themes and counter themes within a culture that tend to control human behaviour and to arouse activity as approved by society. Naturally, worldviews provide central governing sets of values and basic assumptions by which people perceive and interpret reality. They influence the ways with which people engage with the themes of life, implying that they explain the ways with which people deal with challenges that threaten the achievement of basic and felt needs. Worldviews give the time and space framework of why and how incidents occur and the lens for perceiving, interpreting and evaluating empirical events and life experiences. The frames and structures of defining reality are constructed on the basis of a worldview. For that reason, a key consideration is that the interpretation of the phenomena attributed to supernatural powers is shaped by worldviews. The Pauline concept of supernatural powers has, however, been to a large extent, studied from a Western worldview's perspective. The same applies to anthropological studies on the African belief in supernatural powers. The problem is that African and Western worldviews are different and "differences in worldviews present great difficulty in communication".[87] It is relevant therefore to critically appraise the African and Western worldviews so as to appreciate why people inclined to these worldviews may interpret an agreed set of phenomena differently.

a. The African Worldview

That many changes have occurred in the African worldview is not veiled. In most cases, these changes are received and modified to fit into the framework of the primal African worldview. Several scholars agree that the capacity of the Africans to borrow, re-work and integrate foreign ideas has given traditional knowledge tremendous durability in the face of immense changes that the modern era has brought to the African scene. In that case, some of the common features of the traditional African conceptual world plainly persist in the

---

[86] Edward Sapir, "The Unconscious Patterning of Behaviour in Society" in David G. Mandelbum, *Selected Writings of Edward Sapir in Language, Culture, and Personality* (Berkeley: University of California Press, 1949), p. 546; Hiebert, *Anthropological Reflections*, p. 204.

[87] Marguerite G. Kraft, *Understanding Spiritual Power: A Forgotten Dimension of Cross-Cultural Mission and Ministry* (Maryknoll, New York: Orbis Books, 1995), p. 23.

thinking of most Africans even after modern schooling. The primal worldview has not been entirely changed, neither has it vanished since its thoughts still occupy the Africans mind-set. Where changes seem to appear, it is only at the surface, affecting only the material side of life while traditional concepts form the background of perceived reality.[88] Christian converts too do not change their worldview as a result of conversion. They persistently continue to "share the beliefs of their ancestors in an ontology of invisible beings".[89] If truth be told, belief in ghosts perseveres in modern Africa despite the influx of modern technology and scientific knowledge.[90]

A key feature of the African worldview is the lack of separation between the sacred and the secular, the spiritual and the material since they are regarded as aspects of the same reality. The spiritual lens not only forms the framework through which African people conceive reality but also explains everything that relates to human life. Every happening, including human behaviour however mundane it may appear, is seen through a spiritual lens. The popular belief is that exterior and alien supernatural forces stand behind whatever happens to humankind in history and in their structures of existence. Strange and unrestrained behaviour of wild or domestic animals is allegedly spirit-influenced. According to the Gĩkũyũ of Kenya, when a carnivorous animal eats sacrificial meat (despite the fact that carnivorous animals eat meat), it means that spirits have accepted the sacrifice and so sent one of them in the form of an animal to consume the sacrifice.[91] According to the Ewe of West Africa, whenever a domestic animal behaves strangely, it is killed in order to drive away the evil spirit riding on it.[92] The same is also extended to natural disasters.

---

[88] See Ferdinando, *The Triumph of Christ*, p. 2; Kwame Appiah, *In My Father's House: Africa in the Philosophy of Culture* (New York/London: Oxford University Press, 1992), p. 103; Magesa, *African Religion*, p. 20; Mbiti, *African Religions*, p. xi; E. G. Parrinder, *Religion in Africa* (Harmondsworth: Penguin Books, 1969), p. 26.

[89] Appiah, *In My Father's House*, p. 134. See Bediako, *Primal Religions*, p.16, esp. fn 15, p. 65; J. S. Ukpong, "Towards a Holistic Approach to Inculturation Theology" in *Mission Studies: Journal of the International Association for Mission Studies* Vol.XVI-2 32 (1999), p. 105; Magesa, *African Religion*, p. 18; V. E. Akubueze Okwuosa, *In the Name of Christianity: The Missionaries in Africa* (Philadelphia/Ardmore: Dorrance & Company, 1977), p. 26.

[90] See Sunday Nation, 11.06.2000, p. 16 wherein a leading Kenyan Sociology Professor and a one time head of the civil service and secretary to the cabinet, Prof. Phillip Mbithi disclosed how he battled with a ghost and as he said, this was an episode that changed his life completely. Prof. David Ndeetei, a leading Kenyan Psychiatrist also insists, "medical science had no explanation for the ghosts, but it was recognised globally that they appear to people and interfere with their lives" (Daily Nation 24.07.2000)

[91] L. S. B. Leakey, *The Southern Kikuyu Before 1903* Vol. iii (London: Academic Press, 1977), p. 1102.

[92] Solomon K. Avotri, "The Vernacularization of Scripture and African Beliefs: The Story of the Gerasene Demoniac among the Ewe of West Africa" in Gerald O. West and Musa W. Dube (eds.), *The Bible in Africa: Transactions, Trajectories and Trends* (Leiden: Brill, 2000), p. 323.

If natural phenomena cause destruction of human life and property, it is held that a certain spirit has possessed the elements of nature associated with that natural phenomenon. Spirits are perceived as personal but without a material body. They are conceived as shadows, which exist within or without the material reality. These spirits can occupy animate and inanimate beings, material and non-material objects.[93] For that reason, specific and sanctified objects and animals representing the spirits must be respected to avoid rampant diseases.[94] The universe and its natural features have a life of their own, a personality, will and life forces.[95] This is the premise on which Africans interpret the world as a divine creation. The awe and reverence given to the material reality is a moral requirement since the world is the manifestation of God, His power and benevolence. The big rock where people go to sacrifice is not just a big rock but it reveals and contains God's presence and so is a personification of some supernatural quality of the Divine.[96] This applies to anything that inspires awe, yet these elements are in no way God but creatures that have a spirit in them because they exist by the will and through the power of the Supreme Being.[97] To all intents and purposes, this feature of the African worldview is valuable for the upkeep of the environment, which encompasses a life support system crucial for human survival.

Another feature of the African worldview is that whatever emerges suddenly and which appears not to have roots in the known spirits is attributed to a new spirit or spirits. In agreement with Eliade, "everything unusual, unique, new, perfect, or monstrous at once becomes imbued with magico-religious power and an object of veneration or fear according to the circumstances".[98] The introduction of Western education engendered the recognition of a spirit that was only accessible to the Europeans. Western education and technology were thereby explained as coming from "the spirits of Europeans". Many Africans went to school to learn how these spirits could cause a piece of paper to speak and to produce some effects. It always happened that when European

---

[93] J. S. Mbiti, *New Testament Eschatology in an African Background* (London: Oxford University Press, 1971), p. 137; Mbiti, *African Religions*, pp 3-5; Bolaji E. Idowu, *African Traditional Religion* (Maryknoll, New York: Orbis Books, 1975), p. 4.
[94] Magesa, *African Religion*, p 161.
[95] R. H. Codrington, *The Melanesians* (Oxford: Clarendon Press, 1891), p. 119; Placide Tempels, *Bantu Philosophy* (Paris: Présence Africaine, 1959), p. 31; Burnett, *Unearthly Powers*, p. 26.
[96] See Kibicho, "The Continuity of the African Conception of God", p. 372.
[97] See Magesa, *African Religion*, pp. 61, 73; Aylward Shorter, *African Culture and the Christian Church: An Introduction to Social and Pastoral Anthropology* (Maryknoll, New York: Orbis Books, 1973), p. 54; Aylward Shorter, *African Christian Theology: Adaptation or Incarnation?* (Maryknoll, New York: Orbis Books, 1977), pp. 61-78; Charles Nyamiti, *The Scope of African Theology* (Kampala: Gaba Publications, 1973). p. 66; Burnett, *Earthly Powers*, p. 35.
[98] M. Eliade, *Patterns in Comparative Religions* (London/New York: Sheed and Ward, 1958), p. 13.

missionaries or colonists sent their African servants with a letter to another European, an action would follow after reading the letter. This was seen as a mystery coming from the spirit world that only the Europeans had power to control. To gain that power, the urge to know about "the spirits of European" through Western education taught in mission schools increased. This happened because the African worldview is experimentative and adaptive. As a matter of fact, the African worldview can gain new supernatural powers that ease life and get rid of supernatural powers, which may prove ineffectual. While divinities can be acquired and/or dropped should they prove inept, ancestral spirits are irreplaceable.[99] Western education, technology and science have increased and/or decreased the number of spirits in many African societies.

Another key feature of the African worldview is that benevolent or malevolent actions of human leaders are seen through a spiritual lens. There is an age-old belief that a rapport exists between priesthood/chieftainship and the spirit world. Many African societies regard kings/chiefs and priests as God's special agents and representative in ruling people.[100] When political leaders act for the welfare of the community, benevolent spirits control them and so they should be respected and honoured. Conversely, when political leaders act contrary to the welfare of the society, they are under the influence of malevolent spirits. If a person convinces his/her followers or ethnic group that he/she is under the guidance of benevolent spirits to resist a malevolent political regime he/she easily gains approval.[101] This may be dangerous, since within the same community, there may be some people benefiting from the regime, who deem it to be under the control of benign spirits. It is even more dangerous because the criteria for judging the welfare of a nation can be ethnically oriented.[102] It is plain that imperialism placed different ethnic groups

---

[99] See Kwame Bediako, *Jesus in Africa: The Christian Gospel in African History and Experience*. (Akropong-Akuapem, Ghana: Regnum Africa, 2000), p. 90; .Cf. Mbiti, *African Religions*, p. 77.

[100] J. S. Mbiti, *The Concept of God in Africa* (London: SPCK, 1970), p. 122; Roy Willis, *Some Spirits Heal, Others only Dance* (Oxford, New York: Berg, 1999), pp. 42, 63, 68.

[101] See Heike Behrend, "Power to Heal and Power to Kill: Spirit Possession and War in Northern Uganda" in Heike Behrend and Ute Luig (eds.), *Spirit Possession: Modernity and Power in Africa* (Oxford: James Currey and Madison: University of Wisconsin Press, 1999), pp 20-33.

[102] Allegations made by the Kenyan press of night meetings and tribal caucuses that were taking place in relation to the process of reviewing the Kenyan constitution are indicative. The constitutional review was at a critical stage. Delegates had gathered at the Bomas of Kenya for the National Constitutional Conference from May 2003. The Kenyan press alleged that a whirlwind of ethnic and regional secret night meetings were taking place in what was seen as a heightened tension to control the National Constitutional Conference. It was alleged that political factions and individual politicians had increasingly withdrawn to their region and ethnic groupings in the fight for constitutional advantage and to map out strategies of inserting tribal and regional agenda into the Kenyan constitution. These allegations indicate serious weakness in the

in one geographical area, identifying them as a nation. Most African societies believe that evil spirits are alien, while benevolent spirits are familiar. An ethnic group that a political leader does not belong to may thus consider his/her actions as malevolent, while the ethnic group that he/she comes from and which, purportedly or actually, benefits from his/her leadership may consider his/her actions as benevolent. Perhaps this partly explains the cause of civil wars and political/economic instability in some African states. Even so, the African worldview regards the source of socio-political/economic power, health and success in spiritual terms. It is widely accepted that the royalty and the subjects as well as the priesthood and the worshippers all consult good spirits as intermediaries so that they may get help from the Supreme Being.

Finally, the African worldview identifies some people that have special powers to control spirits but not the Supreme Being. It is believed that such persons have the ability to bring the spirits and the spirit world closer or to drive it far away. In view of this, evil and suffering is finally attached to a wrongdoer, who is a human person. It is people who are evil specifically because they entertain bad intentions, utter bad words and engage in wrong deeds. Such evil persons are perceived as incarnations of evil spirits since they behave in an anti-life manner and frustrate the flowering of life and life-energies. It then follows that misfortunes causing imbalances and disharmony in the universe do not just happen. Since the world ought to be stable, well-balanced and good, there is always somebody responsible for misfortunes. If the physical and spiritual worlds are to co-exist for the benefits of human beings, the preset equilibrium must be maintained at whatever cost through rituals and practices, which are explained in chapter three.

Nevertheless, the African worldview's way of interpreting reality is not entirely innocent. The modern socio-political/economic and religio-cultural milieu does not allow the belief that supernatural powers are liable for all that happens in the physical world. There are incidents for which human beings are directly responsible and for which blame cannot be attributed to supernatural powers. It is not helpful to blame supernatural powers or to conclude it to be an act of God if accidents occur that could have been prevented if people had acted responsibly and complied with the necessary safety measures. Failing to see human responsibility in incidents that are hostile to human life is as good as abusing the African worldview, which holds that spirits act according to human conduct. Persons whose responsibility is to repair the railway and who fail to repair it knowing very well it needs repair must be held responsible for any train related accident. Drivers who knowingly overload and drive defective vehicles and policemen, who allow these vehicles to pass police checks due to corruption, only to cause an accident later, must be answerable for the accident. It could be confusing and clumsy if everything is credited to supernatural

---

African worldview, which can replace national interest with tribal, regional and sectarian interest (see *The Sunday Standard Online Edition*, http://www.eastandard.net accessed on 11.05.2003 and *Sunday Nation on the Web*, http://nationaudio.com, assessed on 11.05.2003).

powers, which require being soothed through sacrifices so that they may not go berserk and make people mad.[103] Chances are that people will fail somehow. But even though such failures could cause evil and suffering, attributing this to supernatural powers renders people helpless.

All together, the African worldview recognises that good spirits cause good governance and bad spirits cause bad governance. Malevolent spirits cause accidents, death, drought, famine and all natural phenomena inimical to human life. Good spirits cause good crops, good harvest, healing, successful business and family existence. Socio-political/economic power, success, health and wealth, all have roots in spiritual power. The decline or misuse of spiritual power is a sign of "broken relationship and consequently of disturbed harmony and peace in the community".[104] There is a great need of spirits and the power they impart in daily life. The major concern of most African people is why and how they should interact with spirits and the spirit world. Since the spiritual permeates and influences the physical and material reality, people need increased strength to survive in a world full of spirit activities. Nonetheless, the contact between Africa and the West during the historical eras of the slave trade, missionary enterprises and colonialism somewhat modified the African worldview. Western education, medicine and technology have also modified the African worldview's basic assumptions. This, as noted above, has sadly left some African Christians with a dual religious heritage. Most Africans do not fully accept the views of the Western worldview that are inconsistent with the way they conceive human situations as their worldview enables them.

b. The Western Worldview

The Western worldview, which pays little attention to spiritual reality, is experiencing changes. But there is a growing discontent with regard to its basic assumptions. There is an emerging paradigm shift in the way some Western people view reality and especially the perception of supernatural powers. Some phenomena are recognised as manifestations of more than human powers, though only demonic in the sense of the evil and suffering they cause in human history. Several episodes may appear demonic albeit not caused by personal demonic powers. As Imasogie notes, supernatural powers are held to be symbols without ontological content or as illusions and imaginations of a primitive age under the influence of an obsolete worldview[105]. This is clear in the words of Walter Wink.

> We moderns cannot bring ourselves by any feat of will or imagination to believe in the real existence of these mythological

---

[103] A Gĩkũyũ maxim wisely says, 'ngoma itũrĩkaga cia thĩnjĩrũo', which literally means, spirits become naughty if they are continually soothed through sacrifices. So rather than sacrificing to the chthonic powers, the Gĩkũyũ people symbolically fought them in order to expel them from their midst (see chapter 3, page 45).

[104] Magesa, *African Religion*, p. 164.

[105] Imasogie, *Guidelines*, p. 52.

entities that traditionally have been lumped under the general category 'principalities and powers'... When we read the ancient accounts of encounters with these Powers, we can only regard them as hallucinations, since they have no real physical referent. Hence we *cannot* take seriously their own description of these encounters–as long as our very categories of thought are dictated by the myth of materialism.[106]

This seemingly spiritual view does not replace the materialistic explanations of events. Although some events are viewed through a spiritual lens, the theoretical framework is still material. The Western worldview, however, has not always provided a dependable framework with which to explain reality to some Western people. Burnett insists that it 'has never been an intellectually satisfying worldview'.[107]

Perhaps what Burnett is referring to could be the 'Western intellectual worldview', which tends to use scientific rationalization as a lens to perceive and interpret reality. Its main feature is to separate the spiritual and the material; hence it works with a dichotomy between the sacred and the secular, the spiritual and the material. Presumably, this is the reason behind the categorisation, compartmentalisation and quantification of the affairs of human life.[108] There are institutions, time and space that cater for diverse areas of life. Religious institutions cater for spiritual issues and this is only in places of worship and on set days and times. Educational institutions like schools, colleges and universities cater for the educational and intellectual aspects of life, and this is only during term time. Medical centres are responsible for the issues affecting human health. There are other institutions that promote agriculture and technology for economic pursuit. The problem is that human existence is not seen as a combination of physical, intellectual, social and spiritual aspects. Though the Western worldview recognises an area of human existence that needs spiritual attention, it separates all other areas of life, which an individual fully controls, from the spiritual. It is generally held that commitment to science enables people to control the material universe. There is little recognition that the spiritual interlocks with the material for good or evil intentions. As a result, the belief that spirits have a place in the universe is marginalised and deemed to be of little relevance in daily life. The idea that people receive protection and providence from spiritual beings has no weight since these could be gained through material means now under human control. This implies that nature can be conquered, improved, or demolished and rebuilt in a better way, but which is however impossible.[109] The worse results could be global warming, climate change such as *El Nino/La Nina* phenomenon and the

---

[106] Wink, *Naming the Powers*, p. 4
[107] Burnett, *Earthly Powers*, p.16. Cf. Os Guinness, *The Dust of Death: A Critique of Counter Culture* (London: Inter-Varsity Press, 1973).
[108] See James F. Cobble Jr., *The Church and the Powers: A Theology of Church Structure* (Peabody, Massachusetts: Hendrickson, 1988), pp. 25-39.
[109] Cf. Cicero, *De Natura Deorum*, 2.87.

destruction of the ozone layer.

The Western worldview allows people to use rules set by science to judge religious phenomena such as belief in miracles and spirits as mythical. Whatever cannot be verified scientifically, such as the phenomena attributed to supernatural powers, are said to be in conflict with the civilized world. Citing several eminent philosophers and theologians, Os Guinness traces the historical cause and the obvious results of this thinking in Western culture convincingly. He notes that the Reformation era (16th–17th century) recognized that occultism and witchcraft were real but stressed they were wrong. The eighteenth century European rationalism scorned them as non-existent and held that witchcraft was simply meaningless.[110] Thus Hughes, writing in 1965 could declare that witchcraft is dying rapidly in the American way of life and as a cult belief in Europe. He held witchcraft as a degenerate form of a primitive fertility belief containing the most archaic instructive wisdom, which is over in the West.[111] Since then, the growing interest in the Harry Potter books/films and the Halloween festival in the modern Western world make the rebuff of occult beliefs suspect. Guinness contends, "now it is in the West and among the young and avant-garde that we are seeing an unmistakeable resurgence in the belief and practice of the occult, ranging from the harmless to the horrifying".[112] There is a renaissance of belief in ghosts and the practice of astrology, despite the unrelenting adherence to the philosophy of materialism. Several scholars agree that there is lively occultism in the West that cannot be relegated in time or distance, though some scholars would want to send it to the ridiculous. Some people turn first to the horoscope page in the newspaper while others get involved with spiritism, witchcraft and new religious movements.[113] The Western world is on the verge of a new age that is bringing a paradigm shift of worldview. This is detaching the West from the fundamental assumptions of the Enlightenment.[114]

Even so, anti-supernaturalistic prejudice exemplifies the Western intellectual community and perhaps some common people as well. Guinness's observation thirty years ago about the supernatural or the occult world is perhaps relevant even at present.

> There is still a patronising disregard for, if not outright disbelief in, any such talk. Probably it would still be virtually impossible to publish an article expressing belief in the reality of this world in any respectable journal of psychiatry in Britain or United States,

---

[110] Guinness, *The Dust of Death*, p. 280).
[111] Pnnetorne Hughes, *Witchcraft* (Harmondsworth: Penguin Books, 1965), pp. 210-217.
[112] Guinness, *The Dust of Death*, p. 279.
[113] See Guinness, *The Dust of Death*, p. 278; Burnett, *Earthly Powers*, p. 57, 77; Guy Daniel, "Astronomy, Astrology and Medicine" in Neil, William (ed.), *The Bible Companion* (London: The Caxton Publishing Company, 1959), p. 310; Clinton E. Arnold, *Powers of Darkness*. (Downers Grove: Intervarsity Press, 1992b), pp. 48, 182.
[114] See Hans Küng, *Theology of the Third Millennium* (New York: Doubleday, 1988).

dominated heavily as they are by a naturalistic framework.[115]

Perhaps this explains why some scholars regard the Western church as having failed to practise a theology of the spiritual and to give sufficient or serious attention to the topic of supernatural powers.[116] According to Guinness,

> This is not atypical nor is it surprising, for even in much theology, where one would expect to find a measure of belief, there is little acknowledgement of the supernatural, either positive or negative. The writings of Paul Tillich or Reinhold Niebuhr may use the word *demonic*, but not to refer to an objective demonic world. The word *demonic* is rather used as a symbol of man's bias toward evil. That a man like Archbishop William Temple should actually have believed in a personal devil was regarded as extraordinary in so prestigious an archbishop and so profound a scholar.[117]

The Western church prefers an intellectual and materialistic theology. This, as Burnett argues, probably fails to meet the spiritual aspirations of people.[118]

Guinness also notes that scepticism towards the supernatural in liberal theology and the rise of Higher Criticism added to a persistent infiltration of secularised philosophy into Christian theology.

> One constant sign of this has been the exorcism of any lingering supernatural ideas. The old and new quest for the historical Jesus and the movement to demythologize the gospel have both foundered on the intrinsic impossibility of dividing the human from the supernatural... In a period when liberal theology appeared to speak for intelligent Christianity, it looked as if Christianity as a whole had succumbed to naturalism disguised by semantic symbolism. Christianity (no longer affirming the occult as real but wrong) lost its balanced position between the sceptics who denied it all and those who accepted it completely.[119]

Likewise, Soskice observes that if biblical imagery is lifeless to the modern person (and it is not obvious that this is so), this is more likely the legacy of historical criticism, of the search for the historical Jesus and the effort by both conservatives and liberals to salvage Jesus' exact words and acts from the dross of allusion and interpretation with which the Gospel writers delimited them. "It is the legacy of a literalism which equates religious truth with historical facts, whatever these might be".[120] Even though the Pauline concept of supernatural

---

[115] Guinness, *The Dust of Death*, p. 278.
[116] Kraft, *Understanding Spiritual Power*, p. x; Arnold, *Powers*, p. 11.
[117] Guinness, *The Dust of Death*, p. 279.
[118] Burnett, *Earthly Powers*, p. 197.
[119] Guinness, *The Dust of Death*, p 280-1.
[120] Janet Martin Soskice, *Metaphor and Religious Language* (Oxford: Clarendon Press, 1985), p. 160.

powers is metaphorical, as it will be seen in chapter six, Paul neither reduces spiritual beings to the structures of human existence and/or existential realities nor denies their existence. Actually, most people in his time held that spiritual beings exist. The question is whether Paul just took over this belief for himself, or referred to supernatural powers, which impinged upon, and pushed people in certain directions, because they were so common so as to address the fears and biases of his readers while he operated with a more complex view of the powers. This will be dealt with in chapter five.

The Western worldview is especially reflected in the Western church in its emphasis on doctrine and a persuasive rationalistic approach to theology.[121] Christ is represented on the basis of rational argument and not by the Gospels' testimony of his power in the lives of people who were sick due to possession by demons and evil spirits. The war against demons and evil spirits, which according to the perceptions of the Gospel writers appeared naturally as part of Christ's ministry, is entirely consigned to the miraculous, far from ordinary events. This, as Ferdinando notes, occurs because Western scholarship is "dominated by anti-supernaturalistic rationalism in which 'spirits' have no place except as constructions of the human mind".[122] Attention given to the material and physical world surpasses that given to the spirit world. Faith in human knowledge and science to resolve the concerns of life pushes the belief that spiritual powers are involved with human existence to the periphery. Apparently, this mind-set may give rise to pastoral and doctrinal problems, among which may be not only the relegation of supernatural powers but also of God to a comfortable out-of-the-way place. As some scholars note, it may be possible to include God's power together with that of supernatural powers and to regard God's power as irrelevant in human life. It may also engender a mind-set that seeks the intervention of the divine only in time of crisis and in events that are beyond human understanding and control.

A critical and besetting feature of the Western worldview is the assumption that scientific theories give an accurate description of the world. Rationalism and empirical evidence are regarded as the ideal means to explain the world and human life. The great stride that science has made in its analysis of nature, most of which pours scorn on religious notions, justifies the diminishing acceptance of spiritual beings and miracles in the modern world. It is supposed that the material perception of the universe is superior to the spiritual perception. Yet the assumption that scientific theories rightly elucidate reality is disputed. The position of Lausanne Continuation Committee is indicative.

> We wish to affirm, therefore, against the mechanistic myth on which the typical Western worldview rests, the reality of demonic intelligences which are concerned by all means, overt and covert, to discredit Jesus Christ and keep people from coming to him.[123]

---

[121] See Kraft, *Understanding Spiritual Power*, pp. 32-33.
[122] Ferdinando, *The Triumph of Christ*, p.70. Cf. Wink, *Naming the Powers*, pp. 3-4.
[123] *The Willowbank Report*, p. 21.

What the Willowbank Report refers to as 'the reality of demonic intelligence' cannot be explained by way of science. Relying on science to judge religious issues is like judging handball with football rules. J. B. Russell notes that the trend to dismiss and disprove the existence of supernatural powers as archaic arises from the error that allows science to judge issues unrelated to it[124]. Arnold notes, "If spirits do not have tangible physical existence, modern science does not have the tools for verifying or denying their real existence. This makes the question of their existence depend not on scientific observation, but upon revelation, world view and human experience".[125]

The inevitable conclusion is that working from the perspective of the Western worldview, missionaries and/or theologians may not grasp some of the African worldview's major questions with regard to supernatural powers. Perhaps as Mulago avers, it is imperative to set aside the dualistic dialect, which characterises the Western thought, whereby the exaltation of man would entail the rejection of God, in order to effectively speak to the majority of African Christians. This is crucial since the African worldview takes God and people as its two basic realities and vital centres. [126]

c. Can the African and Western Worldviews Meet?

The distinguished poet Rudyard Kipling once said, "Oh, East is East and West is West, and never the twain shall meet, Till Earth and Sky stand presently at God's great Judgement Seat".[127] Looking at the obvious and remarkable differences between the African and the Western worldview one would justify Kipling's famed line. The difference between the two worldviews has created a cultural gap as to the perception and interpretation of reality, and especially of the phenomena attributed to supernatural powers. The African worldview regards everything in the created order as living and related to the other such that what affects one affects the other. The Western worldview regards some aspects of the creation as lifeless objects that act upon each other like parts of a greater mechanical system, which can be controlled by human power. The African worldview is persuaded by the spiritual approach to life but the Western worldview is slanted to the material approach. The spiritual viewpoint endows the African worldview with the lens to perceive and interpret daily experiences but the material perspective provides the Western worldview with the lens for understanding experiences. Unlike the African worldview, the Western worldview in most cases does not recognise any other power that has

---

[124] Jeffrey Burton Russell, *Mephistopheles: The Devil in the Modern World* (Ithaca/London: Cornell University Press, 1986), p. 21.
[125] Arnold, *Powers*, p. 178.
[126] M. Mulago gwa Chikala, *La Religion Traditionnelle des Bantu et leur Vision du Monde* (Kinshasa: Faculté de Théologie Catholique, 1980), p. 166.
[127] Rudyard Kipling "The Ballad of East and West" in Rudyard Kipling, *Rudyard Kipling's Verses: Inclusive Edition* 1885–1918, vol. I (London: Hodder & Stoughton 1919), pp. 308, 313.

absolute control of human life and environment apart from people themselves. There is little faith in, and reliance on the spiritual dimension for decision-making, problem analysis, gaining protection, wealth and health. The Western worldview does not recognise the possibility of persons placating or invoking supernatural powers for good or evil intentions. The African worldview explains the cause of evil and suffering in personal terms. Somebody/something always causes evil and suffering, not by choice but by either being manipulated or being under the influence of supernatural powers. The difference between African and Western worldviews is that they have unrelated thoughts as to the nature of humankind and the universe. These intensely shape the way people aligned to each worldview conceive and interpret human situations. Different views as to the created order result in different approaches to issues, for example, how to treat illness, how to make the land produce, how to be safe and secure, how to get promotion or win an election, how to relate to each other and so on.

This leads to the conclusion that the interpretation of the Pauline concept of supernatural powers is certainly shaped by the worldview that the interpreter embraces. Yet by now, it is clear that worldviews have identifiable flaws that may undermine the reading of the Pauline concept of supernatural powers. The good thing, however, is that African and Western worldviews are no longer strangers, especially in the modern era. Christianity as propagated by Western missionaries came with many scientific exploits. Africa's encounter with the West is often explained by three Cs (Civilisation, Commerce and Christianity) advocated by the missionaries. As such, there is no doubt that some Western worldview's values have permeated the Africans' way of life in the form of Western civilisation, commerce and Christianity. Not that the three Cs did not agree with the African mentality, since as Beidelmann notes, "nearly or heathen accepted" a religious truth expressed in the view of some missionaries that "all social life, from religion to agriculture, is of one piece".[128] In fact, the Africans did not dichotomise life and so the three Cs did not contradict their mentality and way of life. However, the problem is that the three Cs did not make the best of the Africans' conception of reality. Africans were expected to conform to the Western worldview's conception of reality. They first needed to be civilised or rather, to abide by the Victorian Christian morality before they could be Christianised.[129] This altered some values enshrined in the African worldview, a process Christianity and Western education devotedly and firmly guided. This, however, did not annul the basic assumptions of the African worldview, though it produced a people between two worlds, one part yielding to some values of the African worldview and another accepting some values of the Western worldview.

It has already been said that the spiritual view of the universe has not entirely vanished from the Western worldview. The quest for supernatural help is on the rise in the West especially through the quasi-religious New Age

---

[128] Beidelmann, *Colonial Evangelism*, p. 119.
[129] See Sugirtharajah, *The Bible and the Third World*, p. 63-4.

Movement and the Pentecostalism and charismatic movement that are now familiar in the Western church. A BBC 1 TV show televised a conversation between supporters of spiritual healers and scientifically trained doctors.[130] During the one hour telecast, it was plain that there are increasing numbers of Western people who turn to spiritual healing. Some people held that spiritual healing works, while others said it never works and regarded it as a deception that should not be allowed to happen *since it has no scientific verification*. Nevertheless, it could be that spiritualistic healing meetings draw large crowds in some Western nations.[131] A BBC 2 TV documentary revealed that every diocese in England employs at least one exorcist to assist families to reclaim their homes and expel the evil that they feel surrounds them.[132] Hiebert admits that the Indo-European cosmic myth[133] dominates modern Western thought and it is the basis for Western detective stories, murder mysteries and science fiction. He maintains that the myth is evident in television programmes like Superman, Spiderman, Super Chicken, and most Western cartoons. The myth is also re-enacted in star war movies, dramatised in video games, and taught by the New Age Movement.[134] Yet the intellectual Western worldview tends to remove people from their world and environment, wherein spiritual reality is fixed. It tends to regard human ingenuity and technical progress as the only direct response to the needs of human survival and as the replacement of the spiritual dimension of reality.[135]

Nonetheless, the Western and the African worldviews are experiencing a transformation that may enable each worldview to adapt the strength and assumptions of the other. This implies that worldviews can be modified, even though they tend to conserve old ways and are resistant to change. Exposure to new information, living in a different society, and experiences that persuade a person to re-evaluate previously held concepts and values facilitate change of one's worldview's basic assumptions if not the framework. This, most likely,

---

[130] The programme 'Kilroy' was on air on Tuesday, 15.01. 2002.

[131] Anthropologist and author Roy Willis (*Some Spirits Heal*, p. 8) claims to have discovered he was a spirit healer during his research on "alternative healing". In his healing practices, he alleges to have "noted a success rate of around eighty-five percent – with patients suffering from a wide range of afflictions, most of which had proved recalcitrant to treatment by orthodox medicine". Cf. Burnett, *Earthly Powers*, p. 192.

[132] The documentary 'The Exorcist' was broadcasted on 16.01.2002.

[133] Several scholars admit that the Indo-European myth conceives of a cosmic spiritual war between good and evil and that this myth has spread from Asia to Europe (Cf. Hiebert, *Anthropological Reflections*, pp.204–208; Gerald J. Larson, C. Scott Littleton and Jaan Puhvel (eds.), *Myth and Indo-European Antiquity* (Berkeley, California: University of Chicago Press, 1974); Puhvel, Jean (ed.), *Myth and Law among the Indo-European: Studies in Indo-European Comparative Mythology* (Berkeley, California: University of California Press, 1970).

[134] See Hiebert, *Anthropological Reflections*, pp. 207-8.

[135] Cf. Lewis Mumford, *The Myth of the Machine* 2 Vols (New York: Harcourt, Brace, Jovanovich, 1964), p 36-7; Cobble, *The Church and the Powers*, pp. 23-4.

has happened to many Western and African people. There is therefore a tension in the attempt to combine the secular and material perception of reality and the spiritual conception of reality both in the West and in Africa. Several scholars have admitted that their work exhibits a change of their basic assumptions that they had long acquired from their worldview.[136] All this therefore seems to have turned Kipling's famous line upside down. East is no longer the east and west is no longer the west and the twain have now met. They have had an interaction and each worldview has lost a portion of what could have made it remain east or west. All the same, Kipling's line continued, "but there is neither East nor West, Border, nor Breed, nor Birth, When two strong men stand face to face, tho' they come from the ends of the earth".[137] Having been nurtured in social worlds that have been historically shaped in isolation from each other, Western and African scholars now stand face to face and perhaps they should communicate with each other. This may radically open new ways, possibilities and opportunities for saying, 'this is how things are done' and lessening the possible apprehension and mistrust among them.

What this means is that even if the culture in which people live deeply influences them to construe human situations differently, this will not lead to criticism but to dialogue. In this dialogue, each worldview will be informed of its weakness. The African and Western worldviews certainly have key weak spots in relation to supernatural powers. The most obvious for the Western worldview is the denial that supernatural powers exist. And for the African worldview, it is the infatuated allegiance given to supernatural powers. Putting too much emphasis on the responsibility of spirits in all human actions is as risky as denying they exist. This may create a danger of reading the Pauline concept to fit into the thought pattern and basic assumptions of the African worldview. It may also create a Christianised form of spiritism, if people fail to admit responsibility for their actions but instead blame supernatural powers. Spiritism allows spirits to dominate reality; hence people must battle to appease them to survive. This may prompt a denial of a Christ-centred life as the Pauline concept of supernatural powers teaches. Commenting on the Western worldview, Burnett insists that it explains supernatural powers from a closed universe. He notes that this could be the basis for the out-and-out denial of miraculous phenomena[138]. Emphasising the material lens for perceiving reality and disregarding the spiritual reduces the spiritual dimension of the so-called 'secular'. Secularised scientific progress presumably has spiritual nuances inasmuch as it shapes the essence of what it means to be human.[139] Using science to reject the notions that spirits can influence and are involved with human events also creates a danger of moulding the Pauline concept of supernatural powers to fit into the thought pattern and the basic assumptions of

---

[136] See Wink, *Naming the Powers,* pp. 4-5; O'Brien, "Principalities and Powers", p. 130; Arnold, *Powers,* p. 210.
[137] Kipling, "The Ballad", pp. 308, 314.
[138] Burnett, *Earthly Powers,* p. 33.
[139] Cobble, *The Church and the Powers,* p. 3.

the Western worldview. This causes the danger of reducing reality into materialistic and scientific explanations. This may finally lead believers to defy a Christ-centred life as the Pauline concept teaches.

It is indeed relevant to take C. S. Lewis's caution on board.

> There are two equal and opposite errors into which our race can fall about the devils. One is to disbelieve in their existence. The other is to believe, and to feel an excessive interest in them. They themselves are equally pleased by both errors and hail a materialist or a magician with the same delight.[140]

It is critical therefore that the African and Western worldview should speak to each other. This would augment the African worldview, which attributes accountability largely to spirits, leaving people powerless. It would also supplement the Western materialistic worldview, which largely denies that supernatural powers exist independently. Perhaps the dialogue between the two worldviews could help people not to fall into the two equal and opposite errors noted by Lewis. The dialogue may also enable people to naturally realise that the physical and the spiritual are two sides of the same coin. Viewed from this perspective, the two worldviews could enhance the formulation of a contextual theology of supernatural powers, whose main theme is that of Christ's supremacy over the created order, which includes spirits and the spirit world.

2:4. Conclusion

We can conclude that neither the African worldview nor the Western worldview treats supernatural powers as the Pauline concept does. Unlike the Western worldview, Paul takes supernatural powers seriously as his letters has many references to them. It will be seen in chapter five that God's power in and through Christ is superior to that of supernatural powers since they were created and exist through and by Christ, and also Christ conquered and shamed the powers of darkness on the cross. The Bible also takes people and the natural world seriously. It holds them liable for their actions, even if such actions could be under the influence of spiritual beings, since they have a will and can make a choice to either obey or disobey.[141] The Bible not only focuses its attention on supernatural powers but also on human history and people's relationship with God. The African worldview stands in close proximity to the biblical worldview but the Bible does not validate the absolute power that the African worldview gives to spirits though it validates their existence. As Guinness notes, the Bible affirms the reality of the occult but rebuts its validity. He also notes, "within the Christian framework there is not so much a natural and supernatural world, as if natural were the real and the supernatural the less real;

---

[140] C. S. Lewis, *The Screwtape Letters* (London: Harper Collins Publishers, 1942), ix.
[141] Cf. Sir 15: 11-20.

A Collision of Two Worldviews

rather there is a seen and the unseen, and both have equal reality".[142] On the other hand, the Western scientific and intellectual worldview directly conflicts the first century CE worldview and the biblical worldview.[143] Burnett, having noted the dangers that may be posed by the Western worldview to Christianity, says there is need to engage the Bible afresh so as to determine how to make Christ relevant within the experiences of primal people. The challenge for Western Bible students is "to formulate a more meaningful worldview than the one which is an adaption of the secular worldview".[144] To do this, we may need a situation where the African, Western and biblical worldviews can interact. But the claim that the first century CE is closer to non-Western worldviews than to the Western worldview leads us to chapters three and four, which looks at the belief in supernatural powers in the African context and in the first century CE context respectively.

---

[142] Guinness, *The Dust of Death*, p. 283.
[143] Arnold, *Powers*, p. 150.
[144] Burnett, *Earthly Powers*, p. 33.

CHAPTER 3

The African Context of Reception: Analysing the Diverse Perceptions of Religious Phenomena Prompting Beliefs in Supernatural Powers

3: 1. Introduction

As noted in chapter two, many Africans believe the universe is made of the spiritual and the material that interlock as one reality. Humans and non-humans reside in the material world, supposedly controlled by supernatural powers. The material is not separate and autonomous but is linked to the spiritual. As in Aristotle, animate and inanimate things, visible and invisible creations influence each other. Whatever affects one equally affects the other.[1] A central idea is that supernatural powers either boost or inhibit human life hence many African people ascribe maximum causation to the spirit world. There are several survival tactics with which many African people manage both life-heartening and life-threatening powers. The purpose of this chapter is to identify the African context of reception in which the Pauline concept of supernatural powers is often read. Suffice to say, there are diverse perceptions, which perhaps reveal how elusive the reading of beliefs, rituals and practices as to supernatural powers can be. This chapter explains the Africans' perception and categorization of supernatural powers and their techniques of communicating with, and controlling them. It also assesses the views of anthropologists and comparative religionists and evaluates the alleged postulate of affinity between the biblical and African worlds and ideas.

3:2. Africans' Perceptions of Supernatural Powers

i. Supernatural Powers as the Cause of Human Existence

As one would expect, the reality and existence of supernatural powers is a controversial issue. But as we have seen in chapter two, there is "an almost

---

[1] Aristotle, *Historia Animalium,* books 7–10.

universal acknowledgement of the reality of the spirit and the spiritual realm"[2] in Africa. Many Africans link the belief in supernatural powers with human existence in a complex world. The common idea is that nothing occurs without some supernatural powers behind it and whatever happens in human existence is determined in the spirit world. Individuals therefore must have a relationship that is sustained by observing religious, moral and ethical rules purportedly formulated in the spirit world. These are also communicated to people through ancestral spirits. This relationship enables people to sort out challenges attributable to supernatural powers, which affect their felt need to survive. Beliefs in supernatural powers cause great value for the fullness of life that goes with the desire to control the life-destroying and life-denying powers. Several rituals and practices are performed so as to control, negotiate, coerce or manipulate the powers. These represent the search for an extraordinary power that supposedly enables people to remove malicious and destructive intentions from and within their milieu. They represent the urge to protect life and events from falling into evil machinations and destructive aims. Belief in supernatural powers and corresponding responses thus occur in specific and concrete life situations. Many modern Africans would agree that human existence derives from a mysterious but active power, which Codrington referred to as *mana*. This power, as he says, belongs to some people but usually to the souls of the dead and all spirits. People possess *mana* only because they receive it from higher beings.[3] Many Africans reach out for supernatural powers so as to achieve the human basic and felt need of existence.

ii. Hierarchical Structures and Categories of Supernatural Powers

In agreement with the hierarchical structure of the African world, most Africans believe supernatural powers are hierarchically structured. The lowest structure includes lifeless creation at the base. Next are the animate non-human creation and then human beings. This lower structure is the arena where supernatural powers exercise their influence. Ancestral spirits are closer to people. They are the link between the lowest and highest structures and occupy the middle structure. The higher structure consists of spirits who are slightly above the ancestors but lower than God who takes the highest position. The Gĩkũyũ of Kenya regard their Supreme Being, *Ngai*, as the only God, who cannot be confused with anything else either in the underworld, in the waters, on earth, or in the air. It is God who allows the spirits to supervise the everyday affairs of humankind. The spirits manifest God's power, wrath and other attributes as his messengers and agents. They personify God in nature, in the earth, cultivatable land, forests, mountains, rocks, rivers, seas and lakes, in

---

[2] Scott A. Moreau, *The World of the Spirits: A Biblical Study in the African Context* (Nairobi: Evangel Publishing House, 1990), p.102.
[3] Codrington, *The Melanesians,* pp. 118-121.

weather, air, wind and hailstorm.[4] The spirits are held to be present in all natural phenomena and features, in all human events and in every human contentment or restlessness. They are the mediators between God and people and are perceived as active beings that are either disincarnate persons or powers residing in natural phenomena which impinge human life in one way or the other.

The spirits exist only through the will of God who is their creator, the spiritual ruler and governor of the universe. As a result, some scholars have argued for monotheism in most African societies.[5] In contrast, as King notes, some anthropologists and "old-fashioned comparative religionists" tag African belief as polytheistic due to the belief in spirits. Spirits are, however, not equal to the Supreme Being.[6] God is the undisputed leader, and as Mbiti notes, 90 per cent of prayers are addressed directly to Him and about 10 percent addressed to Him *through* supernatural powers.[7] People only turn to God if lesser spirits fail to grant their wishes and this seems to somehow separate them from the suggested monotheism. If the Supreme Being is ultimate, far above other supernatural powers, it seems that the African belief system is henotheistic. In this belief system, the Supreme Being is surrounded by subordinate spiritual beings that work for him.

The hierarchical structure of supernatural powers implies that they belong to different categories. But as the progenitor and the power behind their existence, the Supreme Being does not fit into any of these categories and so is not among supernatural powers.

a. The Ancestral Spirits
The Africans generally assume that people ontologically lose their humanness to gain the life of spirits. The departed ancestors or the 'living-dead' "are the benevolent ancestral spirits who are the link between the living and the Supreme Being".[8] They allegedly bestow blessings, fertility, health, prosperity, guard their kinsmen from misfortunes and ensure continuity of the past and the present in the family life of their loved ones. They teach medicine-men and

---

[4] The *Daily nation on the web* http://www.nationaudio.com, accessed on 04.11.2002 reported, "Kipsigis believe that lightning is God's punishment for people who do evil things". This was after some people were struck dead by lightening and therefore there was need to appease the spirits by cleansing the living members of the family.

[5] Noel Q. King, *African Cosmos: An introduction to Religion in Africa* (Belmont, California: Wadsworth Publishing Company, 1986), pp. 8, 9; Bolaji E. Idowu, *Olodumare: God in Yoruba Belief* (London: Longman, 1962), pp, 38, 202, 204; D. Forde, (ed.), *African Worlds: Studies in the Cosmological ideas and Social Values of African People* (London: Oxford University Press, 1954), pp. 211, 222; Kraft, *Understanding Spiritual* Power, p. 77; Mbiti, *The Concept of God*, pp. 121-123.

[6] King, *African Cosmos*, p. 9; Idowu, *Olodumare*, p. 202-204

[7] J. S. Mbiti, *Prayers of African Religion* (London: SPCK, 1975), pp. 3-13.

[8] J. Healey and D. Sybertz *towards an African Narrative Theology* (Nairobi: Pauline Publications-Africa, 1996), p. 211.

diviners, either in dreams or in spiritual trips in the heavens, how to make preventive and curative medicines from recommended herbs, leaves, barks or roots of a tree. They validate political and religious structures by accepting or rejecting leaders. They are liable for the welfare of their progeny on earth. They allegedly maintain a friendly relationship between humans and supernatural powers and also teach the living persons about the moral and ethical issues that must be observed so as to maintain and defend this relationship. They also maintain law and order in the society; hence they are viewed as the police force of the community. They protect the community and give it information concerning the intrigues of their enemies, and rightly so, they are the intelligence and military forces that protect their society from external invasions. If things go wrong within the clan or community they are liable ostensibly because they have failed to give proper instructions. The living members of the community are also blamed for neglecting the ancestors' command. It is also held that ancestral spirits are perilous and threatening if their instructions are not followed and kept. They thus protect when obeyed and cause trouble when disobeyed. Their protective role is only guaranteed when not neglected and if neglected, they could be hostile and callous. It is human faults that invite what may seem as cruelty. This seeming cruelty is to enhance discipline among the family or clan members. It is to uphold the traditional morality and to implant the most cherished values and ideas among their nearest and dearest, therefore a benevolent act. They are thus respected yet feared, wanted yet unwanted.

b. Spirits that were Initially Human but not Ancestral

This category has two divisions. The first one includes spirits of the dead, who unlike the ancestral spirits, have passed out of the memory of the living. Unlike the ancestral spirits, these spirits cannot visit the family but they can assume any shape they want. They make people anxious when too close or when too far from the material world. Preferably, they should not attract remoteness or intimacy. When far-off, most Africans believe that they distress people. They interfere with human life when near, causing madness, possessing and frightening people due to their regular appearances. When these spirits are in their right place, they are benign but when the equilibrium is unstable they are malevolent. The second division consists of the spirits of children who died without proper initiation or adults who departed without children of their own. Also included are the spirits of people who upon death did not receive proper burial, either because wild animals mauled them, or they drowned in rivers, or they were social outcasts such as witches or sorcerers. These spirits are always restless, troubling people who failed to give them proper burial.[9] They are

---

[9] The *Daily Nation on the Web* http://www.nationaudio.com accessed on 04.07.2002 reported of a Kenyan elder/pastor giving evidence in a court of law against a woman who wanted to bury her doctor husband outside their ancestral land. The elder/pastor told the court that according to their culture burial outside the ancestral land would make the spirit of the dead linger in the land and haunt the community. The Semites, and

earthbound, readily available, angry, ruthless and violent. Witches make use of them to bring harm to people who allegedly despised them.

c. Non-human Spirits from the Beginning

The third category consists of non-human spirits whose existence has never been anything else but spirits. Like the spirits in the second category, they occupy either the earth or the air. Those who dwell on earth are referred to as the "spirits of the below" (or spirits of the earth) and those who dwell in the air as the "spirits of the above" (or the spirits of the air).[10] Spirits of below inhabit forests, trees, rivers, mountains, seas, rocks, other natural features, insects, animals (wildlife and domestic), birds, amphibians and reptiles. In every hunting expedition, proper rituals are performed to appease these spirits and specifically the spirit inhabiting the killed animal being addressed as brother.[11] The spirits inhabiting the air are linked with thunder, lightening, sun, rain and other natural occurrences beyond human control. But the spirits inhabiting the earth and those dwelling in the air have an interface with human beings. Those believed to dwell in the air are in practice linked with earthly phenomena and events. "Just as the spirits of the below, they can also posses people, either permanently or temporarily. The possessed may have special powers when this happens, particularly "priestly" powers to sacrifice, to divine or to prophesy".[12] The spirits of the air are generally held to be more powerful than the spirits of the below, which are sometimes identified with the clan and can play the same role as ancestral spirits, that is, to protect and punish the clan members. As Magesa asserts, "they thus render the reality in which they are believed to dwell worthy of great respect by the clan and not to be harmed by it in any way".[13]

These spirits, as the Gĩkũyũ people believe, are merciless and they live in the underworld. They say, 'aria me thĩ nĩ a kĩũnũhũ nĩkĩo tũkayagĩra Ngai' (those [spirits] that are in the underworld are malicious that is why we cry to God).[14] Common to these spirits, whether in the underworld, earth or air, is that they can assume a human form even if they are not flesh and blood. They have abstract bodies like shadows; hence they can possess material or non-material

---

especially the Babylonians, as well as the Graeco–Roman world had similar beliefs (W. O. E. Oesterley, and Theodore H. Robinson *Hebrew Religion: Its Origin and Development* (London: SPCK, 1930), pp. 108-110; George Luck, *Arcana Mundi: Magic and the Occult in the Greek and Roman Worlds* (Baltimore: John Hopkins University Press, 1985), p. 165; E. R. Dodds, *The Ancient Concept of Progress and other Essays on Greek Literature and Belief* (Oxford: Clarendon Press, 1973), p. 206.

[10] E. E. Evans-Pritchard, *Witchcraft, Oracles and Magic among the Azande* (Oxford: Clarendon Press, 1937), pp. 28-105.

[11] Cf. Philo, *De Decalogo* XIV.64, "for all created things are brothers to one another, inasmuch as they are created; since the Father of them all is one, the Creator of the universe".

[12] Magesa, *African Religion*, p. 56.

[13] Magesa, *African Religion*, p. 57.

[14] Leakey, *The Southern Kikuyu*, p. 1104.

reality and disturb people, as they are evil. When neglected they cause mischief to draw attention to their existence thereby receiving sacrifices and offerings. Strangely enough, it is held that these spirits can defy human beings as well as God, yet God does not punish or reward them for their activities. As these spirits inhabit nature, they are also referred to as spirits of nature, which are irritated by any environmental abuse. Ecological abuse is considered extremely hazardous since these spirits can cause nature to withdraw its life-supporting ingredients, thus denying human beings the fullness of life.

Altogether, spirits are benevolent or malevolent. They often seize people for good or for evil but they are judged good or evil in as far as they assist or trouble human life. Good spirits specifically exist to protect people, to curb epidemics, to heal sickness, to assist women in childbirth, to detect and punish thieves and to help in general public needs. Evil spirits not only kill people and steal cattle but also treat people without respect. The cause of evil and suffering is thus attributed to them. Unlike the benevolent spirits, malevolent spirits are generally opposed to people's welfare. They are diffused in nature, always ready to wreak havoc. Malevolent spirits are human in origin and always alien, as they do not belong to the society they attack. Like the evil eyed people,[15] malevolent spirits have anger, envy, sensuality, violence and passion. They can attack people at random without any reason but their attack can be initiated by human error. Nevertheless, people can enter into relationship with the benevolent spirits and so share in their powers and blessings. This relationship is the basis for the protection and security people receive from benevolent spirits, which remain obliging as long as people nurtures a genial relationship with them and with the rest of the non-human creation. It is therefore held that spirits exercise absolute sway over human existence, shaping the perception of evil and suffering. Regrettably, this creates fear and insecurity, making many Africans to be careful not to provoke their wrath. It is believed that people can communicate with these spirits through spirit-possessed mediums so as to maintain and restore the relationship. But the relationship with benign spirits enabling people to resist evil spirits is somewhat difficult to find and maintain, and so, rituals and practices, to which we now turn, are the order of the day.

3:3. Rituals and Practices used to Control Supernatural Powers

Rituals and practices play a leading role in the African context. They uphold the expected equilibrium, avert disaster, restore harmony and ensure that people are in good health and wealth. They give people channels for communicating with, resisting and dominating malevolent supernatural powers. But a faulty

---

[15] The evil eye is perceived as a powerful force, which is a significant factor in the understanding of causality. The evil eyed people cause sickness and bring harm to a person or his/her property just by a mere look. So the evil eyed people are generally perceived as dissenters who are jealous of normalcy. They hurt or destroy good people or their precious property because of envy and jealousy, which is projected through the eye.

relationship hinders communication and ruins the equilibrium, rendering the powers bothersome. Such a situation, so they say, provokes benign supernatural powers to withdraw their protection, leaving people open to the aggression of evil powers. These rituals and practices, which include magic, witchcraft and sorcery, divination, exorcism and domestication of spirits, are often concluded in sacrifices.

i. Magic, Witchcraft and Sorcery

The observations on the ambiguity of magic in chapter one apply to African magic, the practice by which people threatened by witchcraft and sorcery get protection. Witches and sorcerers are inverted characters and are associated with incest and cannibalism.[16] Witchcraft and sorcery are anti-social practices that are frustrated and/or neutralized through magic. But there are two different types of magic. That which protects and counters witchcraft and sorcery is good, acceptable and esteemed by the society.

> It is chiefly the specialists, and particularly the medicine-man, diviner and rainmaker who use the knowledge and manipulation of this mystical power for the welfare of their community. It is used in the treatment of diseases, in counteracting misfortunes, and in warding off or diluting or destroying evil 'power' or witchcraft.[17]

The practitioners of good magic are beneficial to their community, having the ability to use herbs and other concoctions to ward off evil spirits and evil power. They are not like witches and sorcerers who practise and use evil magic to control evil spirits, thereby causing havoc in people's lives. Evil magic involves belief in, and the use of, evil power to harm people and their property and is unacceptable.

> Evil magic is based on, or derives from fear, suspicion, jealous, ignorance or false accusation, which goes on in African villages. People fear to leave around their hair, nails, clothes or other articles with which they are normally in direct contact in case their 'enemies' will use them and work evil against them.[18]

---

[16] But several African societies distinguish witches and sorcerers. Unlike the sorcerers, witches do not use any rituals or incantations or material objects, e.g. human hair, nails or human waste to cause harm to their victims. The witch can cause harm just by looking at a person, hence a witch may be described as one with an evil eye. Yet both are connected with punitive spirits. But while these spirits possess witches, the sorcerer manipulates them. But both can use spirit familiars like animals to cause harm or mischief to human beings. So as Ferdinando, *The Triumph of Christ*, pp. 103, 106 observes, "the distinction cannot be pressed" and "must be applied with flexibility" since in some African cultures "witches are believed also to act like sorcerers".

[17] Mbiti, *African Religions*, p. 198.

[18] Mbiti, *Africans Religions*, pp. 199-200.

It is in evil magic that we find sorcery and witchcraft at work, in addition to other related practices, such as casting the evil eye on children or property.

Medicine-men and diviners can only counteract evil magic if they have more powers than the sorcerer or the witch. As they are supposedly under the direction of benevolent spirits, they usually have more power than witches and sorcerers. They use this power to summon evil spirits, persuading them to talk and reveal the witch who sent them to terrorise their victims. As Mbiti notes, "the principle or logic at work here is that the good use of this power will counteract the evil use, and this keeps the user relatively safe, so long as his 'medicine' is more powerful than that of his enemy".[19] Even if diviners or medicine-men are famous for their protective role and the ability to cure both somatic and psychotic disorders, they may become agents of destruction and death and so dangerous and counterproductive. As a result, they are not only admired and respected but also feared and suspected. Generally, they cause harm and kill those who seek their services with evil intention. Altogether, good magic, even if it causes harm to the offending party, is socially approved as a means of protection and self-defence. It is an offensive and defensive practice that arises from the human need for survival, safety, security and protection. It offers channels and the power to communicate to, and relate with the spirits.

ii. Divination

Divination is the means by which causes and remedies of misfortunes are identified. It also helps in identifying malevolent witches, sorcerers and spirits. As Zahan observes, the diviner "holds the code which allows the decipherment of the various messages intended for man, the society in which he lives, and all else related to his destiny".[20] Numerous techniques are used for divination, and so they may vary from one society to another.[21] Divination provides the means to cope with misfortunes, looking backwards for causes and forward for remedial measures. The diviner's duty is to establish the cause of his/her client's misery and to locate the point at which the equilibrium could have been disturbed to his/her client's disadvantage. As specialized knowledge and/or a way of knowing, divination "uses extraordinary powers of communication to

---

[19] Mbiti, *African Religions*, p. 201.
[20] D. Zahan, *The Religion, Spirituality and Thought of Traditional Africa* (Chicago: The University of Chicago Press, 1979), p. 81.
[21] The Bunyoro of Uganda use mechanical devices, augury and spirit familiars, while the popular *Ifa* divination of West Africa repeatedly manipulates palm nuts (See. J. H. M. Beattie, "Divination in Bunyoro, Uganda" in *Sociologus* 14 (1964), pp. 44-62; J. Middleton, "Oracles and divination among the Lugbara" in J. H. M. Beattie and J. Middleton (eds.), *Spirit Mediumship and Society in Africa* (London: Tavistock, 1969), pp. 220-232; N. S. Booth, "God and the Gods in West Africa", in N. S. Booth, *African Religion: A Symposium* (New York: Nok Publishers, 1977), pp 168-9.

reveal occult realities".[22] It is also a social yardstick for human-to-human relations and the relationship between the individual and society at large. It inspects human relations with the cosmological order, including the seen and unseen reality. The specialized knowledge of divination is not only needed in social life but also in political life. It is central and continues to hold influence in many modern African societies. Politicians competing for political offices reportedly consult diviners to win elections or election petitions in law courts.[23] Divination therefore helps people to identify with what is helpful to the fullness of life and the acquisition of class and status in society. Those who own the secret knowledge of divination hold authority that is not arbitrary as it is attached to the results of their predictions. But their power is only recognized if it boosts communication with good spirits, giving people ways and means of dominating and resisting evil spirits.

It is also held that the diviner's knowledge accumulated in his/her career enables him/her to control other people. However, this knowledge is derived from supernatural powers that allegedly 'catch' a person, inflicting a strange ailment. Such supernatural powers must be identified then the 'caught' person undergoes a rigorous training, which 'opens' him/her up to the secret knowledge of divination. This training also enables the person to know what kind of treatment or sacrifice is appropriate for each divinatory prediction. Training does not invalidate the supernatural and transcendental source of the diviner's knowledge. This supernatural and transcendental source of power is accessible through religious affiliation. The danger is that a diviner can change his/her religious affiliation so as to tap the power given by another religion that their former religion could not give.

The royalty, the priesthood and the populace equally consider divination essential. It precedes all actions and functions, which people fear or believe to have destructive or constructive impact on their social life. It predicts and explains if certain undertakings should be tried for the common good of human life. So it is not only a way of prediction and explanation, but also a means of controlling life-threatening events and experiences. It is a problem-solving ritual and an inoculation against threatening disaster attributable to human *ad hoc* acts that supposedly irritate benevolent supernatural powers, making them withdraw their protection.

iii. Accommodation and Expulsion of Possessing Spirits

It is believed that spirits can possess both animate and inanimate creation for good or evil intentions. A possessed person is described as one having or

---

[22] F. Niyi Akinnaso, "Bourdieu and the Diviner: Knowledge and Symbolic Power in Yoruba Divination" in Wendy James (ed.), *The Pursuit of Identity: Religious and Cultural Formulation* (London and New York: Routledge, 1995), p. 236.

[23] Akinnaso, "Bourdieu and the Diviner", pp. 248-250; Magesa, *African Religion,* p. 20.

caught by spirits.[24] The possessing spirits are revealed by name through rituals such as drumming and dancing, which are meant to induce a state of trance. A specialist purportedly caught by a benign spirit determines if the victim has been caught by, or has benign or malign spirits.[25] If spirits are identified as useful, especially in healing, they are retained or accommodated.[26] This is to establish a lasting relationship between the seizing spirit and the seized person, who finally becomes overpoweringly useful in societal affairs. Such a person becomes a spirit healer, or a diviner or a shaman[27]. He/she could become an advisor of the royalty that is, the king or the chief or ruling class.[28] Accommodation entails retaining supportive benevolent spirits, for instance, the spirits that can heal.

Evil spirits seize animate or inanimate creation with destructive intentions. They cause all manner of troubles, threatening human existence. Such sprits are not accepted. They must be exorcised and subsequently cast either in a hole or into deep waters so as to retain normal life for an individual, family, clan or society.[29] The Gĩkũyũ used to perform a symbolic battle to expel these evil and unwanted spirits. At the sound of the battle horn, as Ikenga-Metuh reveals,

> The entire village rushes out with clubs and sticks and starts to beat down the bushes of both sides of the paths that lead to the stream in the attempt to drive the evil spirits down the stream. At the stream, the war horn is sounded again, and the people throw their sticks into the stream and shout victoriously simultaneously: "Evil spirits and your illness we have crushed you. We now sink you in the river. Let the water drive you far away from us. You will go forever and never return again.[30]

Exorcism thus entails the forced removal of invading and unsupportive malevolent spirits.

Altogether, the aforesaid rituals and practices have a common factor. They are designed to contribute to people's welfare in maintaining or enhancing a

---

[24] See Howell, *The Religious Itinerary of a Ghanaian People,* p. 175; Godfrey Lienhardt, "The Dinka and Catholicism" in J. Davis, *Religious Organization and Religious Experience* (New York: Academic Press, 1982), p. 92.

[25] Willis, *Some Spirits Heal,* pp. 17, 92-115, 171-173.

[26] I. M. Lewis, *Religion in Context: Cults and Charisma* (Cambridge: Cambridge University Press, 1996), pp. 122-138.

[27] I. M. Lewis, *Ecstatic Religion: A Study of Shamanism and Spirit Possession* (London: Routledge, 1989), pp. 49-50; Willis, *Some Spirits Heal,* pp. 92-115.

[28] Lesley A. Sharp, "The Power of Possession in Northwest Madagascar" in Heike Behrend and Ute Luig (eds.), *Spirit Possession: Modernity and Power in Africa* (Oxford: James Currey Ltd; Madison: University of Wisconsin Press, 1999), pp. 6, 13; Willis, *Some Spirits Heal,* pp. 53, 63.

[29] Willis, *Some Spirits Heal,* 1999, pp. 131-2.

[30] E. Ikenga-Metuh, *Comparative Studies of African Traditional Religions* (Onitsha, Nigeria: Imico Publishers, 1987), pp. 75.

sympathetic status quo. They seek to pursue and to maintain harmony in a multifaceted and multidimensional cosmos. They are also meant to keep supernatural powers in their right place for the benefit of human life, which is the centre of operation. Attaining the fullness of life is the desired goal, the ultimate value and concern. When needed, sacrifices, which not only pacify the spirits but also give people assurance that their relationship with supernatural powers is impeccably and fittingly secure, are offered to uphold or restore the propitious status quo. It is generally held that sacrifices are the most effective measures for heartening disturbed spirits. However, they are offered after a successful divination so as to ensure promised blessing if the prediction is positive and also to avert evil if the prediction is negative. This ensures a solid link between the horizontal (human to human) and vertical (divine to human) poles of cosmological order.

Indisputably, Africans interpret the same data that the anthropologists work on and give differing views. Many African societies believe in spirits that are accessible, spirits that can expedite or inhibit human existence. The spirits' all-pervasive power is required for success, guidance, giving order to the universe and meeting crises such as illness, accidents, barrenness and draught. A good relationship with spirits and the spirit world implies that people can access the help and the power of spirits and the spirit world whenever they are in need. As spirits may appear to human beings in various forms of manifestations, such as animals, old people and tiny babies, great care must be taken for no one knows the form they may assume while visiting. They are therefore feared and revered; yet this is injurious to Christianity because fear triumphs where the freedom in Christ should reign.

3:4. Anthropological Interpretations of African Beliefs

Several anthropologists have examined beliefs, rituals and practices about supernatural powers in the African context, but their views differ considerably. Discussions of the phenomena prompting belief in supernatural powers are noticeably multifaceted. This, as the functional approach adopted by most anthropologists would persuasively show, adds vital, didactic and imaginative penetration in understanding these phenomena. The functional approach shows how individuals and society use beliefs in supernatural powers to explain events and experiences in their situation. The approach underlines human ability to build symbolic mediums of perceiving and interpreting the meaning of life. This improves orderliness of personal and communal life. Even so, anthropological views have apparent flaws. As Mary Douglas insists, "any kind of illustrative material is intensely difficult to find for exactly the same reason: no reports are exhaustive; none can avoid bias; there is an enormous subjective element of selection in any ethnographic observation".[31] Below are some of the

---

[31] Mary Douglas, *Natural Symbols*: *Explorations in Cosmology* (London: Barrie Jenkins, 1973), p. 131.

popular anthropological perceptions.

i. Spiritual Powers are Illusions

Some modern anthropologists regard supernatural powers as illusions. The tendency is to deny their existence and that they influence daily life. Evans-Pritchard's magisterial work on witchcraft among the Azande has largely been used to confirm this supposed illusion. The idea is that whatever is not perceptible to the five senses does not exist and that modern people should not explain unstable actions as possession.[32] Since belief in demonic activity negates the scientific perception of reality, it should be rejected. Ferdinando comments, "Western scholarship...tends to accept neither traditional African notions of the spirit world, nor traditional African interpretations of spirit-possession"[33]. Several anthropologists caricature African belief in supernatural powers as a comic strip and the creation of the human mind, hence as a mental pathology. J. Brøgger assertively insists, "There is a fairly general agreement among anthropologists that spirits do not exist"[34]. But as Willis rightly notes,

> although these theories have undoubtedly contributed much to our understanding of the forms taken by 'spirit-possession' in modern Africa and in other parts of the non-Western world, they have also had the effect of diverting attention from the subjective content or experience of 'spirit' agency.[35]

Lewis also observes that while several anthropologists consider witchcraft as all delusion and fantasy, others believe in spirit-possession.[36] At any rate, it is

---

[32] Willis (*Some Spirits Heal*, p. 43) suggests that Evans-Pritchard rejects the reality of the Azande worldview on the basis of an enlightenment informed cosmology, that whatever is not perceptible to the senses does not exist. So for Evans-Pritchard (*Witchcraft, Oracles and Magic*, p. 12), the belief in spirits is mysticism; hence 'mystical notions attribute to phenomena supra-sensible qualities which, or part of which, are not derived from observation or cannot be logically inferred from, and which they do not possess'.

[33] Ferdinando, *The Triumph of Christ*, p. 84.

[34] J. Brøgger, "Spirit Possession and the Management of Aggression among the Sidamo" in *Ethnos* 40 (1975), p. 287. See also E. Bourguignon, *Possession* (San Francisco: Chandler & Sharp, 1976), p. 14; M. Singleton, "Spirits and 'Spiritual Direction': The Pastoral Counselling of the Possessed" in E. R. Fashole-Luke, A. Hastings, R. Gray and G. Tasie (eds.), *Christianity in Independent Africa* (London: Rex Callings, 1978), p. 477; W. van Binsbergen, "Becoming a Sangoma: Religious Anthropological in Francistown, Botswana" in *Journal of Religion in Africa* (1991), p. 336.

[35] Willis, *Some Spirits Heal*, 116.

[36] Lewis, *Religion in Context*, p. 46.

not unanimously held that belief in supernatural powers signify illusions.[37] Farvet-Saada avoided this view in her study of occult action in rural France insisting, "the aim of my book...is to take magic force seriously, and not to be content to describe it as a logical error, or someone else's belief".[38]

However, maintaining that whatever cannot be perceived through the five senses does not exist is delicate. As Dow contends, unless we say that only what is verified empirically exists (in which case God does not), there is no way of disapproving the existence of supernatural powers. The assertion that the present day perception of how things are positively rules out demonic perception is indeed reductionism, and to assume that all possible data can be handled in terms of science and its categories is untenable. Perhaps the societies that believe in spirits do so because they are realities of thought and experience for them. Kwame Appiah rightly points out that anthropologists who deny the existence of spirits ignore the beliefs and intention of the people who invite them to heal and protect. What these people say is that they believe spirits exist and can grant favour to their requests.[39]

ii. Belief in Spirits Symbolizes Lack of Scientific Knowledge

According to Mair, belief in spirits represents lack of scientific knowledge. Central to this assumption is that witchcraft is acknowledged in societies lacking scientific knowledge.[40] Furthermore, witchcraft begins from a mistaken premise even though it explains evil and suffering. But witchcraft and other related beliefs are common in the modern era and are regarded as a resistance to technology and consumer culture. They are the means through which spirit mediums and other specialists demonstrate their authority, reaffirming the society's existing traditions.[41] Spirit mediums therefore "construct the present by pitting the spectre of modernity against the constantly recreated tradition anchored in a mythical past".[42] Consequently, modernity and tradition intersect and interact with each other, making scientific knowledge and mythical

---

[37] P. Stoller and C. Olkes, *Sorcery's Shadow* (Chicago: University of Chicago Press, 1987); Edith Turner, *Experiencing Ritual: A New Interpretation of African Healing* (Philadelphia: University of Pennsylvania Press, 1992).

[38] J. Farvet-Saada, *Deadly Words: Witchcraft in Bocage* (Cambridge: Cambridge University Press, 1980), p. 195.

[39] Appiah, *In My Father's House*, p. 110-115.

[40] L. Mair, *Witchcraft* (London: World University Library, 1969); Cf. Scott, *Domination and the Arts of Resistance*, p. 141.

[41] See Adeline Masquelier, "The Invention of Anti-Tradition: Dodo Spirits in Southern Niger" in Heike Behrend and Ute Luig (eds.), *Spirit Possession: Modernity and Power in Africa* (Oxford: James Currey Ltd; Madison: University of Wisconsin Press, 1999), pp. 34-49, esp.43; Brand Weiss, "Plastic Teeth Extraction: The Iconography of Haya Gastro-Sexual Affliction" in *American Ethnologist* 19 (1992), p. 548.

[42] Masquelier, "The Invention of Anti-Tradition", p. 46.

knowledge cohabit.[43] Even though Mair's intellectual analysis has a certain level of credibility, it is rambling. One of its false allusions is the assumption that witchcraft can disappear just because of increased scientific knowledge. This is unlikely as science and witchcraft work on different levels and with different assumptions. What happens is that scientific knowledge explains *how* things happen while witchcraft and other related beliefs explain *why* things happen. Mbiti avers that Africans are not content with the scientific explanation that a mosquito carrying malaria parasite causes a person to suffer death. The answer sought is why the mosquito stung that particular person and not any other person. The most satisfying answer is that someone sent the mosquito or performed evil magic against the person infected with malaria. "This is not a scientific answer, but it is the reality for the majority of the African people".[44] As such, scientific knowledge does not eliminate theories of witchcraft and spirit attacks, as it does not offer an alternative explanation but one of an incomparable kind. The intellectual approach is therefore faced with difficulties for it fails to explain why in some modern societies "from Africa to the South Seas and from Asia to America",[45] which are surely open to scientific knowledge, people explain misfortunes by means of witchcraft.

iii. Belief in Spirits is an Expression of Psychological Disorders

This view depends on modern medical science, psychology and psychiatry. "Spirit-possessed" people are allegedly mentally sick, deviants or maladjusted. As a result, spirit-possession is any altered or unusual state of consciousness and allied behaviour that some people misunderstand as influence of alien spirits, demons or deities. But it is rightly the projection of the repressed self and a technique of dealing with innate feelings of inferiority, fear, bravery, hatred and/or love.[46] Some anthropologists controvert this view consequently minimizing the assumption that spirit-possession is a symptom of mental disorder or of a maladjusted person.[47] This view having been destabilized, some

---

[43] See Heike Behrend and Ute Luig "Introduction" in Heike Behrend and Ute Luig (eds.), *Spirit Possession: Modernity and Power in Africa* (Oxford: James Currey/Madinson, Wisconsin: University of Wisconsin Press, 1999), pp. xiii-xiv.
[44] Mbiti, *African Religions*, p. 200. See also M Gluckman, *Custom and Conflict in Africa* (Oxford: Basil Blackwell, 1955), p. 85.
[45] M. Marwick (ed.), *Witchcraft and Sorcery* (Harmondsworth: Penguin Books, 1982), p 14. See also Ferdinando, *The Triumph of Christ*, p. 376; E. Bourguignon, (ed.), *Religion, Altered States of Consciousness and Social Change* (Columbus: Ohio State University Press, 1973), pp. 17, 359-376.
[46] See Vincent Crapanzano, "Spirit Possession" in M. Eliade, (ed.), *Encyclopaedia of Religion* Vol. XIV (New York: Macmillan, 1987), pp. 12-16.
[47] Beattie and Middleton, *Spirit Mediumship*, pp. xxiii-xxiv; S. F. Nadel, "A Study of Shamanism in Nuba Hills" in *Journal of Royal Anthropological Institute* 76 (1946), p. 36; F. D. Goodman, *Speaking in Tongues: A Cross-Cultural Study in Glossolalia* (Chicago: University of Chicago Press, 1972), pp. xvii, xxi.

anthropologists regard spirit-possession as the 'abnormal state of consciousness'[48] "which a normal, healthy person could achieve, given the appropriate stimuli".[49] Other anthropologists view spirit-possession cathartically and therapeutically, maintaining it purges out internalised feelings and cures unrelenting health problems.[50] The possessed people are thus regarded as a 'therapy-managing group'.[51] But de Sousa explains that spirit-possession in some societies is non-pathological even if in other societies it could heal and calm individuals. Among the Bijagós, de Souza notes, spirit-possession is a collective non-pathological forum for creating future ancestors and regulating societal life. It also restores concord, allegedly broken by death, between gods and human beings, the forest and the village.[52] Lewis also maintains that the psychiatric and psychoanalytic theories

> only solve part of the problem. They leave out...those possession religions which enshrine morality and where to a large extent the office of shaman is filled ascriptively by candidates who, far from being drawn from the margins of society, are from a perfectly

---

[48] Arnold M. Ludwig, "Altered States of Consciousness" in R. Prince (ed.), *Trance and Possession States* (Montreal: R. M. Bucke, 1968), pp. 69, 70-75. Cf. W. Sargant, *Battle for the Mind* (London: Pan Books, 1959), pp. 92-3; S. S. Walker, *Ceremonial Spirit Possession in Africa and Afro-America* (Leiden: Brill, 1972), p.10; N. G. Holm, "Ecstasy Research in the 20th Century – An Introduction in N. G. Holm (ed.) *Symposium on Religious Ecstasy* (Stockholm: Almqvist and Wicksell, 1982), p. 13.
[49] Ferdinando, *The Triumph of Christ*, p 72. See Walker, *Ceremonial Spirit Possession* pp 16-19, 33-4; Goodman, *Speaking in Tongues*, p. 76.
[50] S. D. Messing, "Group Therapy and Social Status in Zar Cult of Ethiopia" in J. Middleton, *Magic, Witchcraft and Curing* (Austin/London: Texas Press, 1967), p. 285; G. Rouget, *La Musique et la Transe: Esquisse d'une Théorie Générale des relations de la Musique et la Possession* (Paris: Gallimard, 1980), p. 494; Janice Boddy, *Wombs and Alien Spirits: Women and Men in the Zar Cult in Northern Sudan* (Madison: University of Wisconsin Press, 1989); Jean-Paul Colleyn, "Horse, Hunter & Messenger: The Possessed Men of the Nya Cult in Mali" in Heike Behrend and Ute Luig (eds.), *Spirit Possession: Modernity and Power in Africa* (Oxford: James Currey Ltd; Madison: University of Wisconsin Press, 1999), p. 76; Nicole Echard, "The Hausa Bori Possession Cult in the Ader Region of Niger: Its Origin and Present Day Function", in I. M. Lewis, Ahmed Al-Safi and Sayyid Hurreiz (eds.), *Women Medicine: The Zar-Bori Cult in Africa and Beyond* (Edinburgh: Edinburgh University Press, 1991), p. 169; Susan M. Kenyon, "The Case of the butcher's Wife: Illness, Possession & Power in Central Sudan" in Heike Behrend and Ute Luig (eds.), *Spirit Possession: Modernity and Power in Africa* (Oxford: James Currey Ltd; Madison: University of Wisconsin Press, 1999), p. 8.
[51] John Janzen, *The Quest of Therapy in Lower Zaïre* (Berkeley: University of California Press, 1978).
[52] Alexandra O. de Sousa, "Defunct Women: Possession among the Bijagós Islanders" in Heike Behrend and Ute Luig (eds.), *Spirit Possession: Modernity and Power in Africa* (Oxford: James Currey Ltd; Madison: University of Wisconsin Press, 1999), pp. 81-87.

respectable background.⁵³

Again, Lewis notes that modern psychology and psychoanalysis have contributed to the decline of the formerly widespread interest in spirit-possession. He argues that no one would question, "that many of the medical symptoms associated with spiritualism in our own past and in traditional societies are now treated on the psychoanalyst's couch... Certainly in the functional approach to psychiatric medicine so widely adopted today we have an interpretation of psychosomatic disorders".⁵⁴ He adds that his comparison of spirit affliction and modern psychotherapy does not mean that all psychological illness is a response to deprivation.

> The parallel seems best restricted to the incidence and treatment of the neurotic disorders, and particularly to psychosomatic and hysterical afflictions. Whatever other types of malady may be associated with tribal spirit-possession cults, these stand out as the most widely reported symptoms associated with peripheral possession... It is therefore in this field of mental disorder that we should seek correlations between these afflictions and deprivation.⁵⁵

Lewis also finds the psychological analysis confusing. He deems it naïve to place great reliance on the scanty information regarding psychosomatic disorders and hysterical reactions on one hand and social class on the other. He also regards it as naïve to accept the parallel he makes between spirit afflictions and deprivation without reservation.⁵⁶ He consequently concludes,

> I do not believe that social phenomena such as spirit-possession can be explained in terms of psychiatric illness or the malfunctioning of the individual psyches. My approach to the topic (which is no more "psychological"...) assumes that all significant social behavior has an affective (i.e., "psychological") dimension. It is not possible to seek to understand spirit-possession in particular, any more than religion in general, without recognising and acknowledging this.⁵⁷

He comments elsewhere, "All social phenomena which exist in the minds of men have a psychological dimension. This psychological dimension is particularly marked in the case of ideology generally and with those assumptions and beliefs which are invoked to make sense of the universe and to come to terms with affliction and stress".⁵⁸ He eventually regards spirit-

---

⁵³ I. M. Lewis, *Ecstatic Religion: An Anthropological Study of Spirit Possession and Shamanism* (Harmondsworth: Penguin Books, 1971), pp. 202-3.
⁵⁴ Lewis, *Religion in Context*, p. 72.
⁵⁵ Lewis, *Religion in Context*, p. 73.
⁵⁶ Lewis, *Religion in Context*, p. 73.
⁵⁷ Lewis, *Religion in Context*, p. 74.
⁵⁸ I. M. Lewis, *Ecstatic Religion: A Study of Shamanism and Spirit Possession* (London: Routledge, 1989), p. 11.

possession as the result of social deprivation and frustrations (see below).

Yet again, Obeyesekere demonstrates the reciprocity between personal-psychological dimension of the symbol and its public, culturally sanctioned role. He asserts that symbols, which are linked with the spirit-possession, are "generated primarily out of the unconscious; once generated it exists on the public level as a cultural symbol".[59] Thus individual and personal psychological and socio-cultural aspects of the human self intersect and interact to determine what is real for a people. He positively shows that the usual anthropological and psychoanalytical distinction between personal and cultural symbols is inadequate and naïve. In fact, the mental and social framework within which the urge to control spirits lies is psychologically and culturally organised. As a result, psychological and socio-cultural dimensions mutually complement each other, so they need not be separated. It seems that to consider the psychological dimension as the only explanation of spirit-possession invites untenable confusion. While spirit-possession may share similar characteristics with psychological defects, it does not necessarily mean that they are one and the same thing. Rightly stated, "sickness does not reveal the calling of a person and ritual does not transform mental disorder into religious office".[60]

iv. *Belief in Spirits is an Expression of Socio-cultural Identity*

Several anthropologists regard belief in spirits as a socially and culturally determined phenomenon. It is controversial whether societies most open to spirit cults are those with complex and rigid, or less complex and less rigid, cultures. Bourguignon maintains that societies that have a complex and rigid culture approve spirit-possession. He maintains that spirit-possession provides the society with a channel for innovation that would be otherwise unavailable, thus giving people a great degree of elbowroom.[61] Conversely, Mary Douglas argues that the Dinka, whose culture is less rigid and complex, welcome spirit-possession while the Nuer, whose culture is more rigid and complex consider it perilous.[62] She holds that spirit-possession allows loosely structured societies to have an integrated socio-political organisation and group cohesion. The general agreement is that the roles of the spirit cult are to construct, strengthen and reproduce social and individual identity. This in turn produces skills for a larger social formation that guides people to local cultural knowledge and collective identity. As such, spirit-possession represents the origin of a society, which the possessing spirits defend by limiting external pressure. The possessing spirits assist people to accrue and apply new ideas, objects and methods for collective and private empowerment. According to Echard, the value of spirits is sociological, historical and political and very rarely psychological. The spirits

---

[59] G. Obeyesekere, *Medusa's Hair: An Essay on Personal Symbols and Religious Experience* (Chicago/London: University of Chicago Press, 1981), p. 37.
[60] Colleyn, "Horse, Hunter & Messenger", p. 74.
[61] Bourguignon, *Religion, Altered States*, pp. 17-23.
[62] Douglas, *Natural Symbols,* pp. 119-130.

rekindle socio-historical realities, that is, how the society was constituted and the main events that brought about major changes.[63] Consequently, spirit cults meet people where they are, offering "meaningful explanations for the social problems of the time".[64] The idea is that beliefs in spirits relate directly to the socio-cultural conditions.

v. Deprivation and Marginalisation Causes Spirit Possession

A widespread perception among anthropologists is that spirit-possession is caused by deprivation and marginalisation. Lewis supports this view in his reaction to Bourguignon[65] and Mary Douglas.[66] He notes that Bourguignon regards trance as 'an altered state of consciousness', while Douglas considers possession as a 'cultural specific theory of trance and illness'. But Lewis hold that these theories are limited. There is "no compelling evidence to suggest that these [trances and possession] necessarily indicate cultures or civilisations with different infrastructures or at different levels of evolutionary complexity".[67] According to Lewis, there are two types of spirit-possession cults. One deals with ancestral spirits of the community, which upholds traditional social morality. The other deals with peripheral spirits that have nothing to do with morality for they come from outside the society. These spirits are capricious, affecting mainly women and estranged males. However, possession by peripheral spirits is a political protest of the politically and socially sidelined. He insists, "possession works to help the interest of the weak and downtrodden who have otherwise few effective means to press their claims for attention and respect".[68] It is "the shrill voice of protest directed against other more fortunate members of the society".[69] It occurs due to 'deprivation and frustrations' of the sidelined[70] and so "a compensation of their exclusion and lack of authority in other spheres".[71]

Several anthropologists, just like Lewis, regard spirit-possession as a

---

[63] Echard, "The Hausa Bori Possession Cult", p. 70.
[64] Ute Luig, "Constructing Local Worlds: Spirit Possession in the Gwembe Valley, Zambia" in Heike Behrend and Ute Luig (eds.), *Spirit Possession: Modernity and Power in Africa* (Oxford: James Currey Ltd; Madison: University of Wisconsin Press, 1999), p. 137.
[65] E. Bourguignon, *Possession* (San Francisco: Chandler and Sharp, 1976).
[66] Mary Douglas (ed.), *Witchcraft: Confession and Accusation* (London: Tavistock Publications Limited, 1970).
[67] Lewis, *Ecstatic Religion*, p. 9.
[68] Lewis, *Ecstatic Religion*, p. 28. Cf. Scott, *Domination and the Arts of Resistance* pp. 140-142.
[69] Lewis, *Ecstatic Religion: An Anthropological*, p. 203.
[70] Lewis, *Religion in Context*, p. 53.
[71] Lewis, *Religion in Context*, p. 48. Also see W. A. Shack, "Hunger, Anxiety and Ritual: Deprivation and Spirit Possession among the Gurage of Ethiopia" in *Man* 6 (1971), pp. 33-35; Walker, *Ceremonial Spirit Possession*, pp. 79-80, 84-85, 164-168.

marginal response of the weak and the powerless,[72] and so it is a 'bargain from weakness'.[73] It is a means of voicing minority, disfavoured and likely risky opinion and simultaneously avoiding the danger of being chastised. The possessing spirit is blamed for any utterances or actions coming from the possessed person. Spirit-possession is thus related to historical crises and it is recognised as a 'safety valve' that enables the subordinates to assert themselves temporarily without being blamed for their actions. As a result, even if spirit-possession in women is seen as evidence of their subordinate status in contrast to men, it is also the means by which they assert themselves over men. These subordinate women can thereby claim that they have spirits as their spouses, which are superior and more powerful than their human male spouses in ordinary life. This offers women new (though temporary and indirect) forms of leverage with the more powerful male.[74] In that case, belief in spirit is not only an expression of deprivation and frustrations, but also a technique of protesting against social exclusion. It is an empowering device that grants alternative techniques of dealing with the issues considered to be outside the control and discourse of the dominant group.[75] The heretofore marginalised gain individual identity, autonomy and power.

But the Lewisian deprivation theory is contentious and some anthropologists

---

[72] J. Monfouga-Nicolas, Ambivalence et Culte de Possession: Contribution à l'Etude du Bori Hausa (Paris: Anthropos, 1972); Nicole Echard, Bori. Aspects d'un Culte de Possession Hausa dans l'Ader et le Kurfey (Niger) CEA EHESS: Documents de Travail, p. 10; Messing, "Group Therapy and Social Status", pp. 285-293; Boddy, Wombs and Alien Spirits; P. Stoller, The Taste of Ethnographic Things (Philadelphia: University of Pennsylvania Press, 1989).

[73] R. Gomm, "Bargaining from Weakness: Spirit Possession on the South Kenya Coast" in Man 10 (1975), pp. 530-543.

[74] See Laurel Kendall, The Life and Hard Times of a Korean Shaman: Of Tales and the Telling of Tales (Honolulu: University of Hawaii Press, 1988); Brown K. McCarthy, Mama Lola: A Vodou Priestess in Brooklyn (Berkeley/Los Angels: University of California Press, 1991), pp. 248, 306-8; I. M. Lewis, Ahmed Al-Safi and Sayyid Hurreiz (eds.), Women Medicine: The Zar-Bori Cult in Africa and Beyond (Edinburgh: Edinburgh University Press, 1991), p. 3; Vincent Crapanzano, Tuhami: A Portrait of a Moroccan (Chicago: University of California Press, 1983); Boddy, Wombs and Alien Spirits,; Kenyon, "The Case of the butcher's Wife", pp. 89-108; James Wafer, The Taste of Blood: Spirit Possession in Brazilian Candomblé (Philadelphia: University of Pennsylvania Press, 1991), pp. 2-3; Lewis, Religion in Context, p. 48.

[75] Scott's study, Domination and the arts of resistance, powerfully illustrates this point. The powerless feign respect while the powerful assert control carefully and cleverly. He offers an incisive discussion of the respectful and non-vengeful public discourse of the powerless and the powerful that he refers to as the 'public transcript' and the mockery and vengeful discourse they display backstage that he refers to as the 'hidden transcript' (p. xii) He reveals how the subordinate develop a large arsenal of techniques that help to shield their identity while promoting open criticism, threats and attacks to the powerful. Among these techniques is "spirit possession", which gives a free rein to dangerous expressions that may summon hostility from the powerful (p. 2. See his footnote 1).

are opposed to it. Mary Douglas argues that the deprivation theory "is unable to deal with the many cases of people who are obviously and consciously deprived, and yet do not react in the predicted way".[76] The explanation of suffering and deprivation as precursors of spirit-possession, she maintains, does not cover the throng of well-to-do women who so often dominate spirit-possession movements[77]. Kenyon notes that possessed people neither regard themselves as a 'depressed category', 'depraved' or 'frustrated', nor do they try to exert any type of mystical pressure on either spirits or humans. They do not see anyone, either male or female, spirit or human as their superior. They do not feel that they have limited resources at their disposal. However, Kenyon concedes that spirit-possession is complex, though it is an empowering occasion for many women. It fortifies female power and control in the wider social world.[78] Thus the belief in spirits is seen as the expression of women culture, a gender-specific form of interaction and communication in order to overcome women's sickness and suffering.[79]

Sharp disputes the notion that spirit-possession gives women temporary and indirect power. He states that spirit marriages in Madagascar where he did his field research operate as permanent as opposed to temporary form of empowerment.[80] The view that women and men of low status bid for attention through spirit-possession is not unanimously convincing. As Colleyn admits,

> Spirit-possession cannot be seen as an oblique strategy or weapon against humiliation. Mediumship is restricted to men of powerful lineages and seldom used to insinuate grievances. Mediums do not belong to the categories of persons who are most readily prone to possession in the epidemiological trends deployed by I. M. Lewis in his comparative study (1996).[81]

Similarly, Wendl's study challenges the view that belief in supernatural powers attracts the marginalised and the socially deprived. He reveals that in the Tchamba cult amongst the Mina of Togo, "it is the descendants of the former slave masters who are afflicted by the spirits of their former slaves".[82] Wendl notes that belief in spirits does not belong either to the socially or economically marginalised or depressed section of the society. Such beliefs are distributed over diverse and reputable professional groups. He contends that his case study "may thus be considered, in some respect, to be even an antithesis to Lewisian

---

[76] Douglas, *Natural Symbols*, p. 117.
[77] Douglas, *Natural Symbols*, p. 113.
[78] Kenyon, "The Case of the butcher's Wife", p. 100.
[79] Ute Luig, "Besessenheit als Ausdruck von Frauenkultur in Zambia" in *Peripherie* 47/48 (1992), pp. 112, 113-115; Kenyon, "The Case of the butcher's Wife", p. 120.
[80] Sharp, "The Power of Possession", pp. 182-4. Cf. de Sousa, "Defunct Women" p. 87
[81] Colleyn, "Horse, Hunter & Messenger", p. 73.
[82] Tobias Wendl, "Slavery, Spirit Possession & Ritual Consciousness" in Heike Behrend and Ute Luig (eds.), *Spirit Possession: Modernity and Power in Africa* (Oxford: James Currey Ltd; Madison: University of Wisconsin Press, 1999), p. 111.

deprivation theory".[83]

On the basis of available evidence, it could be complex to assume that spirit-possession is marginal and only occurs among the marginalized and deprived people. As it seems, it is not marginal but a central cultural phenomenon and not only an experience of the underprivileged but also of the affluent too. It is widespread despite one's religious link, level of education or cosmopolitan experience. It could be complicated therefore to only link spirit-possession with women, inferior or deviant groups and lower class members of a stratified society. It may be unrealistic to explain spirit-possession as an expression of, and a compensatory technique for marginality, which provides a therapeutic outlet for psychological frustrations. In fact, the idea that spirit-possession is an expertise to command attention, to redress grievances, to gain material benefits and an alternative to gaining some measure of status and power are inadequate explanations about beliefs in spirits. Yet this does not rule out the probability that such ideas might, at least, offer somewhat relevant explanations in some cases.

vi. Beliefs in Spirits are Symbolic Cultural Texts

As Giles notes, several studies regard possession "as a culturally-constructed symbolic medium that must be related to the wider society and its system of meaning".[84] She writes,

> Spirit-possession provides an ideal for the creation of cultural texts. It creates powerful metaphorical dramas that are enacted in human form but attributed to the spirit world. The human actors are not actors in the conventional sense but a stage—the human body becomes a vehicle for the spirits to communicate with and interact with the human world.[85]

Several scholars agree that the human actors often occupy a structural position, which renders them culturally suitable to become vehicles for the spirits.[86] To be involved with spirits is a valuable social function, rather than an indication of social deprivation. It is an "integral part of the whole culture" rather than the

---

[83] Wendl, "Slavery, Spirit Possession", p. 111.

[84] Linda L. Giles, "Spirit Possession & the Symbolic Construction of Swahili Society" in Heike Behrend and Ute Luig (eds.), *Spirit Possession: Modernity and Power in Africa* (Oxford: James Currey Ltd; Madison: University of Wisconsin Press, 1999), p. 142-164.

[85] Giles, "Spirit Possession", p. 143.

[86] Jacqueline Nicholas, *Ambivalence et Culte de Possession* (Paris: Anthropos, 1972); Michael Lambek, *Human Spirits: A Cultural Account of Trance in Mayotte* (Cambridge/New York: Cambridge University Press, 1981); Bruce Kapferer, *A Celebration of Demons: Exorcism and the Aesthetic of Healing in Sri Lanka* (Bloomington: Indiana university Press, 1983); Linda L. Giles, "Possession Cults on the Swahili Coast: A Re-Examination of the Theories of Marginality" in *Africa* 57 2 (1987), pp. 234-258.

isolated "subculture".[87]

Beliefs in spirits function as a symbolic system of conveying meaning and as an embodiment of cultural constructed texts of communication. These texts enable the formulation of other cognitive models that would counteract the dominant models within the society and they are 'written' and 'read' by the societies concerned.[88] They are the stories that a society tells about itself and the language used is exceedingly symbolic. Perhaps the symbolic language reflects ordinarily vague metaphysical aspects of society that are updated into symbolic drama form. It shields the views of society that counter bureaucratic ideological statements without requiring public credit. For that reason, the texts can have different levels of meaning that allow distinct personal interpretations. The text can be interpreted in terms of personal lives of the people involved in spirit-possession. This does not deny the specific interpersonal relations between the individual psyche and societal expectations. It could also be that cultural texts are self-reflective commentary on the socio-cultural structures that focus more on social relations than the wider system of cultural meaning. So belief in spirits delivers a message that is often identified as the dialectical expression of basic societal, cultural or cosmic paradoxes. Therefore possession is the foundation for the symbolic expression of cultural identity and historical consciousness. This cultural identity and historical consciousness are situated at the very heart of the belief in spirits. In this case, spirit-possession does not belong to a periphery cult but it is central to human existence. It is "the central institution of local culture that defines collective identity"[89]. It is not merely an experience of the disenfranchised as it epitomises the place of people in the society.

vii. Beliefs in Spirits are the Basis of Religious and Moral Values

From this view, spirit-possession and witchcraft accusations are perceived as a means of restoring social harmony. Sargant believes that spirit-possession sanctions socially approved behaviour, because the possessed dancers enact the character of their gods.[90] Spirit-possession is regarded as the means of establishing order and moral values in the society.[91] According to Echard, spirit-possession is the management of the unseen world where dialogue between the worshipper and the spirits take place. The spirits express themselves through the human bodies they are possessing. At this time, the spirits answer requests, give advice, make remarks and voice their own

---

[87] Lambek, *Human Spirits,* pp. 63.

[88] Edwin Ardener, "Belief and the Problem of Women" in J. S. La Fontaine (ed.), *The Interpretation of Ritual* (London: Tavistock, 1972), pp. 135-158; Clifford Geertz, "Deep Play: Notes on the Balinese Cockfight" in *Daedalus,* (Winter 1972), pp. 1-37.

[89] Sharp, "The Power of Possession", p. 6.

[90] W. Sargant, *Battle for the Mind* (London: Pan Books, 1959).

[91] Evans M. Zuesse, *Ritual Cosmos: The Sanctification of Life in African Religion* (Athens, Ohio: Ohio University Press, 1979).

demands that form the framework of the community's moral structure and religious values.[92] Hagan holds that spirit-possession illuminates and enables the person to reach the desired end of the religious quest to experience the divine. This enlarges the unseen world by revealing unknown divinities and creating new and relevant relationships between the visible and invisible. Spirit-possession thus regulates and renews the basis of social order. Trance is the means through which people justify their loyalty to particular spirits and establishes the importance of paying reverence to such spirits. It also precludes or purges disruptive forces in society, especially in situations of social change and distress. It assists individuals to make decisions that assist them to stick to their role and status in society. It assures religious certainty in a state of institutional and emotional confusion and uncertainties. It gives positive direction and support in situations where change is needed and transforms a situation of "negative liminality into one of positive liminality".[93]

Zahan recognises the religious significance of the motif of witchcraft accusations,[94] for example the association of witches and sorcerers with the night. She reveals that beliefs in sorcery and witchcraft are accurately understood within the total structures of people's religious traditions.[95] Witchcraft is associated with the perversion of the good, moral and ethical.[96] The general belief is that victims of witchcraft are somehow responsible if they have departed from the expected moral codes. As a result, witchcraft may be perceived as a divine means of punishing people who exhibit anti-social traits. While witchcraft upsets the established order and causes chaos, it also enhances the understanding of morality and ethics.[97] Order requires people to observe all sexual and other taboos of the community so as to avoid being accused as a witch, the representative of amoral and anti-social behaviour such as incest and sodomy. Witchcraft accusations enhance morality in offering the society tools to check untamed desire and the destruction of life. People are often required to conduct their lives religiously and morally, observing acceptable social norms that witchcraft negates. Religious tradition duty-binds a moral person to suppress destructive emotions such as hatred, anger, pride, envy and lust. The stress is on the best ways to suppress destructive emotions by showing love, care, concern and sharing with other people. Then witchcraft accusation warns

---

[92] Echard "The Hausa Bori Possession Cult", p. 69

[93] George P. Hagan, "Divinity and Experience: The Trance and Christianity in Southern Ghana" in Wendy James and Douglas H. Johnson (eds.), *Vernacular Christianity: Essays in Social Anthropology of Religion* (Oxford: JASO, 1988), pp 149, 152.

[94] Witchcraft accusations is a technical anthropological term, which describes forces either human or non-human, which frustrate human beings' attempt to realize the abundant life, as demonic or using demonic supernatural powers (Cf. David G. Horrell, *Social-Scientific Approaches to the New Testament Interpretation* (Edinburgh: T & T Clark, 1999), pp. 29, 33.

[95] Zahan, *The Religion, Spirituality*, pp. 93-98.

[96] Magesa, *African Religion*, pp. 69, 165-174.

[97] Magesa, *African Religion*, pp. 167, 171.

members of a society against known and imagined anti-social behaviours.[98] It vetoes falsified deeds, ultimately increasing social solidarity and conformity.[99] It not only explains and confirms social definitions, but also categorises moral and religious dynamics of society. It is a means through which a society ascertains and enforces its moral code.

viii. Belief in Spirits is a Way of Political and Economic Protest

Some anthropologists regard spirit-possession as a technique for limiting or tolerating change attributed to colonialism, European military power and occupation, dictatorship and authoritarian regimes.[100] In view of the escalating interest in power and political agency, spirit-possession is regarded as a political/economic reaction to evils ingrained in the society but voiced in safer religious voices and skill. According to this view, spirit-possession does not represent archaic forms of traditionalism that arise in times of deprivation and hopelessness. It rather signifies a keen awareness of existing power structures and hegemonic forces. It is an expression of "symbolic discontent",[101] which operates as an indirect and safer form of political protest, a "veiled, safer outlet".[102] This protest reveals spiritual authority and so reasserts the power of the masses, thus destabilizing larger hegemonic forces. The widely held view is that the great majority use spirit-possession for revolutionary and recalcitrant

---

[98] M. H. Wilson, *Good Company: A Study of Nyakyusa Age-Village* (London: Oxford University Press, 1951), p.104; M. Marwick, "The Social Context of Cewa Witch Beliefs" in *Africa* 22 (1952), pp.123-4, 228; T. O. Beidelmann, "Witchcraft in Ukaguru" in J. Middleton and E. H. Winter (eds.), *Witchcraft and Sorcery in East Africa* (London: Routledge and Kegan Paul, 1963), pp. 96-7; C. Haule, *Bantu Witchcraft and Christian Morality: The Encounter of Bantu Uchawi with Christian Morality – An Anthropological and Theological Study* (Schonek –Beckenried: Nouvelle Revue de Science Missionnair, 1969), pp. 96-7; Magesa, *African Religion*, p. 171.
[99] Haule, *Bantu Witchcraft*, p. 99, Magesa, *African Religion*, p. 172.
[100] Beattie and Middleton, *Spirit Mediumship*, pp. xxviii-xxix; S. Barrington-Ward, "'The Centre Cannot Hold …' Spirit Possession as Redefinition" in E. R. Fashole-Luke, A. Hastings, R. Gray and G. Tasie (eds.), *Christianity in Independent Africa* (London: Rex Collings, 1978), pp. 459-61; D. S. Noble, "Demoniacal Possession among the Giryama" in *Man* No 49 Vol. 61 (1961), p. 52; J. H. M. Beattie, "Spirit Mediumship in Bunyoro" in J. H. M. Beattie and J. Middleton (eds.), *Spirit Mediumship and Society in Africa* (London: Routledge and Kegan Paul, 1969), p. 161; E. Colson, "Spirit Possession Among the Tonga of Zambia" in J. H. M. Beattie and J. Middleton (eds.), *Spirit Mediumship and Society in Africa* (London: Routledge and Kegan Paul, 1969), pp. 83-85.
[101] Allan Pred and M. J. Watts, *Reworking Modernity: Capitalism and Symbolic Discontent* (New Brunswick, New Jersey: Rutgers University Press, 1992).
[102] Scott, *Domination and the Arts of Resistance*, p. 141.

actions.[103] Spirit-possession in this sense conveys an urge to speak out satisfying national, political and economic needs. This opposes the widely held view that "all possession cults divert the worshipper from practical actions by transforming social realities into the realm of imaginary".[104] Spirit-possession is therefore not a story of the marginalised and the powerless seeking temporary voice. Mediums do not represent an oblique attempt to control but a vital force in times of deliberate social and economic transformation. They are the true guardians of sacred space who manage and control the means of production where capitalism prevails.[105]

ix. Reactions to the Anthropological Interpretations

The different anthropological interpretations cited above expose the dilemma involved in analysing beliefs in supernatural powers. However, they certainly give a wider scope of understanding the intrinsic worth or futility of such beliefs in relation to human existence. Taken separately, each perception could be somewhat reductionist if spirit cults, as Fritz Kramer avers, have several functions. As such, they perform not only one role but also a whole range of different and numerous functions simultaneously, which can cancel each other. Spirit cults therefore serve as therapy, as entertainment, as social criticism, as art, as means to differentiate oneself from one's society, and sometimes even as a form of performative ethnography.[106] Neither do anthropological views clarify if supernatural powers transcend nature. A clear but puzzling "residue remains, for which there is as yet no psychological explanation, and which continues to leave the question open as to whether certain happenings transcend nature".[107] Twelftree believes that psychologists are still faced with this unexplained residue in the interpretation of their fieldwork. While it is unhelpful to deny the medical, rational and psychological accounts regarding the unexplained residue, the question of demonic influence remains open. Even if diseases have a natural or regular depiction, the demonic need not be ruled

---

[103] Echard "The Hausa Bori Possession Cult", p. 71; Heike Behrend, "Power to Heal and Power to Kill: Spirit Possession and War in Northern Uganda" in Heike Behrend and Luig Ute (eds.), *Spirit Possession: Modernity and Power in Africa* (Oxford: James Currey Ltd; Madison: University of Wisconsin Press, 1999), pp. 20-33.
[104] Echard, "The Hausa Bori Possession Cult", p. 71.
[105] Sharp, "The Power of Possession", p. 65-14; David Lan, *Guns and Rain: Guerrillas and Spirit Mediums in Zimbabwe* (Berkeley: University of Chicago Press, 1985); Masquelier, "The Invention of Anti-Tradition", p. 34; Willis, *Some Spirits Heal*, pp. 42-77.
[106] Fritz W. Kramer, *Der rote Fes. Über Besessenheit und Kunst in Afrika* (Frankfurt am Main: Athenäum, 1987), p. 233.
[107] T. K. Oesterreich, *Possession: Demoniacal and Other Among Primitive Races, in Antiquity, the Middle Ages, and Modern Times* (London: Kegan Paul, Trench, Trubner & Co, 1930), p. 378.

out[108]. Anthropological views may have credibility but the problem, viewed from the perspective of African worldview and religion is that "psychologising the phenomena too much robs it of its essential theological character"[109]. Explaining possession in terms of social function, personal advantage or neurophysiology, "does not necessarily invalidate other possible, including mystical, explanations of the experience".[110]

The general editor of *Churchman* Vol. 94, 3 (1980) noted a general accord among the contributors that illness can have a spiritual dimension, so healing should incorporate such a dimension.[111] Dunn and Twelftree specifically note that mental illness can have a spiritual cause; so effective treatment must take seriously and operate at all different levels or dimensions of illness. They regard it as equally foolish to treat a spiritually rooted malady as a mere physical or mental illness as well as to treat an illness that may be mainly mental as a case of demon possession.[112] Spirit-possession must not be reduced to anthropological or psychological experiences. In fact, a religious experience has clear autonomy to develop its own models, causes and experiences. This fittingly applies to spirit-possession, a complex religious experience that cannot be pegged to a single dimension.

It cannot be denied that some anthropologists reduce belief in supernatural powers to the roles such beliefs play. There is a notable hermeneutical problem as to the belief in, and concept of supernatural powers and which is widened by the modern worldview. The anthropological theories that have been formulated at different historical eras somehow enlarge the problem. As noted above, some of these theories regard spirit-possession as an antediluvian and pre-scientific diagnosis of a condition that can be otherwise explained. But as Borg insists,

> Whatever the modern explanation might be and however much psychological or social factors might be involved, it must be stressed that Jesus and his contemporaries (along with people in most cultures) thought that people could be possessed or inhabited by a spirit or spirits from another plane. Their worldview took for granted the actual existence of such powers.[113]

The problem is that, in assessing religious beliefs of other cultures, it is natural to start from one's own. Regrettably, this contributes to unabated bias and a tendency to deny the experiences of those who believe in spirits. This bias can be minimised or better still avoided if scholars take seriously what those involved say about themselves. As Klauck points out, it is vital to pay heed to

---

[108] Graham Twelftree, *Christ Triumphant: Exorcism Then and Now* (London: Hodder & Stoughton, 1985), p. 156.
[109] Magesa, *African Religion*, pp. 173-4.
[110] Ferdinando, *The Triumph of Christ*, p. 85.
[111] Peter Williams, "Editorial" *Churchman* 94 3 (1980), p. 198.
[112] J. D. G. Dunn and Graham H. Twelftree, "Demon Possession and Exorcism in the New Testament" in *Churchman* 94 3 (1980), p. 233.
[113] Borg, Marcus *Jesus: A New Vision* (San Francisco: Happer & Row, 1987), pp. 63-7.

what people of a specific cultural sphere at a given point in time understood under the headings of religion, faith, piety and the experience of the divine, where they recognised the working of numinous powers and where they saw a transcendence that went beyond interworldly horizons.[114] Perhaps as Kwame Appiah argues, "it is precisely the absence of...our alien, alternative point of view in traditional culture that makes it reasonable to adopt the 'traditional' worldview. The evidence that spirits exist is obvious: priests go into trance, people get better after application of spiritual remedy, people die regularly from the action of inimical spirits".[115]

Equally, the African perception too, somehow magnifies the problem. It is therefore vital not to neglect anthropological, sociological and psychological perceptions in interpreting beliefs in supernatural powers. There are cases where social, political, economic and psychological factors come into play. In concord with Klauck, a solitary concentration on a particular culture's religious beliefs cannot be recommended since it lacks objective criterion for description. The approaches from the outside (anthropological etc) and from the inside (people's beliefs) provide ample parameters to work with.[116] The problem is that there is no criterion for judging whether it is the spiritual or the social, political, economic and psychological at work. Reality can be perceived differently depending on the perspective from which it is approached. It must be admitted, though, that spiritual, social, political, economic and psychological dimensions of human life are interlinked and interrelated. Behavioural traits attributable to one dimension may be influenced by, or may influence other dimensions. But Western anthropologists, like the Africans, seem to favour just one dimension, probably due to their backgrounds and prejudices, which influence their reading of the available data. The data, according to some anthropologists, show that beliefs in supernatural powers are marginal while to others the same data point to its centrality. The same data lead Africans to perceive the significance of the spirits and to belief that they determine their existence. Gunton is probably right in noting that "the language of possession by demonic forces... is used to express the helplessness of human agents in the face of psychological, social and cosmic forces in various combinations".[117] This may imply that, as this book often insists, supernatural powers and the structures of human existence interlock and network to cause evil and distress in human life.

---

[114] Klauck, *The Religious Context*, pp. 8-9.
[115] Appiah, *In My Father's House*, p. 118.
[116] Klauck, *The Religious Context*, p. 9.
[117] Gunton, *The Actuality of Atonement*, p. 70.

3:5. The Views of Comparative Religionists and African Theologians

i. Traditional Beliefs as the Basis of the Postulate of Affinity

The views of W. R. Smith that religion does not start with a *tabula rasa* and that a new scheme of faith can only deliver if it appeals to the religious instincts and susceptibilities that already exist[118] significantly influenced comparative religionists. It is supposed that converts to the major religions of the world do not jettison their traditional beliefs. Devotion to life-long held beliefs arguably continue to provide converts with a style of thinking, which helps them to describe the actual state of affairs as disclosed by their world. Within this style of thinking lie the belief in God and lesser supernatural powers whose mysteries are imperceptible to unaided human intellect. Some 'common threads' supply essential motive power that leads humanity away from the physical and mechanical view of the universe to the spiritual and ethical dimension. Therefore the primal worldview forms the most basic and decisive religious forms, which represent a people's shared religious heritage. For that reason, comparative religionists and African theologians give the African primal worldview positive attention, regarding it as a valid tool for imparting relevant contextual theology and hermeneutics. In this way, African culture and worldview are not only *praeparatio evangelica*, but also *"indispensable resources in the interpretation of the gospel message* and in the development of African Christianity".[119] It is believed that African culture and worldview can make considerable contributions to the universal community of faith.

The most penetrative work suggesting the postulate of affinity between the Bible and African worldview is perhaps Turner's analysis of primal religions.[120] Turner reveals that supernatural powers, which populate the world we live in, can affect and sway human existence. People, Turner states, "can enter into relationship with this benevolent spirit world and so share in its powers and blessings and receive protection from evil forces by these more-than-human helpers".[121] He also notes, "across the primal world there seems to be a longing for the true life of man that is not yet achieved and that can only come from the gods ... the transcendent source of true life and practical salvation".[122] There is also the eschatological hope in which human beings not only share the life and power of spirits in this world but also beyond death. Death is not the end since the departed ancestors are still part of the living

---

[118] W. Robertson Smith, *Lectures on the Religion of the Semites* (London: Adam Charles & Black, 1889)
[119] Ukpong, "Development in Biblical Interpretation in Africa", p. 19.
[120] H. W. Turner, "Primal Religions and their Study", in V. Hayes *Australian Essays in World Religion* (Bedford Park: Australian Association for the Study of Religion, 1977), pp. 27-37.
[121] Turner, "Primal Religions", p. 31.
[122] Turner, "Primal Religions", pp. 31-2.

family, being united in affection and in mutual obligation. This makes life to be full of hope as the living and the dead will reunite and receive the immortality of supernatural powers.[123] Turner's analysis finally conceives the physical as the vehicle for 'spiritual' power and that people live in a sacramental universe where there is no dichotomy between the physical and the spiritual. This happens due to the belief that the physical realm is patterned on the mode of the spiritual world. Thus all things are connected with human existence in a world regarded as a microcosm of the macrocosm.[124] Turner's analysis, as he insists, could be used for understanding other kinds of religion besides the primal and will be found readily applicable to the Christian tradition.[125] He gives a positive rapport between primal religions and Christianity, noting that history reveals that the expansion of Christianity mainly and rapidly occurs in places where people still hold to primal religious systems.[126]

Turner's analysis and what has been said above about the African view of supernatural powers have a lot in common. This may have moved several comparative religionists to identify "surprising parallels between religious practices of the primal societies and some practices described in the Bible".[127] They recognise a postulate of affinity between African belief in supernatural powers and biblical supernaturalism. As in the New Testament, the African worldview presupposes an obvious presence and real existence of unseen spirits that intrude into the world and interact with people. For that reason, the African worldview could be an important asset in expounding the Bible. According to Waliggo, the profundity of the Bible cannot be clearly understood without considering the African worldview.[128] The African worldview is considered as helpful to one seeking to relate biblical supernaturalism to a modern social and religious framework. Bediako notes, "The spiritual universe of African primal world does offer valid perspectives for articulating Christian theological commitment".[129]

ii. Reflecting on the Postulate of Affinity

The postulate of affinity between African and biblical supernaturalism seems

---

[123] Turner, "Primal Religions", p. 32. See Mbiti, *African Religions*, p. 83; Magesa *African Religion,* p. 58; G. Wanjohi, *The Wisdom and Philosophy of the Gĩkũyũ Proverbs* (Nairobi: St. Paul's Publication-Africa, 1997), p.184.
[124] Turner, "Primal Religions", p. 32.
[125] Turner, "Primal Religions", p. 32.
[126] Turner, "Primal Religions", p. 32.
[127] Burnett, *Earthly Powers,* p. 21.
[128] J. M. Waliggo, Arij A. Roest Crollius, T. Nkeramihigo and J. Mutiso-Mbinda (eds.), *Inculturation: Its Meaning and Urgency* (Nairobi: St. Paul's Publication-Africa, 1986), p. 20.
[129] Kwame Bediako, *Christianity in Africa: A Renewal of Non-Western Christianity* (Edinburgh: Edinburgh University Press/ Maryknoll, New York: Orbis Books, 1995), p. 95.

too obvious to be denied.[130] It appears that the African belief is closer to the biblical paradigm than Western rationalistic scepticism. Most Africans still live in the world of the New Testament, where belief in demons and a host of invisible supernatural powers was potent and real. They live in a world similar to that of the Gospels, in which Jesus' ministry was, to a great extent, that of deliverance and restoration of life and health after what was perceived as violent attacks from demonic and evil supernatural powers. It seems as if there is no conflict between biblical and African belief as to the reality and existence of supernatural powers. A Jesus who confronted evil spirits and demons in the Gospel would probably fit in the African thought world. A Jesus emptied of all the supernatural contained in the Gospels would be meaningless in the African context. Many African believers certainly feel at home with a Jesus who is victorious over the spiritual realm and in particular the evil forces. African believers certainly require a Jesus who is above every rule and authority due to their keen awareness of forces and powers at work in the world, threatening the interests of life and harmony. They would thus require a Jesus who is a potent protector both in the physical and spiritual universe. So in biblical terms, as Ferdinando maintains, the African belief in spirits or occult attack should not be simply dismissed.[131]

Even so, the postulate of affinity does not mean a one-to-one link between the Pauline concept of, and the African belief in supernatural powers. This could be a serious misunderstanding since the Pauline concept takes a radically different approach to issues that arose in the context of production. More often than not, it challenges and seeks to change cultural beliefs of the people it addressed. To regard the African worldview and the Bible as identical may lead to the danger of 'parallelomania', which arises when a superficial analysis of two institutions in two different cultures in terms of time and space suggests that they resemble each other.[132] Even though there is considerable similarity between the African worldview and the Bible as to supernatural powers, there is a disparity and they are by no means identical. The definitive and actual response of the Pauline concept is unreservedly opposed to the traditional

---

[130] But building on the postulate of affinity to interpret biblical texts may have serious weaknesses. A major weakness may occur if one fails to draw hermeneutical and theological conclusions that emerge from the text. Another weakness may arise if this approach fails to show concern with issues that need a critical appraisal in the African context because of their apologetic and polemic nature. See Ukpong "Development in Biblical Interpretation in Africa", p. 14.

[131] Ferdinando, *The Triumph of Christ*, p. 5.

[132] Howard Clark Kee, *A Community of the New Age* (London: SCM Press, 1977), p. 176 warns against the perils of parallelomania, which he understands to be the fallacy of assuming that because features of the New Testament resemble phenomena of the Graeco-Roman world in certain formal ways, identical functions are intended. Parallelomania, he maintains, raises aloft slogans and attractive banners, to which many may rally, but it contributes little if anything to the twin task of exegesis and historical reconstruction.

African response. In fact, the Pauline concept underlines Christ's supremacy while the African worldview (as also the Graeco-Roman worldview in the context of production) allows supernatural powers to vie for supremacy. The Pauline concept clearly shows that Christ does not share or compete for supremacy with any visible or invisible supernatural powers. If there is any affinity, it is not with the Pauline view but with the contexts of production and reception. Just as Paul contradicts the idea that supernatural powers were the determining factors of human existence in the context of production, his concept does the same in the African context of reception.

However, the Pauline concept certainly used linguistic and religio-cultural symbols of the environment that produced the Bible so as to effectively speak to its readers. Some of those religio-cultural symbols stand in close proximity with the African world of ideas. The biblical writers' world and the modern African world are detached historically and geographically. This seems to make it reasonable for one to regard the postulate of affinity as inappropriate.[133] If we take the belief in supernatural powers as an example, it will be noted that it echoes the human felt need for continued existence in the first century CE and also in the African context. There is therefore a degree of existential if not elemental affinity. It must not be assumed that the Graeco-Roman supernatural powers had one-to-one likeness with supernatural powers of the African context. If, as we shall see in chapter four, Jewish and Graeco-Roman views of supernatural powers differed and yet they belonged to the same era, why must it be that supernatural powers in the African context have similar elements with supernatural powers in the Graeco-Roman context of production? Yet the postulate of affinity may not be cavalierly dismissed if it only seeks existential and not elemental affinities. Dow rightly notes the link between description of present-day alleged demonic phenomena, as encountered in the present-day practice of exorcism and the practice of exorcism in the New Testament. He contends that there is *prima facie* evidence indicating that we are dealing with the same kind of behavioural reality.[134] But even if the existential postulate of affinity may imply continuity between the African worldview and the New Testament, the New Testament offers radical novelty to the African worldview. For the most part, what the African context needs, however, is not denial or fearful fixation with supernatural powers. It needs the proclamation of Christ the redeemer, who is above every rule and authority. As Kwame Appiah notes, there are theories that can explain the belief in spirits better while not asking people to assume their beliefs are false, for they can always make many sensible moves in defence of their beliefs.[135] African Christians need theories that can persuade them to accept the inferiority of supernatural powers and the supremacy of Christ.

---

[133] See Erich Isaac, "Relations between the Hebrew Bible and Africa" in *Jewish Social Studies* 26 2 (1964), p. 95.
[134] Graham Dow, "A Case for the Existence of Demons" in *Churchman* 94 3 (1980), pp. 199-200.
[135] Appiah, *In My Father's House*, p. 118.

The African Context of Reception

It is regrettable that the existential postulate of affinity has never been fully grasped. As noted in chapter two, the missionaries did not appreciate or even recognize the existential affinity. Where the missionaries appreciated it, they erroneously equated lesser and evil supernatural powers with God.[136] The missionaries' critics have equally not grasped the existential affinity, confusing it with elemental affinity. The problem is that the African situation is regarded as indistinguishable from the Bible. The danger of 'parallelomania' continues unabated without considering the fact that the biblical views do not abet fixated belief in supernatural powers. The postulate of affinity must be handled warily if cross-cultural phenomena could be understood, misunderstood or even not understood at all. But the context of production knew of powers that threatened human existence just as in the African context of reception. And if the Pauline concept was meant to engage the belief in supernatural powers in the context of production, it should perhaps engage the belief in supernatural powers in the context of reception. This could make the cross-cultural approach useful in the interpretation of supernatural powers. At any rate, the subject of supernatural powers is an important point of contact between Africa and the New Testament.

3:6. Conclusion

There is a clear polarisation concerning the belief in supernatural powers in the African context. Many Africans hold that the powers operate in every odd manifestation. There is also a tendency to deny or to be sceptical about the existence of supernatural powers. Anthropologists cite varied reasons why people believe in spirits and the different functions these beliefs play in society. This, however, makes the subject of supernatural powers in the African context of reception more complex. It also means that the concept that African and biblical worlds could easily speak to each other needs to be appraised. As Klauck argues, beliefs and narratives have a character specific to an individual culture and there are expected differences from one culture to another. Yet religious beliefs and narratives function as modes for boosting communication about vital issues of human existence.[137] If the Pauline concept of supernatural powers can enhance communication concerning the crucial questions of human existence, this is the point at which the concept should speak to the African belief in supernatural powers. Anthropological interpretations may supplement efforts to let the Pauline concept and the African context speak to each other. This is tied to the idea that anthropology, sociology, psychology, philosophy and other inter-cultural disciplines are vital in actualising the meaning of a text

---

[136] Okot P'Bitek, (*African Religions in Western Scholarship* (Nairobi/Kampala: East African Literature Bureau, 1970), p. 62 shows how the missionaries translated the Acholi '*Rubanga*' as the Creator God, while for the Acholi *Rubanga* was the malevolent spirit that caused tuberculosis of the spine. Also among the Gĩkũyũ 'ngoma' was translated as the evil spirit. However, *ngoma* only means spirit, which needs to be qualified with the adjective 'good' or 'evil'.

[137] Klauck, *The Religious Context*, p. 8.

or a concept in a concrete life situation.

Yet anthropological views sometimes reduce beliefs in supernatural powers into the roles they play. They also fail to recognise the value of the belief as people treat it in their religious practice. They seem not to acknowledge the perception of many Africans that supernatural powers are entities that operate as ends in themselves. Conversely, the African spirit world is not without its own problems. Bediako's observation is certainly instructive.

> The spiritual universe of the African primal religions is not without *hiatus*. It is not a neat hierarchy of divine beings and spirit-forces held in unitary harmony. The African primal world can be conceived of as a universe of distributed power, perhaps even of fragmented power; it is as much a universe of conflict as the rest of the fallen world. It is a world not of one centre, God, but many centres, and the recognition of unity and multiplicity of the Transcendent in the African world also reveals a deep ambivalence. It is this ambivalence to which a creative Christian engagement must answer and do so in terms of the primal imagination itself.[138]

This complicates the subject of supernatural powers in the African context but must not deter reading the Pauline concept of supernatural powers so as to engage the primal imaginations of African believers. Though this is the subject matter of the final chapter, it behoves us to delve into the context of production to identify the nature of the world from which the Pauline concept emerged. This is the world, which this chapter argues has an affinity with the African context of reception. The next chapter attempts to corroborate this claim.

---

[138] Kwame Bediako, *Jesus in Africa: The Christian Gospel in African History and Experience.* (Akropong-Akuapem, Ghana: Regnum Africa, 2000), p. 91).

CHAPTER 4

The Context of Production: A Critical Appraisal of the First Century CE Beliefs in Supernatural Powers

4: 1. Introduction

This chapter examines how the first century CE Jewish and Graeco-Roman populace envisaged supernatural powers. Several scholars agree that the majority believed in supernatural powers that populated the earth, the heavens and the underworld and that the fear of these powers was widespread.[1] Several rituals and practices such as magic, divination and astrology were performed so as to pacify supernatural powers and receive favours from them. But analysing the first century CE beliefs in supernatural powers can be an intricate and elusive task. Most of the literature that outlined popular beliefs in supernatural powers vanished. It is indeed tragic that there was such a great shipwreck of ancient literature about the spirit world.[2] Nonetheless, sources pre-dating and post-dating the first century CE provide some data to work with. These include the apocalyptic literature, Dead Sea scrolls and the scripts of the elite of that time, who, as this chapter will show, were satirically sceptical of Graeco-Roman popular beliefs, rituals and practices. Also included are the magical papyri, which even though penned before or after the first century CE, were presumably known in oral form before and after they were written down.

It also appears that the first century CE milieu was multicultural and multi-religious, so communication was inevitably cross-cultural and inter-religious. But this may have been complicated as Jewish and Graeco-Roman worldviews were conspicuously at variance. Their religious, social, and ethical stance was diametrically opposed.[3] The Graeco-Roman concept of supernatural powers

---

[1] David George Reese, "Demons (New Testament)" in David Noel Freedman (ed.), *The Anchor Bible Dictionary* Vol. 2 (New York: Doubleday, 1992), p. 140; Arnold, *Powers* pp. 19, 22; Bryon E. Shafer (ed.), *Religion in Ancient Egypt: Gods, Myths, and Persona Practice* (London: Routledge, 1991).

[2] See Hans Dieter Betz (ed.), *The Greek Magical Papyri in Translation Including the Demotic Spells*, Vol. 1 (Chicago: University of Chicago Press, 1986), p. xli; Suetonius, *Augustus* 31.1; Acts 19: 19.

[3] See B. D. Chilton, "Judaism and the New Testament" in Craig A. Evans and Stanley E. Porter (eds.), *Dictionary of New Testament Background* (Leicester: Intervarsity Press,

sharply contrasted Jewish and Christian notions of the same. Judaism itself had a radical multiplicity of sects. The Pharisees and Sadducees differed in regards to the belief in spiritual beings like angels.[4] We cannot therefore assume that Jewish beliefs and practices were identical or that their faith was undiluted.[5] The Graeco-Roman world too was not monolithic since ideas of gods were not similar.[6] The Greek gods could be as fallible as human beings while the Roman deities could be impersonal and remote.[7] For that reason, their religion, as some scholars show, was complex. At times it could be primitive and superstitious and at times earnest and contemplative.[8] Christianity too, as Meeks notes "even in its earliest decades, was already a complex of movements in several directions".[9] It could be that the knowledge and interpretation of supernatural powers differed from place to place.[10] It is also possible that Judaism and Hellenism varied from place to place,[11] though there were points that united each of them.[12] It is also possible that Jews and Graeco-Romans understood

---

2000), pp. 603–616; John Collins, *Between Athens and Jerusalem: Jewish Identity in the Hellenistic Diaspora* (New York: Crossroad, 1986), p. 8.

[4] Josephus, *J.W.* 2.20.3 §§ 564-565; 4.4.1§§ 224-225; 2.13.4-6 §§ 648-655; 2.8.14 § 165; *Ant.* 13. 171f; 18.4.3 §§ 90-95; 20.1.1-2 §§ 6-14; Hans-Josef Klauck, *Magic and Paganism in Early Christianity: The World of the Acts of the Apostle* (Edinburgh: T & T Clark, 2000), p. 48-9.

[5] See 1Macc 1: 14-5; Josephus, *Ant.* 12.5.1 §§ 240-241; Wayne A. Meeks, *The First Urban Christians: The Social World of Apostle Paul* (New Haven/London: Yale University Press, 1983), pp.32-50; Klauck, *Magic and Paganism in Early Christianity*, pp. 48-9; Chilton "Judaism", pp. 610-612.

[6] David E. Aune, "Religion, Greco-Roman" in Craig A. Evans and Stanley E. Porter (eds.), *Dictionary of New Testament Background* (Downers Grove/Leicester: Intervarsity Press, 2000), p. 921.

[7] P. G. Walsh, "Introduction" in Cicero, *The Nature of the Gods*: Translated with Introduction and Explanatory Notes by P. G. Walsh (Oxford: Clarendon Press, 1997), p. xxiii.

[8] N. C. Croy, "Religion, Personal" in Craig A. Evans and Stanley E. Porter (eds.), *Dictionary of New Testament Background* (Downers Grove/Leicester: Intervarsity Press, 2000), p. 930; Martin P. Nilsson, *Greek Popular Religion* (New York: Columbia University Press, 1940), pp. 3-4.

[9] Meeks, *The First Urban Christians*, p. 32.

[10] Cicero, *De Natura Deorum* 1.81-84.

[11] W. T. Wilson, "Hellenistic Judaism" in Craig A. Evans and Stanley E. Porter (eds.), *Dictionary of New Testament Background* (Downers Grove/Leicester: Intervarsity Press, 2000), p. 478; John M. G. Barclay, *Jews in the Mediterranean Diaspora from Alexander to Trajan* (323 BCE–117 CE) (Edinburgh: T & T Clark, 1996), pp. 4-9, 19-39; Jonathan Smith, "Some Contours of Early Judaism" in W. S. Green (ed.), *Approaches to Ancient Judaism* II (Chico: Scholars Press, 1980), pp. 19-20; Meeks, *The First Urban Christians*, pp. 32-39.

[12] Aune, "Religion", p. 918; Barclay, *Jews in the Mediterranean Diaspora*, pp. 26-7, 271, 305, 415-443.

The Context of Production

each other's beliefs "since they shared many of the same terms and concepts"[13] as to supernatural powers. Altogether, it seems that in the first century CE, there may have been conflicting beliefs even within the same group of people.

4:2. Jewish Perceptions of Supernatural Powers

Jewish beliefs in supernatural powers witnessed a steady historical development that enabled them to handle problems they faced despite their belief that they were God's portion and inheritance. Some Jews performed forbidden practices, for instance magic, witchcraft, sorcery, divination and astrology. This section will investigate the historical development of Jewish perceptions of supernatural powers from the Old Testament era into the Second Temple era. The idea is to help us establish, especially in chapter five, whether the Jewish perceptions in both eras influenced the thinking of Paul and his first century CE audience. As a result, it is significant to ask, what was the dominant Jewish attitude as to beliefs, rituals and practices with regard to supernatural powers?

i. Jewish Beliefs

a. The Heavenly Court

Undeniably, Jews believed in Yahweh's supreme control and authority that dominated every sphere of human life. It is therefore tempting to characterise the Jewish people as monotheistic. Yet looking at Jewish literature, we are confronted with the possibility of the henotheistic belief among the Jews. This is well attested in the first commandment, 'You shall have no other gods before me'.[14] This implies that the Jews knew other supernatural powers, which did not have the same level of existence as Yahweh as they operated by Yahweh's edict. Like angels, they belonged to a heavenly court, over which Yahweh presided. A few Jewish texts identify the members of this court as בְּנֵי הָאֱלֹהִים ('The Sons of God') or קְדֹשִׁים ('holy ones').[15] Satan too was privy to this heavenly court and appears as one who accomplished God's purpose (Job 1–3). In the Second Temple era, Satan was however associated with the fallen angels, evil spirits and demons as their leader. Genesis 6: 1–4 is often used to account for the prehistoric nature of the angelic fall. The fall was caused by the pride and desire of a senior angel to be exalted at the level of God. This ultimately corrupted the angelic order placed under this angel.[16] These, according to some apocalyptic texts, are the sons of God who, due to lust, entered into a marriage relationship with the daughters of men. This marriage relationship defiled the

---

[13] Arnold, *Powers*, p. 27.
[14] Exd. 20: 3; Dt. 5: 7.
[15] Dt. 33: 2-3; Job 5: 1; 15: 5; Ps 68: 17; 89: 5-8; Zech 14: 5.
[16] 2 En 29: 4-5.

angels such that they could not do their God-given duties—to instruct people on righteousness. On the contrary, these corrupted angels taught the women they married abominable practices that were forbidden among the Jews for instance astrology, magic and sorcery. Their gigantic progeny were responsible for the escalation of aggression in the world.[17] Due to the fall and having been 'hurled out of the height', it could be tellingly possible that in the Second Temple period, the fallen angels and their leader ceased to belong to the heavenly court,[18] though their leader could complain to God on their behalf.[19]

b. The Angel of Nations

The Jews also believed in special angels who supervised other nations. Deuteronomy 32: 8-9 apportioned the nations to בְּנֵי הָאֱלֹהִים, while Israel was Yahweh's portion and heritage. But the fate of the angel was both archetypal and symbolic of what happened to the nations they presided over. They were responsible for the rule and dispensation of justice among the nation and so the agents of God's will. Thus when they failed to ensure that justice was properly dispensed; God could charge and punish them with death like mortal human beings.[20] The Jews held these angels responsible for the evils attributable to the nations.[21] This continued into the Second Temple period but with some developments. As in the past, but now tracing this tradition to Abraham, the nations were under the rule of celestial beings like angels while the Jewish nation was still God's portion.[22] This tradition is preserved in Philo, who recognises the Most High as having "divided the nations, dispersed the sons of Adam, and fixed the boundaries of the nations according to the numbers of the angels of God. And the portion of the Lord was his people Jacob, the limitation of the inheritance of Israel".[23] The angels appointed to rule the nations led these nations astray, deterring them from following the Lord and making them to be against the Jews, God's own chosen people.[24] By intentionally exceeding the limit God had set for them, the angels of nations were evil and defiant as opposed to the good angels who assisted the Jews.[25] Thus the threats posed to

---

[17] 1 En 6: 1-8: 4; 69: 1-12; Jub. 4: 15; 5: 1-11.

[18] 2 En 29: 5; Jub. 5: 6, 10; L.A.E 12: 1; 16: 1f; 1 En 10: 4-6. Cf. Jude 6.

[19] Jub. 10: 6-8.

[20] Ps. 82: 1-7.

[21] See Dan 10: 10-13, where the prince of the kingdom of Persia opposed God's messenger to Daniel but Michael, one of the chief priest, came and helped this messenger.

[22] *Testament of Naphtali* 8–9, esp. 9: 4.

[23] Philo, *De Posteritate Caini* xxv.89. The same tradition is also preserved in the rabbinic writings. *Deuteronomy Rabbah* 2: 34, a Midrash interpreting Song of Solomon 3: 24, which likens the election of Israel to the reception of a king and his entourage. While some citizens chose the king's officials as patrons, Israel, the smartest of all, settles for nothing less than the King.

[24] Jub. 15: 30-32; 48: 9-19.

[25] 1QM 13: 9-13; 17: 5-8; 1QS 3: 20-25; *Testament of Levi* 5: 3-6.

The Context of Production

Israel by the pagan nations were interpreted as the work of the angels, having stirred the kings of these nations to unrest.[26] Yet the suffering experienced by the Jews, which was attributable to the nations, was seen as God's verdict against wayward Jews. Then again, the Jews equated their neighbours' gods with the angels of nations. This was probably the basis of the polemic against angel worship in the rabbinic texts, linking it with idolatry.[27]

c. Evil Spirits and Demons

The Jews also believed in evil spirits and demons that were able to possess people and cause distress. A well-known evil spirit in Mesopotamia לִילִית is documented in Jewish non-canonical texts and in some Aramaic incantations.[28] It is also mentioned in Isaiah. 34:14 (translated by the RSV 'Night Hag') as a demon that will inhabit Edom after God's severe judgment. God's shattering judgment shall contribute to the fading of Babylon's glory, making it to be haunted by 'goat spirits' and other animal demons.[29] The Jews believed demons existed in animal form ('theriomorphic demons') or in human form ('anthropomorphic demons') or a form between the animal and human form.[30] They could have strongly linked wild animals with evil spirits and demons, which, however, were totally under God's control and who sanctioned their evil performance so as to achieve his purpose. Several Old Testament texts indicate that evil spirits (רוּחַ־רָעָה) and lying spirits (רוּחַ שֶׁקֶר), which could inspire chaotic deeds and false prophecy, came from God.[31]

During the Second Temple era, the Jews believed in a complex world, which had varied orders of demons.[32] A section of the Jewish people could have held that demons caused evil and suffering as well as teaching unrighteousness on earth.[33] The leader of these demons otherwise known as Beliar or Mastema or Abaddon or Melchiresha or Beelzebub[34] was also the satanic personage that preached apostasy and waged active war in the present age, though he would be defeated in the final war.[35] The demons, like their leader, sought to overthrow

---

[26] 1 En 56: 5-6.
[27] See *Mek. Rabbi Ishmael, Bahodeš* 6 to Exd. 20: 4-5; *t. Hul.* 2: 18; *b. Hul.* 40a; *y. Ber.* 9: 13a-b; *b. Sanh.* 38b; *Exodus Rabbah.* 32: 4 cited in L. T. Stuckenbruck, "Angels of the Nations" in Craig A. Evans and Stanley E. Porter (eds.), *Dictionary of New Testament Background* (Leicester: Intervarsity Press, 2000), pp 29-31, esp. p 30.
[28] Targum Pseudo-Jonathan on Num 6: 24-26 cited in D. W .Watts, "Excursus on Lilith" in *Isaiah 34–66* WBC 25 (Waco, Texas: Word, 1987), p. 13.
[29] Isa. 13: 21.
[30] W. O. E. Oesterley and Theodore H. Robinson, *Hebrew Religion: Its Origin and Development* (London: SPCK, 1930), pp.110-121.
[31] 1 Sam 16: 14-23; 18: 10; 19: 9; Jdg. 9: 22-25; 1 Kgs. 22 1-28.
[32] 4Q 510 1: 5; 4Q511 10: 1-2; 11Q11 2: 3-4.
[33] See 1En 6: 1-10: 1-22; 11QT 26: 3-13 (Cf. Lev. 16: 7-10).
[34] Jub. 10: 8; 1QM 13:11; 1QS 1: 16-28; 1QM 1: 4-5, 13-16; 11QPs[a] 19: 15; 4Q280 1 2, 4Q560 1:1; 11Q11 4:10 and 4QBer[a] 10 ii 7.
[35] CD 23: 2-3; 1QH and 4Q286; 1QM 13: 11; 14: 9; 17: 4-9.

the sons of light. They personified antipathy towards God and caused physical suffering, sickness and death.[36] In that case, it may have been a Jewish belief that Beliar and his demons had substantial power over people and the material world.[37] According to the *Martyrdom and Ascension of Isaiah* Beliar was the independent agent who influenced King Manasseh to lead the Jewish nation to a reign of terror and evil.

> And Manasseh abandoned the service of the Lord of his father, and he served Satan and his angels, and his powers. And he turned his father's house, which had been in the presence of Hezekiah, away from the words of wisdom and the service of the Lord. Manasseh turned them away so that they served Beliar; for the angel of iniquity who rules this world is Beliar, whose name is Matanbukus. And he rejoiced over Jerusalem because of Manasseh, and he strengthened him in causing apostasy, and the iniquity that was disseminated in Jerusalem... Sorcery and magic, augury and divination, fornication and adultery, and the persecution of the righteous increased...[38]

This interpretation suggests that several Jews believed supernatural powers could use high-ranking persons, "to create a reign of terror and evil"[39] in the structures of human existence. It also implies that several Jews believed the structures of human existence had close link with demonic influences.

The demons were identified with the progeny of the union between the 'sons of God' and 'daughters of men' recorded in Genesis 6: 1-4.[40] It was believed that demons originated from fallen angels, who are referred to as fathers of demons as well as being demons themselves.[41] The association of demons with corrupted angels may suggest that a section of Jewish people believed demons could cause impurity and pollution. This was perhaps one of the reasons why purification rites took a central place among the Qumran society. These rites were meant to defend the holy fellowship and holy space from the incursions of impure demons.[42] The Qumran society probably saw itself as being engaged in a desperate struggle against Mastema and his minions. It defended itself with a spiritual action consisting of prayers and incantations to exorcise demons.[43]

---

[36] Josephus, *Antiquities* 8:46-7; *Assumption of Moses*; Geza Vermes, *Jesus the Jew* (New York: Macmillan, 1973), p. 61

[37] *The Martyrdom and Ascension of Isaiah* 2: 4; Jub 12: 20-1.

[38] *The Martyrdom and Ascension of Isaiah* 2.2-5.

[39] Arnold, *Powers*, p. 203.

[40] 1 En 15: 11–16: 1.

[41] Jub. 10: 5.

[42] Philip S. Alexander, "The Demonology in the Dead Sea Scrolls" in Peter W. Flint and James C. Vanderkam *The Dead Sea Scrolls after Fifty Years: A Comprehensive Assessment* Vol. 2 (Leiden: Brill, 1999), p. 348.

[43] 4Q510; 4Q511, which Philip S. Alexander ("Incarnations and Books of Magic" in E. Schürer, *The History of the Jewish People in the Age of Jesus Christ* (Edinburgh: T & T

Some Jews also held that demons caused problems to human existence but this was not their own doing. It was a God-given task even if God does not like the spirit of darkness epitomised by the demons.[44] God could use evil spirits to protect his chosen people[45] and He alone had the power to control and to remove demons from the face of humanity.[46] Demons will thus continue destroying people unchallenged "until the great judgment, in which the great aeon will be completed".[47] Altogether, many Jews held that God's power is superior to that of Mastema and his minions. Mastema and his minions have a function in the divine economy since evil people are given to their power to be punished. This perhaps developed due to Jews' experiences of suffering and tyranny from alien nations, intensifying the need of a theodicy.

It then seems that the majority of the Jewish people, from the Old Testament era through to the first century CE, believed in the existence of a plethora of evil spirits and demons. Yet this was through a historical development through which the belief in evil spirits and demons gained some nuanced shades. In fact, the interaction between the Jews and their Ancient Near East neighbours added to the Jews' perception of supernatural powers. Besides, several Jews accepted some of their neighbours' beliefs and practices despite having been overtly forbidden to offer sacrifice to the goat demon/idol.[48] They thus stirred Yahweh to jealousy when having mingled with the Gentiles, they learned their works and sacrificed their children to demons (לַשֵּׁדִים) that were not gods but analogous to the idols of Canaan.[49] The LXX translation of Ps. 96: 5 outlines this Jewish view, which regarded the pagan gods as demonic. While the Hebrew text suggests that all the gods of the nations are idols, the LXX text suggests that they are demons. It is likely that the LXX, which was of course translated by Greek speaking Jews, reflects the Jewish belief that pagan gods had a close link with the demonic realm.[50] Could it be that there is a close link between Jewish belief in demons, evil spirits and magic? Oesterley & Robinson note, "The supernatural agencies which were supposed to be controlled by magical rites were really believed to exist".[51] Drawing from Rabbi Huna's exegesis of Ps. 91: 7, 'every one among us has a thousand demons on his left hand and ten thousands on his right', Penney and Wise aver that magic offered

---

Clark, 1987) pp. 318-337, esp. p. 321 argues presents a special liturgy recited by the Maskil as the spiritual mentor to and guardian of the community to keep the demons at bay.

[44] 1QS 3: 15-26.
[45] 1Qap Gen^ar. 20: 8-32. See also 4Q213^a Levi.
[46] Jub. 10: 6-8.
[47] 1 En 15: 11-16: 1.
[48] Lev. 17: 7.
[49] Ps. 106: 37; Dt. 32: 16-17
[50] See 1Cor. 10: 19-21.
[51] Oesterley and Robinson, *Hebrew Religion*, p. 71.

a tangible material defence against invisible demons.[52]

ii. Jewish Rituals and Practices

a. Magic and Divination

As noted in chapter one, magic is a controversial subject. In Jewish circles, there was a considerable overlap between magic and divination, the art of discerning the future.[53] To what extent were the Jews involved in magic and divination? Belief in, and practice of magic and divination certainly thrived in the Ancient Near East and they may have been a great attraction to some Jewish people.[54] The mention of magic and divination in the Old Testament implies that some Jews were accustomed to them. Even so, the Old Testament gives intense emphasis to Yahweh's supremacy over magicians and diviners who sought to control supernatural powers.[55] The Jews were strictly and clearly forbidden to consult magicians and diviners by the legal and prophetic texts.[56] At the same time, the Old Testament does not describe magic and divination in detail. Rather, it contains details of sins committed by key Jewish powerful personalities and the penalty thereafter because of getting involved in these practices.[57] Rather than isolating the Jews from these practices, the prohibition and condemnation reveal that some Jews participated in the same. Altogether, magicians and diviners had some power[58] but this was lower than Yahweh's exalted power and sovereign control.[59] God alone shaped the destiny of Jewish people and so no magical practices could thwart the divine intention.

Though it seems that divination by the oracle of the lot was tolerable during the Second Temple era,[60] it also seems that the Jews relegated magic and some specific forms of divination to the dominion of Beliar.[61] Yet some Jews may

---

[52] D. L. Penney and M. O. Wise "By the Power of Beelzebub: An Aramaic Incantation Formula from Qumran (4Q560) in *Journal of Biblical Literature* 113 (1994), p. 627.

[53] Arnold, *Powers*, p. 21-2; Alexander, "Incarnations and Books", p. 342; Klauck, *Magic and Paganism in Early Christianity*, pp. 14-19, 47-52, 65-70, 97-102; Klauck, *The Religious Context*, p. 213-4.

[54] Oesterley and Robinson, *Hebrew Religion*, p. 72; J. A. Scurlock, "Magic (ANE)" in David N. Freedman (ed.), *The Anchor Bible Dictionary* Vol. 5 (New York: Doubleday, 1992), pp. 464-468.

[55] In Gen 41: 1-8; Exd. 7-9; Dan. 1: 20; 2: 1-49 the wise men, sorcerers and magicians could not cope with Yahweh's power.

[56] Lev 19: 26-28; Dt. 18:10-14; Isa 2–3, esp. 2: 6; Jer. 14: 4, 27: 9; Ezek 13:17-18, 23; Mal 3:1-5.

[57] Dt. 18: 10-12; 1 Sam 28; 2 Chr. 33: 1-13; 2 Kgs. 17: 7-23; 21: 9-15.

[58] Oesterley and Robinson, *Hebrew Religion*, p 71.

[59] *Wisdom of Solomon* 17: 7

[60] 1QS 5: 3; 6: 16–22; 9: 7; 4Q164 1, 5; 4Q176 frg 16: 3; 4Q181 frg 1: 5.

[61] See A. Lange, "The Essene Position on Magic and Divination" in M. Bernstein, F. García Martínez and J. Kampen (ed.), *Legal Texts and Legal Issues: Proceedings of the*

The Context of Production

have practised magic, which Blau criticises as a superstitious mania that was not part of true Judaism. He notes that the Babylonian exile stirred the Jews to hold on to the mania of demons and spirits, making them practise magic against the clear wording of the law and vocal prohibition ensuing from it.[62] Blau's criticism may have been based on the trend that separates magic and divinatory phenomena from religion. Time and space do not allow us to analyse Blau's criticism fully but one of its implications is that some Jews in Palestine and in the Diaspora during the Second Temple period practised magic. As Brashear states, "the repute of Jewish magicians exceeded even that of Egyptian sorcerers".[63] Some scholars agree that some magical papyri may have been created by the Jews,[64] and probably attest to Jewish magical skill. The *Greek Magical Papyri (Papyri Graecae Magicae)* – PGM IV 3007–3086 is a case in point, wherein demons are conjured by "the God of the Hebrews" and it concludes with an advice to its users, "keep yourself pure, for this charm is Hebraic and is preserved among pure men". It also mentions leading Jewish personalities, the exodus and other events in the history of Israel. Commenting on Jewish magical texts, Alexander avers that they were an indicator of the spiritual atmosphere in which a large section of the populace lived, rich and poor, educated and ignorant.[65]

There is also substantial evidence supporting Jewish involvement in magical practices in the Pseudepigrapha and Apocalyptic literature, Qumran texts and Josephus.[66] A notable example is the *Testament of Solomon*, which records how Solomon directed demons to build the temple using magical skills. Another example could be the incantations found in 4Q560 and in the Book of the Watchers (4QEn^{a-e}). Alexander insists that the prayers in 4Q560 said to keep the demons at bay were apotropaic in character and took the form of magical rituals.[67] Penney and Wise insist that these incantations and adjurations must be seen as early witness of Jewish magic.[68] The Book of the Watchers records how 'the chiefs of the chiefs of tens' taught the women they married sorcery and magical skills and how to undo magic.[69] Though the Qumran society may have

---

Second Meeting of the International Organization for Qumran Studies, Cambridge 1995, Published in the Honour of Joseph M. Baungearten STDJ (Leiden: Brill, 1997), pp. 397-433, esp. 411.

[62] L. Blau, *Das altjüdische Zauberwesen* (Budapest: Landesrabbinerschule in Budapest, 1898), p. 19.

[63] William M. Brashear, "The Greek Magical Papyri: An Introduction and Survey; Annotated Bibliography (1928 – 1994)" in *ANRW* II 18.5 (1995), 3426.

[64] See Alexander, "Incarnations and Books", p 357-359; Arnold, "Magical Papyri", p. 668.

[65] Alexander, "Incarnations and Books", p 342.

[66] Jub. 8: 3; 10: 12-4; 11: 8; 12: 6-21; Tob. 6: 6-7, 16-17; 8: 2f; 4Q197 4i 12-13; 4Q197 4ii 14-15; Josephus, *J. W.* 2.8.136; *Ant.* 8.2.5.

[67] Alexander, "The Demonology", p. 345.

[68] Penney and Wise, "By the Power of Beelzebub", p. 628.

[69] 1 En. 6: 1-8: 3; 4Q 201-202.

used magic to deal with maladies purportedly caused by demons, it is not very clear whether this practice played a fundamental role in their healing ministry. Divination by the oracle of the lot was, however, used for administrative purposes such as admitting new members into the society, making decisions and was probably part of the priestly tradition.[70] Even so, the Scrolls disconnect divination by the oracle of the lot from auguries and they heavily condemn necromancy as part of divination.[71] So magic and divination were resolutely disapproved and persistently deplored by Jewish religious authorities.

Even so, magic and divination flourished among the Jews. Some of the pious Jews who fought against the governor of Idumea seem to have used protective magical charms. The soldiers who survived found sacred tokens of the idols of Jamnia, which the law forbids the Jews to wear, under the tunic of dead soldiers.[72] Archaeological discovery of magical papyri, amulets, tablets, incantations and bowls almost certainly reveal Jewish interest in magic.[73] Jewish celebrities like Moses and Solomon were really famous for their magical skills[74], perhaps in the sense of what Philo knew as genuine magic.[75] Thomas was depicted as a righteous magician since he performed deeds of mercy and healings without taking any fee.[76] Klauck insists that Judaism was "far from being utterly immune to the adoption of magical practices, and even without any activity on the part of the Jews, the Hebrew and Aramaic divine names were widely employed among non-Jews as a well-tried magical instrument".[77] Probably as Lange states, "magic and divination were not perceived as independent entities but were an integral part of Jewish belief and thought".[78] Perhaps as indicated by Arnold, nothing reflects the Jewish popular belief in demons, spirits and the powers of evils more than the Jewish involvement in magic, contrary to the official Jewish restrictions against the practice.[79]

---

[70] 1QS 6: 16, 18, 21–22; 1QS 5: 3, 9: 7; 1QSa 1: 16;

[71] 4Q270, frg 2 col. I; 4Q271: 18-9.

[72] 2 Macc. 12: 32-45, esp. v 40.

[73] For a perfect illustration concerning the continuation of Jewish magical tradition, see Margalioth's publication of *Sepher Ha–Razim* translated by Morgan (1983); Josephus *Ant* 8.45–48; 20.142; Juvenal, *Satire* 6. 542-548; Celsus, *apud*, Origen, *Contra Celsum* 1.26; Acts 13: 6-12; 19: 11-17.

[74] See J. G. Gager, *Curse Tablets and Binding Spells from the Ancient World* (Oxford: Oxford University Press, 1992), pp. 134-161; M. Simon, *Verus Israel: A Study of the Relations between Christians and Jews in the Roman Empire AD 135–423* The Littmann Library of Jewish Civilization (Oxford: Oxford University Pres, 1986), pp. 339-368.

[75] Philo, *De Specialibus Legibus* 3.xxviii.100.

[76] *The Acts of Thomas* 20.

[77] Klauck, *The Religious Context*, p. 213.

[78] Lange, "The Essene Position", p. 408. Cf. J. C. VanderKam, *Enoch and the Growth of an Apocalyptic Tradition* CBQMS 16 (Washington: Catholic Biblical Association of America, 1984), p. 75.

[79] Arnold, *Powers*, p. 71.

b. Astrology

Astrology is the practice of observing celestial phenomena for the purpose of predicting human events. It is based on the belief that heavenly bodies are linked by a kind of global sympathy. Like magic and divination, the prophetic tradition urged the Jews not to take notice of the unbridled worship of heavenly hosts.[80] Isaiah predicted the discontent of the enchantments, the sorcerers, the astrologers, the stargazers and the monthly prognosticators by the power of the flame.[81] The Deuteronomist outlawed the idolatrous worship of the luminaries and participating in it was on pain of death.[82] Despite this warning, the worship of the luminaries was rife, probably having begun in the reign of Manasseh.[83] Perhaps it was during the Babylonian exile that the Jews were influenced to believe that stars affected human life. Even if some Jews may have worshipped the luminaries, the clear wording against it may have made them conscious that the practice was heathen and idolatrous.

It also seems that the Qumran Jews accepted a specific type of astrology. Altogether, 4Q186 and 4Q561 illustrate that the Qumran Jews practised astrology to determine if the candidates likely to join them had more darkness than light. Davidson suggests that it is not clear to what extent the Qumran texts represent the general astrological beliefs and practices of the Qumran society[84]. Conversely, Charlesworth acknowledges that it would be wrong to assume that astrology was an improper idea at Qumran.[85] The evidence in some apocalyptic texts, which the Qumran Jews may have been aware of, indicates an existing belief that angels governed the stars and the four physical elements (wind, air, earth and fire) and other aspects of creation.[86] However, celestial rulers such as Mastema were not always under God's control.[87] Yet God elected angels to watch against evil activity and to reinstate orderly working, instructions and commandments for cosmic stability.[88] It could be that some Jews were

---

[80] See Jer. 10:2 and especially Jer. 44:15-19 where the Jews ascribe the national disaster that befell them to the failure to give the queen of heaven the honour and worship she requires, a view that Jeremiah contested (44:20-23) declaring that the national disaster was a result of the Jews' worship of the queen of heaven.

[81] Isa. 47: 12-15.

[82] Dt. 4: 19; Dt. 17:3-5.

[83] 2 Kgs. 21:5.

[84] Maxwell J. Davidson, *Angels at Qumran: A Comparative Study of 1 Enoch 1–36, 72–108 and Sectarian Writings of the Qumran* JSPSup 11 (Sheffield: JSOT Press, 1992), pp.161-2.

[85] J. H. Charlesworth, "Jewish Interest in Astrology During the Hellenistic and Roman Period" in *Aufstieg und Niedergang der Römischen Welt II,* Band 20.2 (Berlin/New York: De Gruyter, 1987), p. 939.

[86] 1 En 43: 3; 60: 11-25; 72:1; 75: 1-3; 80: 1, 6; Jub. 2: 2, 8: 3; 2 En 16: 7.

[87] Jub. 48: 9, 12.

[88] 2 En 4: 1f; 19: 1-3.

interested in astrology, albeit with a critical slant.[89] They believed that the heavenly watchers, the offspring of the "sons of God" and "daughters of men", taught astrological, magical and divinatory skills.[90] Their opposition to the worship of the luminaries was an explicit opposition to astrology as practised by pagans and 'unorthodox' Jews.

The effect of Babylonian astrology was felt during Second Temple Judaism, though the Qumran Jews may have followed what they deemed as the orthodox approach to the luminaries.[91] Jewish astrology focused on calendrical matters, devoid of the belief that the luminaries influenced human destiny. The course of the luminaries followed fixed laws, which could not lead to predictions of the future.[92] Yet the *Treatise of Shem*'s narration about the beginnings of the year and the events that would happen, contrasts this position. Its contention that things occurred according to the sign of the zodiac in which the year began contradicts Jewish paramount belief in God's sovereignty, providence and protection.[93] In contrast, the book of *Jubilees* (albeit not written against the *Treatise of Shem*) rejects the belief that zodiac determined yearly rainfall.[94] In relating the movement of the luminaries and linking the lunar with the solar calendar, 1Enoch 72–75 perhaps explains Jewish thoughts with regard to the true calendar. Eventually, Jewish interest in astrology could have been an effort to gather evidence so as to reveal the sinful pedigree astrology conveyed.

4:3. Graeco-Roman Perceptions of Supernatural Powers

Graeco-Roman culture and religion were inseparable.

> The *religio* of the Roman surrounded his entire daily life and his every act with casuistry of sacred law... The Roman priestly list (*indigitamenta*) contained an almost infinite number of gods, particularized and specialized. Every act and indeed every specific element of an act stood under the influence of special *numina* (spirits). It was therefore the part of discretion for one engaged in an important activity to invoke and honor...various ambiguous gods (*incerti*) whose jurisdiction was uncertain... The Roman interest in keeping the *numina* satisfied had the effect of producing a conceptual analysis of all individual actions into their components, each being assigned to the jurisdiction of a particular *numen* whose special protection it enjoyed.[95]

---

[89] Jub.8: 3; 1 En 8: 3; 33: 3; 72: 1; 74: 2; 75: 3f; 78: 10; 79: 2, 6; 80: 1-8; 82: 7; *Wis.* 13: 2f.
[90] 1 En 8: 3; Jub. 8: 1-4; 11: 7-8.
[91] See Jub 12: 17-20; 1 En 72–82.
[92] 1 En 74: 2-3; 75: 1-3; 78: 9; 79: 2.
[93] TrShem 1:1–12: 9.
[94] Cf. TrShem 5:1 with Jub 12: 4, 16-18.
[95] Max Weber, *The Sociology*, pp. 11-12.

Weber's treatise, however, is an analysis of the role of religion in social change and the connection of religious institutions and practices to other aspects of social structures. It is mainly an evolutionary reading of the relations between religion, society and culture and how they impact on each other. His analysis does show however that the Graeco-Romans believed in a host of supernatural powers. It also suggests that they performed several rituals and practices so as to enjoy favour and protection from spirits or gods.

i. Graeco-Roman Beliefs

The populace believed that supernatural powers could be anti-human or pro-human. They not only went berserk and made human beings mad, but also they could be sensible and give humanity peace of mind. Many Graeco-Romans feared and venerated them. This in most case fused superstitious and religious beliefs; though drawing a dividing line between what was religious and superstitious at that time can be intricate. The Greek word δεισιδαιμονεστέρους translated 'religious' can also be translated 'superstitious'.[96] Klauck notes that the word can imply a range from the pious fears of gods to crass superstition.[97] He argues that the altar of the unknown god in Acts 17: 23 aimed to embrace many divine names. This minimised the fear of neglecting one god since to overlook a god would make it react in anger and punish the people.[98] For the most part, people believed in supernatural powers such as gods and goddesses, demons, spirits and ghosts of dead heroes some of whom were reliable and benign but others erratic and malicious. The masses sought a fixed relationship with supernatural powers in order to conciliate them.

a. Gods and Goddesses

The Graeco-Romans believed in the existence of many gods and goddesses. Unlike the Jews who gave Yahweh supremacy in all areas of life, each god or goddess seems to have been supreme only in a specific area of life. Perhaps the creation of gods was inevitable due to the usual divinisation and personification of abstract moral values and human innate feelings. *Dikē* (Greek for justice or judicial punishment) was divinised and personified as Zeus' daughter and goddess of justice or revenge. *Peithō* (Greek for the art of persuasion) was

---

[96] See Acts 17: 22; 25: 19.
[97] Klauck, *Magic and Paganism in Early Christianity*, p. 81. See also Hans-Josef Klauck, "Religion without Fear: Plutarch, on Superstitions and Early Christian Literature" in *Skrif en Kerk* (1997), p. 111-126 for detailed discussions on δεισιδαιμονία and δεισιδαιμονῶν. But Cicero makes a distinction between religion and superstitions. In *De Natura Deorum* 2.72, superstitious persons were those who spent all their days praying and sacrificing in the hope of having their children survive them, while the religious persons were those who scrupulously rehearsed and studied afresh all the ritual involved in divine worship. So 'the word "superstitious" described something deficient and "religious" something praiseworthy'.
[98] Klauck, *Magic and Paganism in Early Christianity*, pp. 82-3.

personified and divinised as the goddess of persuasion.[99] Other abstract and impersonal qualities such as faith, virtue, justice, concord, honour, wealth, safety, freedom, victory, discipline, providence, prudence, desire, pleasure and sexual joy could be deified and awarded a public shrine.[100] The Graeco-Romans could also divinise innate human feelings and emotions, regarding them as gods or goddesses. However, human innate feelings and emotions were not in reality gods or goddesses, though the inexplicable nature by which they seized individuals, leading them to act was reason enough to divinise them. Human innate feelings and emotions became mysterious powers that controlled human conduct.[101] It is therefore not surprising that human beings divinised and gave life to the intuitive feelings and emotions such as love and desire for love, pangs of guilt and lust of war. It may have been normal to identify Love with the goddess Aphrodite and probably to identify Strife with Ares. These human feelings and emotions, now having been made strange and alien, could sway people to commit acts of indescribable terror.

The Graeco-Roman worldview therefore not only exemplified the belief in gods but also outlined a variety of gods and the central role they played in human life.[102] For instance, Artemis not only influenced religious life but also civic and economic institutions. Her cult was an indispensable economic pillar in the cultural structures and life of Asia and a key factor in the lives of the people Christianity hoped to convert. Its sway extended beyond the religious sphere into the whole Asian life and culture.[103] Challenging the cult of Artemis was an enormous threat to the economic and religious structures of human existence. The riot in Acts 19: 23-41 is indicative. The silversmiths, who depended on the cult for the sale of their merchandise, realized they could lose their clients hence their business. What ensued was a riot based on the claim that Paul's preaching not only jeopardised their business, but also despised the temple of the great goddess and destroyed all her splendour.[104] Paul in Acts 16: 16-24 is reported as having exorcised a spirit from a female slave that enabled her to prophesy for her masters' financial gain. The masters, aiming to boost their profit and having noticed the loss they were to incur, accused Paul and Silas before the rulers. The charge sheet read, "These men being Jews, exceedingly trouble our city; and they teach customs which are not lawful for

---

[99] Klauck, *The Religious Context*, p. 28.
[100] Cicero, *De Natura Deorum* 2.58, 61; Walsh, "Introduction", p. xxiv.
[101] See Lowes G. Dickinson, *The Greek View of Life* (London: Methuen, 1986), p. 6.
[102] Cicero, *De Natura Deorum* 2.63–69; Klauck, *The Religious Context*, p. 29.
[103] See Richard Oster, "The Ephesian Artemis as an Opponent of Early Christianity" in Jahrbuch für Antike und Christentum 19 (1976), p. 34; Clinton E. Arnold, *Ephesians: Power and Magic. The Concept of Power in Ephesians in light of its Historical Setting*. SNTSMS 63 (Cambridge: Cambridge University Press, 1989), pp. 20-21; Arnold, *Powers*, p. 208
[104] Pausanias, *Description of Greece* 4.31.4; Xenophon, *Ephesius Ephesiaca* 1.2.3; Xenophon, *Anabasis* 5.3.4, verify Demetrius' claim that Artemis (Diana) of Ephesus was worshipped by all Asia and the world (Acts 19: 27).

The Context of Production

us being Romans, to receive or observe" (Acts 16:20-1). Paul and Silas were apparently not charged because of teaching different customs but because of shattering the slave girl owners' hope to gain economic security (Acts 16: 19). We can thus conclude that gods and goddesses were directly linked to religious and economic structures of human existence.

Plutarch, whose attitude towards the gods is not *sui generis* but represented the spirit of the age, insists that gods were antithetical.[105] One god created everything good while another created everything evil and ruled the cosmos. The gods did not have equal power since primacy belonged to the better one; though to destroy the evil power was utterly impossible.[106] At the same time, the great majority believed and worshipped gods who by their own providence cared for individuals and cities.[107] The gods were also adored for their ability to heal the sick, having been induced through magic, divination or astrology. Human desire and felt need for bodily health and fear of illness, pain and death were key motivating factors for human conduct and identification with gods or goddesses. The gods and divinised heroes who promised healing captured the attention of people[108] who held that the gods communicated their intent to heal through dreams and visions. What was ideal for the one seeking healing was to avoid lack of faith, mockery and scepticism. Equally decisive was the person's belief in the healing power that resided within the human person. The masses held that gods could use gifted people to heal the sick. Apollonius of Tyana (c 4–96 CE) is an ideal representative of such people. He allegedly spent some time in the sanctuary of Asclepius,[109] who had directed his first patient to him through a dream and whom he cured by good counsel and appropriate warning. He was a well-known wonder worker, who performed miracles to help the sick and the dead. He gave magical amulets and/or recipes to exorcise demons that

---

[105] It should be noted that Plutarch,'s dualistic understanding of the divine is specifically about Egyptian religion. But he also noted that other people knew the Egyptian gods although not by their Egyptian names (*De Iside et Osiride* 66.377d. Cf. 47.396–48.370d; 67.377-8). He held that the gods were not really different among peoples and despite the varying modes and addresses assigned to them, the one supreme reason and providence was the same everywhere and so are the powers that serve them in their respective spheres. So according to Greek thought, Osiris was the same as Dionysus (*De Iside et Osiride* 13.356b). Plutarch, also believed that several philosophers were aware of the antithetical gods (*De Iside et Osiride* 48.370d-371a).

[106] Plutarch, *De Iside et Osiride* 45.369b–49.371a.

[107] Cicero, *De Natura Deorum* 2.120–167; Seneca, *De Providentia* 1.1.

[108] See Strabo, *Geography* 8.6.15; Pausanias *Graec. Descr* 2.27.3.

[109] Asclepius was previously the mortal son of the healing god Apollo (See Homeric Hymns no.16), who worked as a mortal doctor among human beings. But after his death he was raised to the rank of a hero before finally attaining the status of a god (See Klauck, *The Religious Context*, p. 156-7.

possessed people without their knowledge.[110]

This does not mean that medical science, which can be traced to Hippocratic medicine, was never practised. The Hippocratic texts (penned c 450–250 BCE), which deal with a variety of medical topics, are known for "their rejection of supernatural explanation for disease, and their insistence on the importance of careful observation".[111] This may have continued into and beyond the first century CE. Galen (129–c 210 CE), who perhaps followed the Hippocratic tradition faithfully, was the most influential doctor of late Graeco-Roman antiquity.[112] It may not be easy though to draw a precise boundary between medicine and popular practices of healing in Graeco–Roman culture. "There was probably little rivalry between such places of healing and medical skills, since each had its own sector and knew that they depended on each other".[113] Perhaps the majority regarded medicine (which depended on science and philosophy) and the popular practices and cults of healing as mutually linked, complementing and indeed sometimes influencing each other. Even if Galen may have followed the Hippocratic tradition that deplored supernatural explanation of disease, he may have used dreams for diagnosis and also prescribed forms of treatment that were dream inspired.[114] He desired to blend the best work of his predecessors with his own logic and so it appears he used the Aristotelian idea[115] that dreams were helpful in medical diagnosis.[116] Cicero also linked dreams with healing of soldiers injured in battle.[117] On the other hand, he held that a physician could diagnose sickness from the condition of the pulse, breath and many other symptoms.[118]

b. *Demons and Spirits*

Demons were known in Greek religion prior to the first century CE, though the term was probably used to refer to supernatural beings inferior to the famed and unparalleled gods. During the Platonic period, *daimones* were intermediary beings that contacted people on behalf of the gods. They were spiritual beings between gods and humanity,[119] later on held to enhance the visionary power of

---

[110] Flavious Philostratus, *Life of Apollonius of Tyana* 3.38–39. But Lucian depicted a follower of Apollonius as one who knew "his whole bag of tricks" (Lucian, *Alexander* 5) and who became an expert in this particular brand of "pretentious nonsense".

[111] R. J. Hankinson, "Hippocratic Medicine", in *Concise Routledge Encyclopaedia of Philosophy* (London/New York: Routledge, 2000), p. 355.

[112] R. J. Hankinson, "Galen (AD 129–c210)" in *Concise Routledge Encyclopaedia of Philosophy* (London/New York: Routledge, 2000), p. 304.

[113] Klauck, *The Religious Context*, p. 167.

[114] Paul Turner, *Lucian Satirical Sketches* – Translated with an introduction by Paul Turner (Harmondsworth, Middlesex: Penguin Books, 1961), p. 10.

[115] Hankinson, "Galen", p. 304.

[116] Aristotle, *Parva Naturalia* 464b-7f.

[117] Cicero, *De Divinatione* 2.lxvi.137.

[118] Cicero, *De Divinatione* 2.lxx.145.

[119] Plato, *Symposium* 23.202d-e.

the oracles.[120] According to Plutarch, when the oracles were in decline, it was believed that the demons had departed. When they returned, the oracles "sound forth again like musical instruments when the artist comes and play them".[121] Plato classified demons as those in the heavens, in the air and in the human soul. Demons in the air included disembodied souls of the dead, especially dead heroes. Xenocrates (died about 315 BCE), adding to Platonic demonology, distinguished between good and evil demons with the latter haunting the air and the human world. This was probably for apologetic reasons so that there would be no need to blame the gods for evil, suffering, immoral actions, human sacrifice and dismembering of living animals. Demons, whose nature was now inferior, were henceforth blamed for all anti-human and anti-social qualities.[122]

Plutarch clearly shows that demons were known in philosophical circles in and beyond the first century CE.[123] Now regarded as evil supernatural powers, they belonged to popular religion, which from the distant past associated the untamed nature, mountains and forest with demons, the spirits of nature and nymphs. Sometimes these could be kind, but in most cases cruel, angry and threatening, seizing people and making them mad.[124] This perhaps continued into and beyond the first century CE, especially among Christians who recognized Greek gods as demons, purportedly because they caused evil and suffering,[125] inspired idolatry, magic, astrology and Greek wisdom[126] and haunted people, desiring to enslave them and to lead them to error by practising deceit on them.[127] Allen aptly notes that at that time, people were born and bred within a milieu of superstitious terror and the majority believed in demons.[128] Perhaps the masses held that demons could influence the structures of human existence. This seems likely if, as stated by Plutarch, demons are spiritual beings that think intensely and produce vibrations in the air. These vibrations enable other spiritual beings and highly sensitive individuals to receive their thoughts as through antennae.[129] All in all, demons and spirits were violent and vindictive, but magical amulets, verbal skills for instance incantations and other

---

[120] Plutarch, *Ser.Num.Vind.* 30; *De.Def.Orac* 10.409e-483e.

[121] Plutarch, *Def. Orac.* 13-15, especially 418d.

[122] See Plutarch, *Def. Orac.*13-15, especially 417b-e.

[123] Plutarch, *Ser.Num.Vind.* 30; *De Defectu Oraculorum* 417b–425a. See P. G. Bolt, "Jesus, the Daimons and the Dead" in Anthony N. S. Lane (ed.), *The Unseen World: Christian Reflection on Angels, Demons and the Heavenly Realm* (Carlisle, Cumbria: Paternoster/ Grand Rapids, Michigan: Baker Book House, 1996), pp 81-86.

[124] Nilsson, *Greek Popular Religion*, pp. 13, 15.

[125] Justin Martyr, *1 Apol.*5; Tatian, *Orat.* 16-20.

[126] Justin Martyr, *1 Apol.* 41, 56; Tertullian, *de Spect.* 9; *de Test.an.*2; *ad. Scap.* 2; *de Idol.* 4; Origen, *Contra Cels.* 1.60-4; 7.5-9.

[127] Tatian, *Orat.* 7, 14, 16-19; Justin Martyr, *Dial.* 41.1, 77.9-10; Origen, *Contra. Cels.* 4.29, 5.5; *de Princi.* 3.3.4.

[128] R. Allen, *Missionary Methods: St Paul's or Ours* (Grand Rapids, Michigan: Eerdmans, 1962), p. 28.

[129] Plutarch, *De Genio Socratis* 589b.

precautionary techniques were helpful to counter their noxious effects.[130]

c. Spirits of Dead Heroes

Next to the demons, were dead heroes deemed as ghosts, and so supernatural powers. These dead heroes were individuals who in their human lifetime did exceptional deeds and who were alleged to possess mystical power after death. They were thus divinised upon death and they received libation at the site of their tomb.[131] Mandatory funeral rites were performed to honour the departed ancestors and to avoid them was to invite disaster.[132] Tombs of dead heroes were thus the centres of hero cults. The Athenians, notes Plutarch, venerated Theseus, the famed founder of democracy. Slaves and ordinary people terrified of powerful human or spiritual beings often sought refuge in Theseus' grave because he protected and assisted the oppressed and graciously received their petition during his earthly life.[133] Prior to the first century CE, Nilsson notes that the dead heroes could also be revered as healers of diseases and helpers in the time of war. Venerating a dead hero by the side of his tomb was like calling him up to protect his family, and so the cult of the heroes related to popularly felt needs.[134]

It seems that during the first century CE, the Graeco-Romans believed that dead heroes or those who died untimely changed into disembodied spirits.[135] It was believed that after death, a person could become a hero, then a demon and finally a god. Plutarch extols Hesiod as the first person to have hierarchically listed four types of rational beings, namely, gods, demons, heroes, and humans. He also held that an ordinary person could be transformed to a hero, a hero to a demon and a demon to a god. It is only few demons, thanks to their ability, that could be purified to share in the divinity.[136] As it was possible for a person to become a god through the transformation stages, it was likewise possible for demons to sink back into mortal bodies and finally die.[137] The boundaries between gods, spirits, demons and ghosts of dead heroes were somewhat porous. Just like gods and demons, ghosts of dead heroes could be capricious, vengeful and full of wrath and they could sometimes attack or punish the living.[138] The spirits of the dead were restless and moved around like ghosts and as the personification of natural forces and powers.[139] They could exhibit evil intentions, cause illnesses and harm people if commanded via magic. This shows the extent to which the dead were concurrently deified, feared, revered

---

[130] Pliny, *Nat. Hist.* 28.5.23-29.
[131] Aune, "Religion", p. 921.
[132] Sophocles, *Antigone.*
[133] Plutarch, *Thes.* 35.5–36.3.
[134] Nilsson, *Greek Popular Religion*, p. 20.
[135] Plutarch, *Parallela Graeca et Romana* 380a.
[136] Plutarch, *Def. Orac.* 10
[137] Plutarch, *Def.* Orac. 17.419a-e.
[138] Plutarch, *Quaestiones Romanae* 51.277a.
[139] Plutarch, *Ser. Num.Vind;* Klauck, *The Religious Context*, p. 423.

The Context of Production

and required as protectors.[140]

Ordinary Graeco-Romans held supernatural powers responsible for whatever happened in the world and in human life. Seneca informs us that when human beings and natural phenomena took an out of the ordinary nature, it was a divine power that had descended upon the human or natural phenomena, causing the resultant deeds. He notes that a spirit indwells human beings, marking good and bad deeds. As the guardian of human life, the indwelling spirit moves in accordance with how people treat it[141]. So, even if attributing evil and suffering and all human undertakings to supernatural powers could have been the conclusive thread that tied together whatever happened, human action determined the course the events would take. But the great majority always sought to be on the right side with supernatural powers. They could not tell when supernatural powers could be reliable and benevolent, or unreliable and malevolent. It was thus essential to perform several rituals and practices that enabled individuals to manage and maintain their links with supernatural powers.

ii Graeco-Roman Rituals and Practices

a. Magic and Witchcraft

It is vital to recall the discussion in chapter one that illustrates that the subject of magic and related practices of witchcraft and sorcery are complex. It is possible however to trace Graeco-Roman magic to the early age, when Greek life mainly depended on agriculture and the popular belief was that gods were responsible for good crops or poor harvest. It was supposed that the goddess Artemis loved the hills and groves and well-watered places and promoted natural fertility, which never depended on human effort. Magical rites were performed to obliterate vermin and evil powers like wind that endangered the vines. Magic was thus enduring and closest to the earth and was "the source of all religion from which the great gods sprang".[142] Hermes, the great god who guided the souls[143], was linked to magic. He was pictorially illustrated holding a magic rod as he permitted the souls of small winged human figures to ascend and to descend from the mouth of a large jar.[144] The Greeks adopted Hekate from Caria in Asia Minor as they wanted a goddess of witchcraft and a leader of ghosts.[145] The magical papyri innately link great goddesses like Artemis,

---

[140] Cicero, *De Natura Deorum* 2.62.
[141] Seneca, *Epistulae Morales* 41.1-5.
[142] Nilsson, *Greek Popular Religion*, p. 21.
[143] Franz Cumont, *Astrology among the Greeks and Romans* (New York: Dover, 1960), p. 105.
[144] Nilsson, *Greek Popular Religion*, p. 9.
[145] Nilsson, *Greek Popular Religion*, pp. 90, 111.

Selene, and Hekate with magic.[146] Magic was thus linked to the belief in the existence of supernatural powers. It was also linked to the belief that everything in the cosmos was caringly or callously related to human existence.

Magic gave the Graeco-Romans the skills to control and communicate with supernatural powers. This does not mean that magic was popular even if it flourished during the first century CE perhaps as a result of the decay of old religions which, in modern terms, the state had secularised and which the Sophists attacked.[147] Pliny notes how magical spells and medicine were used to cure diseases[148] but rubbished magic[149] describing it as a "thing detestable in itself", which "frivolous and lying as it is ...still bears some shadow of truth upon it".[150] During the second century CE, Lucian doubted the efficacy of magic and ridiculed the belief that something external and quite unconnected with internal causes of disease, plus a few magical words could bring about cure.[151] The widely held belief that a foreign language could scare a swelling or drive away fever and practices of magic and exorcism were only old wives tales and a pack of lies, even if the gods did exist.[152] He poured scorn on ghosts and the beliefs that dead people's ghosts wander about the earth and reveal themselves to anyone they like. He denied that ghosts existed or were seen by anybody or they could be invoked through magic to heal the sick. Yet he respected the gods who could cure and restore people to health through proper medical treatment.[153]

Nevertheless, the practice of magic was taken seriously in the first century CE. Plutarch affirms the grip with which it had held on to the masses. He notes that magicians instructed people possessed by demons to recite the Ephesian writings and to pronounce the names therein correctly.[154] The magical texts contained recipes and names of supernatural powers that supposedly made charms active. Jesus' name seems to have been used to bind demons. A spell preserved in a magical papyrus read, "*By the God of the Hebrews, I adjure you, Jesus, you who appear in fire, you who are in the midst of field and snow and*

---

[146] See PGM IV. 2520–2620, 2622–2707, 2708–2784, 2785–2890. See also PGM LXXVIII 11–12, which has a drawing of Artemis Multi-mammaea.

[147] Nilsson, *Greek Popular Religion*, p. 115; Kraft, *Understanding Spiritual Power*, pp. x, 33, 39; Burnett, *Earthly Powers*, p. 232 attests that religion has historically decayed due to secularisation and attacks, which were probably rampant during the first century CE.

[148] Pliny, *Nat. Hist.*28.21.

[149] Pliny, *Nat. Hist.*30.1-20.

[150] Pliny, *Nat. Hist.*30.6.

[151] Lucian, 'The pathological liar' or 'The unbeliever' in Turner, *Lucian Satirical Sketches*, p. 200.

[152] Lucian, 'The pathological liar' or 'The unbeliever' in Turner, *Lucian Satirical Sketches*, p. 201.

[153] Lucian, 'The pathological liar' or 'The unbeliever' in Turner, *Lucian Satirical Sketches*, p. 201.

[154] Plutarch, *Quaestiones Convivialium* 7.5,4 (760E).

The Context of Production 113

mist. *May your inexorable angel descend and bind fast the wandering demon of this creature*".[155] Clearly, even if detestable, magic thrived in the first century CE. It obsessed Emperor Nero whose "greatest wish was to command the gods" and he desired the magicians' capability to control and command the gods.[156] Other Roman Emperors too had private astrologers whom they largely consulted before performing any task.[157] Perhaps the vitriol against magic persuaded people to practise it clandestinely due to the fear of being ostracised and/or victimised. But the masses held that through magic, the inexplicable and inexorable supernatural powers could be accessed for personal benefit and protection. Luck rightly notes, "We can no longer idealize the Greeks and their 'artistic genius' or the Romans and their 'sober realism.' Magic and witchcraft, the fear of daemons and ghosts, the wish to manipulate invisible powers—all were very much part of the ancient world".[158]

b. Astrology

F. Cumont, the eminent historian of religion, rightly narrates the irresistible triumph of astrology during the Graeco-Roman era, which originated from Mesopotamia, most likely during the era of Babylonian Empire.[159] He depicted it as "this erroneous belief, so long universally accepted, which up to modern times has exercised an endless influence on the creeds and the ideas of the most diverse people".[160] He also notes, "Its starting-point was faith, faith in certain stellar divinities who exerted an influence on the world".[161] Plato (427–347 BCE) seems to have been aware of this faith, whose pinnacle was the reverence of dazzling luminaries in the heavenly places, in claiming that stars were gods.[162] Talented astrologers, also known as *mathematikoi*,[163] allegedly presaged future events by observing the location and movement of the luminaries. Nevertheless, astrology spread fast during the Graeco-Roman era, probably due to the Stoics' influence. On Stoics' astrological beliefs, Cumont writes, "above the old native beliefs the doctrine of Stoicism in particular exercised dominion over men's mind".[164] The Stoics' astral divination was

---

[155] PGM IV.3007-3027.
[156] Howard Clark Kee, M*edicine, Miracle and Magic in New Testament Times* (Cambridge: Cambridge University Press, 1986), p. 6.
[157] Bar-Jesus (Elymas) was attached to a major political figure, Sergius Paulus (Acts 13: 4-12). Josephus identifies a Jewish magician named Atomos who Felix, the Roman governor of Judea asked for help when he fell in love with Drusilla (*Ant.* 20, 142). But on the contrary, Emperor Augustus loathed magic and ordered two thousand magical books to be burnt (Suetonius, *Augustus* 31.3).
[158] Luck, *Arcana Mundi*, p. xiii.
[159] Cumont, *Astrology*, pp. xv, 3-10, 14, 17-8, 38. See also Cicero, *De Divinatione*
[160] Cumont, *Astrology*, p. xi.
[161] Cumont, *Astrology*, p. xiii.
[162] Plato, *Timaeus* 40
[163] Cicero, *De Natura Deorum* 2.51, 103.
[164] Cumont, *Astrology*, p. 46.

anchored in the concept of sympathy between macrocosm and microcosm and of a deterministic worldview. Their cosmology precisely built on two sources—the belief that the universe was ordered by the providence of gods and the belief that destiny was fated and amplified by the stars.[165] They reckoned fate as the decree of stars that ruled the world and could not be altered in any way.[166]

However, the Stoics' cosmology and the popular belief of the populace were at variance. The masses held that fate could be altered because they looked at astrology from a religious rather than a logical persuasion. The Stoics and the popular astrological beliefs were however based on a worldview that saw the universe as an integrated unit without any dichotomy.[167] What affected one part affected the other, so the motion of the stars directly affected the fate of the people on earth. This emerged from the belief that a single divine principle permeated all life, which was identified with Zeus, the powerful divine spirit that governed the mutual relationship of all life. This divine principle caused civility or crudity in the cosmos wherein the part could affect the whole or vice-versa.[168] For the populace, astrology was closely linked with other forms of popular devotion to the gods, like magic and divination/oracles.[169] The masses most likely used magic to invoke the assistance of astral spirits hence altering the astrological fate. It was also believed that the world of human habitation was considerably lower and inferior to the celestial world of the luminaries.[170] This motivated the masses to fear stars, which supposedly possessed the power of gods and could afflict people just because they lived on earth.[171] The masses not only sought protection but also redemption from the luminaries. Considering that modern people have a space in the daily papers dealing with what the stars foretell, it is unsurprising that the luminaries received religious consecration in classical antiquity.[172]

The luminaries were like gods and spirits that allegedly affected and influenced events in the human world. It was believed that stars had power over human affairs and that they could 'indicate' or 'cause' what could shape human destiny. The moon also regulated the tides of the sea and altered the day and

---

[165] Cicero, *De Natura Deorum* 2.73-80.

[166] Manilius 1.25-112, Luck, *Arcana Mundi,* pp. 325, 340, 349. But the Epicureans opposed the Stoics doctrine of the necessity of fate. Gaius Velleius, the Epicurean leading light in Cicero,'s *De Natura Deorum* (1.15) asks, 'how much respect can be accorded to this school of philosophy, which like a pack of ignorant old women regards all that happens as the cause of fate?' (*De Natura Deorum* 1.55).

[167] Cicero, *De Natura Deorum* 2.30.

[168] Cicero, *De Natura Deorum* 2.132.

[169] Cicero, *De Divinatione* 1.lvi.128.

[170] Cicero, *De Natura Deorum* 2. 56.

[171] Cicero, *De Natura Deorum* 2.17, 55.

[172] Guy Daniel, "Astronomy, Astrology and Medicine" in William Neil, (ed.), *The Bible Companion* (London: The Caxton Publishing Company Limited, 1959), p. 310; Arnold, *Powers*, p. 48; Klauck, *The Religious Context*, p. 232.

night while the position of the sun controlled the rhythm of the seasons of the year.[173] It seems that political leaders and the masses alike held that the motion and place of the luminaries directly symbolised the course of events on earth.[174] A particular configuration of stars that came to existence at the birth of a person was assigned to that individual. Learning the secrets of the stars revealed if human fate as ordained by them would be a happy one or not.[175] This perhaps resulted from the belief that gods were apathetic and lacked spiritual vibrancy to address the basic and felt human needs like consolation, protection and atonement. Astrology, which was related to magic, was duly used to command and control the spiritual/celestial world. It guaranteed the masses a blessed destiny as they struggled with hostile evil powers.

Even so, astrological beliefs were not absolutely watertight. The Academics questioned the Stoics' and the masses' belief that whatever happens is fated to happen and can be foretold by divination. Pliny refuted the belief that stars were assigned to an individual at birth to determine the destiny of that person and that the bright stars belonged to the rich while lesser stars to the poor. He did not see commonality between the sky and human destiny hence the widespread belief about stars controlling human destiny was the human attempt to allot great worth to themselves.[176] He rejected the accounts of astrologers maintaining, "no one has better established the relationship between man and the stars or shown more clearly that our souls are particles of heavenly fire".[177] The Academics also doubted the integrity of the Stoics' teaching that the luminaries were divine. In Cicero's *De Natura Deorum*, an Academic asked a Stoic, "is it self-evident and universally agreed that the heavenly bodies are divine, when Velleius (an Epicurean) and many more besides refuse to grant you that they are even alive"?[178] Cicero follows the traditional Academic doubt on astrology expressed before him especially by Carneades (2nd century BCE). He insists that reliance should not be placed on astrologers when they profess to forecast the future from the setting of stars on the day of a person's birth. He castigated astrology, as inconceivable madness for it is not enough to call an

---

[173] Cicero, *De Divinatione* 2.34; Plotinus *Enn.* 2.3.1-8.

[174] Arnold, *Powers*, p. 48, 52-3; Klauck, *The Religious Context*, p. 238. Cumont, *Astrology*, pp. 49, 53 suggests that Augustus and Tiberius were devotees of astrology, though they were hostile to the popular form of foreign worship. But it is not certain to what extent they were devoted to it since they also opposed it. Augustus in 33BCE restricted the future activity of astrologers and in 11 BCE he forbade the populace from consulting them in relation to a person's date of birth. Tiberius expelled the *mathematici* from Rome and Italy in 19CE, but not those who promised to give up their art (Suetonius, *Tiberius* 30). So not all and not always were leaders sympathetic to astrology. Even so, the attacks on astrology, which had now become a world power, rejuvenated and strengthened it to face a new phase of its history and new struggles.

[175] Cicero, *De Divinatione* 1.1.2.

[176] Pliny, *Nat. Hist.* 2.28-9.

[177] Pliny, *Nat. Hist.* 2.26.95.

[178] Cicero, *De Natura Deorum* 3.11.

opinion 'foolishness' when it is utterly devoid of reason. He also disapproved the Stoics' yielding to Chaldean astrology, considering it unintelligible.[179] The disrespect for astrology obviously continued beyond the first century CE. Sextus Empiricus (c 200 CE), a sceptically-minded medical doctor, used empirical expertise in his polemics against astrology.[180] Nonetheless, astrology quickly gained outstanding popularity among the ordinary people who believed the heavenly bodies were either representatives of, or real supernatural powers. They worshiped, invoked, propitiated and manipulated the luminaries and sought their favours via religious rituals.

c. Divination, Oracles and Dreams

Divination is the art of interpreting symbolic messages from the gods and the means by which the gods enabled human beings to have foresight and knowledge of future events. It was an age-old practice that was known during the Homeric era[181] and which probably blossomed in the Graeco-Roman era.[182] It is possible that first century CE divination was the natural progeny of Homeric polytheism, which imagined gods as enslaved by the decrees of fate.[183] Fate allegedly caused things to happen, so nothing occurred arbitrarily without its efficient cause in nature.[184] However, divination could prognosticate what was bound to happen, since by its means individuals could approach near to the very power of gods.[185] The rationale for divination rested on the theory that if gods exist and they do not reveal to people in advance what the future will be, then they do not love human beings, or they do not know what the future will be, or they think it not advantageous for human beings to know what the future will be, or finally they, though being gods, could not give intelligible signs of the coming future. Yet this could not be true because the gods loved human beings and they were their friends and benefactors.[186] The centrality of divination was thus linked with the emphasis on the existence of gods and the necessity to make peace with them. The apparent belief during this period was that peace with the gods and the maintenance of a cordial relationship with them was the basis of temporal prosperity and success. It was generally held that all public and personal disasters were caused by the breach of the relationship between people and gods. Thus, it was critical to identify and rectify the reason for this breach through socially acceptable cultic practices that were known through divination/oracles. The measures included calming

---

[179] Cicero, *De Divinatione*. 2.xlii.88-xlii.91, xlv.94.

[180] Sextus Empiricus, *Adversus Astrologos; Adversus Mathematicos*; Also see Klauck, *The Religious Context*, p. 235.

[181] Homer, *The Odyssey* 1.231-238; 2.177-198; 10.222-229, 492; *The Iliad* 13.663; Cicero, De *Divinatione* 1.xl.89.

[182] Cicero, *De Divinatione* 1.i.1.

[183] Homer, *Iliad* 23.433; Cicero, *De Divinatione* 2.x.25.

[184] Cicero, *De Divinatione* 1.lv.125-lvi.128.

[185] Cicero, *De Divinatione* 1.i.1-2; lvi.127-130.

[186] Cicero, *De Divinatione* 1.xxxviii.82, li.117.

The Context of Production

the gods through sacrifice and prayers and the exact fulfilment of vows and oaths. The cities too were purified and preserved from the hostile influences through established ritual revealed through divination. As Aune notes, strict attention was paid to divination by which outward signs of the gods were revealed.[187] The Stoics were its most fervent supporters. However, Cicero depicted them as "pitiably and distressingly superstitious and so prone to believe everything they heard" and insisted their "view of divination smacked too much of superstitions".[188]

The masses may have been fascinated by divination by which a good or bad omen could be known. They took an omen seriously as it was held that anything involuntary including a sneeze made up an omen that was divinely caused.[189] Divination was also essential during military expeditions and decisions hence the army officially recognized sacred birds and chickens as divinatory paraphernalia.[190] This was perhaps influenced by the Stoics' belief that some birds, which the augurs called "birds of flight" and "birds of utterance", were created to presage the future.[191] With the help of such birds, oracles, prophecies and dream augurs predicted future events and revealed prophetic signs and portents.[192] The casting of dice and the interpretation of the luminaries also helped the diviners to foretell the future. So divination was not only linked with magic, but also with astrology. Dreams were also linked with divination/oracles by which they were received and interpreted.[193] Plutarch referred to dreams as our "oldest, most venerable oracle",[194] a view acknowledged by others.[195] The popular belief was that the gods sent dreams and so they had the same rank as oracles.[196] As a result, the gods were sought for divinatory and oracular purposes because the masses believed divination fulfilled human aspirations and repulsed many dangers.[197] This quickened its domination in the Graeco-Roman cities. In Rome, there was an official board of diviners (augurs), whose duty was to interpret daily events and phenomena.[198] Aune states, "Oracles and divination played an important role in the lives of Greeks from the archaic period until the triumph of Christianity in the fourth century A.D.".[199] Perhaps divination was also popular among the royalty. The

---

[187] Aune, "Religion", p. 920-1.
[188] Cicero, *De Divinatione* 2.xli.87, xlviii.100.
[189] Xenophon, *Anab.* 3.2.8-9; *Mem* 4.3.12; *Eq. Mag.* 9.9; *Symp.* 4. 47f; Cicero, *De Divinatione* 1.xlv.102–104.
[190] Cicero, *De Divinatione* 1.i.2; Livy *Hist.* 10.40.1-5; Suetonius *Tiberius* 2.2.
[191] Cicero, *De Natura Deorum* 2.160.
[192] Cicero, *De Natura Deorum* 2.163.
[193] Cicero, *De Divinatione* 1.xx.39–xxx.65.
[194] Plutarch, *Sept.Sap.Conv* 15.159A.
[195] Aeschylus, *Ag.* 978–981; *Prom.* 485f; Euripides *IPh.Taur.* 1259-1268.
[196] Cicero, *De Natura Deorum* 3.93, 95; *De Divinatione* 1.xxiv.48–xxix.60.
[197] Cicero, *De Natura Deorum* 2.163.
[198] Croy, "Religion", p. 927.
[199] Aune, "Religion", p. 920.

Stoics' voice in Cicero's *De Divinatione* attests that the royalty employed augurs and that no public business was transacted at home or abroad without first taking the auspices from the augurs and soothsayers.[200]

Divination was however confusing because sometimes it could be truthful and sometimes it misled.[201] While the Academics could not scoff at the augural staff, they questioned the origin of divination and observed that the diviners could mislead.[202] The chance that it could mislead probably stirred the elite to criticise it. In the Homeric period, dreams were regarded as false, awkward and confusing.[203] Aristotle interpreted dreams physiologically and psychologically and stated that a god could not send them. He claimed they could be demonic since nature as a whole has a demonic facet.[204] Cicero regarded dreams as the means by which people assumed many false apparitions to be true.[205] He concluded that obscure messages through dreams were utterly inconsistent with the dignity of gods.[206] If god was not the originator of dreams and there was no link between them and the laws of nature, then it followed that no reliance could be placed on them.[207] Cicero also noted that the interpreters of dreams were erratic, and for that reason, their art was nothing but the means of using one's wit to cheat. As such, the Stoics' collection of dreams proved nothing except the shrewdness of men who employ slight inconsistencies in order to draw "now one inference and now another".[208] Cicero held that divination was not applicable where knowledge was gained through the senses and that there was no need of divination in matters within the domain of science and art. He maintained that when people are sick, it was not a prophet or a seer who was summoned but a physician. On the other hand, a person wishing to learn to play a harp or a flute did not take lessons from a soothsayer but from a musician.[209]

Cicero also differentiated diviners, philosophers and astrologers. He asserted that the movement of the luminaries was the work of mathematicians (astrologers), while diviners resolved the questions of what was morally right or wrong. He emphasised that the fame given to divination was inflated since it could not answer all questions of life. Thus issues of dialectic or of physics were not solved by divination since they belonged to the science of physics. There was no place for divination in matters perceived by the senses, so there was no need for it anywhere.[210] There was also no need for divination if everything was ruled by fate and what the diviner forecast depended on chance

---

[200] Cicero, *De Divination* 1.ii.3-5, xliii.95-97.
[201] Cicero, *De Divinatione* 1.xiv.25–lviii.132.
[202] Cicero, *De Natura Deorum* 3.14-5.
[203] Homer, *Iliad* 2.1-40; *Odyssey* 19.603-680.
[204] Aristotle, *Parva Naturalia* 463b.13-15.
[205] Cicero, *De Divinatione* 2.lviii.120.
[206] Cicero, *De Divinatione* 2.lxiv.135.
[207] Cicero, *De Divinatione* 2.lxx.147.
[208] Cicero, *De Divinatione* 2.lxx.144.
[209] Cicero, *De Divinatione* 2.iii.9-10.
[210] Cicero, *De Divinatione* 2.iv.11-12.

The Context of Production

and not on the guidance of the gods or divine agency.[211] It was useless to believe that the crowing of a fowl and the flight of birds could help divination when it was the business of fowls to crow and of birds to fly. Likewise, to base divination on the fact that a snake coiled itself on posts was futile because that is what snakes naturally do. However, if it was a fish that crowed or a post that coiled itself to a snake, then that could call for divination through an omen.[212] He wondered if it is not enough just to admit that some aspects of divination were based on a little error, little superstitions and a good deal of fraud.[213] So even if Cicero belonged to the priestly college of augurs, he was sceptical about these practices. Still, he endorsed divination for reasons of political expediency and for the sake of state religion.[214]

Pliny the Elder also recognized the subjective nature of the oracular interpretations since the meaning of the omens largely resided in the eyes of the diviner.[215] Epicurus scoffed at divination more than anything else, and Cicero depicted him as the only exception among philosophers who did not approve divination.[216] Xenophanes, while backing the existence of gods, repudiated divination in its entirety.[217] Plutarch also rejected the usual perception that whenever seers or oracular priests gave answer to oracles they were speaking with a voice not their own. It was erroneous and "simple-minded, indeed childish to believe that a god himself ... enters the bodies of prophets and speaks from within them, employing their mouth and tongue as his instruments".[218] Lucian depicted Alexander, whom he regarded as a false prophet or a bogus oracle, as a charlatan who shamelessly tricked people with his private oracles.[219] He ridiculed oracles and concluded that hearing stories about oracles given by certain gods was appalling, and the only antidote for such stories was truth and common sense.[220] The Epicureans also spoke of divination spitefully. Even so, this scepticism was not the general rule since the Stoics vigorously defended divination. But being hesitant on the proper judgment on divination could have been credible seeing that some Stoics, despite the fact that the Stoics by and large upheld divination, doubted it on some points.[221] Though several philosophical schools approved divination, it was not to the same degree.[222] Divination through the oracle was popular

---

[211] Cicero, *De Divinatione* 2.vii.19–viii.21, x.25-6.
[212] Cicero, *De Divinatione* 2.xvii.38–xl.84.
[213] Cicero, *De Divinatione*. 2.xxxix.83.
[214] Cicero, *De Divinatione*. 2.xii.28, xviii.42-3.
[215] Pliny, *Nat. Hist.* 28.4.17.
[216] Cicero, *De Natura Deorum* 2.162; De Divinatione 1.iii.5, xxxix.87.
[217] Cicero, *De Divinatione* 1.iii.5, xxxix.87.
[218] Plutarch, *De Defectu Oraculorun* 9.441E.
[219] Lucian, *Alexander* in Turner, *Lucian Satirical Sketches*, p. 221-248.
[220] Lucian, 'The pathological liar or *The unbeliever*' in Turner, *Lucian Satirical Sketches*, pp. 212-13, 217-18.
[221] Cicero, *De Divinatione* 1.iii.7–v.8.
[222] Cicero, *De Divinatione* 1.iii.5f, lviii.132.

despite the negative sentiments it received. The oracle through his god communicated vital religious values to the populace. The oracles gave those oppressed by fear and hope what they wanted, the information about the future.[223] Luck concurs that one must not forget soothsaying was a form of psychotherapy. It helped people who believed in a multiplicity of supernatural powers to cope with fears, and compelled them to make decisions when all possible ideas had been exhausted.[224]

4:4. Graeco-Roman Reservations about Supernatural Powers

Several philosophical schools such as Stoics, Academics, Middle Platonism, Peripatetics and Pythagoreans included a strong religious element. They believed in the existence of divine providence that controlled human affairs via the agency of demons or spirits. But on the other hand, there were some reservations in relation to the religious phenomena prompting people to believe in the existence of supernatural powers. The elite mainly faulted popular teachings and the beliefs in the gods these teachings propagated. This is well attested in Epicurus' letter to Menoikeus.[225] Epicurus believed in the imperishability and blessedness of the gods and held that whatever was not attuned to the gods' imperishability and blessedness should not be attributed to the gods.[226] To do this was an error that led to atheism; an error that people committed by identifying gods with perishable natural phenomena and experiences that terrified them. This error led them to partake in rituals and practices that could not impress the gods that lived outside time and were not involved with what happened in the material world. Epicurus held that the gods were wholly inactive and inattentive and even if endowed with human limbs, they could not make use of them.[227] Sacrifices and prayers could not reach the gods because they were least attracted to events on earth. They experienced no trouble and they caused problem to nobody.[228] So popular beliefs, rituals and practices about gods were onerous and made life to appear shameful for encouraging undue fear of the gods.[229] Naturally the Epicureans (and possibly the Cynics and Euhemerism) regarded the popular beliefs in gods as the basis of atheism.[230] The Academics held that Epicurus' god had no reality, but was a mere likeness of reality.[231] Epicurus himself had acquired the bad name of an

---

[223] Lucian, *Alexander* in Turner, *Lucian Satirical Sketches*, p. 224.
[224] Luck, *Arcana Mundi*, p. 327.
[225] This letter is in Diogenes Laertius, *Vit. Phil.* 10.122–135. (See. Klauck, *The Religious Context*, p. 390).
[226] Diogenes Laertius, *Vit. Phil.* 10.123; Cicero, *De Natura Deorum* 1.45, 55-6.
[227] Cicero, *De Natura Deorum* 3.3.
[228] Cicero, *De Natura Deorum* 1.85.
[229] Titus Lucretius, *De Rerum Natura* 1.62-72.
[230] Cicero, *De Natura Deorum* 1.45.
[231] Cicero, *De Natura Deorum* 1.75.

atheist and a libertine due to his teachings on the gods.[232] The Epicureans thrived in the first century CE and they may represent a tradition that denied the popular belief that supernatural powers influenced human life.

The Epicureans' view was perhaps a minority as the popular spirit of the age recognised supernatural powers that were not remote. The Epicureans were held to be spreading atheism. Plutarch, one of the famous Middle Platonists, was their avowed opponent. He simultaneously scorned superstitions and atheism insisting that superstitious emotions could lead to atheism.[233] He also claimed that superstitious beliefs about the gods were perpetuated through myth. He never denied the validity of myth, but interpreted its mysteries philosophically.[234] His philosophical monotheism elevated the deity above the finite world and so demons were agents of gods' influence in the world.[235] Inasmuch as myth brought the gods to the finite world, he insisted that myths did not happen as reported and enacted in popular belief. For that reason, myths must not be accepted literally but reverently and philosophically. He thus read myth as an image of reality, which enables the minds of people to understand trouble and suffering. He deemed it annoying to believe what myth says about gods as if it really happened.[236] Plutarch therefore rejected the popular idea about gods insisting that the divine is not blessed through wealth and physical power, but through knowledge and intelligence.[237] Certainly, he referred to the gods respectfully and encouraged longing for the truths about them. For him, this was yearning after divinity and was better than public worship such as sacrifices or ritual enactment, ceremonial purification, and temple service.[238] He held that gods were not pleased by public worship but by true belief about them that helped to avoid superstition, no less an evil than atheism.[239]

Nevertheless, the popular belief was that the gods were made happy by public worship. It was the public worship and the form and experience in which piety was practised that generated the criticism of the popular beliefs, rituals and practices related to the gods. Public worship would in most cases include anointing, decorating and clothing the graven images of the gods with precious garments and then placing them on banqueting settees, setting meals before them to eat. Seneca attacked such practices and that of saluting gods in the morning, thronging the doors of the temples and that of lighting lamps on the Sabbath as if gods needed light. He also scorned the practice of bringing towels and flesh-scrapers to Jupiter and proffering mirrors to Juno. He scorned the practices by which people took possession of the gods so as to use them for

---

[232] Cicero, *De Natura Deorum* 1.123.
[233] Plutarch, *De Iside et Osiride* 11.355d; 22.359d–23.260b; 66.377e-378f; *De Supersitione* 1.165a-b; 1.166d-e; 1.167a; 1.169d-e; 1.171b, f.
[234] Plutarch, *De Iside et Osiride* 11.355b; 68.378a.
[235] Plutarch, *De Iside et Osiride* 46.369d.
[236] Plutarch, *De Iside et Osiride* 20.358e–359b.
[237] Plutarch, *De Iside et Osiride* 1.351d; 45.369a.
[238] Plutarch, *De Iside et Osiride* 2.351e; 20.358e.
[239] Plutarch, *De Iside et Osiride* 11.355d.

personal ends. These, as he maintained, were mere ceremonies that attracted mortal ambitions, not the attention of the god, who can only be worshipped by those who truly know him. He insisted that the gods do not need human servants since they order the universe, serve people and maintain their existence. Seneca did not scold the veneration of gods though he criticised the naïve and excessive anthropomorphic images people made for gods. He summoned human beings to recoil from burdensome superstitions insisting that they could progress if they grasp the idea that god possesses all things, allots all things and bestows them without price. He insisted that it was the nature of the gods to do deeds of kindness and thereby rejected the popular notion that the gods could inflict injury, though they could chasten and restrain certain persons, impose penalties and sometimes punish by bestowing that which seems good outwardly.[240]

Seneca also maintained that while trees, forests, caves, mountains, rivers, streams of hot water could prove the presence of the deity, they should not be viewed on a footing of equality with the gods. The gods also should not be equated with people who are terrified in the midst of danger since the quality of the gods is too great and too lofty to resemble the body in which it dwells. He considered it foolish and insane to praise the qualities in a person, which came from without and may be passed to someone else in the next instance. He thereby maintained that there was no need to either lift one's hands to heaven or to beg the keeper of a temple to let human beings approach his idol's ear, as if the prayers were more likely to be heard. Secondly, there was no need for prayers since god is near human beings and he is with them and in them. He insisted that a holy spirit indwells human beings, and as they treat this spirit so does the spirit treat them.[241] Generally, the Stoics could not figure out a god with veins and sinews and bones and who could eat and drink. Neither could they appreciate a god in bodily form since this would make a god afraid of tumbling down, of receiving blows, or be afraid of illness owing to physical fatigue.[242] The Stoics and the Academics censured "the naïve public—and philosophers similarly naïve—who out of shallow-mindedness cannot visualise immortal gods without forming them in human shape".[243] The Stoics could not understand why splendid and useful discoveries of the natural world led people to create false and fictitious deities. They thus rebuked false beliefs, confused misconceptions and superstitions as close to old wives' tales, which reduced gods to the level of human frailties.[244] Pliny also chided the search for the image and form of the divinity as a sign of human frailty.[245] Plutarch too censured the masses for confusing gods with graven images, seasons and

---

[240] Seneca, *Epistulae Morales* 95.47-50.
[241] Seneca, *Epistulae Morales* 41.1-6.
[242] Cicero, *De Natura Deorum* 2.59.
[243] Cicero, *De Natura Deorum* 1.77-83; 2.45.
[244] Cicero, *De Natura Deorum* 2.70.
[245] Pliny, *Nat. Hist.* 2.14.

animals.[246]

The Academics faulted the attempt to dignify properties in nature, which are not personal deities, with the titles of gods. They regarded this as a fallacy gone too far even to assign destructive things like fever, bereavement and misfortune names of gods and to dedicate shrines for such impersonal abstractions.[247] Several other sources reveal that the idea of a person representing a deity could have been offensive.[248] Although most philosophical schools believed in the existence of gods, they could not agree on the nature of the gods[249] hence beliefs about them were not homogeneous.[250] The Academics refuted the Stoics' teaching that since nothing is better than the universe, then it is divine. They also rejected the notion that the motion of the luminaries made them divine. The Academics scorned the Stoics as those whose beliefs were not different from the beliefs of the ignorant since they deified nature and even the animal kingdom.[251] So the belief that the universe and the heavenly bodies were divine was not the faith of all and sundry.[252] The Academics also denied divinity to impersonal and abstract qualities such as faith, righteousness, justice, order, prudence, providence, safety, unity, victory, honour, wealth, freedom, desire, pleasure and sexual joy. They insisted that these were either qualities that reside within human beings or aims to which human beings aspire.[253]

The tradition of despising the Graeco-Roman gods continued beyond the first century CE. Justin Martyr defended Christianity to the emperor[254] insisting that Christians disbelieved pagan gods just like some ancient philosophers and poets did and were honoured. He identified Christians undergoing persecution with Socrates who regarded Greek gods as demons and was sentenced to death as an atheist.[255] Socrates, just like the others cited above could have been the fathers of this tradition, which Lucian of Samosata, otherwise known as the blasphemer adopted. Lucian lived and worked in the second century CE, but his views are highly indebted to previous writers. Lucian, it is said, belonged to the Second Sophistic, whose aim was no longer to express experiences of his time

---

[246] Plutarch, *De Iside et Osiride* 69.378a-379d.
[247] Cicero, *De Natura Deorum* 3.63.
[248] Diodorus Siculus, *bib.Hist.*14.117.6; Livy, *Hist.*5.23.5; Plutarch, *Cam.* 7.1; Dio Cassius, *Hist.*52.13.3.
[249] Cicero, *De Natura Deorum* 1.14; 3.93
[250] Cicero, *De Natura Deorum* 3.11-13, 15-19, 25-28, 40-50.
[251] Cicero, *De Natura Deorum* 3.39-40.
[252] Cicero, *De Natura Deorum* 3.20-25, 51-60, 64.
[253] Cicero, *De Natura Deorum* 3.61, 88.
[254] Justin Martyr *1st Apology* in A. Roberts and J. Donaldson (eds. and Eng. Tr.) *The Anti-Nicene Fathers* Vols. i, iii, iv and x (Edinburgh: T & T Clark, Grand Rapids, Michigan: Eerdmans, 1989), p. 164.
[255] Xenophon, *Memorabilia* 1.1.1.

but to create literature that was a worthy continuation of previous literature.[256] He was following a steady tradition in doubting the gods, who like human beings and everything else were controlled by fate.[257] He argued that there was nothing to gain by offering prayers and sacrifices to Zeus and by honouring the gods.[258] Additionally, the gods should not punish people even if they dishonour them and rob their temples because both obey the orders of fate.[259] Lucian not only derided the gods, but also mocked and likened them to greedy flies that licked sacrificial blood and gulped smoke from the sacrificial meat as if it was something delicious.[260] Though he believed in the existence of the gods, the bronze idols remained just bronze and the work of human hands, which could not intimidate him.[261] Like Epicurus, Lucian admitted that the gods existed while denying that they interfere with human life.

Altogether, during the Graeco-Roman time, "divinities assumed a double character, the one traditional and based on ancient beliefs, the other adventitious and inspired by learned theories".[262] The sober elite rejected the popular beliefs and sought to correct the flawed conclusion that the masses derived from the popular belief. But the insatiable curiosity of the masses seems to have rendered the attempts of the elite ineffective. As it seems, the masses valued magic, divination and astrology since they enabled them to deal with the spiteful supernatural powers.

4:5. Conclusion

Jews and Graeco-Romans believed in supernatural powers but their beliefs conflicted. The Gentiles could not restrict their worship to only one cult and so the Jews castigated them as polytheistic. In contrast, the Gentiles regarded the Jews as atheist and impious people.[263] The Jews too were not consistent with their beliefs because some of them seem to have been totally attracted to the Graeco-Roman way of life,[264] while others, even though attracted, seemed to have retained their uniqueness as Jews. The latter were most likely and in

---

[256] Turner, *Lucian Satirical Sketches*, pp. 12-14. Lucian, *Fishing for Phonies* or *Philosopher's Day Out* in Turner, *Lucian Satirical Sketches*, p. 169-70.

[257] Lucian '*Some Awkward Questions for Zeus*' in Turner, *Lucian Satirical Sketches*, p 137; Homer, *Iliad* XX.336; XXIV.209 –210; Hesiod, *Theogony* 217-219, 904-906.

[258] Lucian, '*Some Awkward Questions for Zeus*' in Turner, *Lucian Satirical Sketches*, p 139.

[259] Lucian, '*Some Awkward Question to Zeus*' in Turner, *Lucian Satirical Sketches*, pp. 139–146.

[260] Lucian, *On Sacrifices* 9.

[261] Lucian, '*The pathological liar*' or '*The unbeliever*' in Turner, *Lucian Satirical Sketches*, p. 208.

[262] Cumont, *Astrology*, p. 15.

[263] Philo, *De Spec Leg 2.165f*; Josephus, *Ant* 3.7.7. 179; 4.6.8.137f; 12.3.2.126; 19.5.3.290; *Against Apion* 1.34.309; 2.6.65–67, 7.79, 10.117..

[264] Josephus, *Against Apion* 1.22.161-175; 1.22.176-181.

certain respects Jewish to the core and Hellenised to the same core. Also, it would be incredibly naïve to assume that Graeco-Roman beliefs, rituals and practices were solid while they were the subject of ongoing doubts and escalating discussion. Although Jewish and Graeco-Roman beliefs were not identical, this does not mean that each group was ignorant of each other's beliefs. The letter of Aristeas implies that the Jews and Graeco-Romans worshipped the same God under the guise of different names.[265] But the letter also differentiates Jews and Greeks insisting that the Jews believe 'God is one', while other people think that 'there are many gods'.[266] The Jews were preserved and separated from false beliefs and honoured one God who is powerful above the whole creation.[267]

The question as to what extent Jews and Graeco-Romans admitted or practised each other's beliefs is elusive. Most of the cited evidence is controversial. The inscriptions attesting the cult of Theos Hypsistos (the highest god) and Sabazius does not provide strong and convincing evidence of the origin of these cults. There is no unanimity as to whether these cults were Jewish or Graeco-Roman since they could have been either or both.[268] The epitome of Valerius Maximus, which insists that the expulsion of Jews from Rome was connected to the cult of Sabazius Jupiter, cannot be used decisively to establish whether the adherents of the cult were Jewish or Graeco-Roman.[269] Of note, the designation 'the Highest God' is not only attested in the LXX, Philo and Josephus as Jewish, but also the predicates 'Zeus Hypsistos' or

---

[265] *Letter of Aristeas* 15-6. However, it is the Graeco-Romans who recognised the God whom the Jews worshipped but this does not mean the Jews recognised the validity of Graeco-Roman worship (See Barclay, *Jews in the Mediterranean Diaspora*, p. 143).

[266] *Letter of Aristeas* 134.

[267] *Letter of Aristeas* 139.

[268] See Clinton E. Arnold, *The Colossian Syncretism*, pp. 31-2, 71-2, 152, 154-5, 195, 197; A. T. Kraabel, "ὕψιστος and the Synagogue at Sardis" in *Greek, Roman, and Byzantine Studies* 10 (1969), pp. 81-93; Paul Trebilco, *Jewish Communities in Asia Minor* SNTSMS 69 (Cambridge: Cambridge University Press, 1991), pp. 127-144, especially 131-133; Franz Cumont, "Les Mystères de Sabazius et le Judaïsme" in *CRAIBL* (1906), pp. 63-79; Franz Cumont, *Oriental Religions in Roman Paganism* (New York: Dover, 1956), pp. 64, 162; A. D. Nock, C. Roberts and T. C. Skeat, "The Guild of Zeus Hypsistos" in Z. Stewart (ed.), *Arthur Darby Nock: Essays on Religion and the Ancient World I* (Oxford: Clarendon, 1972), pp. 422-427.

[269] Valerius Maximus, *Epitome* 1.3.2f. Lane, Eugene N., "Sabazius and the Jews in Valerius Maximus: A Re-Examination" in *Journal of Roman Studies* 69 (1979), pp. 35-38 insists that the text accounts for the expulsion of two distinct groups: Jews as well as worshippers of Sabazius. But this text is historically dubious since textual uncertainties are preserved in the two epitomes. One epitome says the Jews and the Chaldeans were ejected from Rome because 'they tried to transmit their sacred rites to the Romans'. The other says the Jews were compelled to return to their homes because they tried 'to infect Roman customs with the cult of Jupiter Sabazius' (Barclay, *Jews in the Mediterranean Diaspora*, pp. 285-6, 298). So it is difficult to tell if the adherents of Sabazius cults were Jews or pagans or both.

'Theos Hypsistos' were known and used by Graeco-Romans.[270] Therefore, Cumont's theory that Jews in Asia Minor were involved in a detailed syncreticism is now rendered unfounded by this evidence.[271] Barclay maintains that the inscriptions of the Most High God bear no proof of Jewish syncretism.[272] But they may prove that each group knew the beliefs, rituals and practices of each other.

The magical papyri, as noted above include some Hebrew and Aramaic spells and sacred names, and could provide possible evidence of an affinity between Jewish and Graeco-Roman beliefs, rituals and practices. However, the use of the Jewish divine name, the appearance of Hebrew angels and reference to Jewish key personalities like Moses and the patriarchs in the magical papyri is not sufficient proof that Jews participated in Graeco-Roman magic. It is certainly not the same thing to discern whether such texts originated from the Jews and whether the Jews used them in their present syncretistic form.[273] This also does not rule out the possibility that some Jews created and used magical texts. Juvenal the Roman satirist knew a Jewish woman who interpreted dreams with her spells and magic portions.[274] It seems that some Jews were able to compromise their prestige and appeal with beliefs, rituals and practices that would provoke God. The Jews may have used spells and worn amulets containing images and names of Graeco-Roman gods and that of Iao Sabaoth,[275] probably a Graecised version of the Jewish יְהוָה צְבָאוֹת.

Altogether, there is reason to believe that some Jewish and Graeco-Roman beliefs intersected and interacted with each other and possibly influenced each other. Probably neither the Jews nor the Graeco-Romans were ignorant of each other's beliefs, rituals and practices.[276] Arnold insists that regardless of the particular worldview (with regard to cosmogony—that is, origins or eschatology), both Jews and Gentiles could understand what Paul had to say on the topic of supernatural powers.[277] Most people in the first century CE agreed

---

[270] Homer, *Iliad* 8.22; Plutarch, *De Iside et Osiride* 51.371e.
[271] See Trebilco, *Jewish Communities*, pp. 127-144; J. T. Sanders, *Schismatics, Sectarians, Dissidents, Deviants: The First One Hundred Years of Jewish –Christian Relations* (London: SCM Press, 1993), pp. 191-196; Barclay, *Jews in the Mediterranean Diaspora*, pp. 333-4.
[272] Barclay, *Jews in the Mediterranean Diaspora*, pp. 33-4.
[273] Barclay, *Jews in the Mediterranean Diaspora*, p. 121.
[274] Juvenal, *Sat.* 6.553-62.
[275] PGM V.96-172. See also PGM IV.1169-1226; XIII.335-340;XXIIa.17-27; XXIIb.1-26; XXV.1-42. See also Erwin R. Goodenough, *Jewish Symbols in the Graeco-Roman Period* Vol. 2 (New York: Pantheon, 1953), pp. 291-294; Barclay, *Jews in the Mediterranean Diaspora*, p. 122.
[276] J. D. G. Dunn, *The Epistles to the Colossians and to Philemon: A Commentary on the Greek Text* (Grand Rapids, Michigan: Eerdmans; Carlisle, Cumbria: The Paternoster Press, 1996), p. 30; Josephus, *Against Apion* 2.29.210; Philo, *De Praemiis et Poenis* XXVI.152.
[277] Arnold, *Powers*, pp. 27, 171

The Context of Production

that there were supernatural powers but disagreed on how to conceive them. However, the levels at which both the Jews and Gentiles were assimilated and/or syncretistic to the other's beliefs is a subject surrounded by numerous ambiguities and hitherto remains elusive and open-ended.[278] Nonetheless, the masses believed in supernatural powers and considered it necessary to pacify them. Cicero illustrates that superstitious beliefs about supernatural powers were "widespread among the nations and had taken advantage of human weakness to cast a spell over the mind of almost every person".[279] Jewish and Graeco-Roman beliefs, rituals and practices certainly formed the background against which the Pauline concept of supernatural powers was articulated.[280] Was Paul exposed to different influences or a fusion of influences? This will be the subject of the next chapter, which seeks to evaluate the Pauline concept of supernatural powers within its first century CE background.

---

[278] Barclay, *Jews in the Mediterranean Diaspora*, p. 335.
[279] Cicero, *De Divinatione* 2.lxxii.148.
[280] Kenneth Grayston, "The Life and Thought of St. Paul" in Neil, William (ed.), *The Bible Companion* (London: The Caxton Publishing Company Limited, 1959), pp. 196, 205.

CHAPTER 5

The Context of the Literary Genre: Evaluating the Pauline Concept of Supernatural Powers within its First Century CE Milieu

5: 1. Introduction

What milieu gave Paul a terminological and conceptual framework as he responded to the belief in supernatural powers within the context of production? In chapter four, we noted that the context of production was complex. This makes it exacting to determinedly endorse a precise milieu, Jewish or Graeco-Roman, as the sole contributing factor to the terminological and conceptual framework within which Paul developed his theology of supernatural powers. Most of the Pauline terms identified as supernatural powers could ambiguously refer to spiritual beings and also to earthly human rulers.[1] Some of the sources from which we can deduce the everyday usage of these terms are often later (for example most of the Greek Magical Papyri) and unique (for example Philo) and so they may not represent the views of all and sundry. It is also possible that each specific term did not have a range of usage known to every one and implied in every use of the term. As Bauer notes, some Greek word forms could be "indistinct in meaning",[2] while others may have developed "new possibilities of usage".[3] It may be critical to "reckon with the possibility that what, for instance, Paul said, conditioned as he was by his Jewish past, was not always understood in the same terms by his gentile Christian hearers, who were also unable to dissociate themselves entirely from their previous ways of thought".[4] As already noted in chapter four, it is possible that both Jews and Gentiles could understand what Paul had to say about supernatural powers as most people agreed on the idea that they influenced human affairs. Could it be that Paul creatively fused the current Jewish

---

[1] Wink, *Naming the Powers*, pp. 9-10.
[2] Walter Bauer, "An Introduction to the Lexicon of the Greek of the New Testament", in Walter Bauer, W. F. Arndt and F. W. Gingrich, *A Greek-English Lexicon of the New Testament and Other Early Christian Literature* (Chicago: University of Chicago Press, 1957), p. xiv.
[3] Bauer, "An Introduction", p. xv.
[4] Bauer, "An Introduction", p. xxi.

The Context of the Literary Genre 129

apocalyptic and Graeco-Roman academic and polemical depiction of popular gods? Was Paul using usual terms and concepts or were the terminology and concepts his own creation? The focal points of this chapter are exegetical and theological, which may help us identify the message Paul communicated to his hearers, "who may have heard these words before, but with different connotations and associations".[5]

5:2. An Exegetical Treatise

i. *'Εξουσίαι / ἄρχοντες*

Outside the New Testament, ἐξουσίαι and ἄρχοντες not only refer to spiritual beings but also to human rulers[6]. Philo speaks about the emperor as both divine and human in the fragments preserved by Antonius.[7] Perhaps both terms referred to spiritual beings ruling the cosmos using human power or agency. Hellenistic Judaism and the Graeco-Roman mind-set accepted that rulers were divinely chosen and the state had its place in the divine cosmic order. The Graeco-Roman mind-set honoured human rulers with divine attributes and regarded them as divine ministers for the care and safety of humankind. Ἐξουσίαι and ἄρχοντες could thus indicate spiritual or material entities and also signify the inseparable link between the spiritual and material. The boundary between the spirit and the material worlds was fluid and often loose so that human rulers and supernatural powers may have had as much in common as they had differences. The New Testament often uses ἐξουσία in reference to the right or authorisation to use power conferred by an office but uses it only eight times in reference to spiritual beings. The majority of these references are in Paul, six times in the disputed epistles and only once in an undisputed epistle.[8] When the New Testament uses ἄρχοντες as reference for spiritual beings, it usually has a modifying clause for example, ruler of demons, ruler of this world or age or prince of the power of the air.[9]

There is controversy as to whether ἐξουσίαι and ἄρχοντες in Romans 13:1-7, to whom (as the context of the literary genre attest) every soul should submit and pay tax, refer to human or spiritual rulers. Some scholars suppose a double reference, upon which the terms refer both to human rulers and spiritual beings.[10] Other scholars maintain that the context of Romans 13:1-7 does not

---

[5] Bauer, "An Introduction", p. xxi.
[6] Dan. 7: 27 (LXX); 1QM 15: 2–3; Test. Levi. 3: 8; Jub. 48; 1 En. 8: 1; 61:10; 2 En. 20: 1.
[7] Philo, *Frag. Ser. CIV*.
[8] Col 1: 16; 2: 10, 15; Eph 1: 20-1; 3: 10; 6: 11-2; 1Cor 15: 24; 1 Pt 3: 22.
[9] Mt. 9: 34; Jn. 12: 31; 1 Cor 2: 6-8; Eph. 2: 2.
[10] Wink, *Naming the Powers* pp. 45-47; Oscar Cullmann, *Christ and Time*. (Philadelphia, Pennsylvania: The Westminster Press, 1951), pp. 139-43,185-210; Oscar

require any spiritual interpretation since the authorities to which tax is paid (v 6) are human.[11] Cranfield not only attests how these terms refer to civil power but also acknowledges the considerable dispute among scholars as to whether the terms have a double reference to the civil authority and also to the powers, which stand behind and act through the civil authorities.[12] However, the general context in most cases never detached religion and politics and the government derived its authority from spiritual beings.[13] The state was categorically recognized within the sacred order and rulers were somehow divine. They were the earthly provisions for universal harmony, immediate bearers and mediators of divine power. The terms assigned to the deity that allegedly gave human rulers power over their subjects could be used for these rulers.[14] There is an enticing probability of reading ἐξουσίαι and ἄρχοντες in Romans 13:1-7 as spiritual beings even if the immediate context favours human rulers. Perhaps Paul wanted to convey a message that embraced civil power in its human aspect without discarding the spiritual powers that instituted it. Yet Romans 13:1-7 is complicated given that the immediate context verifies a human interpretation while the general context provides liberty for a reading that includes human rulers and spiritual beings.

The literary and rhetorical context of Colossians 1: 16; 2: 10, 15; Ephesians 1: 20-1; 3: 10; 6: 11-2; 1 Corinthians 15: 24 suggests that ἐξουσίαι solely refers to evil spiritual beings. Ephesians 1: 20 and 1 Corinthians 15: 24 use an Old Testament citation (Ps. 110), which is often regarded as a reference to nations believed to have been Israel's enemies. Now the enemies of the new Israel cannot be pagan nations, for the reason that believers from pagan nations have been assimilated into the commonwealth of Israel in Christ through his blood (Eph 2: 1-22). It is probable that the enemies mentioned in 1Corinthians 15: 24, such as ἀρχήν, ἐξουσίαν and δύναμιν[15] and Ephesians 1: 21-2.[16] such as ἀρχῆς,

---

Cullmann, *The State in the New Testament* (London: SCM Press, 1957), pp. 95-114; Clinton D. Morrison, *The Powers That Be: Earthly Rulers and Demonic Powers in Romans 13.1-7* (London: SCM Press, 1960), p. 130.

[11] Joseph Fitzmyer, *Romans: A New Translation with Introduction and Commentary* – The Anchor Bible (New York: Doubleday, 1993), p. 666; J. D. G. Dunn, *Romans 9–16* 38b, WBC (Dallas, Texas: Word Books Publishers, 1988), p. 760.

[12] C. E. B. Cranfield, *The Epistle to the Romans* ICC (Edinburgh: T & T Clark, 1979), p. 656.

[13] See Bauer, "An Introduction", p xxii; Rom 13: 1.

[14] Cicero, *De Natura Deorum* 2.60; Origen, *Against Celsus* 8.63.

[15] The literary and rhetoric context of 1 Cor 15 deals with the resurrection of the dead and treats death as an enemy that will be conquered when Christ hands over the kingdom to God the Father. Just as Christ was raised from the dead, the dead too will be raised. However, θάνατος is not necessarily a spiritual power like ἀρχήν καὶ ἐξουσίαν καὶ δύναμιν. But like the spiritual powers identified as ἀρχήν, ἐξουσίαν and δύναμιν, θάνατος will be destroyed at the eschaton (see chapter 6, pp. 208–211).

[16] The literary/rhetorical context of Eph 1: 20–23 affirms and demonstrates the decisive power of God that occurs in the resurrection and exaltation of Christ. This prepares the

The Context of the Literary Genre 131

ἐξουσίας, δυνάμεως, κυριότητος and ὀνόματος ὀνομαζομένου, are spiritual beings that were the enemies of Christ and his church rather than the pagan nations. As the Davidic kingship would crush the enemies of Israel, so Christ's rule vanquishes the enemies of the new Israel.[17] There are no conceivable supernatural powers outside the dominion of Christ, including those invoked in magical rituals and practices. Despite the views of Carr and Yates,[18] Paul in Ephesians and Colossians (as in 1Corinthians) seems to have been saying that ἐξουσίαι refer to evil spiritual beings that Christ conquered through his death and resurrection.

The literary and rhetorical context of 1Corinthians 2: 6-8 is unclear as to whether ἄρχοντες refer to spiritual or human rulers; hence a double reference has been suggested. There is evidence supporting the interpretation of spiritual rulers outside the Pauline letters. Both the LXX and Theodotion (late second century but relying on a much earlier Greek text) readings of Daniel 10: 13 refer to archangel Michael as εἷς τῶν ἀρχόντων τῶν πρώτων ('one of the pre-eminent rulers'). Theodotion also uses ἄρχων (singular) in reference to Michael in Daniel 10: 21 and 12: 1, while the LXX has ἄγγελος. While the LXX uses στρατηγός for the spiritual rulers of Persia and Greece in Daniel 10: 20-21, Theodotion unswervingly uses ἄρχων. The Masoretic text uses the Hebrew term שַׂר for angelic rulers. Perhaps the Hebrew term שָׂרִים translated 'chiefs' or 'princes' or 'rulers', which could be positively compared with the angelic ruler/prince of light appointed for Israel's defence against the angel of darkness,[19] may have stood behind Paul's usage of ἀρχόντων in 1Corinthians 2: 6-8. The context seems to necessitate the reading of ἀρχόντων as spiritual beings. Paul speaks of τῶν ἀρχόντων τοῦ αἰῶνος τούτου who are coming to nothing (τῶν καταργουμένων) and who did not know the wisdom of God and so crucified the Lord of glory. The modifying clause τοῦ αἰῶνος τούτου enables the identification of ἀρχόντων with spiritual beings. If Paul knew the Danielic

---

way for the significant affirmation about the raising and enthronement of believers with their Lord in Eph 2: 4–7. Having been exalted at the right hand of God, Christ now possesses the full authority of the Father. His position is superior to every imaginable hostile "supernatural power" not only in the present age but also the age to come (see P. T. O'Brien, *The Letter to the Ephesians* (Grand Rapids, Michigan: Eerdmans/Leicester: Apollos, 1999), pp. 139-152. The literary and rhetorical context of this passage seems to suggest that the power of God, which raised Christ from the dead and exalted him at the right hand of God, is also available to believers.
[17] This was the early Christians' interpretation of Psalm 110. See David M. Hay, *Glory at the Right Hand: Psalm 110 in early Christianity* (Nashville: Abingdon, 1973).
[18] Wesley Carr, *Angels and Principalities. The Background, Meaning and Development of the Pauline Phrase hai archai kai hai exousiai*. SNTSMS 42. (Cambridge: Cambridge University Press, 1981), p. 132; Yates, Roy "Christ and The Powers of Evil in Colossians". In E. A. Livingstone (ed.), *Studia Biblica 1978: 111: Papers in Paul and other New Testament Authors* JSNTSup 3. (Sheffield: JSOT Press, 1980).
[19] 1QM 13: 10–12; 1QS 3:20-26.

cosmology of angelic powers lying behind the nations, then it could be that he used ἀρχόντων to refer to spiritual beings, which, as the architects of the wisdom of this age, were oblivious of God's wisdom and plan for the ages and so crucified the Lord of glory. Several Jewish apocalyptic texts depicts ἄρχοντες as beings that did not know Israel were God's children since they had not received the revelation of all mysteries even if they were in heaven.[20] Such literature supports the view that ἀρχόντων τοῦ αἰῶνος τούτου refer to supernatural powers. The synoptic Gospels also support this reading. Beelzebub, the alias of Satan, is described as the chief ruler (ἄρχων) of demons.[21] It is possible then, that τῶν ἀρχόντων τοῦ αἰῶνος τούτου refer to Satan and his minions who could perhaps control human behaviour and also the religio-cultural and socio-political/economic order.[22] If we may correlate John's distinctive usage of the Greek word κόσμος, which refers to human society in its organised opposition to God and if Satan's rule extends to ὁ κόσμος,[23] it is certainly possible that ἀρχόντων refer to evil spiritual beings.[24] For that reason, Herod, Pilate and the Jewish authorities could not bear the weight of the phrase, τῶν ἀρχόντων τοῦ αἰῶνος τούτου. Noticeably, Satan in 2 Corinthians 4: 4 is referred to as ὁ θεὸς τοῦ αἰῶνος τούτου and in John 14: 30-31 as 'ὁ τοῦ κόσμου ἄρχων·' and his coming appears to refer to the crucifixion. It seems that Satan and his minions were regarded as the real architects of Christ's death.

However, the preference of reading ἀρχόντων as human rulers is surprisingly strong. The rulers of this age who crucified the Lord of glory were political and religious human leaders. An early Christian tradition held the chief priest and the rulers accountable for delivering Christ for judgment and subsequent crucifixion. The Jewish people and their leaders were ignorant in delivering Jesus to death.[25] It is therefore possible that ἀρχόντων in 1 Corinthians 2: 6-8 refer to religious and political human leaders as the physical agents of Jesus' death. The context seemingly supports this reading, for Paul has already referred to the 'wise', the 'scribe', the 'powerful' and the 'well-born', whom God is bringing to nothing (1 Cor 1: 18-30). These are certainly human beings, who are the powers of this age (1 Cor 1: 20). Humanity, not demonic powers, is symbolised by ὁ κόσμος (1 Cor 1: 21) that διὰ τῆς σοφίας did not know God. In the Johannine writings, ὁ κόσμος stands in opposition to God (1 Jn. 2: 15) and so incapable of knowing God (Jn. 17: 25). Perhaps it is human wisdom and not the spiritual beings that prevent people from knowing God's power and spiritual truth (1 Cor 2: 5, 13). The context certainly supports a human reading

---

[20] 1 En. 16: 1-3; *Jub* 1: 25; *Asc. Isa* 8: 7.
[21] Mk. 3: 22; Mt. 9: 34; 12: 24; Lk. 11: 15.
[22] See chapter 4, pp. 98 and 106.
[23] Jn. 12: 31, 16: 11; 1 Jn 5: 19; 1 Jn 2: 15. See Walter Bauer, W. F. Arndt and F. W. Gingrich *A Greek-English Lexicon of the New Testament and Other Early Christian Literature* (Chicago: University of Chicago Pres, 1957), pp. 447-8.
[24] Tertullian, *adv. Marc* 5.6; Origen, *de Princ*.3.2.
[25] Lk 24: 20; Acts 3: 13-18.

The Context of the Literary Genre

seeing that the direct opposite in 1 Corinthians 1–2 is not between saved human and lost angels but between two groups of human beings.

It is possible therefore to read ἀρχόντων in 1 Corinthians 2: 6–8 either as spiritual beings or as human rulers. If ἀρχόντων include every power that was involved in Christ's death, then both human rulers and spiritual beings are intended. The *Ascension of Isaiah* and the *Acts of Thomas* depict Satan as the one who stirred people to cause Christ's death.[26] The same tradition is preserved in Ignatius[27] and according to the Nag Hammadi library (dated in the 4th century CE but which has materials that go back to the Second Temple period), men and angels desired to rule the universe, so they killed Jesus.[28] Perhaps the early Christians saw the influence of spiritual beings behind human hostility that led to Christ's death. It could be that 1 Corinthians 2: 6–8 describe how religious and political leaders and institutions, now under the control of spiritual powers, caused the death of Christ. Ἀρχόντων may refer to spiritual beings that worked with and through human beings, or to spiritual beings and human rulers who worked together to bring the death of Christ. To regard τῶν ἀρχόντων τοῦ αἰῶνος τούτου purely as a reference to spiritual beings or purely as a reference to earthly rulers is equally defective. The phrase most likely represents an immediate coincidence of heavenly and earthly activity when Pilate, Herod, Caiaphas and the Jews acted under the control of their spiritual superiors. In that case, human powers could be the unconscious agents of spiritual powers.

ii. Δυνάμεις

Δυνάμεις refer to a sweeping range of powers, such as political or military forces.[29] It could also refer to God's angelic army or host. The LXX identifies δυνάμεις with the powers of heaven, angels, stars and even gods.[30] Several Second Temple texts regard δυνάμεις as heavenly beings as well as human.[31] Philo frequently (about 75 times) uses δυνάμεις to refer to angelic and other heavenly beings, though not in the evil sense[32]. He also uses δυνάμεις in various

---

[26] *Ascension of Isaiah* 9: 13-15; 10: 10-12; *Acts of Thomas* 32
[27] Ignatius, *Symr.* 1; *Mag.* 11 *Trall.* 9: 1.
[28] *Tri. Trac.* 121-122.
[29] See Bauer, Arndt and Gingrich, *A Greek-English Lexicon* pp. 206-7; Wink, *Naming the Powers*, pp. 59-61.
[30] LXX Dan. 8: 10 (for powers of heaven); LXX Ps. 103: 21 (for angels); Isa. 34: 4 (for stars); Ps. 29: 1; 89: 5-8 (for gods).
[31] Jub. 1: 29, 1 En 61: 10; 2; *L.A.E* 25: 1; 48: 4; *Test. Abr.* 9, 14; *2 En.* 20: 1-3.
[32] Philo, *De cher.* 20, 27f, 51, 106; *De sac.* 59-60; *De post.* 20, 167-169; *De mig.* 181, 220; *Quod deus.* 3, 77-8, 109, 100; *De plant.* 14, 129; *De conf.* 137, 166, 171-2, 175, 182; *Quis rer.* 166, 170, 172, 312; *De fuga.* 69-70; 95, 97-8, 100-1; *De mut.* 14-5, 28-9; *De som.* I. 62, 70, 163, 185, 240; II. 254; *De Abr.* 121f, 125, 143, 145-6; De vit.*Mos.* II. 99; 291; *De spec. leg.* I. 45 –49; 209, 307, 329; II. 45; *De virt.* 49.

ways and in most cases idiomatically. Some of his passages depict δύναμις as a human attribute. Others regard δυνάμεις as abstract and impersonal categories such as force (military force), strength, ability, mastery or influence, faculty, might, value, function, potentiality, capacity and as an attribute of number. In some texts, it seems that Philo's understanding of δυνάμεις as angelic and other heavenly beings is a fusion of Jewish monotheism and the Neo-Platonic idea of divine emanations.[33]

The term is also frequently used in the New Testament for miracles and in a few cases to denote spiritual entities and attributes. In some Pauline texts, δύναμις is often used in reference to the power of God, Christ and the Holy Spirit. It is also used in reference to miracles, human ability, power or strength and the meaning or significance of words.[34] However, in Romans 8: 38 and Ephesians 1: 21 δυνάμεις conveys the idea of evil spiritual powers opposed to God probably in the military sense. But the literary context of Romans 8: 38-9 in which δυνάμεις appears should be taken into consideration since not everything that is mentioned alongside δυνάμεις is necessarily evil. The literary context begins with a rhetorical question, εἰ ὁ θεὸς ὑπὲρ ἡμῶν, τίς καθ' ἡμῶν This question is followed by loud and clear assertion that God is not against us and nothing, human or spiritual, good or evil can separate us from Christ's love (Rom 8: 31–39) In fact, neither human powers (v. 35) nor life (whether its experiences are good or evil) nor supernatural powers – δυνάμεις, ἀρχαὶ, ἄγγελοι and οὔτε ὕψωμα οὔτε βάθος, perhaps representing cosmic and astronomical powers, (vv. 39-40) could not stand between Christ and those he has emancipated.[35] The powers cited here could be evil but this must be applied with caution since not everything mentioned here for instance, 'life', 'things present' and 'things to come', may necessarily refer to evil powers. Perhaps the inclusion of terms that may have evil connotation with others that may not, means that Paul's intention was to create an impression that nothing that happens in human life, now or in the future, not even that which may be allegedly caused by human or cosmic or astronomical powers whether good or evil could separate believers from the love of God in Christ Jesus. The context in which δύναμιν appears in 1 Corinthians 15: 24 most likely implies that the term refers to evil spiritual beings, as it is listed among the enemies Christ will destroy at the end of time. The enemies of Christ certainly convey an evil connotation. Perhaps like most of the Jewish people, Paul ranked δυνάμεις as evil and demonic. The Old Testament firmly rebuked Israel for forsaking Yahweh to worship all the host (LXX δυνάμεις) and censures all the host of

---

[33] In *De Conf.* 171–175 God is one, but surrounded by a number of δυνάμεις. In *De Mig.* 181 the whole is held together by chains of invisible powers that cannot be broken.
[34] Rom 1: 16, 20; 9: 17; 1 Cor 1: 18, 24; Eph 3: 20; Phil 3: 10; 2 Tim 1: 8; 3: 5; I Cor 12: 28-9; Gal 3: 5; 1 Cor 4: 19; 2 Cor 1: 8; 8: 3; 1 Cor 14: 11.
[35] Cf. 1 En. 41: 9, "surely, neither angel nor Satan (no authority or power) has the power to hinder; for there is a judge to all of them, he will glance, and all of them are before him, he is the judge".

heaven, who will rot away.[36]

iii. Κυριότης

There is no evidence of pre-Christian use of κυριότης, translated as 'dominion' or 'lordship' or ruling power.[37] The term appears in Colossians 1: 16 (in plural – κυριότητες) and Ephesians. 1: 21 (in singular – κυριότητος). The image supplied by κυριότης is that of the realm or territory over which a κύριος rules.[38] Κυριότης seems to have represented angelic power believed to have had some control over human fate.[39] It is still not clear if the term lies behind the Slavonic term for 'dominion' as part of the heavenly army of the seventh heaven in 2 Enoch 20: 1. It is also not clear whether the pre-Christian sources in favour of 'dominion' used κυριότης or ἐξουσία (Col 1: 13) or ἡγεμονίας (Josephus, J. W 6.330; Lk 3: 1) or even ἀρχῆς (Dt 17: 20,–LXX).[40] The term appears in Jude 8 and 2 Peter 2: 10 as a reference to 'authority' or possibly 'limit'. Later usage of the term is surrounded with ambiguity for while some used it to refer to heavenly beings,[41] others used it in the sense of ruling power.[42] The Hebrew term ממשלת used for the dominion of Beliar in Dead Sea Scrolls (1QS 1: 18; 2: 19; 1QM 14: 9; 18: 1) could possibly be linked with κυριότης. The dominion of Beliar could also be paralleled to τῆς ἐξουσίας τοῦ σκότους in Colossian. 1: 13. Perhaps κυριότης represents a sphere of spiritual influence formerly ruled by the 'gods many and lords many' (1 Cor. 8: 5). Perhaps there is continuity between κυριότης and Paul's reference to the 'many lords' and the 'so-called gods'.

iv. Θρόνοι

Several sources outside the Pauline letters use θρόνοι as a reference to dominion or sovereignty, to the throne of human rulers, God, Satan and other supernatural beings.[43] The term occurs in some Jewish texts next to other terms that refer to spiritual beings.[44] It is also used to refer to angelic beings in several

---

[36] 2 Kgs. 17: 16, Isa. 34: 4.
[37] Bauer, Arndt and Gingrich, *A Greek-English Lexicon*, p. 461
[38] See Bauer, Arndt and Gingrich, *A Greek-English Lexicon*, p. 461.
[39] See the GNM Morphology and Barclay-Newman Greek Dictionary as represented in the BibleWorks for Windows Copyright © (1998), BibleWorks, LLC.
[40] See also Jub. 5:6; I En. 82: 10, 16, 17, 20, 1QH 1, 11,19, 20, 24; 1Q 34 bis; 1QS 1, 2, 10; 1QM 10, 12, 13, 14, 18; 4Q 169.2, 184, 286-7; 1QM 1; 1QpHab 2.
[41] Cyril of Jerusalem, *Epist. Apost.* 13; Nag Hammadi Library, *Treat. Res.* 44: 35-38.
[42] Shepherd of Hermas, *Herm. Sim.* 5.6.1.
[43] See Bauer, Arndt and Gingrich, *A Greek-English Lexicon*, pp. 364-5.
[44] Dan 7: 9 (LXX); *Asc. Isa* 7–8; *Test. Abr* 13: 10; *2 En* 20: 1; *Test. Lev* 3: 8; *Test. Sol* 3: 5.

magical texts.⁴⁵ One of the Greek Magical Papyri gives seven magical names to seven thrones that were invoked in the time of need.⁴⁶ In the New Testament, θρόνοι appears once (Col 1: 16) with other terms that also refer to animate, personal and wilful spiritual beings. The literary context where θρόνοι appears is a hymn celebrating Christ's supremacy and pre-existence above and before all things, including spiritual beings. The hymn's stress on the supremacy and pre-eminence of Christ seems to pre-empt the "false heretical definition of the relationship of Christ to the powers",⁴⁷ which Paul challenged. Other scholars insist that θρόνοι and other terms listed here were associated with the worship of angels or worship through angels (Col 2: 18),⁴⁸ which Paul equally disputed.

v. Κοσμοκράτορας

Κοσμοκράτορας continues to puzzle scholars. It does not appear in Jewish writings until the *Testament of Solomon*.⁴⁹ Wink implies that Ephesians could have influenced the use of κοσμοκράτορας in the *Testament of Solomon*.⁵⁰ In contrast, Conybeare holds that it reflects Jewish demonology and cannot be regarded as an import from Ephesians into the *Testament of Solomon*.⁵¹ Could it be that the author of Ephesians created the term? Alternatively, could it be that the later use of κοσμοκράτορας accurately reflects an earlier usage pre-dating the time of Paul? The latter seems more likely since κοσμοκράτορας was popular in magical tradition and astrology, which almost certainly thrived in Paul's time. Κοσμοκράτωρ is used in the magical texts as a title for Serapis and various gods/spirits that were summoned by the supplicant for help.⁵² It is also found in some magical papyri that have some astrological elements⁵³ and was used by

---

[45] Augustus Audollent, *Defixionum Tabellae*, p. 65, Def. Tab 35: 37; p. 320, Def. Tab. 240: 1-4.

[46] See PGM CI 40

[47] Hans-Martin Schenke, "Der Widerstreit gnostischer und kirchlicher Christologie im Spiegel des Kolosserbriefes in *Zeitschrift für Theologie und Kirche* (1964), p. 391.

[48] Martin Dibelius, "The Isis Initiation in Apuleius and Related Initiatory Rites" in F. O. Francis and W. A. Meeks (eds.), *Conflict at Colossae* SBLSBS 4 (Missoula: Scholar's Press, 1973), pp. 82, 90; Günther Bornkamm, "The Heresy of Colossians" in F. O. Francis and W. A. Meeks (eds.), *Conflict at Colossae* SBLSBS 4 (Missoula: Scholars Press, 1973) pp. 123, 130-1: Arnold, *The Colossian Syncretism*, pp. 158-9; 254.

[49] *Test. Sol.* 8: 2; 18: 2.

[50] Wink, *Naming the Powers*, p. 85.

[51] F. C. Conybeare, "The Testament of Solomon" in *Jewish Quarterly Review* 11 (1896), p. 6.

[52] Betz (ed.), *The Greek Magical*, PGM III. 35; PGM IV.166, 1599, 2198f; PGM XIII.618-640.

[53] PGM XVIIb. 1-4, V. 400-1. See also F. Cumont and L. Canet, "Mithra ou Serapis ΚΟΣΜΟΚΡΆΤΟΡ?" in *Comptes rendues l' Académie des Inscriptions et belles-lettres* 1919), pp. 313-328.

Pseudo-Petosiris for planets in the second century BCE.[54] Cumont and Canet link the term with the Roman god Mithras, conferring on it cosmic and astrological significance that depicted the god it was applied to as the master of the universe and of time.[55]

Κοσμοκράτορας could thus refer to world-ruling gods or spirit beings that had parts of the cosmos under their control.[56] It occurs only one time in the New Testament (Ephesians 6: 12) and it is obvious that κοσμοκράτορας τοῦ σκότους τούτου refer to evil spiritual beings. The phrase τὰ πνευματικὰ τῆς πονηρίας ἐν τοῖς ἐπουρανίοις, underlines the evil nature of these 'world rulers' and so there is no other likely interpretation except the demonic. Therefore, κοσμοκράτορας, with other terms in the passage, indicate a world engulfed by an invisible spiritual network of powers unsympathetic to human existence. But the term is controversial. Wink avers that it represented the powerful spirit of the empire that upheld itself through a succession of rulers.[57] Arnold doubts if the term was applied to the Roman emperors in the first century CE. He maintains that the earliest evidence for such usage is found in a second century CE Egyptian inscription that referred to Caracalla as κοσμοκράτωρ.[58]

vi. Ἄγγελοι

Several sources use ἄγγελοι as a referent to human or angelic messengers sent either by God or by humans.[59] Other sources use it as a referent to evil spirits and to intermediary beings, now as the opposite of human beings, without indicating their relation to God.[60] Famous angels known in Judaism appear in the magical papyri, perhaps revealing a link between Jewish angelology and pagan magic.[61] Due to the influence of magic, ἄγγελοι can be linked to spiritual beings populating the underworld[62] and to astral spirits assumed to be holding the key to cruel fate.[63] The use of ἄγγελοι in Greek magical texts reveals the apotropaic role of angelic powers as guardians, protectors and intermediary

---

[54] *Anthologies* of Vettius Valens cited in Cumont and Canet, "Mithra ou Serapis", p. 318 fn. 3. See also Arnold, *Ephesians: Power and Magic*, p. 66.

[55] Cumont and Canet, "Mithra ou Serapis", pp. 320-1.

[56] Bauer, Arndt and Gingrich, *A Greek-English Lexicon*, p. 446.

[57] Wink, *Naming the Powers*, p. 85.

[58] Arnold, *Ephesians: Power and Magic*, p. 67, 193 fn 86.

[59] Jud. 1: 11; 3: 1; 1 Macc: 44; 7: 10; LXX Hag 1: 13; Mal 2: 7; 3: 1; Gen 32: 4, 7, Jos 7: 22; Josephus, *Ant* 14.15.11.451; Bauer, Arndt and Gingrich, *A Greek-English Lexicon*, p. 7

[60] *Testament of Joseph* 19: 9; *Testament of Asher* 6: 4; 1Cor 4: 9; Philo, *De Gigantibus* IV.16; PGM IV 2701; Bauer, Arndt and Gingrich, *A Greek-English Lexicon*, p. 8

[61] Arnold, *The Colossian Syncretism*, pp. 24-29.

[62] See Bauer, Arndt and Gingrich, *A Greek-English Lexicon*, p. 7.

[63] PGM IV. 571; 1190–1205. See also *PGM I*. 214–216.

spirits.[64] "Άγγελοι were invoked to convey favours, prosperity, success[65] and revelation to the supplicant.[66] Since some magical amulets are essentially Jewish in character, it is likely that Jewish magical tradition invoked angels for apotropaic intent. There was concord between some Jews and pagans if both could have invoked angelic powers for various reasons through magical recitals. From the perspective of magic, ἄγγελοι could thus refer to self-motivated spiritual beings.

In the Pauline letters, ἄγγελοι is used as a reference for spiritual beings, which could have an evil disposition and even go wrong consequently inviting judgement. In Romans 8: 38, the context suggests that ἄγγελοι are evil spiritual powers that could attempt to thwart God's plan. In 1 Corinthians 6: 3, ἄγγελοι appear to be at fault and are subject to the judgment of believers. In 2 Corinthians 12: 7, the thorn in Paul's fresh was ἄγγελος Σατανᾶ harassing him so as to keep him from being too elated by the abundance of revelations. However, the more problematic usage of ἄγγελοι in the Pauline letters is in Colossians 2: 18, which is caused by the ambiguity of the genitive in the phrase θρησκείᾳ τῶν ἀγγέλων. If τῶν is an objective genitive, it means angel worship. If it is a subjective genitive, it refers to the angelic worship of God, or worship led by angels. Could it be that the author of Colossians intended the objective genitive? There may have been a cult of angels in Asia Minor and it is people rather than angels who performed the worship. Allowing for the popular belief that angels were powerful celestial beings who could protect or harm people, it may be that θρησκεία τῶν ἀγγέλων refers to worship directed to angels for invoking protection. However, θρησκεία τῶν ἀγγέλων is a *crux interpretum*. All in all, people were involved in "angelic worship" at Colossae.

vii. Τὰ Στοιχεῖα τοῦ Κόσμου

The noun στοιχεῖα could refer to the letters that made up a word, whether silent or vocal, the basic components of learning a language (e.g. letters, syllable and words) and musical notes. It could also refer to the basics of a subject e.g. ABC, the basic elements of the physical world e.g. earth, air, water, fire and the heavenly bodies.[67] Stars were allegedly made of the chief and purest element, fire. It was assumed that they were visible gods, who by some account

---

[64] Betz (ed.), "*The Greek Magical Papyri*", PGM IV 1932–1954; PGM V. 96–172; PGM XXXVI. 170–176. See Arnold, "*Powers*", P. 140; *The Colossian Syncretism*, 1995 p. 20-1, 31

[65] Betz (ed.), "*The Greek Magical Papyri*", PGM IV, 3165–3167; PGM XXXVI. 35-68.

[66] Betz (ed.), "*The Greek Magical Papyri*", PGM I. 296-327; PGM VII. 795-845.

[67] Xenophon, *Memorabilia* 2.1.1; Plato *Theaet.* 201c; Plutarch, *De Liberis Educandis* 16.2; Diogenes *Laertius* 7: 136, 137; 2 Macc. 12: 13; Wis. 7: 17; 19: 18; 4 Macc 12: 13; PGM 4.440, 1303; Philo, *De Cherubim* 2.XXXV.127.

The Context of the Literary Genre 139

influenced the events and fate of human beings.⁶⁸ They were also regarded as celestial demons or spirits inimical to humankind.⁶⁹ Consequently, scholars read τὰ στοιχεῖα τοῦ κόσμου differently as (a) basic principles, (b) essential components of the universe and (c) spiritual beings. These readings have found their way into several Bible translations, with the RSV and NEB preferring spiritual beings and the NIV and NASB favouring the basic/elemental principles of the world.

Στοιχεῖα appears three times outside the Pauline corpus. One reference indicates the basic teachings of Christian faith (Heb 5: 12), and two the natural substances of which the world is made (2 Pt. 3: 10, 12). The Pauline letters uses τὰ στοιχεῖα four times (Gal. 4: 3; Gal 4: 9; Col. 2: 8, 20), three times with the qualifying genitive τοῦ κόσμου and one time (Gal 4: 9) without it, but which may be an abbreviated reference. The contentious issue among scholars is whether τὰ στοιχεῖα τοῦ κόσμου in Paul refer to basic principles or essential components of the universe or to spiritual beings. Several scholars regard τὰ στοιχεῖα τοῦ κόσμου as basic principles. They are of the opinion that τὰ στοιχεῖα τοῦ κόσμου refer to the basic set of religious and philosophical principles, which sent out their claim upon people prior to and apart from Christ, and which still threaten to supplant Christ.⁷⁰ Several other scholars consider τὰ στοιχεῖα τοῦ κόσμου as a reference to the essential components of the world,⁷¹ which are in a mighty strife.⁷² The idea is that the four elements were in 'strife', causing imbalance that could bring deluge upon the world.⁷³ So the elements of the world are not worshiped but feared, they were not deities or spirits but earth,

---

⁶⁸ Cicero, *De Natura Deorum* 2. 42-3; Ps –*Calisthenes* 1:12:1. See also GNM Morphology and Barclay-Newman Greek Dictionary rendering of στοιχείων in the BibleWorks for Windows Copyright © (1998), BibleWorks, LLC.

⁶⁹ *Test. Sol.* 8:2; Gerhard Delling "στοιχεῖον" in G. Kittel and G. Friedrich, *Theological Dictionary of the New Testament* Vol. VII (Grand Rapids, Michigan: Eerdmans, 1971), pp. 670-687.

⁷⁰ C. F. D. Moule, *The Epistle to the Colossians and Philemon* CGTC (Cambridge: Cambridge University Press, 1957), p. 92; Richard E. DeMaris, " Element, elemental Spirit" in David N. Freedman (ed.), *The Anchor Bible Dictionary* Vol. 2 (New York: Doubleday, 1992), p. 444; Richard N. Longenecker, *Galatians* WBC 41 (Dallas: Word, 1990), p. 166; A. J. Bandstra, *The Law and the Elements of the World* (Kampen: J. H. Kok N. V., 1964), pp. 57, 70; Wink, *Naming the Powers,* pp. 74-78; Walter Wink, *Unmasking the Powers: The Invisible Forces that Determine Human Existence* (Philadelphia: Fortress Press, 1986), pp 133-4, 148-9.

⁷¹ E Schweizer, *The Letter to The Colossians* (Minneapolis: Augsburg, 1982); E. Schweizer, "Slaves of the Elements and Worshipers of Angels" in *Journal of Biblical Literature* 107 (1988), p. 456; J. D. G. Dunn, *The Theology of Paul the Apostle* (Edinburgh: T & T Clark, 1998), p 108; J. D. G. Dunn, *The Epistles to the Colossians and to Philemon: A Commentary on the Greek Text* (Grand Rapids, Michigan: Eerdmans; Carlisle, Cumbria: The Paternoster Press, 1996), pp. 149-50.

⁷² Aristotle, *Metaphysics* II. 4 [1000].

⁷³ See Philo, *DeSpecialibus Legibus* 2. XXXI. 190–192.

water, air and fire.⁷⁴

Most scholars insist τὰ στοιχεῖα τοῦ κόσμου refers to spiritual beings,⁷⁵ although they tag them differently as astral spirits, star deities, evil angels and demons, elemental spirits, angels of the nations or local tribal and national deities.⁷⁶ Whatever the tagging, the reading that τὰ στοιχεῖα τοῦ κόσμου refers to spiritual beings is consistent. The linguistic context associates τὰ στοιχεῖα του κοσμου with other spiritual beings such as principalities and powers, angels, beings that by nature are not gods and sets them in contradistinction to Christ. Further, the old popular belief that the luminaries were celestial divinities that controlled the cosmos and human destiny⁷⁷ links τὰ στοιχεῖα τοῦ κόσμου to spiritual beings. The false teaching at Colossae that was according to τὰ στοιχεῖα τοῦ κόσμου rather than to Christ probably implies a proximity of τὰ στοιχεῖα τοῦ κόσμου to principalities and powers (Col. 2: 8–10), allowing a correlation of the two categories of supernatural powers. The hint at spiritual discipline linked to the 'worship of angels' perhaps allows for a parallel between τὰ στοιχεῖα τοῦ κόσμου and angelic powers. Paul in Colossians 2: 20 speaks of Christians having died with Christ from τῶν στοιχείων τοῦ κόσμου, which by implication are linked with burdensome and ineffective regulations.

---

⁷⁴ Philo holds that the four elements had "transcendent powers" (*De Aet. Mund.* 107). They could be identified with gods or spirits and given names of deities (*De Vita Contemplativa* 3; *De Decalogo* 53). Wink (*Naming the powers*, 74) suggests that the divinisation of the elements was commonplace during the Graeco-Roman era. F. Cumont (*Astrology and Religion among the Greeks and the Romans* (New York/London: G. P. Putnam's, 1912), p. 34 asserts that long before the first century CE, earth, fire and water were worshipped as divine cosmic powers. Herodotus (1.31) and Strabo (15.3.13) also attest the worship of the four physical elements. Then the Pauline audience could have read τὰ στοιχεῖα τοῦ κόσμου as spiritual beings (Arnold, *The Colossian Syncretism*, pp. 163-183).

⁷⁵ See Arnold, *The Colossian Syncretism*, p. 159-60, esp. note 4.

⁷⁶ Arnold, *The Colossian Syncretism*, pp. 162, 185-193; D. G. Reid, "Elements/Elemental Spirits of the World." in G. F. Hawthorne, R. P. Martin and D. G. Reid (eds.), *Dictionary of Paul and His Letters* (Downers Grove, Illinois/Leicester: Intervarsity Press, 1993), p. 232; R. P. Martin *Ephesians, Colossians and Philemon* (Louisville: Westminster/John Knox, 1991), pp. 90-96; J. D. G. Dunn, "The theology of Galatians: The Issue of Covenantal Nominism" in J. M. Bassler (ed.), *Pauline Theology* Vol. 1; *Thes. Phil. Gal.* (Minneapolis: Fortress Press, 1991), p. 136; J. D. G. Dunn, *The Epistles to the Colossians and to Philemon: A Commentary on the Greek Text* (Grand Rapids, Michigan: Eerdmans; Carlisle, Cumbria: The Paternoster Press, 1996), pp. 149-50; N. T Wright, *Colossians and Philemon* (Leicester: Inter-Varsity Press, 1986), pp. 101-2, 155-6.

⁷⁷ Plato *Tim.* 40a, 40c, 40d, 41a; Diogenes Laertius 8.28; 6.102; PGM 39. 18-2; 1En. 43: 1-2; 60: 11-12, 72-82; Jub. 2: 2; *Test. Sol.* 8: 1-4; Josephus *J. W.* 5.5.4.212-5.218; Acts 7: 42-3; Amos 4: 25-27 Jdg 5: 20. See also F. Rochberg-Halton, "Astrology in the Ancient Near East" in David N. Freedman (ed.), *The Anchor Bible Dictionary* Vol. 1 (New York: Doubleday, 1992), pp.504-507.

In Galatians 4: 3 τὰ στοιχεῖα τοῦ κόσμου are paralleled to Jewish experiences under the law described in Galatians 3: 23-25. In Galatians 4: 8 τὰ στοιχεῖα τοῦ κόσμου are linked to the Gentile religious past when they did not know God and were subjected to 'beings that by nature are no gods'. Apparently, there is a parallel between Colossians 2: 8, 20 and Galatians 4: 8-10 provided by the polemical nature of both contexts. The contexts link τὰ στοιχεῖα τοῦ κόσμου with spiritual beings and religious rules. Perhaps this reveals the long-held belief that τὰ στοιχεῖα τοῦ κόσμου could work with and through people and religious institutions. Both the law and paganism, distinguishable from τὰ στοιχεῖα τοῦ κόσμου, allow spiritual beings that were local, national and tribal identities[78] to impose bondage on individuals. It is thus unsurprisingly credible that τὰ στοιχεῖα τοῦ κόσμου are spiritual beings, which exploited the principles of religion to lead people and institutions astray. Paul may have followed the popular reading of τὰ στοιχεῖα τοῦ κόσμου as cosmic powers.[79] He may have relied on Graeco-Roman philosophers and Jewish apocalyptic scorn of idolatry as the mistaken worship of air, fire and water as gods to challenge his readers' spiritual ignorance.[80]

viii. Δαίμων

In the New Testament, the term δαίμων could refer to malevolent demonic spirits and also to heathen gods.[81] However, the Pauline epistles contain very few references to δαίμων. In 1 Timothy 4: 1, Paul regards demons as the source of false teachings and in 1 Corinthians., which is discussed in a separate section below, he links demons with idol worship. Could it be that the association of demons with the false teachings and pagan religions echoes Paul's idea that Satan inspires religious deception? Again, are demons and "principalities and powers" interrelated? According to Ferdinando, "the exact relationship between demons and powers remains unresolved in the Pauline epistles, as indeed is the case elsewhere in the New Testament".[82] Yet demons and "principalities and powers" have a similar relationship of subservience to Satan and all are under attack with the coming of Christ. This however requires us to consider how Paul understood Satan and whether he viewed supernatural powers as similar to the Synoptic Gospels' perception of demons as evil beings under the authority of Satan.

---

[78] Dunn, "The Theology of Galatians", p. 136.
[79] Philo, *De Aeternitate Mundi* XXI.107f; Shepherd of Hermas, *Herm. Vis.* 3.13.3.
[80] *Wis. Sol* 12: 2-3; DeMaris, " Element, Elemental Spirit", p. 445.
[81] See Mt 7: 22; 8: 31; 9: 33-34; 10: 8; 12: 24; Mk 5: 12; Lk. 8: 29; Acts 17: 18; 1 Cor 10: 10, 20-21; Rev. 9: 20; 16: 14; 18: 2.
[82] Ferdinando, *The Triumph of Christ*, p. 266.

ix. Σατανᾶς/διάβολος

Wink observes that Satan is a spirit and he is evil. But this has been compromised by the modern worldview, which excludes spirits from rational discourse and resolutely refuses to accept the existence of evil, "preferring to regard it as a kind of systems breakdown that can be fixed with enough tinkering"[83]. As a result, the idea that Satan is an evil spirit has almost faded away.

> Although mythologically true, the devil is intellectually indefensible and once it was realized the concept of the powers of evil was 'only' a representation of people's experience, no matter how accurate, the devil began to fade away... With only sense experience and reason to go on and with no rational place for an evil cause, enlightened people simply dropped the devil from consideration. With direct psychic experience no longer admissible as evidence of his reality, the devil was as good as dead[84].

How do Paul in particular and the Bible in general understand Satan? In the Old Testament, שָׂטָן often refers to a human adversary[85]. But שָׂטָן is also used as a reference to a supernatural adversary. In Numbers 22: 22 מַלְאַךְ יְהוָה is שָׂטָן, the adversary whose purpose is to confront Balaam[86]. In Job 1–3 and Zech 3, הַשָּׂטָן appears in the divine council to accuse the righteous before God but on both occasions, the accusations are dismissed. In 1 Chronicles 21: 1, שָׂטָן opposes Israel and seduces their king to commit evil but that seems to be a latter development. In an earlier version of this text (2 Sam 24: 1), it is the anger of the Lord that was kindled against Israel inciting David to count Israel and Judah. 1 Chronicles 21: 1 seems to be correcting 2 Samuel 24: 1 by avoiding the implication that God incited David to sin and consigning blame to הַשָּׂטָן. Most scholars agree that Satan in the Old Testament is indeed God's servant and his role is to oppose people[87]. Von Rad regards Satan as "an official prosecutor" and his "task is to go through the earth and consider men"[88]. It appears, however, that the idea of Satan as supernatural adversary "indicates a serious conflict between the Satan on the one hand and God and the righteous

---

[83] Wink, *Unmasking the Powers*, p. 9.

[84] Morton Kelsey, "The Mythology of Evil" in *Journal of Religion and Health* 13, No. 1 (1974), p. 16.

[85] See 1 Sam 29: 4; 2 Sam 29: 17-24; 1 Kgs. 5: 16, 20; 11: 14, 23; Ps. 109: 6.

[86] See R. S. Kluger, *Satan in the Old Testament* (Evanston: Northwestern University Press, 1967).

[87] G. B. Caird, *Principalities and Powers: A study in Pauline Theology* (Oxford: Clarendon Press, 1956), pp. 31-2; J. Kallas, *The Significant of Synoptic Miracles* (London: SPCK, 1961), p. 48; Wink, *Unmasking the powers*, p. 11; H. G. M. Williamson, *1 and 2 Chronicles* (London: Marshall, Morgan & Scott, 1982), pp. 143-144.

[88] Gerhard von Rad, "Διάβολος" in G. Kittel and G. Friedrich, *Theological Dictionary of the New Testament* Vol. II (Grand Rapids, Michigan: Eerdmans, 1964), p. 73.

on the other".[89] In the book of Job, Satan is a troublemaker and the natural enemy of the upright since Job's righteousness is firmly affirmed. In fact, God allows Satan to test Job after he insists that Job is only righteous because God provides for him and protects him (Job 1: 7-12; 2: 1-6).

The New Testament does not understand ὁ σατανᾶς in physical terms as a persecutor but in moral terms as an accuser and tempter, albeit a supernatural adversary. Again, the New Testament always subjects ὁ σατανᾶς to divine authority. This is a precise and consistent development from the Old Testament references of הַשָּׂטָן. In the Pauline epistles, like the rest of the New Testament, ὁ σατανᾶς refers to a spirit also known as ὁ διάβολος. There is no clear distinction between ὁ σατανᾶς and ὁ διάβολος apart from their different etymology. Σατανᾶς is Semitic for accuser whereas διάβολος is Greek for slanderer. It is very likely that both terms are used interchangeably in the Pauline epistles and they were so used during the New Testament period. Several other Pauline phrases are probably used interchangeably to refer to the one malignant spirit, generally known as ὁ σατανᾶς or ὁ διάβολος. These include, τὸν ἄρχοντα τῆς ἐξουσίας τοῦ ἀέρος, and τοῦ πνεύματος τοῦ νῦν ἐνεργοῦντος ἐν τοῖς υἱοῖς τῆς ἀπειθείας (Eph 2: 2). Also included are phrases such as ὁ θεὸς τοῦ αἰῶνος τούτου (2 Cor 4: 4), ὁ πειράζων (1 Thes.3: 5) and τοῦ πονηροῦ (Eph 6: 16; 2 Thes 3: 3).

Paul therefore depicts Satan as a supernatural being that wields considerable power and if τὸν ἄρχοντα τῆς ἐξουσίας τοῦ ἀέρος (Eph 2: 2) refers to Satan, then he could be the ruler of supernatural powers. It was considered, before and during the time of Paul, that the air was the dwelling place of evil spirits.[90] If τοῦ ἀέρος (Eph 2: 2) could be referring to the same sphere as τοῖς ἐπουρανίοις, (Eph 6: 12) then Satan is the ruler of supernatural powers ἐν τοῖς ἐπουρανίοις. If this is possible, then ἐξουσίας in Ephesians 2: 2 describes "the sphere of the ruler's authority rather than… that authority itself".[91] This probably echoes the tradition of the Synoptic Gospels, which depict Satan as the 'ruler of demons'.[92] For that reason, the spiritual conflict in Ephesians 6: 10-20 presupposes Satan's rule over the heavenly realm. With supernatural powers listed in Ephesians 6: 12 as spiritual beings, could it be that in juxtaposing them to τὰς μεθοδείας τοῦ διαβόλου (Eph 6: 11), the author is defining more closely the means by which Satan operates? As Schnackenburg states, "the following enumeration of the evil powers bring to view the spiritual world subordinate to the devil, inspired and directed by him".[93] It is legitimately credible to conclude that supernatural powers "are part of Satan's empire, the agency by which he wages war against

---

[89] Ferdinando, *The Triumph of Christ,* p. 145.
[90] See Bauer, Arndt and Gingrich, *A Greek-English Lexicon,* p. 19; C. L. Milton, *Ephesians* (London: Olipha, 1976), p. 83; Arnold, *Ephesians: Power and Magic* pp. 60-1; R. Schnackenburg, *Ephesians: A Commentary* (Edinburgh: T & T Clark, 1991), p. 91.
[91] Andrew T. Lincoln, *Ephesians* WBC 42 (Waco, Texas: Word Books, 1990), pp. 95-96.
[92] See Mk. 3: 22; Mt. 12: 24; Lk. 15.
[93] Schnackenburg, *Ephesians,* p. 273.

the people of God".⁹⁴ For that reason, supernatural powers have a relationship with Satan, having been cited in the same context as spiritual beings engaged in similar activities (Eph 6: 10-20). This probably implies an identity of nature and purpose.⁹⁵ So, did Paul regard Satan and his powers of darkness as spiritual beings that could impede human survival contrary to God's intentions?

According to Paul, Satan exercises his authority in the human world. The phrase ὁ θεὸς τοῦ αἰῶνος τούτου (2 Cor 4: 4) follows "the apocalyptic notion of two ages and asserts that Satan is the god of the present age, unbelievers being subjected to him".⁹⁶ That ὁ θεὸς τοῦ αἰῶνος τούτου blinds τὰ νοήματα τῶν ἀπίστων εἰς τὸ μὴ αὐγάσαι τὸν φωτισμὸν τοῦ εὐαγγελίου τῆς δόξης τοῦ Χριστοῦ, implies that the devil can prevent the liberation of unbelievers from his dominion typified as 'this evil age' (Gal 1: 4) and so hinder their transfer to the kingdom of God's Son (Col 1: 13). Some scholars agree that the phrases περιεπατήσατε κατὰ τὸν αἰῶνα τοῦ κόσμου τούτου, κατὰ τὸν ἄρχοντα τῆς ἐξουσίας τοῦ ἀέρος and τοῦ πνεύματος τοῦ νῦν ἐνεργοῦντος ἐν τοῖς υἱοῖς τῆς ἀπειθείας (Eph 2: 2) refer to how Satan directs the life of the godless.⁹⁷ The exact meaning of the second phrase in Ephesians 2: 2 is controversial, but it is likely that πνεύματος parallels ἐξουσίας hence referring to a spiritual sphere of influence but not to a spiritual being. Some scholars agree that Satan is not only τὸν ἄρχοντα τῆς ἐξουσίας τοῦ ἀέρος but also the ruler of τοῦ πνεύματος τοῦ νῦν ἐνεργοῦντος ἐν τοῖς υἱοῖς τῆς ἀπειθείας, which is perhaps a spiritual sphere of influence that animates unbelieving humanity.⁹⁸

In the New Testament, the term Βελιάρ, which is another term for Satan, occurs only in 2 Corinthians 6: 15. It also occurs once in the LXX (Jdg 20:13), though it often occurs in some Qumran texts as a reference to the prince of evil.⁹⁹ The sharp contrast between Βελιάρ and Christ (2 Cor 6: 15) and the perception of Satan as ὁ θεὸς τοῦ αἰῶνος τούτου (2 Cor 4: 4) may prompt a conclusion that Paul was operating with a cosmological dualism. As Barrett argues, if the Pauline language is dualistic, it is only superficially so.¹⁰⁰ In fact, Paul's thinking was clear that God is one (1Cor 8: 6; 1 Tim 1: 17). He had no doubts on God's reign as believers had been delivered from Satan's control and transferred to the kingdom of Christ (Eph 2: 4–22; Col 1: 13; Gal 1: 4). He

---

⁹⁴ Ferdinando, *The Triumph of Christ*, p. 249.
⁹⁵ See Bandstra, *The Law and the Elements*, p. 166; Ferdinando, *The Triumph of Christ*, p. 265.
⁹⁶ Ferdinando, *The Triumph of Christ*, p. 250.
⁹⁷ Markus Barth, *Ephesians 1–3* (New York: Doubleday, 1974), p. 214; Ferdinando, *The Triumph of Christ*, p. 250; O'Brien, *The Letter to the Ephesians*, p. 158.
⁹⁸ Barth, *Ephesians*, p. 215; Wink, *Naming the Powers*, p. 83; Lincoln, *Ephesians*, pp. 96-7, Ferdinando, *The Triumph of Christ*, p. 150.
⁹⁹ 1QM 13:11; 14: 9; 17: 4–9 1QS 1: 16–28; 1QM 1: 4–5, 13–16; 11QPsᵃ 19: 15; 4Q280 1 2, 4Q560 1:1; 11Q11 4:10 and 4QBerᵃ 10 ii 7; CD 23: 2–3; 1QH; 4Q286. Cf. Jub. 10: 8; *Asc. Isa* 2.2-5.
¹⁰⁰ C. K. Barrett, *A Commentary to the Second Epistle to the Corinthians* (London: A & C Black, 1973), pp. 197-8.

could not doubt God's sovereignty given that Satan could be used by God to accomplish His plan (1 Cor 5: 5; 2 Cor 12: 7). The ideas that Christ conquered evil spiritual forces (Col 2: 15; Eph 1: 20) and Satan faces an imminent defeat (Rom 16: 20) do not seem to favour a dualistic worldview. In Paul's thinking, the role of Satan is that of a tempter, who entices believers so as to undermine their relationship with God and establish his own control over them. Satan is thus ὁ πειράζων, who Paul feared could undermine believers' faith (1 Thes 3: 5). Some younger widows had been drawn from Christ by satanic incentive (1 Tim 5: 15). Satan could also take advantage of believers if they lacked self-control as to the consummation of conjugal rights (1Cor 7: 5).

Noticeably, believers are the ones who give ὁ διάβολος a chance to penetrate their moral life. This thinking is clear in Ephesians 4: 27, where believers may give the devil a chance to access their individual and communal life. Rightly noted, Ephesians 4: 27 can be translated: "do not give the devil a chance to exert his influence".[101] J. A. Robinson suggests that μηδὲ δίδοτε τόπον τῷ διαβόλῳ signify an "opportunity for the entry of an evil spirit", implying spirit-possession.[102] The verse, however, does not explain what kind of 'chance' or 'foothold' or 'opportunity' the devil can gain in the life of believers. For that reason, Robinson's claim that this verse signifies the entry of an evil spirit is improbable. Even if the verse does not explain what kind of opportunity, it does suggest that the devil can gain access to a person's life. *The Testament of Dan* explains how God's people could give Beliar a chance to control their lives due to anger. "Anger and falsehood together are a double-edged evil, and work together to perturb the reason. And when the soul is continually perturbed, the Lord withdraws from it and Beliar rules it".[103] Although Paul did not say that believers could be demon-possessed and that Satan produced the anger, he did say that anger could give the devil a chance to cause strife within the life of an individual and the community. The source of this anger is to be found in the person but if we consider the immediate context of Ephesians 4: 27, it is not only anger that could give the devil a chance but also falsehood, stealing, evil speech, bitterness, wrath, commotion, slander, malice and failure to forgive. O'Brien asserts, "the temptation to do any of these, or for that matter, to behave in a manner that is characteristic of the 'old person' (v. 22), is presumably the occasion of a spiritual battle which the devil is able to exploit to his own advantage".[104]

Paul also regarded Satan as an architect of moral seduction, who incites people to depart from the truth. In 2 Corinthians 11: 14-5, Satan stands behind the false apostles, who seek to lead believers away from Christ. With the activity of the false apostles having been compared to the serpent's deception of Eve (2 Cor 11: 3), was Paul establishing an essential identity between the

---

[101] Bauer, Arndt and Gingrich, *A Greek-English Lexicon*, p. 823.
[102] J. Armitage Robinson, *St. Paul's Epistle to the Ephesians* (London: Macmillan, 1907), p. 112.
[103] *The Testament of Dan* 4: 7.
[104] O'Brien, *The Letter to the Ephesians*, p. 341.

activity of the false apostles, Satan and the serpent? Does this imply that Paul regarded Satan as the real source of the serpent's seduction as well as the operations of the false apostles? In 2 Timothy 2: 25-6, the conduct of those against the truth (τοὺς ἀντιδιατιθεμένους) is explained as ἐκ τῆς τοῦ διαβόλου. Also, ὁ ἄνθρωπος τῆς ἀνομίας (2 Thes 2: 4) seems to refer to the manifestation of Satan's activity. Ridderbos suggests that ὁ ἄνθρωπος τῆς ἀνομίας will come as a 'religious seducer' but this time not for those inside but outside the church.[105] In some way, ὁ ἄνθρωπος τῆς ἀνομίας seems to be replicating the manifestation of Christ at the end of the times. There will be the παρουσία of Christ (2 Thes 2: 1) but it will not happen before the παρουσία of the rebel by the working of Satan ἐν πάσῃ δυνάμει καὶ σημείοις καὶ τέρασιν ψεύδους (2 Thes 2: 9). Paul seems to be saying that just as Christ came as the incarnation of God, ὁ ἄνθρωπος τῆς ἀνομίας is the ultimate incarnation of Satan or satanic power. Paul again avoids giving the impression that those who followed ὁ ἄνθρωπος τῆς ἀνομίας are simply his victims. God allows those who are to perish to be deceived and to believe falsehood for the purpose of their condemnation due to their own stubbornness to believe and love the truth (2 Thes 2: 10-12; Cf. Rom 1: 18-32).

While it is not clear how Satan hindered Paul from visiting Thessalonica believers (1 Thes 2: 18–though it could be through illness or opposition of civil authority,[106]) he certainly attributed his failure to Satan. The apparent and problematic implication here is that Satan might occasionally frustrate God's purpose and sometimes get the upper hand. Is this not to oversimplify Paul's understanding of supernatural causation? We have seen that Paul strongly stresses God's sovereignty, so it is improbable that he implied Satan would ever get an upper hand (see Rom 8: 28; 2Cor 2: 14; Eph 1: 11). Paul does not doubt that the activity of Satan is real but logically concludes that Satan's deeds are subject to God's supreme authority, thus fulfilling God's purpose. While scholars are not unanimous what σκόλοψ (2 Cor 12: 7) refers to,[107] it was surely recurrent and personal. Perhaps it was a physical ailment that caused frailty and humiliation.[108] Of special significance is that σκόλοψ τῇ σαρκί is attributed to

---

[105] Herman N. Ridderbos, *Paul: An Outline of His Theology* (London: SPCK, 1977), p. 523.

[106] Cf. Ernest Best, *The First and Second Epistles to the Thessalonians* (London: A & C Black, 1972), p. 126; I. H. Marshall, *1 and 2 Thessalonians* (London: Marshall, Morgan & Scott, 1983), p. 86-7.

[107] Cf. P. E. Hughes, *Paul's Second Epistle to the Corinthians* (Grand Rapids, Michigan: Eerdmans, 1962), p. 447; Ralph P. Martin, *2 Corinthians* (Milton Keynes: Word Publishing, 1991), p. 412; R. M. Price, "Punished in Paradise" in *Journal for the Study of the New Testament* 7 (1980), p. 37.

[108] See J. Wilkinson, *Health and Healing: Studies in New Testament Principles and Practice* (Edinburgh: The Handsel Press, 1980), pp. 114-116, 123; Price "Punished in Paradise", p. 36; F. F. Bruce, *The Epistle to the Galatians* (Exeter: Paternoster Press, 1982), p. 208; Hans Dieter Betz, *Galatians* (Hermenia, Philadelphia: Fortress Press, 1979), p. 224.

Satan. This presumes Satan's ability to impose physical affliction even upon a believer. However, the use of the passive ἐδόθη μοι indicates that Paul did not see Satan as the ultimate cause of his affliction. It was God who had allowed σκόλοψ τῇ σαρκί to attack Paul for the purpose of subduing any tendency to boast due to the abundance of revelation. Martin notes that ἐδόθη should be read as an example of the *passivum divinum*.[109] So if Satan afflicted Paul, he did so subject to God's sovereign control and permission and the pain he imposed was meant to fulfil God's plan.[110] Also, Paul depicts Satan as one who employs subtle techniques to attack the church and believers. This is overtly seen in the idea that the opponents of the Gospel were to repent so that they may escape ἐκ τῆς τοῦ διαβόλου παγίδος, ἐζωγρημένοι ὑπ' αὐτοῦ εἰς τὸ ἐκείνου θέλημα (2 Tim 2: 26). It is also clear that one who desires to be ὁ ἐπίσκοπος in the church must not be a novice and must be of good report ἵνα μὴ τυφωθεὶς εἰς κρίμα ἐμπέσῃ τοῦ διαβόλου (1 Tim 3: 6). The expressions ἵνα μὴ πλεονεκτηθῶμεν ὑπὸ τοῦ σατανᾶ· οὐ γὰρ αὐτοῦ τὰ νοήματα ἀγνοοῦμεν (2 Cor 2: 11) and ὑμᾶς στῆναι πρὸς τὰς μεθοδείας τοῦ διαβόλου (Eph 6: 11) equally convey the idea that Satan deviously and subtly attacks the church.

Did Paul regard Satan as an agent who enforces church discipline? In 1 Corinthians 5: 1-5, the man having a relationship with his stepmother was to be delivered to Satan for the destruction of his flesh so that his spirit may be saved. The context is not very clear whether ὄλεθρος carries the idea of physical death or excommunication from the church. The flesh, as usual in Paul, does not refer to the man's physical body but to the way he conducted his life contrary to the life in the spirit. The flesh refers to his actions, which showed him to be living in a world limited only to sensual indulgence. Satan was to work on him εἰς ὄλεθρον τῆς σαρκός, ἵνα τὸ πνεῦμα σωθῇ ἐν τῇ ἡμέρᾳ τοῦ κυρίου. Here Satan does some good work. He augments the purpose of Christ, to save sinners. If this man is the same as the one cited in 2 Corinthians 2: 5-11, then Satan succeeded in destroying his flesh, and so allowing for the salvation of his spirit immediately and not at least on Christ's return. To the believers who had tolerated his sin but refused to forgive and to receive him back, Paul cautions that failure to forgive and re-admit the repentant sinner would give Satan advantage over them. It seems as if Satan could gain advantage through the tolerating of sin and refusal to forgive. In all this, and like in Ephesians 4: 27, Satan is neither good nor evil. If the man's preferred choice had been to continue living in sin, Satan would have been blamed for his damnation. If the church had refused to forgive and receive him back, Satan would have caught them in self-righteousness. Apparently, it is human choice that may have made Satan good or evil.

It appears that the Satan who acts as God's instrument only perpetuates evil and suffering so that people can come to their senses and turn to God or avoid wicked actions. This makes the role of Satan ambiguous; hence Satan the

---

[109] Martin, *2 Corinthians*, p. 412.
[110] Ferdinando, *The Triumph of Christ*, p. 278-9; Martin, *2 Corinthians*, p. 412.

servant of God could also be the epitome of evil. According to Wink, Satan "evolved from a trustworthy intelligence-gatherer into a virtually autonomous and invisible suzerain within a world ruled by God".[111] With Satan portrayed in the book of Job and in Paul as one who can cause evil and suffering, it is not surprising that he is epitomized as an evil spirit. In view of this, Satan would rather be called a chameleon for he "is never quite the same from moment to moment, but changes his colors according to circumstances".[112] He is revealed as the power of evil or as the servant of God. In every situation, evil or not, Paul saw God working for good to those who trust in, and belong to Him. "We know that in everything God works for good with those who love him who are called according to his purposes" (Rom 8: 28). Perhaps this thinking was always at the back of Paul's mind and so he depicted the devil as an agent who fulfils God's plan with regard to the elect. Therefore, there are two competing and mutually allied understandings of Satan. But the context is clear when Satan is God's servant and when evil. We cannot, therefore, explicitly say that Paul depicted Satan as entirely evil without any good use for God's redemptive purpose. But Satan could disguise himself as the angel of light (2 Cor 11: 14).

Therefore, we must not only avoid straitjacketing "Satan in rigid doctrinal categories", but also the "rejection of Satan altogether". This "induces blindness to the radicality of evil, trivializes the struggle for conscious choice, and denies the satanic underground, converting the conscious into a cesspool of erupting nightmares".[113] But in denying Satan a personality,[114] is Wink giving more weight only to the biblical view that depicts Satan as God's servant who acts upon us due to the choices we make? Is he undermining the other biblical view that depicts Satan as a powerful force capable of hindering unbelievers from turning to God? Wink may be right to say that we do not create Satan by our choices since Satan is an autonomous spirit and it is only by our choice we decide which side Satan is on.[115] Yet it is questionable if it is right to deny Satan a personality and to instead argue Satan did not begin as an idea but as an experience.[116] Altogether, Paul distinguishes between the position of believers and that of unbelievers with regard to Satan's activity. Non-believers are subjected to Satan's power in a way that believers are not. While people are responsible for their actions whether tempted by Satan or not, there is an inevitability of satanic inspiration as to their conduct. As such, believers must struggle against ὁ πονηρός as they have been promised supernatural assistance (Eph 6: 10-20). In fact, "spiritual victories and defeats are the results of the way in which everyday temptations are handled".[117] Nevertheless, Paul considered

---

[111] Wink, *Unmasking the Powers*, p. 22-3.
[112] Wink, *Unmasking the Powers*, p.30.
[113] Wink, *Unmasking the Powers*, p. 33.
[114] Wink, *Unmasking the Powers*, p. 33.
[115] Wink, *Unmasking the Powers*, p. 34.
[116] Wink, Unmasking *the Powers*, p. 10.
[117] S. H. T. Page, *Powers of Evil: A Biblical Study of Satan and Demons* (Grand Rapids, Michigan: Baker/Leicester: Apollos, 1995), p.189.

Satan as the great opponent of the Kingdom of God and the personification of evil.[118]

The above-mentioned Pauline terms and phrases probably imply that Paul did not exhaust the possibilities of names describing supernatural powers. Consequently, it must not be construed that in using supernatural powers as a general term indicates that the diverse Pauline terms refer to similar entities. Ἀρχή καὶ ἐξουσία are not similar to τὰ στοιχεῖα τοῦ κόσμου. Citing Cicero, the diverse names for gods denote their differences because if the gods are look-alikes, there is no point of the plurality of names.[119] Even so, while these names are varied, they also expose the activities of the devil. O'Brien consequently argues, "despite the variety in nomenclature, the overall picture is the same: a variety of evil forces under a unified head".[120] As a result, the different Pauline terms and phrases refer to evil spiritual powers differently understood, though they communally indicate a mysterious and invisible phenomenon, a single all-pervading evil spiritual force working in the world and operating in human thought.[121] Could it be that the Pauline terms and phrases identified in this study as supernatural powers are metaphors explaining the working of this evil spirit, otherwise referred to as Satan or the devil? The Pauline terms identified as supernatural powers were obviously and widely used not only in Jewish apocalyptic, but also in the magical texts and by different Greek philosophical schools. From this, suspicion begins to rise as to whether Paul's terminological framework exclusively depended on Jewish apocalyptic terms, which he demythologised.[122]

x. The Pauline Terminological Framework

Rather than demythologising the apocalyptic terminology, could it be that Paul saw an affinity between abstract and personified divinities of Greek philosophical thought and personal spiritual beings mentioned in Jewish apocalyptic texts?[123] Forbes seems to answer the above question affirmatively

---

[118] Ragnar Leivestad, *Christ the Conqueror: Ideas of Conflict and Victory in the New Testament.* (London: SPCK, 1954), pp. 85-92.
[119] Cicero, *De Natura Deorum* 1.84.
[120] O'Brien, "Principalities and Powers", p. 137.
[121] Cf. Cicero, *De Natura Deorum* 2.19
[122] Hendrik Berkhof, *Christ and the Powers* (Scotdale, PA: Herald Press, 1962), p. 23; J. Y. Lee, "Interpreting the Demonic Powers in Pauline Thought" in *Novum Testament* 12 (1970), p. 54; J. C. Becker, *Paul the Apostle: The Triumph of God in Life and Thought* (Edinburgh: T & T Clark; Philadelphia: Fortress Press, 1980), pp. 189-192; Wink, *Naming the Powers,* pp. 61-2, 100; Dunn, *The Theology of Paul,* p. 110.
[123] Chris Forbes, "Principalities and Powers: Demythologizing Apocalyptic"? in *Journal for the Study of the New Testament* 82, (June 2001), pp. 61-88; Chris Forbes "Pauline Demonology and/or Cosmology? Principalities and Powers and the Elements of the World in their Hellenistic Context" in *Journal for the Study of the New Testament* 85, (March 2002), p. 51.

in his two articles.[124] In the first article, Forbes looks at the Pauline terminology and concept of the 'spirit world' within a Jewish setting. Paul does not deny that the world is populated by personal spiritual beings but they are not central to his thinking. Personified abstractions played a greater role than the personal demons and angels defined in the Gospels and in Acts.[125] Also the paucity of references to angels and demons in the Pauline texts reveals too little about their role. The texts tell us more about what angels cannot do than what they can do. Other Pauline terms, which may not fully give a clear picture of the Pauline spirit world include devil/Satan or spirit, which are used in a personal sense and/or in an impersonal sense. These terms are not only used in few places, but also they do not disclose the active role for spirits and Satan in Pauline theology beyond the general-purpose role of opposition.[126] Even though the Pauline texts exhibit belief in angels, demons, spirits and Satan, his terminology is largely made up of impersonal and abstract ideas, not solely influenced by Jewish pre-Christian apocalyptic. The apocalyptic writers did not present spiritual powers in abstract terms as they often attributed names and personality to them. The Pauline terms are surprisingly abstract and impersonal even where names or types of personal spirits might have been expected. Could it be that Paul favoured abstract terms because he belonged to a new wave that used abstract terminology to refer to spiritual beings?[127]

In his second article, Forbes shows that the Pauline terminology has some elements of Greek philosophy, especially that of Philo and Plutarch's Middle Platonism. Terms like ἀρχή, δύναμις and στοιχεῖα were standard terms, which early Greek philosophy had long personified for over five hundred years.[128] The early Greek philosophy used στοιχεῖα widely in reference to the types of matter; ἀρχή in reference to matter or forces depending on definition; δύναμις in reference to forces or potentials, and not to matter.[129] The early Greek philosophy allegorised these terms (especially Theagenes of Rhegium, c 525 BCE) so as to understand Homeric mythology.[130] According to K. Dowden, Theagenes regarded Homer's warring Olympians as mythical figures that actually represented the basic qualities of matter, that is, the hot, the wet, the dry and the cold or aspects of human psychology.[131] During the Platonic era,

---

[124] Forbes, "Principalities and Powers", pp. 61-88; Forbes, "Pauline Demonology", pp. 51-73.

[125] Forbes, "Principalities and Powers", pp. 61-63.

[126] Forbes, "Principalities and Powers", pp. 64-67.

[127] Forbes, "Principalities and Powers", pp. 67-81.

[128] See Forbes, "Pauline Demonology", pp. 52-55 esp. footnote 2, p. 52.

[129] Plutarch *Mor.* 276f, 360e, 390a, 419a, 1051c; Philo *Quis rer* xxx.154, lvii.281; *De Aet.Mun.*xxi.108-9, *De Vit.Mos.*1, xxviii.156; Albinus/Alcinous *Didaskalikos* 13; Diogenes Laertius 3. 73. 3, 5.33.2, 7.134, 147. See also Forbes, "Pauline Demonology" p. 55.

[130] Forbes, "Pauline Demonology", pp. 55-6.

[131] Ken Dowden, *The Use of Greek Mythology* (London/New York: Roultedge, 1992), pp. 40-1.

use of allegory to make myths intellectually credible and socially useful was well-established but Plato himself doubted if allegory really resolved the problems of myth.[132] Yet "by the first century allegory was the universally accepted way of dealing with the problems of ancient mythic text".[133] Philo was the best-known first century CE exponent of allegory[134] but his "allegorical reading is designed to overcome some embarrassment with, or oddity in, the sacred text".[135] Plutarch also was inclined to allegorical reading but for him the question was not whether the texts were to be taken allegorically but what kind of allegory they were.[136] Forbes insists that for the erudite first century CE reader, allegorization made it rationally permissible to interpret gods, demigods and heroes as mythical personifications of natural forces. Most people did not regard this as reductionism, but as the actual intention of ancient poets and mythologers. Allegory gave a more 'scientific' framework to integrate traditional myths and rituals and mythical personalities were abstracted into cosmic principles.[137]

Perhaps Philo's and Plutarch's Middle Platonic metaphysics are a probable framework with which to understand the Pauline abstract and personified terminology. Philo was however aware of the ancient cosmology that conceptualised good and evil, rational and imperishable demons and angels, which differed only in name but not in identity[138]. Forbes insists that Philo's cosmology had a key element of earlier thinking and now under the influence of allegory, re-emerged in a new form that personalises δύναμις.[139] The evidence in Philo demonstrates that abstract terms like δύναμις and ἀρχή could be personalised to refer to spiritual beings such as angels. They could also refer to the faculties of body and soul, to the potentialities of matter, to God's personal power and to abstract and personified powers of God.[140] For Plutarch

---

[132] Plato, *Republic* 378d; Forbes, "Pauline Demonology", p. 56.
[133] Forbes, "Pauline Demonology", p. 56.
[134] See *De Mig.Abr*.xvi.89-93, where Philo argues for both the allegorical understanding and the literal practice of both the keeping of Sabbath and circumcision.
[135] Forbes, "Pauline Demonology", p. 57.
[136] Plutarch *Mor*.20a, 360e. Also see Forbes, "Pauline Demonology", pp. 56-7.
[137] Forbes, "Pauline Demonology", pp. 57-7.
[138] Philo *De Gig*.iv.16; *De Conf.Ling*.xxxv.176-7.
[139] Forbes, "Pauline Demonology", pp. 58-67.
[140] Philo *De Som*.1, xxv.157; *De Spec.Leg*.1, viii.45,xii.66, lx.329; *De Vit.Mos*.1, i.3, xii.70; 2, xxvi.132; *De Plant*. iv.14, xii.46, xx.86, xxiv.141, xxix.125; *Leg. Alleg*.1, ix.22, xxx.96; 2, xxi.86; 3, x.35, xxii.73, xxix.88, xxxii.97, lxii.177-8; *De Conf.Ling*.xxxiv.171-175, xxxv.179; *Quis rer*.xli.205; *De Abr*.iv.26, xii.59, xxxix.228, xxiv.121–xxv.130; *De Ebr*.vi.22, lx.32; xxvii.106; *Quod.Det.Pot.Ins.Sol*. xxii.81-2, xxiv.89, xxv.92, 95; *De Post. Cai*. v.14–vi.20, ix.27, xix.66, xxiv.89; *De Sobr*.ix.43; *De Agr*.v.22, xiv.63, xxi.94, xxxiii.167, xxxvii.162; *De Op.Mun*.ii.7, v.20, vi.23, xiv.46, xxiv.72; *De Cher*.vi.20, viii.29; *De.Gig*.x.47; *Quod deus*.xvii.78, 80f, xxxiv.109-10, xxv.116; *De Fuga*.xii.69, xviii.94-105; *De Leg.Ad.Gai*.i.6; *De Sac*.xxv.59; *De Mig. Abr*. xxxi.170.

δύναμις and ἀρχή were not truly personal, yet he deemed it appropriate to personalise them and to recognize them in mythological personalities.[141] It appears that δύναμις and ἀρχή could be used to refer to nature or abstract or semi-abstract forces. The terms could be personified and named differently by diverse cultural traditions to refer to the variety of gods that concerned Plutarch. Then behind the abstract terminology were the differing names from culture to culture of different spiritual beings, which even if they were not truly personal, could be personified and identified in mythical narratives.[142] This probably allows us to read the Pauline abstract terminology metaphorically, probably helping us to discover how spiritual beings work with, and through people and human institutions.

Taken together, the evidence from early Greek Philosophy and Middle Platonism (Philo and Plutarch) seems to offer a possible terminological framework for Paul's thinking with regard to supernatural powers. Paul's preferred abstract and personified terminology therefore does not supplant the apocalyptic terms.[143] The abstract terminological parallels between Paul, Philo and Plutarch do not favour such an idea. This leaves the previously held idea that Paul demythologised the apocalyptic terms to such an extent that his use of them was different open to doubt.

xi. The Pauline Conceptual Framework

In chapter four, it came out clearly that the belief in supernatural powers was rife during the first century CE. But what shaped the conceptual framework through which Paul read supernatural powers? Was it the satirical remarks on false gods, hateful idolatry, making of idols and animal worship in the Wisdom of Solomon 13: 1–16: 4? Was it the Graeco-Roman elitist scepticism that, as demonstrated in chapter four, derided some beliefs about gods and behaviour exhibited in public worship? Was the Pauline conceptual framework tied to a particular Jewish or Graeco-Roman expression? Perhaps we can only know Paul's viewpoint as to supernatural powers if we understand what shaped the conceptual framework with which he perceived Graeco-Roman "pagan" gods. Were they just 'beings that by nature were no gods', 'the so-called gods' or idols or demons? Alternatively, was Paul referring to the same reality, but in different ways? This is what we intend to find out by considering and correlating three of the undisputed Pauline texts, that is, Galatians 4: 8; 1 Corinthians 8: 4–6; 10: 14–22. These could be the most useful texts as to the Pauline conceptual framework of supernatural powers.

In Galatians 4: 8, Paul tells the Galatians that when they did not know God, or rather when they were not known by God, they were slaves 'to beings that

---

[141] Plutarch, *De Is.et Os.*25.360e; 33.364a; *Mor.*366c, 367b, 368d-e, 369a, b-e, 372b, 375f–376a, 377d, 377f–378a; 425e–426b, 1014e, 1015b, 1017a; Also see Diogenes Laertius 7.147

[142] Forbes, "Pauline Demonology", pp. 68-71.

[143] See Forbes, "Principalities and Powers", p. 85.

by nature are no gods'. Did Paul at that time deny the existence of pagan deities? What did he mean in stating that the pagan deities were beings that by nature are no gods? Paul at that time spoke from a Jewish perspective.[144] It was a characteristic Jewish belief that they alone were privileged to have the knowledge of God[145]. The Jews maintained that other nations did not know God,[146] meaning that these nations had no experience of God's covenantal grace and they did not realise He was the only God. Consequently, they worshipped gods that were 'no gods',[147] and so Galatians 4: 8 is thoroughly Jewish. The term φύσις (translated 'by nature') is not a Jewish concept but may show Paul's alertness to the distinction made within Graeco-Roman philosophy between 'gods in reality' and 'gods by human convention'.[148] Dunn insists that Paul was evoking a whole sweep of Greek philosophical (particularly Stoic) thought in its attempt to speak about the nature of reality, the true nature of things.[149] It should be noted that according to the Stoics the gods existed, they were alive and endowed with reason, united with each other in concord and fellowship and as animate beings, with joint control over the cosmos as a single unit.[150] The Stoics held that all except out-and-out unbelievers generally agreed that gods exist.[151] So any argument "against the existence of gods, whether from sincerity or the sake of argument, is a debased and impious practice".[152] Perhaps the populace regarded the beings that for Paul were by nature not gods along the lines of Stoic teachings about the true gods. Could it be that the beings that by nature are no gods qualify to be the so-called gods thought to exist and were worshipped as gods though they were not?[153] We shall shortly try to link the beings that by nature are no gods with the so-called gods in 1 Corinthians 8: 4-6. But for now, suffice to say that the phrase τοῖς φύσει μὴ οὖσιν θεοῖς cannot be used to conclude that Paul denied the existence of pagan supernatural powers. The phrase also does not provide clear-cut answer as to whether Paul considered these gods to be non-existent or as demonic powers.[154]

A key consideration, however, may be that the phrase denies those beings

---

[144] J. D. G. Dunn, *A Commentary on the Epistle to the Galatians* (London: A & C Black, 1993), p. 224.
[145] Dt. 5: 39; 1 Sam. 3: 7; Ps. 9: 10; 45: 10; Isa. 43: 10; Hos. 8: 2; Mic. 6: 5; Wis. 2: 13.
[146] Ps. 79: 6; Jer. 10: 25; Wis. Sol. 13: 1; Jud 9: 7; 2 Macc. 1: 27.
[147] 2 Chr. 13: 9; Isa. 37: 19; Jer. 2: 11; 5: 7; 16: 20; Wis. 12: 27.
[148] Hans Dieter Betz, *Galatians* (Hermenia, Philadelphia: Fortress Press, 1979), pp. 214-5.
[149] Dunn, *A Commentary on the Epistle to the Galatians*, p. 224.
[150] Cicero, *De Natura Deorum* 2.78-9.
[151] Cicero, *De Natura Deorum* 3.7.
[152] Cicero, *De Natura Deorum* 2.168.
[153] Bruce Winter, "Theological and Ethical Response to Religious pluralism – 1 Corinthians 8–10" in *Tyndale Bulletin* 41 2 (November 1990), pp. 209-226, esp. p. 214.
[154] Ernest de Witt Burton, *A Critical and Exegetical Commentary on the Epistle to Galatians* (Edinburgh: T & T Clark, 1921), p. 227-8; Dunn, *A Commentary on the Epistle to the Galatians*, p. 224.

that by nature are no gods the nature of the deity, even if it does not affirm or deny their existence. Even if Paul may have been less clear about their existence, the phrase viewed from a Jewish perspective, may imply that they were real beings though not gods. Alternatively, Paul referred to them because his hearers believed them to be gods and so worshipped them. Paul could have been speaking to the feelings and/or prejudices of his audience. Paul shows himself here to be a citizen of two cultures, able to integrate two worldviews and to angle his argument so as to have impact on his readers,[155] and his goal was to change the Galatians' mind. This may imply that Paul believed the beings that the Galatians Christian converts previously worshipped existed and were real but they were not equal to God. Perhaps he wanted the Galatians to come face to face with the ultimate reality of the only and real God who had now known them or whom they had now come to know. There is no doubt that Paul, as a Christian held that there was by nature only one God and Father who raised Jesus Christ. So Paul probably endorsed the reading favoured by Hellenistic Judaism that the pagan gods by nature did not exist as gods but as inferior demonic beings. This might become clearer if we correlate Paul's view of idols and demons in 1 Corinthians with the 'beings that by nature are no gods' but works of human hands.

In 1 Corinthians 8: 4–6, Paul states that 'an idol has no real existence' even if there are the 'so-called gods in heaven or on earth—as indeed there are many gods and many lords'. The setting of this passage must be fully understood, if we are to grasp the Pauline conceptual framework as to supernatural powers. A crucial starting point must be the Ancient Near East, where it was generally believed that idols were significant since they were living, feeling beings in which the deity was actually present.[156] But the Jewish official position, as depicted by the Old Testament, stands in striking contrast to their Ancient Near East neighbours. For the Jews, idols were lifeless and human-made objects. They were neither living, feeling beings nor the abode of the deity. The second commandment not only barred Jews from making graven images, but also from worshipping them.[157] The Shema (Dt. 6: 4), which firmly reminded the Jews that they could only worship Yahweh, reinvigorated the second commandment. Yahweh is the One and only God who reveals himself through his word and nature and not via images made by human hands. Unlike the non-Jewish gods, Yahweh's "self-disclosure came through a revelation in words and the Sinai experience constituted a paradigm of God's self-disclosure to Israel; thus images were prohibited".[158] While the second commandment prohibited the making and worshiping of idols, the Shema sanctioned faith in one God, who alone was worthy of worship. This positively distinguished the Jews from their

---

[155] Dunn, *A Commentary on the Epistle to the Galatians*, p. 225.
[156] Edward M. Curtis, "Idol, Idolatry" in David N. Freedman (ed.), *The Anchor Bible Dictionary* Vol. 3 (New York: Doubleday, 1992), p. 377.
[157] Exd. 20: 4-5; Dt. 5: 8. See also Exd. 34: 17; Lev. 19: 4; 26: 1; Dt. 4: 15-19, 25.
[158] Curtis, "Idol, Idolatry", p. 379.

The Context of the Literary Genre

'pagan' neighbours and the polytheistic culture.[159]

That the Jews regarded the idols derisively and derogatorily is clear from the vocabulary used to describe them. Noticeably, the Old Testament vocabulary portrays the idols as entities shaped, formed and patterned by human hands. The vocabulary also depicts them as weak, worthless, dumb, impotent and detestable even if they are worshipped. Even so, the detestable idol could pollute the people participating in its worship, rendering them unclean before God.[160] As a result, the prophetic tradition regarded the idol as an abomination that could pollute the land,[161] even if they were insubstantial or worthless, false and the work of delusion, ineffective or empty.[162] Since the first commandment depicts Yahweh as the unrivalled God and so no image could fittingly represent Him, the prophetic tradition ridiculed the worship of non-existent, lifeless and impotent objects made by human hands.[163] The song of Moses (Dt. 32: 15-6) makes it clear that to worship strange gods was to disown God, to stir him to jealousy and provoke him to anger. For that reason, the prohibitions are not only directed to the elimination of idol making, but also to curtail the assimilation of foreign religious values to the worship of Yahweh.[164]

The idolatry of the Ancient Near East was certainly present in the Graeco-Roman world, since making and worshipping idols were widespread in the emperor, fertility and mystery cults.[165] Philo in his interpretation of the second commandment elaborates the folly and wickedness of idol worship. He also shows the imprudence of idolaters, who worshipped the elements and carved images believing they were gods, while they were lifeless creatures unworthy even to be compared to beasts.[166] With Christianity having its root in Judaism, this underscored the purging of idolatry. As such, a Christian leader like Paul was almost certainly influenced by the official Jewish derisive and derogatory attitude towards the idols. The use of images and statues by Graeco-Roman cults therefore represented idolatry in the eyes of Paul. It is notable that Paul regarded idol worship as originating from human rejection of God's self-revelation and so idolatry substitutes the worship of the Creator with the worship of the creature (Rom 1: 18-32). So Paul, in keeping with the Jewish perspective, asserts that idols made with human hands are no gods and so they do not exist as God does.[167] The claim that no idol exists in the world and there

---

[159] Num 23: 9; Philo *De Vit. Mos.* 1.L (50).278; Josephus, *Ant.* 4. 114-117. See also Barclay, *Jews in the Mediterranean Diaspora*, pp. 1-4.
[160] Curtis, "Idol, Idolatry", p. 378.
[161] Isa. 44: 19; Jer. 16: 18; Ezek. 5: 11.
[162] Jer. 10: 14-5; 51: 17-8; Jonah 2: 8; Ps. 31: 6.
[163] Isa. 40: 18, 25; 42: 17; Jer. 5: 17.
[164] Cf. J. Gutman, "The 'Second Commandment' and the Images in Judaism", in *Hebrew Union College Annual* 32 (1961), pp. 161-174; Curtis, "Idol, Idolatry", p. 379.
[165] J. E. Stambaugh, and D. L. Bauch *The New Testament in its Social Environment* (Philadelphia: The Westminster Press, 1986), pp. 41-46; 138-167.
[166] Philo, *De Decalogo* xiv.65-xvi.81; xxix. 156; *De Vita Contemplativa* i.1-8.
[167] Stambaugh and Balch, *The New Testament*, pp, 149-154.

is no God except one is thoroughly Jewish and consistent with the prophets and the psalmist who equally mocked the lifeless idols of the heathens.[168] The claim that idols do not have real existence and the assertion that there is no God but one have a polemical thrust and are a confession of faith respectively.[169] It is probable therefore that Paul's perception of the so-called gods echoed *Wisdom of Solomon* 13: 1–19, which takes to task those who respect the natural elements as gods and those who make idols. Even so, a second century CE account of Corinth that cites the deities Corinthians worshipped,[170] may imply that Paul's audience believed that the so-called gods existed in heaven and earth. These could have included natural objects like stars, sun, fire, sea, or wind now worshipped as gods[171] and the divinised human leaders for instance Julius Caesar and Augustus Caesar.[172] Paul could not have denied these existed but affirmed they were erroneously understood to exist as gods. Paul here advocates the continuity of Israel's faith in one God into Hellenistic Christianity, laying the basis of the theological and historical affirmation of the Christian creed in one God.[173]

The first commandment, "You shall have no other gods before me", may imply that the Jews recognized the existence of other gods beside Yahweh, albeit not having the same existence as Yahweh. It seems that the Jews believed not so much in monotheism as to what is called henotheism. This is the belief in one God who is supreme over all spiritual beings, but which exist as means of his supreme power.[174] For Paul, these were the so-called gods and it is worth noting that the term λεγόμενοι translated 'so-called' is perhaps used here in a derogatory sense.[175] Even so, the so-called gods existed and could control those who worshipped them. Paul may have been saying that the so-called gods existed in the imaginations of the worshipper and they could influence human actions.[176] Perhaps the idols and the so-called gods (1Cor 8: 4-6) were similar entities to the beings that by nature are no gods (Gal. 4: 8) and which enslaved believers. They may have the appearance of gods but, in the real sense, were non-existent for they were not gods and lords qua the One God and One Lord

---

[168] Isa. 44: 9-20; Ps. 115: 3-8.

[169] Raymond F. Collins, *First Corinthians* – Sacra Pagina Series edited by David J. Harnington, S. J. (Collegeville, Minnesota: The Liturgical Press, 1999), p. 313. See also Acts 17: 24–29.

[170] See Pausanias, *Description of Greece*, 1-5; Collins, *First Corinthians*, p. 314.

[171] Wis. Sol. 13: 2–3.

[172] Collins, *First Corinthians*, p. 314.

[173] Cf. Gordon D. Fee, *The First Epistle to the Corinthians* (Grand Rapids, Michigan: Eerdmans, 1987), p. 370.

[174] James Moffatt, *The First Epistle of Paul to the Corinthians* (London: Hodder & Stoughton, 1938), p. 139. See also Josephus, *J. W.* 5.5.218.

[175] Collins, *First Corinthians*, p. 319.

[176] Betz, *Galatians*, p. 15; Fee, *The First Epistle to the Corinthians*, pp. 372-3, 471; Frank J. Matera, *Galatians*, in Sacra Pagina Series edited by Daniel J. Harrington, S. J (Collegeville, Minnesota: The Liturgical Press, 1992), p. 152.

of Christian faith.[177] Certainly for Paul any idol or any spiritual power, known or unknown that is theoretically equated to the one and only God, is a mere non-entity.[178] But an idol may not be a non-entity if it is the equivalent of a demon.

In 1 Corinthians 10: 14-22, Paul advises believers to eschew the worship of idols, which are categorised as demons. He draws a lesson from the wilderness generation for the Corinthian church.[179] During the first century CE, δαιμονίων was a reference to an evil supernatural being that caused physical harm in all sorts of ways.[180] The Jews identified the pagan gods with idols that were no gods,[181] which at best were characterised as demons[182] wrongly worshiped by the apostate Jews. As noted in chapter four, while the Hebrew text suggests that all the gods of the nations are idols, the LXX text suggests that they are demons. It is possible that the Jews who translated the LXX conveyed a Jewish belief that pagan gods were closely linked to the demonic realm, a belief that was indeed widespread in the New Testament times.[183] We have already seen in chapter four that the Second Temple Jewish literature regarded demons as the fallen angels or spirits. They were often linked with the work of Satan.[184] Paul recognised the many gods and many lords but he probably transformed their status and classified them as demons.[185] It is apparent in 1Corinthians 10: 14-22 that even if idols and food offered to them is nothing, pagan sacrifices are offered to demons and not to God. Paul was perhaps bringing to contemporary use the Song of Moses, wherein to participate in the worship of demons that were not gods is to reject the one and only true God (Dt. 32: 15–22). So to partake in the sacrifice offered to idols was to have communion with demons. In that case, if we link the beings that by nature are not gods, the so-called gods and an idol that has no real existence with demons, then according to Paul, there is a devilish reality behind them.

Robertson and Plummer suggest that if εἴπερ εἰσίν and ὥσπερ εἰσίν in 1 Corinthians 8: 5 refers to what really exist, the meaning will be, 'If you like to

---

[177] Larry W. Hurtado, *One God, One Lord: Early Christian Devotion and Jewish Monotheism* (Philadelphia: Fortress Press, 1988), pp. 97-99.

[178] Moffatt, *The First Epistle of Paul to the Corinthians*, p. 106.

[179] See T. Paige, "Demons and Exorcism" in G. F. Hawthorne, R. P. Martin and D. G. Reid (eds.), *Dictionary of Paul and His Letters* (Downers Grove, Illinois/Leicester: Intervarsity Press, 1993), p. 210.

[180] See Mk. 5: 12; Mt. 8: 31; Lk. 8: 29; Rev. 16: 14; 18: 2.

[181] 2 Chr. 13: 9; Isa 37: 19; Jer 2: 11; 5: 7; 16: 20.

[182] Pss. 96: 5; 106: 37-9; Dt. 32: 16-17.

[183] According to 1 Tim 4: 1 and 2 Tim 4: 3-4, demons tempted people to idolatry, witchcraft, magic, war and other anti-social vices that could keep people away from God.

[184] Paige, "Demons and Exorcism", p. 210.

[185] Joop F. M. Smit, *About the Idol Offerings: Rhetoric, Social Context and Theology of Paul in 1st Corinthians 8: 1-1:1* (Bondgenotenlaan, Leuven/Sterling, Virginia: Peeters, 2000), p. 75.

say that, because there are supernatural beings in abundance, as we all believe, therefore the so-called gods of the heathens really exist, nevertheless for us Christians, there is only one God'. Paul here seems to be saying that *to the worshipper*, the idol *is* an object of adoration. Yet while they actually worship a non-entity, ethically they are worshippers of demons (1 Cor 10: 20). The thinking behind Paul may be that of Deuteronomy 10: 17 and Psalms. 136: 2-3 wherein Yahweh is God of gods and Lord of lords. This may imply that the second εἰσὶν refers to actual existence. While pagan sacrifices were offered to beings that did not exist as God does, there were supernatural powers behind the idols although not the gods depicted by the idols.[186] Graeco-Roman pagan idols were then gods of another kind; the 'so-called gods' who by nature were not gods but demons,[187] but which were feared as they allegedly ruled nature.[188] It follows then Paul followed his Jewish heritage that idols were man-made but could steer believers' loyalty away from the Lord.[189] Even if idols are the product of human hands they are non-entities for Christians (1Cor 8: 4–6). They represent malevolent supernatural beings that can control those who participate in their worship (1Cor 10: 16f). It appears that Paul is telling the Corinthians that they cannot have it both ways and there is no neutrality between Christian celebration and demonic rites for it is either one or the other.[190] The reality and existence of supernatural powers may have not been an issue for Paul. They are nothing compared to God but a reality nevertheless, as they exert influence over those who fellowship with them. The food offered to the idol and the idol itself is obviously nothing but there is something behind the idol although not what was believed to be there.[191] Paul appears to be forbidding any kind of relationship with the demonic, a relationship that cannot be with a non-entity, as some scholars would wish to believe. In other words, Paul is saying that idols are not God but in fact demons (1 Cor 10: 20)[192] and to have alliance with them would renew the earlier bondage to 'beings that by nature are no gods' or the 'so-called gods', thereby depriving believers of their newly found freedom in Christ (Gal 4: 8–9).

---

[186] Archibald Robertson and Alfred Plummer, *A Critical and Exegetical Commentary on the First Epistle of St. Paul to the Corinthians*, ICC, (Edinburgh: T & T Clark, (1999 originally 1911), p. 167. See also Moffatt, *The First Epistle of Paul to the Corinthians*, p. 235-6; Smit, *About the Idol Offerings*, p. 75.

[187] George Duncan, *The Epistle of Paul to the Galatians* (London: Hodder & Stoughton, 1934), p.133; J. B. Lightfoot, *St. Paul's Epistle to the Galatians* (London: MacMillan & Co Ltd, 1910), pp.170-1.

[188] See chapter 4, pp. 104-120.

[189] Moffatt, *The First Epistle of Paul to the Corinthians*, p. 139; Smit, *About the Idol Offerings*, p. 77.

[190] Smit, *About the Idol Offerings*, p.77.

[191] Robertson and Plummer, *A Critical and Exegetical Commentary* p. 215; Paige, "Demons and Exorcism", p. 210.

[192] Gregory J. Lockwood, *1 Corinthians* – Concordia Commentary (St. Louis: Concordia Publishing House, 2000), p. 344.

We can conclude that Paul's conceptual framework was that of a Jew with regard to Graeco-Roman gods.[193] On the other hand, his conceptual framework could have been that of a Graeco-Roman philosopher. As noted in chapter four, some Graeco-Roman philosophers vilified popular beliefs, rituals and practices with regard to supernatural powers. They censured superstitious beliefs and fears that led people to call human-made idols and mountains, trees and shapeless stones gods "although such things bear no resemblance to the gods than does the human form".[194] Paul may have built on the critique of these Graeco-Roman thinkers. So his conceptual framework was an imaginative blending of his Jewish heritage and Graeco-Roman philosophical views.[195] It could be that Paul was creatively working with the angelology and demonology of his Jewish heritage and the worldview of the Graeco-Roman philosophers. In fact, Paul was a product of decades of intellectual interaction between Judaism and Graeco-Roman culture. His thinking could have been shaped by his own effort to fuse his Jewish legacy and understanding of pagan supernatural powers with the contemporary Graeco-Roman philosophical appraisal of the same so as to communicate his cosmological and Christological ideas.[196] While Paul's terminological framework built on abstract personifications, his conceptual framework allowed the existence of spiritual beings, not the abstracts, which some scholars, as Gordon Fee notes, would wish us to believe.[197]

5:3. Theological Reflections: The Evidence for Christ's Supremacy over Supernatural Powers

i. Christ is Pre-eminent, Supernatural Powers are Created

A key Pauline text depicts Christ as the image of the unseen God and all things in heaven and on earth, seen or unseen, were created ἐν αὐτῷ, δι' αὐτοῦ and εἰς αὐτόν (Col 1: 16). If τὰ ὁρατὰ καὶ τὰ ἀόρατα include the full sweep of evil spiritual powers identified as θρόνοι, κυριότητες, ἀρχαί, ἐξουσίαι, then God created supernatural powers perhaps to serve His own purpose and will. The need for Christ to reconcile all things in heaven or on earth and to make peace (Col 1: 20) indicates that all is not well. It seems that some powers that were originally good had become hostile to God's plan, causing confusion among

---

[193] Paige, "Demons and Exorcism", p. 210.
[194] Dio Chrysostom, *Olympian Discourse* 12.60.
[195] Forbes, "Pauline Demonology", p. 73. Cf. Barclay (*Jews in the Mediterranean Diaspora*, p. 393) who states, "by an extraordinary transference of ideology, Paul deracinates the most culturally conservative forms of Judaism in the Diaspora and uses them in the service of his largely Gentile communities".
[196] Forbes, "Principalities and Powers", pp. 73, 88
[197] Fee, *The First Epistle to the Corinthians,* p. 475.

believers. Apparently, believers at Colossae erroneously regarded supernatural powers as rivals to Christ (Col 2: 8, 20) and they probably held that they had an independent ontological existence, though not in the same sense as Paul. So Paul makes it clear that since the pre-existent Christ brought the powers into existence in his creative role (Col. 1: 16), then they are not equal to Him. Neither do they exist on their own because all things hold together in Christ (Col. 1: 17). The text unmistakably indicates that the Son of God is not part of the creation. Neither is he on the top of the hierarchy of supernatural powers, as the Hellenistic culture would have assumed. This Christological hymn suggests that supernatural powers were created through him, in him, and for him.

It is unmistakable that like any other creation, supernatural powers are subservient to the Creator and to the principle by which they exist, that is, Jesus Christ. These created supernatural powers must include the ones implied in the spatial image enumerated as οὔτε ὕψωμα οὔτε βάθος (Rom 8: 39). This image perhaps refers to the zenith and nadir of heavenly bodies and it embraces the full sweep of celestial powers. Consequently, οὔτε ὕψωμα οὔτε βάθος could have been a reference to all astrological powers, visible or invisible, which were believed to determine and control fate and human destiny.[198] The image may also refer to the powers that could occupy the height of heaven or the underworld—or any space between.[199] Irrespective of the fact that supernatural powers aim to separate believers from the love of Christ, unlike Christ, they are not pre-existent. Even if they are invisible and spiritual, this does not mean that they are eternal since they were created. Although they are invisible this does not mean they are only heavenly since some earthly realities such as air and wind are invisible too. In fact, Colossian 1: 15-20 distinguishes the Creator and the creation, which is both material and spiritual. As Noble avers, "the word 'invisible'... is therefore of the highest significance... since it seems to insist that everything that is not God, everything 'spiritual' as well as everything material... is to be placed clearly into the category of creation".[200]

According to Philippians 2: 6-11, supernatural powers are subservient to Jesus, who has been given the name above all names that every knee in heaven, on earth and under the earth should bow and every tongue confess that Jesus Christ is Lord. This assertion seems to include every rational being, human and

---

[198] J. D. G. Dunn, *Romans 1-8* WBC 38a, (Dallas, Texas: Word Books Publishers, 1988), p. 513; Bauer, Arndt and Gingrich, *A Greek-English Lexicon*, p. 128.

[199] D. G. Reid "Principalities and Powers" in G. F. Hawthorne, R. P. Martin and D. G. Reid (eds.), *Dictionary of Paul and His Letters* (Downers Grove, Illinois/Leicester: Intervarsity Press, 1993), p. 749; Arnold *Powers* p. 120; Bruce J. Long, "Demons: An Overview" in M. Eliade (ed.), *The Encyclopaedia of Religion* Vol. 4 (New York: Macmillan, 1987), 4 p. 285. See also *PGM* IV. 2694-2704, which has reference to the demons of the air, of the earth and of the underworld.

[200] Thomas A. Noble, "The Spirit World: A Theological Approach" in Anthony N. S. Lane (ed.) *The Unseen World: Christian Reflection on Angels, Demons and the Heavenly Realm* (Carlisle, Cumbria/Grand Rapids, Michigan: Paternoster Press/Baker Book House, 1996), p. 193.

spiritual, good and evil, as ultimately and presently submissive to Christ's rule.²⁰¹ In Ephesians 1: 21 supernatural powers are linked with παντὸς ὀνόματος ὀνομαζομένου. Perhaps the mention of ὄνομα in Philippians 2: 9 and Ephesians 1: 21 addressed a cultural milieu, wherein it was popularly held that successful magical manipulation of evil powers was to be attested or affirmed in the knowledge of the power's name. The phrases τὸ ὄνομα τὸ ὑπὲρ πᾶν ὄνομα (Phil 2: 9) and ὑπεράνω πάσης... καὶ παντὸς ὀνόματος ὀνομαζομένου (Eph 1: 21) certainly stress the supremacy and sovereignty of Christ over every power known or unknown, real or imagined, present or future. Having been resurrected and exalted, Christ re-asserted his supremacy over supernatural powers, which they already knew during his earthly life (Mk. 1: 23-25; Lk. 4: 33-25). The supremacy of Christ is well attested by the existence of all things that originate from Him, including supernatural powers.

ii. The Existence and Resistance of the Church

One cannot speak of supernatural powers without mentioning Christ and the church. Even if Paul is silent on the fall of supernatural powers, some are fallen and have become the enemies of Christ and the church. Nevertheless, Christ's church exists amidst her enemies, which are not flesh and blood but supernatural powers. According to Ephesians 3: 10, it is διὰ τῆς ἐκκλησίας that the manifold wisdom of God is made known to supernatural powers. How does the church do this? It is not by preaching as Wink claims.²⁰² Most scholars agree that Paul never intended the church to carry out any evangelism, social action or any other activity to supernatural powers.²⁰³ In all probability, the phrase διὰ τῆς ἐκκλησίας signifies the existence of the church, now seen as a multiracial community made of Jews and Gentiles. In that case, the existence of the church is the means by which the manifold wisdom of God is made known to supernatural powers. The church therefore does not play an active role but a passive one, not "in the sense of failing to resist the influence of the "powers" but in the sense that it does not act as a dispatched agent to proclaim the message of God's dominion to the "powers".²⁰⁴ In fact, the passive γνωρισθῇ implies that it is God himself who make his wisdom (through the mystery hidden in Him v.9) known to supernatural powers. In that case, the church passively and visibly testifies to God's wisdom by *her very existence*. However, the powers to which the manifold wisdom of God is made known are in the heavenly places just like the powers hostile to the church in Ephesians 6: 10-20.

---

[201] Cf. Isa. 45: 23; 24: 21.
[202] See Wink, *Naming the Powers*, pp. 93, 95-96.
[203] See O'Brien, *The Letter to the Ephesians*, p. 246; S. E. Porter, *Idioms of the Greek New Testament* (Sheffield: Academic Press, 1994), pp.149-50; Arnold, *Ephesians: Power and Magic*, p. 63; Martin Dibelius, *Die Geisterwelt im Glauben des Paulus* (Göttingen: Vandenhoeck & Ruprecht, 1909), p.161, note 1.
[204] Arnold, *Ephesians: Power and Magic*, p. 63.

Through her own existence, the church makes known the manifold wisdom of God to the enemies of Christ and his church. This is an encouragement to a people who lived in a background where supernatural powers were greatly feared. As Arnold contends, "the readers would find great encouragement in knowing that the 'powers' can see that they have been devastatingly foiled by the emerging of the body of Christ, the church. This would also give the readers added assurance of victory over the 'powers' as they engage in spiritual warfare and await the consummation of the age to come".[205]

The church not only exists amidst enemies but she also resists the same enemies through the power of the Lord and the strength of his might. Could it be that the language of the church vis-à-vis her enemies is metaphorical, having been drawn from the experiences of the Jewish people, so as to explain the supremacy of Christ? During the Second Temple era, Palestinian Judaism faced a historic but acute theological problem as to the Roman occupying power, which endangered the purity of the Temple and Torah as well as their sacred history. This, more than a socio-political problem, was a religio-cultural dilemma, which required a theodicy. The Qumran War Scrolls (1QM; 4QM 491-496) provide the apocalyptic perspective with which this doctrinal problem was voiced. The scrolls, perhaps being dependent on the eschatological battle in Daniel 11: 40–12: 3, depicts the war in which the righteous Jews (referred to as the Sons of Light) are assisted by Michael and other angelic forces to defeat the 'sons of darkness' who are assisted by Beliar and his powers of darkness.[206] This synthesis of the language and imagery of divine warfare with the traditional names of Israel's foes and the participation of angelic powers, probably anticipates a tradition that would, henceforth, metaphorically swap the ancient enemies of Israel with supernatural powers as the enemies of Christ and his church. This may have been the start of a developing tradition by which the Pauline theology of supernatural powers can be mirrored.

Paul's conversion to Christianity definitely transformed his Jewish theology, which regarded the nations as the enemies of Israel. The Gentiles, who once were 'far off' aliens and enemies (Eph. 2: 17; Col 1: 21-22) had now become the focus of God's emancipating grace. The Gentile nations therefore could not and cannot be the enemies and the subject of the Old Testament divine warfare imagery. Through the death of Christ on the cross (Gal 3: 10–14), an opening was created for Jews and Gentiles to form the one new eschatological person in Christ (Eph 2: 11–22). The true enemies were no longer the Romans, but spiritual powers behind human authority and empires of this world. This is a worldview that Paul and many other Jews probably shared[207] and may provide the framework for discerning the enemies of Christ and of the church. It is clear that these foes are not flesh and blood but supernatural powers that could, according to the views of that time, control socio-political and religio-cultural

---

[205] Arnold, *Ephesians: Power and Magic*, p. 64.
[206] 1QM 1: 1-17. See Reid, "Principalities and Powers", p. 750.
[207] Jub. 15: 30-32; 1 En. 89: 59-61; 90: 20-25, where the seventy shepherds seem to represent the angels of the nation.

institutions. Since Christ will finally destroy every rule, authority, power and death, it is plausible that ἀρχὴ, ἐξουσίαι, δύναμις and θάνατος (1Cor 15: 24-26) are real enemies of Christ and the church. That these powers play the role of probable hinderers of the love of Christ (Rom 8: 38-9) in the redemption drama implies they are the antagonists of Christ and the church. The hostility of supernatural powers to the church is therefore unmistakable.

As noted above, the church's existence testifies the supremacy of Christ, who strengthens her to resist supernatural powers despite their opposition to her existence (Eph 6: 10-20). The church resists supernatural powers by putting on the whole armour of God. The earthly resistance of the church is set against a metaphor reminiscent of the Jewish holy war. However, a major difference between the church's struggle and the Jewish holy war is that the church does not fight against flesh and blood but against intangible principalities, powers, world rulers of this present darkness and spiritual forces of evil ἐν τοῖς ἐπουρανίοις (Eph 6: 12). The weapons of the church are both for attacking and defending but the power of the militant church is "in the Lord and in the strength of his might". The church resists the enemy from the position of power founded on Christ's defeat of supernatural powers, which also testifies to Christ's supremacy. While the archetype of the warfare is unmistakably Jewish, the terminology and military paraphernalia are taken from the Graeco-Roman world. This indicates that even if the Pauline concept of supernatural powers is Jewish, it was meant to interact with the hearts of his Graeco-Roman audience. Is shifting domination and resistance from tangible nations to intangible spiritual powers an attempt to move from the known to the unknown by way of metaphor? This will be discussed in chapter six but now we turn to the defeat of supernatural powers as evidence of Christ's supremacy.

iii. The Defeat of Supernatural Powers

The limited knowledge of supernatural powers regarding God's plan of redemption (1Cor 2: 6–8) contributed to their defeat. The rulers of this age could not understand God's wisdom so they crucified the Lord of glory expecting to frustrate God's salvific plan. They did know that by crucifying Christ, they were being reduced from hero to zero and so sealing their own fate. The verb καταργέω used here not only means 'destroy' but also 'render powerless or ineffective', 'abolish', 'nullify', 'cease' and 'wipe out'.[208] It is most likely that Paul did not intend to convey the idea of total annihilation but that of destroying or depriving the ability of supernatural powers to work

---

[208] See F. W. Danker and F. W. Gingrich *A Greek-English Lexicon of the New Testament and Other Early Christian Literature* (Chicago: University of Chicago Press, 1979), p. 417; GNM Morphology and Barclay-Newman Greek Dictionary as represented in the BibleWorks for Windows Copyright © (1998) BibleWorks, LLC.

evil.[209] Thus even if the powers may seemingly appear very active in opposing the church, their fate is fixed. The death and resurrection of Christ marked the start of the destruction of their ability to work evil as implied in 1 Corinthians 2: 6-8. Their ultimate destruction awaits the eschaton, before Christ 'hands over the Kingdom to God the Father' (1Cor 15: 24). The debate among scholars, however, is whether supernatural powers have been stripped of their powers and brought into the service of Christ or whether they have been absolutely defeated or will be finally destroyed. Since the powers are still opposed to God's purpose and to the church, their ultimate defeat is yet to come and so the language of 1 Corinthians 15: 24 suggest their end. The context powerfully suggests the out-and-out defeat of supernatural powers, with no possibility of redemption.[210]

Colossians 2: 15 exposes rebellious and evil supernatural powers that God conquered in Christ or by the cross. The powers were disarmed and publicly exposed in a triumphal procession. At the cross, Christ's death stripped from supernatural powers the ability they may have had against him and his church. For that reason, supernatural powers cannot exert their potent influence over the people whom Christ has claimed for himself. The participle ἀπεκδυσάμενος (translated 'disarmed') although in the middle voice, should be interpreted in the active voice.[211] In that case, Christ did not strip from himself[212] but God stripped off the ability of supernatural powers through Christ or in the cross of Christ. Thus ἐν αὐτῷ (v. 15) can either refer to Christ or to the cross of Christ. It follows therefore that God is the subject and so the accusative phrase τὰς ἀρχὰς καὶ τὰς ἐξουσίας must be the object of the participle ἀπεκδυσάμενος.[213] It was in the cross of Christ or in Christ that the powers were publicly exposed as weak and a disgrace or even a mockery. The aorist indicative verb ἐδειγμάτισεν that holds the idea of public exposure can also be translated as 'disgraced' or even 'mocked'. The notion of exposure in relation to the displaying and disgracing of demonic powers is clearly articulated in Jewish tradition.[214] The triumphal procession, to be fair, was a celebration of Christ's victory and reign over supernatural powers.

Such a triumphal procession (θριαμβεύω) was regular when Roman generals defeated the opposing forces and won a battle. The disheartened and subjugated opponent and his army became a public spectacle for ridicule and were paraded for all to see. Similarly, God put the conquered supernatural powers on public display, revealing their weakness before Christ and indicating the supremacy of

---

[209] Arnold, *Powers*, p. 163; C. K. Barrett, *The First Epistle to the Corinthians* HNTC (San Francisco: Harper & Low, 1968), p. 358.
[210] Reid, "Principalities and Powers", p. 751.
[211] It is notable that the same participle is used in the active sense in Col 3: 9.
[212] Against Carr, *Angels and Principalities*, p. 61.
[213] Arnold, *The Colossian Syncretism*, pp. 278-280.
[214] See *Ascension of Isaiah* 3: 13; *Acts of Peter* 32[3].

Christ.²¹⁵ Yet a minority of scholars have rejected the traditional interpretation, to argue instead that τὰς ἀρχὰς καὶ τὰς ἐξουσίας are not evil powers but good angels from the throne of God who worshipped Christ in the celebration of his majesty.²¹⁶ This interpretation is not tenable and does injustice to the context of Colossians, which does not portray supernatural powers as adoring Christ. The context points to the supremacy of Christ as the creator of, and the *raison d'être* of supernatural powers' existence. In fact, the text and context expose τὰς ἀρχὰς καὶ τὰς ἐξουσίας as spiritual beings behind the written code and its regulations, which were against human efforts to attain the fullness of life.²¹⁷ Carr and Yates seem to ignore that Paul's theology resolutely upholds the supremacy of Christ over supernatural powers. They overlook the idea that most of the Pauline references to ἀρχὰς καὶ ἐξουσίας indicate evil spiritual beings. They specifically fail to notice that Ephesians 1: 21-22 explains Christ's never-ending supremacy over supernatural powers. God, having raised Christ from the dead, exalted and installed Him to a position of power far above all conceivable supernatural powers.

Christ's death and resurrection is not only effective for acquiring the forgiveness of sins but also for defeating supernatural powers that could impede God's redemptive plan. The forgiveness of sins and the defeat of τὰς ἀρχὰς καὶ τὰς ἐξουσίας are closely linked, since it is through the forgiveness of sins that believers are transferred from the kingdom of darkness to the Kingdom of God (Col 1: 13). It is clear that through Christ's death and resurrection, the forgiveness of sins, including the wiping out of τὸ χειρόγραφον,²¹⁸ was ended. The forgiveness of sin and the wiping out of τὸ χειρόγραφον (Col 2: 13-14) mean that supernatural powers have been disarmed (2: 15).²¹⁹ Their disarming sums up the thoughts in the avowal of the forgiveness of τὰ παραπτώματα and the annulment of τὸ χειρόγραφον. Does this imply that supernatural powers could work with and through sin and the legal demands to inhibit human efforts to attain the fullness of life in Christ? Altogether, the zenith of the forgiveness of τὰ παραπτώματα, the annulment of τὸ χειρόγραφον and the disarming of the powers is accomplished in and through the death, resurrection and exaltation of Christ.

---

²¹⁵ Eduard Lohse, *Colossians and Philemon* (Philadelphia: Fortress Press, 1971), p. 112; Arnold, *Powers*, p. 106.

²¹⁶ See Carr, *Angels and Principalities*. pp. 47-85; Roy, "Christ and the Powers", pp. 461-8.

²¹⁷ Forbes, "Principalities and Powers", p. 70.

²¹⁸ Χειρόγραφον refers to a record of one's debts. See Adolf Deissmann, *Bible Studies* (Edinburgh: T & T Clark, 1901), p. 247; Roy Yates, "Colossians 2: 14: Metaphor of Forgiveness" in *Biblica* 90 (1990), pp. 248-259; Arnold, *The Colossian Syncretism*, pp 292-3; T. J. Sappington, *Revelation and Redemption at Colossae* JSNTSup 53 (Sheffield; JSOT Press, 1991), pp. 214-220; P. T O'Brien, *Colossians, Philemon* WBC 44 (Waco, Texas: Word Books, 1982), p. 125; Petr Pokorný, *Colossians: A Commentary* (Peabody, Massachusetts: Hendrickson, 1991), p. 139.

²¹⁹ Sappington, *Revelation and Redemption*, pp. 211-223.

Christ has therefore defeated supernatural powers (Col 2: 15), reclaiming his own from the kingdom of darkness (Col 1: 12–14). Supernatural powers are now subjected to the rule and authority of the exalted Christ, who is reigning as the heavenly king (Phil 2: 9; Col 3: 1; Eph 1: 21) and receives praise and obeisance (Phil 2: 10).[220] Yet the other side of Paul's theology indicates that supernatural powers are still opposed to Christ and his church (Eph 6: 10-18) even with the claims that they have been conquered. There is an anticipated victory at the end when Christ will deliver the kingdom to God the Father (1Cor 15: 24). So how does the claim that Christ has defeated and shamed supernatural powers make sense? Perhaps this can be explained through the typical New Testament tension between a "now" and a "not yet" eschatology. Between now and the eschaton the powers will persistently seek to undo what Christ has done. But Christ empowers his own church to unflinchingly resist their attacks. At the end, like the kings of the Gentiles nations who were enemies of the Davidic kingship (cf. Ps 110), Christ's enemies (supernatural powers and death) that exercise authority and dominion in this age will be finally placed under Christ's feet (1 Cor 15: 24-28). For now, Christ reigns in the midst of his enemies (cf. Ps 110: 2), which include supernatural powers, sin and death. Oscar Cullmann sought to solve this tension with the analogy of D-Day and V-Day based on the events of the Second World War.[221] This analogy may very well relate to the conflict between Christ's church and all her enemies.

5:4. Conclusion

The Pauline texts recognize the existence of spiritual beings, which operate in a cosmic theatre. The texts suggest their domain is in heaven and earth, this age, in the heavenly and the underworld.[222] Nevertheless, Christ's supremacy permeates the three-tiered universe and so spiritual beings in the heavens, on the earth and in the underworld, have no sovereign status as they are subject to Christ.[223] But it is also evident that the Pauline terminology and concept of supernatural powers do hold some common features. The texts noticeably introduce and explain supernatural powers in relation to Christ and the life of the church. The primary concerns of the concept are Christological and pastoral.[224] The concept frequently uses Jewish ideas and Graeco-Roman imagery and paraphernalia, perhaps metaphorically, to drive the point home. The Pauline terminological framework somewhat differed from that of Jewish apocalyptic and Greek magical texts, which some exegetes believe influenced

---

[220] Reid, "Principalities and Powers", p. 751.
[221] Oscar Cullmann, *Christ and Time*. (Philadelphia, Pennsylvania: The Westminster Press, 1951), pp.139-143.
[222] Eph. 2: 2; 3: 10; 6: 12; Phil. 2: 10.
[223] M. Barth and H. Blanke, *Colossians* (AB, New York: Doubleday, 1994), p. 202; Forbes, "Pauline Demonology", p. 72.
[224] Ferdinando, *The Triumph of Christ*, p 241.

him. The Jewish conceptual understanding of pagan gods agrees with Paul's depiction of the same. In the same way, his conceptual framework agrees with several Graeco-Roman philosophers, who disparaged Graeco-Roman gods, as understood by the populace, as no gods.

It is clear as to what the Pauline terms and concept of supernatural powers meant to the author and what they communicated to the readers. Even if the terms could refer to human agents, in most of the Pauline texts, they refer to animate and personal spiritual beings inimical to Christ and his church. The concept clearly reveals that supernatural powers can work in and through other external and internal forces to keep people under control and in disobedience to God. These powers could exploit the flesh and the world, and it follows that supernatural powers such as 'the god of this world' (2 Cor 4: 4) and τὰ στοιχεῖα τοῦ κόσμου (Gal. 4: 3; Col 2: 8, 20) could exert tremendous sway in the socio-political and religio-cultural structures of human existence. But the capability of the powers is provisional since they are still under the control of God even if inimical to Christ and his church. Though they might appear powerful in this age, the church can withstand them and by her existence in and through Christ, let them know the manifold wisdom of God. Because the church exists, the powers do not have the ability to thwart what Christ has instituted. Christ has now immobilized their genius to deny believers the fullness of life. Their power will be finally destroyed in the eschaton, when Christ will give the kingdom to God (1Cor 15: 24). Paul's message to his first century CE audience was that of Christ's supremacy over and against his enemies and those of the church. Still, it is critical to interact with some selected scholars who interpret supernatural powers from the perspective of myth, claiming that Paul demythologised the Jewish apocalyptic and mythological terminology.

CHAPTER 6

Previous Interpretations: Interacting with Some Selected Scholars Who Deal with Supernatural Powers from the Perspective of Myth

6:1. Introduction

Is myth, and by extension demythologisation, a suitable tool with which to interpret the Pauline concept of supernatural powers? This question has been motivated by the fact that many modern interpreters deal with the concept of supernatural powers from the perspective of myth. The dominant nineteenth century view was that myth was part of an antediluvian worldview, which modern people could dispense with, so as to come up with a message of timeless value. Little attention was paid to supernatural powers and the prevailing mind-set was that they were vestiges of ancient mythology, so insignificant in Paul's thinking. Otto Everling acknowledged that Paul believed in the existence of a multitude of devilish beings that inhabit the air under the command of Satan[1] but he regarded them as absolutely of inferior significance in Paul's view; hence they should receive trifling attention.[2] The idea that the New Testament's cosmology was essentially mythical contributed to an anti-supernaturalistic mentality, leading liberal scholars such as Harnack, to claim that there was no such thing as miracles.[3] What Harnack did was to reduce the kerygma to some basic principles of religion—love of God and neighbour—which are timeless and eternal. It was thus critical to distinguish between the core of religion and the temporary garb with which Christianity was clothed during the New Testament era. As with miracles, Harnack, as O'Brien notes, regarded references to supernatural powers as part of the temporary garb that must be discarded.[4]

Dibelius, though following Everling, maintained that a world dominated by supernatural forces was central to Paul's thinking. He admitted that in Paul's

---

[1] Otto Everling, *Die Paulinische Angelologie und Dämonologie* (Göttingen: Vandenhoeck & Ruprecht, 1888), p. 109.
[2] Everling, *Die Paulinische,* p. 4.
[3] Adolf von Harnack, *What is Christianity?* Vol. IV (New York: G. P. Putnam's Sons, 1901), p. 27.
[4] O'Brien, "Principalities and Powers", p. 111.

view these forces were hostile to human existence and this was the framework within which Paul developed his view about human existence and the work of Christ. He insisted that the distinctiveness of Paul's message was his belief that Christ had conquered these powers. He thus identified a special significance of supernatural powers in relation to eschatology and Christology. He held that rejecting this significance was to jettison a part of the Pauline faith. He also held that with the concept of spirits and devils disappearing, the language and concept of supernatural powers was insignificant for a modern Christian.[5] For that reason, it was critical to ascertain the real meaning of Paul's message concerning human existence. Evidently, the claims that supernatural powers were trivial in Paul's thoughts and irrelevant for modern people somewhat impelled an existentialist and structuralist interpretation of supernatural powers. It is clear that after Dibelius the Pauline concept of supernatural powers received little or no attention and became a neglected emphasis in New Testament theology.[6]

Several years after the first quarter of the twentieth century, a new interest in supernatural powers in Pauline thinking began to emerge. Schlier, as cited by Berkhof, wondered if "we have generally neglected even to ask whether Scripture and Christian tradition might be thinking of definite life experiences when they speak of the devil and the demons".[7] Schlier interpreted supernatural powers not as objective realities but as projections of what Bultmann would later call self-understanding. Schlier somehow contributed to the existentialist interpretation of supernatural powers. Rudolf Bultmann, who reacted to the nineteenth century view that myth could be discarded so as to discern a message of eternal value,[8] might be credited as the one who revolutionalized the study of supernatural powers in the modern era. Concerning the heavenly powers in Paul's theology, as Dunn notes, "this whole area of ancient belief has regularly been identified as a prime example of "myth," and since Bultmann it has been a prime candidate for his programme of demythologisation".[9] Bultmann understood supernatural powers as the expression of human inability to control their world and the future and also in terms of the New Testament's

---

[5] Dibelius, *Die Geisterwelt*, p. 5.
[6] James Stewart, "On a Neglected Emphasis in New Testament Theology" in *Scottish Journal of Theology* 4 (1951), pp. 292-301; Abijole, "The Pauline Concept of Principalities and Powers", pp. 118-129.
[7] Berkhof, *Christ and the Powers*, p. 73.
[8] Rudolf Bultmann, "New Testament and Mythology" in H. W. Bartsch (ed.), *Kerygma and Myth* Vol.1 (London: SPCK, 1964), p. 9; O'Brien, "Principalities and Powers", p. 114; Anthony C. Thiselton, *The Two Horizons* (Exeter: Paternoster Press, 1980), pp. 205-208; J. D. G. Dunn, "Demythologizing – The Problems of Myth in the New Testament" in I. H. Marshall (ed.), *New Testament Interpretation: Essays in Principles and Method* (Exeter: The Paternoster Press, 1977), p. 289.
[9] Dunn, *The Theology of Paul*, p. 110.

call for existential liberation.[10] He contends that Paul was "only expressing a certain understanding of existence: The spirit powers represented the reality into which man is placed as one full of conflicts and struggle, a reality which threatens and tempts".[11] Central to Bultmann's hermeneutics is his understanding of myth. In his opinion, myth was all-encompassing and it could not be simply discarded. With the Gospel suffused with myth, to discard the myth was to discard the Gospel. He regarded myth as the pre-scientific view of the world that modern man could no longer accept. But demythologisation could not simply strip the mythical worldview away. Rather, the message of the New Testament had to be re-appreciated and re-interpreted in modern terms. To demythologise therefore was not to reject the Christian Gospel but the mythic worldview with which it was clothed. Walter Wink, following a structuralist reading embraced to some extent by other scholars before him,[12] maintains that Bultmann's demythologisation was a move in the right direction but from the wrong foundation. His quest, like that of Bultmann and other modern interpreters, has been to extract a relevant message for the modern era from the myth through "demythologisation", a programme which is claimed to have originated from Paul and other New Testament writers such as John.

This chapter will focus mainly on Bultmann and Wink, who are regarded as the most influential twentieth century scholars with regard to the subject of supernatural powers. It is important to identify how these scholars understood myth because demythologisation largely depends on each scholar's working definition of myth. Nevertheless, the idea of demythologising the myth of supernatural powers is a complex issue that a chapter cannot adequately handle, for this would require at least a monograph. The big issues are the definition of myth, the truth of myth and whether mythology is expendable or indispensable. This chapter will first look at the problems of myth, which perhaps make it a less useful tool than metaphor in dealing with supernatural powers. Secondly, the chapter will interact with Bultmann's and Wink's handling of supernatural powers. This will be followed by some key considerations with regard to demythologisation. Thirdly, the chapter will look at metaphor, attempting to demonstrate that metaphor could be a more useful tool to deal with supernatural powers in Paul than myth. It will be seen that metaphors too have problems that may widen the referential problem of supernatural powers.

---

[10] Rudolf Bultmann, *Theology of the New Testament* Vol. 1 (London: SCM Press, 1952), pp. 258-9. Cf. L. Bautista, H. B. Garcia and Sze-Kar Wan "Asian Way of Thinking in Theology" in *Evangelical Review of Theology* 6 (1982), pp. 37-49, esp. p. 43.
[11] Bultmann, *Theology of the New Testament*, p. 259.
[12] See R. J. Sider, "Christ and Powers" in *International Review of Mission* 69 (1980), p. 12; Gordon Rupp, *Principalities and Powers: Studies in the Christian Conflict in History* (London: Epworth, 1952), p. 11-2; Berkhof, *Christ and the Powers*, p. 23; Amos N. Wilder, *Kerygma, Eschatology and Social Ethics* (Philadelphia: Fortress Press, 1966), pp. 23-30; G. B. Caird, *Principalities and Powers*, pp. 90-110; J. H. Yoder, *The Politics of Jesus* (Grand Rapids, Michigan: Eerdmans, 1972), pp. 137-142; Richard Mouw, *Politics and the Biblical Drama* (Grand Rapid, Michigan: Eerdmanns, 1976), pp. 87-115.

6:2 Understanding Myth and Its Truth

i. The Problem of Definition

The subject of myth and its truth are elusive, exceedingly slippery, vast and complicated. Different views as to what myth is and its reality presents a wide-ranging perspective of understanding myth and its truth.[13] To do justice to the definition of myth, one, as Dunn notes, would require an extensive competence in such different fields such as early Greek literature and drama, the comparative study of religion, philosophy of history, anthropology and psychoanalysis.[14] Caird, after scrutinizing no less than nine views and definitions of myth from various schools of thought[15] judiciously writes, "Faced with this array of opinion, we shall be wise to conclude that myth has a complexity which defies all attempts of the foolhardy to reduce it to a single origin or function".[16] What complicates myth from the very beginning is the problem of definition. "There is no one definition of myth, no platonic form of a myth against which all actual instances can be measured".[17] Indeed the problem of defining myth goes back to the ancient usage of μύθος, which etymologically, as several sources suggests, can mean 'a word' or 'a story'. Of note is that in ancient Greek literature, the meaning of μύθος could vary from a "true story", "an account of facts" to an invented story, legend, fairly story, fable or poetic creation.[18] It is also noteworthy that in later Greek thought, μύθος was regarded as the antithesis of rational thought (*logos*) and history.[19] The understanding was that myth signified "what cannot really exist" and anything which is opposed to reality. This was a Graeco-Roman legacy that dominated Western academic thinking. Moreover, as Dunn demonstrates, the precise meaning of myth became a subject of vigorous debates from different schools of thought, resulting in three competing views. The first view is that myth is a story whose subject is the primeval age and whose role is to provide a

---

[13] See Dunn, "Demythologizing", pp. 285-307; Caird, *The language and Imagery,* 1980 pp. 219-242.

[14] Dunn, "Demythologizing", p. 285.

[15] See Caird, *The language and Imagery,* pp. 221-4

[16] Caird, *The language and Imagery,* p. 223.

[17] G. S. Kirk, *Myth: Its Meaning and Function in Ancient and Other Cultures* (Cambridge: Cambridge University Press, 1970), p. 7.

[18] See *The Analytical Greek Lexicon,* (London: Samuel Bagster and Sons, n.d.), p. 273; Bauer, Arndt and Gingrich, *A Greek-English Lexicon,* pp. 530-1; Dunn, "Demythologizing", p. 285; G. Stählin " μύθος ", in G. Kittel and G. Friedrich (eds.), *Theological Dictionary of the New Testament* Vol. IV, (Grand Rapids, Michigan: Eerdmans, 1992), pp. 766-769.

[19] According to Plato (*The Republic* 376-7), even if traditional myths were false (ψεῦδος) they had value in teaching children and they were an indispensable complement to rational thought.

basis for the present world and social order in primordial times.[20] The second view is that myth is a primitive conceptual form, the mode of conception and expression in the childhood of the human race, exposing the structures of primitive consciousness as yet untouched by modern science. Yet "the growth of myth has been checked by science, it is dying of weights and measures, of proportions and specimen".[21] This view is in fact foremost in the debate on the relevance of demythologisation as a hermeneutical solution to the New Testament.[22] The third view portrays myth as poetry, belonging to a sphere where it is judged by standards other than that of its understanding of the world. It is thus a symbol and drama able to awaken feelings, invite thought and evoke response.[23]

The issue about the truth of myth is as controversial as the issue of what it is. Reading the pages of Dunn and Caird, one would find no fewer than six views on its truth. One view implies that myths tell something about how primitive people speculated on the natural and strange phenomena and how they coped with the fears of the unknown such as death and the afterlife. It also explains how primitive people discerned mysteries surrounding their experiences allegedly caused by gods, demons and spirits and how to control these powers by ritual of magic.[24] Another view supposes that myth developed as an appendix to ritual performance and is closely related to social structure. Its truth is explicit in legitimising the cult since it takes the place of dogma. In this sense, the truth of myth lies in its attempt to justify a people's rights, loyalties and beliefs. These could be traced back to the primeval times and which hitherto continue to influence the world and human destiny.[25] Thirdly, according to the psychoanalytic view, the truth of myth is to tell something about human nature. This, as in dreams, occurs through the expression of the subconscious, the archetypal images rising from the depths of humanity. Myth therefore is "the natural and indispensable intermediate stage between

---

[20] See Mircea Eliade, *The Myth of the Eternal Return* (Princeton, New Jersey: Princeton University Press, 1954), p. 5.
[21] Tylor, *Primitive,* p. 317.
[22] See Dunn, "Demythologizing", pp. 285, 302 footnote 5.
[23] See Paul Ricoeur, *The Symbolism of Evil* (New York: Harper & Row, 1967).
[24] See Tylor, *Primitive,* p. 317.
[25] See Smith, *Lectures on the Religion,* pp. 17-21; Bronsilav Malinowski, *Myth in Primitive Psychology* (London: Kegan Paul, Trench, Trubner & Co, 1927), pp. 92, 100; Bronsilav Malinowski, "Primitive Religion and Primitive Science" in Julian Huxley, J. Arthur Thomson, J. S. Haldane and others, *Science and Religion: A Symposium* (London: Gerald Howe, 1931), pp. 65-81; Bronsilav Malinowski, "The Problem of Meaning in Primitive Languages" in C. K. Ogden and I. A. Richards (eds.), *The Meaning of Meaning* (London: Kegan Paul, 1946), pp. 296-336. Cf. Kirk, *Myth: Its Meaning,* pp. 12-29; Pannenberg, *Basic Questions in Theology* (London: SCM Press, 1973), pp. 5-8; Dunn, "Demythologizing", p. 287; Caird, *The language and Imagery,* p. 221.

unconscious and conscious cognition",[26] the "original revelation of the preconscious psyche, and involuntary statements about unconscious psychic happenings".[27] In that case, the operative value of myth is in its expression of "deep-seated and permanent human needs, and at the same time as a means of directing the flood of emotion into socially acceptable channels".[28]

A fourth view concerning the truth of myth originates from the idea of the uniformity of the structure of the mind. Anthropologist C. Lévi-Strauss regards the structure of myth as identical with the structure of the human mind. Human thinking is a process of binary analysis, so myth is a model in which the binary division in society, the contradictions in humankind's view of the world (between village and jungle, male and female, life and death, earth and sky) can be resolved and overcome. The general idea is that the truth of myth reveals human striving to create order out of the contradictions in which people find themselves.[29] Its truth therefore lies in its function as "an instrument for social manipulation and control, the means with which social movements win support by presenting themselves to the imagination as struggles for an eventually victorious cause".[30] It "carries the lines of logos organically beyond the frontiers of conceptual knowledge... It arises when there is need to express something which can be expressed in other way".[31] Even if myth "always refers to events alleged to have taken place in time: before the world was created, or during its first stages...what gives the myth an operative value is that the specific pattern described is everlasting; it explains the present and the past as well as the future".[32] Lévi-Strauss maintains that the true message of myth has nothing to do with the context, as it is a piece of algebra about the working of human mind in the abstract.

Fifthly, the truth of myth is also viewed from the poetic perspective, where myth is regarded as the expression of a whole area of human experience and awareness of values and truths presented only in symbolic language. Myth, according to Tylor, shapes "those endless analogies between man and nature which are the soul of all poetry...so full to us of unfading life and beauty", though they "are the masterpiece of an art belonging rather to the past than to the present".[33] Tylor recognises the affinity between myth and poetry, even with his view that myth has been checked by science and it is not only dying

---

[26] Carl Jung, *Memoirs, Dreams and Reflection* (London: Collins and Routledge & Kegan Paul, 1963), p. 343.
[27] Kirk, *Myth: Its Meaning*, p. 279.
[28] Caird, *The language and Imagery*, p. 223.
[29] C. Levi-Strauss, *Structural Anthropology* (Harmondsworth: Penguin Books, 1963), esp. chapter 4; Kirk, *Myth: Its Meaning*, pp. 42-83; Dunn, "Demythologizing", p. 287.
[30] Caird, *The language and Imagery*, p. 222, paraphrasing sociologist Georges Sorel's view of myth.
[31] Stählin, "μύθος", p. 774.
[32] C. Lévi-Strauss "The Structural Study of Myth" in T. A. Sebeok, *Myth—A Symposium* (Bloomington: Indiana University Press, 1958), p. 85.
[33] Tylor, *Primitive*, p. 317.

but also half dead. He recognises its use of analogies, the symbolic language, which Jasper contends is "the cipher language of myth".[34] Myth therefore is "the poet's awareness of a "moreness" to life than eating, sleeping, working, loving, without wishing or attempting to define that "moreness" except by means of evocative images and symbols".[35] The sixth view, now from the perspective of comparative religion, regards myth as a distinct religious experience. It would seem the truth of myth is in its ability to convey the awareness of the numinous. Its significance, according to Ricoeur, is in its power to discover and to reveal the bond between people and what they consider sacred.[36] As Rudolf Otto asserts, myth is not just a human response to what they think of as divine, but is itself somehow revelatory of the divine. In this sense, "stories about gods" may not always and simply be the expression of a primitive and unscientific age. They are mainly the product of religious consciousness, "the vestibule at the threshold of the real religious feelings, an earliest stirring of the numinous".[37] Myth is therefore an entrance to the innate religious experiences. But Eliade seems to be enlivening the view that religious experiences generated by myth belong to the so-called primitive era of human society in maintaining, "For all *primitive mankind*, it is religious experience which lays the foundation of the world".[38]

It is apparent that most views on myth decisively consign myth to the so-called primitive era of human society. Testifying how the "which came first?" controversy in relation to ritual and myth may be wrongly conceived, Dunn insists that the reason for this is the fact that "the roots of both *myth* and *ritual* may lie in *primitive man's* attempts to express an irreducibly religious experience".[39] According to Kirk, "the *primitive mentality* does not invent myths, it expresses them".[40] However, it could be problematic to relegate myth to the so-called primitive mentality faced with such varied views of myth especially if myth is indispensable. It could be even more complex especially at this time when the primal worldview, which most people would agree is full of myths, is emerging as a significant tool facilitating the spread and reception of biblical teachings especially in the African context.[41] Yet Dunn's view that

---

[34] K. Jasper, "Myth and Religion", in H. W. Bartsch (ed.), *Kerygma and Myth* Vol.1 (London: SPCK, 1964), p. 145.
[35] Dunn, "Demythologizing", pp. 287, 302 footnote 13.
[36] Ricoeur, *The Symbolism*, p. 5.
[37] Rudolf Otto, *The Idea of the Holy* (London: Oxford University Press, 1923), p. 126.
[38] Mircea Eliade, *Myths, Dreams and Mysteries*, (New York: Harper Torchbooks, 1960), p. 19, emphasis mine.
[39] Dunn, "Demythologizing", p. 287, emphasis mine.
[40] Kirk, *Myth: Its Meaning,* p. 229, emphasis mine.
[41] J. S. Mbiti, *The Bible and Theology in African Christianity* (Nairobi: Oxford University Press, 1986), p.7; J. S. Mbiti "The Bible in African Culture" in Rosino Gibellini (ed.) *Paths of African Theology* (London: SCM Press, 1994), pp. 27-39; Bediako, *Primal Religions*; Gillian M. Bediako, "Primal Religion and Christian Faith: Antagonists or Soul-mates? In *Journal of African Christian thought* Vol. 3 No.1 (June

myth is a human effort to express an irreducible religious experience is pertinent. It may imply that demythologisation, in its attempt to reduce or replace myth, could be a sort of reductionism.

ii. The Indispensability of Myth

Jung states, "No science will ever replace myth, and a myth cannot be made out of any science. For it is not that God is a myth, but that myth is the revelation of a divine life in man. It is not we who invent myth, rather it speaks to us as a word of God".[42] Caird adds that it is a fallacy that science is hostile to myth since both are systems of explanation.[43] If as Ricoeur maintains, myths are narratives about the origin and end of things, could it be that every human society, ancient or modern, operates in a mythical framework? Indeed, Ricoeur asserts that myths "are not fables but a particular way in which man places himself in relation to the fundamental reality, whatever it may be".[44] This specifically conveys the primary function of myth without judging its precision. The key point is that myth plays a vital role in human society for it is through it that a society gives an account of its origin. Myth forms a common thread that runs through all religions from the most primal to the most modern. It gives the indispensable motivation that enables people to turn away from physical and mechanical perception of the world to the spiritual and ethical. Myths report realities and events from the origin of the world that remain valid for the basis and purpose of all human activity, societal wisdom and knowledge. It seems

---

2000), pp. 12-16; A. F. Walls, "Towards Understanding Africa's Place in Christianity" in J. S. Pobee, (ed.) *Religion in a Pluralistic Society* (Leiden: Brill, 1976), pp. 180-189. A. F. Walls, "Africa and Christian Identity" in *Mission Focus* Vol. iv, No 7 (November 1978), pp. 11-13; A. F. Walls, *The Missionary Movement in Christian History: Studies in the Transmission of Faith* (Maryknoll, New York: Orbis Books, 1996); A. F. Walls, "Of Ivory Towers and Ashrams: Some Thoughts on Theological Scholarship in Africa" in *Journal of African Christian Thought* Vol. 3, No.1, (June 1998), pp. 1-4; A. F. Walls, "In Quest of the Father of Mission Studies" in *International Bulletin of Missionary Research*. Vol. 23 No.3 (July 1999), pp. 98-102, 104-5; Lamin Sanneh, *Translating the Message: The Missionary Impact on Culture* (Maryknoll, New York: Orbis Books, 1989); D. B. Barrett (ed.), *World Christian Encyclopedia* (Nairobi: Oxford University Press, 1982); H. W. Turner, "Primal Religions and their Study" in V. Hayes, *Australian Essays in World Religion* (Bedford Park: Australian Association for the Study of Religion, 1977), p. 32; J. L. Cox, "The Classification Primal Religions as a Non-Empirical Christian Theology", in *Studies in World Christianity*, Vol.2 Pt.1 (1996), p. 52; Ninian Smart, *The Phenomenon of Religion* (New York: The Seabury Press, 1973), pp. 79-120 have shown how myths and rituals preserve a religion from generation to generation and how useful they have been in spreading Christianity in primal societies.
[42] Jung, *Memoirs*, p. 373.
[43] Caird, *The language and Imagery*, p. 221.
[44] Paul Ricoeur, *Freud and Philosophy: An Essay on Interpretation* (New Haven/London: Yale University Press, 1970), p.7.

then that people and all religions operate in a mythical framework, tell sacred stories and express aspects or meanings of the myth in rituals.[45]

This suggests that myths cannot be dismissed as ancient stories that are irrelevant to the modern world. It is overwhelmingly probable that myth is not only irreplaceable but also indispensable and so it plays a key role in human society. Wink notes, "the myth literally replays itself, without any awareness on the part of those who repeat it, under the guise of completely secular stories".[46] He also notes, "the mythic dimension—the atemporal, cosmic, supernatural aspect of the story…has accompanied us from the outset…the mythic is not the residue left over and discardable after everything meaningful has been explained"[47]. Arnold therefore may be right in observing that every society operates in a mythical framework and that in the West, the myths of evolution and materialism have replaced the creation account of Genesis.[48] According to Caird, "the imagination of our own age has been gripped by the myth of the arrival of explorers from outer space, which owes its wide popularity to the fact that it decks out with the apparatus of sophisticated technology the ancient myth of visitants from another and better world".[49] Myth may not be archaic and outdated after all and it could be foundational to human thinking.

The problem is that the advocates of demythologisation seem to evaluate myth and the truth it conveys from the perspective that myth is prehistoric and unscientific and that it carries false notions, though indispensable. It is regrettable and puzzling when the word 'myth' is used to cover the whole range of theological language, implying that anything like speaking about God or spirits is mythical. In this sense, and according to Bultmann, myth is just an imagery to express the otherworldly in terms of this world and the divine in terms of human life, the other side in terms of this side.[50] This view of myth, as nearly all critics of Bultmann's demythologisation would agree, can reduce theology to silence.[51] Dunn's pertinent caution should therefore be taken on board.

It is important, however, that the problem of myth in the New

---

[45] See O'Brien, "Principalities and Powers", p. 116; Thiselton, *Horizons,* p. 289; Bediako, *Primal Religions,* p. 348; Kees W. Bolle, " Myth: An Overview", in Mircea Eliade (ed.), *The Encyclopedia of Religion* Vol. 10 (New York: MacMillan, 1987), p. 261; Ricoeur, *The Symbolism,* p. 5; Ricoeur "Myth and History" in M. Eliade (ed.), *The Encyclopaedia of Religion* Vol. 10 (New York: Macmillan, 1987), pp. 273-4; Cox, "The Classification Primal Religions", p. 62; Caird, *The language and Imagery,* pp. 220, 224.
[46] Walter Wink, *Engaging the Powers: Discernment and Resistance in a World of Domination.* (Minneapolis: Fortress Press, 1992), p. 21.
[47] Wink, *Naming the Powers,* p. 103.
[48] Arnold ,*Powers,* p. 173.
[49] Caird, *The language and Imagery,* p. 221.
[50] See Bultmann, "New Testament and Mythology", p. 16
[51] Caird, *The language and Imagery,* p. 217; O'Brien, "Principalities and Powers", p. 116; Ferdinando, *The Triumph of Christ,* pp. 107-8.

Testament—that is whether there is myth in the New Testament and if so what the exegete does with it—should not be tackled on too narrow a front, but rather should be set in the wider context of the investigation and treatment of myth in other disciplines.[52]

Dunn adds that it is unfair to peg the understanding of myth and its truth on one level of definition. Fairly and appropriately, he notes that the failure of demythologisation is to work on one level of understanding myth, without realising that the New Testament myth can move on all levels of definition.[53] This, in fact, makes demythologisation a complex issue. It implies that demythologising the Pauline concept of supernatural powers, and indeed the entire New Testament, could be contentious, bearing in mind the problem of defining myth.

iii. The Problem of Myth as to the New Testament

It is important to look at the problem of myth from the perspective of the New Testament. The inevitable question is whether there is myth in the New Testament and how it should be defined. In fact, the few times the word μύθος appear in the New Testament (all in the Pauline pastoral epistles except once),[54] though used in a negative sense, does not apply to the teachings of the New Testament but to what opposed its teachings. Generally, the New Testament and particularly the Pauline epistles repudiate myths as "invented and untrue stories". As such, if the New Testament writers were asked if they were dealing with myth defined as the primitive way of looking at reality or invented and untrue stories, their answer would be a straightforward and definite no.[55] It is clear that the New Testament writers did not regard what they were teaching and which they conceived as the right doctrine for the church as mythical in the sense of being fictitious. But as Dunn observes, New Testament writers rejected only one genre of myth. The question whether other levels of myth and mythical thinking are present in the New Testament is not posed or answered. He remarks, "Subsequent attempts to wrestle with myth at this deeper level reveals something of its complexity". What Dunn considers as the 'deeper level' of dealing with myth is "the long and respected tradition of biblical interpretation by means of allegorizing". He seems convinced that in turning to allegory, the allegorizers were expressing dissatisfaction with the obvious meaning, hence treating the biblical narrative as a type of myth whose literal meaning could be ignored.[56] Still, it is not clear whether the New Testament writers knew the other genres of myth known to modern scholars. This leaves the claim that the process of demythologisation began with Paul and other New

---

[52] Dunn, "Demythologizing", p. 285.
[53] Dunn, "Demythologizing", p. 288.
[54] 1 Tim 1: 4; 4: 7; 2 Tim 4: 4; Tit 1: 14; 2 Pt 1: 16.
[55] See Dunn, "Demythologizing", p. 288.
[56] Dunn, "Demythologizing", p. 288.

Testament writers open-ended. In turning to allegory, "is it possible to argue that much of the so-called 'mythological language' of the New Testament is metaphor"?[57] Here, as Ricoeur asserts, it is true that "paradoxical as it may seem, the myth, when it is thus demythologized through contact with scientific history and elevated to the dignity of a symbol, is a dimension of modern thought".[58]

Paul did not have doubts on the Jewish view as to the existence of evil powers. As a man of his own time, he

> never showed any sign of doubt regarding the real existence of principalities and powers. He saw them as angelic beings belonging to Satan's kingdom. Their aim is to lead humanity away from God through direct influence of individuals as well as through wielding control over the world religions and various other structures of our existence.[59]

If myths relate to worldview, being the way by which a society narrates its origin, Paul was definitely indebted to the Old Testament accounts of creation but which he understood in the light of Christ as the new Adam. Yet it is impossible to categorically state the extent to which Paul accepted the Jewish view contained in several apocalyptic texts, which as noted in chapter four, read Genesis 6: 1-4 as an account of the origins of demons. The Pauline texts do not expose Paul as embracing such views. Rather they show that the existence of supernatural powers and their onslaught against believers occupied his thoughts. It might be said with certainty that even if Paul may have worked from the perspective of myth (a story of origin and end), the details of the myth are neither clear nor did they appear to be important to him. If myths are indispensable and Paul was operating in a mythological framework, perhaps he was not demythologising but recalling a myth (a story of origin and end) to metaphorically explain the means with which Satan works and how believers should identify with Christ so as to resist a wide range of supernatural powers, which they believed could inhibit them from attaining the fullness of life. For that reason, the issue is whether Paul's conscious understanding is normative or whether modern scholars can see more clearly what Paul was referring to by turning to a myth or even using metaphorical terms to explain supernatural powers. While the context and background within which we interact with the Pauline concept may enable us to see more clearly what Paul was alluding to, our interpretations should not be regarded as the equivalent of what he was saying. Our interpretations only seek to make what Paul was saying intelligible in our own contexts. It behoves us therefore to interact with some scholars who deal with supernatural powers from the perspective of myth, insisting that Paul himself was engaged in his own kind of demythologisation.

---

[57] O'Brien, "Principalities and Powers", p. 116.
[58] Ricoeur, *The Symbolism*, p. 5.
[59] Arnold, *Powers*, p. 169.

6:3. The Twentieth Century Treatment of Supernatural Powers in Paul

i. Rudolf Bultmann: Interpreting the Myth Existentially

We have mentioned that Bultmann regarded the New Testament cosmology as essentially mythical and the New Testament records as suffused with myth. He depicted myth as a primitive way of explaining strange, curious, surprising, or frightening phenomena and events by attributing their cause to supernatural powers such as gods or demons. Myth therefore expresses the knowledge that human beings are neither the masters of the world nor of their lives. It offers another way of speaking about gods and demons in terms of powers, which humankind suppose they depend on, whose favours they need and whose wrath they fear. Myth enables people to explain riddles and mysteries that abound in their world and life. Bultmann regarded a mythical cosmology as one that depicts the world as a three-tiered structure. The earth is at the centre, above is the heaven, which is the abode of God and celestial beings and below the underworld, which is hell. In this structure, the earth is the scene of the supernatural activities of God and his angels on one hand and of Satan and his minions on the other. These supernatural forces interfere with the course of nature and in all that people think, will and do.[60] Supernatural powers are mythological entities that must be demythologised for modern persons. He justified demythologisation as a process that partially began with Paul and radically with John; so to demythologise is not to discard the myth but to interpret it along existential lines,[61] which was necessary for hermeneutics and exegesis.

Having associated myths to the primitive and pre-scientific worldview, Bultmann suggested that modern scientific and technological advancement forbid belief in miracles and the world of spirits. It is not feasible therefore, to use electric light and the wireless and to take advantage of modern medical and surgical discoveries, and at the same time believe in the New Testament world of spirits and miracles. Discovery of the forces and laws of nature mandates modern people to no longer believe in spirits whether good or evil.[62] These are mythological formulations and allegations representing uncritical thinking and projections of human uneasiness in the cosmos.[63] On the assumption that spirits are mythical, Bultmann maintained that they should be demythologised, that is,

---

[60] Bultmann, "New Testament and Mythology", pp. 1-10.
[61] Rudolf Bultmann, *Jesus Christ and Mythology* (New York: Charles Scribner's Sons, 1958), pp. 18, 32, 34, 45. See also Thiselton, *Horizons*, pp. 205-8; Dunn, "Demythologizing", p. 295.
[62] Bultmann, "New Testament and Mythology", pp. 5, 10.
[63] Reid, "Principalities and Powers", p. 747; O'Brien "Principalities and Powers", pp. 112-115.

interpreted anthropologically or existentially but not cosmologically.[64] Yet, to demythologise is not to deny the Bible or the Christian message, but the worldview of Scriptures, which all too often is retained in Christian teachings and preaching. To demythologise is to deny that the message of Scripture and of the church is bound to an obsolete ancient worldview.[65] Clinging to this worldview would only mean, "Accepting a view of the world in our faith and religion which we should deny in our every day life".[66] In that case, demythologisation eliminates false stumbling blocks and brings "into sharp focus the real stumbling-blocks…"[67]

Bultmann's idea that myths allow supernatural powers to intervene in the affairs of the world and of human existence did not convince all and sundry. According to Pannenberg, every religious understanding of the world basically believes in divine intervention in the course of events. He strongly argues that the belief in demons in the New Testament era was part of their worldview, but it must not be regarded and identified specifically with myth.[68] Similarly, Thiselton argues, "belief about supernatural intervention in the affairs of men…is not necessarily primitive or pre-scientific, as the enlightenment view of myth would imply".[69] So Bultmann's idea of myth, as Dunn suggests, is too all-embracing, confusing myth and analogy. What Bultmann regards as mythical language is in reality metaphorical, symbolical and analogical.[70] It seems that Bultmann's demythologisation illustrates radical reductionism for it reduces and removes not only the activity of Satan and his minions but also the working of God in human life. Was Bultmann's existential interpretation meant to straitjacket supernatural powers into the assumptions of a modern worldview?[71] Bultmann seems to have been a committed Christian scholar, who sought to make the Gospel message relevant to his "modern man", who is not universally representative. Fee maintains that Bultmann's "modern man", who cannot believe in such realities, is the true "myth", not the gospel he set out to "demythologise".[72]

Despite its flaws, demythologisation has a pertinent offer to hermeneutics. Bultmann asserts that hermeneutics is not independent from the interpreters' pre-understanding or a prior life-relation to the subject matter of the text.[73] He

---

[64] Bultmann, "New Testament and Mythology", pp. 10-11. See G. H. C. MacGregor, "Principalities and Powers: The Cosmic Background of Paul's Thought" in *New Testament Studies* 1, (1954-1955), pp. 26-27; Dunn, "Demythologizing", p. 295.
[65] Bultmann, *Jesus Christ and Mythology*, pp. 35-6.
[66] Bultmann, "New Testament and Mythology", p. 10.
[67] Bultmann, *Jesus Christ and Mythology*, pp. 35-6.
[68] Pannenberg, *Basic Questions* pp. 14 (n. 32), 67); Thiselton, *Horizons*, p. 290.
[69] Thiselton, *Horizons*, p. 289.
[70] Dunn, "Demythologizing", p. 297.
[71] Thiselton, *Horizons*, pp. 283, 289; O'Brien, "Principalities and Powers", p. 116.
[72] Fee, *The First Epistle to the Corinthians*, p. 472.
[73] Rudolf Bultmann, "The Problem with Hermeneutics" in J. C. G. Greig, *Essays Philosophical and Theological* (London: SCM Press, 1955), pp. 234-261, esp. pp. 242-

insists that pre-understanding implies not a prejudice but a way of raising questions.[74] Even so, pre-understanding could probably restrain interpreters, if all pre-understandings are like the computer default settings that might need to be altered so as to understand biblical texts in the light shed by the context of production.[75] Individual pre-understandings specially belong to a cultural or theological tradition[76] that may not be universally applicable. Pre-understanding is not only significant but also inevitable because it reveals the impossibility of having a neutral stance in hermeneutics. It positively elicits the significance of encounter and dialogue between the interpreter, the context of production, the context of the literary genre and the context of reception. This encounter makes the theory that interpreters can only achieve a contextual finality in hermeneutics dependable. For that reason, Bultmann's crucial emphasis on pre-understanding must not be rejected due to its link with other assumptions delineating demythologising.[77]

ii. Walter Wink: Structuralist Reading of the Powers

a. The Powers are Structures in Disguise

As mentioned above, Wink insists that Bultmann's programme of demythologisation was a move in the right direction but from the wrong foundation. This is because Bultmann defined myth as a falsifying objectification of reality and sought to discard myth through an existentialist interpretation. Wink maintains that had Bultmann worked with a more positive understanding of myth, like that of Carl Jung, Mircea Eliade, or Paul Ricoeur,[78]

3; Rudolf Bultmann, "Is Exegesis without Presuppositions Possible?" in S. M. Ogden, (ed), *Existence and Faith* (London: Hodder & Stoughton, (1961 [1964]), pp. 342-351. See G. N. Stanton, "Presuppositions in New Testament Criticism" in I. H. Marshall (ed.), *New Testament Interpretation: Essays in Principles and Method* (Exeter: The Paternoster Press, 1977), pp. 60-71; B. J. Nicholls, "Towards a Theology of Gospel and Culture" in J. Scott & Coote R. T (eds.), *Gospel and Culture* (Pasadena: William Carey Library, 1979), pp. 69-82 for a discussion on pre-understanding in relation to hermeneutics.

[74] Bultmann, Is Exegesis", p. 346.
[75] Cf. J. D. G. Dunn, "Altering the Default Setting: Re-envisaging the Early Transmission of the Jesus Tradition" in *New Testament Studies* 49 (2003), pp. 139-175.
[76] See Arnold, *Powers*, 176.
[77] Anthony C. Thiselton, "The New Hermeneutic" in I. H. Marshall (ed.), *New Testament Interpretation: Essays in Principles and Method* (Exeter: The Paternoster Press, 1977), p. 313.
[78] C. G. Jung ,"Synchronicity: An Acausal Connecting Principle" in C. G. Jung and W. Pauli, *The Interpretation of Nature and the Psyche* (New York: Pantheon Books, 1955) regards myth as part of projections to the collective unconsciousness. He does not advocate discarding religious myths involving evil spirits since they are powerful psychological realities. His concept of the "shadow" as the negative side of personality

his quite proper concern for making the text intelligible and existentially meaningful could have been achieved without sacrificing myth to the interpretation.[79] Nevertheless, like Bultmann, Wink is approaching supernatural powers from the perspective of myth, which modern people cannot take seriously "as long as our very categories of thought are dictated by the myth of materialism".[80] Wink believes that he is not demythologising the myth but transporting it into a new key and juxtaposing the ancient myth with the emerging postmodern (mythic) worldview, asking how they may equally illuminate each other.[81] He highlights the impossibility of simply discarding myth in "favour of our demythologized interpretation" since "all our "explanations" of myth are dispensable and time-bound and will soon be forgotten, but the myth lives on, fed by its continual interplay with the very reality it "presents".[82] For Wink, it seems that the very reality that the ancient myths presents, that is, evil and suffering are attributable to supernatural powers is now perpetuated by the structures of human existence.

Wink therefore argues that supernatural powers are structures in disguise. He describes the powers as the intangible "inner and outer aspects of any given manifestation of power... the spirituality of an institution".[83] As the inner aspect, the powers are the spirituality of institutions, the 'within' of corporate structure systems, the inner essence of outer organizations of power. As the outer aspect, the powers are the political system, appointed officials, the chair of an organisation, laws, and all tangible manifestations that power takes.[84] He holds that the powers, unlike the assumptions of ancient myths, do not have independent spiritual existence outside the material. They are encountered primarily in the material or "earthly" reality of which they are the innermost essence.[85] Wink rightly avers that the atrocities perpetuated and sanctioned by political and religious authorities in human history have a demonic nature and may warrant their being seen as demonic. He is unable, however, to imagine the demonic apart from the structures and people who operate them. As a result, he depicts Satan "as the actual power that congeals around idolatry, injustice, or inhumanity".[86] Satan is also the collective symbolization of evil and it is human

---

is close to the idea of an evil power, which is collective. Eliade, (*Myths, Dreams*, 19) regards myth as a religious experience for all *primitive mankind*, which lays the foundation of the world. Ricoeur regards myth as a symbol and drama, which is distinct from history since it narrates the founding events that occur before time but which is able to awaken feelings, invite thought and evoke response (Ricoeur, *The Symbolism*, p 5; Ricoeur "Myth and History", pp. 273-4.

[79] Wink, *Naming the Powers*, p. 143, note 44.
[80] Wink, *Naming the Powers*, p. 4
[81] Wink, *Naming the Powers*, p. 104.
[82] Wink, *Naming the Powers*, pp. 142-3.
[83] Wink, *Naming the Powers*, p. 5
[84] Wink, *Naming the Powers*, p. 5. See also pp. 10, 109, 100-1, 118, 139-40.
[85] Wink, *Naming the Powers*, pp. 104-113.
[86] Wink, *Naming the Powers*, p. 105.

beings who have made Satan, "the God of this world" (2 Cor 4: 4).[87] He holds that people have been slow to identify the complex institutions and forces in the Domination System that has besieged them and which is as old as human life. He regards Satan, demons and the powers as late arrivals that entered the world but were visible after human societies reached a certain threshold of density, complexity, and conflict.[88] Wink maintains that even though Paul believed in the reality of an invisible spirit world, he demythologised the powers such that their spiritual essence was no longer in his mind.[89]

However, as Dunn asserts, Wink "overpresses his argument" though "the main thrust of his interpretation needs to be taken with utmost seriousness".[90] Similarly, Rasmussen maintains "You are not among the living if you have no arguments of your own with the author, but you'll be much the poorer if you fail to join him where he excels: ...engaging the powers and ourselves in the process".[91] Wink rightly cautions against the excessive use of the term 'personification', acknowledging that personification could be an illusion because the spirituality of an institution is something real.[92] His view that myth cannot be dispensed with and that our explanations of myth are dispensable is significant. There is no doubt whatsoever that Wink unmasks how the powers of evil access human life and structures of human existence. His research undeniably illustrates that evil, which afflicts the entire society including the church, cannot be fully explained in materialistic terms. He persuasively unmasks the spiritual realities within and underneath the social, political, economic and religious crisis human beings face in daily life. He rightly emphasises that every economic system, state apparatus and power elite has an intrinsic spirituality, an inner essence, a collective culture or ethos that cannot be directly deciphered from its outer manifestations.[93] In this way, the determinants of human existence are "more", and this "holds the clue to their profundity... They are both visible and invisible, earthly and heavenly, spiritual and institutional". It is the spiritual aspect "that is hard for people inured in materialism to grasp".[94] So his discernment of the nature of structural evil in light of biblical evidence provides another way of grasping the problem of evil and suffering. Wink has greatly contributed to the way in which the church can differentiate and engage both the structures and spirituality of oppressive institutions.

Even so, Wink's views are simultaneously fascinating and baffling, flaunting a potent bias most likely informed by the Western worldview. He confesses that he cannot believe in the real existence of evil spirits and

---

[87] Wink, *Unmasking the Powers*, p. 24.
[88] Wink, *Engaging the Powers*, p. 39.
[89] See Wink, *Naming the Powers*, pp. 82-84.
[90] Dunn, *The Theology of Paul*, p. 110, note 42.
[91] Cited in Wink, *Engaging the Powers*, p. iii.
[92] Wink, *Naming the Powers*, pp. 105, 136.
[93] Wink, *Unmasking the Powers*, p. 4. Cf. Wink, *Engaging the Powers*, p. 3.
[94] Wink, *Engaging the Powers*, p. 3.

whatever cannot fit into the material categories he labels superstitious.[95] As observed, "This bias constrains him to find another explanation for the phenomena that Paul refers to as 'principalities and powers'",[96] which he regards as institutions, social systems, and political structure.[97] Apparently, he applies Jung's view of myth to preserve something uniquely 'spiritual to the powers'.[98] His use of Jung's psychological category of myth to interpret the meaning of the powers could be biblically and theologically unpersuasive. As Osborn observes,

> in speaking of heaven as the inwardness of creation and relating spiritual entities to Jungian archetypes, he tempts us to interpret the relationship between heaven and earth on the analogy of the relationship of mind (or soul) and body. Thus Wink's approach opens up the possibility of treating heaven as the world-soul. Such reading of the dual nature of creation owes more to Plato than Scripture. It is theologically dangerous because it lends our view of the world a wholeness that does not need God.[99]

And according to Moltmann, "if the earth is the body of heaven, and if heaven is the soul of the earth, the result is the image of the macranthropos, a self-sufficient, divine-human entity which revolves around itself".[100]

Wink's structuralist reading raises several questions. Is it logical to equate supernatural powers with the manifestations of power, structures of human existence and the "inner spirituality" of an institution? How could it be that the 'angels of nature' are identical to nature itself? Why are the 'principalities and powers' similar to the inner and spiritual essence or gestalt of an institution or state? Why are the 'demons' identical to the psychic or spiritual power emanated by organisation or individuals or subaspects of the individuals whose energies are bent at overpowering others? Why should the 'gods' be the same as the archetype or ideological structures that determine reality and mirror the human brain? Why is Satan identical to the degree of collective refusal to choose higher values?[101] It seems as if Wink's perception of power is somewhat

---

[95] Wink, *Naming the Powers*, p. 4.
[96] Arnold, *powers*, 198.
[97] Wink, *Naming the Powers*, p. 5.
[98] According to Caird (*The language and imagery*, p. 223), Jung's psychoanalytical theory of the universe archetypes arising from the collective unconscious has influenced the treatment of myth as the expression of deep-seated and permanent human needs, and at the same time as a means of directing the flood of emotions into socially acceptable channels.
[99] Lawrence Osborn, "Angels: Barth and Beyond" in Anthony N. S. Lane (ed.), *The Unseen World: Christian Reflections on Angels, Demons and the Heavenly Realm* (Carlisle: Paternoster Press; Grand Rapids, Michigan: Baker Book House, 1996), p. 44.
[100] J. Moltmann, *God in Creation: An Ecological Doctrine of Creation* (London: SCM, 1985), p. 161.
[101] Wink, *Naming the Powers*, pp. 104-5.

materialistic, which he paradoxically covers with a cryptic understanding of the spiritual dimension of power. Wink himself regards his remarks as 'cryptic',[102] a word, which according to *Chambers Dictionary*, indicates that which is 'mysteriously obscure'.

Of course, the subject of supernatural powers is mysteriously obscure and Wink excels because he does not deny the reality of supernatural powers. It does seem however, that Jungian archetypes may not rightly explain the link between supernatural powers and the social structures of human existence. As Osborn observes,

> the Jungian depth psychology appropriated by Wink to lend intelligibility to the notion of spiritual entities is not, in spite of its trappings, a theologically neutral science. On the contrary, Jung and his disciples are engaged in the rediscovery and appropriation of Gnostic and hermetic spiritualities.[103]

Jung himself is cited by Raschke as having said, "I am on the best way to deliver up the Christian concept of the spirit to the chaos of Gnosis again".[104] Apparently, Wink's view that the powers do not have an independent spiritual existence, and that spiritual and material reality are identical leads to some kind of Gnostic *panentheism*. He admits this view in his abridged volume of the powers.[105] He attains *panentheism* (which he describes as everything in God and God in everything) through what he refers to as the 'integrated worldview', that is, a mixture of the ancient worldview, the spiritualistic worldview, the material worldview and the theological worldview.[106] In accepting *panentheism*, Wink seems to have "taken a significant step towards the divinisation of the cosmos".[107]

Wink regards other worldviews, from which the integrated worldview that "affirms spirit at the core of every created thing"[108] emerges, as having dualistic proclivity. But granting supernatural powers independent existence and insisting that they can work with, and through the social structures of human existence does not lead into dualism. As explained in chapter five, Paul insists on Christ's supremacy over supernatural powers and that all things, seen or unseen, spiritual or material are under God's rule through Christ. God is ultimate and He alone is worthy of worship. In Paul's worldview, God is surrounded by lesser powers that do his bidding and are unworthy of worship. Wink accepts this as the framework by which Jewish people envisaged evil

---

[102] Wink, *Naming the Powers*, p. 105.
[103] Osborn, "Angels", p. 44.
[104] C. Raschke, *The Interruption of Eternity: Modern Gnosticism and the Origins of the New Religious Consciousness* (Chicago: Nelson Hall, 1980), p. 145.
[105] Walter Wink, *The Powers that Be: Theology for a New Millennium* (New York: Doubleday, 1998), p. 20.
[106] Wink, *The Powers that Be*, pp. 13-36.
[107] Osborn, "Angels", p. 44.
[108] Wink, *The Powers that Be*, p. 20.

spirits, referring to it as a 'secure henotheistic framework', which imposed itself on Israel due to institutionalised evil.[109] Nevertheless, institutionalised evil, according to some Jewish apocalyptic texts as noted in chapter four, could be the visible results of supernatural powers working *with*, and *through* the visible reality. Institutionalised evil does not allow rejecting the independent existence of supernatural powers. Could it be that, even in modern times, these powers not only work *with*, and *through* physical and material reality, but also *with* and *through* powerful personages to cause chaos in the structures of human existence? Russell notes that the devil is "a mighty person with intelligence and will whose energies are bent on the destruction of the cosmos and on the misery of its creatures".[110] While Wink laudably unmasks the spiritual reality within and underneath the structures of human existence, he leaves open the question whether it is right to deny supernatural powers independent existence. Even so, Wink's study wields considerable influence on scholars working on the area of social ethics.

b. Supernatural Powers as Death, Sin, Law and the Flesh

Notably, supernatural powers are closely associated with other Pauline themes such as the world, death, sin and redemption. In fact, Paul largely uses literary personifications to explain the powers that distress people and push them in certain directions. He seems to have been operating with a more sophisticated understanding of the powers of Sin and Death. Some Pauline texts regard sin as an animate entity that could seize human beings in almost the same way as demons could. As it were, the law of sin rules the body so that it acts contrary to the will of God (Rom 7: 14–25). Thus the demonic nature of sin is revealed in the very fact that it uses what was by itself good and promised life and which by nature was spiritual, as a tool for trapping and destroying humanity. Death is also personified as a tyrannical power that holds humanity in bondage, though it is something alien and evil. Having entered the world through sin, it has continuously reigned as a cruel power over the whole creation (Rom. 5: 12-14; 8: 20-23).[111] It is still not conclusive that the law and the flesh should be viewed as powers in the same way as Sin and Death are.[112] Dunn rightly notes, "The law as the ally of the powers of sin and death should not be regarded as itself a cosmic power".[113] Equally, could it be that the powers of sin and death should not be regarded as cosmic powers?

Nevertheless, Wink seems to include the law and the flesh among the powers. He follows J. C. Beker in his discussion on Paul's view as to the

---

[109] Wink, *Naming the Powers*, p. 132; Wink, *Unmasking the Powers*, pp. 109-111.

[110] Jeffrey Burton Russell, *Mephistopheles: The Devil in the Modern World* (Ithaca/London: Cornell University Press, 1986), p. 301.

[111] See the discussion on sin, law and death as powers from which Christ delivers human being in Ragnar, *Christ the Conqueror*, pp. 92-138.

[112] See the insightful discussion on the differing views as to the flesh and law in Dunn, *The Theology of Paul*, pp. 62-72 and 128-161 respectively.

[113] Dunn, *The Theology of Paul*, p. 161.

Previous Interpretations

powers that determine human life.[114] Beker states that Paul interpreted the apocalyptic forces anthropologically to show that human situations are influenced by ontological powers of law, sin, death, and the flesh and not by mythological demons and angels. He claims that Paul personalised death, sin and flesh (Rom 5: 21; 6: 9; 1Cor 15: 26; Gal 5: 17) and gave each of these forceful realities a specific reign or dominion.[115] Wink insists that we should follow Paul's lead to reinterpret the mythic language of the powers, since Paul "has already taken key steps towards "demythologizing" or at least depersonalising it by means of the categories of sin, law, the flesh, and death".[116] And even if Paul used traditional Jewish apocalyptic terms (1 Cor 15: 24-28; Rom 8: 38f; 1Cor 2: 6-8), "he prefers elsewhere to speak of those ontological powers that determine the human situation within the context of God's created order and comprise the 'field' of death, sin, law and the flesh".[117] Moreover, "Paul developed a quite unique manner of dealing with the determinants of human existence, *substituting* such quasi-hypostatised words as sin, law, flesh and death for the terms more frequently encountered in Jewish apocalyptic: Satan, Azazel, Beliar, evil spirit, demons".[118] Wink also argues, "The length to which Paul has already carried this process of demythologizing is visible especially in his treatment of wisdom and law". Therefore, "demythologizing" is simply withdrawing the "mythic projection of the real determinants of human existence out onto the cosmos and their identification as the actual physical, psychic, and social forces at work in us, in society, and in the universe".[119] Like Beker, he maintains that these were the powers that Christ defeated by his death on the cross.[120]

However, looking at a key Pauline text (Eph. 2: 1-3), the compelling nature of evil influence stems from the world ('the ways of this world'), the devil ('the ruler of the power of the air') and the flesh ('the cravings of our sinful nature ... its desires and thoughts').[121] It is likely that 'the ways of this world' included the whole range of societal and institutional behaviour and attitudes fashioned by set codes that are at odds with God. 'The flesh' may embrace innate drives that stir people to act in deviance to God's righteousness. For Paul, the flesh is the stimulus of many sins linked with sexual promiscuity, anger, envy and other emotions.[122] Nevertheless, the essential features of 'the devil' can and should be differentiated from the world, sin and death, although all are hostile to God's redemptive plan for human beings and so enemies of

---

[114] Wink, *Naming the Powers*, p. 62, footnote 58.
[115] J. C. Beker, *Paul the Apostle: The Triumph of God in Life and Thought* (Edinburgh: T & T Clark & Philadelphia: Fortress Press, 1980), pp. 189-192.
[116] Wink, *Naming the Powers*, p. 104.
[117] Wink, *Naming the Powers*, pp. 61-2.
[118] Wink, *Naming the Powers*, p. 100.
[119] Wink, *Naming the Powers*, pp. 62-3.
[120] Wink, *Naming the Powers*, p. 63. See Beker, *Paul the Apostle*, pp. 205-209.
[121] Cf. Rom 8: 5-8; Gal 6: 8. See O'Brien, *The Letter to the Ephesians*, p. 158.
[122] Gal 5: 19-21; Col 3: 5-10; 1 Cor 6: 9-10.

Christ. Supernatural powers are certainly and persuasively separate powers, but which, in tandem with the world and the flesh, can influence human actions. As noted above, Paul was aware of the existing belief that the world was populated by supernatural powers inimical to human existence. Paul may have also been aware of the influential force of innate feelings and emotions (see chapter four), capable of altering human deeds. It is probable that supernatural powers and the innate human feelings and emotions were distinct and yet related forces that could hinder human efforts to attain the fullness of life. Death too is a power among other personified powers, which sought to separate believers from the love of Christ and which will be destroyed at the end.[123] There is no doubt therefore that for Paul, the enemies that believers withstand are internal (flesh and sins associated with it, which at times derive from innate feelings and emotions such as lust, anger, malice, covetousness and fear), external (the world and all the societal and institutional behaviour sanctioned by laws inimical to God's plan) and supernatural (the devil and all his minions). Paul's theology of the powers is thus balanced if the powers that determine human existence can operate as personifications of inner feelings (human nature), impersonal institutions (structures) and personal supernatural powers (the devil and his powers of darkness). For Paul, these were different but related powers without and within, bearing upon us in an adverse and oppressive way.

Yet, as noted above, Satan and his minions if given a chance could take advantage over individual and communal life. This may imply that supernatural powers can take advantage of the world and the flesh to sway human beings and the structures of their existence. As already noted, τὰ στοιχεῖα τοῦ κόσμου worked with and through the structures of human existence, such as Jewish law and Gentile religion, so as to enslave believers and to hold non-believers in bondage. Perhaps the false teaching at Colossae was created and transmitted by people under the influence of supernatural powers (Col 2: 8-20).[124] It seems that Jewish and Graeco-Roman structures of human existence, through their leaders, could give supernatural powers a chance to exploit Jewish law, pagan religion and human frailty to deny people fullness of life. It is overwhelmingly probable therefore that Paul was aware of distinct but related enemies of Christ and the church, which Christian theology describes as the devil, the world and the flesh, and none can be a substitute for the other. Even if we may grant the possibility that in Paul, rulers and authority are existential realities that include law, sin and death, these "are not seen as merely existential, but are precisely personified and/or hypostatised, and projected out into the scene as opponents of Christ".[125] For Paul, principalities and powers are always heavenly powers. Therefore, as Arnold states, "one must be cautious of seeing Paul as engaging in a process of demythologising his apocalyptic tradition. Though he is not enamoured with speculations about the demonic realm, he does maintain a firm

---

[123] Rom. 8: 38-9, 1 Cor 15: 24-5.
[124] See Arnold, *The Colossian Syncretism*, pp. 188-9.
[125] Forbes, "Principalities and Powers", p. 85.

belief in the reality of hostile spiritual powers".[126]

Dunn also looks at the heavenly powers, which Paul envisaged as threatening believers. Having examined the passages wherein the heavenly powers appear, he writes, "in every case what seems clearly to have been in mind were heavenly beings, subordinate to God and his Christ, with the potential to intervene between God and his creation, and hostile to his purpose and people".[127] He also notes that the full sequence of the common Pauline terms such as *archai and exousiai* confirms their status as supramundane powers. Again, *angeloi* (Rom 8: 38) are obviously thought of as agents of heaven or intermediaries between heaven and earth, and since "the assurance is that they cannot come between God and his people, the thought is presumably of hostile angels".[128] Commenting on the spatial image and reference of "height and depth" (Rom 8: 38-9), which denotes the space below the horizons from which the stars arise, Dunn comments, "not very far is the thought that the heavenly bodies might influence human conduct, or at least the thought that the forces which influence planets and stars may also influence human destiny".[129] He also notes that Paul shared a common belief that there were several heavens and what was presumably a "common belief that the lower heavens were populated by various hostile powers or that the hostile heavenly powers mounted a kind of roadblock to prevent access to the higher heavens..."[130]

Dunn however regards it as puzzling that Paul says so little about the heavenly powers, stating that the two references in the undisputed Pauline epistles (Rom 8: 38-9; 1Cor 15: 24) look as if they were added almost for effect. "Suspicion begins to mount, therefore, that Paul himself did not have a very strong, or at least very clear, belief regarding these heavenly powers".[131] Nonetheless,

> that they were real powers, supraindividual, suprasocial forces, spiritual realities which influenced events and conducts, he had no doubts. But he never thought it of relevance to define these powers in any detail...it would seem that Paul refers to such heavenly beings as opposed to God's purpose, not so much because he had clear beliefs about them...but because he needed terms to speak of the all too real supraindividual, suprasocial forces of evil which he experienced and saw at work, and because these were the terms which expressed widely held current beliefs.[132]

Dunn rightly argues that Paul's views "were probably largely *ad hominen*, with

---

[126] Clinton E. Arnold, "Returning to the Domain of the Powers: *Stoicheia* as Evil Spirits in Galatians 4: 3, 9 in *Novum Testamentum* 38 1 (1996), p. 68.
[127] Dunn, *The Theology of Paul*, p. 106.
[128] Dunn, *The Theology of Paul*, p. 106.
[129] Dunn, *The Theology of Paul*, p. 107.
[130] Dunn, *The Theology of Paul*, p. 108.
[131] Dunn, *The Theology of Paul*, pp. 108-9.
[132] Dunn, *The Theology of Paul*, p. 109.

a view to reassuring those for whom such heavenly powers were all too real and inspired real fear... It was the powers that his converts experienced and still feared which had been overcome and rendered ineffective".[133]

Consequently, Dunn maintains that Paul's relative detachment from the issue, or lack of commitment to it as a matter of pressing urgency implies that the mythological gap is much narrower.

> Perhaps we have to say that Paul himself engaged in his own demythologisation at this point. For he did believe in spiritual powers and treated the subject with immense seriousness. But the spiritual powers he focused his theological and pastoral concern were not the "rulers and authorities" but the powers of sin and death. And these are existential more than ontological realities, the personifications or reifications, or, better, recognition of powers which were (and are) nevertheless all too real in human experiences.[134]

It would be futile to deny that Paul's theological and pastoral concerns were focused on the power of sin and death, especially in Romans. But also the effects that rulers and authorities, which Dunn recognises as supramundane powers in Paul's thought brought to human life and to the church, were certainly Paul's theological and pastoral concern. It could be right that the real problem for Paul was sin and death and he referred to supernatural powers because his contemporaries thought in these terms. Paul may have not treated them as a major feature of his theology and therefore his relative disregard of could be seen as a kind of demythologisation. Still, this leaves open the question and activity of Satan, whom Paul, as we have seen in chapter five, regarded as the chief opponent of the Gospel. As shown above, the Pauline depiction of the powers of evil is well balanced. He reckons several powers that are distinct but also allied since what they produce links with the realities that engender, constrain and pressure within and upon people and human society. However, if we are interpreting Dunn rightly, he differentiates heavenly powers from sin and death. This is clearly identifiable in his observation that the heavenly powers lost any effective power they had over those who belong to Christ and their destiny and that the same theme is implicit in references to the particular powers of sin and death.[135] So while Ephesians and Colossians strongly underline supernatural powers, Romans prominently deal with flesh, sin, law and death. But in Galatians the law and 'the elemental spirits of the universe' could enslave human beings. Could it be that the different emphasis in these epistles emerged due to the different experiences of Paul's listeners, which he equally regarded as his theological and pastoral concerns?

The idea that Paul demythologised supernatural powers is then open to doubt. Why should Paul demythologise what was perfectly intelligible to a

---

[133] Dunn, *The Theology of Paul*, p. 109.
[134] Dunn, *The Theology of Paul*, p. 110.
[135] Dunn, *The Theology of Paul*, p. 230.

people who regarded supernatural powers as "the effective agents of powerful effects in the world" and who treated them as "conscious, willing beings"?[136] If the Pauline supernatural powers, "like those of Philo are spiritual beings created by God and immanent within the world, but unlike those of Philo and like the princes of the nations, they frequently act in defiance of God's purpose and to the enslavement of mankind",[137] then why should it be that supernatural powers are only the political, social, economic and religious structures of power? Seeing the differences between ancient and modern worldviews, as Lincoln poses in reaction to Wink's claims that he is juxtaposing the two worldviews so that they may illuminate each other with regards to the powers,

> Why not simply allow the two worldviews to be different? Why try so hard to find the elements of the new cosmology in the ancient cosmology... Why not be content to claim that in the dialogue between ancient and postmodern worldviews the language about spiritual powers in the former provides a convenient tool which, in the Gospel's interaction with present society, enables the analysis of evil not to be materialistically reductionist?[138]

We cannot then be sure that Paul demythologised supernatural powers into structures of human existence or into law, sin, death and the flesh. Could it be that the idea that Paul demythologised supernatural powers at least belongs to the interpreters' view and can only serve a contextual purpose?[139] Should the idea that the New Testament cosmology is essentially mythical be a problem if myth is indispensable and every society operates within a mythical framework? It then follows that interacting with the Pauline concept of supernatural powers from the perspective of myth, and mainly that which regards myth as irrelevant for the modern world, continues to be problematic.

iii. Some Key Considerations as to Demythologisation

The most commendable thing about demythologisation is to make the Pauline concept of supernatural powers explicable for the Western worldview, which as we saw in chapter two, is sceptical as to the existence of supernatural powers. The rule seems to be that a people's worldview, religio-cultural and socio-political issues arising in the context of reception shape the hermeneutical horizons of understanding supernatural powers. Interpreters react to current situations from the perspective of the decisive thought system within their

---

[136] Wink, *Naming the Powers*, p. 3.
[137] Caird, *The language and Imagery*, p. 242.
[138] Andrew T. Lincoln, "Liberation from the powers: Supernatural Spirits or Societal Structures" in R. D. M. Carroll, David J. A. Clines and Philip R. Davies, *The Bible in Human Society* (Sheffield: Sheffield Academic Press, 1995), pp. 346-7.
[139] See Lincoln, "Liberation from the powers", pp. 345-7.

contexts.[140] As noted, Bultmann held that to demythologise was not to reject the content of the Gospel but the worldview from which it emerged, which was at odds with and irrelevant for modern people. Dunn observes that Bultmann's distinction between kerygma and myth was "the heritage of German idealism".[141] O'Brien notes that the rise of Nazism provoked German theologians to start "reading the relevant Pauline text in a new way".[142] Wendland & Hachimba avers that a "rationalistic, secularised, anti-supernatural worldview" influences demythologisers to hermeneutically contextualize supernatural powers for the modern worldview.[143] According to Ferdinando, such contextualisations are "hermeneutical manoeuvres" that often identify supernatural powers with tangible realities in the material world.[144] The result, as Imasogie notes, is that the ontic reality of references to demons is effectively denied in favour of a symbolic interpretation that demythologises the text, removing all traces of the supernatural from it.[145] Ferdinando rightly insists demythologisation is "exegetically anachronistic" since it fails "to reflect the concerns of the original authors and readers, despite the claim of some demythologisers to be identifying the sense which the author originally intended".[146] For that reason, demythologisation is a contextual hermeneutical method by which scholars have sought to make supernatural powers meaningful within a specific context.

Following Wink's claim that modern people can no longer believe in what the ancients referred to as the powers, one could say the issue is whether to accept the so-called mythical worldview or a scientific worldview. Demythologisation is clearly a corollary of science, in that modern people cannot believe in mythological beings due to scientific and technological progress. It is also an outcome of science, if as Kwame Appiah notes, "one powerful reaction among Christian intellectuals has been to retreat in the face of science into demythologization of the doctrines whose central theme...they cannot escape".[147] But it could be confusing to judge religious beliefs by means of scientific laws. Dunn observes that the 'law' of cause and effect is obvious in all scientific investigations and its operation can be easily recognized. The issue is more complicated when dealing with human relationships or the link between

---

[140] Arnold, *Powers,* p. 195; Keith Ferdinando, "Screwtape Revisited: Demonology, Western, African and Biblical" in Anthony. N. S. Lane, *The Unseen World: Christian Reflections on Angels, Demons and the Heavenly Realm* (Carlisle, Cumbria: Paternoster Press & Grand Rapids, Michigan: Baker Books, 1996), p. 107.
[141] Dunn, "Demythologizing", p. 299.
[142] O'Brien, "Principalities and Powers", p. 112.
[143] E. R. Wendland and Salimo Hachimaba, "A Central African Perspective on Contextualizing the Ephesian Potentates, principalities and powers" in *Missiology: An International Review* Vol. 28 No 3 (July 2000), p. 342.
[144] Ferdinando, "Screwtape Revisited", p. 105.
[145] Imasogie, *Guidelines,* p. 52
[146] Ferdinando, "Screwtape Revisited", p. 108
[147] Appiah, *In My Father's House,* p. 114.

the physical world and the psyche.[148] If spiritual forces contradict scientific laws, it does not mean that they do not indicate an existing reality, if reality can be spiritual as well as physical. Imposing modern assumptions so as to tolerate that which is deemed pre-scientific and ancient often clogs the effort to understand the experiences and the real life situations of ancient people.[149] Arnold notes that the temptation to interpret biblical texts "through our own cultural lenses" could hinder efforts to understand the nature and magnitude of the issues facing first century CE Christians.[150] Therefore, scholars' attempts to develop a relevant meaning for the powers should not be made to appear universally decisive. It has been noted that both untrained and trained readers of the Bible in Africa and Asia have no problem with the Pauline language and concept of supernatural powers. Yet they are disillusioned by some Western commentaries that fail to accept the existence and reality of supernatural powers and their defeat in Christ.[151] So, as Fee suggests, demythologisation may "isolate Western academics from the realities that many Third World people experience on a regular basis",[152] hence hindering dialogue between Western and African Bible readers, which we argued in chapter two is greatly needed.

Even if there could be no other way to deal with supernatural powers except myth, demythologisation is still complex and so it may not apply to every context. Dunn notes its complicatedness and dialectical nature as to modern conditionedness and first century conditionedness. He recognises the need for a continuing dialogue that must be taken up afresh by each believer and believing community. The dialogue should not just involve the interpreter's own voice and the voice of the past. Other voices should break in posing other questions and offering other answers. For that reason, dialogue cannot reach finality of form or expression because each person's question is peculiar and each generation has its own agenda.[153] If it is significant to make biblical texts understandable, meaningful and relevant in every context, should we not be talking of contextualisation, the attempt to translate biblical themes and concepts so that they may speak to modern situations? Contextualisation seems to agree with the principle of 'dynamic equivalence', which, as *The Willowbank Report* states, involves changing the form so as to preserve the meaning. Even so, form and meaning go together if meaning includes what we say and form

---

[148] Dunn, "Demythologizing", p. 291.
[149] See Jeffrey Burton Russell, *The Prince of Darkness: Radical Evil and the Power of God in History* (Ithaca, New York: Cornell University Press, 1988), p.260.
[150] Arnold, *Powers*, p. 150.
[151] See O'Brien, "Principalities and Powers", p. 130; Fee, *The First Epistle to the Corinthians*, p. 472, note 49; Arnold, *Powers*, pp. 176-182; Paul G. Hiebert, "The Flaw of the Excluded Middle" in *Missiology* 10 (1982), pp. 35-37.
[152] Fee, *The First Epistle to the Corinthians*, p. 472.
[153] Dunn, "Demythologizing", p. 301.

includes how we say it.[154] Then it follows that, contextualisation may be a more useful framework for reading the New Testament, which "presents events critical to Christian faith in language and concepts which are often outmoded and meaningless"[155] to modern people.

On a positive note, demythologisation compels interpreters to pay attention to their pre-understandings and assumptions as they read the text within its religio-cultural and socio-political context. It is by appreciating the context of production that we can re-contextualise the Pauline texts in the context of reception without sneaking our default setting into the text and the context of production. This certainly agrees with what Thiselton regards as the continuing dialogue with the text by which the text gradually corrects and reshapes the interpreter's questions and assumptions.[156] So, even if the New Testament can be interpreted today within a particular frame of reference, which may differ radically from what the text initially addressed,[157] this does not mean today's interpretation is what the text originally meant. The view that "in a changed situation the traditional phrases, even when recited literally, do not mean what they did at the time of their original formulation"[158] does not allow us to say that what they may mean to us today is what they meant to the first century CE writer or reader. That the same word can be read in another time differently[159] does not invalidate the way it was read initially. Although it is crucial to interpret the New Testament so that the past becomes alive, illuminating our present with new possibilities for personal and social change[160], this does not allow us to impose our theories into the context of production. This has been a major flaw of biblical studies in the academy, which Wink regards as a trained inability to deal with the real problems of actual living persons as they unfolded in their context in their everyday life. The danger, as Wink puts it, is that of asking questions that are not "raised by the text, but those likely to win a hearing from the professional guild of academicians".[161] One would therefore want to ask, has it been successful to deal with the subject of supernatural powers from the perspective of myth?

---

[154] Lausanne Committee for World Evangelisation: *The Willowbank Report: Report of a Consultation on Gospel and Culture*, held at Willowbank, Somerset Bridge Bermuda from 6th-13th January 1978 (Wheaton: Lausanne Committee for World Evangelisation, 1978), p. 8. See the NIV Bible explanation of "ten thousand talents" as "that is, millions of pounds" and "a hundred denarii" as "that is, a few pounds" (Mt. 18: 24, 28). This explanation is perfectly understandable to people who use the pound as their currency.
[155] Dunn, "Demythologizing", p. 300.
[156] Thiselton, *Horizons*, p. 439.
[157] Thiselton, "The New Hermeneutic", p. 308-9.
[158] Pannenberg, *Basic Questions*, p. 9.
[159] G. Ebeling, "Time and Word" in J. M. Robinson (ed.), *The Future of our Religious Past: Essays in Honour of Rudolf Bultmann* (London: SCM Press, 1971), p. 265.
[160] Walter Wink, *The Bible in Human Transformation: Towards a New Paradigm for Biblical Studies* (Philadelphia: Fortress Press, 1973), p. 2.
[161] Wink, *The Bible in Human Transformation*, pp. 6, 10.

6:4. Understanding Metaphor

i. The Relationship between Myth and Metaphor

As we turn to the subject of metaphor, it is critical to realise that the relationship between myth and metaphor could raise a considerable debate. According to Soskice, there is "a terminological imprecision" that links and often confuses metaphor with myth and uses them as synonyms.[162] She is of the opinion that "myth is all too often not distinguished in theological discussions from metaphor" despite that, "myth has its locus in textual or narrative analysis, and not on discussions of figures of speech".[163] The problem, citing Turbayne, is that "when things are called by the same name they are often thought to be the same thing or the same kind...when things are said to be of the same kind, they often have some of the same properties or are alike in some respect".[164] The question for us therefore is whether myth and metaphor is the same thing, the same kind, whether they have the same property or whether they are alike in some respect. According to Caird, the Bible uses myth as a metaphor system for the theological interpretation of historical events. So, myth is a specialised kind of metaphor and its use in the Bible is particularly metaphorical.[165] He adds that the explanation in Colossians 2: 15 concerning Christ's triumph over cosmic powers in the cross is a mythological statement,[166] but which, as will be argued below, could be best understood as a metaphorical statement. But Caird also admits that there is no purpose served "by obliterating the distinction between myth and metaphor in general".[167] According to other scholars, the abuse of metaphor occurs when metaphor is taken literally, transforming it into a myth.[168] It therefore seems that there is a problem as to the relationship of myth and metaphor. This may create a language problem, making language fail to live up to its communicative role, namely, connecting us with images and to bring us in touch with what is remote in time and space.[169] And as Caird observes, "if language is the indispensable vehicle of communication, it follows that its breakdown must bring thoughts to standstill".[170]

It is significant, however, to make a distinction between myth and metaphor,

---

[162] Soskice, *Metaphor*, pp. x, 17.
[163] Soskice, *Metaphor*, p. 56.
[164] Collin Murray Turbayne, *The Myth of Metaphor* (New Haven/London: Yale University Press, 1962), p. 75.
[165] Caird, *The language and Imagery*, p. 219.
[166] Caird, *The language and Imagery*, pp. 212-3.
[167] Caird, *The language and Imagery*, p. 220.
[168] Douglas Berggren, "The Use and Abuse of Metaphor" 16. 2 & 16.3, in *The Review of Metaphysics* (1962), pp. 238, 244, 458; Turbayne, *The Myth of Metaphor* pp. 59-60; Gunton, *The Actuality of Atonement*, p. 64.
[169] See Bertrand Russell, *The Analysis of Mind* (London: Allen & Unwin, 1921), p. 203; Turbayne, *The Myth of Metaphor*, pp. 92-3.
[170] Caird, *The language and Imagery*, p. 19.

if language or words can be used properly or misused especially if the referents, perhaps as intended by the author are not very clear. Turbayne rightly insists, "we know a thing when we understand it, and we understand it when we can interpret or tell what it signifies".[171] It will be shown below that metaphor is referential, and so it has advantage over myth. The use of metaphor with regard to supernatural powers evades the almost unavoidable negative implications and overtones of myth. As noted above, myth classically has been understood as the antithesis to history since it is non-historical. Even if one would want to defend the idea of myth having referentiality, it is more amorphous and unclear than metaphor since metaphor, as will be shown below, takes into consideration the tension between sense and referent. In that case, the metaphorical "is" both signify "is like" and "is not". The referentiality of myth, as we have seen above, especially in the Bultmannian thinking, is primitive and so a misunderstanding and misrepresentation of reality. The language content of metaphor takes into account analogies, similes and other figures of speech. So, metaphor is more positive in the use of language to define reality than myth, which looks back to the primitive mentality. But if as Ricouer notes, myth "is not a false explanation but a traditional narration which relates to events that happen at the beginning of time and which has the purpose of providing grounds for the ritual actions of men today, and in general manner, establishing all form of expression and thought by which man understands himself in his world", then myth, like any other narrative can use metaphor to achieve its goal. As such, myth has "its symbolic function—that is to say, its power of discovering and revealing the bond between man [sic] and what he considers sacred".[172] Apparently, there is a complex relationship between myth and metaphor. Yet as will be shown below, even if metaphor has problems, to which we now turn, it is better placed to deal with supernatural powers than myth.

ii. *The Problems of Definition and Distinction*

The topic of metaphor, seeing that metaphors have given rise to diverse and still unsolved problems, would require a monograph, if justice were to be done to it. This is not because metaphors have been greatly and deeply analysed and are wide-ranging and ever-present in time and space. The problems are those of definition and distinction, or rather, how to clearly identify a metaphor. Indeed, a definition useful to one discipline may be useless to another.[173] But from its Greek origin, metaphor has the connotation of "transferring" or "carrying" a thing or concept across. In that case, a metaphor is a referential trope, which takes an object or a concept or an image and turns it into an unexpected use and

---

[171] Turbayne, *The Myth of Metaphor*, p. 73.
[172] Ricoeur, *The Symbolism*, p. 5.
[173] See J. J. A. Mooij, *A Study of Metaphor: On the Nature of Metaphoric Expression, with Special Reference to their Reference* (Amsterdam/New York/Oxford: North Holland Publishing Company, 1976), p. 1-2, 6; Berggren, "The Use and Abuse of Metaphor", p. 237; Soskice, *Metaphor*, pp. 15-22.

reference. It does this by saying what cannot be simply changed into a literal description, or rather, what cannot be said in other ways.[174] It is its unexpected use and referential character that stuns and provokes the reader/hearer to pay attention to the metaphor and its referent. Perhaps this unexpected use and referential nature is a factor that generates a variety of its definitions. These include a *comparison* between two objects, or a *substitution* of one expression for another, or the *identification* of one thing with another or the *interaction* of two opposed thoughts or objects where a new meaning is developed.[175] The definition theories of comparison, substitution, identification and interaction are not free from error or narrow limitation. They seem to fuse metaphor with other tropes, for instance, simile, catachresis, chiasmus, oxymoron, metonymy, synecdoche, tmesis, and analogy.[176] This is probably because metaphors and the aforesaid figures of speech are in each other's way. But there is no agreement as to what *kinds* of linguistic phenomena may exactly qualify as metaphorical.[177]

Soskice explains that even if the discussion of the literal/metaphorical distinction centres on dead metaphor, that is, when words or phrases lose their metaphorical character and are used literally, there are good reasons for regarding dead metaphor as being in some sense still metaphor.[178] The problem, if Gunton is right that "metaphors die, but may also be recalled to life, and over a period of time reveal a wide spectrum of movement to and from the metaphorical",[179] is how to draw a line between dead and living metaphors. It is also hard to distinguish metaphor from metonymy and metaphor from simile.[180] It seems plausible to agree that a metaphor is "neither a kind of substitution of terms nor a matter of simple one-for-one comparison".[181] But this becomes complicated if tropes are in each other's way and are functionally the same but only different textually or in their grammatical form.[182] This begs the question

---

[174] Soskice, *Metaphor*, p. 63.
[175] See Paul Ricoeur, *The Rule of Metaphor: Multi-Disciplinary Studies of the Creation of Meaning in Language* (London/Henley: Routledge & Kegan Paul, 1977), pp. 3, 65-100; Soskice, *Metaphor*, pp. 38-43; Northrop Frye, *Myth and Metaphor: Selected Essays 1974-1988* (Charlottesville/London: University Press of Virginia, 1990), p. 111; Michael Whitworth, *Einstein's Wake: Relativity, Metaphor and Modernist Literature* (Oxford: Oxford University Press, 2001), p. 10.
[176] Turbayne, *The Myth of Metaphor*, pp. 11-2; Caird, *The Language and Imagery*, pp. 133-143; Soskice, *Metaphor*, pp. 43, 54-66.
[177] See Mooij, *A Study of Metaphor*, p. 8.
[178] Soskice, *Metaphor*, pp. 71-83.
[179] Gunton, *The Actuality of Atonement*, p. 35.
[180] Ricoeur, *The Rule of Metaphor*, pp. 179-187; Paul Ricoeur, *Hermeneutics and Human Science* edited and translated by John B. Thompson (Cambridge: Cambridge University Press, 1981), p. 172; Soskice, *Metaphor*, pp. 7-10, 25-6.
[181] Soskice, *Metaphor*, p. 40.
[182] See Soskice, *Metaphor*, p. 59; Stephen Ullmann, "Smile and Metaphor" in Davies, Anna Morpurgo and Wolfgang Meid (eds.) *Studies in Greek, Italic, and Indo-European*

of when a comparison becomes a simile and when it becomes a metaphor. According to Caird, if a comparison is explicit, it is a simile and should be taken literally. If it is implicit, it is a metaphor, which is non-literal.[183] On the other hand, Ricoeur notes that it is only comparable things that are compared, so it is tempting "to say that metaphor is a planned category mistake".[184] According to Ryle, a 'category mistake' occurs when facts belonging to one category are presented in the idioms suitable to another category.[185] The mistake is however valid if it obliterates the logical and established frontiers of language so as to expose new similarity, which would have remained obscure.[186] Thus comparing the incomparable is a "category mistake that clears the way to a new vision".[187] As such, metaphor overtly but through conflict between identity and difference, represents a process, which covertly generates semantic grids that fuse differences into identity.[188]

The distinction between metaphor and other tropes must be accepted but not overstated. Soskice is of the view that while there may be a natural reluctance to ditch the distinction, there are good reasons why the distinction should be kept.[189] Should this also apply to the distinction between metaphorical and literal statements? If Caird is correct that metaphor and other related tropes and the terms they use could have been intended literally, then the distinction between literal and metaphorical might be blurred.[190] It is in fact hard to distinguish metaphorical attribution from the literal attribution because the same word is sometimes one, sometimes the other.[191] Yet those who make the distinction base it on the truth or falsity of a metaphorical statement and its referents. The tendency is to speak of something being 'only metaphorically true', or in contradistinction, 'literally true'. Whatever cannot be translated from metaphorical into 'literal' is held to be untrue; hence metaphor is depicted as an irrational interaction with the world—*unless it ceases to be metaphorical, it cannot tell the truth*. The trend is to regard metaphorical statements as the most junior of literal statements.[192] This, however, is untenable since any statement, literal or metaphorical, may be true or false, and its referents may be real or unreal. As truth or meaning can be expressed through a metaphor, it is not enough to say that what has been expressed is metaphorical truth or

---

Linguistics Offered to Leonard R. Palmer (Innsbruck: Innsbruck Beiträge zur Sprachwissenschaft, 1976), p. 429.

[183] Caird, *The Language and Imagery*, p. 144.
[184] Ricoeur, *The Rule of Metaphor*, p. 197.
[185] Gilbert Ryle, *The Concept of Mind* (Harmondsworth: Penguin, 1963), p. 10.
[186] Ricoeur, *The Rule of Metaphor*, p. 197.
[187] Ricoeur, *The Rule of Metaphor*, p. 230.
[188] Ricoeur, *The Rule of Metaphor*, p. 198.
[189] Soskice, *Metaphor*, pp. 60-62.
[190] Caird, *The Language and Imagery*, pp. 133-143.
[191] See Ricoeur, *The Rule of Metaphor*, p. 252; Gunton, *The Actuality of Atonement*, p. 35.
[192] See Soskice, *Metaphor*, p. 67; Gunton, *The Actuality of Atonement*, p. 30

meaning, which is distinct from and inferior to literal truth or meaning. If literal and non-literal have very little to do with the truth or falsity of what we say and with the existence or non-existence of the things they refer to, it could be misleading to contrast literal and metaphorical in terms of the truth or falsity of their referents.[193] Yet debate on "the relation between the literal and figurative use of language is an academic battleground".[194]

To apply a word figuratively to something beyond its literal meaning is at the same time to appeal to what is known about the literal meaning. The literal meaning does not disappear but plays a significant part in the interpretation of the metaphor. The rule seems to be that something must exist so that something else may be identified with it. In that case, the postulate of existence is the basis of identification.[195] Metaphor first functions literally as a rule for pinpointing the object or situation and then functions metaphorically by indirectly assigning another similar situation. As a result, and if it is the context that might enable one to decide what is figurative and what is not, the distinction between literal and metaphorical is unclear.[196] Tension exists between literal and metaphorical, which according to Ricoeur is a tension in the relational function of the verb "to be", where the metaphorical "is" at once signifies both "is not" and "is like".[197] Consequently, "tension, contradiction, and controversion are nothing but the opposite side of the reconciliation in which metaphor 'makes sense'".[198] Besides, if a concept or object signifies the other, each retains its independent status. So resemblance operates between the same terms that contradiction sets. The tension is between identity and difference, which are opposed and yet united if the similarity is perceived despite the difference and contradiction.[199] "Through this specific trait", says Ricoeur, "enigma lives on in the heart of metaphor".[200]

The possible indistinctness of the referent of metaphor may imply that metaphor is open-ended and inarticulate. Does this go along with Ayer's claim that what is unintelligible cannot be described meaningfully and any attempt to describe it must be nonsense?[201] Ayer is only right if we object to reliance on non-literal speech and assume that what is not literally true does not have value. This is Ayer's assumption and so he avers, "if what they (metaphors) are said to

---

[193] See Caird, *The Language and Imagery*, p. 131; Soskice, *Metaphor*, p. 70.
[194] Lewis S. Mudge, "Paul Ricoeur on Biblical Interpretation" in Paul Ricoeur, *Essays in Biblical Interpretation* (Philadelphia: Fortress Press, 1980), p. 5.
[195] See Mooij, *A Study of Metaphor*, p. 13; Ricoeur, *The Rule of Metaphor*, p. 217.
[196] See Ricoeur, *The Rule of Metaphor*, p. 189; Paul Henle, "Metaphor" in Paul Henle (ed.), *Language, Thought and Culture* (Ann Arbor: University of Michigan Press, 1958), pp. 183-185.
[197] Ricoeur, *The Rule of Metaphor*, pp. 7, 247.
[198] Ricoeur, *The Rule of Metaphor*, p. 195.
[199] See Ricoeur, *The Rule of Metaphor*, pp. 195-198.
[200] Ricoeur, *The Rule of Metaphor*, p. 196.
[201] A. J. Ayer, *Language, Truth and Logic* (Harmondsworth: Penguin Books, 1971), p. 156.

establish does not make sense or, on any literal interpretation, is obviously false, then at the very least the case for their being cognitive has not been made out".[202] In the light of the aforesaid, is Ayer's opinion justified? Soskice rightly contends that Ayer stands in an empiricist framework that leads to religious scepticism, at a time when the same empiricism has been shown to be bankrupt in other areas of philosophy.[203] Ayer's opinion is puzzling if the same phrase can be said at one time literally and at another time metaphorically. It seems that literal and metaphorical are different ways of expressing the same state of affairs and not two kinds of states of affair. Concurring with Soskice, it is particular usages that are literal or metaphorical, and not particular facts.[204] Saying that the metaphorical 'is' signifies both 'is like' and 'is not' is a way of alerting the reader/listener to the potential ambiguity of a statement. This must be expected if "language itself is from the outset and for the most part distorted: it means something other than what it says, it has a double meaning, it is equivocal".[205] But there is a problem if a metaphor has dual meaning, which calls for interpretation.[206] Interpretation helps us to understand the meaning of a statement or a concept. But the hermeneutical discourse has problems, which get deeper if the "metaphorical use must be solely contextual, that is, a meaning which emerges as the unique and fleeting result of a certain contextual action".[207]

iii. The Problems of Interpreting Metaphor

The aforesaid problems of metaphor go beyond literary analysis if they present us "with a significantly new interpretative web which may affect further analyses".[208] This occurs due to differing theories, opinions and theoretical background. The existing definitions of metaphor have caused different interpretations. Moreover, the distinction between literal and metaphorical exists as a result of different interpretations and the different ways of using words in discourse. But to determine the literal sense of words is not as simple as it might seem due to 'polysemy', the case in which words have a number of related yet different senses. However, the interpretative task becomes more complex if what makes a word literal or metaphorical depends on the

---

[202] A. J. Ayer, *The Central Question of Philosophy* (Harmondsworth: Penguin Books, 1976), pp. 5-4.

[203] Soskice, *Metaphor*, pp. 97-141.

[204] Soskice, *Metaphor*, p. 70.

[205] Paul Ricoeur, *Freud and Philosophy: An Essay on Interpretation,* translated by Denis Savage, (New Haven/London: Yale University Press, 1970), p. 7.

[206] Ricoeur, *Freud and Philosophy*, pp. 7-19; Ricoeur, *Hermeneutics*, p. 169. See Caird, *The Language and Imagery*, p. 149 for biblical metaphors with multiple meaning.

[207] Ricoeur, *Hermeneutics*, p. 169.

[208] Soskice, *Metaphor*, p. 62.

Previous Interpretations

context.²⁰⁹ Karin notes that metaphors are culturally and socially defined and that they are context-sensitive. They reflect social and cultural ways of understanding and self-definition.²¹⁰ Lakoff and Johnson note that metaphors are grounded in human experience of space, time and physical objects.²¹¹ Yet a theoretical background given by one socio-cultural context could differ from that given by another socio-cultural context. Human experience could also differ from place to place and time to time. If metaphors aid people to organise their thinking, people operate under different metaphors, which express their worldview. It seems plausible to hold that a metaphor can only illuminate the reality of its referents to those who order their thinking and life through it. In that case, metaphors can only be assessed in terms of the context in which they are formulated and in the descriptive language and traditional beliefs of a specific community.²¹² This makes the interpretation of metaphor tricky yet it is within an interpretation that the literal sense and metaphoric sense can be distinguished and articulated.²¹³ Despite this, it is critical not to neglect cultural, contextual and experiential aspects of metaphor, which are nevertheless helpful tools for its interpretation.

So what do we make out of the above problems of metaphor? It seems that "metaphors constitute the indispensable principle for integrating diverse phenomena and perspectives without sacrificing their diversity".²¹⁴ The problems of metaphor make it what it is and these problems could be windows shedding light on it. Ricoeur is right that metaphor requires the polarity between sense and reference, reference and reality and reference to self.²¹⁵ The tension between literal and metaphorical must be preserved if it is critical to the meaning of a metaphor and if metaphors create and discover meanings from the clues in the literal meaning.²¹⁶ Then, as Turbayne comments, "it is not necessarily a confusion to present items belonging to one sort in the idioms

---

²⁰⁹ Mooij, *A Study of Metaphor*, p. 10; Ricoeur, *The Rule of Metaphor*, pp. 113, 291; Ricoeur, *Hermeneutics*, p. 170; Soskice, *Metaphor*, p. 83.
²¹⁰ Karin S. Moser, "Metaphorical Analysis in Psychology—Method, Theory, and Fields of Application" [Paragraphs 5-6, 15] in *Forum: Qualitative Socialforschung/Forum: Qualitative Social research* (Online Journal Vol. 1 No. 2, 2000), http://www.qualitative-research.netfqs-texte/2-00/2-00moser-e.htm, accessed on 15:11:03.
²¹¹ G. Lakoff and M. Johnson, *Metaphors we Live By* (Chicago: University of Chicago Press, 1980).
²¹² See Gunton, *The Actuality of Atonement*, p. 28; Soskice, *Metaphor*, p. 151; John Haynes, "Metaphors and Mediation", http://www.mediate.com/articles/metaphor.cfm accessed on 15:11:03.
²¹³ Ricoeur, *The Rule of Metaphor*, p. 221.
²¹⁴ Berggren, "The Use and Abuse of Metaphor", p. 237.
²¹⁵ Ricoeur, *Hermeneutics*, p. 171.
²¹⁶ Paul Ricoeur, "Biblical Hermeneutics" in *Semeia* 4 (1975), p. 143; Ricoeur, *The Rule of Metaphor*, pp. 188, 221; Paul Ricoeur, *Interpretation Theory* (Fort Worth: Texas University Press, 1977b), p. 46; David Klem, *The Hermeneutical Theory of Paul Ricoeur* (London/Toronto: Associated University Press, 1983), pp. 98, 148.

appropriate to another. If it were, we should have to say that the making of every myth, of every metaphor and almost every theory involved a confusion".[217] Yet Ricoeur is right.

> The paradox consists in the fact there is no other way to do justice to the notion of the metaphorical truth than to include the critical incision of the (literal) 'is not' within the ontological vehemence of the (metaphorical) 'is'... In the same way that logical distance is preserved in metaphorical proximity, and in the same way as the impossible literal interpretation is not simply abolished by the metaphorical interpretation but submits to it while resisting, so the ontological affirmation obeys the principle of tension and the law of 'stereoscopic vision'. It is this tensional constitution of the verb *to be* that receives its grammatical mark in the 'to be like' of metaphor elaborated into simile, at the same time as the tension between *same* and *other* is marked in the relational copula.[218]

Although metaphor has problems, it is a more useful tool than myth in dealing with the subject of supernatural powers. Working from the perspective of myth, scholars tend to dispense with the literal meaning. Metaphor may not allow this, if as noted above, it finds the literal meaning relevant for interpretation and if it first functions literally and then metaphorically to designate another similar situation. The problems of metaphor need not deter the quest to identify the metaphor of supernatural powers, which is nonetheless complicated by its referential problem.

iv. The Referential Problem of Supernatural Powers

The question of whether the Pauline concept of supernatural powers is metaphorical or literal is not trivial. According to the concept, Christ's victory on the cross was/is against supernatural powers (Col 2: 15), to which the church makes known the manifold wisdom of God (Eph 3: 10). Again, supernatural powers cannot separate believers from the love of Christ (Rom 8: 38-9) and believers must resist them by being strong in the Lord and in the power of his might (Eph 6: 10-20). The issue here is whether the Pauline terms, identified in this study as supernatural powers, are metaphorical or literal. What complicates the whole issue is the ambiguity and fluidity of these terms. As noted in chapter five, the terms could literally refer to spiritual powers or to human rulers in the first century CE. It is, however, the context that determines if the referents of a given term are spiritual or material. It follows that the referents of these terms could be spiritual or material and also the literal sense could be spiritual or material. As Caird asserts, it is important to note that biblical writers use metaphors derived from human and non-human realms.[219] Does this mean that

---

[217] Turbayne, *The Myth of Metaphor*, p. 4.
[218] Ricoeur, *The Rule of Metaphor*, p. 255-6.
[219] Caird, *The Language and Imagery*, p. 174.

the metaphorical tension between 'is' and 'is not' of supernatural powers could be never-ending, vast and open-ended? If supernatural powers belong to the category of metaphors that do not have "specifiable referents" and which are "irresolvably vague",[220] could it be difficult to exactly identify their referents? If the terms identified as supernatural powers could refer to both material and spiritual entities, is it not difficult to ascertain if the literal or the metaphorical is spiritual or material? Given the ambiguity of the terms and sometimes of the context wherein the terms appear, it might be safer to accept that the Pauline concept points to a reality, which cannot be expressed suitably in any other than metaphorical terms. As a result, the concept describes the activity of different but related devilish forces that upset human efforts to attain the fullness of life. These forces could move in various dimensions such as, moral, spiritual, social, psychological or anthropological, thus influencing people and their structures of existence. It could be naïve therefore to reduce the referents of supernatural powers to a single predicate. It is likely that the concept of supernatural powers describes forces that upset human life but which cannot be explained except in tropes and figures.

Perhaps supernatural powers fall under Soskice's category of confusing and radically irreducible metaphors. She avers that three ideas help to distinguish irreducible metaphors.

> The first is that irreducible metaphors are incorrigibles which are susceptible of no elaboration or explanation whatsoever; the second is that they can only be redescribed in terms of other metaphors; and the third is that they are metaphors which purport to be referential, but for which no ostensively identifiable referent is independently available.[221]

Irreducible metaphors are therefore inexplicable but if metaphors are naturally extendable, an irreducible metaphor is identifiable if the sense suggests that the referred reality is possible. So, "to say that Jesus is the true vine suggests that life and growth are possible in union with him, that new branches can be grafted... If no such expansion were possible, we should not identify the passage as being metaphor".[222] Therefore, irreducible metaphors "must be those which can only be redescribed by other metaphors and/or those which lack identifiable referents".[223] Given the complicatedness to identify the referents of supernatural powers, then, it is an extendable and irreducible metaphor. If Paul used metaphors drawn from the battlefield (Col 2: 15), military weaponry (Eph 6: 10-20) and that of slavery (Gal 4: 3-11), these could be the "other metaphors" that help us to identify the referents of supernatural powers.

The idea that Christ's death on the cross entails victory against supernatural powers may be extended to mean that believers, by being strong in the Lord

---

[220] Soskice, *Metaphor*, p.124.
[221] Soskice, *Metaphor*, p. 94.
[222] Soskice, *Metaphor*, p. 94.
[223] Soskice, *Metaphor*, p. 94.

and in the power of His might, can share in Christ's victory. Comparing or identifying God with a victorious Roman general could be the "other metaphor" re-describing supernatural powers, bearing in mind that the metaphorical 'is' signifies both 'is like' and 'is not'. In Colossians 2: 15, Christ is compared to or identified with a Roman general who defeats and leads the captives in a triumphal procession. This does not warrant any conclusion to the effect that the metaphor and its referent have a one-to-one link. The literal triumphal procession of the Roman general was noticeable to the naked eye and in the streets of Roman cities, while Christ's metaphorical triumphal procession was hardly noticeable to the naked eye and was in Christ or in the cross of Christ. The idea that Christ's death on the cross was/is victory is indeed startling to those who know that in normal circumstances, death and especially crucifixion is not victory. Yet if "anyone who wants to understand a poet must go to the poet's country",[224] the metaphor is instantly recognizable since Roman generals used to lead their defeated foes in a triumphal procession. The metaphor is also clear if a metaphor transfers a concept from one context to another and uses familiar and ordinary concepts to imply something unusual.[225] Because of the tension between the metaphorical "is like" and "is not", Christ is not a Roman general, but he is like a Roman general since He acts like one.[226] It should be recalled that comparison, identification and substitution could limit the understanding of metaphor, including the metaphor of supernatural powers.

However, is it hard to identify the referent of the metaphor of supernatural powers from the perspective of first century CE worldview? As noted above, several scholars identify the structures of human existence or law, sin and death as the referents of supernatural powers. While it is true that some forces that frustrate human life are social, political, economic, psychic and religious, there are invisible powers that go beyond material, physical, psychic, sociological and psychological descriptions. These powers cannot be aptly "described in every day empirical terms"[227] devoid of celestial appeal. Seeing that the idea of victory and struggle (Col 2: 15; Eph 6: 10-20) implies some sort of person-to-person encounter, could it be that the referents of supernatural powers are animate, personal and wilful spiritual beings? In the first place, it might be crucial not to detach the Pauline concept of supernatural powers from the tradition and culture on which it initially stood and the experience on which it was grounded. As observed, "a concrete image drawn from one part of human experience of the world to a new context" turns out to be "the means of expressing truth about the way the world is".[228] So, could it be that the experience and what was/is believed to be the cause of that experience can be perceived metaphorically, that is, giving the alleged source of what was/is experienced some human qualities such as, the power, influence and control

---

[224] J. W. Goethe, cited in Caird, *The Language and Imagery*, p. 145.
[225] Cf. Gunton, *The Actuality of Atonement*, p. 28.
[226] Cf. Caird, *The Language and Imagery*, p. 145.
[227] Gunton, *The Actuality of Atonement*, p. 65.
[228] Gunton, *The Actuality of Atonement*, p. 32.

exerted by human rulers? If the Pauline concept initially handled experience grounded on evil and suffering, then according to the popular tradition of the time, evil and suffering were attributed to personal spiritual beings. There is an enticing probability, if based on the first century CE context of production and on the African context of reception that supernatural powers refer to personal and animate spiritual beings, which were/are believed to have the ability to upset human existence.

Could it be that the first century CE world personalised abstract terms like sin, law, flesh and death while the African world personalises natural phenomena since the forces that upset human existence could only be explained through metaphors drawn from human experience, hence explaining supernatural powers as personal spiritual beings? Does it follow therefore that to regard supernatural powers as personal beings is to deny they are metaphorical? Soskice asserts,

> it does not follow that such irreducibly metaphorical discourse is thereby unintelligible, devoid of cognitive meaning, or that it fails to be referential. And as for eliminating as insignificant any metaphor whose referent was unspecifiable apart from metaphor, this would eliminate a great part of physical theory which relies on metaphor and concomitant models to discuss entities and state of affairs beyond direct observation.[229]

Is it not possible to read the Pauline terms identified as supernatural powers as personal spiritual beings if the context of the literary genre allows it?[230]

Soskice comments, "No metaphor is completely reducible to a literal equivalent without consequent loss of content, not even those metaphors for which one can specify an ostensive referent".[231] If the metaphor of supernatural powers is irreducible, then it ought to be figured out if the literal or metaphorical is the material or the spiritual. Well, it has already been said that it could be difficult to categorically state that the literal is spiritual or material or vice-versa. Yet the first century CE context of production and the African context of reception seem to allow the referents of supernatural powers to be personal spiritual beings. This of course is not a paradox but an affirmation of what has been noted above that metaphors are culturally and socially defined and that they are context-sensitive. Noting how tricky it could be to firmly state that the literal is spiritual or material is to recognise that the metaphor of supernatural powers reveals a networking of evil forces and the structures of human existence. So it could be illogical to speak of one without reference to the other. This is most likely clear in the Pauline guidance that believers must put on the whole armour of God so that they may be able to stand against the wiles of the *devil* (Eph 6: 11). Noteworthy is that believers must put away falsehood, not to sin due to anger, not to dwell on anger if they are to avoid

---

[229] Soskice, *Metaphor*, p. 94.
[230] See chapter 5.
[231] Soskice, *Metaphor*, pp. 94-5.

giving the *devil* an opportunity (Eph 4: 25-32). In that case, the idea of believers fighting against supernatural powers 'in the heavenly places' and to avoid giving the *devil* a chance, metaphorically alerts them that their resistance "is not different from their daily struggle to live the new life of faith in the hostile environment of pagan society"[232] or in the hostile structures of their existence.

It is very important to steer a middle course between a naïvely supernaturalistic view of the demonic and a reductionist one, where it is construed as a way of speaking of merely finite or psychological influences. The Pauline concept of supernatural powers does not present us "with superhuman hypostases trotting about the world but *with the metaphorical characterization of moral and cosmic realities which would otherwise defy expression*".[233] This implies that the literal oppression, evil and suffering experienced within the socio-political/economic and religio-cultural structures of human existence go beyond these structures. In fact, the Pauline concept does not reduce the idea of personal spiritual beings. Paul's opponents could disguise themselves as servants of righteousness while they were the servants of Satan (2 Cor 11: 13-15). His ailment was a thorn in the flesh and a messenger of Satan (2 Cor 12: 7). The reference of ἄγγελος σατανᾶ could be a circumlocution indicating the satanic origin of Paul's σκόλοψ τῇ σαρκί.[234] This was certainly a Jewish view, which according to several apocalyptic texts, as noted in chapter four, depicted Satan as a spiritual being that could cause suffering in real life situations.

The major problem is not that the metaphor of supernatural powers is vague and can refer to "psychological or other forces within the individual or society" or to "something more dualistic, an alien reality which enslaves the person or group believed to be so afflicted".[235] The problem is to determine whether the metaphor of supernatural powers only refers to suprahuman realities that must be demythologised, or if it is an irreducible metaphor, which fittingly describes suprahuman realities that upset human existence. To all intents and purposes, the latter option seems more reasonable than the former because it allows us to hold in tension both the personal and extra-personal manifestations of evil and suffering. It also allows us to recognise the metaphorical 'is' signifies both 'is like' and 'is not', thus realising that the forces that determine human existence are not just material or psychological or sociological or anthropological but more. However, this "more" has complexity and obscurity, and probably indicates an independent spiritual existence of forces believed to cause evil and suffering.[236] This assertion may appear as a resort to the language of myth, but it sounds more satisfactory than the theories that explain evil and suffering only

---

[232] Caird, *The Language and Imagery*, p. 239.
[233] Gunton, *The Actuality of Atonement*, p. 67.
[234] See Martin, *2 Corinthians*, p. 413.
[235] Gunton, *The Actuality of Atonement*, p. 67.
[236] Cf. Gunton, *The Actuality of Atonement*, pp. 67-74.

in terms of human motives.[237] It follows that even if those who were *literally* liable for Christ's death were human political and religious leaders (1 Cor 2: 6-8), we saw in chapter five that ἀρχόντων τοῦ αἰῶνος τούτου could not have been Caiaphas, Herod and Pilate who were already dead. The phrase could be a metaphorical expression, referring to the invisible and real rulers behind the thrones of visible rulers.[238] It must be unremittingly said that the metaphor of supernatural powers is "not reducible to a single atomistic predicate".[239]

The referential problem of supernatural powers is complicated. It is theologically and philosophically controversial but unavoidable.[240] But like any other metaphor, the question of the referents of supernatural powers has nothing to do with truth or falsity. The dilemma reaches its apex in the case of religious expression, especially in decoding the meaning of the reality to which a trope refers.[241] What emerges in some rare cases is the fear of forfeiting the right to believe in the reality that the metaphor expresses.[242] This fear can only be justified on two assumptions, "either that metaphor is an optional embroidery which adds nothing substantial to the meaning of a sense; or that metaphor can be used only in emotive and evocative utterances which have no true value" but which are absolutely ungrounded.[243] As Gunton asserts, truth does not "depend upon whether it is expressed in literal or metaphorical terms, but upon whether language of whatever kind expresses human interaction with reality successfully (truthfully) or not".[244] Even if metaphors can be interpreted "in a purely subjective way – speaking primarily of *our* minds and *our* usage, not of the world outside – a more plausible account is that it is the way by which we are enabled to speak about the real world".[245] Unlike myth, metaphors, biblical or otherwise, as Gunton notes, are ways of describing realistically what can be described only in the indirect manner of this kind of language but an indirect description is still a description of what is really there. New Testament metaphors are not just literary constructions of myths, or perspectives of the primitive mind. The writers mean us to understand the demonic realistically but in an appropriately indirect manner.[246] Then, is it not

---

[237] See Stewart R. Sutherland, "Language and Interpretation" in *Crime and Punishment*", *Philosophy and Literature*, (1978), pp. 223-236.
[238] See Caird, *The Language and Imagery*, p. 192.
[239] Soskice, *Metaphor*, p. 95.
[240] Cf. Gunton, *The Actuality of Atonement*, pp. 43-47
[241] Mudge, "Paul Ricoeur", p. 4; Caird, *The Language and Imagery*, p. 132.
[242] Cf. J. A. T. Robinson, *The Body* SBT 5 (London: SCM Press, 1952), p. 51; E. L. Mascall, *Christ, the Christian and the Church: A Study of the Incarnation and Its Consequences* (London: Longmans, Green, 1946), pp. 112, 161 who suggests that the description of the church as "the body of Christ" is not a metaphorical but a literal truth.
[243] Caird, *The Language and Imagery*, pp. 132, 131-197. Cf. Gunton, *The Actuality of Atonement*, pp. 27-52.
[244] Gunton, *The Actuality of Atonement*, p. 35.
[245] Gunton, *The Actuality of Atonement*, p. 36.
[246] Gunton, *The Actuality of Atonement*, pp. 65-6.

right to conclude that metaphor is a more useful tool in dealing with the subject of supernatural powers than myth?

6:6. Conclusion

The chief problem confronting modern scholars with regard to the Pauline concept of supernatural powers is the problem of language. The previous interpretations with a preference for demythologisation are indeed a worthy effort to grapple with this problem. It appears that the best hope of a solution is to come at the problem from the perspective of metaphor rather than that of myth. Perhaps this may have minimised the complications that arise when beliefs in supernatural powers are relegated to the ancient worldview and so considered irrelevant for modern people. If, as noted above, metaphor allows us to hold in tension both the personal and extra-personal manifestations of evil and suffering, then demythologisation, which according to Wink is the withdrawal of mythic projection of the real determinants of human existence out of the world so as to identify them as the actual physical, psychic, and social forces at work in us, in society, and in the universe, might not be necessary. As noted above, the causes of evil and suffering are more than physical, social and psychological. Wink himself allows that the determinants of human existence are spiritual and institutional but he recognises that the spiritual aspect is hard for people inured in materialism to grasp.[247] Could it be that people accustomed to materialism find it hard to grasp the spiritual aspect since the subject is approached from the perspective of myth and not metaphor?

To all intents and purposes, myth proves to be a less useful tool in dealing with supernatural powers; from which it follows that demythologisation goes out of the window with myth. But if demythologisation goes out the window with myth, is this not to create a hermeneutical vacuum, which may cause other problems in relation to the subject of supernatural powers? If we do away with demythologisation, what other theoretical framework could be relevant to deal with the subject of supernatural powers? Perhaps turning to an inculturation framework and recognising that metaphor would allow us to hold in tension both the personal and extra-personal manifestations of evil and suffering could be the way to avoid creating a hermeneutical vacuum. Perhaps handling supernatural powers from the perspective of metaphor and turning to the inculturation framework could contextualise the Pauline concept in the African context. Contextualising the Pauline teaching about supernatural powers in the African context is an important issue that the African church cannot ignore. Could it be that the effort to contextualise Paul's teaching, to which we now turn in the next chapter, must be based on the theme of Christ's supremacy over supernatural powers?

---

[247] Wink, *Engaging the Powers*, p. 3.

CHAPTER 7

Conclusion: The African Church and Supernatural Powers with Regard to Christ's Supremacy

7:1. Towards a Retrospective Glance

In this final chapter, it is important to have a glance in the rear-view mirror. It can be asserted with certainty that Paul's teachings about supernatural powers engaged the first century CE context of production where people believed in, and feared supernatural powers as people in the African context of reception do. Paul, however, unlike the Western worldview, does not deny the existence of supernatural powers. Unlike the African worldview, Paul's teaching does not permit believers to give supernatural powers phobic allegiance or to allow them to determine human life. Unlike the anthropological perceptions, the Pauline concept does not reduce beliefs in supernatural powers into social functions they purportedly play in society. Some modern anthropological and theological treatises unlike the Pauline concept do not recognise the significance of meeting people at the point of their beliefs and practices. While Paul may not have shared the popular beliefs of his first century audience, he built on these beliefs to *ad hominen* address the feelings and/or prejudices of his readers. As such, the Pauline concept engages its readers from the perspective of their beliefs.[1] This means that Paul's teaching on the subject of supernatural powers should engage African belief in, and fear of supernatural powers from the perspective of an African worldview.

The African spirit world is not without problems due to the multiplicity of divine beings and spirits that tend to supplant the supremacy of Christ. The problem is that the earlier readings that advocate demythologising supernatural powers do not engaged the full measure of African belief in, and fear of supernatural powers. There is need therefore to re-visit the Pauline concept so that it may speak to the African context afresh. Yet the effort to make the Pauline concept and the African belief in supernatural powers speak to each other could be complicated. This follows from the discovery that the concept of supernatural powers in the context of production and of the literary genre is not as straightforward as one would expect. The same applies to the African context of reception as a result of the different perceptions attached to the belief

---

[1] See the discussion in chapter 5, pages 152-159 especially pp. 153-4.

in supernatural powers. Many Africans believe that spirits and the spirit world inhibit or expedite human existence. As noted earlier, the problem is that the African belief system creates fear and inspires people to give supernatural powers an angst-ridden religious zeal, thus allowing them to determine human existence. This negates Paul's teaching with regard to Christ supremacy over the powers and that Christ provides fullness of life.

According to a first century CE popular belief, supernatural powers hindered people's attempt to attain the fullness of life using the structures of human existence. Even so, the idea that supernatural powers work with and through structure of human existence was not acceptable to every one. Some Graeco-Roman thinkers doubted and vilified the gods expressed in myths and rebuffed the behaviour exhibited in public worship. Despite that, many ancient people agreed that supernatural powers could use, control and shape human life and institutions.[2] The same is true for the African context. This begs the question of whether the African church should consider educating believers on how to survive in a hostile milieu purportedly dominated by the powers of darkness as an option for her theological and hermeneutical agenda. To all intents and purposes, this is inevitable if the African church is to avoid a shallow but wide growth comparable to a two thousand miles wide river, but which is two inches deep. The problem is that believers must not be conformed to this world (Rom 12: 2), yet they are subject to the governing authorities for there is no authority except from God (Rom 13: 1). They should not take their lawsuits before the unrighteous because they will not only judge the world, but also the angels (1 Cor 6: 1-8). They must be separated from unbelievers as there is no fellowship between light and darkness and there is no accord between Christ and Beliar (1 Cor 6: 14-18).

In chapter six, it was emphasised that it would be unwisely restrictive to reduce supernatural powers into a single predicate, such as, the structures of human existence. Equally, it would be imprudently limited to view the cause of events only from a spiritual dimension. The spiritual and physical reality

---

[2] The human mind most likely works on a framework that interprets supernatural powers as having influence over human life and institutions. This is probably clear in Lewis's *Screwtape Letters*, which creatively envisage a demon having been assigned to every 'patient'. The demon's responsibility is to ensure the 'patients' attention is drawn away from anything that would lead the person to the kingdom of God. It is also clear in Peretti's *This Present Darkness*, which explains the strategy and networking of hostile and evil opponents who come from the realm of spirit, demons and powers. These forces rally to specifically gain control of a typical small American town and eventually the whole nation primarily by drawing people away from Christ. There is a demonic activity behind human struggles and difficulties, showing the likelihood of perverting institutions on account of demonic influences. C. S. Lewis shows how evil supernatural powers may influence a person's day-to-day life. Peretti describes the individual workings of demonic powers, but he also shows their unified collective purpose. Lewis and Peretti show how the powers of darkness unleash their influence both on individuals and institutions (see Arnold, *Powers*, pp. 205-207).

interlocks and produces forces that work with and through the structures to influence and shape human existence. This perspective may help us to interpret social realities in the African context, taking into consideration that for the Africans, human existence is inseparably linked to the idea that supernatural powers influence and use the structures of human existence.[3]

7:2. What Can the African Church Do Concerning Supernatural Powers?

The above question is significant and in an attempt to answer it, this chapter proposes two related points that the African church should consider. The African church should also consider a third point that supplements the first two related points. Suffice to say that the two related points are based on Ferdinando's observation, which one would indeed say is the final word for the African context with regards to supernatural powers.

> The proclamation of the Gospel in the African context should take seriously the existential felt need of protection from spirits, just as the epistles to the Colossians and Ephesians responded to the somewhat similar concerns of the intended recipients. Accordingly the significance of Christ's death for the demonic realm should be stressed more than has been the case in the West, but without obscuring its primary significance in effecting reconciliation of sinners to God by making atonement for their sin. The context must be addressed but should not be allowed to control or distort the message.[4]

Several scholars agree that Paul was largely interested in the faith and life of the churches in the context of production[5]. The churches emerged from and spread within a milieu that believed in the existence of supernatural powers. This belief has persistently caused pastoral and doctrinal problems for the worldwide church in every phase of her existence[6]. This is credited to what we

---

[3] Andrew Olu Igenoza, "Contextual Balancing of Scripture with Scripture: Scripture Union in Ghana and Nigeria" in Gerald O. West and Musa W. Dube (eds.) *The Bible in Africa: Transactions, Trajectories and Trends* (Leiden: Brill, 2000), p. 292.

[4] Ferdinando, "Screwtape Revisited", p. 131

[5] See Morrison, *The Powers That Be*, p. 18; Arnold, *Powers*, pp. 126-7

[6] The council of Laodicea (held at about 350 CE) took time to issue decrees prohibiting Christians and the clergy from getting involved in rituals and practices linked with supernatural powers. The 35th decree admonished Christians not to forsake the church of God and turn to the worship of angels, thus introducing the cult of angels. The 36th decree forbade the higher and lower clergy from becoming magicians, conjurors, mathematicians, or astrologers. To be shut out from the church was the punishment of those who failed to adhere to the prohibitions. (See C. J Hefele, *A History of the Councils of the Church* Vol. II: A.D. 326–429 (Edinburgh: T. & T. Clark, 1896); J. B Lightfoot, *St. Paul's Epistle to the Colossians and to Philemon: A Revised Text with introduction, notes and Dissertations:* (Lynn, Massachusetts: Hinderckson Publishers,

have noted as two opposed but related errors; to deny the reality and existence of supernatural powers and to believe in their existence, giving them fixated allegiance and as a result, allowing them to determine human existence. These errors contributed to the commencement and continuation of the pastoral and doctrinal problems with regard to supernatural powers encumbering the African church. How can the African church respond to the opposite but related errors? This leads to a reflection on the two related points the African church should consider.

i. Underline Christ's Supremacy

First and foremost, the Pauline teaching underlines Christ's supremacy over supernatural powers and the structures of human existence, both of which may work together to threaten individual and social life. The teaching seeks to stabilise and shape the believers' life in Christ through the right doctrine. Berger and Luckmann note that the development of Christian theological thought occurred as a result of heretical challenges to the official tradition.[7] The official Christianity and popular Christianity[8] in the African context, as already noted in chapter two, follow different paths in matters of faith and practice. Ordinary believers pretend to follow what their church leaders teach and demand. Nevertheless, unity of faith and practice between official Christianity and popular Christianity is desirable, as it would help believers to withstand supernatural powers and receive Christ's victory as their own. What O'Brien notes in relation to the unity of Jews and Gentiles may, in reverse angle, apply to church leaders and ordinary believers in the African context. God's intention "is to bring all things together in unity in Christ (vv. 9-10)" but "two obstacles need to be overcome before the divine purposes would reach their fulfilment—the subjection of the powers (representing 'the things in heaven'), and the church, particularly the relationship of Jewish and Gentiles (representing the 'things on earth')".[9] Now the unity of Jews and Gentiles has been won and what emerged is a distinctive group that is neither Jew nor Gentile but believers, who soon after regarded themselves a third race or new race.[10] The unity of believers significantly indicates the fulfilment of God's eternal plan. The existence of the body of Christ, now made of Jews and Gentiles (or with regard to the African context, now made of theologically trained believers and

---

1875), p. 69; Arnold, *The Colossian Syncretism*, p. 86. That the church sanctioned the hunt and persecution of witches in Europe that was eventually abolished in 1737 (Guinness, *The Dust of Death*, p. 280) is another pointer to the pastoral and doctrinal problems that the belief in supernatural powers has caused in the history of the church.

[7] Berger and Luckmann, *The Social Construction of Reality*, p. 125.

[8] See page 42, footnote 79. It should be noted that church leaders and theologically trained believers represent official Christianity. The ordinary believers and theologically untrained believers represent popular Christianity.

[9] O'Brien, *The Letter to the Ephesians*, p. 183.

[10] See. Clement, *Stromateis* 6.5.41.6; *Epistle to Diognetus* 1.

theologically untrained believers), uniquely witnesses to supernatural powers in heavenly places the manifold wisdom of God (Eph 3: 10).[11] This brings about a realisation that the unity of faith and practice between theologically trained and theologically untrained believers in the African context is vital for the life and faith of the church. As a result, as Boff and Boff note with regard to liberation theology, trained theologians should have one foot in the centre of study and the other foot in the community of believers.[12]

Rather than condemning the practice of popular Christianity, church leaders should instead emphasise the supremacy of Christ over supernatural powers. This would bring popular Christianity into the fold of official Christianity, forging a unity that would enable believers to come to terms with the fact that they have been delivered from the domain of darkness and transferred to the kingdom of God's Son. This deliverance and transference is critical in relation to believers' present life.

> Because believers are already taken unto Christ's dominion where they enjoy immunity from sin's tyranny and are given the assurance of the Lord's present reign as they are raised with him (see Col 3: 1), they need no longer suffer doubt and fear on account of malevolent spirit-forces. They have known emancipation from past bondage, (Col 2: 20; 3: 3). These hostile powers were forced to release their grip as the crucified Christ overcame them in his hour of seeming defeat (Col 2. 15) and dereliction. How much more does his triumph in the resurrection prove that He is "the head of all rule and authority"! And the Colossians have "come to the fullness of life in him" (Col 2: 10) as they are risen with Him (Col 2: 13).[13]

In view of this, believers should no longer live κατα τὰ στοιχεῖα τοῦ κόσμου but κατὰ Χριστόν (Col 2: 8). They should create and maintain social structures that reinforce their existence.

Paul's teaching can help African believers to identify false teaching that is at variance with Gospel truth and would relegate the supremacy of Christ to a

---

[11] O'Brien, *The Letter to the Ephesians*, pp. 200-1.
[12] L Boff and C. Boff, *Introducing Liberation Theology* (Tunbridge: Kent, Burns and Oates; Mary Knoll, New York: Orbis Books, 1987), p. 19. See also Gerald West, "Being Partially Constituted by Work With Others: Biblical Scholars Becoming Different" *In Journal of Theology for Southern Africa* No 104 (July 1999), p. 44-53; A. K. wa Gatumu, "Primal Worldview and The Bible: An African Christian Contribution to a Hermeneutical Method from the Perspective of the Primal Worldview, with Particular Reference to the Gĩkũyũ of Kenya" (Unpublished M. Th. Dissertation, University of Kwa-Zulu Natal, Pietermaritzburg, South Africa, 2000), p. 98, 128.
[13] Ralph P. Martin, *Colossians: The Church's Lord and Christian's Liberty* (Exeter: The Paternoster Press, 1972), p. 39.

downward spiral.¹⁴ If Paul's teaching acted upon the context of production and educated believers on how to shape their lives despite the false teachings, it should act upon believers in the African context of reception, educating them about Christ's supremacy. As MacDonald asserts, "The symbol of the crucified and the resurrected Messiah calls for a certain life-style; it stands at the centre of the effort to build communities".[15] The African church must encourage believers to base their life and faith in Christ and to reject any other teaching (philosophy and empty deceits) κατὰ τὴν παράδοσιν τῶν ἀνθρώπων, κατὰ τὰ στοιχεῖα τοῦ κόσμου (Col 2: 8). The supremacy of Christ is an indication that believers should no longer accept teachings that are contrary to what they were taught. Christ is supreme and they have been raised with him. Self-abasement and worship of angels and living as if they still belonged to the world would undermine their status in Christ. MacDonald rightly notes, "In stating that by dying and raising with Christ, believers had been delivered once and for all, the author sought to illustrate the misguided nature of their activity".[16]

As mentioned in chapter five, Satan and his hosts inspire false doctrines and religious deception. Believers must choose either to live according to the elemental spirits of the universe or according to Christ.[17] Living according to Christ is to participate in the power of his death and resurrection. This is to die and to be raised with Christ, to live a life of moral purity, devoid of fornication, impurity, passion, evil desire, covetousness and idolatry that marked the former life of believers. It is to put away destructive emotions and unethical tendencies such as anger, wrath, malice, slander and foul talk (Col 3:5-9) that can give the devil a chance to sway believers according to his impulses (Eph 4: 25-32). Believers therefore should not take part in the unfruitful works of darkness, but instead expose them. They should walk as wise people, making the most use of the time because the days are evil (Eph 5: 11-16). The "general statement with respect to acting wisely in the face of evil days does presuppose that caution is necessary with one's dealing with an evil world".[18] African believers must detach themselves and their God from the doings of unbelievers. They must understand and differentiate their present and former lives.[19]

The theology of supernatural powers in the African context brings to the forefront what Meeks refers to as "soteriological contrast pattern" that reminds believers "that 'once' their life was characterized by vices and hopelessness,

---

[14] Cf. Margaret Y. MacDonald, *The Pauline Churches: A Socio-historical Study of Institutionalisation in the Pauline and Deutero-Pauline Writings* (Cambridge: Cambridge University Press, 1988), p. 17.

[15] MacDonald, *The Pauline Churches*, p. 72.

[16] MacDonald, *The Pauline Churches*, p. 152.

[17] See Lohse, *Colossians and Philemon* pp.130-1; MacDonald, *The Pauline Churches*, p. 151.

[18] MacDonald, *The Pauline Churches*, p. 102.

[19] Cf. Gal 4: 3-9; Eph 2: 1-22; Col. 1: 21-2; 2: 13-14. See also Rom 6: 17-22; 7: 5-6; 11: 30.

Conclusion

but 'now' by eschatological security and life of virtue".[20] Paul's teaching should persuade African believers to live a life that does not contradict Christ's supremacy. One would thus regard the Pauline concept as an *aide memoire* to the African believers' as to the 'then' and 'now' schema of conversion, which invites right actions for those transferred to the kingdom of God's Son. The transference of believers from the dominion of darkness to the kingdom of God's Son means that they now share Christ's supremacy. They have not only been made alive and raised up with Christ but also they have been made to sit with him in the heavenly places (Eph 2: 5-6). They have been reconciled to God in one body through the cross of Christ (Eph 2: 11-22). Consequently, "along with the description of the cosmic reconciliation encompassed within the body of Christ", Paul's teaching describes "a kind of heavenly enthronement of Christ which is presently shared by the believers... Through their sharing in his death and resurrection, they themselves were lifted into the realm of salvation".[21] In the same way God exalted Christ, He similarly exalts the joint heirs with Christ. The believers' source of strength, that is, God's mighty power, enables them to enjoy the victory gained by Christ as they withstand supernatural powers.

Realising the struggle is not against flesh and blood (i.e. humanity in its weakness and frailty[22]) but against more powerful supernatural powers is also to acknowledge that believers do not resist against equals. As O'Brien notes, "the notion of going to battle with Satan and the powers of darkness 'may seem a frightening prospect' and indeed to take on such formidable foes simply with 'one's own resources would be to court disaster'. Believers would be fatally unprotected and exposed".[23] Yet Paul's teaching is that by virtue of being 'in Christ', believers are spiritually strong, stable and robust to face the challenge of the more-than-human opponents. To be in Christ to a greater extent is to be endowed with superior power that however belongs to Christ.[24] Believers, who are flesh and blood, do not take the challenge on their own strength and might. The Lord, by the power of his might, strengthens them. This idea agrees with the prophecies of Isaiah, which depict Yahweh as the Lord of hosts and as a warrior dressed up for battle. Believers are now being strengthened and being provided with God's own armour, worn before by God and his Messiah.[25] This

---

[20] Meeks, *The First Urban Christians*, p. 95.
[21] MacDonald, *The Pauline Churches*, p. 143.
[22] O'Brien, *The Letter to the Ephesians*, p. 466.
[23] O'Brien, *The Letter to the Ephesians*, p. 464.
[24] See Walter Grundmann, *Ber Begriff der Kraft in der Neutestamentlichen Gendankenwelt* BWANT 8 (Stuttgart: Kohlhammer, 1932), p. 108.
[25] Arnold (*Ephesians: Power and Magic*, pp.108-9) believes Ephesians 6: 10-20 heavily depends on Isaiah 11: 5; 40: 26; 52:1-7; 57: 19. So "the book of Isaiah appears to be the author's primary source for his presentation of the metaphoric weaponry". He also insists, "it is possible that the author was thinking of Wis 5: 17–particularly because of πανοπλία (absent from Isaiah)" (p.109). See also Carr, *Angels and Principalities*, p. 111;

interpretation is allowed, as the imperative verb ἐνδυναμοῦσθε is preferably passive[26] as opposed to the middle voice advocated by some scholars.[27]

In putting on the whole armour of God, believers are now the vehicles of God's mighty power. This is understandable in a context where human beings are perceived as vehicles that transport the benevolence of supernatural powers. The theology of supernatural powers in relation to Christ's supremacy ought to enable believers to recognise that they are the vehicles of God's mighty power so as to aptly engage supernatural powers that work with or through structures of human existence in a spiritual warfare. African believers are thus on God's side and against the god of this world and his powers of darkness. Now the believers' public life, like that of military soldiers, must demonstrate "practical obedience to commands",[28] that is, to put on God's full amour so as to become indispensable. Putting on God's full armour implies a living relationship with God in Jesus Christ. Maintaining the relationship is metaphorically comparable to 'putting on the new nature, created after the likeness of God in true righteousness and holiness' (Eph 4: 24). By putting on the whole armour of God, believers imitate God. O'Brien states, "some of the weapons believers are to don, namely, truth, righteousness and salvation suggest that we put on God himself, or at least his characteristics, and this idea is close in meaning to the distinctive exhortation of Ephesians 5: 1, "Be imitators of God".[29] Then, as Snodgrass asserts, "in the end all the armour language is a way to talk about identification with God and his purpose".[30] Ephesians 6: 10-20 give African believers hope and confidence that evil supernatural powers can be defeated.[31] Believers must know that "their chances of success are more than possible or probable: victory will be a reality given their dependence upon the divine

---

Robert A. Wild, "The Warrior and the Prisoner: Some Reflections on Ephesians 6: 10-20 in *Catholic Biblical Quarterly* (1984), p. 287.

[26] See Heinrich Schlier, *Christus und die Kirche im Epheserbrief* BHT (Tübingen: Mohr, 1930), p. 289; Bauer, Arndt and Gingrich, *A Greek-English Lexicon*, p. 263; Andrew T. Lincoln, *Ephesians* WBC 42 (Waco, Texas: Word Books, 1990), p. 441; Arnold, *Ephesians Power and Magic*, p. 107; O'Brien, *The Letter to the Ephesians*, p. 460; GNM Morphology and Barclay-Newman Greek Dictionary as represented in the BibleWorks 4.0 for Windows Copyright © 1998 BibleWorks, LLC.

[27] See F. F. Bruce, *The Epistle to the Colossians, to Philemon, and to the Ephesians* (Grand Rapids, Michigan: Eerdmans, 1984), p. 403; S. E. Porter, *Verbal Aspects in the Greek of New Testament, with Special Reference to Tense and Mood* (New York: Lang, 1989), p. 359; T. Y. Neufeld, *Put on the Armour of God: The Divine Warrior from Isaiah to Ephesians* (Sheffield: Sheffield Academic Press, 1997), p. 112.

[28] Scott, *Domination and the Arts of Resistance*, p. 29.

[29] O'Brien, *The Letter to the Ephesians*, p 463.

[30] K. Snodgrass, *Ephesians: The NIV Application Commentary* (Grand Rapids: Zondervan, 1996), p. 339.

[31] See Page, *Powers of Evil*, p. 187; John R. W. Stott, *The Message of Ephesians* (Leicester: Inter-varsity Press, 1979), p. 266; O'Brien, *The Letter to the Ephesians*, p. 464.

Conclusion

power".³² Depending upon God's power and putting on His armour, believers can keep Satan from gaining advantage over them since they now know his designs (2 Cor 2: 11).

The African church should be aware that supernatural powers seek to undo what Christ has done. Believers are flesh and blood and not equal to supernatural powers. And since they do not empower themselves, this implies that they are not the ones being challenged. The powers of darkness want to undo what God has done in Christ and so the challenge is directed to the one who empower believers. Several scholars agree that supernatural powers cited in Ephesians 6: 10-20 seek to undo what God has done in Christ. G. D. Fee explains that this final section of the letter most likely outlines Paul's chief concern for his readers. The placing of this material in the emphatic final position suggests that he has been purposely building the letter toward this climax all along.³³ Similarly, O'Brien notes that the passage is

> a crucial element to which the rest of the epistle has been pointing. Here the apostle looks at the Christian responsibility of living in the world from a broader, that is, cosmic perspective. The moral issues with which he deals are not simply a matter of personal reference, as many within our contemporary and postmodern world contend. On the contrary, they are essential elements in a larger struggle between the forces of good and evil.³⁴

So the passage is the conclusion of the whole Epistle, a *peroratio* summing up the main themes and prompting its readers to action.³⁵ The epistle first shows how great is the purpose of God in Christ, which goes with the glory of his high calling and the standard of life that should ensue from it. This transpires in a life of fellowship observed by the community of believers, whose intimate circle is the family. Yet, the life of fellowship is not devoid of fierce spiritual battle.

The rationale for resisting the evil one is to preserve what Christ has achieved through God's mighty power. The rationale for the attacks of the evil one and his spiritual host of wickedness is to destroy the new community God is building through Christ. The invisible forces intend to re-build the walls of hostility that Christ demolished. God has successfully thwarted their effort to

---

³² Arnold, *Ephesians: Power and Magic*, p. 107.

³³ Gordon D. Fee, *God's Empowering Presence: The Holy Spirit in the Letters of Paul* (Peabody, Massachusetts: Hendrickson, 1994), p. 723.

³⁴ O'Brien, *The Letter to the Ephesians*, p. 457.

³⁵ Cf. Francis Foulkes, *The Epistle of Paul to the Ephesians: An Introduction and Commentary* (Leicester: Inter-varsity Press, 1989); Stott, *The Message of Ephesians*, p. 266; O'Brien, *The Letter to the Ephesians*, p. 457; Arnold, *Ephesians: Power and Magic*, pp. 103, 105; Lincoln "Liberation from the powers", pp. 99-114; Neufeld, *Put on the Armour of God*, pp. 110-1; C. B. Kittredge, *Community and Authority: The Rhetoric of Obedience in the Pauline Tradition* (Harrisburg, PA: TPI, 1998), p. 144-5; Snodgrass, *Ephesians*, p. 335.

undo what he has done in Christ. Believers must therefore come to terms with the fact that the decisive victory over the powers has already been won by God through Christ (Eph. 1: 19-22 cf. 4: 8). Their defeat is certain considering the success of God's purpose of reconciling Jews and the Gentiles through the death of Christ. This guarantees the existence of the church as the united body of Christ, victoriously moving towards its climax; to make known to the powers the wisdom of God (Eph. 3: 10) by means of her existence. For that reason, the powers of darkness cannot hinder the progress of God's purpose now and in the eschaton, when their ultimate defeat will be achieved. Christ's defeat of the powers through his death and resurrection is the reason for his exaltation at a place of honour in God's right hand.

In view of the aforesaid, *the African church should underline Christ's supremacy in her faith and life.* The issue is what the African church should believe and teach with regard to supernatural powers. The African church needs a theology of supernatural powers in relation to Christ's supremacy. But this theology must not contravene the framework of Christian theology, which as Noble points out,

> is the articulation of our knowledge of the Lord God who has revealed himself to us. Our understanding of the world or the penumbra of Christian belief, those areas which are controversial even among Christians, must be centred in our doctrine of the God and Father of our Lord Jesus Christ.[36]

Consequently, the controversial subject of supernatural powers should be sorted out in line with the Christocentric faith that shapes Christian theology. This would enable the church to avoid a doctrine that is eccentric and out of perspective. The African church must therefore put supernatural powers in the perspective of historical faith affirmed by the creeds and authenticated by the Bible.

The hermeneutical framework for interpreting supernatural powers must agree with the doctrine of creation, which states that God created all things by his word. The Pauline concept attests that all things, in heaven or earth, visible or invisible, were created 'in', 'through' and 'for' Christ (Col 1: 16). This includes supernatural powers, the enemies of Christ and his church. On the cross, Christ's death cancelled the bond that stood against us with its legal demand and disarmed supernatural powers, humiliating them publicly and triumphing over them (Col 2: 15). Due to Christ's decisive defeat and victory over supernatural powers attained at the cross once and for all, the supremacy of Christ dominates the visible and invisible creation. Yet the final defeat will be realised at the eschaton, and as Arnold rightly concludes, is assured. Until then, the church exists in a dangerous time and there are many battles to be fought. Satan and his minions continue to attack the church, hold unbelieving humanity in bondage and promote every kind of evil throughout the world.

---

[36] Noble, "The Spirit World", p. 187.

Conclusion

Believers will continue to suffer the painful effects of evil such as war, morally deplorable public policies, crimes, gang violence and the like, spurred on by the powers of darkness,[37] though perpetuated by human beings. As a result, the spiritual warfare against supernatural powers continues until the final and decisive victory day.

As the African church awaits the inauguration of this day, the important thing will be to propagate a Christ-centred theology of supernatural powers that would unite believers in matters of faith and practice. Of special notice is that Jews and Gentiles believers are now one new person seeing that Christ has demolished the wall of hostility (Eph 2: 11-22), redeeming them from the dominion of darkness ruled by the prince of the power of the air (Col 1: 13; Eph 2: 2). "There cannot be Greek and Jew... but Christ is all and in all" because believers "have put off the old nature and put on the new nature" (Col 3: 10-1). Believers no longer follow the course of this world as they have been reconciled to God in one body through the cross (Eph 2: 12-22). While underlining the supremacy of Christ, the theology of supernatural powers taught by the African church must emphasise the unity of faith and practice, especially between ecclesiastical leadership and ordinary Christians. The unity of faith and practice between the official Christianity and popular Christianity in the African context is imperative for the development of a spontaneous theology of supernatural powers in relation to Christ's supremacy.

The new life in Christ should be reflected in the households of believers in which Christ should be perfectly imitated (Eph 5: 21-6:1-9; Col 3: 18–4: 1).

> A strong belief in Christ as the head of all things becomes reflected in the ethos where the subjection of individuals to the authoritative members of the household is demanded. The love/authority of Christ becomes a reference point according to the designs of the ethos of love-patriarchalism. For example, the union of man and woman becomes linked with the cosmic symbol of the union of Christ and the church, while traditional definitions of masculine and feminine roles are at the same time reinforced (Eph 5: 21-33).[38]

The exemplary living within the Christian households is probably a prerequisite for the believers being strengthened in the spiritual warfare. The supremacy of Christ is thus unmistakable in the structures of human existence. This should create awareness to the believers that even as they exist in the structures of human existence; they belong to the kingdom of God's son. They are separated from the domain of darkness. Their devotion to God must be through Christ and not through intermediary supernatural powers. These powers are not equal to Christ, neither can they facilitate access to the heavenly places, where Christ is seated at the right hand of God having been given the name above all names.

The African church ought unambiguously, through her life and faith, to teach that despite Christ having defeated supernatural powers (Col 2: 15), it is

---

[37] Arnold, *Powers*, p. 123.
[38] MacDonald, *The Pauline Churches*, pp. 145-6.

vital for believers to take the whole armour of God to resist the attacks of the evil one. The battle is to be fought bearing in mind that, "neither death, nor life, nor angels, nor principalities, nor powers, nor height, nor depth, nor anything else in creation, will be able to separate us from the love of God in Jesus Christ our Lord" (Rom 8:38-9). With such a promise, African believers must not revert to the state of "once" when they were without Christ and followed the course of this world and the prince of the power of the air. They must always remain and operate within the state of "now", being in Christ and having been reconciled to God. This summons believers to be vigilant and perceptive in the spiritual warfare, for in so doing they accept Christ's supremacy in their faith and life. They admit that supernatural powers have no authority to take them captive, separate them from God or keep them in sin. This means those physical afflictions credited to supernatural powers are still under God's overriding sovereignty. As Ferdinando comments, "Christ's present exaltation to the right hand of God indicates that it is he who exercises that sovereignty... It means that Satan and his forces harm believers only by God's permission and within limits He defines".[39] As noted in chapter five, the African church therefore must not have a simplistic view on how Satan and his minions work. Yet it must be put into perspective that Christians are not removed from the sphere ruled by the god of this world through his minions such as principalities and powers in the heavenly places. Their being delivered from the dominion of darkness and transferred to the kingdom of God's Son does not remove them from physical affliction. Physical affliction, as it was with Paul (2 Cor 12: 7), could be the way in which God achieves his purpose that is always for the good of believers.

The theology of supernatural powers in relation to Christ's supremacy must be built on the framework of the historical faith affirmed by creeds and explicit in the Pauline concept. However, as discussed in chapter two, this was undermined by the missionary legacy and the African response to it. The pioneer missionaries did not take the African belief in supernatural powers seriously, so they failed to proclaim the total supremacy of Christ. What captured the African mentality was that the God of the missionaries was only active on Sunday, specifically in the church building during the one-hour service. This made the Christian God and His Christ appear too small and less interested in spirits and the spirit world. The assumption was that since Christ was only active on Sundays, the other days were to be lived according to the traditional way. As a result, supernatural powers received too much attention not because there was "little conception of a supreme and reigning God" as Ferdinando erroneously asserts[40] but because Christ was not introduced as one who could deliver the African people from the powers of darkness, transferring them to God's kingdom. As Imasogie notes,

> Christians could talk of Christ's power to save from sin but not of

---

[39] Ferdinando, *The Triumph of Christ,* pp. 393-4
[40] Ferdinando, "Screwtape Revisited", p. 130.

his power to destroy the works of the devil and to save, to the utmost, those who are committed to him. For instance, the nineteenth century theologian could still quote Ephesians 6: 12, 'for we are not fighting against human beings, but against the wicked spiritual forces in the heavenly world, the rulers, authorities and cosmic powers of this dark age' but not with the same meaning Paul gave them when he penned those lines in Ephesians".[41]

Similarly, Walls notes, "in the missionary period, Christianity could protect innocent people from terrorizing accusations of witch activity; but its power to deal with the fear that such activity was taking place was limited. Still less obviously was there any help for the person who feared that they themselves possessed witch powers".[42] Jesus was only introduced as one who saves people from sins but not from spirits and the spirit world. Africans could not understand some of the sins from which Christ was to save them because in their view the Bible did not condemn the alleged sins.[43]

Incidentally, failing to locate supernatural powers in proper perspective vis-à-vis Jesus Christ could be damaging for the theological and spiritual growth of the church.

> A Christianity which refuses to acknowledge, confront and harness these chthonic powers will remain vulnerable to its young people leaving the church in favour of New Age spirituality, to its most eminent pastors just finding themselves 'helpless' falling in love with married congregation members, to the atrocities of a Rwanda where many of the butchers were faithful church goers, and to the paranoia which delights in uncovering imagined world conspiracies bent on destroying the Christian church.[44]

---

[41] Imasogie, *Guidelines*, p. 52.
[42] A. F. Walls, *The Cross-Cultural Process*, p. 132.
[43] The missionaries regarded some Gĩkũyũ practices such as polygamy and female circumcision as sin. But after reading '*Ibuku rĩa Ngai*' (literary translated as 'the book of God', meaning the Bible) the Gĩkũyũ people found that most of the respected characters of the Bible had more than one wife. They also found that the Gĩkũyũ term 'mũiritu' (that is, a circumcised girl) used as the equivalent of the Greek term παρθένος translated in English as 'virgin' described Mary's condition before her marriage to Joseph (See Kenyatta, *Facing* pp. 271-2; Karanja, *Founding an African Faith*, p. 153). Had the Bible translators done more research, they would have discovered that when the term 'mũiritu' referred to a virgin, it was qualified with the verb 'kathirange', hence, 'mũiritu kathirange', meaning a girl who had never known a man. However, it should be said that polygamy and female circumcision are no longer popular among the Gĩkũyũ people. In particular, those who practise female circumcision do it clandestinely and if known, they become the laughing stock in their area. Polygamy is also regarded as a weird practice that could impoverish the society.
[44] Robert Cook, "Devils & Manticores: Plundering Jung for a Plausible Demonology" in Anthony N. S. Lane (ed.) *The Unseen World: Christian Reflection on Angels, Demons*

Equally, it is detrimental for the African church if supernatural powers are assigned decisive and absolute power, which the Pauline concept denies them. As indicated above, the victory of Christ over supernatural powers also belongs to those 'in Christ'. It must be proclaimed openly, in words and deeds, that the existence of the church amidst the challenges that Africans credit to these chthonic powers illustrates that Christ's victory is extendable to believers. The errors of disbelieving supernatural powers exist and of believing they exist and giving them ultimate and absolute power that are common in the Western and African worldviews should be avoided. In fact, supernatural powers are real and they exist but the most important thing is to acknowledge that they are not sovereign, they do not have autonomous power and they are created just as we are.

The African church must therefore have a theology that directs her members "to live in the light of Christ's victory over the powers of darkness, demonstrating *confidence and boldness*".[45] Sadly, many African believers have not agreeably shown the confidence and boldness the Pauline concept demands because they frequently revert to traditional practices to solve life-threatening problems. "The usual resort of the African Christian in crisis is reversion to the traditional African religious practices".[46] Church leaders might frown on this reversion but they frequently fail to offer an alternative. This leaves many believers "feeling exposed and helpless in the face of hostile forces. In such circumstances, a reversion to traditional approach is almost inevitable".[47] Denials and condemnation are laughable; as they do not meet the felt needs traditional practices sorted out. They only enlarge the pastoral problem since "in times of crisis professing Christians adopt traditional solutions in large measures because they are unaware of an adequate and positive biblical response". Yet,

> the solution to such ignorance lies in teaching which goes beyond condemnation and which deals with the traditional concerns in the light of the gospel of Christ. It was in this way that Paul responded to the possibly rather similar fears of the Colossians, not denying their validity but demonstrating the absolute sufficiency of Christ to meet them (cf. Col 2:9-10).[48]

Perhaps the African church should use the traditional African religious practices to teach believers to shift their faith from supernatural powers to the belief that Christ is the one who guarantees adequate protection and the fullness of life.

The African church must deliberately and decisively emphasise Christ's

---

and the Heavenly Realm (Carlisle, Cumbria: Paternoster Press; Grand Rapids, Michigan: Baker Book House, 1996), p. 183.

[45] O'Brien, "Principalities and Powers", p. 143.
[46] Imasogie, *Guidelines*, p. 11.
[47] Ferdinando, *The Triumph of Christ*, p. 399.
[48] Ferdinando, *The Triumph of Christ*, p. 400.

supremacy over supernatural powers and their human agents. What is required is a teaching that goes beyond condemnation, systematically and penetratingly handling traditional fears on supernatural powers and exposing their inferior status in comparison to Christ. This, in fact, is the way in which Paul responded to the fears of supernatural powers within the context of production. He did not deny their reality but underscored Christ's supremacy over them. In this sense, underlining the theme of Christ's supremacy is crucial so as to incorporate the same into the African worldview as its central pillar. This effort could certainly bring essential changes to the African worldview, having created a model that responds to traditional concerns in an authentic Christian way that is also creatively African and devotedly biblical. Transforming the African worldview insinuates that believers will live out their life and faith without reverting to traditional remedies for as Hiebert states, the conception of the world to which people adhere shapes their decisions and behaviour.[49] How will the church explain the supremacy of Christ in the African context? O'Donuhue suggests this is only feasible if Africa returns to the real roots of her traditional philosophy, where the vision of humanity as a joyful partner in communion with all that is, prevailed.[50] This observation leads us to the second point that the African church should observe.

ii. Use of and Reliance on Cultural Resources and Tools

To explain Christ's supremacy in the African context, *the African church should use and rely on cultural resources/tools*. This begs two vital questions. Does the African culture and worldview have apposite and adequate resources or tools to sustain the teaching on Christ's supremacy? Is it possible to have a genuine theology that underlines Christ's supremacy over supernatural powers and which seeks a synthesis between Christianity and cultural continuity? The assumption is that if Paul relied on Jewish and Graeco-Roman cultural resource and tools to explain Christ's supremacy over supernatural powers, this, then, is what the African church may need to do. If the Bible identifies with "each culture as its natural destination and as a necessity of its life",[51] African culture and worldview must shape the teaching on the supremacy of Christ over supernatural powers for the African church. As A. F. Walls notes, "By their translation into Greek and use by converted Hellenistic Gentiles, the Hebrew Scriptures took on a new purpose and were applied within a new universe of thought. They became an authoritative sourcebook for Greek Christians seeking to build a coherent world view".[52] So the message of the Bible has *ad infinitum*

---

[49] Paul G. Hiebert, *Cultural Anthropology* (Grand Rapids, Michigan: Baker Book House, 1976), pp. 14-16.
[50] John O'Donuhue, *Spirits and Magic–A Critical look* Spearhead No. 68 (Eldoret: Gaba Publication, 1981), p. 49.
[51] Sanneh, *Translating the Message*, p. 69.
[52] Walls, *The Missionary Movement in Christian History*, p. 33.

"discovered a compatibility with indigenous cultures"[53] receiving it. In that case, African Christians would want to build a coherent worldview in which Jesus is above everything and so a genuine *Christus Victor* over every spiritual rule and authority. Chapter three exposed the African intense awareness of forces and powers at work in the world that threatens the interest of life and harmony. The victory of Jesus over the spiritual realm, particularly over evil forces would perfectly meet the need for a powerful protector. This message is consistent with African culture and worldview and it would enable Christians to recognize the supremacy of Christ.

Noticeably, the Graeco-Roman philosophical culture provided words to explain Christ's supremacy over supernatural powers. If the Graeco-Roman concept of κύριος was used for Christ through whom supernatural powers came into being, hence denoting Christ's Lordship over them, perhaps the African concept of ancestor could apply to Christ as the Supreme Ancestor by whom the African ancestors find their life and reason to exist. If "principalities and powers" were created to serve Christ the same could apply to African ancestral spirits. Perhaps the African healing tradition can offer a model for explaining Christ's supremacy. In many African communities, the spiritual healer was highly exalted when he successfully healed the sick or the one possessed by evil spirits. Jesus is known to have effectively healed sick and spirit-possessed people. Therefore, as Bujo notes, "another Christological model might be derived from the African healing tradition. Jesus might be conceived of as 'Healer of Healers'".[54] He has not only conquered supernatural powers but also diseases/defilement the majority of Africans fear most.[55] It is noticeable that the Gĩkũyũ people identified themselves with a diviner who could heal sickness and whom they exceedingly exalted.[56] African Christians can thus identify with Christ on the basis of his exaltation, which is linked to his victory over the

---

[53] Sanneh, *Translating the Message*, p. 71. Cf. Walls, *The Missionary Movement*, pp. 7-6, 40; Bediako, *Christianity in Africa*, p. 121.

[54] B. Bujo, *African Theology in its Social Context* (Nairobi: St Paul's publication-Africa, 1992), p. 85.

[55] The Gĩkũyũ people fear defilement, mistakes and taboos, which they believe originate from supernatural powers. For that reason, they visited diviners for purification rites and as Kĩama Gathigira observes, *"ningĩ tondũ Agĩkũyũ nĩmetigagĩra mathahu mũno, nĩkĩo maathiaga kurĩ andũ ago nĩguo merwo kĩrĩa kĩngĩnina thahu."* [Since the Gĩkũyũ people feared defilement exceedingly, they went to diviners to inquire what would purify defilement] (S. K. Gathigira, *Mĩĩkarĩre ya Agĩkũyũ. [The Gĩkũyũ People's Way of Life]* (Karatina: Scholars Publishers, 1933), p. 57.

[56] If the diviner managed to purify a defiled person, the Gĩkũyũ people highly exalted him. As Gathigira informs, *"maũndũ macio maarĩka gwĩkwo, nake mũndũ mũrũarũ ahone mũndũ mũgo ũcio akagathwo mũno"* [After these things (cleansing rituals), and the sick (defiled) person is healed, the medicine man is highly praised [exalted]. (Gathigira, *Mĩĩkarĩre*, p. 58).

Conclusion

supernatural.[57]

However, it must be stressed that Christ is not one among the ancestors and healers but the Lord of creation and so superior to anything created, visible or invisible. He is the indubitable Lord of reconciliation, who reconciles all things in heaven or earth to himself, making peace (Col 1: 20). Christ is above supernatural powers and he does not belong to any hierarchical structure or category of supernatural powers known in the African context.[58] Likewise, Christ's Lordship is not on the same level with the 'lords many and gods many' of the Hellenistic religion and worldview. So even if Christ may be acclaimed as an Ancestor or a Healer in the African context, he is not on the same level with the African healers and ancestors. Just as the Colossians *"received Jesus Christ as Lord"* and were to continue *"living in him, rooted and built up in him, strengthened in the faith as* (they*) were taught, and overflowing with thankfulness"* (Col. 2: 6–7), the African Christians, having *"received Jesus Christ"* as Ancestor and Healer must *"continue to live in him rooted and built up in him, strengthened in the faith as* they *were* (or are being) *taught, and overflowing with thankfulness"*.

The Christian faith confirms belief in the 'communion of saints', which includes the living and the dead in Christ. Healey and Sybertz identify saints as "special Christian ancestors and that all the deceased people participate in the communion of saints".[59] They further note, "In the complex African cosmology the living dead are the benevolent ancestral spirits who are the link between the living and the Supreme Being".[60] As stated in chapter three, the ancestors' care is assured by a sound relationship and practical obedience to their instructions. When people remained loyal to their inheritance, making the experiences of their ancestors their own, they remained in living communion not only with their ancestors but also with fellow humans, continually re-living the history of their people. When people conduct themselves according to the patterns established by the ancestors, they strengthen the tribe or clan as a whole and contribute to the well-being of each individual member.[61] In fact, beliefs in spirits in the African context constitute an inclusive exploration and integration of the natural and the spiritual. This especially revolves around the observance of distinctive moral values, norms and principles that are hospitable to the realisation of abundant life for all and sundry. The observance of these distinctive moral values, norms and principles infuses meaning and harmony to societal life in Africa.[62] Ferdinando's comments on Africans' concerns, "which do not recognise the moral and spiritual dimension of spirits' power but are

---

[57] wa Gatumu "Primal Worldview and The Bible", p. 86; Ukpong, "Development in Biblical Interpretation in Africa", p. 18.
[58] See chapter 3, pp. 60-65.
[59] Healey and Sybertz, *Towards an African*, p. 28.
[60] Healey and Sybertz, *Towards an African*, p. 211
[61] Bujo, *African Theology*, p. 22
[62] Magesa (*African Religion*, esp. pp. 14, 16-7, 37-8, 41-2, 59-71) discusses this view persuasively arguing that the basis of African morality is the promotion of human life.

preoccupied with the physical suffering they inflict"[63] is unfounded. The African mind-set takes into account the spiritual and the moral aspect of human deeds and the world. "The world as a sacred abode of the life forces of God, the ancestors and diverse spirits is what gives human action its necessarily sacred character".[64] As such, it would not be a big issue for African Christians to put their loyalty to Christ as their Supreme Ancestor, as their worldview demands them to be spiritually and morally aligned to the benevolent ancestral spirits for individual and communal welfare. Indeed the African context of reception has rich resources that would offer a paradigm shift in the African worldview, consequently sustaining the theme of Christ's supremacy over the powers of darkness. Faith in, and a cordial relationship with Christ would be enough to protect believers from malignant supernatural powers.

The belief in supernatural powers in the African context is linked to the desire for the abundant life. This belief is a significant cultural tool that would enable African believers to accept Paul's teaching that the fullness of life is found ἐν Χριστῷ and in a community centred on Christ.

> It seems that when Paul uses 'ἐν Χριστῷ', he means both that salvation is attained through attachment to the Messiah – participation in his death and resurrection – and that salvation is to be found in the community of believers which is centred around Christ. The participation in the Christ event is central for Paul, but the individual must become part of the community of others rooted in the same experience. The expression ἐν Χριστῷ reinforces the boundaries separating the body of those who will be saved from those on the outside; it connects the revelation of Christ with the existence of the community of believers.[65]

Paul's teaching encourages believers to intersect and interact with each other amidst the forces that may frustrate their attempt to realise the meaning of their existence in Christ. These, using Berger's words, are the "forces of chaos", which "threaten" the construction of the meaning of their existence in this world.[66] But the community of believers must unite as they seek to gain the fullness of life in Christ.[67] As stated above, Healey and Sybertz identify saints as the special ancestors of the Christian community and the majority of African societies understand the community to include the departed ancestors and the living. The issue that the theology of supernatural powers in the African context must persistently handle is whether the ancestral spirits belong to the community of believers. This for many African people is the logical

---

[63] Ferdinando, *The Triumph of Christ*, p. 393.
[64] Magesa, *African Religion*, p. 59.
[65] MacDonald, *The Pauline Churches*, p. 74.
[66] Cf. P. L. Berger, *The Social Reality of Religion* (London: Penguin Books, 1969), p. 61.
[67] Eph 2: 1-22; 3: 4-6; 4: 8-16; Col 3: 11; Gal 3: 28.

Conclusion

conclusion.⁶⁸

As members of the living community, we have noted that the ancestors guarantee protection and providence of their loved ones in a world full of spirit activities. This central belief of the African worldview would help African believers to realise that life in Christ does not remove them from the world ruled by the god of this age and dominated by supernatural powers. It also reminds them of the necessity to live a different life-style from the past one when they did not know Christ. The challenge for the first century CE believers was to observe a new life in a pluralistic pagan setting. As Marshall argues, "It was impossible to be a Christian and live as one had formerly lived. The new faith led to a new way of life".⁶⁹ African believers are thus expected to no longer live as if they belonged to the world. Their former existence has no value in checking the indulgences of the flesh (Col 2: 23). They must put off the old nature with its practices and put on a new nature renewed in the knowledge of the image of its creator (Col 3: 9-10). Life in Christ, which is synonymous with life in the Spirit, is the new mode of existence that is opposed to life in the flesh (Gal 5: 16-25). Life in Christ or in the Spirit is the tactic to flee from the present intimidating reality attributed to supernatural powers. MacDonald's observation in relation to Paul's original audience is relevant to Paul's audience in the African context. "In a society where demons could cause considerable havoc (1 Cor 10: 20-1) and where Satan was an agent to contend with (2 Cor 2: 11), the body where life was lived in Spirit offered protection from destructive forces in the universe".⁷⁰ The new life in Christ guarantees the safety and existence of believers in a hostile world under the dominion of the spirit of this age.

The spontaneous prayers and praises of Jesus by an ordinary Ghanaian Christian woman and traditional midwife, intensely deriving from images of her primal worldview, are instructive to the point being made. Fr. John Kirby has faithfully translated the prayers and praises, originally documented in Akan mother tongue, into English, "to give the reader a good indication of their depth of Christian experience conveyed in the thought-forms of Akan world view".⁷¹ Concerning these prayers and praises, Bediako notes that in the setting of ubiquitous forces and mysterious powers, a Christian who has understood that

---

⁶⁸ In 1994 the Anglican Church in Kenya cerebrated the 150th anniversary of its existence since the arrival of John Ludwig Krapf, the first CMS sponsored missionary, who arrived in Kenya in 1844. The Rt. Rev. David Gitari, the then bishop of ACK Diocese of Kirinyaga, electrified the congregation in acknowledging that people who died before baptism rightly belonged to the community of believers since they had demonstrated their faith in Christ by enrolling for the baptismal catechism classes but died before the actual baptism. Many people regarded this to be in agreement to the African worldview, in which the departed ancestors are still part of the community.
⁶⁹ I. H. Marshall, "Culture and the New Testament" in J. Scott and R. T. Coote (eds.), *Gospel and Culture* (London, SCM, 1979), p. 37.
⁷⁰ MacDonald, *The Pauline Churches*, p. 82.
⁷¹ Bediako, *Jesus in Africa*, p. 9

Jesus Christ is a living reality, can be at home, assured in faith that Jesus alone is Lord, Protector, Provider and Enabler. He further notes that the prayers deeply reflect a well-known and main feature of African primal religion.[72] They recognise the struggles and battles of life, in which 'Jesus of the deep forest' is capable of fighting, conquering and leading his people to triumph. 'Jesus of the deep forest' rescues the hunter from the attacks of wild beasts believed to be the agents of invisible supernatural powers that are active in the natural order. Jesus fights the evil powers, reducing their leader Satan into a mouse; hence Christians have no fear of the devil. Jesus fights for Christians in such a way that by the time they reach the edge of the battle the war has already ended. The prayers and praises represent Jesus as the "Hero Incomparable" whose followers do not need a sword in battle if they go with him. The word of his mouth is the weapon that makes enemies turn and run. Walking with Jesus therefore rules out the possibility of fear, even when there is trouble and even when the devil charges like a lion. Jesus reverses the terrors that threaten human life and above all, the terror of death. Jesus has tied the terror of death to a tree so that his followers may be happy.[73]

The metaphors with which the prayers and praises describe Jesus as he manifests and discloses himself and his power in threatening conditions and structures of human existence are of startling quality. These prayers and praises reveal the all-powerful Jesus performing marvellous deeds. They also describe Jesus as the Saviour of the poor and a dependable friend who ensures healthy growth. He is the unrivalled diviner and the saviour of all nations. As a benign provider, Jesus breaks down barriers between people and transforms enemies into brothers and sisters. For that reason, all classes and groups of people find their longings met in him.[74] The titles ascribed to Jesus in these prayers were traditionally and presently ascribed to the Akan rulers.[75] Jesus is the Chief of all chiefs, and as Bediako maintains, the picture here is of the Akan king, who sits on the throne of the ancestors, receiving the homage of all his subjects during the annual New Year *Odwira* Festival.[76] Jesus is the Chief of all chiefs and according to the prayers, the chiefs are wise men.[77] This preserves social and political relationship that sustains the community. The ancestral and royal titles that the prayers and praise of Afua accredit to Jesus allows the apprehension of the all-pervasive Lordship of Jesus in the realm of ancestral spirits and in the human realm ruled by human kings. According to Bediako, "the powers of the biblical world can also be experienced here and now, even in the uncertainties

---

[72] Bediako, *Jesus in Africa*, p. 9

[73] John Kirby, *Jesus of the deep forest: Prayers and Praises of Afua Kuma*, Translated by John Kirby from Akan to English, (Accra: Asempa Publishers, 1980), pp. 7, 17-19, 30, 46.

[74] Kirby, *Jesus of the deep forest*, pp. 577, 14-5, 22-25, 35-39; Bediako, *Jesus in Africa*, pp. 8-15.

[75] Bediako, *Jesus in Africa*, p. 14.

[76] Bediako, *Jesus in Africa*, p. 14.

[77] Kirby, *Jesus of the deep forest*, p. 25.

of modern African politics".[78]

Certainly, this unschooled Ghanaian woman had heard the stories of the Gospel read and preached in her own life. Yet it is the richness of the African religious past that enabled her to identify Jesus of the Gospels with Jesus of the deep forest, the miracle worker who does the impossible and wins over nature. And as noted in chapter three, according to the African worldview, supernatural powers reside in natural phenomena and more so in the deep forest. Jesus of the deep forest like Jesus of the Gospels provides food to the hungry and water to the thirsty, delivers people from all manners of ailments. He grants salvation, even when strange malign creatures with superhuman powers (*Mmoatia*) and their leader (*Sasabonsam*) threaten the fullness of life. The prayers and praises show that the African context has adequate tools that the church can use to explain Christ's supremacy over supernatural powers. These prayers make the defeat and disgrace of supernatural powers meaningful for the African context. Jesus has destroyed the power of invisible supernatural powers and the power of visible wild creatures that can suddenly attack a village. Jesus is

> The hunter gone to the deep forest. *Sasabonsam*, the evil spirit has troubled the hunters for many years. They ran in fear, leaving their guns behind. Jesus has found those guns, and brought them to the hunters to go and kill the elephant. Truly Jesus is the Man among men, the most stalwart of men. He stands firm as a rock.[79]

This celebration of Jesus is historical since evil spirits have troubled the hunters for many years. But Jesus has come and he is acclaimed where he was not known before. While the defeat of evil supernatural powers is a living and abiding reality it was, however, a definite event in the past, which now lives in the local memory[80]. It is apparent the African primal religious experience can allow a deeper consciousness of Christ's supremacy over supernatural powers. This would undo the angst-ridden loyalty given to supernatural powers by some African Christians. As the prayers and praises insist,

> Our ancestors did not know *Onyankpon*, the great God. They served lesser gods and spirits and became tired. But for us, we have seen holy men and prophets. We have gone to tell the angels how Jehovah helped us reach this place. Jehovah has helped us come this far; with gratitude we come before Jesus, the one who gives everlasting life.[81]

Perhaps the African church should preach a message similar to the one Ignatius preferred for Ephesus believers. Ignatius emphasised that with the

---

[78] Bediako, *Jesus in Africa*, p. 15.
[79] Kirby, *Jesus of the deep forest*, p. 19.
[80] Bediako, *Jesus in Africa*, p. 10.
[81] Kirby, *Jesus of the deep forest*, p. 30.

coming of Christ, all magic and every kind of spell were dissolved.[82] In the same way, through the incarnation, death, resurrection and exaltation of Christ, the power of supernatural powers over believers was destroyed. Now, supernatural powers are the defeated enemies and believers have no fears as they await the eschatological glorification. Bediako notes, "One aspect of the relevance of the achievement of early Hellenistic Christian thought for the modern African context has to do with the possibility of a genuine theology which seeks a synthesis between Christian religious commitment and cultural continuity".[83] However, cultural continuity must not be understood as an effort to compromise biblical teaching and demands with the cultural traits that are repugnant to the truth of the Gospel. Paul did not recklessly rely on the Graeco-Roman culture and worldview. This means that the African church cannot just use the African culture and worldview uncritically.[84] As noted in chapter two, African culture and worldview impeded the initial reception of biblical teachings and have continually undermined the Pauline teachings on Christ's supremacy over supernatural powers. The synthesis that Bediako calls for must not be construed as a summons to syncretism. It is not fusing African beliefs in supernatural powers with biblical teaching so as to come up with a different message from that which the Pauline concept upholds. The idea is to transform culture. This does not mean to wipe out culture but to give it a new outlook, a new worldview. This implies the conversion of culture, a conversion of what is already there and which needs no substitute.

So, rather than being against culture and worldview, the Pauline concept would engage the ultimate dynamism of culture, transforming what is already there, and not imposing what is outside that culture and worldview. This would require a "positive commendation of what is good in the world as being worthy of the attention of the Christian".[85] Bediako rightly points out, "The significant transforming impact of the Gospel upon the Non-Western world arises from the Non-Western response to the Gospel in its own terms and not in terms of Western expectations".[86] Just as the Pauline concept sought to change the culture and worldview encircling the Graeco-Roman context of production, it ought to transform the culture and worldview encasing the African context of reception. Perhaps the Pauline concept can only transform culture if it receives a cultural response. For that reason, the African church ought to rely on cultural tools, creatively and critically engaging with the same, so as to underline the theme of Christ's supremacy.

---

[82] Ignatius, *Ephesians* 19: 3.
[83] Kwame Bediako, *Theology and Identity: The Impact of Culture upon Christian Thought in the Second Century and Modern Africa*. (Oxford: Regnum Books, 1992), p. 432.
[84] Cf. Walls "In Quest", p. 104; wa Gatumu "Primal Worldview and The Bible", p. 28-9.
[85] Marshall, "Culture and the New Testament", p. 38.
[86] Bediako, *Christianity in Africa*, p. 174.

iii. Coming to Terms with Other Dimensions of Supernatural Powers

The two related points discussed above specifically relate to the African belief that places spirits at the core of everything that happens in human life. This belief, as already mentioned, is detrimental to the life of the African church because fear of spirits prevails where freedom in Christ should reign. This belief, as discussed in chapter two, makes people appear as the-who-cannot-help-it-lot. Too much stress is given to the spiritual causation of events, without considering the fact human involvement also adds to the causation of such events. The African church should therefore consider a third point: to *come to terms with other dimensions of supernatural powers*. In chapter six, it was stated that supernatural powers are irreducible metaphors which are explainable through other metaphors and in that sense they are also extendable. It was also noted that even though irreducible metaphors are inexplicable, the fact that metaphors are typically extendable make irreducible metaphors identifiable if the sense suggests that the referred reality is possible.[87] However, a key observation was that the metaphor of supernatural powers could not be reduced to a single predicate. The African church must take into consideration the positive implications the metaphor of supernatural powers might offer for the education of her members so as to come to terms with other dimensions of supernatural powers. The use of metaphor may enable the African church to underline the supremacy of Christ in the structures of human existence. This, as we noted in the close of chapter six, would be the way forward to contextualise the Pauline concept of supernatural powers in the African context.

It is important for the African church to recognise that, as stated in chapter one, the major problem that confronts human beings with regard to supernatural powers is the problem of language. This has led to the recognition that people "cannot describe the reality of the Numinous except by imaginatively using the symbols, images and signs of their own existence and experience, and stretching them to the limit".[88] Human awareness of the authority and control human leaders have over their subjects has been metaphorically transferred or identified or substituted or interacted with the alleged authority and control supernatural powers have over human existence. As noted in chapter six, the literal meaning does not disappear but plays a critical part in the interpretation of the metaphor. Metaphor first functions literally as a rule for pinpointing the object or situation and then functions metaphorically by indirectly designating another similar situation. The rule seems to be that something must exist in order that something else may be identified with it. This allows metaphor to minimise the problem of language with regards to supernatural powers. For this to happen, it is critical to recognise that the metaphorical 'is' signifies both is like and is not; hence the forces that determine human existence have spiritual, physical, psychological, sociological, anthropological and other dimensions. As noted in chapter three, the aforesaid dimensions of human life are interlinked

---

[87] See chapter 6, pp. 204-206.
[88] Magesa, *African Religion*, p. 37.

and interrelated. Behavioural traits attributable to one dimension may be swayed by, or may sway other dimensions. These dimensions of human existence and which are also the dimensions that metaphors can take, make the understanding of the metaphor of supernatural powers more nuanced. Due to the tension between literal sense and metaphorical referent, people may agree on the reality and existence of supernatural powers but it is not given that they may conceive the metaphor in similar ways. For this reason, the African church should make an effort to educate her members that the concept of supernatural powers does not depend on a too naïve view of spirits. Also it does not depend on anti-supernaturalistic view of the reality and existence of spirits. Believers ought to engage with all dimensions of the powers, yet cautiously. In fact, metaphorical language like any other figurative language may not engage fully a people's belief system. However, it minimises the problem of language with regards to supernatural powers.

As already noted, the African worldview allows the beliefs in supernatural powers to revolve around human existence. The African church should realise that supernatural powers and the structures of human existence work together to impede human life. Even so, the struggle for human survival is against spiritual forces that use the structures of human existence and powerful personage to create a reign of terror, which entangles people in a way they cannot untangle themselves. The big issue is whether the people who allow themselves to work with or to be used by supernatural forces inimical to human existence should be held responsible for the suffering that befalls humanity. This demands an explicit and critical application of the metaphorical tension of is like and is not. In so doing, the church will recognise the dehumanising values of the structures of human existence that should be credited to human and not to spirit forces. It is human beings, according to Ephesians 4: 27 who can give the devil a chance. Humans are therefore accountable for allowing forces outside themselves to control their life and the structures within which they exist.

According to the Lewisian deprivation theory, the marginalised, deprived and frustrated female and male are more prone to spirit-possession.[89] In reality, this means that social marginalisation, deprivation and exclusion can provide an opening for supernatural powers to sway, control and shape human continued existence negatively. It is not a secret that women in most African societies are excluded in the ownership of property. Regrettably, they form a minority in religious leadership, albeit constituting large numbers supporting religious institutions. Lewis believes this male-dominated scenario creates many cases of spirit-possession and causes many diseases among the marginalised women.[90] He contends, "The role of women in spirit-possession is a compensation for their exclusion and lack of authority in other spheres".[91] The exclusion of women in the management of religio-cultural and socio-political institutions

---

[89] See chapter 3 pp 77-79.
[90] Lewis, *Religion in Context*, p. 50.
[91] Lewis, *Religion in Context*, p. 48.

Conclusion

damages the development of African societies.[92] If claims of spirit-possession by the less empowered people in the society is a means of dominating the empowered[93], this may dreadfully affect development if, for instance, possessed women make costly demands that their husbands struggle to meet and cannot resist as spirits demand them.[94] Spirit possession can also serve the interests of men by confirming that women are vulnerable to evil spirits, so they abet economic and social disparity.[95] Either way, this is to give the devil or his host of supernatural powers a chance to sway the structures of human existence. Deprivation and frustrations may cause anger and other adverse emotions by which the devil and his hosts could gain a chance to deny people the fullness of life.

It is not a secret that some leaders and institutions in the African context use their status to deny human beings what is rightly theirs. Several institutions and their human leaders have deprived the poor and the hungry. As an example, a newspaper reports how coffee farmers in Kenya lost Kshs. 337 million (about £3.37 million) from 1995 to 1999 because of corruption.[96] Another newspaper report exposed the state of hunger and food deprivation in Northern Kenya. "In the midst of this abject misery, there are reports of widespread theft of relief food by some administration officials and head teachers. The food is then sold in shops in Lodwar or transported back to Kitale according to the Catholic Peace and Justice Commission".[97] In both illustrations, poor and hungry peasants were denied their right to enjoy the fullness of life. In accordance with the African worldview, malevolent spirits inspire leaders and institutions that deny people the abundant life. But this does not allow us to overlook the fact that human leaders aligned to these institutions bring about a situation where corruption and oppression boost marginalisation, deprivation and frustrations of poor and hungry peasants. In such a situation, an odd desire for status in society by whatever means seems inevitable. The structures of human existence create a competitive mood only explicable in terms of Machiavellian principle, where expediency rather than morality rule and where the catchphrase is "survival of

---

[92] The findings of a New York based human rights lobby group indicates that Kenyan women are among the world's most discriminated against through the violation of their property rights. The devastating effects of the violations, says the human right's lobby group, are not only discriminatory but also fatal since they not only harm women and children, but also Kenya's growth (Daily Nation online, http://www.nationaudio.com, accessed on 05.03.2003).

[93] Lewis, *Religion in Context,* p. 61.

[94] Cf. Lewis, *Religion in Context,* pp. 52, 54, 57-6, 64.

[95] Cf. Gomm, "Bargaining from Weakness", pp. 304-5. The Gĩkũyũ refer to the whirlwind as "spirits of women". Since the whirlwind can cause destruction of precious property, this loss may be attributed to women. As a result, women can be sidelined with the argument that they bring in destructive spirits. Invoking spirits therefore can be misused in order to justify a human attempt to cope with a social situation.

[96] *Sunday Nation,* "Coffee Board Lost Millions to Bosses" (21.11.1999), pp. 1-2.

[97] *Sunday Nation* "Famine in Northern Kenya: The shocking truth" (21.11.1999), p. 1.

the fittest".⁹⁸ This is a situation in which supernatural powers create a spirit of improvising African families and society. Believers are summoned to avoid such situations by not giving the devil a chance. The African church should use this belief to alert believers that resisting a spiritual devil and his host of spiritual powers is metaphorical and so, as we saw in chapter six, not different from resisting the physical sources of oppression, evil and suffering.

A further analysis would imply that people give the devil a chance through the ideologies they create. These ideologies having been created somehow outlive their creators, gaining a somewhat divine status and autonomy. Berger and Luckmann maintain that language and available knowledge are socially constructed, stocked within the society and largely shape people's perception and interpretation of reality. Reality is also based and defined in a socio-cultural setting, where people relate to each other through institutions. These institutions transmit the language and available knowledge to persons as soon as they are born. The habitual human activity is related to the institutionalised setting while the institutional norms regulate human behaviour. This happens because institutions have a history that precedes the history of the individual. It also occurs since individuals stand as part of the institution despite their attitude about the institution. Berger and Luckmann note that, though individuals create institutions, these institutions outlive their founders and develop their own reality. Eventually, institutional reality shapes individuals' natural and reflexive attitudes. What the institution's language and available knowledge define as the objective truth is learned and internalised as the subjective reality that has power to shape the individual.⁹⁹

It is crucial for the church to understand how the powers and structure of human existence interlock and network. The unavoidable question, especially for the African context is what causes institutions to outlive their founders and develop their own reality that shapes the individual's natural and reflexive instincts. Wink would call this the Domination System, which is prehistoric and traceable to what he calls the myth of redemptive violence. He builds upon the conflicts of the gods in the Enuma Elish, where Marduk gained supremacy above other gods.¹⁰⁰ By implication, the Domination System has a supernatural origin. In that case, supernatural powers confer to an institution a spirituality that makes the institution outlive its founders. It follows that if the god of this world bring about a spirit of corruption, those aligned to its sphere of influence

---

⁹⁸ Joe Babendreier observes that Niccolo Machiaveli argued that might make right and rejected social justice in favour of political opportunism. Machiaveli believed success depended on being dubious and ruthless and the most powerful government not only gets away with deceiving its citizen and other nations but also survives by cunningness. (Lifestyle Magazine, Sunday Nation online, http://www.nationaudio.com, accessed on 04.05.2003).
⁹⁹ Berger and Luckmann, *The Social Construction of Reality*, pp. 33-85.
¹⁰⁰ Wink, *Engaging the Powers*, pp. 9, 13-104; Wink, *The Powers that Be*, pp. 37-62.

become corrupt.[101] This perhaps explains why individuals of upright character and international fame appointed to purposely eradicate corruption and other social evils in institutions become corrupt. They get entangled in a web of a spirituality inimical to human existence. This makes corruption a mysterious and alien spirituality that manifests the link between the god of this world and the structures of human existence. The same applies to tribalism or ethnic rivalry for political and resource control. Perhaps anti-human and anti-social conduct allied to corruption, tribalism, nepotism and other social evils come from supernatural powers behind institutions.[102] Whatever these forces are, it seems that they act for a reality that generates its own force that sweeps persons to its power. Perhaps these forces, now having their own spiritual existence, form a matrix that seeks to restrain human beings, a matrix that enslaves and from which people cannot redeem themselves on their own. In tandem with Gunton, "the point is that human beings do in different ways appear to fall into the grip of alien forces, which leave them not only incapable of acting morally but also of distinguishing good and evil".[103]

Religious institutions are also subject to the sway of the god of this world, especially in leadership rivalry.[104] Like any other human institution, the church can give the god of this world a chance to derail the fullness of life in Christ.[105] In the words of A. F. Walls, if principalities and powers work within the human system, they can also work within Christianity, for it is not Christianity that saves but Christ.[106] The god of this world can therefore control the church's language and available knowledge and so suppress the understanding of God's mystery revealed in Jesus Christ through which people attain the fullness of

---

[101] Wink (*Engaging the Powers*, p. 15) building from Ricoeur recalls how Marduk and Era killed one of the gods imprisoned for siding with Tiamat and used the blood of the assassinated god to create human beings. He then asserts, "the implication is clear: humanity is created from the blood of a murdered god. Our very origin is violence. Killing is in our blood. Humanity is not the originator of evil, but merely finds evil already present and perpetuates it. Our origins are divine, to be sure, since we are made from a god, but from the blood of an assassinated god". Cf. Ricoeur, *The Symbolism* pp.178-183.

[102] Cf. Ward Ewing, *The Power of the Lamb* (Cambridge, Massachusetts: Cowley Publications, 1990), p. 47.

[103] Gunton, *The Actuality of Atonement*, p. 73.

[104] As informed by the leaders of the East African Revival Fellowship in a personal dialogue, demonic powers 'visit' the fellowship after every thirty years or so, causing chaotic rivalry. The fellowship emphasizes personal testimony and commitment to Jesus Christ. Its members are drawn from mainline protestant churches. For an elongated period, the leaders of the fellowship, popularly known as Team were involved in a power struggle, which they believed was inspired by supernatural powers. In June 2000, when I was the Director of Communications and acting Administrative Secretary of ACK. Diocese of Kirinyaga, they sent a delegation to me for prayers and arbitration.

[105] See Cobble, *The Church and the Powers*, p. 39.

[106] Walls, *The Missionary Movement*, p. 62.

life. This recognition is perhaps an inoculation to stop the church from being enslaved and victimised by a religious enthusiasm that outwardly has the form and sense of God but inwardly denying its power (2 Tim 3: 5). Unfortunately, such enthusiasm, if allowed to infiltrate the church's spirituality, may block the church's deliberate and preferential option of addressing social, economic, political and religious forces that are hostile to God's plan for human beings as revealed in Jesus Christ. The African church in particular must acknowledge the possibility that the god of this world stands behind oppressive institutions that deny people the fullness of life[107]. She must also admit that where people give supernatural powers an opening to control the institution's language and available knowledge, blame must be credited to such people. Above all, and since the struggle is not against flesh and blood, the African church must take Arnold's observation on board. "The work of the evil one moves far beyond the simple notion of tempting an individual to sin. Satan appears to have a well-organized strategy. He aims strongly at the people with power and influence".[108]

Apparently, the structures of human existence impede the fullness of life in so far as the people involved in running these structures are inclined towards the possibility of evil. This gives supernatural powers a chance to exert control over individuals and institutions and to keep people in bondage to legalism, social ideologies and moral compromises.[109] The structures of human existence finally hold people hostage, pollute human mind and make people's attitude and deeds hostile to God's salvific purposes. The irony is that the structures are integral to human survival for the reason that they not only enslave but also liberate.[110] Their liberating nature enables people to enjoy ultimate freedom in Christ while their enslaving nature brings about fear and terror of the god of this world. Arguably, their enslaving nature results from hostile ideologies, whose creation is probably influenced by supernatural powers. People transmit these ideologies through and within the structures of their existence. But instead of liberating, the ideologies burden people with a suprahuman force as destructive as the god of this world. Subsequently, the ideologies operate on the level of supernatural powers, having the status of a god. Cobble demonstrates that such ideologies exist in every society, are present in symbols, motivations and structures of social groups. Citing examples from the American context, he detects the spirit of capitalism and spirit of competition that have no sovereign existence without the people who create them.[111]

---

[107] Ferdinando, *The Triumph of Christ*, pp. 247-257 maintains that Satan's goal is to seduce believers so as to undermine their relationship with God. By so doing, he intends to re-establish his own control over human beings.

[108] Arnold, *Powers*, p. 204.

[109] Cf. Thomas B. White, *The Believer's Guide to Spiritual Warfare* (Ann Arbor, Michigan: Servant Publications, 1990), p. 35.

[110] Stephen C. Mott, *Biblical Ethics and Social Change* (New York/London: Oxford University Press, 1982), p. 15.

[111] Cobble, *The Church and the Powers*, pp. 20-1.

Conclusion

Nevertheless, ideologies have a concealed potential to condition and to shape life through individuals and institutions that create them. To attain total control, they encircle human life, acquire spiritual value, and subordinate individuals to their authority. They become "invisible forces that determine human physical, psychic and social existence".[112] While it is persuasive that an ideology cannot exist without the people who create it,[113] it may not be credible that it is the equivalent of apocalyptic supernatural powers. Nevertheless, an ideology, which cannot exist separately without the people who create it and for whom it is created, somehow becomes a terror to human life. The rulers of this age, who now work against God's plan are responsible for worsening ideologies that people create with good intentions.[114] Nevertheless, these good intentions become oppressive if people who transmit them chose to follow the way of the god of this world. Such people allow the god of this world or the rulers of this age to control the spirituality of an institution. The reverse angle is that supernatural powers use such people to control human and institutional life. According to Jung people have unconsciously ingested the demons of nature that they had overcome, consequently becoming the devil's maisonette. Demons no longer inhabit rocks, woods, mountains and rivers but use human beings as a more dangerous dwelling place.[115] This indicates the interlocking and networking of human leaders and supernatural powers. It also gives a clue as to what makes human leaders and the ideologies that finally cause division and chaos in human life absolute. The absolutised regimes in human history should be responsible for indefinable evil and suffering they cause to human existence. Such regimes could be regarded as demonic, though not demons in the literal sense of the word, because they are under the control of, and reveal the networking between supernatural powers and the structures of human existence.[116]

Supernatural powers work behind the scenes, making use of hostile values so as to control the structures of human existence and to cause oppression and

---

[112] Wink, *Unmasking the Powers*, p. 4.

[113] Arnold, *Powers*, p. 204 rightly insists, "just as a glove has no authority on its own to carry out a task, ideologies, economic systems and the like have no power apart from the people who subscribe to them and enforce them. A tradition ceases to be a tradition when people no longer pass it on".

[114] Nyerere created Ujamaa philosophy to enable equitable distribution of resources among the Tanzanian people, but it contributed to rampant poverty among the ordinary people. Kenyatta created Harambee philosophy for Kenyan people to assist each other so as to fight poverty, ignorance and disease, but it became a source of corruption (see http://www.kentimes.com accessed on 05.03. 2003). Moi's Nyayo Philosophy (Nyayo means footsteps) of peace, love and unity and being concern with general welfare of others did not live up to its vision. The legacy of the Nyayo era includes insecurity, tribal animosity, ethnic cleansing and corruption.

[115] Jung, "Synchronicity", p. 593-4.

[116] Cf. C. Ngcokovane, *Demons of Apartheid: A Moral and Ethical Analysis of the NGK, NP, Broerderbond Justification of Apartheid*. (Braamfontein: Skotaville, 1989).

marginalisation. But this must not be viewed with a simplistic one-dimensional naïvety. If human deeds move supernatural powers to act benignly or malignly, such people are responsible for events hostile to human existence. In fact, τῶν ἀρχόντων τοῦ αἰῶνος τούτου (1 Cor 2: 6-8) refer to spiritual powers and human rulers who were responsible for Christ's death. Early Christian tradition held supernatural powers and human political and religious leaders accountable for Christ's death.[117] What the metaphor of supernatural powers does to the African church is to open up the understanding that spiritual beings inspire evil plotting, which if internalised by human leaders, make institutions and ideologies they create inimical to human existence.[118] This generates complex institutions that have conceited inner logic or spirituality inimical to fundamental human needs and general welfare. What matters is the existence of the institution, as it is arguably clear in some political parties in Africa (and in the world) whose leaders condone the loss of life and property in order to remain in power.[119] It is also clear in some religious institutions, which propagate beliefs injurious to human existence. Such institutions communicate to people illusions of peace, hope and security, which besiege life and which they cannot evade.[120]

7:3. A Summing-up Analysis

From the aforesaid it would be naïve to exonerate humans of responsibility in events where people equally and willingly participate in the creation of what makes human existence unbearable. The metaphorical "is", signifying both is like and is not rules out a too naïve view of spirits and allows African believers to consider other dimensions of power. It would be foolhardy to neglect the fact that, as noted in chapter three, spiritual, social, political, economic and psychological dimensions of human existence are interlinked and interrelated. Behavioural traits attributable to one dimension may be influenced by, or may influence other dimensions. For that reason, The African church should regard the metaphorical understanding of supernatural powers beneficial. Does Paul not refer to his ailment as a thorn in the flesh, a messenger of Satan? Paul's ailment was like a literal thorn pricking the flesh, but it was more than a thorn as it was a messenger of Satan. This shows different levels of metaphor, which could allow the understanding that leaders who frustrate human existence by denying people what is rightly theirs are literally human beings. Yet they can

---

[117] See chapter 5, page 131-133.

[118] See Heinrich Schlier, *Principalities and Powers in the New Testament* (Freiburg: Herder; London: Burns & Oates, 1961), p. 31; Wink, *Naming the Powers,* p. 84.

[119] Investigations by the East African Standard (http://www.eastandard.net, accessed on 08.03.2003) revealed how several state corporations in Kenya deposited taxpayers' money in unclear circumstances in an insolvent bank. According to investigations, the government owned institutions deposited the colossal amount as a result of political intrigues and manipulation so that the then ruling party might get tribal support from the tribe of the person who owned this bank.

[120] See Wink, *Engaging the Powers,* pp. 96-104.

be identified or compared with malignant powers hostile to human existence since they misuse available resources at the expense of the great majority. They choose demonic values that are a setback to human life and they encourage fraud and all kinds of deceit. Rather than challenging rampant corruption and other social vices that frustrate human existence, they condone them in word and deed. Rather than always acting in the interest of the public, they reject public trust to pursue selfish interests. By so doing, the public disapprove them, meaning that they, not supernatural powers are accountable for their conduct. The theology of supernatural powers in relation to Christ's supremacy in the African context ought to move believers a step further. Other dimensions that explain constraints and pressures that impinge upon us must not be neglected at the expense of the spiritual dimension. Indeed, it is awful to only emphasise a spiritual dimension with regards to healing an illness that obviously requires medical dimension.[121] It is equally appalling to emphasise a medical dimension when affliction plainly requires a spiritual dimension.

More important, the root of what makes people think and act the way they do must be identified so as to engage their acts of commission and/or omission. Paul's teaching liberates believers from the fear of, and unwarranted allegiance given to supernatural powers. Paul offers encouraging evidence to the constant supreme reign of God's kingdom on earth and the victory over evil.[122] He definitely displays Christ's supremacy over supernatural powers in a world dominated by the fear of the same. His teaching validates the reality of Christ's reign, sovereignty and subjugation of supernatural powers. By accentuating the supremacy of Christ, Paul restores confidence to a people whose existence is eclipsed by fears and suspicions caused by erroneous beliefs in supernatural powers. His teaching on Christ's supremacy and victory should annul denials about the existence, and fearful obsessions of supernatural powers. As Dunn avers, "Christ's death and resurrection mean that any and all heavenly powers have lost any effective power over those who belong to Christ and any effective say in their destiny".[123] As such, it is determinedly critical to address existential fears of African Christians from the perspective of their culture and worldview.

> Each culture perceives Jesus Christ through the spectacles of its own needs. Western cultures for example, tend to be guilt ridden and so are generally attracted to Jesus as the sacrifice for sin… Another culture which focuses more on enhancing life forces because of fear of being overcome by evil powers will perceive that same Jesus as a

---

[121] The East African Standard Newspaper (online edition http://www.eastandard.net , accessed on 20.05.2004) reported an incident where a 15-year-old Kenyan boy died in Embu distict because his parents would not take him to hospital. The parents follow the doctrine of Kavonokia religious sect. The sect teaches its adherents not to go for modern medicine but only for spiritual remedy for the purpose of healing every sickness.
[122] Cf. Margaret A. Umeagudosa, "The Healing of the Gerasene Demoniac from a Specifically African Perspective" in *African Christian Studies* 12/4 (1986), pp. 35-6.
[123] Dunn, *The Theology of Paul*, p. 230.

long sought after protective shield.[124]

Probably, for a culture that seeks protection from inimical supernatural powers, without redemption from these powers and without depicting Jesus as a protective shield from the powers of evil, there would be no salvation from sin. Yet the redemption from supernatural powers does not substitute salvation from sins. It does not undermine the fact that defeat of the powers culminated with forgiveness of sins (Col 2: 13-15).

Underlining redemption from supernatural powers in the African context does not render human responsibility for their sins irrelevant as Ferdinando assumes.[125] This is to address the existential concerns of African believers, so that they may appreciate the supremacy of Christ. The theology of supernatural powers in relation to supremacy of Christ points to the rather secondary significance of Satan and his minions in human life. At the same time the aim of supernatural powers is to discontinue or compromise believers' relationship with God using human institutions. "Through coordinating the activity of his innumerable powers, Satan attempts to permeate every aspect of life in his indefatigable attempts to oppose God and his kingdom".[126] As Marshall notes with regard to the context of production, "the only way for Christianity to spread was by demonstrating that the power of Jesus was superior to that of the demons",[127] the same must be said as to the African context. Undoubtedly, the supremacy of Christ in the African context should be the top theme, and which must be constantly and clearly developed in theological and hermeneutical agenda as well as in pastoral and preaching programmes of the African church. Indeed, despite some of his noted flawed assumptions, Ferdinando has the final word.

> In the traditional African situation, the theme of his (Christ's) triumph over the supernatural powers of darkness is of special importance and therefore demands particular attention in order that it may be proclaimed as an integral part of the salvation he (Christ) came to accomplish.[128]

The supremacy of Christ must not be limited only to supernatural powers of darkness since these powers work with and through the structures of human existence. Not only that, they operate in other dimensions that resonate with human life. All in all, a theology of supernatural powers where Christ subdues the powers that upset life is what African believers have been waiting for.

---

[124] D. Jacobs, "Commenting on C. R. Taber, 'Is There More than One Way to Do Theology?'" in *Gospel in Context* (1978), p. 24.
[125] Ferdinando, *The Triumph of Christ*, pp. 396-7.
[126] Arnold, *Powers,* p. 204.
[127] I. H. Marshall, *Acts* (Leicester: Inter-Varsity Press, 1980), p. 312.
[128] Ferdinando, *The Triumph of Christ*, p. 403.

Bibliography

Primary Sources: Text and Translations

Aland, Barbara, Kurt Aland, Johannes Karavidopoulos, Carlo M. Martini and Bruce M. Metzger (eds.), *The Greek New Testament* 4th ed. (Stuttgart: Deutshe Bibelgesellschaft, 1993).
Audollent, Augustus, *Defixionum Tabellae* (Frankfurt/Main: Minerva, 1967 [1904]).
Barnard, William Leslie (Tr.), *St. Justin Martyr: The First and Second Apologies* (New York and Mahwah, New Jersey: Paulist Press, 1977).
Barnes, Jonathan, (ed.), *The Complete Works of Aristotle*, 2 Vols. (Princeton, New Jersey: Princeton University Press, 1995).
Barrett, C. K. (ed.), *The New Testament Background: Selected Documents* (London: SPCK, 1961).
Black, Matthew, *Apocalypsis Henochi Graece* (Leiden: Brill, 1970).
Blank, D. L. (Tr.), *Sextus Empricus: Adverse Mathematicos* (Oxford: Clarendon, 1998).
Bellenden, John and Craige William A., *Livy: The History of Rome* (Scottish Text Society Publication, 1903).
Betz, Hans Dieter (ed.), *The Greek Magical Papyri in Translation Including the Demotic Spells*, Vol. 1 (Chicago: University of Chicago Press, 1986).
Bowen, A. J. (Tr.), *Xenophon: Symposium* (Warminster: Aris & Phillips, 1998).
Bowersock, G. W. (ed.), *The Life of Apollonius of Tyana* (Harmondsworth, Middlesex: Penguin Books, 1970).
Bury, R. G. (Tr.), *Sextus Empiricus Vol. 4: Against the Professors* (Cambridge/Massachusetts: Harvard University Press; London: Heinemann, 1971).
Butterworth, G. W. (Tr.), *Origen on First Principles* (London: SPCK, 1936).
Campel, Archibald (Tr.), *The Agamemnon of Aeschylus* (London: University Press and Hodder & Stoughton, 1940).
Capps, E., T. E. Page and W. H. D. Rouse (eds.), *The Apostolic Fathers* 2 Vols. (London: William Heinemann, 1925 [1930]).
Carter, John M. (ed.), *Suetonius: Divus Augustus* (Bristol: Bristol Classical Press, 1982).
Chadwick, Henry (Tr.), *Origen: Contra Celsum* (Cambridge: Cambridge University Press, 1953).
Charles, R. H., *The Apocrypha and Pseudepigrapha of the Old Testament*, Vol. 2 (Oxford: Claredon, 1913).
Charlesworth, J. H. (ed.), *The Old Testament Pseudepigrapha: Apocalyptic Literature and Testaments* Vol.1 (London: Darton, Longman & Todd, 1983).
——— (ed.), The *Old Testament Pseudepigrapha: Expansion of the Old Testament Legends, Wisdom and Philosophical Literature, Prayers, Psalms and Odes, Fragments of Lost Judeo-Hellenistic Works* Vol.2 (London: Darton, Longman & Todd, 1985).
Cropp, M. J. (Tr.), *The Plays of Euripides: Iphigenia in Taurus* (Warminster, Wiltshire: Aris & Phillips, 2000).

Dakyns, H. G. (Tr.), *The Works of Xenophon* 4 Vols. (London: Macmillan & Co, 1890-1897).
Di Lella, Alexander A., *The Old Testament in Syriac 2.5 – Wisdom of Solomon* (Leiden: Brill, 1979).
Emerton, John A., *The Peshitta of the Wisdom of Solomon* (Leiden: Brill, 1959).
Evans, Craig, Robert, L. Webb and Richard A. Wiebe (eds.), *Nag Hammadi Texts and the Bible* (Leiden: Brill, 1993).
Evans, Ernest (ed. and Tr.), *Tertullian Adversus Marcionem* Books 1-5 (Oxford: Clarendon Press, 1972).
Fagles, Robert (Tr.), *Homer: The Iliad* –Introduction and Notes by Bernard Knox (The Softback Preview, 1997).
———— (Tr.), *Homer: The Odyssey* –Introduction and Notes by Bernard Knox (The Softback Preview, 1997).
Ferguson, John (Tr.), *Clement of Alexandria: Stromateis* (Washington, D.C: Catholic University Press, 1991).
Frazer, J. G. (Tr.), *Pausanias' Description of Greece* 6 Vols. (London: Macmillan & Co, 1898).
Hamilton, W. (Tr.), *Plato: The Symposium* (Harmondsworth, Middlesex: Penguin Books, 1951).
Henderson, Jeffrey (ed.), Xenophon: *Anabasis* (London: William Heinemann, 1998).
Horace, *Satires and Epistles*. (Harmondsworth: Penguin Classics, 1973).
Hude, Carolus (ed.), *Thucydides Historiae* (Lipsiae: B.G. Teubner, 1913).
Gent, H. C. (Tr.), *The History of Diodorus Siculus* (London: John Macock, 1653).
Goold, G. P. (Tr.), *Manilius: Astronomica* (London: William Heinemann, 1977).
Gordon, C. H., "Two Magic Bowls in Teheran" in *Orientalia* 20 (1951), pp. 306-315.
Griffiths, J. Gwyn (ed.), *Plutarch's De Iside Et Osiride*, edited with an introduction, translation and commentary by J. Gwyn Griffiths (University of Wales Press, 1970).
———— *The Isis-Book* (*Metamorphoses Book XI*) EPRO 39 (Leiden: Brill, 1975).
Griffiths, Mark (ed.), *Aeschylus: Prometheus Bound* (Cambridge: Cambridge University Press, 1983).
———— (ed.), *Sophocles: Antigone* (Cambridge: Cambridge University Press, 1999).
Kirby, John, *Jesus of the Deep Forest: Prayers and Praises of Afua Kuma*, Translated by John Kirby from Akan to English (Accra: Asempa Publishers, 1980).
Klijn, A. F. J., *The Acts of Thomas: Introduction, Text and Commentary* (Leiden: Brill, 2003).
Mackenna, Stephen (Tr.), *Plotinus: The Enneads* (London: Faber, 1969).
Martínez, Florentino García and Eibert J. C. Tigchelaar, *The Dead Sea Scrolls: Study Edition* Vol. 1, 1Q1–4Q273 (Leiden: Brill/Grand Rapids, Michigan: Eerdmans, 1997).
———— *The Dead Sea Scrolls: Study Edition* Vol. 2, 4Q274–11Q31 (Leiden: Brill; Grand Rapids, Michigan: Eerdmans, 1998).
MeeCham, Henry G. (Tr.), *The Epistle to Diognetus* (Manchester: Manchester University Press, 1949).
Owen, S. G. (Tr.), *Thirteen Satires of Juvenal* (London: Methuen, 1924).
Page, T. E., E. Capp.s and W. H. D. Rouse (eds.), *Plutarch's Moralia: De Liberis Educandis* Vol. 1, *De Superstitione* Vol. 2, *Septum Sapientium Convivum* Vol. 2, *Parallela Graeca et Romana* Vol. 4, *Questiones Romanae* Vol. 4, *De Defectu Oraculorum* Vol. 5, *De Sera Numinis Vindicta* Vol. 7, *Degenio Socratis* Vol 7, *Questiones Convivialum* Vol. 8 (London: William Heinemann, 1927-1929).

Bibliography

———— (eds.), *The Geography of Strabo*, 8 Vols. (London: William Heinemann, 1927-1931).
———— (eds.), *Plato: Timeaus* Vol. 7 (London: William Heinemann, 1929), pp. 1-244).
———— (eds.), *Plutarch's Lives* Vol. 2 [*Camillus*] (London: William Heinemann, 1929).
———— (eds.), *Plato's Republic* Vol. 1 (London: William Heinemann, 1930).
———— (eds.), *Cicero: De Natura Deorum* (London: William Heinemann, 1933).
———— (eds.), *Plato's Republic* Vol. 2 (London: William Heinemann, 1935).
———— (eds.), *Seneca: Moral Essays – De Providentia* (London: William Heinemann, 1938).
———— (eds.), *Dio Crysostom: Olympic Discourse* Vol. 2 (London: William Heinemann, 1939).
———— (eds.), *Diogenes Laertius* Vol. 1, Book 3 [*Plato*]; Book 5 [*Aristotle*] (London: William Heinemann, 1925).
———— (eds.), *Diogenes Laertius* Vol. 2, Book 7 [*Zeno*] (London: William Heinemann, 1925).
Page, T. E., et al (eds.), *Plutarch's Lives* Vol. 1 [*Theseus*] (London: William Heinemann, 1914).
———— *Cicero: Pro A. Licinio Archia Poeta Oratio* (London: William Heinemann, 1923).
———— *Seneca: Epistulae Morales* 3 Vols. (London: William Heinemann, 1924-1927).
————*Dios Roman History* Vols. 1-8 (London: William Heinemann, 1951).
———— *Cicero: De Divinatione* (London: William Heinemann, 1953).
Preisendanz, Karl, *Papyri Graecae Magicae: Die Griechischen Zauberpapyri* (Leipzig/Berlin: Verlag und Druck von B. G. Teubner, 1928/31/42).
Rhodes, P. J. (ed., Tr.), *Thucydides Historiae* 4.1 –5. 24 (Warminster: Aris & Phillips, 1998).
Roberts, A. and J. Donaldson (eds., and Eng. Tr.), *The Writings of Tertullian* Vol. 1 (Edinburgh: T & T Clark, 1872).
———— (eds. and Eng. Tr.), *The Anti-Nicene Fathers* Vols. i, iii, iv and x (Edinburgh: T & T Clark/ Grand Rapids, Michigan: Eerdmans, 1989).
Roberts, A. and F. Crombie (eds.), *The Writings of the Apostolic Fathers* (Edinburgh: T & T Clark, 1867).
Robinson, J. M. (ed.), *The Nag Hammadi Library in English* (Leiden/New York: Brill, 1996).
Rolfe, J. C. (Tr.), *Suetonius* (Cambridge, Massachusetts: Harvard University Press, 1997-1998).
Rooke, John (Tr.), *Xenophon's Ephesian History* (London: J. Millan, 1727)
Ross, W. D. (Tr.), *The Works of Aristotle* Vol. VIII *Metaphysica* (Oxford: Clarendon Press, 1908).
———— (Tr.), *Aristotle: Parva Naturaria* (Oxford: Clarendon Press, 1955).
Rouse, W. H. D (Tr.), *Lucretius Carus Titus: De rerum Natura* (Cambridge, Massachusetts: Harvard University Press, 1992).
Schaff, P. and H. Wace (eds., Eng. Tr.), *Nicene and Post-Nicene Fathers of the Christian Church* Vol.1 (Edinburgh: T & T Clark, 1991).
Tho Lodge, D. (Tr.), *The Workes of Lucius Annaeus Seneca: Both Morrall and Naturall* (London: William Stansby, 1614).
Turner, Paul, *Lucian Satirical Sketches* – Translated with an introduction by Paul Turner (Harmondsworth, Middlesex: Penguin Books, 1961).

Taylor, Thomas (Tr.), *The Works of Plato* 5 Vols. (Frome, Somerset: The Prometheus Trust, 1995-1996).

―――― (Tr.), *Iamblichus on the Mysteries of the Egyptians, Chaldeans, and Assyrians and Life of Pythagoras* (Frome: The Prometheus Trust, 1999).

Wake, W. (Tr.), *The Genuine Epistles of Ignatius* (Edinburgh: n.p, 1708.)

Walsh, P. G., *Cicero, The Nature of the Gods: Translated with Introduction and Explanatory Notes by P. G. Walsh* (Oxford: Clarendon Press, 1997).

West, M. L. (Tr.), *Hesiod: Theogony and Works and Days* (Oxford: Oxford University Press, 1988).

Whiston, William (Tr.), *The Works of Josephus* (Peabody, MA: Hendrickson Publishers, 1987).

Whittaker, Molly (ed., Tr.), *Tatian: Oratio ad Graecos and Fragments* (Oxford: Clarendon Press, 1982).

Yonge, C. D. (Tr.), *The Works of Philo* (Peabody, MA: Hendrickson Publishers, 1993).

Secondary Sources: Dictionaries and Encyclopaedias

Bauer, Walter, W. F. Arndt and F. W Gingrich, *A Greek-English Lexicon of the New Testament and Other Early Christian Literature* (Chicago: University of Chicago Press, 1957).

Bromiley, G. W. (ed.), *The International Standard Bible Encyclopaedia* Vols. I, III and IV (Grand Rapids, Michigan: Eerdmans, 1979).

Brown, Colin (ed.), *The New International Dictionary of New Testament Theology*. (Exeter: The Paternoster Press, 1975).

Buttrick, G. A. et al (eds.), *The Interpreter's Dictionary of the Bible,* Vol. I (Nashville: Abingdon Press, 1962).

Craig, Edward, *Concise Routledge Encyclopaedia of Philosophy* (London/New York: Routledge, 2000)

Danker, F. W. and F. W. Gingrich, *A Greek-English Lexicon of the New Testament and Other Early Christian Literature* (Chicago: University of Chicago Press, 1979).

Douglas, J. D. (ed.), *The New Bible Dictionary* (Wheaton: Tyndale House Publishers, 1991).

Eliade, M. (ed.), *Encyclopaedia of Religion* Vols. 4, 6, 9, 10, 14 (New York: Macmillan, 1987).

Evans, C. A and S. E. Porter (eds.), *Dictionary of New Testament Background* (Downers Grove/Leicester: Intervarsity Press, 2000).

Freedman, David N. (ed.), *The Anchor Bible Dictionary* 6 Vols (New York: Doubleday, 1992).

Hammond, N. G. L. and H. H. Scullard (eds.), *The Oxford Classical Dictionary* (Oxford: Oxford University Press, 1970).

Hawthorne, Gerald F, R. P. Martin and D. G. Reid, *Dictionary of Paul and His Letters* (Downers Grove, Illinois/Leicester: Intervarsity Press, 1993)

Kittel, G. and G. Friedrich (eds.), *Theological Dictionary of the New Testament* Vols. 1, 2, 3, 4, 7 (Grand Rapids, Michigan: Eerdmans, 1992).

Liddell, H. G. and R. Scott, *A Greek-English Lexicon* (Oxford: Claredon, 1940).

March, Jenny, *Dictionary of Classical Mythology* (London: Cassell, 1998).

Neil, William (ed.), *The Bible Companion* (London: The Caxton Publishing Company Limited, 1959)

Bibliography

van der Toorn, K. B. Becking and P. W. Van der Horst (eds.), *Dictionary of Deities and Demons in the Bible* (Leiden: E. J Brill, 1995).
Vine, W. E., *An Expository Dictionary of New Testament Words* (Nashville: Thomas Nelson Publishers, 1985).
The Analytical Greek Lexicon, (London: Samuel Bagster and Sons, n.d.)

Secondary Sources: Commentaries, Books and Articles

Abbot, T. K., *A Critical and Exegetical Commentary on the Epistle to the Ephesians and to the Colossians*, ICC (Edinburgh: T & T Clark, 1901)
────── *The Epistle to the Ephesians and to the Colossians*. ICC. (Edinburgh: T & T Clark, 1987)
Abijole, Bayo, "The Pauline Concept of Principalities and Powers in the African Context" in *African Theological Journal* Vol.19, No.2 (1988), pp. 118-129.
Abogunrin, Samuel O., "The Total Adequacy of Christ in the African Context (Col. 1: 13-23; 2: 8-3: 5)" in *Ogbomoso Journal of Theology* 1 (1986), pp. 9-16.
────── "The Synoptic Gospel Debate: A Re-Examination in the African Context" in *African Journal of Biblical Studies* 2/1 and 2 (1987), pp. 25-51.
Adamo, David Tuesday, "The Use of Psalms in African Indigenous Churches in Nigeria" in Gerald O. West and Musa W. Dube (eds.), *The Bible in Africa: Transactions, Trajectories and Trends* (Leiden: Koninklijke Brill), pp. 336-349.
Addo-Fening, R., *Akyem Abuakwa 1700-1943: From Ofori Panim to Sir Ofori Atta*. (Trondheim: Norwegian University of Science and Technology-NTNU, 1997).
Adegbola, E. A. Adeolu, "The Theological Basis of Ethics" in K. A. Dickson and P. Ellingworth (eds.), *Biblical Revelation and African Beliefs* (Maryknoll, New York: Orbis Books, 1969), pp. 116-136.
Adkins, A. W. H., *Merit and Responsibility* (Oxford: Clarendon, 1960).
Adler, G. M. Fordham and H. Read (eds.), *The Collected Works of C. G. Jung* Vol. 18, English tranlslation by R. F. C. Hull, (Princeton: Princeton University Press, 1978).
Akinnaso, F. Niyi, "Schooling, Language and Knowledge in Literate and Nonliterate Societies" in *Comparative Studies in Society and History* 34 (1992), pp. 68-109.
────── "Bourdieu and the Diviner: Knowledge and Symbolic Power in Yoruba Divination" in James, Wendy (ed.), *The Pursuit of Identity: Religious and Cultural Formulation* (London and New York: Routledge, 1995), pp. 234-284.
Albani, Matthias, "Horoscopes in the Qumran Scrolls" in Peter W. Flint and James C. Vanderkam, *The Dead Sea Scrolls after Fifty Years: A Comprehensive Assessment* Vol. 2 (Leiden: Brill, 1999), pp. 279-330.
Albright, W. F. and David, N. F. (eds.), *Ephesians – The Anchor Bible* (New York: Doubleday, 1960).
Alexander, Philip S., "Incarnations and Books of Magic" in E. Schürer, *The History of the Jewish People in the Age of Jesus Christ* (Edinburgh: T & T Clark, 1987), pp. 342-379.
────── "'Wrestling against Wickedness in High Places': Magic in the Worldview of the Qumran Community" in S. E. Porter and C. A. Evans (ed.), *The Scrolls and the Scriptures: Qumran Fifty years After* JSPSup 26/RILP 3 (Sheffield: Sheffield Academic Press, 1997), pp. 318-337.
────── "The Demonology in the Dead Sea Scrolls" in Peter W. Flint and James C.

Vanderkam, *The Dead Sea Scrolls after Fifty Years: A Comprehensive Assessment* Vol. 2 (Leiden: Brill, 1999), pp. 331-353.

Alexander, W. M., *Demonic possession in the New Testament* (Grand Rapids: Baker Books Publishing House, 1980).

Allen, R., *Missionary Methods: St Paul's or Ours* (Grand Rapids, Michigan, Eerdmans, 1962).

Anderson, B. W., "Hosts of Heaven" in G. A. Buttrick, *(et al.,* eds.), *The Interpreter's Dictionary of the Bible,* Vol. I (Nashville: Abingdon Press, 1962), pp. 654-656.

Appadurai, Arjun ,"The Production of Locality" (Unpublished Manuscript: ASA Fourth Decennial Conference, Oxford, 1993).

Appiah, Kwame, *In My Father's House: Africa in the Philosophy of Culture* (New York/London: Oxford University Press, 1992).

Apter, Andrew, *Black Critics and Kings: The Hermeneutics of Power in Yoruba Society* (Chicago: University of Chicago Press, 1992).

Ardener, Edwin, "Belief and the Problem of Women" in J. S. La Fontaine (ed.), *The Interpretation of Ritual* (London: Tavistock, 1972), pp. 135-158.

Arnold, Clinton E., "The 'Exorcism of Ephesians 6: 12 in Recent Research: A critique of Wesley Carr's View of the Role of Evil Powers in the First-Century AD Belief in *Journal for the Study of the New Testament* 30, June (1987), pp. 71-87.

─────── *Ephesians: Power and Magic. The Concept of Power in Ephesians in light of its Historical Setting.* SNTSMS 63 (Cambridge: Cambridge University Press, 1989).

─────── "'Principalities and Powers' in recent Interpretation." *Catalyst* 17.2 (February 1991), pp. 4-5.

─────── "Principalities and Powers" in David N. Freedman (ed.), *The Anchor Bible Dictionary* Vol. 5 (New York: Doubleday, 1992), p. 467.

─────── *Powers of Darkness* (Downers Grove: Intervarsity Press, 1992).

─────── "Magic" in Hawthorne, Gerald F, R. P. Martin and D. G. Reid, *Dictionary of Paul and His Letters* (Downers Grove, Illinois/Leicester: Intervarsity Press, 1993), pp. 580-583.

─────── *The Colossian Syncretism: The Interface Between Christianity and Folk Belief at Colossae,* WUNT. 77 (Tübingen: J. C. B. Mohr [Paul Siebeck], 1995).

─────── "Returning to the Domain of the Powers: *Stoicheia* as Evil Spirits in Galatians 4: 3, 9 in *Novum Testamentum* 38.1 (1996), pp.71-87.

─────── "Magical Papyri" in Craig A. Evans and Stanley E. Porter, *Dictionary of New Testament Background* (Downers Grove/Leicester: Intervarsity Press, 2000) pp. 666-670.

Ashley, M. J., *The House of Phalo: A History of the Xhosa People in the Days of Their Independence* (Johannesburg: Ravan Press, 1981).

─────── "Universes in Collision: Xhosa Missionaries and Education in the 19th Century South Africa" in *Journal of Theology for Southern Africa* No 32, (Sept. 1998), pp. 28-38

Asimpi, Kofi, "European Christian Missions and Race Relations in Ghana: 1826–1970" (Unpublished Ph.D. Dissertation, Boston University, 1996).

Assimeng, Max, *Religion and Social Change in West Africa* (Accra: Ghana University Press, 1989).

Attwel, D., "The Transculturation of English: An Exemplary Case of the Rev. Tiyo Soga, African Nationalist" (Inaugural Lecture, 12th Oct. 1984 University of Natal, Pietermaritzburg, 1984).

Aune, David E., "Demon; Demonology" in G. W. Bromiley (ed.), *The International Standard Bible Encyclopaedia* Vol. 1 (Grand Rapids, Michigan: Eerdmans, 1986), pp. 919-923.

Bibliography

―――――― "Magic; Magician" in G. W. Bromiley (ed.), *The International Standard Bible Encyclopaedia* Vol. 3 (Grand Rapids, Michigan: Eerdmans, 1986), pp. 213-219.
―――――― "Night Hag" in G. W. Bromiley (ed.), *The International Standard Bible Encyclopaedia* Vol. 3 (Grand Rapids, Michigan: Eerdmans, 1986), p. 536.
―――――― "Religion. Greco-Roman" in Craig A. Evans and Stanley E. Porter, *Dictionary of New Testament Background* (Downers Grove/Leicester: Intervarsity Press, 2000), pp. 917-926.
Avotri, Solomon K., "The Vernacularization of Scripture and African Beliefs: The Story of the Gerasene Demoniac among the Ewe of West Africa" in Gerald O. West and Musa W. Dube (eds.), *The Bible in Africa: Transactions, Trajectories and Trends* (Leiden: Brill, 2000 pp. 311–325.
Ayer, A. J., *Language, Truth and Logic* (Harmondsworth: Penguin Books, 1971).
―――――― *The Central Question of Philosophy* (Harmondsworth: Penguin Books, 1976).
Balcomb, A., "Of Radical Refusers and Very Willing Victims: Interpretation of Missionary Message in the Stories of Nongqawuse, Nxele, Ntiskana, and Soga in *Bulletin for Contextual Theology in Southern Africa and Africa*. Vol. 5 No 1 and 2, (1998), pp. 4-15.
Baldwin, J. G., *Haggai, Zechariah and Malachi* (Leicester: Intervarsity Press, 1972).
Bamberger, B. J., *Fallen Angels* (Philadelphia: The Jewish Publication Society of America, 1952).
Bandstra, A. J., *The Law and the Elements of the World* (Kampen: J. H. Kok N. V, 1964).
Barclay, John M. G., *Jews in the Mediterranean Diaspora from Alexander to Trajan (323 BCE–117 CE)* (Edinburgh: T & T Clark, 1996).
Barker, M. G., "Possession and the Occult – A Psychiatrist's View" in *Churchman* 94 3 (1980), pp. 246-253.
Barrett, C. K., *A Commentary on the Epistle to the Romans* (A & C Black: London, 1957).
―――――― *The Epistle to the Romans* (London: Adam & Charles Black, 1962 [1971]).
―――――― "Christianity at Corinth" in *Bulletin of the John Rylands Library* 46 (1963), pp. 269-297.
―――――― *The First Epistle to the Corinthians* HNTC (San Francisco: Harper & Low, 1968).
―――――― *A Commentary to the Second Epistle to the Corinthians* (London: A & C Black, 1973).
―――――― *Ephesians*, 2 Vols. (Garden city, New York: Doubleday & Company, 1974).
―――――― *The Epistle to the Romans* Vol. II (Edinburgh: T & T Clark, 1975).
Barrett, D. B., *Schism and Renewal in Africa* (Addis Ababa/Lusaka: Oxford University Press, 1968).
―――――― (ed.), *World Christian Encyclopedia* (Nairobi: Oxford University Press, 1982).
Barrington-Ward, S., "'The Centre Cannot Hold …' Spirit Possession as Redefinition" in Edward W. Fashole-Luke, R. Gray, A. Hastings and G. Tasie (eds.), *Christianity in Independent Africa* (London: Rex Collings, 1978), pp. 455-470.
Barth, Karl, *Church Dogmatics* Vol 3.3: *The Doctrine of Creation* – ed. by G. W. Bromiley and Thomas Forsyth Torrance, English translation by R. J. Ehrlich (Edinburgh: T & T Clark, 1960).
Barth, M. and H. Blanke, *Colossians* (AB, New York: Doubleday, 1994).
Barth, Markus, *The Broken Wall: A Study of the Epistle to the Ephesians.* (Chicago: Judson

Press, 1959).

———— *Ephesians 1–3* (New York: Doubleday, 1974).

———— *Ephesians 4–6* (New York: Doubleday, 1974).

Bauer, Walter, "An Introduction to the Lexicon of the Greek of the New Testament" in Bauer, Walter, W. F Arndt and F. W Gingrich, *A Greek-English Lexicon of the New Testament and Other Early Christian Literature* (Chicago: University of Chicago Press, 1957), pp. ix-xxv.

Bautista, L., H. B. Garcia and Sze-Kar Wan, "Asian Way of Thinking in Theology" in *Evangelical Review of Theology* 6 (1982), pp. 37-49.

Bayart, J–F, *Religion et Modernité: Politique en Afrique Noire* (Paris: Karthala, 1993).

Beattie J. H. M. and J. Middleton (eds.), *Spirit Mediumship and Society in Africa* (London Routledge & Kegan Paul, 1969).

Beattie, J. H. M., "Initiation into the Cwezi Spirit Possession Cult in Bunyoro" in *African Studies* 16 (1957), pp. 150-161.

———— "Sorcery in Bunyoro" in J. Middleton and E. H. Winter (eds.), *Witchcraft and Sorcery in East Africa* (London: Routledge and Kegan Paul, 1963 pp. 27-55).

———— "Spirit Mediumship and Hunting in Bunyoro" in *Man* 63 (1963), pp. 188-189.

———— "Divination in Bunyoro, Uganda" in *Sociologus* 14 (1964), pp. 44-62.

———— "Spirit Mediumship in Bunyoro" in Beattie, J. H. M. and J. Middleton (eds.), *Spirit Mediumship and Society in Africa* (London: Routledge and Kegan Paul, 1969), pp. 159-170)

———— "Spirit Mediumship as Theatre" in *Royal Anthropological Institute News*, (June 1977), pp. 1-6.

Beckwith, R. T., *Calendar and Chronology, Jewish and Christians: Biblical, Intertestamental and Patristic Studies* AGJU 33 (Leiden: Brill, 1996).

Bediako, G., *Primal Religions and the Bible* (Sheffield: Sheffield Academic Press, 1997)

———— "Primal Religion and Christian Faith: Antagonists or Soul-mates? In *Journal of African Christian thought* Vol. 3 No.1 (June 2000), pp. 12-16.

Bediako, Kwame, "Epilogue" in Ype Schaaf, *On Their Way Rejoicing: The History and Role of the Bible in Africa* (Carlisle: Paternoster Press, 1984), pp. 243-254).

———— *Jesus in an African Culture: A Ghanaian Perspective* (Accra: Asempa publishers, 1990).

———— *Theology and Identity: The Impact of Culture upon Christian Thought in the Second Century and Modern Africa* (Oxford: Regnum Books).

———— 1995 *Christianity in Africa: A Renewal of Non-Western Christianity* (Edinburgh: Edinburgh University Press/ Maryknoll, New York: Orbis Books, 1992).

———— "A Half Century of African Christian Thought: Pointers to Theology and Theological Education in the Next Half Century" in *Journal of African Christian thought* Vol. 3 No.1 (June 2000), pp. 5-11.

———— *Jesus in Africa: The Christian Gospel in African History and Experience* (Akropong-Akuapem, Ghana: Regnum Africa, 2000).

Behrend, Heike and Ute Luig (eds.), "Introduction" in Heike Behrend and Ute Luig (eds.), *Spirit Possession: Modernity and Power in Africa* (Oxford: James Currey/Madinson, Wisconsin: University of Wisconsin Press, 1999), pp. xiii-xxii.

———— (eds.), *Spirit Possession: Modernity and Power in Africa* (Oxford: James Currey/Madinson, Wisconsin: University of Wisconsin Press, 1999).

Behrend, Heike, "Power to Heal and Power to Kill: Spirit Possession and War in Northern Uganda" in Heike Behrend and Ute Luig (eds.), *Spirit Possession:*

Modernity and Power in Africa (Oxford: James Currey Ltd/Madison: University of Wisconsin Press, 1999), pp. 20-33).

Beidelmann, T. O.,"Witchcraft in Ukaguru" in J. Middleton and E. H. Winter (eds.), *Witchcraft and Sorcery in East Africa* (London: Routledge and Kegan Paul, 1963), pp. 57-98.

────── "Towards more Open Theoretical Interpretations" in M. Douglas (ed.), *Witchcraft Confession and Accusations* (London: Tavistock Publications, 1970), pp. 353-356.

────── *Colonial Evangelism: A Socio-Historical Study of an East African Mission at the Grassroots* (Bloomington: Indiana University Press, 1982).

Beker, J. C., *Paul the Apostle: The Triumph of God in Life and Thought* (Edinburgh: T & T Clark; Philadelphia: Fortress Press, 1980).

Benson, Stanley, "The Conquering Sacrament: Baptism and Demon Possession among the Maasai of Tanzania" in *The African Theological Journal* 9/2 (1980), pp. 28-41.

Berends, William, "The Biblical Criteria for Demon-Possession "In *Westminster Theological Journal* 37 (1975), pp. 342-365.

Berger, P. L and T. Luckmann, *The Social Construction of Reality: A Treatise in the Sociology of Knowledge* (London: Penguin Books, 1967).

Berger, P. L., *The Social Reality of Religion* (London: Penguin Books, 1969).

Berggren, Douglas, "The Use and Abuse of Metaphor" in *The Review of Metaphysics* 16.2 and 16.3 (1962-1963), pp. 237-258; 450-472.

Berglund, A-I., *Zulu Thought-Pattern and Symbolism* (London: C. Hurst, 1989 [1976]).

Berkhof, Hendrik, *Christ and the Powers* (Scotdale, PA: Herald Press, 1962).

Bernstein, M, Florentino García Martínez and J. Kampen (ed.), *Legal Texts and Legal Issues: Proceedings of the Second Meeting of the International Organization for Qumran Studies, Cambridge 1995, Published in the Honour of Joseph M. Baumgarten* STDJ (Leiden: Brill, 1997).

Best, Ernest, *The First and Second Epistles to the Thessalonians* (London: A & C Black, 1972).

Betz, Hans Dieter, *Galatians* (Hermenia, Philadelphia: Fortress Press, 1979).

────── "The Formation of Authoritative Tradition in the Magical Papyri" in B. F. Meyers and E. P. Sanders *Jewish and Christian Self-Definition III* (London: SCM Press, 1982), pp.161-170.

────── "Introduction to the Greek Magical Papyri" in Betz, Hans Dieter, *The Greek Magical Papyri in Translation Including the Demotic Spells*, Vol. 1 (Chicago: University of Chicago Press, 1986), pp. xli-liii).

────── "Magic and Mystery in the Greek Magical Papyri" in *Hellenismus und Urchristentum* Gesammelte Aufsätze I (Tübingen: Mohr, 1990), pp. 209-229.

────── "Paul" in David N. Freedman (ed.), *The Anchor Bible Dictionary* Vol. 5 (New York: Doubleday, 1992), pp. 186-201).

Bishop, E. F. F., "Angelology in Judaism, Islam and Christianity" in *Anglican Theological Review* 46 (1964), pp. 142-154.

Bjerke, S., *Religion and Misfortune: The Bacwezi Complex and Other Spirit Cults of Zinza of North Western Tanzania* (Oslo: Universistetsforlaget, 1981).

Black, Matthew, *The Book of Enoch or 1 Enoch: A New English Edition with Commentary and Textual Notes* (Leiden: Brill, 1985).

Black, Max, *Models and Metaphors* (Ithaca: Cornell University Press, 1962).

Blau, L., *Das altjüdische Zauberwesen* (Budapest: Landesrabbinerschule in Budapest, 1898).

Bloomhill, G., *Witchcraft in Africa* (Cape Town: Howard Timmins, 1962).

Bockmuehl, Markus N., *A Revelation and Mystery in Ancient Judaism and Pauline Christianity* WUNT 2.36 (Tübingen: Mohr, 1990).
Boddy, Janice, *Wombs and Alien Spirits: Women and Men in the Zar Cult in Northern Sudan* (Madison: University of Wisconsin Press, 1989).
─────── "Managing Tradition: Superstitions and the Making of National Identity Among Sudanese Women Refugees" in Wendy James (ed.), *The Pursuit of Certainty: Religious and Cultural Formulations* (London/New York: Routledge, 1995), pp. 17-44.
Boff, L and Boff, C., *Introducing Liberation Theology* (Tunbridge: Kent, Burns and Oates/Mary Knoll, New York: Orbis Books, 1987).
Bolle, Kees W., "Myth: An Overview" in Mircea Eliade (ed.), *The Encyclopedia of Religion* Vol. 10 (New York: MacMillan, 1987), pp. 261-273).
Bolt, P. G., "Jesus, the Daimons and the Dead" in Anthony N. S. Lane (ed.), *The Unseen World: Christian Reflection on Angels, Demons and the Heavenly Realm* (Carlisle, Cumbria: Paternoster/ Grand Rapids, Michigan: Baker Book House, 1996), pp. 75-102.
Bonner, C., *Studies in Magical Amulets Chiefly Greaco-Egyptian* (Ann Arbor: University of Michigan Press and London: Cambridge University Press, 1950).
Booth, N. S., "God and the Gods in West Africa", in N. S. Booth *African Religion: A Symposium* (New York: Nok Publishers, 1977), pp. 159-182.
Borg, Marcus, *Jesus: A New Vision* (San Francisco: Happer & Row, 1987).
Bornkamm, Günther, "μυστήριον" in Kittel, G. and G. Friedrich (eds.), *Theological Dictionary of the New Testament* Vol. 4, (Grand Rapids, Michigan: Eerdmans 1965), pp. 802-827.
─────── "The Heresy of Colossians" in F. O. Francis and W. A. Meeks (eds.), *Conflict at Colossae* SBLSBS 4 (Missoula: Scholars Press, 1973), pp. 123-145.
Bourguignon, E., "The Self, the Behavioural Environment and the Theory of Spirit Possession" in Milford E. Spiro, *Context and Meaning in Cultural Anthropology* (New York: The Free Press, 1965), pp. 39-60.
─────── (ed.), Religion, *Altered States of Consciousness and Social Change* (Columbus: Ohio State University Press, 1973).
─────── *Possession* (San Francisco: Chandler and Sharp, 1976).
Boyer, P., *The Naturalness of Religious Ideas: A Cognitive Theory of Religion* (Berkeley: University of California Press, 1994).
Bradbury, R. E., *The Benin Kingdom and the Edo-Speaking Peoples of South Western Nigeria.* (London: International African Institute–Oxford University Press, 1957).
Brashear, William M., "The Greek Magical Papyri: An Introduction and Survey, with Annotated Bibliography (1928 – 1994)" in *ANRW* II 18.5 (1995), 3380-3603.
Brain, R., "Child-Witches" in M. Douglas (ed.), *Witchcraft Confession and Accusations* (London: Tavistock Publications, 1970), pp. 161-179.
Brenk, F. E., *In Mist Apparelled: Religious Themes in Plutarch's Moralia and Lives* – Mn. S 48, (, Leiden: Brill, 1977).
Brøgger, J., "Spirit Possession and the Management of Aggression among the Sidamo" in *Ethnos* 40 (1975), pp. 285-290).
Brown, Karen McCarthy, *Mama Lola: A Vodou Priestess in Brooklyn* (Berkeley: University of California Press, 1991).
Brown, Raymond E., *The Semitic Background of the Term 'Mystery' in the NT*

Bibliography

(Philadelphia: Fortress Press, 1968).
Bruce, F. F., *The Epistle to the Ephesians* (London: Pickering & Inglis, 1961)
——— *Paul: Apostle of the Heart Set Free* (Grand Rapids, Michigan: Eerdmans, 1977).
——— *The Epistle to the Galatians* (Exeter: Paternoster Press, 1982).
——— *The Epistle to the Colossians, to Philemon, and to the Ephesians* (Grand Rapids, Michigan: Eerdmans, 1984).
——— *The Book of Acts*, in *The New International Commentary on the New Testament* (Grand Rapids: Eerdmans, 1992).
——— and E. K. Simpson, *Commentary on the Epistle to the Ephesians and the Colossians* in *The New International Commentary on the New Testament* (Grand Rapids: Eerdmans, 1957).
Brunt, P. A., *The Fall of the Roman Empire* (Oxford: Clarendon, 1988).
——— *The Roman Imperial Themes* (Oxford: Clarendon, 1990)
Bube, Richard H., "Penetrating the Word Maze" in *Perspective on Science and Christian Faith*, (1989) available at http://www.asa3.org/ASA/PSCF/1989/PSCF6-89Bube.html, accessed on 22.06.04.
Bubeck, Mark I., *Overcoming the Adversary* (Chicago: Moody Press, 1984).
Buck, C. and G. Taylor, *Saint Paul: A Study of the Development of His Thoughts* (New York: Charles Scribner's Sons, 1969).
Bujo, B., *African Theology in its Social Context* (Nairobi: St Paul's publication-Africa, 1992).
Bultmann, Rudolf, "The New Testament and Mythology: The Problem of Demythologizing the New Testament Proclamation" in Schubert Ogden (ed.), *The New Testament and Mythology and Other Basic Writings* (London: SCM Press, 1941), pp. 1-43.
——— *Theology of the New Testament* Vol. 1 (London: SCM Press, 1952).
——— "The Problem with Hermeneutics" in J. C. G. Greig (Tr.), *Essays Philosophical and Theological* (London: SCM Press, 1955), pp. 234-261.
——— *Jesus Christ and Mythology* (New York: Charles Scribner's Sons, 1958).
——— "Is Exegesis without Presupp.ositions Possible?" in Ogden, S. M. (ed., Tr.), *Existence and Faith* (London: Hodder & Stoughton (1961 [1964]), pp. 342-351).
——— "New Testament and Mythology" in H. W. Bartsch (ed.), *Kerygma and Myth* Vol.1 (London: SPCK, 1964), pp. 1-44.
Burkert, Walter, *Ancient Mystery Cults* (Cambridge: Harvard University Press, 1987).
Burnett, David, *Unearthly Powers: A Christian Perspective on Primal and Folk Religion* (Eastbourne, Sussex: MARC, 1988).
Burton, Ernest de Witt, *A Critical and Exegetical Commentary on the Epistle to Galatians* (Edinburgh: T & T Clark, 1921).
Busia K. A., "The Ashante of the Gold Coast" in Daryll Forde (ed.), *African Worlds: Studies in the Cosmological Ideas and Social Values of African People* (London: Oxford University Press – International African Institute (1954), pp. 190-209.
Buswell III, J. Oliver, "Contextualisation: Is it Only a New Word for Indigenization"? in *Evangelical Missions Quarterly* 14 (1978), pp.13-20.
Buxton, Thomas *The African Slave Trade and Its Remedy* (London: Murray, 1939-40).
Cagnolo, C *The Akikuyu* (Nyeri: The Mission Printing School, 1933).
Caird, G. B., *Principalities and Powers: A study in Pauline Theology* (Oxford: Clarendon Press, 1956).

────── *The language and Imagery of the Bible* (London: Duckworth, 1980).
Cannon, George E., *The Use of Traditional Material in Colossians* (Macon: Mercer University Press, 1983).
Caplan, Lionel, *Class and Culture in Urban India: Fundamentalism in a Christian Community* (Oxford: Clarendon Press, 1987).
────── "Introduction" in L. Caplan, *Studies in Religious Fundamentalism* (London: Macmillan, 1987) pp. 1-24.
────── (ed.), *Studies in Religious Fundamentalism* (London: Macmillan, 1987).
────── "The encounter of Global Fundamentalism and the Local Christianity in Urban South India" in Wendy James (ed.), *The Pursuit of Certainty: Religious and Cultural* Formulations (London/New York: Routledge, 1995), pp. 92-111.
Caragounis, Chyrs C., *The Ephesian Mysterion: Meaning and Context* ConB. 8 (Lund: Gleerup, 1977).
Carcopino, Jérôme, *Daily life in Ancient Rome* (Harmondsworth, Middlesex: Penguin Books, 1941).
Carr, Wesley, "The Rulers of this Age – 1 Corinthians II. 6-8" in *New Testament Studies* 23 (1976), pp. 20-35.
────── *Angels and Principalities. The Background, Meaning and Development of the Pauline Phrase hai archai kai hai exousiai* SNTSMS 42 (Cambridge: Cambridge University Press, 1981).
Carson, D. A, Douglas J. Moo and Leon Morris, *An Introduction to the New Testament* (Leicester: Apollos, 1992).
Cerulli, Ernesta, *Peoples of South-West Ethiopia and Its Borderlands* (London: International African Institute, 1956).
Charles, R. H., *The Book of Enoch* (Oxford: Claredon, 1893).
Charlesworth, J. H., "Jewish Interest in Astrology During the Hellenistic and Roman Period" in *Aufstieg und Niedergang der Römischen Welt II*, Band 20.2 (Berlin and New York: De Gruyter, 1987), pp. 926-950.
Chidester, D., *Religion of South Africa* (London, Rouledge, 1992).
Chilton, B. D., "Judaism and the New Testament" in Craig A. Evans and Stanley E. Porter, (eds.), *Dictionary of New Testament Background* (Leicester: Intervarsity Press, 2000), pp. 603-616.
────── "Rabbis" in Craig A. Evans and Stanley E. Porter, (eds.), *Dictionary of New Testament Background* (Leicester: Intervarsity Press, 2000), pp. 914-917.
────── "Purity" in Craig A. Evans and Stanley E. Porter, (eds.), *Dictionary of New Testament Background* (Leicester: Intervarsity Press, 2000), pp. 874-882.
Cobble, James F. Jr., *The Church and the Powers: A Theology of Church Structure* (Peabody, Massachusetts: Hendrickson, 1988).
Codrington, R. H., *The Melanesians* (Oxford: Clarendon Press, 1891).
Cole, Victor, "Africanising the Faith: Another Look at the Contextualisation of Theology in S. Ngewa, M. Shaw and T. Tienou (eds.), *Issues in African Christian Theology* (Nairobi: East African Educational Publishers, 1998), pp. 12-23).
Colleyn, Jean-Paul, "Horse, Hunter & Messenger: The Possessed Men of the Nya Cult in Mali" in Heike Behrend and Ute Luig (eds.), *Spirit Possession: Modernity and Power in Africa* (Oxford: James Currey Ltd; Madison: University of Wisconsin Press, 1999), pp. 68-78.
Collins, John, *Between Athens and Jerusalem: Jewish Identity in the Hellenistic Diaspora* (New York: Crossroad, 1986).
Collins, Raymond F., *First Corinthians* – Sacra Pagina Series edited by David J. Harnington, S. J. (Collegeville, Minnesota: The Liturgical Press, 1999).

Bibliography

Colson, E. "Spirit Possession among the Tonga of Zambia" in J. H. M. Beattie and J. Middleton (eds.), *Spirit Mediumship and Society in Africa* (London: Routledge and Kegan Paul, 1969), Pp. 69-103.

Comaroff, Jean, *Body of Power, Spirit of Resistance: The Culture and History of South African People* (Chicago: University of Chicago Press, 1985).

Comaroff, Jean and John Comaroff, *Of Revelation and Revolution: Christianity, Colonisation and Consciousness in South Africa* (Chicago/London: University of Chicago Press, 1991).

———— (eds.), Modernity *and its Malcontents: Ritual and Power in Postcolonial Africa* (Chicago: University of Chicago Press, 1993).

Congdon, G. Dal, "An Investigation into the Current Zulu Worldview and its Relevance to Missionary Work" in *Evangelical Missions Quarterly* 21 (July 1985), pp. 296-299.

Conn, Harvie M., "Contextualisation: A New Dimension for Cross-Cultural Hermeneutic" in *Evangelical Missions Quarterly* 14 (1978), pp. 39-46.

Conybeare, F. C., "The Testament of Solomon" in *Jewish Quarterly Review* 11 (1896), pp. 1-45.

Cook, Robert, "Devils & Manticores: Plundering Jung for a Plausible Demonology" in Anthony N. S. Lane (ed.), *The Unseen World: Christian Reflection on Angels, Demons and the Heavenly Realm* (Carlisle, Cumbria: Paternoster Press; Grand Rapids, Michigan: Baker Book House 1996), pp. 165-184.

Cory, H., "The Buswezi" in *American Anthropologist* 57 (1955), pp. 923-952.

Coser, Lewis, *The Function of Social Conflict* (New York: Free Press, 1956).

Cox, J. L., *Expressing the Sacred: An introduction to the Phenomenology of Religion* (Harare: University of Zimbabwe Publication, 1992).

———— "The Classification Primal Religions as a Non-Empirical Christian Theology", In *Studies in World Christianity*, Vol.2, Pt.1 (1996). pp. 55-76.

Cranfield, C. E. B., *The Epistle to the Romans* ICC (Edinburgh: T & T Clark, 1979).

Crapanzano, Vincent, *The Hamadsha: A Study in Moroccan Ethnopsychiatry* (Berkeley: University of California Press, 1973).

———— *Tuhami: A Portrait of a Moroccan* (Chicago: University of California Press, 1983).

———— "Spirit Possession" in M Eliade (ed.), *Encyclopaedia of Religion* Vol. XIV (New York: Macmillan, 1987), pp. 12-19.

Crapanzano, V and V. Garrison (eds.), *Case Studies in Spirit Possession* (London: Wiley, 1977).

Crawford, J. R., *Witchcraft and Sorcery in Rhodesia* (London: Oxford University Press, 1967).

Crenshaw, J. L., "Job, Book of" in David N. Freedman (ed.), *The Anchor Bible Dictionary* Vol. 3. (New York: Doubleday, 1992), pp. 858-868.

Croy, N. C. "Religion, Personal" in Craig A. Evans and Stanley E. Porter, *Dictionary of New Testament Background* (Downers Grove/Leicester: Intervarsity Press, 2000), pp. 926-931.

Cullmann, Oscar, *Christ and Time.* (Philadelphia, Pennsylvania: The Westminster Press, 1951).

Cullmann, Oscar *The State in the New Testament* (London: SCM Press, 1957).

Cumont, F and L. Canet, "Mithra ou Serapis ΚΟΣΜΟΚΡΑΤΟΡ?" in *Comptes rendues l' Académie des Inscriptions et belles-lettres* 1919), pp. 313-328.

Cumont, Franz, *Die Orientalischen Religionen im Römischen Reich* (Darmstadt: Wissenschaftliche Buchgesell schaft, 1975).

———— "Les Mystères de Sabazius et le Judaïsme" in *CRAIBL* (1906), pp. 63-79.

——— *Astrology and Religion among the Greeks and the Romans* (New York/London: G. P. Putnam's, 1912).
——— *Oriental Religions in Roman Paganism* (New York: Dover, 1956).
——— *Astrology among the Greeks and Romans* (New York: Dover, 1960).
Curtis, Edward M., "Idol, Idolatry" in David N. Freedman (ed.), *The Anchor Bible Dictionary* Vol. 3 (New York: Doubleday, 1992), pp. 376-381.
Daniel, Guy, "Astronomy, Astrology and Medicine" in William Neil (ed.), *The Bible Companion* (London: The Caxton Publishing Company Limited, 1959), pp. 309-321).
Daniélou, Jean, "Christianity as a Jewish Sect" in Arnold Tonybee, *The Crucible of Christianity: Judaism, Hellenism and the Historical Background to the Christian Faith* (London: Thames & Hudson, 1969), pp. 261-274.
Danker, F. W., *Benefactor: Epigraphic Study of a Graeco-Roman and New Testament Semantic Field* (St. Louis: Clayton, 1982).
Davidson, Maxwell J., *Angels at Qumran: A Comparative Study of 1 Enoch 1–36, 72–108 and Sectarian Writings of the Qumran* JSPSup 11 (Sheffield: JSOT Press, 1992).
Davies, Douglas James, *Meaning and Salvation in Religious Studies* (Leiden: Brill, 1984).
——— *Religious Organisation and Religious Experience* (New York: Academic Press, 1982).
Day, P. L., *An Adversary in Heaven: Śāṭān in the Hebrew Bible* (Atlanta, Georgia: Scholars Press, 1988).
de Heusch, Luc, "Cultes de possession et religions initiatiques de salut en Afrique" in *Annales du Centre d'Etudes des religions* Vol. 2 (Brussels: Institut de sociologie de l'Université libre de Bruxelles, 1962), Pp. 127-167.
——— *Pourquoi l'épouser?* (Paris: Gallimard, 1971).
deSilva, D. A., "Honor and Shame" in Craig A. Evans and Stanley E. Porter, *Dictionary of the New Testament Background* (Downers Grove/Leicester: Intervarsity Press, 2000), pp. 518-522.
de Sousa, Alexandra O., "Defunct Women: Possession Among the Bijagós Islanders" in Heike Behrend and Ute Luig (eds.), *Spirit Possession: Modernity and Power in Africa* (Oxford: James Currey Ltd; Madison: University of Wisconsin Press, 1999), pp. 81-88.
De Villiers, P. G. R.., *Like a Roaring lion: Essays on the Bible, the Church, and Demonic powers* (Pretoria: University of South Africa, 1987).
Debrunner, H., *Witchcraft in Ghana* (Kumasi: Presbyterian Book Deport, 1959).
Dehn, G., "Engel und Obrigkeit; ein Beitrag zum Verständnis von Rom. 13: 1-7" in E. Wolf (ed.), *Theologische Aufsätze für Karl Barth* (Munich: Chr. Kaiser, 1936), pp. 90-109.
Deissmann, Adolf, *Bible Studies* (Edinburgh: T & T Clark, 1901).
Delling, Gerhard, "ἀρχή" in G. Kittel and G. Friedrich, (eds.), *Theological Dictionary of the New Testament* Vol. 1 (Grand Rapids, Michigan: Eerdmans, 1971), pp. 481-488).
——— "ἄρχων" in G. Kittel and G. Friedrich, (eds.), *Theological Dictionary of the New Testament* Vol. 1 (Grand Rapids, Michigan: Eerdmans, 1971), pp. 488-489.
——— "στοιχεῖον" in G. Kittel and G. Friedrich, *Theological Dictionary of the New Testament* Vol. VII (Grand Rapids, Michigan: Eerdmans1971), pp. 670-687.
DeMaris, Richard E., "Element, elemental Spirit" in David N. Freedman (ed.), *The Anchor Bible Dictionary* Vol. 2 (New York: Doubleday, 1992), pp. 444-5.

────── *The Colossian Controversy: Wisdom in Dispute at Colossae* JSNTSup 96 (Sheffield: JSOT Press, 1994).

Dibelius, Martin, *Die Geisterwelt im Glauben des Paulus* (Göttingen: Vandenhoeck & Ruprecht, 1909).

────── "The Isis Initiation in Apuleius and Related Initiatory Rites" in F. O. Francis and W. A. Meeks (eds.), *Conflict at Colossae* SBLSBS 4 (Missoula: Scholar's Press, 1973 Originally published in 1917), pp. 61-121.

Dickason, C. Fred, *Demon Possession and the Christian* (Chicago: Moody Press, 1987).

Dickinson, G. Lowes, *The Greek View of Life* (London: Methuen & Co Ltd, 1896).

Dickson, K and P. Ellingworth (eds.), *Biblical Revelation and African Beliefs* (Maryknoll, New York: Orbis Books, 1969).

Diehl, C. G., *Church and Shrine: Intermingling Patterns of Culture in the Life of Some Christian Groups in South India* (Upp.sala: Hakan Ohlssons Boktryckeri, 1965).

Dodds, E. R., *Pagan and Christian in an Age of Anxiety* (Cambridge: Cambridge University Press, 1965).

Dodds, E. R., *The Ancient Concept of Progress and other Essays on Greek Literature and Belief* (Oxford: Clarendon Press, 1973).

DomNwachukwu, Chinaka S., *Demons are Real* (Lagos: Integrated Press, 1990).

Donavans, W., *Umfundisi: A Biography of Tiyo Soga 1829-1871* (Lovedale Press, 1978).

Douglas, Mary, *Purity and Danger: An Analysis of the Concept of Pollution and Taboo* (London: Routledge & Kegan Paul, 1966).

────── "Witch Beliefs in Central Africa" in *Africa* 37 (1967), pp. 72-80.

────── (ed.), *Witchcraft: Confession and Accusation* (London: Tavistock Publications Limited, 1970).

────── *Natural Symbols: Explorations in Cosmology* (London: Barrie Jenkins, 1973).

Dovlo, Elom, "Ancestors and Soteriology in Africa and Japanese Religions" in *Studies in Interreligious Dialogue* 33 1 (1993), pp. 48-57.

Dow, Graham, "A Case for the Existence of Demons" in *Churchman* 94 3 (1980), pp. 199-209.

Dowden, Ken, *The Use of Greek Mythology* (London/New York: Roultedge, 1992).

Dube, W. Musa, "Towards a Post-Colonial Reading of the Bible" In *Semeia*, 78 (1997), pp. 56-68).

Duffield, Guy P. and Nathaniel M. van Cleave, *Foundations of Pentecostal Theology* (Los Angeles: L.I.F.E. Bible College, 1987).

Duncan, George, *The Epistle of Paul to the Galatians* (London: Hodder & Stoughton, 1934).

Dundas, C., *Kilimanjaro and its People* (London: Frank Cass & Company Limited, 1924).

Dunn, J. D. G. and Graham H. Twelftree, "Demon Possession and Exorcism in the New Testament" in *Churchman* 94 3 (1980), pp. 210-225.

Dunn, J. D. G., "Demythologizing – The Problems of Myth in the New Testament" in I. H. Marshall (ed.), New *Testament Interpretation: Essays in Principles and Method* (Exeter: The Paternoster Press 1977), pp. 285-307).

────── *Romans 1–8* 38a, WBC (Dallas, Texas: Word Books Publishers, 1988).

────── *Romans 9–16* 38b, WBC (Dallas, Texas: Word Books Publishers, 1988).

────── "The theology of Galatians: The Issue of Covenantal Nominism" in J. M. Bassler (ed.), *Pauline Theology* Vol. 1; Thes. Phil. Gal. (Minneapolis: Fortress Press, 1991), pp. 125-146.

────── *A Commentary on the Epistle to the Galatians* (London: A & C Black, 1993).

―――――― *The Epistles to the Colossians and to Philemon: A Commentary on the Greek Text* (Grand Rapids, Michigan: Eerdmans / Carlisle, Cumbria: The Paternoster Press, 1996).
―――――― *The Theology of Paul the Apostle* (Edinburgh: T & T Clark, 1998).
―――――― "Altering the Default Setting: Re-envisaging the Early Transmission of the Jesus Tradition" in *New Testament Studies* 49 (2003), pp.139-175.
Dzobo, Noah, "References to the Next World (Bome) in the Daily Life of the Ewe of West Africa" in J. M. Agossou (ed.), *L'Experience Religiuse Africaine Et Les Relations Interpersonelles* (Abidjan: Savanes – Fortes, 1982), pp. 339-358.
Eadie, John, *A Commentary on the Greek text of the Epistle of Paul to the Colossians* (Grand Rapids, Michigan: Baker Books, 1979).
Ebeling, G. "Time and Word" in J. M. Robinson (ed.), *The Future of our Religious Past: Essays in Honour of Rudolf Bultmann* (London: SCM Press, 1971), pp. 247-266.
Echard, Nicole, *Bori: Aspects d'un Culte de Possession Hausa dans l'Ader et le Kurfey (Niger)* (CEA EHESS: Documents de Travail, 10, 1989).
―――――― *Bori: Genies d'un Culte de Possession Hausa de l'Ader et du Kurfey (Niger)* (Paris: Institut d'Ethnologie, 1989).
―――――― "The Hausa Bori Possession Cult in the Ader Region of Niger: Its Origin and Present Day Function" in Lewis, I. M, Ahmed Al-Safi, and Sayyid Hurreiz (eds.), Women *Medicine: The Zar-Bori Cult in Africa and Beyond* (Edinburgh: Edinburgh University Press, 1991), pp. 64-80.
Eckel, Paul T., "Expository Article: Ephesians 6:10-20" in *Interpretation: Journal of Bible and Theology* Vol. 45 (Jul. 1991), pp. 288-293.
Eitel, Keith, *Transforming Culture: Developing a Biblical Ethic in an African Context* (Nairobi: Evangel Publishing House, 1986).
―――――― *Myth and Reality* (New York: Harper & Row, 1963).
―――――― *Shamanism* (London: Arkana, 1989).
Eliade, Mircea, *Le chamanisme et les techniques archaïques de l'extase* (Paris: Libraire Payot, 1951).
―――――― *The Myth of the Eternal Return* (Princeton, New Jersey: Princeton University Press, 1954).
―――――― *Patterns in Comparative Religions* (London/New York: Sheed and Ward, 1958).
―――――― *Birth and Rebirth: The Religious Meaning of Initiation in Human Culture* (New York: Harper, 1958).
―――――― "Methodological Remarks on the Study of Religious Symbolism" in M. Eliade and J. M. Kitagawa, *The History of Religious Essays in Methodology"* (Chicago/London: The University of Chicago Press, 1959), pp. 86-107.
―――――― *Myths, Dreams and Mysteries*, (New York: Harper Torchbooks, 1960).
Eliade, M and L. E. Sullivan, "Hierophany" in M. Eliade (ed.), *The Encyclopaedia of Religion* Vol. 6 (New York: Macmillan, 1987), pp. 313-317.
Elliott, J. H., *A Home for the Homeless* (London: SCM Press, 1982).
―――――― *Social-Scientific Criticism of the New Testament* (London: SPCK, 1995)
Ellis, Earle E., *Pauline Theology: Ministry and Society* (Grand Rapids, Michigan: Eerdmans, 1989).
Evans-Pritchard, E. E., *Witchcraft, Oracles and Magic among the Azande* (Oxford: Clarendon Press, 1937 [1976]).
―――――― *Theories of Primitive Religion* (Oxford: Clarendon Press, 1965).
Everling, Otto, *Die Paulinische Angelologie und Dämonologie* (Göttingen: Vandenhoeck & Ruprecht, 1888).

Ewing, Ward, *The Power of the Lamb* (Cambridge, Massachusetts: Cowley Publications, 1990).
Fashole-Luke, Edward W., "Introduction" in Edward W. Fashole-Luke, R. Gray, A. Hastings and G. Tasie (eds.), *Christianity in Independent Africa* (London: Rex Collings, 1978), pp. 357-363.
────── R. Gray, A. Hastings and G. Tasie (eds.), *Christianity in Independent Africa* (London: Rex Collings, 1978).
Farvet-Saada, J., *Deadly Words: Witchcraft in Bocage* (Cambridge: Cambridge University Press, 1980)
Fee, Gordon D., "II Corinthians vi. 4 –vii. 1 and Food Offered to Idols" in *New Testament Studies* 23 (1977), pp. 140-61.
────── *The First Epistle to the Corinthians* (Grand Rapids, Michigan: Eerdmans, 1987).
────── *God's Empowering Presence: The Holy Spirit in the Letters of Paul* (Peabody, Massachusetts: Hendrickson, 1994).
Ferchiou, Sophie, "Survivances Mystique et Culte de Possession dans le Maraboutisme Tunisien" in *L'Homme* 12 (1972), pp. 47-69.
Ferdinando, Keith, "Screwtape Revisited: Demonology, Western, African and Biblical" in Lane, *The Unseen World: Christian Reflections on Angels, Demons and the Heavenly Realm* (Carlisle, Cumbria: Paternoster Press; Grand Rapids, Michigan: Baker Books, 1996), pp. 103-132.
────── "The Great Dragon: The Nature and Limits of Satan's Power" in *African Journal of Evangelical Theology* 16 1 (1997), pp. 17-30.
────── "The Dragon Hurled Down: The Victory of Christ over the Dominion of Darkness" in *African Journal of Evangelical Theology* 16 2 (1997), pp. 113-136.
────── *The Triumph of Christ in African Perspective: A study of Demonology and Redemption in the African context* (Carlisle, Cumbria: Paternoster Press, 1999).
Ferguson, Everett, *Demonology of the Early Christian World.* (Lewiston: The Edwin Mellen Press, 1984).
────── *Background of Early Christianity* (Grand Rapids, Michigan: Eerdmans, 1993).
Field, M. J., *Religion and Medicine of the Ga People* (London: Oxford University Press, 1937).
Filson, F. V., *The New Testament Against Its Environment: The Gospel of Christ the Risen Lord* (London, SCM Press, 1950).
Finley, Noses I, *The World of Odysseus* (New York: Penguin, 1979).
Firth, Raymond, *Essays on Social Organisation and Values* (London: Athlone Press, 1964).
────── *Tikopia Ritual and Beliefs* (London: Allen & Uwin, 1967).
Fitzmyer, Joseph, *Romans: A New Translation with Introduction and Commentary –* The Anchor Bible (New York: Doubleday, 1992).
Flint, Peter W. and James C. Vanderkam, *The Dead Sea Scrolls after Fifty Years: A Comprehensive Assessment* Vol. 2 (Leiden: Brill, 1999).
Foerster, W., "κυριότης" in G. Kittel and G. Friedrich, (eds.), *Theological Dictionary of the New Testament* Vol. III (Grand Rapids, Michigan: Eerdmans, 1965), pp. 1096-7.
────── "σατανᾶς" in G. Kittel and G. Friedrich, (eds.), *Theological Dictionary of the New Testament* Vol. VII (Grand Rapids, Michigan: Eerdmans, 1971), pp. 151-163.

Forbes, Chris, "Principalities and powers: Demythologizing Apocalyptic"? in *Journal for the Study of the New Testament* 82 (June 2001), pp. 61-88.

─────── "Pauline Demonology and/or Cosmology? Principalities and Powers and the Elements of the World in their Hellenistic Context" in *Journal for the Study of the New Testament* 85 (March 2002), pp. 51-73.

Forde, D. and Jones, G. I., *The Ibo and Ibibio-Speaking Peoples of South-Eastern Nigeria* (London: Oxford University Press– International African Institute, 1950).

Forde, D. (ed.), *African Worlds: Studies in the Cosmological ideas and Social Values of African People* (London: Oxford – University Press International African Institute, 1954).

─────── "Spirits, Witches and Sorcerers in the Supernatural Economy of the Yakö" in *Journal of the Royal Anthropological Institute* 88, 1958), pp.165-178.

Fortes, M., *Religion, Morality and the Person: Essays on Tallensi Religion* (Cambridge: Cambridge University Press, 1987).

Foulkes, Francis, *The Epistle of Paul to the Ephesians: An Introduction and Commentary* (Leicester: Inter-varsity Press, 1989).

─────── "Epistle to the Ephesians" in J. D. Douglas (ed.), *The New Bible Dictionary*. (Wheaton: Tyndale House Publishers, 1991), pp. 379-80.

Francis, F. O., and W. A. Meeks (eds.), Conflict *at Colossae* SBLSBS 4 (Missoula: Scholar's Press, 1973).

Francis, Fred O., "Humility and Angelic Worship in Col 2: 8" in F. O. Francis and W. A. Meeks (eds.), *Conflict at Colossae* SBLSBS 4 (Missoula: Scholar's Press, 1973), pp. 163-195.

France, R. T., *Divine Government* (London: SPCK, 1990).

Frankfort, Henri, John A. Wilson, Thorkild Jacobsen and William A. Irwin, *The Intellectual Adventure of Ancient Man: An Essay on Speculative Thought in the Ancient Near East* (Chicago: Chicago University Press, 1946).

Frazer, J. G., *The Golden Bough: A Study in Magic and Religion* Vol. 1 (London: Macmillan, 1926).

Freedman, David Noel (ed.), *The Anchor Bible Dictionary* Vol. 2 (New York: Doubleday, 1992).

Frye, Northrop, *Myth and Metaphor: Selected Essays 1974–1988* (Charlottesville/London: University Press of Virginia, 1990).

Friedson, S. M., *Dancing Prophets: Musical Experience in Tumbuka Healing* (Chicago: Chicago University Press, 1996).

Fuller, D. P., "Satan" in G. W. Bromiley (ed.), *The International Standard Bible Encyclopaedia* Vol. IV (Grand Rapids, Michigan: Eerdmans, 1988), pp. 340-344).

Gaba, C. R., "Man's Salvation: Its Nature and Meaning in African Traditional Religion" in Edward W. Fashole-Luke, R. Gray, A. Hastings and G. Tasie (eds.), *Christianity in Independent Africa* London: Rex Collings, 1978, 1978), pp. 389-401.

Gager, J. G., *Curse Tablets and Binding Spells from the Ancient World* (Oxford: Oxford University Press, 1992).

Gairdner, W. H. T., *Edinburgh 1910: An Account and Interpretation of the World Missionary Conference* (London: Oliphant, Anderson & Ferrier, 1910).

Ganusah, Rebecca Yawa, "Pouring Libation to Spiritual powers Among the Ewe-Dome of Ghana: An Indigenous Religious and Biblical Perspective" in Gerald O. West and Musa W. Dube (eds.), *The Bible in Africa: Transactions, Trajectories and Trends* (Leiden: Brill, 2000), pp. 278-291.

Bibliography

Gaster, T. H., "Angel" in G. A. Buttrick (et al., eds.), *The Interpreter's Dictionary of the Bible*, Vol. I (Nashville: Abingdon Press, 1962), pp. 128-134.

Gathigira, S. K., *Mĩĩikarĩre ya Agĩkũyũ. [The Gĩkũyũ People's Way of Life]* (Karatina: Scholars Publishers, 1933).

Geertz, Clifford, "Ethos, Worldview and the Analysis of Sacred Symbols" in A. Dundes, (ed.), *Every Man his Way: Reading in Cultural Anthropology* (Englewood Cliffs, New Jersey: Prentice Hall, 1968), pp. 301-315.

———— "Deep Play: Notes on the Balinese Cockfight" in *Daedalus* (Winter 1972), pp.1-37.

———— "Suq: The Bazaar Economy in Sefrar" in C. Geertz, H. Geertz and L. Rosen *Meaning and Order in Moroccan Society. Three essays in Cultural Analysis* (Cambridge: Cambridge University Press, 1979), pp. 123-313).

Gelfand, M., *The African Witch* (Edinburgh/London: E. & S. Livingston, 1967).

Gibellini, Rosino, (ed.), *Paths of African Theology* (London: SCM Press, 1994).

Giles, Linda L., "Possession Cults on the Swahili Coast: A Re-Examination of the Theories of Marginality" in *Africa* 57 2 (1987), pp. 234-258.

———— "The Dialectic of Spirit Production: A Cross-Cultural Dialogue" in *Mankind Quarterly* 33 3 (1989), pp. 243-265.

———— "Spirit Possession on the Swahili Coast: Peripheral Cults of Primary Texts?" (Unpublished Doctoral Dissertation, University of Texas, Austin, 1989).

———— "Spirit Possession & the Symbolic Construction of Swahili Society" in Heike Behrend and Ute Luig (eds.), *Spirit Possession: Modernity and Power in Africa* (Oxford: James Currey Ltd/Madison: University of Wisconsin Press, 1999), pp. 142-164.

Gluckman, M., *Custom and Conflict in Africa* (Oxford: Basil Blackwell, 1955).

Gomm, R., "Bargaining from Weakness: Spirit Possession on the South Kenya Coast" in *Man* 10 (1975), pp. 530-543.

Goodenough, Erwin R., *By Light, Light: The Mystic Gospel of Hellenistic Judaism* (New Haven: Yale, 1935).

———— *Jewish Symbols in the Graeco-Roman Period* Vol. 2 (New York: Pantheon, 1953).

Goodman, F. D., *Speaking in Tongues: A Cross-Cultural Study in Glossolalia* (Chicago: University of Chicago Press, 1972).

———— *How About Demons: Possession and Exorcism in the Modern World* (Bloomington/Indianapolis: Indiana University Press, 1988).

Goody, E., "Legitimate and Illegitimate Aggression in a West African State" in M. Douglas (ed.), *Witchcraft Confession and Accusations* (London: Tavistock Publication, 1970), pp. 207-244.

Grayston, Kenneth, "The Life and Thought of St. Paul" in Neil, William (ed.), *The Bible Companion* (London: The Caxton Publishing Company, 1959), pp. 196-209.

Green, R. M., "Religion and Morality in the African Traditional Setting" in *Journal of Religion in Africa* 14 (1983), pp. 1-23.

Grosheide, F. W., *Commentary on the First Epistle to the Corinthians* (Grand Rapids, Michigan: Eerdmans, 1953).

Grundmann, Walter, *Ber Begriff der Kraft in der Neutestamentlichen Gendankenwelt* BWANT 8 (Stuttgart: Kohlhammer, 1932).

Guillaume, A., *Studies in the Book of Job, with a New Translation* (Leiden: Peter Brill, 1968).

Guinness, Os, *The Dust of Death: A Critique of Counter Culture* (London: Inter-Varsity Press, 1973).

Gundel, W and H. G. Gundel, *Astrologumena: Die Astrologische Literatur in der Antike*

und ihre Geschichte– SAHM.B6 (Wiesbaden: F. Steiner, 1966).
Gunton, Colin E., *The Actuality of Atonement: A Study of Metaphor, Rationality and the Christian Tradition* (Edinburgh: T & T Clark, 1988).
Guthrie, Donald, "Colossians." In Donald Guthrie and J. A. Motyer (eds.), *The New Bible Commentary* (Leicester: Intervarsity Press, 1970), pp. 1139-1153.
——— *New Testament Introduction* (Leicester: Apollos/Downers Grove, Illinois: Intervarsity Press, 1990).
Gutman, J., "The 'Second Commandment' and the Images in Judaism, in *Hebrew Union College Annual* 32 (1961), pp. 161-174.
Hafemann, Scot, *Suffering and the Spirit: An Exegetical Study of II Cor 2: 14–3: 3 Within the Context of the Corinthian Correspondence* WNUT II/19 (Tübingen: J. C. B. Mohr [Paul Siebeck], 1986).
——— "Roman Triumph" in Craig A. Evans and Stanley E. Porter, *Dictionary of New Testament Background* (Downers Grove/Leicester: Intervarsity Press, 2000), pp. 1004-1008.
Hagan, George P., "Divinity and Experience: The Trance and Christianity in Southern Ghana" in Wendy James and Douglas H. Johnson (eds.), *Vernacular Christianity: Essays in Social Anthropology of Religion* (Oxford: JASO, 1988), pp. 146-156.
Hammond-Tooke, W. D., "The Witch Familiar as a Mediatory Construct" in M. Marwick (ed.), *Witchcraft and Sorcery* (Harmondsworth: Penguin Books, 1982), pp. 365-375.
Hankinson, R. J., "Galen (AD 129–c210)" in *Concise Routledge Encyclopaedia of Philosophy* (London/New York: Routledge, 2000), p. 304.
——— "Hippocratic Medicine" in *Concise Routledge Encyclopaedia of Philosophy* (London/New York: Routledge, 2000), pp. 354-5.
Harnack, Adolf von, *What is Christianity?* Vol. IV (New York: G. P. Putnam's Sons, 1901).
Harner, Michael J., *The Way of the Shaman* (New York: Bantum, 1980).
Harris, G., "Possession 'Hysteria' in A Kenya Tribe" *American Anthropologist* 59 (1957), pp. 1046-1066.
Hartley, J. E., *Job* (Grand Rapids, Michigan: Eerdmans, 1988).
Harwood, A., *Witchcraft, Sorcery and Social Categories among the Safwa* London: Oxford University Press, 1970).
Haule, C., *Bantu "Witchcraft and Christian Morality: The Encounter of Bantu Uchawi with Christian Morality – An Anthropological and Theological Study* (Schonek –Beckenried: Nouvelle Revue de Science Missionnair, 1969).
Hay, David M., *Glory at the Right Hand: Psalm 110 in early Christianity* (Nashville: Abingdon, 1973).
Haynes, John, "Metaphors and Mediation" available at http://www.mediate.com/articles/metaphor.cfm accessed on 15:11:03.
Hayford, Jack W. (ed.), Spirit *Filled Life Bible.* (Nashville: Thomas Nelson Publishers, 1991).
Healey, J. and Sybertz D., *Towards an African Narrative Theology* (Nairobi: Pauline Publications-Africa, 1996).
Healey, J. F., "Thanatos" in van der Toorn, K. B. Becking and P. W. Van der Horst (eds.), *Dictionary of Deities and Demons in the Bible* (Leiden: Brill, 1995). Cols.1122-1132.
Heelas, Paul and Anna Marie Haglund-Heelas, "The Inadequacy of 'Deprivation' as a Theory of Conversion" in Wendy James and Douglas H. Johnson (eds.), Vernacular *Christianity: Essays in the Social Anthropology of Religion*

(Oxford: JASO, 1988), pp. 112-119.
Hefele, C. J., *A History of the Councils of the Church* Vol. II: A.D. 326-429 (Edinburgh: T & T Clark, 1896).
Heintze, Beatrix, *Besessenheitsphänomene im Mittleren Bantu-Gebiet* (Wiesbaden: Franz Steiner Verlag, 1970).
Hemer, J. Colin, "Tarsus" in Bromiley, Geoffrey (et al), *International Standard Bible Encyclopedia* Vol. 4 (Grand Rapids, Michigan : Eerdmans, 1979-1988) pp. 734-736.
Hendriksen, W., *New Testament Commentary: Exposition of Colossians* (Grand Rapids: Baker Book House, 1964).
———— *New Testament Commentary: Exposition of Ephesians* (Grand Rapids Baker Book house, 1967).
Hengel, M., *Judaism and Hellenism: Studies in their Encounter in Palestine during the Early Hellenistic Period* 2 vols (London: SCM Press / Philadelphia: Fortress Press, 1974).
———— *Jews, Greeks and Barbarians* (London: SCM Press, 1980).
Henle, Paul, "Metaphor" in Paul Henle (ed.), *Language, Thought and Culture* (Ann Arbor: University of Michigan Press, 1958), pp. 173-195.
Hesselgrave, D., *Communicating Christ Cross-Culturally.* (Grand Rapids, Michigan, Zondervan, 1991).
Hester, Marcus B., *The Meaning of Poetic Metaphor: An Analysis in the Light of Wittgenstein's Claim that is Use* (The Hague: Mouton & Co, 1967).
Hiebert, Paul G., *Cultural Anthropology* (Grand Rapids, Michigan: Baker Book House, 1976).
———— "The Flaw of the Excluded Middle" in *Missiology* 10 (1982), pp. 35-47.
———— *Anthropological Insights for Missionaries* (Grand Rapids, Michigan: Baker Book House, 1985).
———— *Anthropological Reflections on Missiological Issues* (Grand Rapids, Michigan: Baker Books, 1994).
Hobley, Charles Williams, *Ethnology of A-kamba and Other East African Tribes* (Cambridge: The University Press, 1910).
Hodge, Charles, *Commentary on the Epistle to the Ephesians* (London: Banner of Truth Trust, 1964).
Hodgson, J., "A Study of the Xhosa Prophet Nxele" [Pt. i] in *Religion in South Africa* Vol. 6, No.2, (July 1985), pp. 11-36..
Hollander, H. W. and M. de Jonge, *The Testaments of the Twelve Patriarchs* (Leiden: Brill, 1985).
Holm, N. G., "Ecstasy Research in the 20th Century – An Introduction in N. G. Holm (ed.), *Symposium on Religious Ecstasy* (Stockholm: Almqvist and Wicksell, 1982), pp. 7-26.
Holmberg, Bengt, *Paul and Power: The Structure of Authority in the Primitive Church as Reflected in the Pauline Epistles* (Philadelphia: Fortress Press, 1980).
Horrell, David, G., *Social-Scientific Approaches to the New Testament Interpretation* (Edinburgh: T & T Clark, 1999).
Horton, Robin, *Patterns of Thought in Africa and the West: Essays on Magic, Religion and Science* (Cambridge: Cambridge University Press, 1993).
Howell, A. M., *The Religious Itinerary of a Ghanaian People: The Kasena and the Christian Gospel.* (Frankfurt am Main, Peter Lang, 1997).
Hughes, P. E., *Paul's Second Epistle to the Corinthians* (Grand Rapids, Michigan: Eerdmans, 1962).
Hughes, Pnnetorne, *Witchcraft* (Harmondsworth: Penguin Books, 1965).

Hull, J. M., *Hellenistic Magic and the Synoptic Tradition* (London: SCM Press, 1974).
Hume, David, *Essays: Moral, Political and Literary*, 2 Vols edited with preliminary dissertation and notes by T. H. Green and T. H. Grose (London: Longmans, Green & Co, 1875).
Huntingford, G. W. B., "Nandi Witchcraft" in J. Middleton and E. H. Winter (eds.), *Witchcraft and Sorcery in East Africa* (London: Routledge and Kegan Paul, 1963), pp. 175-186).
Hurtado, Larry W., *One God, One Lord: Early Christian Devotion and Jewish Monotheism* (Philadelphia: Fortress Press, 1988).
Hurvitz, A., "The Date of the Prose Tale of Job Linguistically Reconsidered" in *Harvard Theological Review* 67 (1974), pp. 17-34.
Idowu, Bolaji E., *Olodumare: God in Yoruba Belief* (London: Longman, 1962).
————— *African Traditional Religion* (Maryknoll, New York: Orbis Books, 1975).
Igenoza, Andrew Olu, "Contextual Balancing of Scripture With Scripture: Scripture Union in Ghana and Nigeria" in Gerald O. West and Musa W. Dube (eds.), *The Bible in Africa: Transactions, Trajectories and Trends* (Leiden: Brill, (2000), pp. 292-310.
Ikenga-Metuh, E., *Comparative Studies of African Traditional Religions* (Onitsha, Nigeria: Imico Publishers, 1987).
Imasogie, Osadolor, *Guidelines for Christian Theology in Africa* (Achimota, Ghana: African Christian Press, 1993).
Isaac, Erich, "Relations between the Hebrew Bible and Africa" in *Jewish Social Studies* 26 2 (1964), pp. 87-98.
————— *The Concept of Spirit* (London: Heythrop College, 1976).
Jacobs, D., "Commenting on C. R. Taber, 'Is There More than One Way to Do Theology?'" in *Gospel in Context* (1978), pp. 4-10, 24.
James, Wendy, "Introduction: Whatever Happened to the Enlightenment?" in Wendy James (ed.), *The Pursuit of Certainty: Religious and Cultural Formulations* (London: Routledge, 1995), pp. 1-14.
————— (ed.), *The Pursuit of Certainty: Religious and Cultural Formulations* (London: Routledge, 1995).
Janzen, John, *The Quest of Therapy in Lower Zaïre* (Berkeley: University of California Press, 1978).
————, *Ngoma: Discourses of Healing in Central and Southern Africa* (Berkeley: University of California Press, 1992).
Jasper, K., "Myth and Religion" in H. W. Bartsch (ed.), *Kerygma and Myth* Vol.1 (London: SPCK, 1964), pp. 133-180.
Jewett, Robert, *A Chronology of Paul's Life* (Philadelphia: Fortress, 1979).
Johnson, R. A., *The Origins of Demythologisation: Philosophy and Historiography in the Theology of Rudolf Bultmann* (Leiden: Brill, 1974).
Jonsson, Thomas, *Pastor: You can get Your Church to Prosper: The Law of Giving and Reaping* (Upp.sala: TJTM, 1998).
Jung, Carl, "Synchronicity: An Acausal Connecting Principle". In C. G. Jung and W. Pauli, *The Interpretation of Nature and the Psyche*. New York: Pantheon Books, 1955).
————— *Memoirs, Dreams and Reflection* (London: Collins and Routledge & Kegan Paul, 1963).
Kallas, J., *The Significant of Synoptic Miracles* (London: SPCK, 1961).
Kapferer, Bruce, *A Celebration of Demons: Exorcism and the Aesthetic of Healing in Sri Lanka* (Bloomington: Indiana university Press, 1983).
————— *A Celebration of Demons* (Oxford: Berg Publishers, 1991).

Bibliography

Karanja, John K., *Founding an African Faith: Kikuyu Anglican Christianity 1900–1945* (Nairobi: Uzima Press, 1999).
Käsemann, E., *Romans* (London: SCM Press, 1980).
Kato, Byang, *The Spirits: What the Bible Teaches*, booklet NO.5 (Achimota Ghana: African Christian Press, 1976).
Kee, H. C and Young, F. W., *The Living World of the New Testament* (London: Darton, Longman & Todd, 1960).
Kee, Howard Clark, *A Community of the New Age* (London: SCM Press, 1977).
───── *Jesus in History* (Harcourt Brace: Jovanovich, 1977).
───── *Christian Origin in Sociological Perspectives* (London: SCM Press, 1980).
───── *Medicine, Miracle and Magic in New Testament Times* (Cambridge: Cambridge University Press, 1986).
───── "From the Jesus Movement toward Institutional Church" in Robert W. Hefner (ed.), *Conversion to Christianity: Historical and Anthropological Perspective on a Great Transformation* (Berkeley, Los Angeles – California –, Oxford: University of California Press, 1993), pp. 47-63.
Keegan, T. J., *Interpreting the Bible: A Popular Introduction to Popular Hermeneutics* (Mahwa, New Jersey: Paulist Press, 1985).
Keek, Leander E., *Paul and his Letters*, Proclamation Commentaries (Philadelphia: Fortress Press, 1979).
Kehoe, Alice B. and Dody A. Gilleti, "Women's Preponderance in Possession Cults: The Calcium Deficiency Hypothesis Extended" in *American Anthropologist* 83 3 (1981), pp. 549-561.
Kelsey, Morton, "The Mythology of Evil" in *Journal of Religion and Health* 13 No. 1 (1974), pp. 7-18.
Kendall, Laurel, *The Life and Hard Times of a Korean Shaman: Of Tales and the Telling of Tales* (Honolulu: University of Hawaii Press, 1988).
Kennedy, J. G., "Nubian Zar Ceremonies as Psychotherapy" in *Human Organization* 26 (1967), pp.185-194.
Kenyatta, Jomo, *Facing Mount Kenya* (London: Secker & Warburg, 1938).
Kenyon, Susan M., "The Case of the butcher's Wife: Illness, Possession & Power in Central Sudan" in Heike Behrend and Ute Luig (eds.), *Spirit Possession: Modernity and Power in Africa* (Oxford: James Currey Ltd; Madison: University of Wisconsin Press, 1999), pp. 89-108.
Kerenyi, C., *The Religion of The Greeks and The Romans* (London: Thames & Hudson, 1962).
Kibicho, Samuel G., "The Continuity of the African Conception of God Into and Through Christianity: A Kikuyu Case Study" in Edward W. Fashole-Luke, R. Gray, A. Hastings and G. Tasie (eds.), *Christianity in Independent Africa* (London: Rex Callings, 1978), pp. 370-388.
Kim, Seyoon, *The Origin of Paul's Gospel* WUNT 2/4. (Tübingen: Mohr, 1981).
King, Noel Q., *Religions of Africa* (New York: Harper & Row, 1970).
───── *African Cosmos: An introduction to Religion in Africa* (Belmont, California: Wadsworth Publishing Company, 1986).
Kinsler, Ross F., "Mission and Context: The Current Debate about Contextualisation" in *Evangelical Missions Quarterly* 14 (1978), pp. 23-29.
Kirk, G. S., *Myth: Its Meaning and Function in Ancient and Other Cultures* (Cambridge: Cambridge University Press, 1970).
Kitagwa, J. M. (ed.), *Understanding and Believing* (New York, 1968).
Kittredge, C. B., *Community and Authority: The Rhetoric of Obedience in the Pauline Tradition* (Harrisburg, Pennsylvania: TPI, 1998).

Klass, M., *Ordered Universe: Approaches to the Anthropology of Religion* (Boulder, Colorado: Westview Press, 1995).
Klauck, Hans-Josef, "Religion without Fear: Plutarch on Superstitions and Early Christian Literature" in *Skrif en Kerk* (1997), pp.111-126.
────── *Magic and Paganism in Early Christianity: The World of the Acts of the Apostle* (Edinburgh: T & T Clark, 2000).
────── *The Religious Context of Early Christianity* (Edinburgh: T & T Clark, 2000).
Klem, David, *The Hermeneutical Theory of Paul Ricoeur* (London/Toronto: Associated University Press, 1983).
Kluger, R. S., *Satan in the Old Testament* (Evanston: Northwestern University Press, 1967).
Knibb, M .A., *The Ethiopic Book of Enoch* (Oxford: Oxford University Press, 1978).
Knox, John, *Chapters in a Life of Paul* (London: Adam & Charles Black, 1954).
Knox, Wilfred L., "Jewish Liturgical Exorcism" in *The Harvard Theological Review* 31 (1938), pp. 191-203.
Knutsson, K. E., "Possession and Extra-Institutional Behaviour: An Essay on Anthropological Micro-Analysis" in *Ethos* 40 (1975), pp. 244-272.
Koester, Helmut, *History, Culture, and Religion of the Hellenistic age* (Berlin: Walter de Gruyter, 1982).
Koritschoner, H., "Ngoma ya Shetani: An East African Native Treatment of Psychical Disorder" in Journal *of the Royal Anthropological Institute* 66 (1936), pp. 209-219.
Kraabel, A. T., "ὕψιστος and the Synagogue at Sardis" in *Greek, Roman, and Byzantine Studies* 10 (1969), pp. 81-93.
Kraft, Charles H., *Christianity with Power: Your Worldview and Your Experience of the Supernatural* (Ann Arbor: Vine Books, 1989).
──────*Christianity in Culture* (Maryknoll, New York: Orbis Books, 1981).
Kraft, Marguerite G., *Worldview and the Communication of the Gospel: A Nigerian Case Study* (Pasadena: William Carey Library, 1978).
────── "Reaching out for Spiritual Powers: A Study in the Dynamics of Felt Needs and Spiritual Power" (Ph. D. Dissertation, School of World Mission, Fuller Theological Seminary, Pasadena, 1990).
────── Understanding *Spiritual Power: A Forgotten Dimension of Cross-Cultural Mission and Ministry* (Maryknoll, New York: Orbis Books, 1995).
Kramer, Fritz W., *Der rote Fes. Über Besessenheit und Kunst in Afrika* (Frankfurt am Main: Athenäum, 1987).
Krigie, D. J., "The Social Function of Witchcraft" in M. Marwick (ed.), Witchcraft *and Sorcery* (Harmondsworth: Penguin Books, 1982), pp. 263-275.
Krigie, E. J. and D. J. Krigie, *The Realm of a Rain Queen: A Study of the Patterns of Lovedu Society* (London: Oxford University Press, 1943).
Krug, Antje, *Heilkunst und Heilkult: Medizin in der Antike* (Munichen: C. H. Beck, 1993).
Kuemmerlin-McLean, Joanne K., "Magic (Old Testament)" in David N. Freedman (ed.), *The Anchor Bible Dictionary* Vol. 5 (New York: Doubleday, 1992), pp. 468-471.
Küng, Hans, *Theology of the Third Millennium* (New York: Doubleday, 1988).
Kuukure, E., *The Destiny of Man: Dagaare Beliefs in Dialogue with Christian Eschatology* (Frankfurt am Main: Peter Lang, 1985).
La Fontaine, J. S., "Witchcraft in Bagisu" in J. Middleton and E. H. Winter (eds.), *Witchcraft and Sorcery in East Africa* (London: Routledge & Kegan Paul, 1963), pp. 187-220.

Bibliography

La Potterie, Ignace de, *The Hour of Jesus: The Passion and the Resurrection of Jesus* (Slough: St. Paul Publications, 1989).
Ladd, George Eldon, *A Theology of the New Testament* (Grand Rapids, Michigan: Eerdmans, 1994).
Lähnemann, Johannes, *Der Kolosserbrief: Komposition, Situation und Argumentation* SNT 3 (Gütersloh: Mohn, 1971).
Laing, R. D., *The Politics of Experience* (Harmondsworth: Penguin Books, 1967).
Lakoff, G., "The Contemporary Theory of Metaphor" in A. Ortony (ed.), *Metaphor and Thought* (Cambridge: Cambridge University Press, 1993), pp. 202-251.
────── and M. Johnson *Metaphors we Live By* (Chicago: University of Chicago Press, 1980).
Lambek, Michael, *Human Spirits: A Cultural Account of Trance in Mayotte* (Cambridge/New York: Cambridge University Press, 1981).
Lan, David, *Guns and Rain: Guerrillas and Spirit Mediums in Zimbabwe* (Berkeley: University of Chicago Press, 1985).
Lane, Anthony N. S. (ed.), *The Unseen World: Christian Reflections on Angels Demons and the Heavenly Realm* (Carlisle, Cumbria: Paternoster Press; Grand Rapids, Michigan: Baker Book House, 1996).
Lane, Eugene N., "Sabazius and the Jews in Valerius Maximus: A Re-Examination" in *Journal of Roman Studies* 69 (1979), pp. 35-38.
Lange, A. "The Essene Position on Magic and Divination" in M. Bernstein, F, García Martínez and J. Kampen (ed.), *Legal Texts and Legal Issues: Proceedings of the Second Meeting of the International Organization for Qumran Studies, Cambridge 1995, Published in the Honour of Joseph M. Baungearten* STDJ (Leiden: Brill, 1997), 377-435.
Langley, Myrtles S., "Spirit Possession and Social Context: An Anthropological Perspective with Theological Implications" in *Churchman* 94 3 (1980), pp. 226-245.
Langton, E., *Satan, a Portrait* (London: Skeffington & Son, 1945).
Larson, Gerald J., C. Scott Littleton and Jaan Puhvel (eds.), *Myth and Indo-European Antiquity* (Berkeley, California: University of Chicago Press, 1974).
Leakey, L. S. B., *The Southern Kikuyu Before 1903* Vol. iii (London: Academic Press, 1977).
Lease, Gary, "Nag Hammadi – Archaeology" in David N. Freedman (ed.), *The Anchor Bible Dictionary* Vol. 4 (New York: Doubleday, 1992), pp. 982-984.
Lee, J. Y., "Interpreting the Demonic Powers in Pauline Thought." *Novum Testament* 12 (1970), pp. 54-69.
Leenhardt, Godfrey, *Divinity and Experience: The religion of the Dinka* (Oxford: Clarendon Press, 1961).
Leivestad, Ragnar, *Christ the Conqueror: Ideas of Conflict and Victory in the New Testament* (London: SPCK, 1954).
LeMarquand, Grant, "New Testament Exegesis in (Modern) Africa" in Gerald O. West and Musa W. Dube (eds.), *The Bible in Africa: Transactions, Trajectories and Trends* (Leiden: Brill, 2000), pp. 72-102.
LeVine, R. A., "Witchcraft and Society in a Gusii Community" in J. Middleton and E. H. Winter (eds.), *Witchcraft and Sorcery in East Africa* (London: Routledge & Kegan Paull, 963), pp. 221-255.
Levi-Strauss, C., "The Structural Study of Myth" in T. A. Sebeok 1958 *Myth—A Symposium* (Bloomington : Indiana University Press, 1958), pp. 81-95.
────── *Structural Anthropology* (Harmondsworth: Penguin Books, 1977).

Lewis, C. S., *The Screwtape Letters* (London: Harper Collins, 1942).
Lewis, I. M., "Spirit Possession and Deprivation Cults" in *Man* 1 3 (1966), pp. 307-329.
———— "A Structural Approach to Witchcraft and Spirit-possession" in M. Douglas (ed.), *Witchcraft Confession and Accusations* (London: Tavistock Publications, 1970), pp. 393-309.
———— *Ecstatic Religion: An Anthropological Study of Spirit Possession and Shamanism* (Harmondsworth: Penguin Books, 1971).
———— *Social Anthropology in Perspective* (Cambridge: Cambridge University Press, 1985).
————*Ecstatic Religion: A Study of Shamanism and Spirit Possession* (London: Routledge, 1989).
———— *Religion in Context: Cults and Charisma* (Cambridge: Cambridge University Press, 1996).
———— Ahmed Al-Safi and Sayyid Hurreiz (eds.), *Women Medicine: The Zar-Bori Cult in Africa and Beyond* (Edinburgh: Edinburgh University Press, 1991).
Lienhardt, Godfrey, *Divinity and Experience: The religion of the Dinka* (Oxford: Clarendon Press, 1961).
———— "The Dinka and Catholicism" in J. Davis, *Religious Organisation and Religious Experience* (New York: Academic Press, 1982), pp. 81-95.
———— "Constructing Local Worlds: Spirit Possession in the Gwembe Valley, Zambia" in Heike Behrend and Ute Luig (eds.), *Spirit Possession: Modernity and Power in Africa* (Oxford: James Currey Ltd/Madison: University of Wisconsin Press, 1999), pp. 124-141.
Lightfoot, J. B., *St. Paul's Epistle to the Colossians and to Philemon: A Revised Text with introduction, notes and Dissertations:* (London: MacMillan, 1875 [Reprint1981]).
———— *St. Paul's Epistle to the Galatians* (London: MacMillan, 1876).
———— "The Colossian Heresy" in F. O. Francis and W. A. Meeks *Conflict at Colossae* SBLSBS 4 (Misoula: Scholar's Press, 1975), pp. 13-59.
Lijadu, E. M., *Orunmla!* (Nottingham: S. Richards, 1908 [Reprint 1972]).
Lincoln, Andrew T., "A Re-Examination of "The Heavenlies" in Ephesians" in *New Testament Studies* 19 (1972-73), pp. 468-483.
———— *Paradise Now and Not Yet: Studies in the Role of Heavenly Dimension in Paul's Thought with Special Reference to Eschatology* SNTSMS 43 (Cambridge: University Press, 1981).
———— *Ephesians* WBC 42 (Waco, Texas: Word Books, 1990).
———— "The Theology of Ephesians" in A. T. Lincoln and A. J. M Wedderburn, *The Theology of the Later Pauline Letters* (Cambridge: Cambridge University Press, 1993), pp. 75-166.
———— "'Stand, Therefore...': Ephesians 6: 10-20 as *Peroratio*" in *Biblical Interpretation* 3 (1995), pp.99-114.
———— "Liberation from the powers: Supernatural Spirits or Societal Structures" in R. D. M. Carroll, David J. A. Clines and Philip R. Davies, , *The Bible in Human Society: essays in honour of John Rogerson :* essays in honour of John Rogerson (Sheffield: Sheffield Academic Press, 1995).
———— and A. J. M. Wedderburn. *The Theology of the Later Pauline Letters* (Cambridge: Cambridge University Press, 1993).
Lindblom, G. *The Akamba in British East Africa* (Upp.sala: Appelbergs Boktrykeri Abtieblolag, 1920).
Ling, Samuel, "An Independent, Pioneering Spirit: Christian Individualism West and East" (available at http://www2.ccim.org/~reformata/Individualism.htm, accessed on 16.05.03

Little, Kenneth, "The Mende in Sierra Leone" in Daryll Forde (ed.), *African Worlds: Studies in the Cosmological Ideas and Social Values of African People* (London: Oxford University Press – International African Institute, 1954), pp. 111-137.

Littlewood, Roland, *Pathology and Identity: The Work of Mother Earth in Trinidad* (Cambridge: Cambridge University Press, 1992).

Lloyd-Jones, D. M., *The Christian Soldier: An Exposition of Ephesians 6:10 to 20* (Edinburgh: the Banner of Truth Trust, 1977).

Lockwood, Gregory J., *1 Corinthians* – Concordia Commentary (St. Louis: Concordia Publishing House, 2000).

Lohmann, Roger Ivar, "The Supernatural is Everywhere: Defining Qualities of Religion in Melanesia and Beyond" in *Anthropological Forum* Vol. 13 No 2 (2003), pp. 175-185.

Lohse, Eduard, *Colossians and Philemon* (Philadelphia: Fortress Press, 1971).

Long, Bruce J., "Demons: An Overview" in M. Eliade (ed.), *The Encyclopaedia of Religion* Vol. 4 (New York: Macmillan, 1987), pp. 282-288.

Long, E., *The History of Jamaica* Vol. 2 (London: Frank Cass & Co, 1774).

Longenecker, Richard N., *Paul, Apostle of Liberty* (Grand Rapids: Baker, 1976).

────── *Galatians* WBC 41 (Dallas: Word, 1990).

Loram, C. T., "Education in Africa" in *Church Missionary Review* 74 (1923), pp. 156-160.

Luck, George, *Arcana Mundi: Magic and the Occult in the Greek and Roman Worlds* (Baltimore: John Hopkins University Press, 1985).

────── *Magie und andere Geheimlehren in der Antike* – KTA 489 (Stuttgart: Kröner, 1990).

Lüdemann, Gerd, *Paul, Apostle to the Gentiles: Studies in Chronology* (Philadelphia: Fortress, 1984).

Ludwig, Arnold. M., "Altered States of Consciousness" in R. Prince (ed.), Trance *and Possession States* (Montreal: R. M. Bucke, 1968), pp. 69-95.

Lugira, A. M., *Ganda Art: A Study of the Ganda Mentality with Respect to Possibilities of Acculturation in Christian Art* (Kampala,: Osasa Publications, 1970).

Luig, Ute, "Besessenheit als Ausdruck von Frauenkultur in Zambia" in *Peripherie* 47/48 (1992), pp. 111-128.

────── "Gesellschaftliche Entwicklung und ihre individuelle Verarbeitung in den affliktinen Besessenheitskulten der Tonga" in *Tribus* 42 (1993), pp. 109-120.

────── "Constructing Local Worlds: Spirit Possession in the Gwembe Valley, Zambia" in Heike Behrend and Ute Luig (eds.), *Spirit Possession: Modernity and Power in Africa* (Oxford: James Currey Ltd/Madison: University of Wisconsin Press, 1999), pp. 124-141.

Lyonnet, Stanislaus, "Paul's Adversaries in Colossae" in F. O. Francis and W. A. Meeks (eds.), *Conflict at Colossae* SBLSBS 4 (Missoula: Scholar's Press, 1973), pp. 147-161.

Lystad, Robert Arthur, *The Ashanti: A Proud People* (New Brunswick, New Jersey: Rutgers University Press, 1958).

MacArthur, John Jr., *Ephesians – The MacArthur New Testament Commentary Series*. (Chicago: Moody Press, 1986).

MacDonald, Margaret Y., *The Pauline Churches: A Socio-historical Study of Institutionalisation in the Pauline and Deutero-Pauline Writings* (Cambridge: Cambridge University Press, 1988).

MacGregor, G. H. C., "Principalities and Powers: The Cosmic Background of Paul's Thought" in *New Testament Studies 1* (1954-1955), pp. 17-28.

Mackay, Alexander M, *The Story of A.M. Mackay—Pioneer Missionary of the C.M.S to*

Uganda—Told by His Sister (London: Hodder & Stoughton, 1878).
MacMullen, Ramsay, *Paganism in the Roman Empire* (New Haven: Yale University Press, 1974).
Magesa, Laurenti, "Death as a Moral Maturity: A Synthesis of Three Theological Theories" in *Journal for African Christian Studies CHIEA* 4 2 (June 1988), pp. 25-48.
─────── "From a Privatized to Popular Hermeneutics in Africa" in H. Kinoti and J. Walligo (eds.), *The Bible in African Christianity* (Nairobi: Acton press, 1997), pp. 25-39.
─────── *African Religion: The Moral Traditions of Abundant Life* (Maryknoll, New York: Orbis Books, 1997).
Mair, Lucy Philip, *Witchcraft* (London: Weidenfeld & Nicolson, 1969).
Malina, B. J. and Jerome H. Neyrey, "Honour and Shame in Luke-Acts: Pivotal Values of the Mediterranean World" in J. H. Neyrey (ed.), *The Social World of Luke-Acts: Models for Interpretation* (Peabody, Massachusetts: Hendrickson, 1991), pp. 25-66.
─────── Conflict in Luke-Acts: Labelling and Deviance Theory" in J. H. Neyrey (ed.), The *Social World of Luke-Acts: Models for Interpretation* (Peabody, Massachusetts: Hendrickson, 1991), pp. 97-124.
─────── "Jesus the Witch: Witchcraft Accusations in Matthew 12" in Horrell, David G *Social-Scientific Approaches to New Testament Interpretation* (Edinburgh: T & T Clark, 1999), pp. 29-67.
Malina, Bruce J., *The New Testament World: Insight from Cultural Anthropology* (London: SCM Press, 1981).
─────── *Christian Origins and Cultural Anthropology: Practical Models for Biblical Interpretation* (Atlanta, Georgia: John Knox Press, 2001).
Malinowski, Bronsilav, *Myth in Primitive Psychology* (London: Kegan Paul, Trench, Trubner & Co, 1927).
─────── "Primitive Religion and Primitive Science" in Julian Huxley, J. Arthur Thomson, J. S. Haldane and others, *Science and Religion: A Symposium* (London: Gerald Howe, 1931), pp. 65-81.
─────── "The Problem of Meaning in Primitive Languages" in C. K. Ogden and I. A. Richards (eds.), *The Meaning of Meaning* (London: Kegan Paul, 1946), pp. 296-336.
Manaoukian, M., *Akan and Ga-Adangme Peoples of the Gold Coast* (Oxford: International African Institute–Oxford University Press, 1950).
Maquet, J., *Africanity: The Cultural Unity of Black Africa* (New York: Oxford University Press, 1972).
Marshall, I. H., "Culture and the New Testament" in J. Scott and R. T. Coote (eds.), Gospel *and Culture.* (London, SCM Press, 1979), pp. 21-46.
─────── *Acts* (Leicester: Inter-Varsity Press, 1980).
─────── *1 and 2 Thesalonians* (London: Marshall, Morgan & Scott, 1983).
Martey, Emanuel, *African Theology: Inculturation and Liberation* (Maryknoll, New York: Orbis Books, 1995.)
Martin, Ralph P., *Colossians: The Church's Lord and Christian's Liberty* (Exeter: The Paternoster Press, 1972).
─────── *Colossians and Philemon* NCB (London: Marshall, Morgan & Scott, 1974).
─────── *Ephesians, Colossians and Philemon* (Louisville: Westminster/John Knox, 1991).
─────── *2 Corinthians* (Milton Keynes: Word Publishing, 1991).

Bibliography

Martyn, J. L., "Christ and the Elements of the Cosmos" in his *Theological Issues in the Letters of Paul* (Edinburgh: T & T Clark, 1997), pp. 125-140.

Marwick, M "The Social Context of Cewa Witch Beliefs" in *Africa* 22 (1952), pp. 120-135; 215-133.

Marwick, M., (ed.), *Witchcraft and Sorcery* (Harmondsworth: Penguin Books, 1982).

Mascall, E. L., *Christ, the Christian and the Church: A Study of the Incarnation and Its Consequences* (London: Longmans, Green, 1946).

Masenya, M., "Proverb 31: 10-31 in a South African Context: A Reading for the Liberation of African (Northern Sotho) Woman" in *Semeia* 78 (1997), pp. 55-67.

Masquelier, Adeline, "Encounter with a Road Siren: Machines, Bodies and Commodities in the Imaginations of a Mawri Healer" in *Visual Anthropology Review* 8 (1992), pp. 56-69.

———— "The Invention of Anti-Tradition: Dodo Spirits In Southern Niger" in Heike Behrend and Ute Luig (eds.), *Spirit Possession: Modernity and Power in Africa* (Oxford: James Currey Ltd/Madison: University of Wisconsin Press, 1999), pp. 34-49.

Matera, Frank J. *Galatians* in Sacra Pagina Series edited by Daniel J. Harrington, S. J (Collegeville, Minnesota: The Liturgical Press, 1992).

Mbiti, J. S., *African Religions and Philosophy* (London/Nairobi: Heinemann Educational Books, 1969).

———— *The Concept of God in Africa* (London: SPCK, 1970).

———— *New Testament Eschatology in an African Background* (London: Oxford University Press, 1971).

———— *Prayers of African Religion* (London: SPCK, 1975).

———— "Theological Impotence and the Universality of the Church" in Gerald H. Anderson and Thomas F. Stransky, *Mission Trends, 3: Third World Theologies* (Grand Rapids, Michigan: Eerdmans, 1976), pp. 6-18.

———— *The Bible and Theology in African Christianity* (Nairobi: Oxford University Press, 1986).

———— "The Bible in African Culture" in Rosino Gibellini (ed.), *Paths of African Theology* (London: SCM Press, 1994), pp. 27-39.

McCarthy, Brown K., *Mama Lola: A Vodou Priestess in Brooklyn* (Berkeley/Los Angels: University of California Press, 1991).

McCown, C. C., "The Christian Tradition as to the Magical Wisdom of Solomon" in *Journal of Palestine Oriental Society,* 2 Jerusalem (1922), pp. 11-24.

———— *The Testament of Solomon* – Untersuchungen zum Neuen Testament 9 (Leipzig: J. C. Heinrichs, 1922).

———— "The Ephesian Grammata in Popular Belief" in *Transactions of the American Philological Association* 54 (1923), pp.128-140.

McGarry, Cecil S. J., "Preface" in J. M. Waliggo, Arij A. Roest Crollius, T. Nkeramihigo and J. Mutiso-Mbinda (eds.), *Inculturation: Its Meaning and Urgency* (Nairobi: St. Paul's Publication-Africa, 1986).

McGavaran, D., *The Clash between Christianity and Cultures* (Washington DC: Canon, 1974).

McVeigh, M. J., *God in Africa* (Cape Cod, Massachusetts/Hartford, Vermont: Claude Stark, 1974).

Meeks, Wayne A., "In One Body: The Unity of Humankind in Colossians and Ephesians" in Wayne Meeks and Jacob Jervell (eds.), *God's Christ and His People: Studies in Honour of Nils Alstrup Dahl* (Oslo, Bergen and Tromsö: Universitetsforlaget, 1977), pp. 209-221.

———— *The First Urban Christians: The Social World of Apostle Paul* (New Haven/London: Yale University Press, 1983).

Mercier, P., "The Fon of Dahomey" in Daryll Forde (ed.), *African Worlds: Studies in the Cosmological Ideas and Social Values of African People* (London: Oxford University Press – International African Institute, 1954), pp. 210-234.

Merkelbach, R. "Mithras, Mithraism" in David N. Freedman (ed.), *The Anchor Bible Dictionary* Vol. 4 (New York: Doubleday, 1992), pp. 877-8.

Messing, S. D., "Group Therapy and Social Status in Zar Cult of Ethiopia" in J. Middleton, *Magic, Witchcraft and Curing* (Austin/London: Texas Press, 1967) pp. 285-293.

Meyer, M. "Mysteries" in Craig A. Evans and Stanley E. Porter, *Dictionary of New Testament Background* (Downers Grove/Leicester: Intervarsity Press, 2000), pp. 720-724.

Meyers, C. L. and E. M. Meyers *Haggai and Zechariah 1–8* (New York: Doubleday, 1987)

Middleton, J. and E. H. Winter, *Witchcraft and Sorcery in East Africa* (London: Routledge and Kegan Paul, 1963).

Middleton, J. (ed.), *Magic, Witchcraft and Curing* (Austin/London: Texas Press, 1967).

———— "Oracles and divination among the Lugbara" in J. Beattie and J. Middleton (eds.), *Spirit Mediumship and Society in Africa* (London: Tavistock, 1969), pp. 220-232.

————*Lugbara Religion:* Ritual and Authority among an East African People (Washington, D. C/London: Smithsonian Institution Press, 1987 [1960]).

———— "Theories of Magic" in M. Eliade (ed.), *The Encyclopaedia of Religion* Vol. 9 (New York: Macmillan, 1987), pp. 82-89.

Miegge, G., *Gospel and Myth in the Thought of Rudolf Bultmann* (London: Lutterworth Press, 1960).

Milik, J. T., *The Books of Enoch: Aramaic Fragments of Qumran Cave 4* (Oxford: Oxford University Press, 1976).

Miller, Elmer S., "The Christian Missionary: Agent of Secularisation" in *Missiology* Vol. 1 (January 1973), pp. 99-107.

Miller, G., " ΟΓ ΑΡΧΟΝΤΕΣ ΤΟΥ ΑΙΩΝΟΣ ΤΟΥΤΟΥ"– A New Look at 1 Corinthians 2: 6-8 " in *The Journal of Biblical Literature* 91 (1972), pp. 522-528.

Miller, Patrick D., *The Religion of Ancient Israel* (London: SPCK, 2000).

Milton, C. L., *Ephesians* (London: Oliphants, 1976).

Moffatt, James, *The First Epistle of Paul to the Corinthians* (London: Hodder & Stoughton, 1938).

Mofokeng, T., "Black Christians, the Bible and Liberation" in *Journal of Black Theology* 2 (1988), pp. 34-42.

Moltmann, J., *God in Creation: An Ecological Doctrine of Creation* (London: SCM Press, 1985).

Monfouga-Nicolas, J., *Ambivalence et Culte de Possession: Contribution à l'Etude du Bori Hausa* (Paris: Anthropos, 1972).

Montgomery, J. (ed.), *Demon Possessing* (Minneapolis Bethany Fellowship, 1979).

Moila, M. P., "The Effects of Belief in the Living Dead on the Church in South Africa" in *Africa Theological Journal*, Vol. 18 No.1 (1989), pp. 140-150.

Mooij, J. J. A., *A Study of Metaphor: On the Nature of Metaphoric Expression, with Special Reference to their Reference* (Amsterdam/New York/Oxford: North Holland Publishing Company, 1976).

Moreau, A. Scott, *The World of the Spirits: A Biblical Study in the African Context* (Nairobi: Evangel Publishing House, 1990).

Morgan, M. A., *Sepher Ha–Razim: The Book of Mysteries* (Chico: Scholars Press, 1983).
Morris, H., "The Relations of Missions to Government" in *Church Missionary Review*, 62 (1911), pp.129-136.
Morris, Leon, *The Epistle to the Romans* (Grand Rapids, Michigan: Eerdmans, 1988).
Morrison, Clinton D., *The Powers That Be: Earthly Rulers and Demonic Powers in Romans 13.1-7* (London: SCM Press, 1960).
Morsy, Soheir, "Sex Roles, Power and Illness in an Egyptian Village" in *American Ethnologist* 5 (1978), pp. 137-150.
Mosala, Itumelang J., "The use of the Bible in Black Theology" in J. Mosala and B. Tlhagale *The Unquestionable Right to be Free: Essays in Black Theology* (Johannesburgh: Skotaville, 1986), pp. 175-199.
────── *Biblical Hermeneutics and Black Theology in South Africa* (Grand Rapids, Michigan: Eerdmans, 1989).
────── "Race, Class, and Gender as Hermeneutical Factors in African Independent Churches" in *Semeia* 73 (1996), pp. 43-57.
Moser, Karin S., "Metaphorical Analysis in Psychology—Method, Theory, and Fields of App.lication" in *Forum: Qualitative Socialforschung/Forum: Qualitative Social research* (Online Journal Vol. 1 No. 2, 2000), available at http://www.qualitative-research.netfqs-texte/2-00/2-00moser-e.htm, accessed on 15.11.03.
Mott, Stephen C., *Biblical Ethics and Social Change* (New York/London: Oxford University Press, 1982).
Moule, C. F. D., *The Epistle to the Colossians and Philemon* CGTC (Cambridge: Cambridge University Press, 1957 [1982]).
────── *The Birth of the New Testament* (London: Adam & Charles Black Limited, 1962).
Moule, H. C. G., *Ephesian Studies* (S.l.: Hodder and Stoughton, n.d.).
Mouw, Richard, *Politics and the Biblical Drama* (Grand Rapid, Michigan: Eerdmanns, 1976).
Moxnes, Halvor, "Honour and Shame", in Rohrbaugh, Richard L. (ed.), The *Social Science and New Testament Interpretation* (Peabody, Massachusetts: Hendrickson Publishers, 1996), pp. 19-40.
Mudge, Lewis S., "Paul Ricoeur on Biblical Interpretation" in Paul Ricoeur, *Essays in Biblical Interpretation* (Philadelphia: Fortress Press, 1980), pp. 1-40.
Mugambi J. N. K., *From Liberation to Reconstruction: African Christian Theology After the Cold War* (Nairobi: E. A. E. P, 1995).
Mulago, gwa Chikala M., *La Religion Traditionnelle des Bantu et leur Vision du Monde* (Kinshasa: Faculté de Théologie Catholique, 1980).
Mumford, Lewis, *The Myth of the Machine* 2 Vols. (New York: Harcourt, Brace, Jovanovich, 1964).
Murillo, Mario, *Fresh Fire* (Danville: Anthony Douglas Publishing, 1991).
Murray, Gilbert, *Five Stages of Greek Religion* (Oxford: Clarendon Press, 1925).
Murray, John, *The Epistle to the Romans* (London: Marshall, Morgan & Scott, 1967).
Mussies, G., "Pagan, Jews and Christians at Ephesus" in P. W. van der Horst and G. Mussies (eds.), *Studies in the Hellenistic background of the New Testament* (Utrecht: Faculteit der Godgeleerdheid, Rijksuniverstiet Utrecht, (1990), pp. 177-194.
Myers, Ched, *Binding the Strong Man: A political Reading of Mark's Story of Jesus* (Maryknoll: Orbis Books, 1988).
Nadel, S. F., "A Study of Shamanism in Nuba Hills" in *Journal of Royal Anthropological Institute* 76 (1946), pp. 25-37.

Nash, June, *We Eat the Mines and the Mines Eat Us: Dependency and Exploitation in Bolivian Tin Mines* (New York: Columbia University Press, 1979).

Naveh, J., "Fragments of an Aramaic Magic Book from Qumran" in *Israel Exploration Journal* 48 (1998), pp. 252-261.

Ndung'u, Nahason, "The Role of the Bible in the Rise of the African Instituted Churches: The Case of the Akurinu Churches in Kenya" in Gerald O. West and Musa W. Dube (eds.), *The Bible in Africa: Transactions, Trajectories and Trends* (Leiden: Brill, 2000), pp. 236-237.

Nebechukwu, A., "Third World Theology and the Recovery of African Identity" in *Journal of Inculturation Theology* Vol.2 No. 1 (June 1995), pp. 17-27.

Neil, S., "Religion and Culture: A historical Introduction" in J. Scott and R. T. Coote (eds.), *Gospel and Culture* (London, SCM Press, 1979), pp. 1-17.

Neil, William, (ed.), The *Bible Companion* (London: The Caxton Publishing Company Limited, 1959).

Neufeld, T. Y., *Put on the Armour of God: The Divine Warrior from Isaiah to Ephesians* (Sheffield: Sheffield Academic Press, 1997).

Neugebauer, O., "The 'Astronomical' Chapters of the Ethiopic Enoch (72–82): Translation and Commentary", with Additional Notes on the Aramaic Fragments by Matthew Black, in Matthew Black *The Book of Enoch or 1 Enoch: A New English Edition with Commentary and Textual Notes* (Leiden: Brill, 1985), pp. 386-419.

Newbigin, Lesslie, *Honest Religion for Secular Man* (Philadelphia: Westminster Press, 1966).

Neyrey, Jerome H., "Clean/Unclean, Pure/Polluted and Holy/Profane: The Idea of the System of Purity" in Richard L. Rohrbaugh (ed.), *The Social Sciences and New Testament Interpretation* (Peabody, Massachusetts: Hendrickson Publishers, 1996), pp. 80-104.

Ngcokovane, C., *Demons of Apartheid: A Moral and Ethical Analysis of the NGK, NP, Broerderbond Justification of Apartheid*. (Braamfontein: Skotaville, 1989).

Ngulube, Naboth, *Some Aspects of Growing up in Zambia* (Lusaka: Kenneth Kaunda Foundation, 1989).

Nicholas, Jacqueline, *Ambivalence et Culte de Possession* (Paris: Anthropos, 1972).

Nicholls, B. J., *Contextualization: A Theology of Gospel and Culture* (Illinois: Intervarsity press/Exeter: Paternoster Press, 1979).

────── "Towards a Theology of Gospel and Culture" in Scott. J. and Coote R. T (eds.), Gospel *and Culture* (Pasadena: William Carey Library, 1979), pp. 69-82.

Niebuhr, H. R., *Christ and Culture*. (New York, Harper & Brothers, 1951).

Nilsson, Martin P., *Greek Popular Religion* (New York: Columbia University Press, 1940).

──────*Greek Piety* (Oxford: Clarendon Press, 1948).

────── *The Dionysiac Mystery of the Hellenistic and Roman Age* (Lund: C. W. K. Gleerup, 1957).

────── *Geschichte der Griechischen Religion* (Munich: Beck, 1974).

Noble, D. S., "Demoniacal Possession among the Giryama" in *Man* Vol. 61 No 49 (1961), pp. 50-52.

Noble, Thomas A., "The Spirit World: A Theological Approach" in Anthony N. S. Lane (ed.), *The Unseen World: Christian Reflection on Angels, Demons and the Heavenly Realm* (Carlisle, Cumbria: Paternoster Press and Grand Rapids, Michigan: Baker Book House, 1996), pp. 185-223.

Nock, A. D., "Studies in Graeco-Roman Beliefs of Empire in Z. Stewart (ed.), Arthur

Darby Nock: Essays on Religion and the Ancient World I (Cambridge: Cambridge University Press, 1972a), pp. 34-41.

———— "Greek Magical Papyri" in Z. Stewart (ed.), Arthur *Darby Nock: Essays on Religion and the Ancient World I* (Oxford: Clarendon, 1972), pp. 176-194.

———— C. Roberts and T. C. Skeat "The Guild of Zeus Hypsistos" in Z. Stewart (ed.), Arthur *Darby Nock: Essays on Religion and the Ancient World I* (Oxford: Clarendon, 1972), pp. 422-427.

North, R., "Separated Spiritual Substances in the Old Testament" in *Catholic Biblical Quarterly* 29 (1967), pp. 419-449.

Nthamburi, Zablon and Douglas Waruta, "Biblical Hermeneutics in African Instituted Churches" in H. Kinoti and J. Waliggo (eds.), The *Bible in African Christianity* (Nairobi: Acton press, 1997), pp. 40-57.

Nürnberger, K., *MODIMO: The Sotho Notion of the Supreme Being and the Impact of the Christian Proclamation, Journal of Religion in Africa*, Vol. II (1974), pp. 179-199.

Nyamiti, Charles, *The Scope of African Theology* (Kampala: Gaba Publications, 1973).

———— *Christ our Ancestor: Christology from an African Perspective* (Gweru: Mambo Press, 1984).

O'Brien, P. T.., *Colossians, Philemon* WBC 44 (Waco, Texas: Word Books, 1982).

———— "Principalities and Powers: Opp.onents of the church" in Carson D. A (ed.), Biblical *interpretation and the church: Text and Context* (Exeter: Paternoster Press, 1984), pp. 110-150.

———— *The Letter to the Ephesians* (Grand Rapids, Michigan: Eerdmans/Leicester: Apollos, 1999).

O'Donovan, Wilber, *Biblical Christianity in African Perspective* (Carlisle: Paternoster Press, 1996).

O'Donuhue, John, *Spirits and Magic: A Critical look* Spearhead No. 68 (Eldoret: Gaba Publication, 1981).

Obeng, Emanuel, "The Use of Biblical Critical Methods in Rooting the Scriptures in Africa" in H. Kinoti, and J. Waliggo (eds.), *The Bible in African Christianity* (Nairobi: Acton press, 1997), pp. 8-24.

———— "Healing the Groaning Creation in Africa", in M. N. Getui, and E. A. Obeng (eds.), *Theology of Reconciliation: Exploration Essays* (Nairobi: Acton Press, 1999), pp. 10-27.

Obeyesekere, G., *Medusa's Hair: An Essay on Personal Symbols and Religious Experience* (Chicago/London: University of Chicago Press, 1981).

Oesterley, W. O. E. and Theodore H. Robinson, *Hebrew Religion: Its Origin and Development* (London: SPCK, 1930).

Oesterreich, T. K., *Possession: Demoniacal and Other Among Primitive Races in Antiquity, the Middle Ages, and Modern Times* (London: Kegan Paul, 1930).

Okorocha, Cyril C., *The Means of Religious Conversion in Africa: A Case of the Igbo of Nigeria* (Aldershot: Avebury, 1987).

Okwuosa, V. E., Akubueze *In the Name of Christianity: The Missionaries in Africa* (Philadelphia/Ardmore: Dorrance & Company, 1977).

Olowola, Cornelius, *African Traditional Religion and the Christian Faith* (Achimota, Ghana: African Christian Press, 1993).

Olsen, Marvin E., *The Process of Social Organisation* (New York: Holt Rinehart, 1968).

Omoyajowo, A., "What is Witchcraft'? in E. A. A. Adegbola (ed.), *Traditional Religion in West Africa* (Nairobi: Uzima Press, 1983), pp. 317-337.

Ong, Aihwa, *Spirit of Resistance and Capitalist Discipline: Factory Women in Malaysia* (Albany, New York: University of New York Press, 1987).

———— "The Production of Possession: Spirits and the Multinational Corporation in Malaysia" in *American Ethnologist* 15 1 (1988), pp. 28-42.

Onwu, Nlenanya "The Hermeneutical Model: The Dilemma of the African Theologian" in *African Theological Journal* Vol. 14 (1985), pp. 145-160.

Onyango, Symon 1979 *Set Free from Demons* (Nairobi, Evangel Publishing house).

Ortony, Andrew, (ed.), *Metaphor and Thought* (Cambridge: Cambridge University Press, 1993).

———— "Angels: Barth and Beyond" in Anthony N. S. Lane (ed.), *The Unseen World: Christian Reflections on Angels, Demons and the Heavenly Realm* (Carlisle/Grand Rapids, Michigan: Paternoster Press/Baker, 1996), pp. 29-48.

Oster, Richard, "The Ephesian Artemis as an Opponent of Early Christianity" in *Jahrbuch für Antike und Christentum* 19 (1976), pp. 24-44.

———— "Ephesus as a Religious Centre under the Principate I: Paganism before Constantine" in W Haasel (ed.), Principat 18.3 1990), pp. 1661-1728.

Otner, Sherry, "Is Female to Male as Nature is to Culture?" in Michelle Rosaldo and Louise Lamphere (eds.), *Women Culture and Society* (Stanford: Stanford University Press, 1974), pp. 67-87.

Otto, Rudolf, *The Idea of the Holy* (London: Oxford University Press, 1923).

Otto, W. F., *The Homeric Gods: The Spiritual Significance of Greek Religion* (London: Thames & Hudson, 1955).

Owanikin, Rebecca M., "Colossians 2: 18: A Challenge to Some Doctrines of Certain Aladura Churches in Nigeria" in *African Journal of Biblical Studies* 2/ 1 & 2 (1987), pp. 89-96.

Packer, J. "The Gospel: Its Content and Communication" In J. Scott and R. T. Coote (eds.), *Gospel and Culture* (London, SCM Press, 1979), pp. 135-153.

Page, S. H. T., *Powers of Evil: A Biblical Study of Satan and Demons* (Grand Rapids, Michigan: Baker and Leicester: Apollos, 1995).

Paige, T., "Demons and Exorcism" in G. F. Hawthorne, R. P. Martin and D. G. Reid (eds.), *Dictionary of Paul and His Letters* (Downers Grove, Illinois/Leicester: Intervarsity Press, 1993), pp. 209-211.

Painter, John, *Theology as Hermeneutics: Rudolf Bultmann's Interpretation of the History of Jesus* (Sheffield: Almond Press, 1987).

Pannenberg, W., *Basic Questions in Theology* (London: SCM Press, 1973).

———— *The Idea of God and Human Freedom* (Philadelphia: Fortress Press, 1973).

Parfitt, Tudor, *The Lost Tribes of Israel* (London: Weidenfeld & Nicolson, 2002).

Parratt, John, *African Traditional Religion* (London: Sheldon Press, 1974).

———— "African Theology and Biblical Hermeneutics" *in African Theological Journal,* Vol.13 No.4 (1984), pp. 84-90.

———— *Reinventing Christianity: African Theology Today* (Grand Rapids, Michigan: Eerdmans, 1995).

Parrinder, E. G., *West African Psychology: A Comparative Study of Psychological and Religious Thoughts* (London: Lutterworth Press, 1951).

———— *Witchcraft: European and African* (London: Faber & Faber, 1958).

———— *Religion in Africa* (Harmondsworth: Penguin Books, 1969).

———— *African Traditional Religion* (London: Sheldon Press, 1974).

Pattermore, Stephen W., "Principalities and powers in Urak Lawoi. Introduction: Contextualizing Key Terms" in *Bible Translator* 45 1 (1994), pp. 116-129.

P'Bitek, Okot, *African Religions in Western Scholarship* (Nairobi/Kampala: East African Literature Bureau, 1970).

Peake, A. S., "The Epistle to the Colossians" in W. Robertson Nicoll (ed.), *Expositor's Greek Testament,* 3: (London: Hodder and Stoughton, 1903), pp. 475-507.

Pearson, Birger A., "Nag Hammadi Codices" in David N. Freedman (ed.), *The Anchor Bible Dictionary* Vol. 4 (New York: Doubleday, 1992) pp. 984-993.

―――― "Jewish Sources in Gnostic Literature" in M. Stone (ed.), *Jewish Writings of the Second Temple Period* CRINT 2/2 (Assen & Philadelphia, 1984), pp. 443-481.

Pearson, B. W. R., "Associations" in Craig A. Evans and Stanley E. Porter, *Dictionary of New Testament Background* (Downers Grove/Leicester: Intervarsity Press, 2000), pp. 136-138.

Peel, J. D. Y., "The Pastor and the *Babalawo*: The interaction of Religions in Nineteenth-century Yorubaland" in *Africa* 60 (1990), pp. 338-369.

Peires, J. B., "Nxele, Ntiskana and the Origins of the Xhosa Religious Reaction" in *Journal of African History*, 20, 1 (1979), pp. 51-61.

―――― *The Dead Will Arise: Nongqawuse and The Cattle-Killing Movement 1856-57* (Johannesburg: Ravan, 1989).

Penney, D. L. and M. O. Wise, "By the Power of Beelzebub: An Aramaic Incantation Formula from Qumran (4Q560) in *Journal of Biblical Literature* 113 (1994), pp. 627-650.

Percy, Ernest, *Die Probleme der Kolosser – und Epheserbriefe: Skrifter Utigivna av Kungl. Humanistiska Vetenskapssamfundet i Lund* XXXIX (Lund: C. W. K. Gleerup, 1964 [Reprint of 1946 edition]).

Peretti, Frank E., *This Present Darkness* (Westchester, Illinois: Crossway, 1986).

Peristiany, J. G. (ed.), *Honour and Shame: The Values of Mediterranean Society* (London: Weidenfeld and Nicholson, 1966).

―――― and J. Pitt-Rivers (eds.), *Honour and Grace in Anthropology* (Cambridge: Cambridge University Press, 1992).

Pitt-Rivers, Julian, "Spiritual Power in Central America" in M. Douglas (ed.), *Witchcraft Confession and Accusations* (London: Tavistock Publications, 1970), pp. 183-206.

Pobee, J. N., "Political Theology in the African Context" in *Africa Theological Journal* 11 (1982), pp. 168-172.

―――― *West Africa: Christ Would Be an African Too* (Geneva: World Council of Churches, 1996).

Pokorný, Petr, *Colossians: A Commentary* (Peabody, Massachusetts: Hendrickson, 1991).

Porter, S. E., *Verbal Aspects in the Greek of New Testament, with Special Reference to Tense and Mood* (New York: Lang, 1989).

―――― *Idioms of the Greek New Testament* (Sheffield: Academic Press, 1994).

Prasch, Thomas, "Which God for Africa: The Islamic-Christian Debate in Late Victorian England" in *Victorian Studies* 22 (1989), pp. 51-73.

Pred, Allan and M. J. Watts, *Reworking Modernity: Capitalism and Symbolic Discontent* (New Brunswick, New Jersey: Rutgers University Press, 1992).

Price, E, "The Defeat of M'Bona, the Rain Chief" in *The South African Pioneer* XXIX (1916), pp. 82-84.

Price, R. M., "Punished in Paradise" in *Journal for the Study of the New Testament* 7 (1980), pp. 33-40.

Price, S. R. F., *Rituals and Power: The Roman Imperial Cult in Asia Minor* (Cambridge: Cambridge University Press, 1984).

Puhvel, Jean (ed.), *Myth and Law among the Indo-European: Studies in Indo-European Comparative Mythology* (Berkeley, California: University of California Press, 1970).

Quarshie, B. Y., "The Significance of Biblical Studies for African Christian Theology" In

Journal of African Christian Thought Vol. 3 No. 1 (June 2000), pp. 17-26.

Rabin, Chaim, "The Uniqueness of Bible Translation" in Engelbert Mveng and R. J. Z. Werblowsky (eds.), *The Jerusalem Congress on Black Africa and the Bible Congress, April 24-30, 1972 Proceedings* (New York: Anti-Defamation League of B'nai B'rith, 1972), pp. 108-116.

Radin, Paul, *Primitive Religion: Its Nature and Origin* (New York: Dover Publications, 1957).

Ramsay, William M., *The Cities of St. Paul: Their Influence on His life and Thought* (London: Hodder & Stoughton, 1907).

Ranger T. O and John Weller, *Themes in the Christian History of Central Africa* (London/Nairobi/Ibadan/Lusaka: Heinemann Educational Books, 1975).

Raschke, C., *The Interruption of Eternity: Modern Gnosticism and the Origins of the New Religious Consciousness* (Chicago: Nelson Hall, 1980).

Rattray, R. S., *Religion and Art in Ashanti* (Oxford: Oxford University Press, 1963).

Ray, B., "The Story of Kintu: Myth, Death, and Ontology in Buganda" in I. Karp and C. S Birds (eds.), *Explorations in African System of Thought* (Bloomington: Indiana University Press, 1980), pp. 60-79.

Raybeck, D, J. Shoobe and J. Grauberg, "Women, Stress and Participation in Possession Cults: A Re-Examination of the Calcium Deficiency Hypothesis" in *Medical Anthropology Quarterly* 3 2 (1989), pp. 139-161.

Reasoner, M., "Purity and Impurity" in G. F. Hawthorne, R. P. Martin and D. G. Reid (eds.), *Dictionary of Paul and His Letters* (Downers Grove, Illinois/Leicester: Intervarsity Press, 1993), pp. 775-6.

Redfield, Robert, "A Selection from the Folk Culture of Yucatan" in C. Leslie (ed.), *Anthropology of Folk Religion* (New York: Vintage, 1960), pp. 337-388).

─────── *The Primitive World and Its Transformation* (Ithaca, New York: Cornell University Press, 1953).

─────── *The Folk Culture of Yucatan* (Chicago: University of Chicago Press, 1941).

Reed, C., *Pastors, Partners and Paternalists: African Church Leaders and Western Missionaries in the Anglican Church in Kenya, 1850-1900* (Leiden: Brill, 1997).

Reese, David George, "Demons (New Testament)" in David Noel Freedman (ed.), *The Anchor Bible Dictionary* Vol. 2 (New York: Doubleday, 1992), pp. 140-142.

Reicke, Bo, *The Disobedient Spirits and Christian Baptism: A Study of 1 Peter III: 19 and Its Context* (København: Elinar Munksgaard, 1946)

Reid, D. G., "Elements/Elemental Spirits of the World." in G. F. Hawthorne, R. P. Martin and D. G. Reid (eds.), *Dictionary of Paul and His Letters* (Downers Grove, Illinois/Leicester: Intervarsity Press, 1993), pp. 229-33.

─────── "Principalities and Powers" in G. F. Hawthorne, R. P. Martin and D. G. Reid (eds.), *Dictionary of Paul and His Letters* (Downers Grove, Illinois/Leicester: Intervarsity Press, 1993), pp. 746-752.

Reiter, Rayna (ed.), *Toward an Anthropology of Women* (New York: Monthly Review Press, 1975).

Reminick, R. A., "The Evil Eye Belief among the Amhara of Ethiopia" in *Ethnology* 13 (1974), pp. 279-291.

Reynolds, B., *Magic, Divination and Witchcraft among the Barotse of Northern Rhodesia* (London: Chatto & Windus, 1963).

Ribi, Alfred, "Demons: Psychological Perspective" in M. Eliade (ed.), *The Encyclopaedia of Religion* Vol. 4 (New York: Macmillan, 1987), pp. 288-292.

Riches, John, "Interpreting the Bible in African Contexts: Glasgow Consultation" in *Semeia* 73 (1996), pp. 181-188.

Ricoeur, Paul, *The Symbolism of Evil* (New York: Harper & Row, 1967).
——— *Freud and Philosophy: An Essay on Interpretation*, translated by Denis Savage (New Haven/London: Yale University Press, 1970).
——— "Biblical Hermeneutics" in *Semeia* 4 (1975), pp. 29-145.
——— *The Rule of Metaphor: Multi-Disciplinary Studies of the Creation of Meaning in Language* (London/Henley: Routledge & Kegan Paul, 1977).
——— *Interpretation Theory* (Fort Worth: Texas University Press, 1977).
——— *Essays on Biblical Interpretation*, edited with an Introduction by Lewis S. Mudge (Philadelphia: Fortress Press, 1980).
——— *Hermeneutics and Human Science*, edited and translated by John B. Thompson (Cambridge: Cambridge University Press, 1981).
——— "Myth and History" in M. Eliade (ed.), *The Encyclopaedia of Religion* Vol. 10 (New York: Macmillan, 1987), pp. 273-282.
Ridderbos, Herman N., *Paul: An Outline of His Theology* (London: SPCK, 1977).
Ring, Irene, Typische Beziehungen in einigen fremdkulturell gespeisten Therapien und Konsultationen unserer Tage (Unpublished MA Thesis, Philosophical Faculty, University of Cologne, Cologne, 1994).
Ringgren, Helmer, *Word and Wisdom: Studies in the Hypostatization of Divine Qualities in the Ancient Near East* (Lund: H. Ohlsson, 1947).
Roberts, A. D., (ed.), The *Cambridge History of Africa c 1790 – c 1870* Vol. 5 (Cambridge: Cambridge University Press, 1986).
Robertson, Archibald and Alfred Plummer, *A Critical and Exegetical Commentary on the First Epistle of St. Paul to the Corinthians*, ICC, (Edinburgh: T & T Clark, 1999 [1911]).
Robinson, J. Armitage, *St. Paul's Epistle to the Ephesians* (London: Macmillan, 1907).
——— *Commentary on Ephesians: The Greek Text with Introduction Notes and Indexes* (Grand Rapids: Kregel publication, 1979).
Robinson, John Arthur Thomas, *The Bod: A Study in Pauline Theologyy* SBT 5 (London: SCM Press, 1952).
Robinson, S. E, *The Testament of Adam: An Examination of the Syriac and Greek Traditions* (Chico, California: Scholars Press, 1982).
Rochberg-Halton, F., "Astrology in the Ancient Near East" in David N. Freedman (ed.), *The Anchor Bible Dictionary* Vol. 1 (New York: Doubleday, 1992), pp. 504-507.
Rohrbaugh, Richard L. (ed.), The *Social Science and New Testament Interpretation* (Peabody, Massachusetts: Hendrickson, 1996).
Rosaldo, Michele, "Women, Culture and Society: A Theoretical Overview" in Michelle Rosaldo and Louise Lamphere (eds.), *Women Culture and Society* (Stanford: Stanford University Press, 1974), pp. 17-43.
Rosaldo, Michelle and Louise Lamphere (eds.), "Introduction" in Michelle Rosaldo and Louise Lamphere (eds.), *Women Culture and Society* (Stanford: Stanford University Press, 1974), pp. 1-16.
——— (eds.), *Women Culture and Society* (Stanford: Stanford University Press, 1974).
Roscoe, John, *The Bakitara or Banyoro: The First Part of the Report of the Mackie Ethnological Expedition to Central Africa* (Cambridge: Cambridge University Press, 1923).
——— *The Baganda: An Account of Their Customs and Beliefs* (London: Frank Cass & Company Limited, 1965).
——— *The Northern Bantu* (London: Frank Cass, 1966).
Rose, H. J., Les *Maîtres Fous* (Paris: Comité du Film Ethnographique, 1954).

──────── *Les Songay* (Paris: Presses Universitaires de France – International African Institute, 1954).
──────── *Notes on Migration into the Gold Coast: First Report on the Mission Carried in Gold Coast from March to December 1954* (Accra:s.n.)
──────── *The Roman Questions of Plutarch* (Oxford: Clarendon Press, 1924).
──────── "Hades" in N. G. L. Hammond, and H. H. Scullard (eds.), *Oxford Classical Dictionary* (Oxford: Oxford University Press, 1970), p. 484.
──────── "Jean Rouch Talks about his Films to John Marshall and John W. Adams" in *American Anthropologist* 80, 1978), pp.1005-1022.
Rouget, G., *La Musique et la Transe: Esquisse d'une Théorie Générale des relations de la Musique et la Possession* (Paris: Gallimard, 1980).
Rowland, Christopher, "Apocalyptic Visions and the Exaltation of Christ in the Letter to the Colossians" in *Journal for the Study of the New Testament* 19 (1983), pp. 73-83.
Ruel, Malcolm, "Christians as Believers" in Davis, J *Religious Organisation and Religious Experience* (New York: Academic Press, 1982), pp. 9-31.
Rupp, Gordon, *Principalities and Powers: Studies in the Christian Conflict in History* (London: Epworth, 1952).
Russell, Bertrand, *The Analysis of Mind* (London: Allen & Unwin, 1921).
Russell, Jeffrey Burton, *Mephistopheles: The Devil in the Modern World* (Ithaca/London: Cornell University Press, 1986).
──────── *The Prince of Darkness: Radical Evil and the Power of God in History* (Ithaca, New York: Cornell University Press, 1988).
Russell, D. S., *The Method and Message of Jewish Apocalyptic: 200 BC–AD 100* (London: SCM Press, 1964).
Ryle, Gilbert, *The Concept of Mind* (Harmondsworth: Penguin, 1963).
Saler, B., "Supernatural as a Western Category" in *Ethos* 5 1 (1977), pp. 31-52.
──────── *Conceptualizing Religion: Immanent Anthropologists, Transcendent Natives and Unbounded Categories* (Leiden: Brill, 1993).
Sabourin, L., "The Mystery of Jesus (11): Jesus and Evil powers" in *Biblical Theology Bulletin*, 4 (1974), pp. 115-175.
Sanders, J. T., *Schismatics, Sectarians, Dissidents, Deviants: The First One Hundred Years of Jewish–Christian Relations* (London: SCM Press, 1993).
Sandmel, Samuel, "Parallelomania" in *Journal of Biblical Literature* 81 (1962), pp.1-13.
──────── *The First Christian Century in Judaism and Christianity: Certainties and Uncertainties* (New York: Oxford University Press, 1969).
Sanneh, Lamin, *Translating the Message: The Missionary Impact on Culture.* (Maryknoll, New York: Orbis Books, 1989).
Sapir, Edward, "The Unconscious Patterning of Behaviour in Society" in David G. Mandelbum, *Selected Writings of Edward Sapir in Language, Culture, and Personality* (Berkeley: University of California Press, 1949), pp. 544-559.
Sappington, T. J., *Revelation and Redemption at Colossae* JSNTSup 53 (Sheffield; JSOT Press, 1991).
Sargant, W., *Battle for the Mind* (London: Pan Books, 1959).
Saunders, C. [ed.), *Black Leaders in South Africa History* (London, Heinemann, 1979).
Schaaf, Y., *On Their Way Rejoicing: The History and Role of the Bible in Africa* (Carlisle: The Paternoster Press, 1994).
Schaeffer, Francis A., *Escape from Reason* (London: Intervarsity Press, 1968).
Schebester, P., *My Pygmy and Negro Hosts* (London: Hutchinson & Co, 1936).
Schenke, Hans-Martin., "Der Widerstreit gnostischer und kirchlicher Christologie im Spiegel des Kolosserbriefes in *Zeitschrift für Theologie und Kirche* (1964),

pp.391-403.
Schlier, Heinrich, *Christus und die Kirche im Epheserbrief* BHT (Tübingen: Mohr, 1930).
──── *Principalities and Powers in the New Testament* (Freiburg: Herder; London: Burns & Oates, 1961).
Schmidt, K. l., "Das Gegenüber von Kirche und Staate in der Gemeinde des Neuen Testaments in *Theologische Blätter* 16, 1937 pp. 1-16.
Schnackenburg, R., *Ephesians: A Commentary* (Edinburgh: T & T Clark, 1991).
Schniewind, J., "Die Archonten dieses Äons: 1 Kor. 2: 6-8" in *Nachgelassene Reden und Aufsätze* (Berlin: A. Töpelmann, 1951), pp. 104-109.
Schoffeleers, Matthew, "The Interaction of the M'Bona Cult and Christianity" in Ranger T. O and John Weller *Themes in the Christian History of Central Africa* (London/Naairobi/Ibadan/Lusaka: Heinemann Educational Books, 1975).
Scholem, Gershom G., *Jewish Gnosticism, Merkabah Mysticism and Talmudic Tradition* (Jewish Theological Seminary, 1960).
──── *Major Trends in Jewish Mysticism* (Schocken Books, 1961)
Schreiter, R. J., *Constructing Local Theologies* (Maryknoll, New York: Orbis Books, 1985).
Schweitzer, Wolfgang, *Die Herrschaft Christi und der Staat im Neuen Testament* (Zürich: Gotthelf–Verlag, 1948).
Schweizer, E., *The Letter to The Colossians* (Minneapolis: Augsburg, 1982).
──── "Slaves of the Elements and Worshipers of Angels" in *Journal of Biblical Literature* 107 (1988), pp. 455-468.
Scott, James C., *Domination and the Arts of Resistance: Hidden Transcript* (New Haven/London: Yale University Press, 1990).
Scroggs, R., "The Earliest Christian Communities as Sectarian Movements" in Morton Smith FS (ed.), Jacob Neusner; Part Two, *Early Christianity* (Leiden: Brill, 1975), pp. 1-23).
Scurlock, J. A., "Magic (ANE)" in David N. Freedman (ed.), *The Anchor Bible Dictionary* Vol. 5 (New York: Doubleday, 1992), pp. 464-468.
Segal, Alan F., *Two Powers in Heaven: Early Rabbinic Reports about Christianity and Gnosticism* SJLA 25. (Leiden: Brill, 1977).
──── "Hellenistic Magic: Some Questions and Definitions" in Brown Judaic Studies 127 *The Other Judaism of Late Antiquity* (Atlanta: Scholar's Press, 1987), pp. 79-108).
Segal, J. B., "Popular Religion in Ancient Israel" in *Journal of Jewish Studies* 27 (1976), pp. 1-22.
Sergio Torres (eds.), *African Theology en Route* (New York: Orbis Books, 1979).
Shack, W. A., "Hunger, Anxiety and Ritual: Deprivation and Spirit Possession among the Gurage of Ethiopia" in *Man* 6 (1971), pp. 30-43.
Shafer, Bryon E. (ed.), *Religion in Ancient Egypt: Gods, Myths, and Persona Practice* (London: Routledge, 1991).
Sharp, Lesley A., *The Possessed and the Dispossessed: Spirits, Identity and Power in a Madagascar Migrant Town* (Berkeley: University of California Press, 1993).
──── "The Power of Possession in Northwest Madagascar" in Heike Behrend and Ute Luig (eds.), *Spirit Possession: Modernity and Power in Africa* (Oxford: James Currey Ltd/Madison: University of Wisconsin Press, 1999), pp. 3-19.
Shorter, Aylward and Edwin Onyancha, *Secularism in Africa: A Case Study: Nairobi City* (Nairobi: Pauline Publications-Africa, 1997).
Shorter, Aylward, "The Migawo: Peripheral Spirit Possession and Christian Prejudice" in *Anthropos* 65 (1970), pp. 110-126.

───── *African Culture and the Christian Church: An Introduction to Social and Pastoral Anthropology* (Maryknoll, New York: Orbis Books, 1973).
───── *Prayers in the Religious Traditions of Africa* (Nairobi: Oxford University Press, 1975).
───── "Problems and Possibilities for the Church's Dialogue with African Traditional Religion" in *Bulletin of the Pontifical Council for Interreligious Dialogue* 28-29 (1975), pp. 111-121.
───── (ed.), *Dialogue with the African Traditional Religion* (Kampala: Gaba Publications, 1975).
───── *African Christian Theology: Adaptation or Incarnation?* (Maryknoll, New York: Orbis Books, 1977).
───── African Traditional Religion: Its Relevance in the Contemporary World" in *Cross Currents* (1978/79), pp. 421-431.
───── *Towards a Theology of Inculturation* (London: Geoffrey Chapman, 1988).
Sibeko, M., and B. Haddad, "Reading the Bible "with" Women in the Poor and the Marginalized Communities in South Africa" in *Semeia* 78 (1997), pp. 83-92.
Sider, R. J., "Christ and Powers" in *International Review of Mission* 69 (1980), pp. 8-20.
Simon, M., *Verus Israel: A Study of the Relations between Christians and Jews in the Roman Empire AD 135–423* The Littmann Library of Jewish Civilization (Oxford: Oxford University Press, 1986).
Singleton, M., "Spirits and 'Spiritual Direction': The Pastoral Counselling of the Possessed" in Edward W. Fashole-Luke, R. Gray, A. Hastings and G. Tasie (eds.), Christianity *in Independent Africa* (London: Rex Callings, 1978), pp. 471-478.
Smart, Ninian, *The Phenomenon of Religion* (New York: The Seabury Press, 1973).
Smit, Joop F. M., *About the Idol Offerings: Rhetoric, Social Context and Theology of Paul in 1st Corinthians* 8: 1–11:1 (Bondgenotenlaan, Leuven/Sterling, Virginia: Peeters, 2000).
Smith, Edwin W., *The Christian Mission in Africa* (London: The International Missionary Council, 1926).
───── (ed.), African *Ideas of God* (London: Edinburgh House, 1950).
Smith, Jonathan, "Some Contours of Early Judaism" in W. S. Green (ed.), *Approaches to Ancient Judaism* II (Chico: Scholars Press, 1980), pp. 1-25).
Smith, N., *The Presbyterian Church of Ghana, 1835-1960* (Accra, Ghana University Press, 1966).
Smith, R. W., *Lectures on the Religion of the Semites* (London: Adam Charles & Black, 1889).
Snodgrass, K., *Ephesians: The NIV Application Commentary* (Grand Rapids: Zondervan, 1996).
Soskice, Janet Martin, *Metaphor and Religious Language* (Oxford: Clarendon Press, 1985).
Stambaugh, J. E and D. L. Bauch, *The New Testament in its Social Environment* (Philadelphia: The Westminster Press, 1986).
Stanton, G. N., "Presuppositions in New Testament Criticism" in I. H. Marshall (ed.), *New Testament Interpretation: Essays in Principles and Method* (Exeter: The Paternoster Press, 1977), pp. 60-71.
Stählin G., "μυθος" in G. Kittel and G. Friedrich (eds.), *Theological Dictionary of the New Testament* Vol. IV, (Grand Rapids, Michigan: Eerdmans, 1992), pp. 762-95.
Stendahl, Krister, *Paul among Jews and Gentiles, and Other Essays* (Philadelphia: Fortress Press, 1976).

Stewart, James, "On a Neglected Emphasis in New Testament Theology" in *Scottish Journal of Theology* 4 (1951), pp.292-301.
Stoesz, Samuel J., *Sanctification: An Alliance Distinctive* (Camp Hill: Christian Publications, 1992).
Stoller, P. and C. Olkes, *Sorcery's Shadow* (Chicago: University of Chicago Press, 1987).
Stoller, P., *The Taste of Ethnographic Things* (Philadelphia: University of Pennsylvania Press, 1989).
Stott, John R. W., *The Message of Ephesians* (Leicester: Inter-varsity Press, 1979).
Strauss, D. F., *The Life of Jesus Critically Examined* (London: SCM Press, 1973).
Strelan, Paul, *Paul, Artemis and the Jews in Ephesus* (Berlin: Walter de Gruyter, 1996).
Stringfellow, W., *Free in Obedience: The Radical Christian Life* (New York: Seabury Press, 1964).
Stuckenbruck, L. T., "The "Angels" and "Giants" of Genesis 6: 1-4 in Second and Third Century BCE Jewish Interpretation: Reflection on the Posture of Early Apocalyptic Traditions" in *Dead Sea Scrolls: A Journal of Current Research on the Scroll and Related Literature* Vol. 7 No. 3 – Angels and Demons (Leiden: Brill, 2000), pp. 354-377.
―――――― "Angels of the Nations" in Craig A. Evans and Stanley E. Porter, *Dictionary of New Testament Background* (Leicester: InterVasity Press, 2000), pp. 29-31.
Sugirtharajah, R. S., *The Bible and the Third World: Precolonial, Colonial and Postcolonial Encounters* (Cambridge: Cambridge University Press, 2001).
Sundkler, Bengt G. M., *Bantu Prophets in South Africa* (London: Oxford University Press, 1961).
―――――― *The World of Missions* (London: Lutterworth Press, 1965).
Sutherland, Stewart R., "Language and Interpretation" in *Crime and Punishment*, *Philosophy and Literature* (1978), pp. 223-236.
Swartz, M. D., *Scholastic Magic: Ritual and Revelation in Early Jewish Mysticism* (Princeton, New Jersey: Princeton University Press, 1996).
Synge, F. C., *Philippians and Colossians* TBC (London: SCM Press, 1951)
Taussig, Michael T., "The Genesis of Capitalism Amongst a South American Pleasantly: Devil's Labor and the Baptism of Money" in *Comparative Studies in Society and History* 19 (1977), pp. 130-155.
Taylor, J. V., *Primal Vision: Christian Presence amid African Religion* (London: SCM Press, 1963).
―――――― (ed.), *Primal Worldviews: Christian Involvement with Traditional Thought Forms* (Ibadan: Daystar Press, 1976).
Tempels, Placide, *Bantu Philosophy* (Paris: Présence Africaine, 1959).
Thiselton, Anthony C. "The New Hermeneutic" in I. H. Marshall (ed.), *New Testament Interpretation: Essays in Principles and Method* (Exeter: The Paternoster Press, 1977), pp. 308-333.
―――――― *The Two Horizons* (Exeter: Paternoster Press, 1980).
―――――― *New Horizons in Hermeneutics: Theory and Practice of Transforming Biblical Reading* (Grand Rapids, Michigan: Zondervan Publishing House, 1992).
Thomas, H. B., "The Doctrine of God in Uganda" in E. W. Smith (ed.), *African Ideas of God* (London: Edinburgh House Press, 1950), pp. 201-207.
Thorndike, L., *A History of Magic and Experimental Science* 8 vols. (New York: Macmillan, 1923-58).
Tidball, Derek, *An Introduction to the Sociology of the New Testament* (Exeter: Paternoster Press, 1983).

Tierney, M., "Ephesus, Pagan and Christian" in *Irish Quarterly Review* 18 (1929), pp. 449-463.
Tippet, A. R., *People of Southwest Ethiopia* (Pasadena: William Carey, 1970).
Tracy, David, *Plurality and Ambiguity: Hermeneutics, Religion, Hope* (San Francisco: Harper & Row, 1987).
Trebilco, Paul, *Jewish Communities in Asia Minor* SNTSMS 69 (Cambridge: Cambridge University Press, 1991).
Turbayne, Collin Murray, *The Myth of Metaphor* (New Haven/London: Yale University Press, 1962).
Turner, Edith, *The Drums of Affliction: A Study of Religious Processes among the Ndembu of Zambia* (Oxford: Clarendon Press, 1968).
———— (ed.), *On the Edge of the Bush: Anthropology as Experience* (Tucson: University of Arizona Press, 1985).
———— *Experiencing Ritual: A New Interpretation of African Healing* (Philadelphia: University of Pennsylvania Press, 1992).
Turner, H. W., *Profile through Preaching* (London: Edinburgh House Press, 1965).
———— *Living Tribal Religions* (London: ward Lock Educational, 1974).
———— "The Contributions of Studies on Religion in Africa to Western Religious Studies" in M. E. Glasswell and E. W. Fashole-Luke (eds.), *New Testament Christianity for Africa and the World* (London: SPCK, 1974), pp. 168-178.
———— "New Religious Movements in Primal Societies" in *World Faiths* No.95, (1975), pp. 5-10.
———— "Primal Religions and their Study" in V. Hayes, *Australian Essays in World Religion* (Bedford Park: Australian Association for the Study of Religion, (1977), pp. 27-37.
———— *Religious Invasion in Africa: Essays on New Religious Movements* (Boston, MA: G. K. Hall, 1979).
———— "The Way Forward in the Religious Study of African Primal Religions" in *Journal of Religion in Africa* 12.1 (1981), pp. 1-15.
Turner, V. W., *Chihamba, the White Spirit: A Ritual Drama of the Ndembu* (Manchester: Manchester University Press, 1962).
———— *The Forest Symbols* (Ithaca: Cornell University Press, 1967).
———— *The Drums of Affliction: A Study of Religious Processes among the Ndembu of Zambia* (Oxford: Clarendon Press, 1968).
Tutu, D. M., "Whither African Theology?" in Edward W. Fashole-Luke, R. Gray, A. Hastings and G. Tasie (eds.), *Christianity in Independent Africa* (London: Rex Collings, 1978), pp. 364-369.
———— "Black Theology and African Theology: Soul Mates or Antagonist" in Parratt, J. *A Reader in African Christian Theology* (London: SPCK, 1987), pp. 46-57.
Twelftree, Graham, *Christ Triumphant: Exorcism Then and Now* (London: Hodder & Stoughton, 1985).
Tylor, E. B., *Primitive Culture* (London: John Murray, 1871).
Ukpong J. S., "Inculturation and Evangelization: Biblical foundations for Inculturation" in *Vidyajyoti* 58.5 (1984), pp. 298-307.
———— "Towards a Renewed Approach to Inculturation Theology" in *Journal of Inculturation Theology* 1 (1994), pp. 3-15.
———— "Re-reading the Bible with African Eyes: Inculturation and Hermeneutics", in *Journal of Theology for Southern Africa.* No 91 (June 1995), pp. 3-14.
———— "The Parable of the Shrewd Manager (Lk. 16: 1-13): An Essay in Inculturation Biblical Hermeneutics" in *Semeia* 73 (1996), pp. 189-210.

Bibliography

———— "Towards a Holistic Approach to Inculturation Theology" in *Mission Studies: Journal of the International Association for Mission Studies* Vol.XVI-2, 32 (1999), pp.100-124.

———— "Development in Biblical Interpretation in Africa: Historical and Hermeneutical Directions" in Gerald O. West and Musa W. Dube (eds.), *The Bible in Africa: Transactions, Trajectories and Trends* (Leiden: Brill, 2000), pp. 11-28.

———— "Bible Reading with a Community of Ordinary Readers" in M. Getui, T. Maluleke and J. Ukpong (eds.), Interpreting *the New Testament in Africa* (Nairobi: Acton Publishers, 2001), pp.188-212.

Ullmann, Stephen, "Smile and Metaphor" in Davies, Anna Morpurgo and Wolfgang Meid (eds.), Studies *in Greek, Italic, and Indo-European Linguistics Offered to Leonard R. Palmer* (Innsbruck: Innsbruck Beiträge zur Sprachwissenchaft, 1976), pp. 425-430.

Umeagudosa, Margaret A., "The Healing of the Gerasene Demoniac from a Specifically African Perspective" in *African Christian Studies* 12/4 (1986), pp. 30-37.

Umoren, U., "Social Cultural Anthropology and the Method of Inculturation" in *Journal of Inculturation Theology* Vol. 2 No 1 (1995), pp. 4-15.

Unger, Merill F., *Biblical Demonology. A Study of the Spiritual Forces Behind the Present Unrest* (Wheaton: Van Kampen press, 1952).

van Binsbergen, W., "Becoming a Sangoma: Religious Anthropological in Francistown, Botswana" in *Journal of Religion in Africa* (1991), pp. 309-343.

Van der Horst, P. W., "Thanatos" in van der Toorn, K. B. Becking and P. W. Van der Horst (eds.), *Dictionary of Deities and Demons in the Bible* (Leiden: Brill, (1995), Col. 1609-1613.

Van Rheenen, Gailyn, "Animism, Secularism and Theism" in *International Journal of Frontier Mission*, Vol 10 4 (October 1993), pp. 169-171.

van Unnik, *Tarsus or Jerusalem: The City of Paul's Youth* (London: Epworth, 1962).

VanderKam, J. C., *Enoch and the Growth of an Apocalyptic Tradition* CBQMS 16 (Washington: Catholic Biblical Association of America, 1984).

———— *The Dead Sea Scrolls after Fifty Years: A Comprehensive Assessment* Vol. 2 (Leiden: Brill, 1999).

Veith, G. Edward, *A Guide to Contemporary Culture* (Leicester: Crossway Books, 1994).

Vera, Diane, *The Existence of the Supernatural*, available at http://www.angelfire.com/ny5/dvera/philos/supernatural.html, accessed on 22.06.04, (© 2003)

Vermes, Geza, *Jesus the Jew* (New York: Macmillan, 1973).

Versnel, H. S., *Triumphus: An Inquiry into the Origin, Development and Meaning of the Roman Triumph* (Leiden: Brill, 1970).

von Rad, Gerhard, "Διάβολος" in G. Kittel and G. Friedrich, *Theological Dictionary of the New Testament* Vol. II (Grand Rapids, Michigan: Eerdmans, 1964), pp. 72-75.

———— *Wisdom in Israel* (Abingdon Press, 1972).

wa Gatumu, A. K "Primal Worldview and the Bible: An African Christian Contribution to a Hermeneutical Method from the Perspective of the Primal Worldview, with Particular Reference to the Gĩkũyũ of Kenya" (Unpublished M. Th. Dissertation, University of Natal, Pietermaritzburg, South Africa, 2000).

wa Wanjau, Gakaara, *Warahuri wa Muhoere wa Gikuyu na Mumbi* [*Reviving the Worship of Gikuyu and Mumbi*] (Karatina: Gakaara Press, 1999).

Wafer, James, *The Taste of Blood: Spirit Possession in Brazilian Candomblé*

(Philadelphia: University of Pennsylvania Press, 1991).
Wagner, C. Peter (ed.), *Engaging the Enemy* (Ventura: Regal Books, 1991).
Wagner, G., *The Bantu of North Kavirondo,* Vol. 1 (Oxford: International African Institute – Oxford University Press, 1949).
Wagner, Roy, *The Invention of Culture* (Chicago: Chicago University Press, 1981).
Waliggo J. M., Arij A. Roest Crollius, T. Nkeramihigo and J. Mutiso-Mbinda (eds.), *Inculturation: Its Meaning and Urgency* (Nairobi: St. Paul's Publication-Africa, 1986).
Walker, S. S., *Ceremonial Spirit Possession in Africa and Afro-America* (Leiden: Brill, 1972).
Walls, A. F., "Towards Understanding Africa's Place in Christianity" in J. S. Pobee (ed.), *Religion in a Pluralistic Society* (Leiden: Brill, 1976), pp. 180-189.
───── "Africa and Christian Identity" in *Mission Focus* Vol. IV No 7 (November 1978), pp. 11-13.
───── *The Missionary Movement in Christian History: Studies in the Transmission of Faith* (Maryknoll, New York: Orbis Books, 1996).
───── "In Quest of the Father of Mission Studies" in *International Bulletin of Missionary Research.* Vol. 23 No.3 (July 1999), pp. 98-102, 104-5.
───── "Of Ivory Towers and Ashrams: Some Thoughts on Theological Scholarship in Africa" in *Journal of African Christian Thought* Vol. 3 No.1 (June 2000), pp. 1-5.
───── *The Cross-Cultural Process in Christian History* (Maryknoll, New York: Orbis Books/Edinburgh: T & T Clark, 2002).
Walsh, George, *The Role of Religion in History* (New Brunswick, New Jersey: Transaction Publishers, 1998).
Walsh, Patrick Gerard, "Introduction" in *Cicero The Nature of the Gods: Translated with Introduction and Explanatory Notes by P. G. Walsh* (Oxford: Clarendon Press, 1997).
Wanjohi, G., *The Wisdom and Philosophy of the Gĩkũyũ Proverbs* (Nairobi: St. Paul's Publication-Africa, 1997).
Warner, Timothy, "Power Encounter" (Lecture Notes, Trinity Evangelical Divinity School 11-15 January Deerfield, Illinois). Available at http://www.missiology.org/animism/AnimisticBook/Chapter05.htm, accessed on 16:04:03, © 1988)
Watts, D. W., "Excursus on Lilith" in *Isaiah 34–66* WBC 25 (Waco, Texas: Word, 1987).
Weber, Max, *The Sociology of Religion* (London: Methuen & Co Ltd, 1965).
Webber, Robert, *The Church in the World* (Grand Rapids: Zondervan, 1986).
Wedderburn, A. J. M., "The Theology of Colossians" in A. T. Lincoln, and A. J. M. Wedderburn, *The Theology of the Later Pauline Letters* (Cambridge: Cambridge University Press, 1993), pp. 3-71.
Weiss, Brand, "Plastic Teeth Extraction: The Iconography of Haya Gastro-Sexual Affliction" in *American Ethnologist* 19 (1992), pp. 538-552.
Wendl, Tobias, "Slavery, Spirit Possession & Ritual Consciousness" in Heike Behrend and Ute Luig (eds.), *Spirit Possession: Modernity and Power in Africa* (Oxford: James Currey Ltd/Madison: University of Wisconsin Press, 1999), pp. 111-123.
Wendland, E. R., *The Cultural factor in Bible Translation: A Study of Communicating the Word of God in a Central African Cultural Context* (New York: United Bible Societies, 1987).
───── "UFITI – Foundation of an Indigenous Philosophy of Misfortune: The

Socioreligious Implication of Witchcraft and Sorcery in a Central African Setting" in *Research in the Social Scientific Study of Religion* 4 (1992), pp. 209-243.

―――― and Hachimba, Salimo, "A Central African Perspective on Contextualizing the Ephesian Potentates, principalities and powers" in *Missiology: An International Review* Vol. 28 No 3 (July 2000), pp. 341-363.

Wendland, von Heinz-Dietrich, *Die Briefe an die Korinther: Paulus Apostulus* (Göttingen: Vandenhoeck & Ruprecht, 1946).

West, Gerald O. and Musa W. Dube, (eds.), The *Bible in Africa: Transaction, Trajectories and Trends* (Leiden: Brill, 2000).

West, Gerald O. *Biblical Hermeneutics of Liberation* (Pietermaritzburg, Cluster and Maryknoll, New York: Orbis books, 1991).

―――― *Contextual Bible Study* (Pietermaritzburg: Cluster, 1993).

―――― "Reading the Bible and Doing Theology in South Africa" in R. D. M. Carroll, David J. A. Clines and Philip R. Davies, *The Bible in the Human Society* (Sheffield: Sheffield Academic Press, 1995), pp. 445-458.

―――― "Reading the Bible Differently: Giving Shape to the Dominated" In *Semeia*, 73 (1996) pp. 21-41.

―――― "Discerning the Contours of Domination and Resistance in Liberation Hermeneutics: Do the Poor and the Marginalised Speak?" in *Bulletin for Contextual Theology in Southern Africa & Africa* Vol.5, Nos. 1 and 2 (1998), pp. 28-35.

―――― "Biblical Scholars Inventing Ancient Israel and the 'Ordinary Readers' of the Bible Re-inventing Biblical Studies", in *Old Testament Essays* 11/3 (1998), pp, 629-644.

―――― "On the Eve of an African Biblical Studies: Trajectories and Trends" in *African biblical studies, TD 46:2* (1999), pp.103-109.

―――― "Being Partially Constituted by Work with Others: Biblical Scholars Becoming Different" *In Journal of Theology for Southern Africa* No 104 (July 1999), pp. 44-53.

―――― *The Academy of the Poor* (Sheffield: Sheffield Academic Press, 1999).

Westerlund, D. *Africa and Christianity* (London: Oxford University Press, 1937).

―――― *African Religions in African Scholarship: A Preliminary Study of the Religious and Political Background* (Stockholm: Almqvist and Wicksell International, 1985).

―――― *Pluralism and Change: A Comparative Approach to African Disease Etiologies* (Stockholm: Stockholm University, 1989).

Whisson, M. G., "Some Aspects of Functional Disorders among the Kenya Luo" in A. Kiev (ed.), *Magic, Faith and Healing* (New York: The Free Press, 1964), pp. 283-304.

White, Thomas B., *The Believer's Guide to Spiritual Warfare* (Ann Arbor, Michigan: Servant Publications and Eastbourne, Sussex: Kingsway Publications, 1990).

Whiteley, D. E. H., "Expository Problems in Ephesians 6:12- Evil Powers" in *Expository Times* 68 (1957), pp.100-103.

―――― *The Theology of St. Paul* (Oxford: Basil Blackwell, 1964).

Whitworth, Michael, *Einstein's Wake: Relativity, Metaphor and Modernist Literature* (Oxford: Oxford University Press, 2001).

Whyte, S. R., "Men, Women and Misfortune in Bunyole" in *Man* 16 (1981), pp. 350-366.

―――― "Knowledge and Power in Nyole Divination" in Peek, P. M. (ed.), African *Divination System: Ways of Knowing* (Bloomington, Indiana: Indiana

University Press, 1991), pp. 153-172.
Wild, Robert A., "The Warrior and the Prisoner: Some Reflections on Ephesians 6: 10-20 in *Catholic Biblical Quarterly* (1984), pp. 284-298.
Wilder, Amos N., *Kerygma, Eschatology and Social Ethics* (Philadelphia: Fortress Press, 1966).
Wilkinson, J., *Health and Healing: Studies in New Testament Principles and Practice* (Edinburgh: The Handsel Press, 1980).
Willetts, R., *Cretan Cults and Festivals* (London: Routledge & Kegan Paul, 1962).
Williams, A Luckyn., "The Cult of Angels at Colossae" in *Journal of Theological Studies* 10 (1909), pp. 413-438.
Williams, Peter, "Editorial" *Churchman* 94 3 (1980), pp. 195-198.
Williamson, H. G. M., *1 and 2 Chronicles* (London: Marshall, Morgan & Scott, 1982).
Willis, Roy, *Some Spirits Heal, Others only Dance* (Oxford, New York: Berg, 1999).
Wilson, B. R., *Magic and the Millennium: A Sociological Study of Religious Movements of Protest among Tribal and Third World Peoples* (New York: Harper & Row, 1973).
Wilson, John A., "Egypt: The Nature of the Universe" in Henri Frankfort (et al.), *The Intellectual Adventure of Ancient Man* (Chicago: Chicago University Press, 1946), pp. 31-61.
Wilson, M. H., *Good Company: A Study of Nyakyusa Age-Village* (London: Oxford University Press, 1951).
Wilson, Michael, "Exorcism" in *The Expository Times* LXXXVI (July 1975) pp. 292-295.
Wilson, W. T., "Hellenistic Judaism" in Craig A. Evans and Stanley E. Porter, *Dictionary of New Testament Background* (Downers Grove/Leicester: Intervarsity Press, 2000), pp. 477-482.
Wimber, John, *Power Evangelism: Signs and Wonders Today* (London: Hodder & Stoughton, 1985).
Wink, Walter, *The Bible in Human Transformation: Towards a New Paradigm for Biblical Studies* (Philadelphia: Fortress Press, 1973).
———— *Naming the Powers: The Language of Power in the New Testament* (Philadelphia Fortress Press, 1984).
———— *Unmasking the Powers: The Invisible Forces that Determine Human Existence* (Philadelphia: Fortress Press, 1986).
———— *Engaging the Powers: Discernment and Resistance in a World of Domination* (Minneapolis: Fortress Press, 1992).
———— *The Powers that Be: Theology for a New Millennium* (New York: Doubleday, 1998).
Winter, Bruce, "Theological and Ethical Response to Religious Pluralism – 1 Corinthians 8-10" in *Tyndale Bulletin* 41 2 (November 1990), pp. 209-266.
Winter, E. H., "The Enemy Within: Amba Witchcraft and Sociological Theory" in J. Middleton and E. H. Winter (eds.), *Witchcraft and Sorcery in East Africa* (London: Routledge and Kegan Paul, 1963), pp. 277-299.
Wood, A., Skevington, "Ephesians" in Frank E. Gaebelein (ed.), *The Expositor's Bible Commentary*, Vol. 11 (London: Pickering & Inglis, 1978), pp. 1-92.
Wood, Peter, "Afterword: Boundaries and Horizons" in Hefner, Robert W. (ed.), *Conversion to Christianity: Historical and Anthropological Perspective on a Great Transformation* (Berkeley & Los Angeles, California/Oxford: California University Press, 1993), pp. 305-321.
Wolter, Michael, *Der Brief an die Kolosser. Der Brief an Philemon* ÖTKNT 12 (Gütersloh: Mohn, 1993).

Wortmann, Dierk, "Neue Magische Texte" in *Bonner Jahrbücher* 168, 1968 pp. 56-111.
Wright, N. T., *Colossians and Philemon* (Leicester: Inter-Varsity Press, 1986).
Yamauchi, E. M., "Magic or Miracle? Disease, Demons and Exorcism" in D. Wenham and C. Blomberg (eds.), *Gospel Perspectives: The Miracles of Jesus* Vol. VI (Sheffield: JSOT, 1986), pp. 89-183.
Yates, Roy, "Christ and the Powers of Evil in Colossians" in E. A. Livingstone (ed.), *Studia Biblica 1978: 111: Papers in Paul and other New Testament Authors* JSNTSup 3. (Sheffield: JSOT Press, 1980), pp. 461-8.
—— "Colossians 2: 14: Metaphor of Forgiveness" in *Biblica* 90 (1990), pp. 249-259.
Yoder, J. H., *The Politics of Jesus* (Grand Rapids: Eerdmans, 1972).
Young, J. U., "Out of Africa: African Traditional Religion and Theology" in D. Cohn-Sherbok, *World Religions and Human Liberation* (Maryknoll, New York: Orbis Books, 1992), pp. 93-112.
Zahan, D., *The Religion, Spirituality and Thought of Traditional Africa* (Chicago: The University of Chicago Press, 1979).
Zempelini, Andras, "From Symptom to Sacrifice: The Story of Khady Fall" in Vincent Caprazano and Vivian Garrison (eds.), *Case Study in Spirit Possession* (New York: Wiley & Sons, 1977), pp. 87-140.
Zola, Irving, "Medicine as an Institution of Social Control" in J. Ehrenreich (ed.), *The Cultural Crisis of Modern Medicine* (New York: Monthly Review Press, 1978), pp. 80-100.
Zuesse, Evans M., "On the Nature of Demonic: African Witchery" in *Numen* 18 (1971), pp. 210-239.
—— *Ritual Cosmos: The Sanctification of Life in African Religion* (Athens, Ohio: Ohio University Press, 1979).

Reports

Lausanne Committee for World Evangelisation: *The Willowbank Report: Report of a Consultation on Gospel and Culture*, held at Willowbank, Somerset Bridge Bermuda from 6th to 13th January 1978 (Wheaton: Lausanne Committee for World Evangelisation, 1978).
Secretariatus Pro Non-Christianis: *Meeting the African Religions*(Rome: Libreria Editrice Ancora, 1968).
World Missionary Conference: 1910: *Report of Commission IV: The Missionary Message in Relation to non-Christian Religions* (Edinburgh & London: Oliphant, Anderson & Ferrier, 1910).
British and Foreign Bible Society: *The Word among the Nations: A Popular Illustrated Report of the British and Foreign Bible Society for the Year* 1908–1909 (London: The Bible House, 1909).

Scripture Index

Genesis
4: 21 18
4: 22 18
6: 1-4 95, 98, 178
32: 4 137
32: 7 137
41: 1-8 100

Exodus
20: 3 96
20: 4-5 97, 154
34: 17 154
7–9 100

Leviticus
16: 7-10 97
17: 17 99
19: 4 154
19: 26-28 100
26: 1 154

Numbers
6: 24-26 97
22: 22 142
23: 9 155

Deuteronomy
4: 19 103
5: 7 95
6: 4 154
10: 17 158
17:3-5 103
17: 20 135
18: 10-12 100
18:10-14 100
32: 8-9 96
32: 15-6 155
32: 15-22 157
32: 16-17 99
33: 2-3 95

Joshua
7: 22 137

Judges
5:20 140
9: 22-25 97
20:13 144

1 Samuel
3: 7 153
16: 14-23 97
Sam 28 100
1 Sam 29: 4 142

2 Samuel
24: 1 142
29: 17-24 142

1 Kings
5: 16 142
5: 20 142
11: 14 142
11: 23 142
22 1-28 97

2 Kings
17: 7-23 100
17: 16 135
21: 9-15 100
21:5 103

1 Chronicles
21: 1 142

2 Chronicles
13: 9 153
33: 1-13 100

Job
1: 7-12 143
2: 1-6 143
1–3 95, 142

5: 1 95
15: 5 95

Psalms
9: 10 153
29: 1 153
31: 6 155
45: 10 133
68: 17 95
79: 6 153
82: 1-7 96
89: 5-8 95, 133
91: 7 99
96: 5 99, 157
103: 21 133
106: 37 99
106: 37-9 157
109: 6 142
110 130, 131, 166
110: 2 166
115: 3-8 156
136: 2-3 158

Isaiah
2: 6 100
2–3 100
13: 21 97
11: 5 215
24: 21 161
34: 4 133, 135
34:14 97
34–66 97
37: 19 153, 157
40: 18 155
40: 25 155
40: 26 215
42: 17 155
43: 10 153
44: 9-20 156
44: 19 155
45: 23 161
47:12-15 103

52:1-7 215
57: 19 215

Jeremiah
2: 11 153, 157
5: 7 153, 157
5: 17 155
10:2 103
10: 14-5 155
10: 25 153
14: 4 100
14: 27 100
16: 18 155
16: 20 153, 157
44:15-19 103
44:20-23 103
51: 17-8 155

Ezekiel
5: 11 155
13:17-18 100
13: 23 100

Daniel
1: 20 100
2: 1-49 100
7: 9 135
7: 27 129
8: 10 133
10: 10-13 96
10: 13 131
10: 20-21 131
10: 21 131
11: 40–12: 3 162
12: 1 131

Hosea
8: 2 153

Amos
4: 25-27 140

Micah
6: 5 153

Zechariah
3 142
14: 5 95

Malachi
2: 7 137
3: 1 137
3:1-5.

Matthew
7: 11 18
7: 22 141
8: 31 141, 157
9: 33-34 141
9: 34 129, 132
10: 8 141
12: 24, 132, 141,143
18: 24 194
18: 28 194

Mark
1: 23-25 161
3: 22 132, 143
5: 12 141, 157

Luke
3: 1 135
4: 33-25 161
8: 29 141, 157
11: 15 132
15 143
24: 20 132

John
12: 31 129, 132
14: 30-31 132
16: 11 132
17: 25 132

Acts
3: 13-18 132
7: 42-3 140
13: 4-12 113
13: 6-12 102
13: 8 13
16: 16-24 106
16: 19 107
16:20-1 107
17: 18 141
17: 22 105
17: 23 105
17: 24-29 156
19: 11-17
19: 19 93, 102
19: 23-41 106
19: 27 106
25: 19 105

Romans
1: 16 134
1: 20 134
1: 18-32 146, 155
8: 5-8 187
8: 28 146, 148
8: 31-39 134
8: 38 134, 138
8: 38-9 134, 163, 188, 220
8: 39 160
9: 17 134
12: 2 210
13: 1 130, 210
13:1-7 129-130
16: 20 145

1 Corinthians
1: 18 134
1: 18-30 132
1: 20 132
1: 21 132
1: 24 134
1–2 133
2: 5 132
2: 6-8 129, 131-133, 163-4, 187, 207, 238
2: 13 132
2: 28-9 134
4: 9 137
4: 19 134
5: 1-5 147
5: 5 145
6: 1-8 210
6: 3 138
6: 14-18 210
6: 9-10 187
7: 5 145
8: 4–6 152-156, 158
8: 5 135, 157

Scripture Index

8: 6 144
10: 10 141
10: 14–22 152, 157-
10: 16-7 158
10: 19-21 99
10: 20 158
10: 20-21 141, 227
14: 11 134
15: 24 129, 130, 134, 163, 164, 166, 167, 189
15: 24-5 188
15: 24-28 166, 187
15: 26 187

2 Corinthians
1: 8 134
2: 5-11 147
2: 11 147, 217, 227
2: 14 146
4: 4 132, 143, 144, 167, 183
6: 15 144
8: 3 134
11: 3 145
11: 13-15 206
11: 14 148
11: 14-5 145
12: 7 138, 145, 146, 206, 220

Galatians
1: 4 144
3: 5 134
3: 10–14 162
3: 23-25 141
3: 28 226
4: 3 139, 141, 167, 189
4: 3-9 214
4: 3-11 203
4: 8 141, 152-3, 156
4: 8-9 158
4: 8-10 141
4: 9 139, 189
5: 17 187
5: 16-25 227
5: 19-21 187
6: 8 187

Ephesus
1: 11 146
1: 19-22 218
1: 20 130, 145
1: 20-1 129, 130
1: 20–23 130
1: 21 134, 135, 161, 166
1: 21–22 165, 226
2: 2 129, 143, 144, 166, 219
2: 1-22 130, 214
2: 4–7 131
2: 4–22 144
2: 5-6 215
2: 11–22 162, 215, 219
2: 12-22 219
2: 17 162
3: 4-6 226
3: 10 129, 130, 161, 166, 213, 218
3: 20 134
4: 8 218
4: 8-16 226
4: 24 216
4: 25-32 214
4: 27 145, 147, 232
5:1 216
5: 11-16 214
5: 21-33 219
5: 21-6:1-9 219
6: 10-18 166
6: 10-20 143, 144, 148, 161, 163, 215, 216, 217
6: 11-2 129, 130
6: 11 137, 143, 147
6: 12 143, 163, 166, 221
6: 16 143

Philippians
2: 6-11 160
2: 9 161, 166
2: 10 166
3: 10 134

Colossians
1: 12-14 166
1: 13 135, 144, 165, 219
1: 13-23 35
1: 15-20 160
1: 16 129, 131, 135, 136, 159, 160, 218
1: 17 160
1: 20 159, 225
1: 21-22 162, 214
2: 6-7 225
2: 8 139, 141, 160, 167
2: 8-10 140, 213, 214
2: 8-20 188
2: 8–3: 5 35
2:9-10 222
2: 10 129, 131, 213
2: 13-14 165, 213, 214
2: 13-13 240
2: 14 165
2: 15 129, 131, 145, 164, 165, 166, 195, 202, 203, 204, 213, 218, 220
2: 18 35, 136, 138
2: 20 139, 140, 141, 160, 167, 213
2: 23 227
3: 1 166, 213
3: 3 213
3: 5-9 214
3: 5-10 187
3: 9 164
3: 9-10 227
3: 10-11 219
3: 11 226
3: 18–4: 1 219

1 Thessalonians
2: 18 146,
3: 5 143, 145

2 Thessalonians
2: 1 146
2: 4 146
2: 9 146

2: 10-12 146
3: 3 143

1 Timothy
1: 4 177
1: 17 144
3: 6 147
4: 1 141, 157
4: 7 177
5: 15 145

2 Timothy
1: 8 134
2: 25-26 146
2: 26 147
3: 5 134, 236

4: 3-4 157
4: 4 177

Titus
1: 14 177

Hebrews
5: 12 140

1 Peter
3: 22 129

2 Peter
1: 16 177
3: 10 141
3: 12 141

1 John
2: 15 132
5: 19 132

Jude
6 96
8 135

Revelation
9: 20 141
16: 14 141, 157
18: 2 141, 157

Author Index

Abijole, Bayo 16, 169
Abogunrin, Samuel O. 35
Adamo, David Tuesday 36, 39, 40
Aeschylus 117
Akinnaso, F. Niyi 68
Al-Safi, Ahmed 74, 78
Alexander, Philip S. 98, 100, 101
Allen, R 109
Anderson, Gerald H. 33
Appiah, Kwame 45, 72, 85, 86, 90, 192
Ardener, Edwin 81
Arnold, Clinton E. 16, 24, 51, 52, 54, 57, 59, 93, 95, 98, 100, 101, 102, 106, 114, 115, 125, 126, 136, 137, 138, 140, 143, 160, 161, 162, 164, 165, 176, 178, 187, 181, 183, 184, 188, 189, 192, 193, 210, 211, 212, 215, 216, 217, 218, 219, 236, 237, 240
Arndt, W. F. 128, 132, 133, 135, 137, 143, 145, 160, 171, 216
Aristotle, 26, 60, 118, 139
Audollent, Augustus 136
Aune, David E. 13, 94, 110, 117
Avotri, Solomon K. 45
Ayer, A. J.199, 200

Bandstra, A. J 139, 144
Barclay, John M. G. 94, 125, 126, 127, 135, 139, 155, 159, 163
Barrett, C. K. 144, 164
Barrett, D. B. 175
Barrington-Ward, S. 83
Barth, Markus 144, 166
Bauch, D. L. 155
Bauer, Walter 128, 129, 130, 132, 133, 135, 137, 143, 145, 160, 171, 216
Bautista, L 170
Beattie J. H. M. 67, 73, 83
Bediako, G. 26, 27, 45, 174, 176, 224, 227, 228, 229, 230
Bediako, Kwame 33, 47, 88, 91, 92
Beker, J. C. 186, 187

Behrend, Heike 47, 69, 72, 74, 77, 79, 80, 83
Benson, Stanley 36
Berger, P. L 43, 212, 226, 234
Berggren, Douglas 195, 196, 201
Berkhof, Hendrik 149, 169, 170
Bernstein, M. 100
Best, Ernest 146
Betz, Hans Dieter 93, 136, 138, 146, 153, 156
Beidelmann, T. O. 30, 31, 55, 82
Blanke, H. 166
Blau, L. 101
Boddy, Janice 74, 78
Boff, C. 213
Boff, L. 213
Bolle, Kees W. 176
Bolt, P. G. 109
Booth, N. S. 9, 67
Borg, Marcus 85
Bornkamm, Günther 136
Bourguignon, E. 71, 73, 76, 77
Boyer, P.. 6
Brashear, William M. 101
Brøgger, J. 71
Bromiley, G. W. 13
Brown, Karen McCarthy 78
Bruce, F. F. 146, 216
Bube, Richard H. 5
Bujo, B. 224, 225
Bultmann, Rudolf 169, 170, 176, 179-181, 182, 192, 194, 196
Burkert, Walter 17
Burnett, David 19, 28, 36, 46, 50, 51, 52, 56, 57, 58, 59, 88, 112
Burton, Ernest de Witt 153
Buxton, Thomas 29, 30, 32

Cagnolo, C 29
Caird, G. B. 1, 8, 142, 170-173, 175, 176, 184, 191, 195- 202, 204-207
Canet, L. 136, 137

Author Index

Caplan, Lionel 35
Charlesworth, J. H 103
Carr, Wesley 131, 164, 165, 215
Carroll, R. D. M. 191
Carson, D. A. 36
Chilton, B. D. 93, 94
Cicero 50, 94, 105- 108, 110-123, 127, 130, 139, 149, 153
Clement of Alexandria, 212
Clines, David J. A. 191
Cobble, James F. Jr. 50, 56, 57, 235, 236
Codrington, R. H. 46, 61
Colleyn, Jean-Paul 74, 76, 79
Collins, John 94
Collins, Raymond F. 156
Colson, E. 83
Congdon, G. Dal, 40
Conn, Harvie M. 22
Conybeare, F. C. 136
Cook, Robert 221
Cox, J. L. 175, 176
Cranfield, C. E. B. 130
Crapanzano, Vincent 73, 78
Crollius, Arij A. 88
Croy, N. C. 94, 117
Cullmann, Oscar 129, 130, 166
Cumont, F. 111, 113, 115, 124, 125, 126, 136, 137, 140
Curtis, Edward M. 154, 155

Daniel, Guy 51, 114
Danker, F. W. 163
Davidson, Maxwell J. 103
Davies, Douglas James 21, 26
Davies, Anna Morpurgo 197
Davies, Philip R. 191
de Sousa, Alexandra O. 74, 79
Deissmann, Adolf 165
Delling, Gerhard 139
DeMaris, Richard E. 139, 141
Dibelius, Martin 136, 161, 168, 169
Dickinson, G. Lowes 106
Dodds, E. R. 64
Donaldson, J. 123
DomNwachukwu, Chinaka S. 41
Douglas, Mary 12, 14, 70, 76, 77, 78, 79
Dow, Graham 72, 90
Dowden, Ken 150

Dube, W. Musa 20, 35, 36, 45, 211
Duncan, George 158
Dunn, J. D. G. 3, 85, 126, 130, 139-141, 149, 153, 154, 160, 169, 171- 174, 176- 181, 183, 186, 189, 190, 192, 193, 194, 239

Ebeling, G. 194
Echard, Nicole 74, 76, 77, 81, 83, 84
Eliade, Mircea 1112, 46, 73, 160, 172, 174, 176, 181, 182
Empiricus, Sextus 116
Evans, Craig A. 93, 94, 97
Evans-Pritchard, E. E. 64, 71,
Everling, Otto 168
Ewing, Ward 236
Euripides 117

Fashole-Luke, Edward 9, 16, 36, 37, 41, 71, 83
Farvet-Saada, J. 72
Fee, Gordon D. 24, 156, 159, 180, 193, 217
Ferdinando, Keith 42, 45, 53, 66, 71, 73, 74, 85, 89, 141, 143, 144, 147, 166, 176, 192, 211, 220, 222, 225, 226, 238, 240
Fitzmyer, Joseph 130
Flint, Peter W. 98
Forbes, Chris 149-152, 159, 165, 166, 188
Forde, D. 62
Foulkes, Francis 217
Francis, F. O. 136
Frazer, J. G. 12
Freedman, David N. 93, 100, 139, 140, 154
Friedrich, G. 139, 142, 171
Frye, Northrop 197

Garcia, H. B. 170
Gager, J. G. 12, 102
Gairdner, W. H. T. 29
Ganusah, Rebecca Yawa 35
Gathigira, S. K. 224
Geertz, Clifford 81
Gingrich, F. W. 128, 132, 133, 135, 137, 143, 145, 160, 163, 171, 216
Glasswell, M. E. 16

Author Index

Goodenough, Erwin R. 126
Goodman, F. D 73, 74
Gray, W. R. 9, 36, 41, 71, 83
Grayston, Kenneth 127
Green, T. H. 27
Green, W. S. 94
Grose T. H. 27
Grundmann, Walter 215
Guinness, Os 50- 52, 58, 212
Gunton, Colin E. 2, 86, 195, 197, 198, 201, 204, 206, 207, 235
Guthrie, Donald 24
Gutman, J. 155

Hachimba, Salimo 19, 192
Haddad, B. 40
Hagan, George P. 81, 82
Hankinson, R. J. 108
Harnack, Adolf von 168
Harrington, Daniel J.156
Hastings, A. 9, 36, 41, 71, 83
Haule, C. 83
Hawthorne, Gerald F. 140, 157, 160
Hay, David M. 131
Haynes, John 201
Healey, J. 62, 225, 226
Hefele, C. J. 211
Henle, Paul 199
Hesiod 110, 124
Hesselgrave, D. 17, 18
Hiebert, Paul G. 26, 28, 33, 35, 44, 56, 193, 223
Holm, N. G. 74
Homer, 116, 118, 124, 126, 150
Horrell, David, G. 82
Horton, Robin, 11
Howell, A. M. 34, 35, 40, 69
Hughes, P. E. 146
Hughes, Pnnetorne 51
Hume, David 27
Hurreiz, Sayyid 74, 78
Hurtado, Larry W. 157

Idowu, Bolaji E. 46, 62
Igenoza, Andrew Olu 211
Ikenga-Metuh, E. 9, 69
Imasogie, Osadolor 28, 39, 49, 192, 220, 221, 222

Ignatius 133, 229, 230
Isaac, Erich 90

Jacobs, D. 240
James, Wendy 35, 68, 82
Janzen, John 74
Jasper, K. 174
Johnson, M. 201
Johnson, Douglas H. 82
Jonsson, Thomas 36
Josephus 94, 98, 101, 102, 113, 124, 125, 126, 135, 137, 140, 155, 156
Jung, C. G. 173, 175, 181, 184, 185, 221, 237
Juvenal 102, 126

Kallas, J. 142
Kampen, J. 100
Kapferer, Bruce 80
Karanja, John K. 38, 221
Kee, H. C. 22, 89, 113
Kelsey, Morton 142
Kendall, Laurel 78
Kenyatta, Jomo 29, 221, 237
Kenyon, Susan M. 74, 78, 79
Kibicho, Samuel G. 36
King, Noel Q. 62
Kinoti, H. 40
Kirby, John 227-229
Kirk, G. S. 171, 172, 173, 174
Kittredge, C. B. 217
Kitagawa, J. M. 11
Kittel, G. 139, 142, 171
Klass, M. 3, 7
Klauck, Hans-Josef 13, 85, 86, 91, 94, 100, 102, 105, 106, 107, 108, 110, 114, 115, 116, 120
Klem, David 201
Kluger, R. S. 142
Kraabel, A. T. 125
Kraft, Marguerite G. 44, 52, 53, 62, 112
Kramer, Fritz W. 84
Küng, Hans 51

La Fontaine, J. S. 81
Laertius, Diogenes 120, 138, 140, 150, 152
Lakoff, G. 201

Lambek, Michael 80
Lan, David 84
Lane, Anthony N. S. 109, 160, 184, 192, 221
Lane, Eugene N. 125
Lange, A. 100, 102
Larson, Gerald J. 56
Leakey, L. S. B. 64
Lee, J. Y. 149
Leivestad, Ragnar 149
Levi-Strauss, C. 173
Lewis, C. S. 58, 210
Lewis, I. M. 14, 69, 71, 74, 75, 77, 78, 79, 232, 233
Lienhardt, Godfrey 69
Lightfoot, J. B. 158, 211
Lincoln, Andrew T. 143, 144, 191, 216, 217
Ling, Samuel 26
Littleton, C. Scott 56
Livy 117, 123
Lockwood, Gregory J. 158
Lohmann, Roger Ivar 6
Lohse, Eduard 165
Long, Bruce J. 160
Long, E 27
Longenecker, Richard N. 140
Loram, C. T. 31
Lucian 108, 112, 119, 120, 123, 124
Luck, George 12, 64, 113, 114, 120
Luckmann, T. 43, 212, 234
Ludwig, Arnold M. 73
Luig, Ute 47, 69, 72, 74, 77, 79, 80, 83

MacDonald, Margaret Y. 214, 215, 219, 226, 227
MacGregor, G. H. C. 180
Mackay, Alexander M. 33
Magesa, Laurenti 9, 37, 41, 45, 46, 49, 64, 68, 82, 83, 84, 87, 225, 226, 231
Mair, Lucy Philip 72
Malinowski, Bronsilav 172
Manilius 114
Matera, Frank J. 156
Marshall, I. H. 146, 169, 181, 227, 230, 240
Martin, R. P. 24, 140, 146, 147, 157, 160, 206, 213
Martínez, Florentino García 100

Martyr, Justin 109, 123
Mbiti, J. S. 9, 14, 15, 16, 33, 35, 40, 45, 46, 47, 62, 66, 67, 73, 87, 174
McCarthy, Brown K. 78
Meeks, W. A. 94, 136, 214, 217
Meid, Wolfgang 197
Messing, S. D. 74, 78
Middleton, J. 12, 67, 73, 74, 83
Miller, Elmer S. 36
Milton, C. L. 143
Moffatt, James 156, 157. 158
Mofokeng, T. 34
Moltmann, J. 184
Mooij, J. J. A. 196, 197, 199, 201
Moreau, Scott A.
Morris, H. 31
Morrison, Clinton D. 130, 211
Moser, Karin S. 202
Mott, Stephen C. 236
Moule, C. F. D. 139
Mouw, Richard 170
Mott, Stephen C. 236
Mudge, Lewis S.199, 207
Mulago, gwa Chikala M. 54
Mutiso-Mbinda, J. 88

Nadel, S. F. 73
Ndung'u, Nahason 35
Neil, William 51, 127
Neufeld, T. Y. 216, 217
Newbigin, Lesslie 36
Ngcokovane, C. 237
Nicholas, Jacqueline 80
Nicholls, B. 181
Niebuhr, H. R. 52
Nilsson, Martin P. 94, 109, 110, 111, 112
Nkeramihigo, Roest, T. 88
Noble, D. S. 83
Noble, Thomas A. 160, 218
Nock, A. D. 126
Nthamburi, Zablon 40
Nürnberger, K. 42
Nyamiti, Charles 46

O'Brien, P. T. 36, 57, 131, 144, 145, 149, 161, 165, 168, 169, 176, 178, 179, 180, 187, 192, 193, 212, 213, 215, 216, 217, 222

Author Index

O'Donuhue, John 223
Obeng, Emanuel 40
Obeyesekere, G. 75, 77
Oesterley, W. O. E. 64, 97, 99, 100
Oesterreich, T. K. 84
Okwuosa, V. E. 45
Olkes, C. 71
Oster, Richard 106
Otto, Rudolf 174

Page, S. H. T. 148, 216
Pannenberg, W. 172, 180, 194
Parfitt, Tudor 27
Parratt, John 37
Parrinder, E. G. 10, 45
Pauli, W. 181
Pausanias 106, 107, 156
P'Bitek, Okot 90
Penney, D. L. 100, 101
Peretti, Frank E. 211
Philo 13, 64, 96, 102, 124, 125, 126, 128, 129, 133, 134, 136, 138, 139, 140, 141, 150-152, 154, 155, 191
Philostratus, Flavious 108
Pitt-Rivers, Julian 12
Plato, 26, 108, 109, 113, 138, 140, 151, 171, 184
Pliny the Elder 110, 112, 115, 119, 121, 122
Plotinus 115
Plummer, Alfred 157, 158
Pobee, John 32
Pokorný, Petr 165
Porter, Stanley E. 93, 94, 97
Powers, Jessica 30
Plutarch, 105, 107, 109-110, 112, 117, 119, 121, 122, 123, 126, 138, 150-152,
Prasch, Thomas 30
Pred, Allan 83
Price, E. 33
Price, R. M. 146
Prince, R. 73
Puhvel, Jaan 56

Ranger T. O. 36
Raschke, C. 186
Reese, David George, 93
Reid, D. G. 140, 157, 160, 162, 164, 166, 179
Ricoeur, Paul 42, 172, 174, 175, 176, 178, 181, 196, 197, 198, 199, 200, 201, 202, 207, 235
Ridderbos, Herman N. 146
Ringgren, Helmer 22
Roberts, A. 123
Roberts, A. D. 27
Roberts, C. T. 126
Robertson, Archibald 157, 158
Robinson, J. A. 145, 207
Robinson, J. A. T. 207
Robinson, J. M. 194
Robinson, Theodore H. 64, 97, 99, 100
Rochberg-Halton, F. 140
Rohrbaugh, Richard L. 21
Rouget, G. 74
Rupp, Gordon 170, 186, 193
Russell, Jeffrey Burton 54
Ryle, Gilbert 198

Saler, B. 3
Sanders, J. T. 126
Sanneh, Lamin 17, 175, 223, 224
Sapir, Edward 44
Sappington, T. J. 165
Sargant, W. 73, 81
Schenke, Hans-Martin. 136
Schlier, Heinrich 169, 216, 238
Schnackenburg, R. 143
Schweizer, E. 139
Scott, James C. 42, 72, 77, 78, 83, 216
Scurlock, J. A. 100
Segal, Alan F. 12
Seneca 107, 111, 121-122,
Shack, W. A. 77
Shafer, Bryon E. 93
Sharp, Lesley A. 69, 79, 81, 84
Shorter, Aylward 41, 46
Sibeko, M. 40
Siculus, Diodorus 123
Sider, R. J. 170
Simon, M. 102
Singleton, M. 72
Smart, Ninian 175
Smit, Joop F. M. 157, 158
Smith, Edwin W. 10
Smith, Jonathan 94

Smith, N. 34
Smith, W. R. 86, 172
Snodgrass, K. 216, 217
Soskice, Janet Martin 52, 195, 196, 197, 198, 199, 200, 201, 203, 205, 207
Stählin G. 171, 173
Stewart, James 169
Stewart Z. 125
Stoesz, Samuel J. 26
Stoller, P. 71, 78
Stott, John R. W. 216, 217
Strabo 107, 140
Stransky, Thomas F. 33
Stambaugh, J. E. 155
Stanton, G. N. 181
Strelan, Paul 21
Stuckenbruck, L. T. 97
Suetonius 93, 113, 115, 117
Sugirtharajah, R. S. 38, 55
Sundkler, Bengt G. M. 10, 30, 32, 34
Sutherland, Stewart R. 207
Sybertz, D. 62, 225, 226
Synge, F. C. 24

Tasie, G. 9, 36, 41, 71, 83
Tatian 109
Taylor, Isaac 30
Taylor, J. V. 10, 11, 16
Tempels, Placide 46
Temple, William 52
Tertullian 109, 132
Thiselton, Anthony C. 169, 176, 179, 180, 181, 194
Thorndike, L. 10
Tillich, Paul 52
Titus, Lucretius Carus 120
Trebilco, Paul 125, 126
Turbayne, Collin Murray 195, 196, 197, 201, 202
Turner, Edith 71
Turner, H. W. 1, 16, 87, 88, 175
Turner, Paul 108, 112, 119, 120, 124
Tutu, D. M. 41
Twelftree, Graham H. 84, 85
Tylor, E. B. 27, 172, 173

Ukpong J. S. 20, 38, 45, 87, 88, 225
Ullmann, Stephen 197

Umeagudosa, Margaret A. 239

van Binsbergen, W. 71
Van Rheenen, Gailyn 40
Vanderkam, James C. 98, 102
Vera, Diane 4
Vermes, Geza 98
von Rad, Gerhard 23, 142

wa Gatumu, A. K. 213, 225, 230
Wafer, James 78
Waliggo, J. 40, 88
Walker, S. S. 73, 74, 77
Walls, A. F. 29, 30, 32, 35, 36, 37, 38, 39, 175, 221, 223, 230, 235
Walsh, George 2
Walsh, Patrick Gerard 94, 106
Wan, Sze-Kar 170
Wanjohi, G. 87
Waruta, Douglas 40
Watts, D. W. 97
Watts, M. J. 83
Weber, Max 21, 105
Weiss, Brand 72
Wendl, Tobias 79
Wendland, E. R 19, 192
Weller, John 36
West, Gerald O. 20, 35, 36, 45, 211, 213
White, Thomas B. 236
Whitworth, Michael 197
Wild, Robert A. 216
Wilder, Amos N. 170
Williams, Peter 85
Williamson, H. G. M. 142
Willis, Roy 47, 56, 69, 71, 84
Wilkinson, J. 146
Wilson, M. H. 82
Wilson, W. T. 94
Wink, Walter 1, 2, 49, 50, 53, 57, 128, 129, 133, 136, 137, 139, 140, 142, 144, 148, 149, 161, 170, 176, 181-187, 191, 192, 194, 208, 234, 235, 237, 238
Winter, Bruce 153
Winter, E. H. 83
Wise, M. O. 100, 101
Wright, N. T. 140

Xenophon 106, 117, 123, 138

Author Index

Yates, Roy 131, 165
Yoder, J. H. 170

Zahan, D. 67, 82
Zuesse, Evans M. 81

Paternoster Biblical Monographs
(All titles uniform with this volume)
Dates in bold are of projected publication

Joseph Abraham
Eve: Accused or Acquitted?
A Reconsideration of Feminist Readings of the Creation Narrative Texts in Genesis 1–3
Two contrary views dominate contemporary feminist biblical scholarship. One finds in the Bible an unequivocal equality between the sexes from the very creation of humanity, whilst the other sees the biblical text as irredeemably patriarchal and androcentric. Dr Abraham enters into dialogue with both camps as well as introducing his own method of approach. An invaluable tool for any one who is interested in this contemporary debate.
2002 / 0-85364-971-5 / xxiv + 272pp

Octavian D. Baban
Mimesis and Luke's on the Road Encounters in Luke-Acts
Luke's Theology of the Way and its Literary Representation
The book argues on theological and literary (mimetic) grounds that Luke's on-the-road encounters, especially those belonging to the post-Easter period, are part of his complex theology of the Way. Jesus' teaching and that of the apostles is presented by Luke as a challenging answer to the Hellenistic reader's thirst for adventure, good literature, and existential paradigms.
***2005** / 1-84227-253-5 / approx. 374pp*

Paul Barker
The Triumph of Grace in Deuteronomy
This book is a textual and theological analysis of the interaction between the sin and faithlessness of Israel and the grace of Yahweh in response, looking especially at Deuteronomy chapters 1–3, 8–10 and 29–30. The author argues that the grace of Yahweh is determinative for the ongoing relationship between Yahweh and Israel and that Deuteronomy anticipates and fully expects Israel to be faithless.
2004 / 1-84227-226-8 / xxii + 270pp

Jonathan F. Bayes
The Weakness of the Law
God's Law and the Christian in New Testament Perspective
A study of the four New Testament books which refer to the law as weak (Acts, Romans, Galatians, Hebrews) leads to a defence of the third use in the Reformed debate about the law in the life of the believer.
2000 / 0-85364-957-X / xii + 244pp

Mark Bonnington
The Antioch Episode of Galatians 2:11-14 in Historical and Cultural Context

The Galatians 2 'incident' in Antioch over table-fellowship suggests significant disagreement between the leading apostles. This book analyses the background to the disagreement by locating the incident within the dynamics of social interaction between Jews and Gentiles. It proposes a new way of understanding the relationship between the individuals and issues involved.

2005 / 1-84227-050-8 / approx. 350pp

David Bostock
A Portrayal of Trust
The Theme of Faith in the Hezekiah Narratives

This study provides detailed and sensitive readings of the Hezekiah narratives (2 Kings 18–20 and Isaiah 36–39) from a theological perspective. It concentrates on the theme of faith, using narrative criticism as its methodology. Attention is paid especially to setting, plot, point of view and characterization within the narratives. A largely positive portrayal of Hezekiah emerges that underlines the importance and relevance of scripture.

2005 / 1-84227-314-0 / approx. 300pp

Mark Bredin
Jesus, Revolutionary of Peace
A Non-violent Christology in the Book of Revelation

This book aims to demonstrate that the figure of Jesus in the Book of Revelation can best be understood as an active non-violent revolutionary.

2003 / 1-84227-153-9 / xviii + 262pp

Robinson Butarbutar
Paul and Conflict Resolution
An Exegetical Study of Paul's Apostolic Paradigm in 1 Corinthians 9

The author sees the apostolic paradigm in 1 Corinthians 9 as part of Paul's unified arguments in 1 Corinthians 8–10 in which he seeks to mediate in the dispute over the issue of food offered to idols. The book also sees its relevance for dispute-resolution today, taking the conflict within the author's church as an example.

2006 / 1-84227-315-9 / approx. 280pp

Daniel J-S Chae
Paul as Apostle to the Gentiles
His Apostolic Self-awareness and its Influence on the Soteriological Argument in Romans

Opposing 'the post-Holocaust interpretation of Romans', Daniel Chae competently demonstrates that Paul argues for the equality of Jew and Gentile in Romans. Chae's fresh exegetical interpretation is academically outstanding and spiritually encouraging.

1997 / 0-85364-829-8 / xiv + 378pp

Luke L. Cheung
The Genre, Composition and Hermeneutics of the Epistle of James

The present work examines the employment of the wisdom genre with a certain compositional structure and the interpretation of the law through the Jesus tradition of the double love command by the author of the Epistle of James to serve his purpose in promoting perfection and warning against doubleness among the eschatologically renewed people of God in the Diaspora.

2003 / 1-84227-062-1 / xvi + 372pp

Youngmo Cho
Spirit and Kingdom in the Writings of Luke and Paul

The relationship between Spirit and Kingdom is a relatively unexplored area in Lukan and Pauline studies. This book offers a fresh perspective of two biblical writers on the subject. It explores the difference between Luke's and Paul's understanding of the Spirit by examining the specific question of the relationship of the concept of the Spirit to the concept of the Kingdom of God in each writer.

2005 / 1-84227-316-7 / approx. 270pp

Andrew C. Clark
Parallel Lives
The Relation of Paul to the Apostles in the Lucan Perspective

This study of the Peter-Paul parallels in Acts argues that their purpose was to emphasize the themes of continuity in salvation history and the unity of the Jewish and Gentile missions. New light is shed on Luke's literary techniques, partly through a comparison with Plutarch.

2001 / 1-84227-035-4 / xviii + 386pp

July 2005

Andrew D. Clarke
Secular and Christian Leadership in Corinth
A Socio-Historical and Exegetical Study of 1 Corinthians 1–6

This volume is an investigation into the leadership structures and dynamics of first-century Roman Corinth. These are compared with the practice of leadership in the Corinthian Christian community which are reflected in 1 Corinthians 1–6, and contrasted with Paul's own principles of Christian leadership.

2005 / 1-84227-229-2 / 200pp

Stephen Finamore
God, Order and Chaos
René Girard and the Apocalypse

Readers are often disturbed by the images of destruction in the book of Revelation and unsure why they are unleashed after the exaltation of Jesus. This book examines past approaches to these texts and uses René Girard's theories to revive some old ideas and propose some new ones.

2005 / 1-84227-197-0 / approx. 344pp

David G. Firth
Surrendering Retribution in the Psalms
Responses to Violence in the Individual Complaints

In *Surrendering Retribution in the Psalms*, David Firth examines the ways in which the book of Psalms inculcates a model response to violence through the repetition of standard patterns of prayer. Rather than seeking justification for retributive violence, Psalms encourages not only a surrender of the right of retribution to Yahweh, but also sets limits on the retribution that can be sought in imprecations. Arising initially from the author's experience in South Africa, the possibilities of this model to a particular context of violence is then briefly explored.

2005 / 1-84227-337-X / xviii + 154pp

Scott J. Hafemann
Suffering and Ministry in the Spirit
Paul's Defence of His Ministry in II Corinthians 2:14–3:3

Shedding new light on the way Paul defended his apostleship, the author offers a careful, detailed study of 2 Corinthians 2:14–3:3 linked with other key passages throughout 1 and 2 Corinthians. Demonstrating the unity and coherence of Paul's argument in this passage, the author shows that Paul's suffering served as the vehicle for revealing God's power and glory through the Spirit.

2000 / 0-85364-967-7 / xiv + 262pp

Scott J. Hafemann
Paul, Moses and the History of Israel
The Letter/Spirit Contrast and the Argument from Scripture in 2 Corinthians 3
An exegetical study of the call of Moses, the second giving of the Law (Exodus 32–34), the new covenant, and the prophetic understanding of the history of Israel in 2 Corinthians 3. Hafemann's work demonstrates Paul's contextual use of the Old Testament and the essential unity between the Law and the Gospel within the context of the distinctive ministries of Moses and Paul.
2005 / 1-84227-317-5 / xii + 498pp

Douglas S. McComiskey
Lukan Theology in the Light of the Gospel's Literary Structure
Luke's Gospel was purposefully written with theology embedded in its patterned literary structure. A critical analysis of this cyclical structure provides new windows into Luke's interpretation of the individual pericopes comprising the Gospel and illuminates several of his theological interests.
2004 / 1-84227-148-2 / xviii + 388pp

Stephen Motyer
Your Father the Devil?
A New Approach to John and 'The Jews'
Who are 'the Jews' in John's Gospel? Defending John against the charge of antisemitism, Motyer argues that, far from demonising the Jews, the Gospel seeks to present Jesus as 'Good News for Jews' in a late first century setting.
1997 / 0-85364-832-8 / xiv + 260pp

Esther Ng
Reconstructing Christian Origins?
The Feminist Theology of Elizabeth Schüssler Fiorenza: An Evaluation
In a detailed evaluation, the author challenges Elizabeth Schüssler Fiorenza's reconstruction of early Christian origins and her underlying presuppositions. The author also presents her own views on women's roles both then and now.
2002 / 1-84227-055-9 / xxiv + 468pp

Robin Parry
Old Testament Story and Christian Ethics
The Rape of Dinah as a Case Study

What is the role of story in ethics and, more particularly, what is the role of Old Testament story in Christian ethics? This book, drawing on the work of contemporary philosophers, argues that narrative is crucial in the ethical shaping of people and, drawing on the work of contemporary Old Testament scholars, that story plays a key role in Old Testament ethics. Parry then argues that when situated in canonical context Old Testament stories can be reappropriated by Christian readers in their own ethical formation. The shocking story of the rape of Dinah and the massacre of the Shechemites provides a fascinating case study for exploring the parameters within which Christian ethical appropriations of Old Testament stories can live.

2004 / 1-84227-210-1 / xx + 350pp

Ian Paul
Power to See the World Anew
The Value of Paul Ricoeur's Hermeneutic of Metaphor in Interpreting the Symbolism of Revelation 12 and 13

This book is a study of the hermeneutics of metaphor of Paul Ricoeur, one of the most important writers on hermeneutics and metaphor of the last century. It sets out the key points of his theory, important criticisms of his work, and how his approach, modified in the light of these criticisms, offers a methodological framework for reading apocalyptic texts.

2006 / 1-84227-056-7 / approx. 350pp

Robert L. Plummer
Paul's Understanding of the Church's Mission
Did the Apostle Paul Expect the Early Christian Communities to Evangelize?

This book engages in a careful study of Paul's letters to determine if the apostle expected the communities to which he wrote to engage in missionary activity. It helpfully summarizes the discussion on this debated issue, judiciously handling contested texts, and provides a way forward in addressing this critical question. While admitting that Paul rarely explicitly commands the communities he founded to evangelize, Plummer amasses significant incidental data to provide a convincing case that Paul did indeed expect his churches to engage in mission activity. Throughout the study, Plummer progressively builds a theological basis for the church's mission that is both distinctively Pauline and compelling.

2006 / 1-84227-333-7 / approx. 324pp

July 2005

David Powys
'Hell': A Hard Look at a Hard Question
The Fate of the Unrighteous in New Testament Thought

This comprehensive treatment seeks to unlock the original meaning of terms and phrases long thought to support the traditional doctrine of hell. It concludes that there is an alternative—one which is more biblical, and which can positively revive the rationale for Christian mission.

1997 / 0-85364-831-X / xxii + 478pp

Sorin Sabou
Between Horror and Hope
Paul's Metaphorical Language of Death in Romans 6.1-11

This book argues that Paul's metaphorical language of death in Romans 6.1-11 conveys two aspects: horror and hope. The 'horror' aspect is conveyed by the 'crucifixion' language, and the 'hope' aspect by 'burial' language. The life of the Christian believer is understood, as relationship with sin is concerned ('death to sin'), between these two realities: horror and hope.

2005 / 1-84227-322-1 / approx. 224pp

Rosalind Selby
The Comical Doctrine
The Epistemology of New Testament Hermeneutics

This book argues that the gospel breaks through postmodernity's critique of truth and the referential possibilities of textuality with its gift of grace. With a rigorous, philosophical challenge to modernist and postmodernist assumptions, Selby offers an alternative epistemology to all who would still read with faith *and* with academic credibility.

2005 / 1-84227-212-8 / approx. 350pp

Kiwoong Son
Zion Symbolism in Hebrews
Hebrews 12.18-24 as a Hermeneutical Key to the Epistle

This book challenges the general tendency of understanding the Epistle to the Hebrews against a Hellenistic background and suggests that the Epistle should be understood in the light of the Jewish apocalyptic tradition. The author especially argues for the importance of the theological symbolism of Sinai and Zion (Heb. 12:18-24) as it provides the Epistle's theological background as well as the rhetorical basis of the superiority motif of Jesus throughout the Epistle.

2005 / 1-84227-368-X / approx. 280pp

Kevin Walton
Thou Traveller Unknown
The Presence and Absence of God in the Jacob Narrative
The author offers a fresh reading of the story of Jacob in the book of Genesis through the paradox of divine presence and absence. The work also seeks to make a contribution to Pentateuchal studies by bringing together a close reading of the final text with historical critical insights, doing justice to the text's historical depth, final form and canonical status.
2003 / 1-84227-059-1 / xvi + 238pp

George M. Wieland
The Significance of Salvation
A Study of Salvation Language in the Pastoral Epistles
The language and ideas of salvation pervade the three Pastoral Epistles. This study offers a close examination of their soteriological statements. In all three letters the idea of salvation is found to play a vital paraenetic role, but each also exhibits distinctive soteriological emphases. The results challenge common assumptions about the Pastoral Epistles as a corpus.
2005 / 1-84227-257-8 / approx. 324pp

Alistair Wilson
When Will These Things Happen?
A Study of Jesus as Judge in Matthew 21–25
This study seeks to allow Matthew's carefully constructed presentation of Jesus to be given full weight in the modern evaluation of Jesus' eschatology. Careful analysis of the text of Matthew 21–25 reveals Jesus to be standing firmly in the Jewish prophetic and wisdom traditions as he proclaims and enacts imminent judgement on the Jewish authorities then boldly claims the central role in the final and universal judgement.
2004 / 1-84227-146-6 / xxii + 272pp

Lindsay Wilson
Joseph Wise and Otherwise
The Intersection of Covenant and Wisdom in Genesis 37–50
This book offers a careful literary reading of Genesis 37–50 that argues that the Joseph story contains both strong covenant themes and many wisdom-like elements. The connections between the two helps to explore how covenant and wisdom might intersect in an integrated biblical theology.
2004 / 1-84227-140-7 / xvi + 340pp

Stephen I. Wright
The Voice of Jesus
Studies in the Interpretation of Six Gospel Parables
This literary study considers how the 'voice' of Jesus has been heard in different periods of parable interpretation, and how the categories of figure and trope may help us towards a sensitive reading of the parables today.
2000 / 0-85364-975-8 / xiv + 280pp

Paternoster Theological Monographs

(All titles uniform with this volume)
Dates in bold are of projected publication

Emil Bartos
Deification in Eastern Orthodox Theology
An Evaluation and Critique of the Theology of Dumitru Staniloae

Bartos studies a fundamental yet neglected aspect of Orthodox theology: deification. By examining the doctrines of anthropology, christology, soteriology and ecclesiology as they relate to deification, he provides an important contribution to contemporary dialogue between Eastern and Western theologians.

1999 / 0-85364-956-1 / xii + 370pp

Graham Buxton
The Trinity, Creation and Pastoral Ministry
Imaging the Perichoretic God

In this book the author proposes a three-way conversation between theology, science and pastoral ministry. His approach draws on a Trinitarian understanding of God as a relational being of love, whose life 'spills over' into all created reality, human and non-human. By locating human meaning and purpose within God's 'creation-community' this book offers the possibility of a transforming engagement between those in pastoral ministry and the scientific community.

2005 / 1-84227-369-8 / approx. 380 pp

Iain D. Campbell
Fixing the Indemnity
The Life and Work of George Adam Smith

When Old Testament scholar George Adam Smith (1856–1942) delivered the Lyman Beecher lectures at Yale University in 1899, he confidently declared that 'modern criticism has won its war against traditional theories. It only remains to fix the amount of the indemnity.' In this biography, Iain D. Campbell assesses Smith's critical approach to the Old Testament and evaluates its consequences, showing that Smith's life and work still raises questions about the relationship between biblical scholarship and evangelical faith.

2004 / 1-84227-228-4 / xx + 256pp

Tim Chester
Mission and the Coming of God
Eschatology, the Trinity and Mission in the Theology of Jürgen Moltmann
This book explores the theology and missiology of the influential contemporary theologian, Jürgen Moltmann. It highlights the important contribution Moltmann has made while offering a critique of his thought from an evangelical perspective. In so doing, it touches on pertinent issues for evangelical missiology. The conclusion takes Calvin as a starting point, proposing 'an eschatology of the cross' which offers a critique of the over-realised eschatologies in liberation theology and certain forms of evangelicalism.
2006 / 1-84227-320-5 / approx. 224pp

Sylvia Wilkey Collinson
Making Disciples
The Significance of Jesus' Educational Strategy for Today's Church
This study examines the biblical practice of discipling, formulates a definition, and makes comparisons with modern models of education. A recommendation is made for greater attention to its practice today.
2004 / 1-84227-116-4 / xiv + 278pp

Darrell Cosden
A Theology of Work
Work and the New Creation
Through dialogue with Moltmann, Pope John Paul II and others, this book develops a genitive 'theology of work', presenting a theological definition of work and a model for a theological ethics of work that shows work's nature, value and meaning now and eschatologically. Work is shown to be a transformative activity consisting of three dynamically inter-related dimensions: the instrumental, relational and ontological.
2005 / 1-84227-332-9 / xvi + 208pp

Stephen M. Dunning
The Crisis and the Quest
A Kierkegaardian Reading of Charles Williams
Employing Kierkegaardian categories and analysis, this study investigates both the central crisis in Charles Williams's authorship between hermetism and Christianity (Kierkegaard's Religions A and B), and the quest to resolve this crisis, a quest that ultimately presses the bounds of orthodoxy.
2000 / 0-85364-985-5 / xxiv + 254pp

Keith Ferdinando
The Triumph of Christ in African Perspective
A Study of Demonology and Redemption in the African Context
The book explores the implications of the gospel for traditional African fears of occult aggression. It analyses such traditional approaches to suffering and biblical responses to fears of demonic evil, concluding with an evaluation of African beliefs from the perspective of the gospel.

1999 / 0-85364-830-1 / xviii + 450pp

Andrew Goddard
Living the Word, Resisting the World
The Life and Thought of Jacques Ellul
This work offers a definitive study of both the life and thought of the French Reformed thinker Jacques Ellul (1912-1994). It will prove an indispensable resource for those interested in this influential theologian and sociologist and for Christian ethics and political thought generally.

2002 / 1-84227-053-2 / xxiv + 378pp

David Hilborn
The Words of our Lips
Language-Use in Free Church Worship
Studies of liturgical language have tended to focus on the written canons of Roman Catholic and Anglican communities. By contrast, David Hilborn analyses the more extemporary approach of English Nonconformity. Drawing on recent developments in linguistic pragmatics, he explores similarities and differences between 'fixed' and 'free' worship, and argues for the interdependence of each.

2006 / 0-85364-977-4 / approx. 350pp

Roger Hitching
The Church and Deaf People
A Study of Identity, Communication and Relationships with Special Reference to the Ecclesiology of Jürgen Moltmann
In *The Church and Deaf People* Roger Hitching sensitively examines the history and present experience of deaf people and finds similarities between aspects of sign language and Moltmann's theological method that 'open up' new ways of understanding theological concepts.

2003 / 1-84227-222-5 / xxii + 236pp

John G. Kelly
One God, One People
The Differentiated Unity of the People of God in the Theology of Jürgen Moltmann
The author expounds and critiques Moltmann's doctrine of God and highlights the systematic connections between it and Moltmann's influential discussion of Israel. He then proposes a fresh approach to Jewish–Christian relations building on Moltmann's work using insights from Habermas and Rawls.
2005 / 0-85346-969-3 / approx. 350pp

Mark F.W. Lovatt
Confronting the Will-to-Power
A Reconsideration of the Theology of Reinhold Niebuhr
Confronting the Will-to-Power is an analysis of the theology of Reinhold Niebuhr, arguing that his work is an attempt to identify, and provide a practical theological answer to, the existence and nature of human evil.
2001 / 1-84227-054-0 / xviii + 216pp

Neil B. MacDonald
Karl Barth and the Strange New World within the Bible
Barth, Wittgenstein, and the Metadilemmas of the Enlightenment
Barth's discovery of the strange new world within the Bible is examined in the context of Kant, Hume, Overbeck, and, most importantly, Wittgenstein. MacDonald covers some fundamental issues in theology today: epistemology, the final form of the text and biblical truth-claims.
2000 / 0-85364-970-7 / xxvi + 374pp

Keith A. Mascord
Alvin Plantinga and Christian Apologetics
This book draws together the contributions of the philosopher Alvin Plantinga to the major contemporary challenges to Christian belief, highlighting in particular his ground-breaking work in epistemology and the problem of evil. Plantinga's theory that both theistic and Christian belief is warrantedly basic is explored and critiqued, and an assessment offered as to the significance of his work for apologetic theory and practice.
2005 / 1-84227-256-X / approx. 304pp

Gillian McCulloch
The Deconstruction of Dualism in Theology
With Reference to Ecofeminist Theology and New Age Spirituality
This book challenges eco-theological anti-dualism in Christian theology, arguing that dualism has a twofold function in Christian religious discourse. Firstly, it enables us to express the discontinuities and divisions that are part of the process of reality. Secondly, dualistic language allows us to express the mysteries of divine transcendence/immanence and the survival of the soul without collapsing into monism and materialism, both of which are problematic for Christian epistemology.

2002 / 1-84227-044-3 / xii + 282pp

Leslie McCurdy
Attributes and Atonement
The Holy Love of God in the Theology of P.T. Forsyth
Attributes and Atonement is an intriguing full-length study of P.T. Forsyth's doctrine of the cross as it relates particularly to God's holy love. It includes an unparalleled bibliography of both primary and secondary material relating to Forsyth.

1999 / 0-85364-833-6 / xiv + 328pp

Nozomu Miyahira
Towards a Theology of the Concord of God
A Japanese Perspective on the Trinity
This book introduces a new Japanese theology and a unique Trinitarian formula based on the Japanese intellectual climate: three betweennesses and one concord. It also presents a new interpretation of the Trinity, a co-subordinationism, which is in line with orthodox Trinitarianism; each single person of the Trinity is eternally and equally subordinate (or serviceable) to the other persons, so that they retain the mutual dynamic equality.

2000 / 0-85364-863-8 / xiv + 256pp

Eddy José Muskus
The Origins and Early Development of Liberation Theology in Latin America
With Particular Reference to Gustavo Gutiérrez
This work challenges the fundamental premise of Liberation Theology, 'opting for the poor', and its claim that Christ is found in them. It also argues that Liberation Theology emerged as a direct result of the failure of the Roman Catholic Church in Latin America.

2002 / 0-85364-974-X / xiv + 296pp

Jim Purves
The Triune God and the Charismatic Movement
A Critical Appraisal from a Scottish Perspective

All emotion and no theology? Or a fundamental challenge to reappraise and realign our trinitarian theology in the light of Christian experience? This study of charismatic renewal as it found expression within Scotland at the end of the twentieth century evaluates the use of Patristic, Reformed and contemporary models of the Trinity in explaining the workings of the Holy Spirit.

2004 / 1-84227-321-3 / xxiv + 246pp

Anna Robbins
Methods in the Madness
Diversity in Twentieth-Century Christian Social Ethics

The author compares the ethical methods of Walter Rauschenbusch, Reinhold Niebuhr and others. She argues that unless Christians are clear about the ways that theology and philosophy are expressed practically they may lose the ability to discuss social ethics across contexts, let alone reach effective agreements.

2004 / 1-84227-211-X / xx + 294pp

Ed Rybarczyk
Beyond Salvation
Eastern Orthodoxy and Classical Pentecostalism on Becoming Like Christ

At first glance eastern Orthodoxy and classical Pentecostalism seem quite distinct. This ground-breaking study shows they share much in common, especially as it concerns the experiential elements of following Christ. Both traditions assert that authentic Christianity transcends the wooden categories of modernism.

2004 / 1-84227-144-X / xii + 356pp

Signe Sandsmark
Is World View Neutral Education Possible and Desirable?
A Christian Response to Liberal Arguments
(Published jointly with The Stapleford Centre)

This book discusses reasons for belief in world view neutrality, and argues that 'neutral' education will have a hidden, but strong world view influence. It discusses the place for Christian education in the common school.

2000 / 0-85364-973-1 / xiv + 182pp

Hazel Sherman
Reading Zechariah
The Allegorical Tradition of Biblical Interpretation through the Commentary of Didymus the Blind and Theodore of Mopsuestia
A close reading of the commentary on Zechariah by Didymus the Blind alongside that of Theodore of Mopsuestia suggests that popular categorising of Antiochene and Alexandrian biblical exegesis as 'historical' or 'allegorical' is inadequate and misleading.
2005 / 1-84227-213-6 / approx. 280pp

Andrew Sloane
On Being a Christian in the Academy
Nicholas Wolterstorff and the Practice of Christian Scholarship
An exposition and critical appraisal of Nicholas Wolterstorff's epistemology in the light of the philosophy of science, and an application of his thought to the practice of Christian scholarship.
2003 / 1-84227-058-3 / xvi + 274pp

Damon W.K. So
Jesus' Revelation of His Father
A Narrative-Conceptual Study of the Trinity with Special Reference to Karl Barth
This book explores the trinitarian dynamics in the context of Jesus' revelation of his Father in his earthly ministry with references to key passages in Matthew's Gospel. It develops from the exegeses of these passages a non-linear concept of revelation which links Jesus' communion with his Father to his revelatory words and actions through a nuanced understanding of the Holy Spirit, with references to K. Barth, G.W.H. Lampe, J.D.G. Dunn and E. Irving.
2005 / 1-84227-323-X / approx. 380pp

Daniel Strange
The Possibility of Salvation Among the Unevangelised
An Analysis of Inclusivism in Recent Evangelical Theology
For evangelical theologians the 'fate of the unevangelised' impinges upon fundamental tenets of evangelical identity. The position known as 'inclusivism', defined by the belief that the unevangelised can be ontologically saved by Christ whilst being epistemologically unaware of him, has been defended most vigorously by the Canadian evangelical Clark H. Pinnock. Through a detailed analysis and critique of Pinnock's work, this book examines a cluster of issues surrounding the unevangelised and its implications for christology, soteriology and the doctrine of revelation.
2002 / 1-84227-047-8 / xviii + 362pp

Scott Swain
God According to the Gospel
Biblical Narrative and the Identity of God in the Theology of Robert W. Jenson
Robert W. Jenson is one of the leading voices in contemporary Trinitarian theology. His boldest contribution in this area concerns his use of biblical narrative both to ground and explicate the Christian doctrine of God. *God According to the Gospel* critically examines Jenson's proposal and suggests an alternative way of reading the biblical portrayal of the triune God.
2006 / 1-84227-258-6 / approx. 180pp

Justyn Terry
The Justifying Judgement of God
A Reassessment of the Place of Judgement in the Saving Work of Christ
The argument of this book is that judgement, understood as the whole process of bringing justice, is the primary metaphor of atonement, with others, such as victory, redemption and sacrifice, subordinate to it. Judgement also provides the proper context for understanding penal substitution and the call to repentance, baptism, eucharist and holiness.
2005 / 1-84227-370-1 / approx. 274 pp

Graham Tomlin
The Power of the Cross
Theology and the Death of Christ in Paul, Luther and Pascal
This book explores the theology of the cross in St Paul, Luther and Pascal. It offers new perspectives on the theology of each, and some implications for the nature of power, apologetics, theology and church life in a postmodern context.
1999 / 0-85364-984-7 / xiv + 344pp

Adonis Vidu
Postliberal Theological Method
A Critical Study
The postliberal theology of Hans Frei, George Lindbeck, Ronald Thiemann, John Milbank and others is one of the more influential contemporary options. This book focuses on several aspects pertaining to its theological method, specifically its understanding of background, hermeneutics, epistemic justification, ontology, the nature of doctrine and, finally, Christological method.
2005 / 1-84227-395-7 / approx. 324pp

Graham J. Watts
Revelation and the Spirit
A Comparative Study of the Relationship between the Doctrine of Revelation and Pneumatology in the Theology of Eberhard Jüngel and of Wolfhart Pannenberg

The relationship between revelation and pneumatology is relatively unexplored. This approach offers a fresh angle on two important twentieth century theologians and raises pneumatological questions which are theologically crucial and relevant to mission in a postmodern culture.

2005 / 1-84227-104-0 / xxii + 232pp

Nigel G. Wright
Disavowing Constantine
Mission, Church and the Social Order in the Theologies of John Howard Yoder and Jürgen Moltmann

This book is a timely restatement of a radical theology of church and state in the Anabaptist and Baptist tradition. Dr Wright constructs his argument in dialogue and debate with Yoder and Moltmann, major contributors to a free church perspective.

2000 / 0-85364-978-2 / xvi + 252pp

www.ingramcontent.com/pod-product-compliance
Lightning Source LLC
Chambersburg PA
CBHW052144300426
44115CB00011B/1514